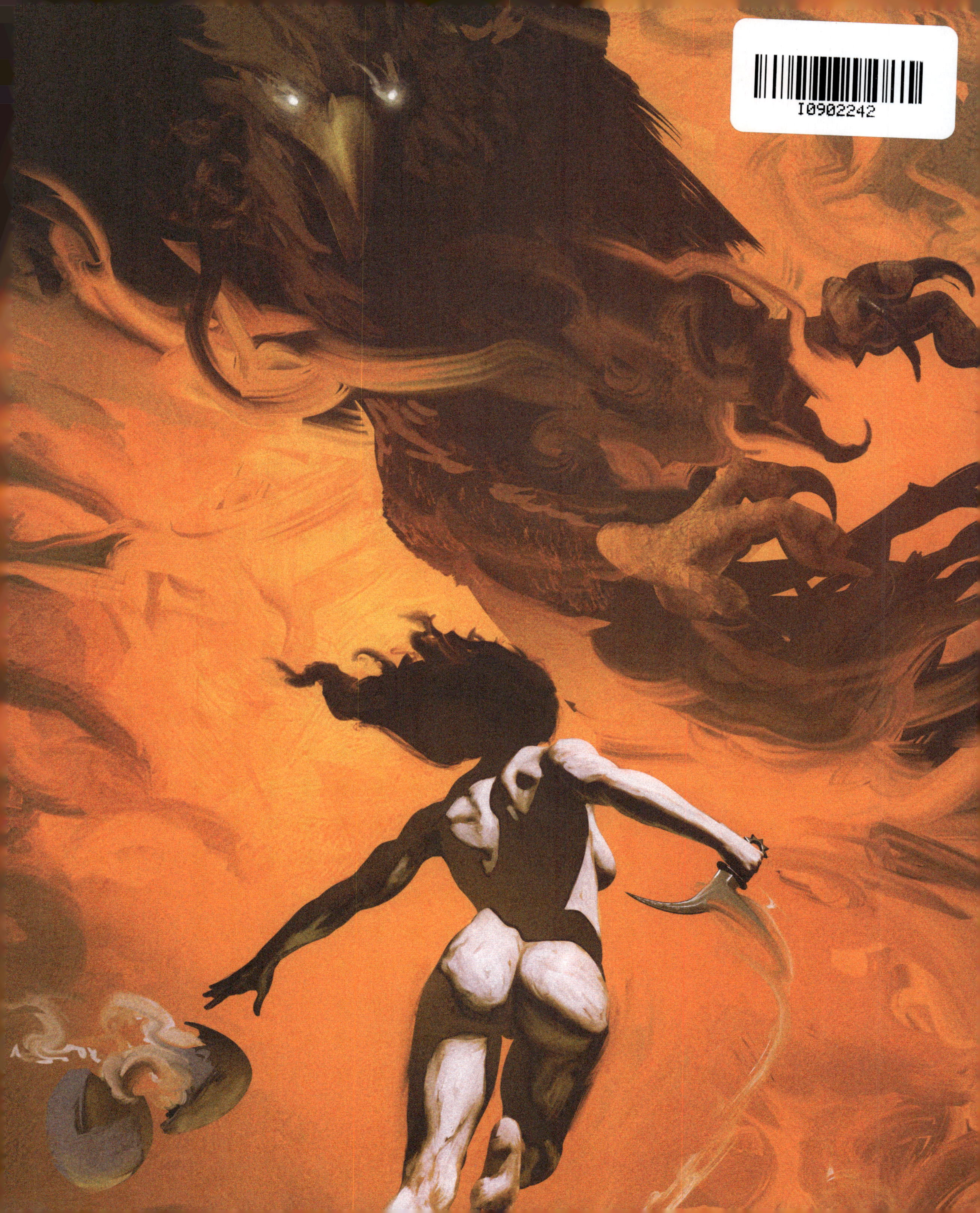

FRANK FRAZETTA

An Artists' Tribute

3dtotal Publishing

Correspondence: publishing@3dtotal.com
Website: store.3dtotal.com

First published in the United Kingdom, 2023, by 3dtotal Publishing.

Address: 3dtotal.com Ltd,
29 Foregate Street, Worcester
WR1 1DS, United Kingdom.

Hard cover ISBN:
978-1-912843-81-7

Printed and bound in China
by C&C Offset Printing Co., Ltd

Visit store.3dtotal.com for a complete list of available book titles.

Editor: Marisa Lewis
Designer: Fiona Tarbet
Lead Editor: Samantha Rigby
Lead Designer: Joseph Cartwright
Studio Manager: Simon Morse
Managing Director: Tom Greenway

Cover artwork: Frank Frazetta

FSC www.fsc.org MIX Paper | Supporting responsible forestry FSC® C008047

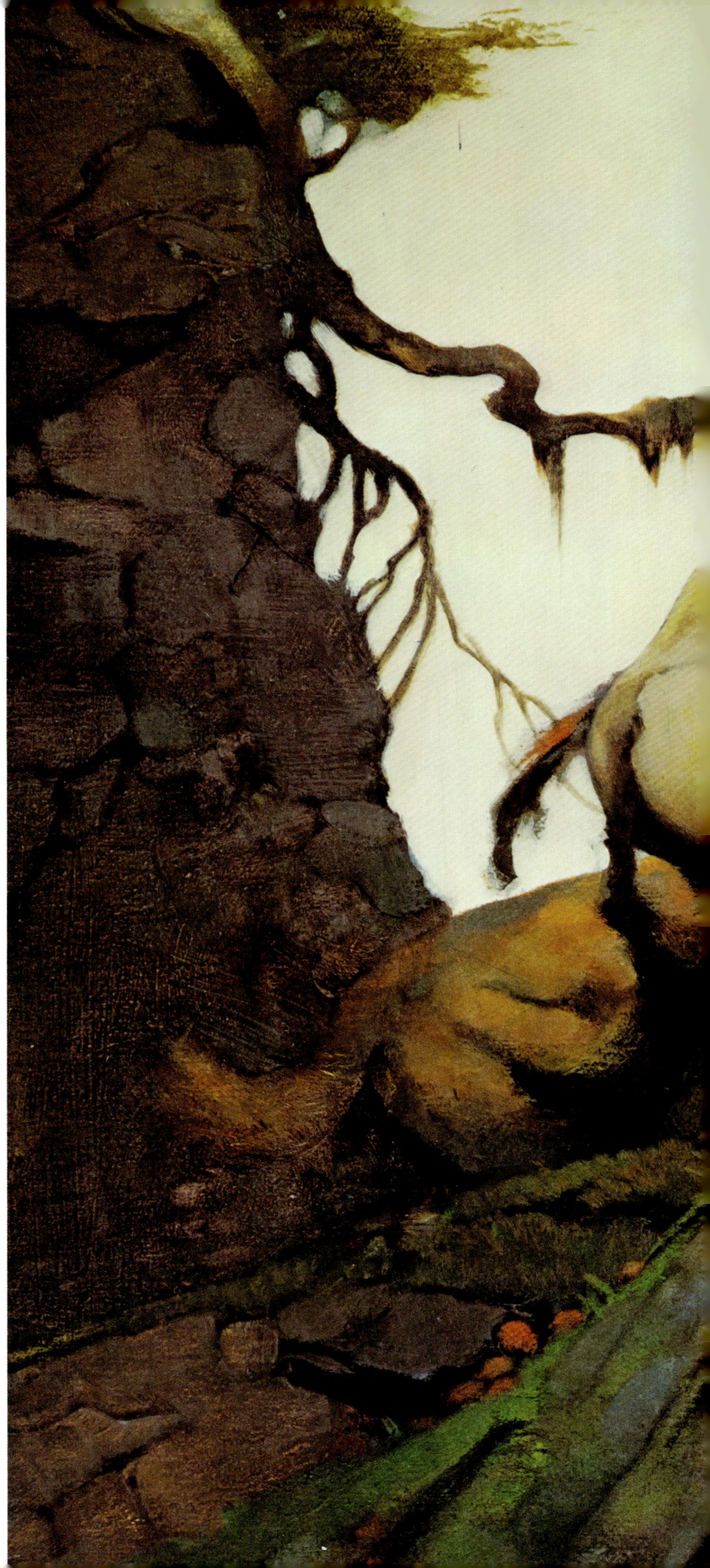

Savage Pellucidar © Frank Frazetta

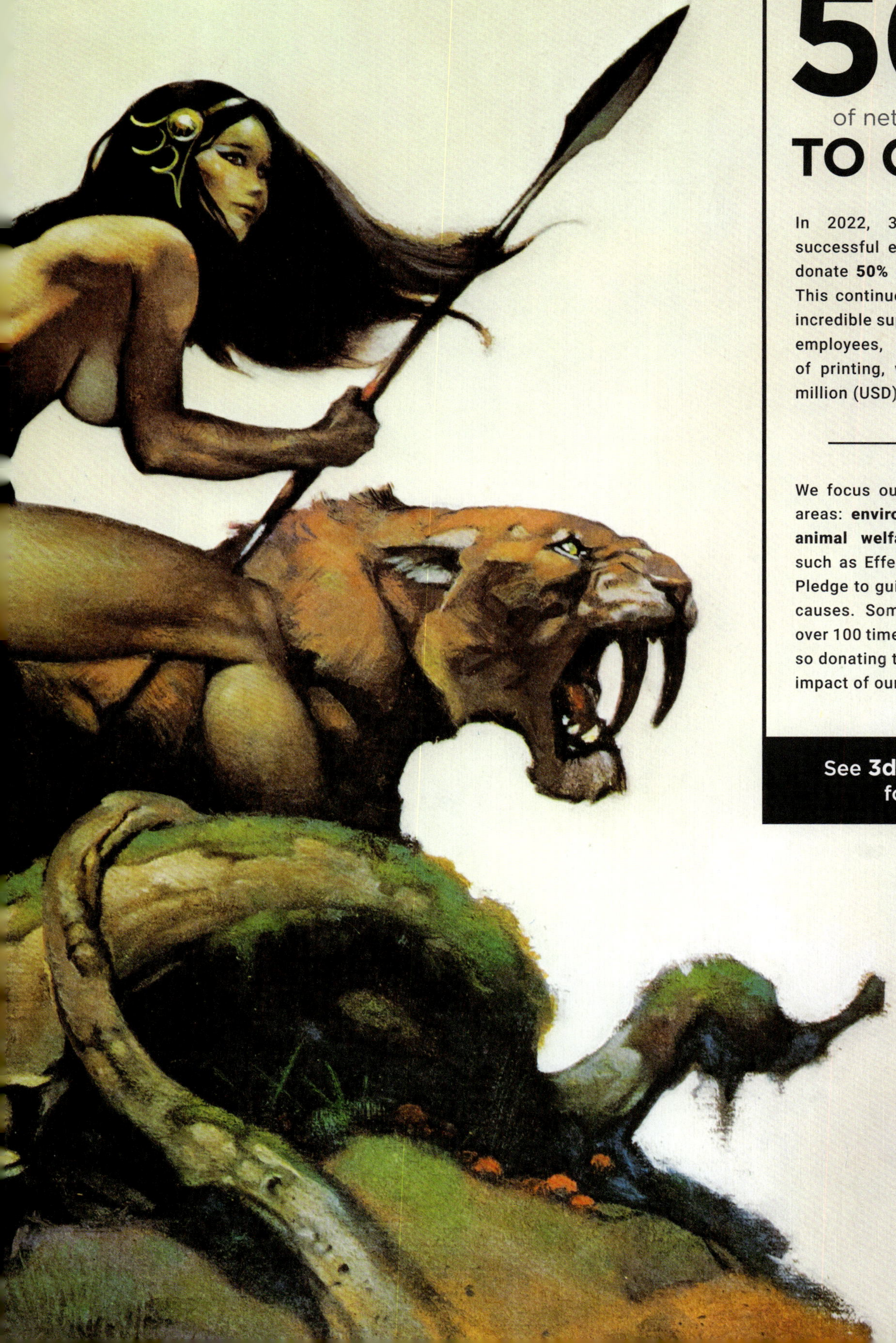

50%

of net profits donated

TO CHARITY

In 2022, 3dtotal Publishing became successful enough to make a pledge to donate **50% of its net profits to charity**. This continues to be possible due to the incredible support from all our customers, employees, and partners. At the time of printing, we have donated over $1.3 million (USD) to charity.

We focus our giving on three charitable areas: **environmental**, **humanitarian**, and **animal welfare**. We use organizations such as Effective Altruism and Founders Pledge to guide who we help within these causes. Some ways of doing good are over 100 times more effective than others, so donating this way hugely increases the impact of our contributions.

See **3dtotal.com/charity** for full details.

This book is an homage to one of fantasy art's most distinctive and enduring icons – Frank Frazetta. His mythic visions of fearsome warriors, voluptuous women, otherworldly monsters, and sweeping battles have helped to define how we see the fantasy genre, and have been an inspiration for countless creators for over fifty years. Within these pages, a selection of such artists share their own visual tributes to Frazetta in fantasy illustration tutorials, as well as reflecting on his influence and spotlighting their favourite paintings from his immense body of work. Perhaps they will encourage you to pick up a pencil, brush, or stylus and craft some epic fantasy worlds of your own.

Special thanks to Frazetta Girls for generously sharing Frank Frazetta's artwork with us for this project.

Marisa Lewis | *Editor*

Contents

Foreword

Flirtin' with Disaster, an album by Molly Hatchet, was my first experience with Frank Frazetta's work. The album showcased a dark, enigmatic character, sitting atop an equally dark steed. To my eleven-year-old self there was nothing cooler on Earth than *Death Dealer*, the name of the piece. Not to be lacking, Molly Hatchet also featured *Dark Kingdom* on a second album, and that piece was equally cool to me. Of course my kid brain exploded when I saw *Conan the Conqueror* on a third album. I still find those pieces to be amazing to this day, though I sadly haven't seen the originals in person. I have seen many other Frazetta originals and none of them disappoint.

Those three images were some of the first that I tried to emulate as a child. At that age, where I lived, no one knew about the concept of master studies. Even if they had, my being would have rebelled at the word 'study' being associated with an activity that was so much fun to try and accomplish. Frazetta was likely my first inspiration, before H.R. Giger, before movies, before almost everything else except comic books (which I bought to look at before I could even read them). I consider his work to be foundational in my love of fantasy, horror, and fiction in general. Seeing that first album awakened my mind to those genres in a very direct way.

From that experience onward, I would look for 'his' kind of art on everything I could find, from comics to magazines to movies. In the time before the internet, it was exceedingly difficult to find anything of a specific artist unless you happened upon one of their contracted illustrations. Certainly not like today. As you might imagine, I still spend a considerable portion of my time finding and looking at artists' work and if, at times, I get lost in the viewing for hours on end, you can blame Frazetta for instilling in me a hunger for all things imaginative.

Allen Williams

rd

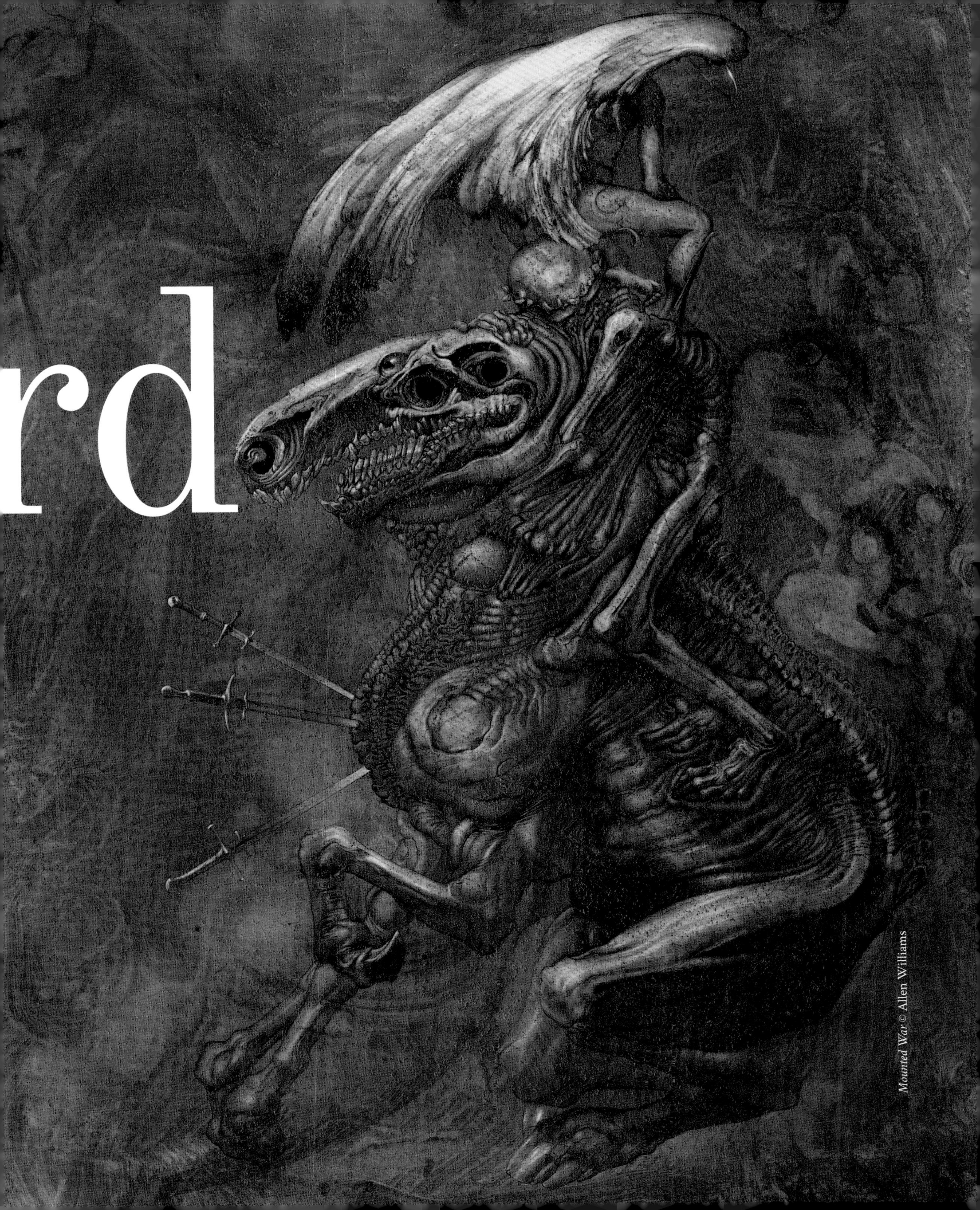

Mounted War © Allen Williams

My Grandpa, Frank

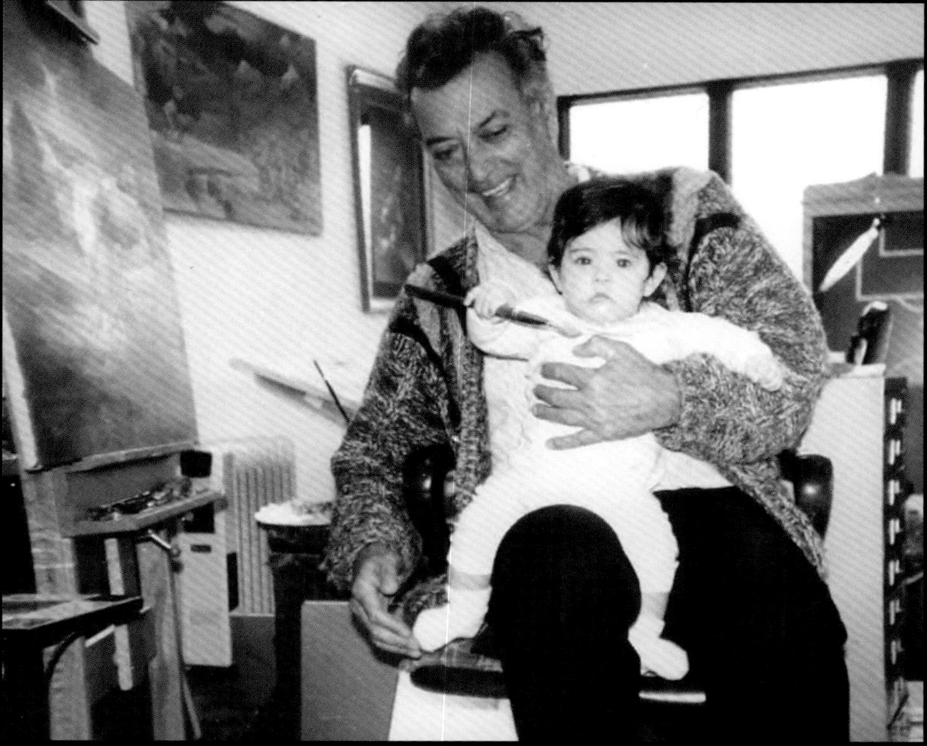

Frank Frazetta and a young Sara Frazetta in the studio

Photographs courtesy of Frazetta Girls

by Sara Frazetta

I remember being surrounded by my grandfather's prolific artworks since I was a child, but I never understood how deeply impactful he was until after he passed away. It took time to truly grasp how important his works were to the world. To me, he was just 'grandpa' for the longest time. We loved listening to music and watching films together – those were our favourite kinds of art to enjoy together. I'm so blessed to have had so many beautiful moments with him in this lifetime.

My grandfather started drawing when he was a very young boy. He copied newspaper strips by Hal Foster, Milton Caniff, Burne Hogarth, Al Capp, and E.C. Segar. These influences are obvious in his early professional comic work. He began attending the Brooklyn Academy of Fine Arts when he was just eight years old, until the age of fourteen, but it was a very informal training – he met with the class once a week and learned the fundamentals. He worked as an apprentice for John Giunta, Ralph Mayo, and Graham Ingels to refine his skills, but otherwise he was largely self-taught.

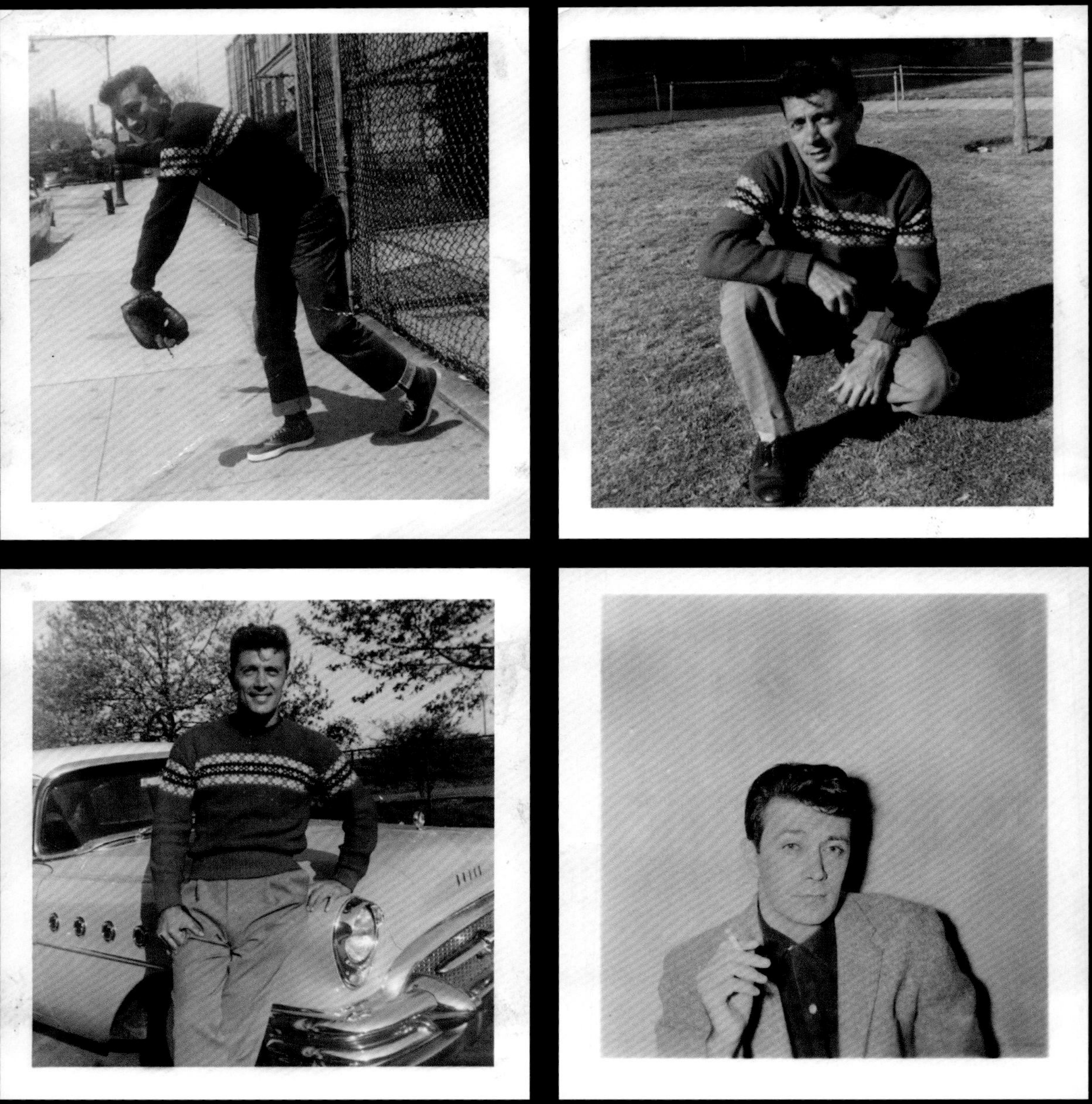

Various photos of Frank Frazetta in the 1950s

He loved to listen to classical compositions by Stravinsky while he painted and the greatest hits of Frank Sinatra while he did everything else. His favourite films, from which he took inspiration, were Disney's *Fantasia*, *Night of the Hunter*, and the original *King Kong*. He was influenced by artists like Hal Foster, Jack Kirby, Joseph Clement Coll, J. Allen St. John, and Howard Pyle. He wasn't a huge fan of most contemporary artworks of his time, including music and film. He was a classics man.

His physical side defined him as a person and artist; he spent most of his days outside on the baseball field, or really anywhere he could exert his intense energy. He loved to let it all out – run like a wild man and swing that bat like there was no tomorrow. You can definitely see his physicality in all of his work. I think it's a huge reason why so many people are attracted to it.

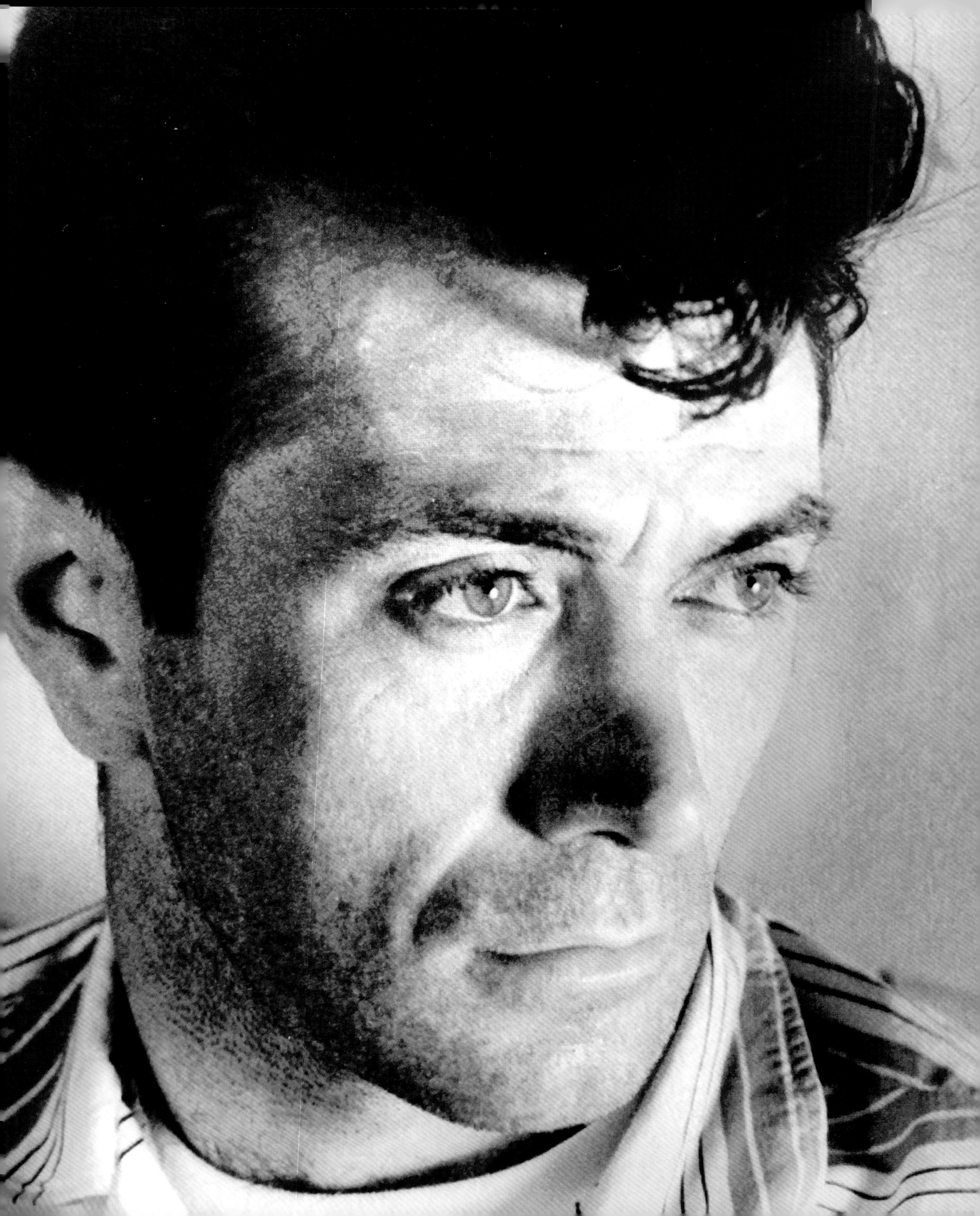

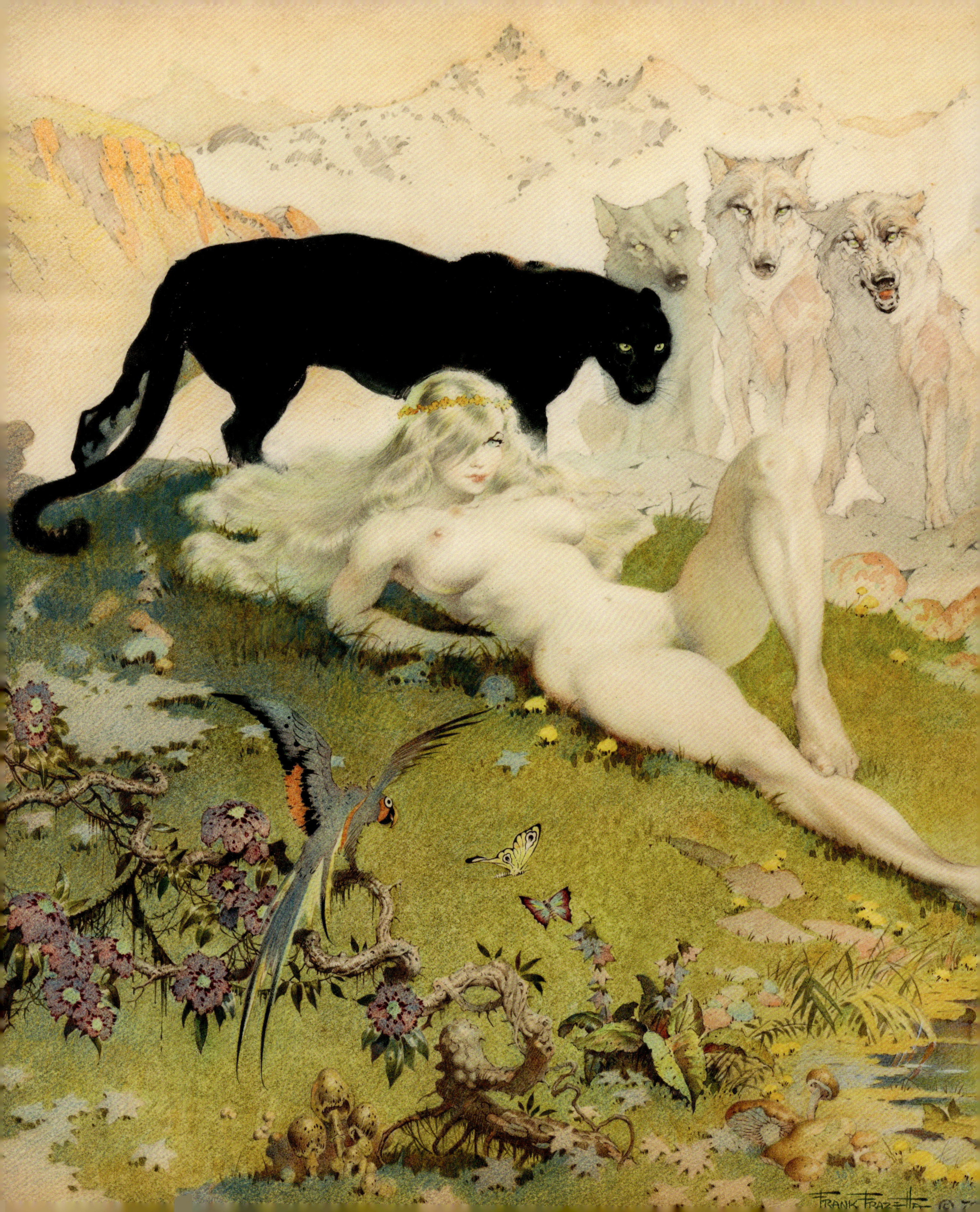
FRANK FRAZETTA

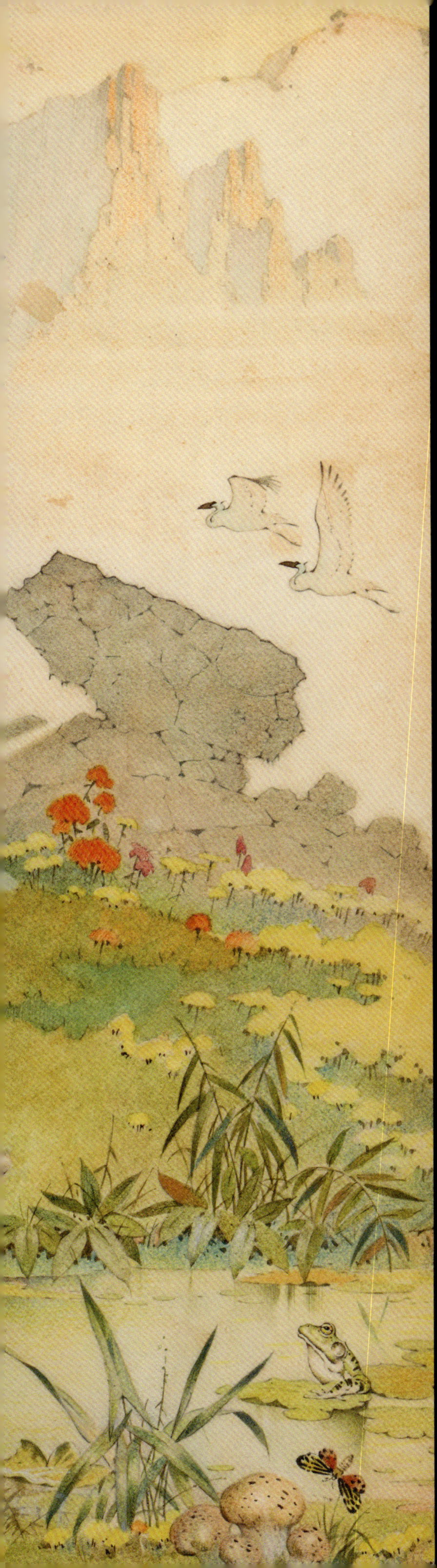

Golden Girl © Frank Frazetta

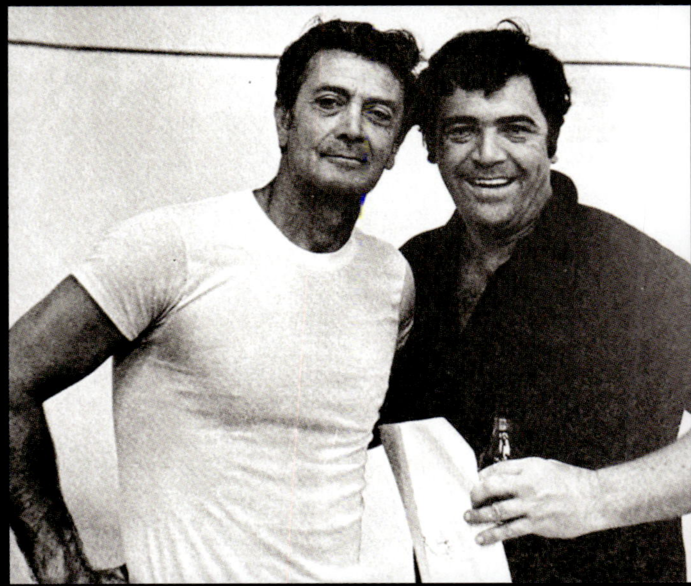

I believe his work endures due to the power of his imagination and his incomparable draughtsmanship. He transports you into a new world where you can just completely lose yourself in one of his paintings. *Silver Warrior* (see on page 243), *Conan the Barbarian*, and *Death Dealer I* have been by far the most inspirational paintings among the fans I have spoken with. Personally, I love his *Golden Girl* watercolour from the 1950s. His depictions of women are so empowering and I feel *Golden Girl* is the quintessential 'Frazetta Girl'.

Many fans have wondered which works were Frank Frazetta's own all-time favourites; on more than one occasion, he declared *Death Dealer I*, *Cat Girl*, and *Weird Science-Fantasy #29* as his top three artworks he admired most.

I believe he was aware of how impactful his work was on popular culture, but he was also very humble about it all and didn't speak about it often.

Frank Frazetta (left) and filmmaker Ralph Bakshi (right) in 1982. The pair collaborated on the epic dark-fantasy animation Fire and Ice, *released in 1983.*

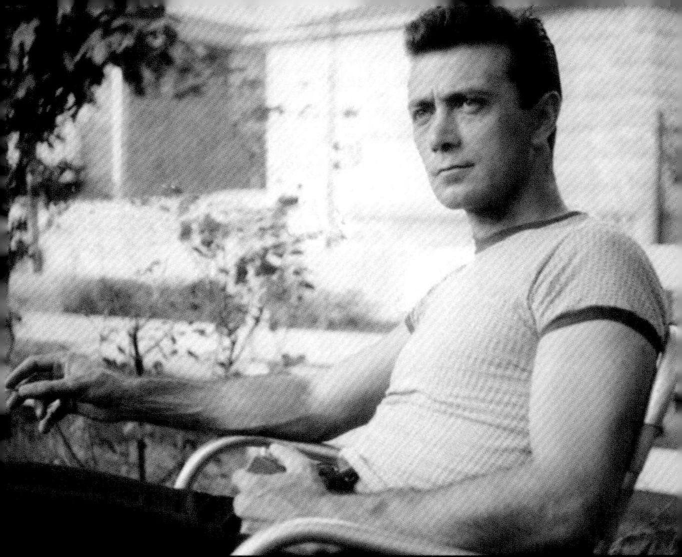

t's pretty incredible where this journey with Frazetta Girls has taken me. I never expected it would be so challenging but, of course, with the biggest challenges come the biggest rewards. It's been such an honour to be able to connect with my grandfather's fans and build upon the enormous legacy he already had. We hope to continue doing everything we are already doing, but better.

Hearing from the artists who are inspired by my grandfather means everything to me, because it highlights the importance of forging your own path in life and being yourself. Those are two important principles he preached. If you can tap into your truth and share who you are with the world through art, it's always going to be inspiring and will keep the creative world evolving. ❖

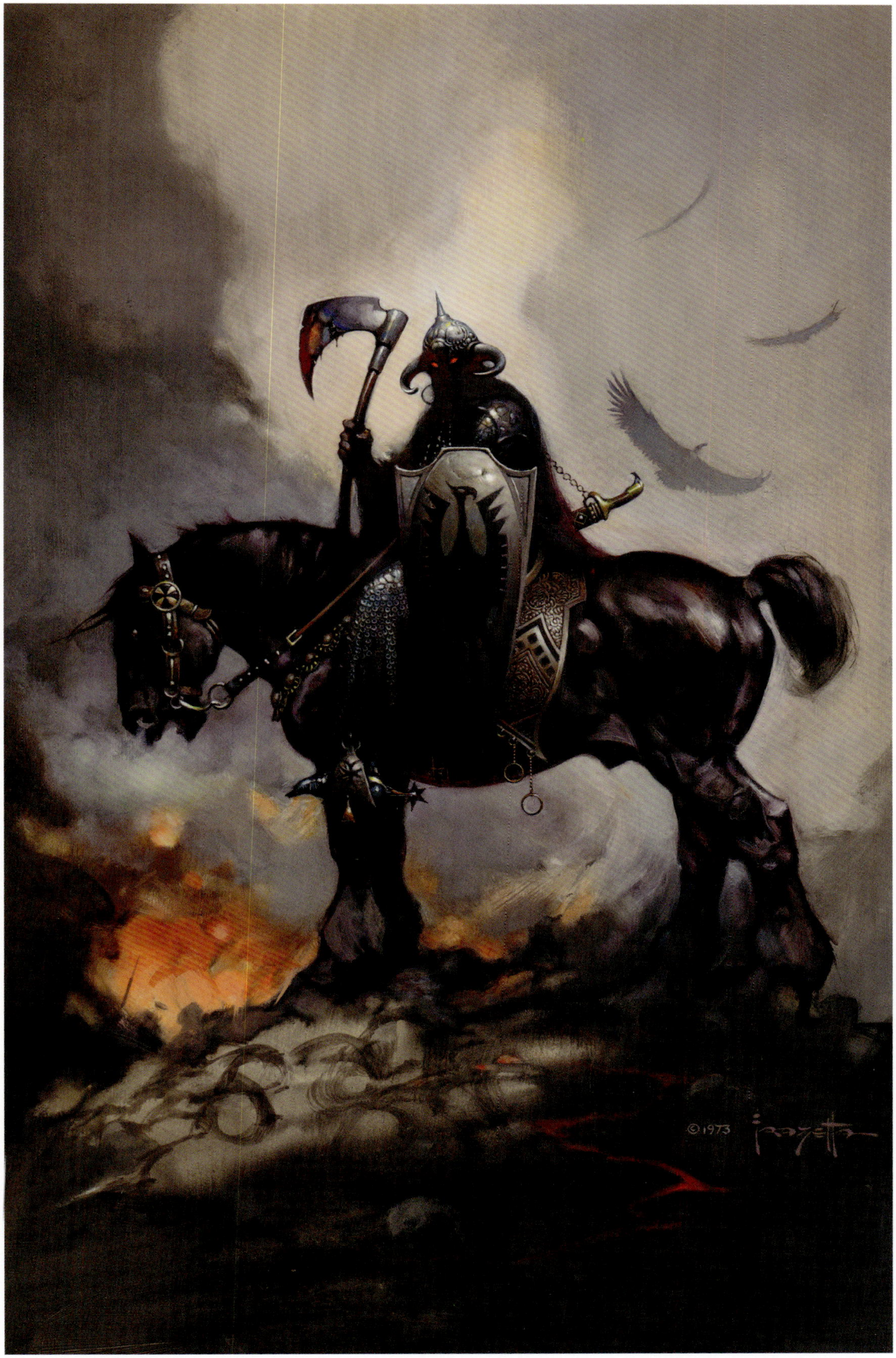

Death Dealer I © Frank Frazetta

1928

Frank Frazetta is born in Brooklyn, New York, on 9th February.

1944

Frazetta becomes a published cartoonist in his mid-teens.

Through the late 1940s and early 1950s, the young Frazetta quickly establishes a professional name for himself as a cartoon and comics prodigy.

1952

Frazetta is offered his own comic strip, which runs daily for over a year, as well as working with renowned cartoonist Al Capp, with whom he continues working for almost a decade.

Through the 1960s and 1970s, Frazetta works freelance, creating many of the book covers, posters, and album artworks for which he is now best known.

1983

The animated cult classic *Fire and Ice* is released – a dark sword-and-sorcery epic created in partnership by Frazetta and filmmaker Ralph Bakshi.

Frazetta experiences numerous health issues from the late 1980s onwards, including a misdiagnosed illness caused by turpentine exposure, and strokes that force him to re-learn painting with his non-dominant hand.

2001

Frazetta receives the World Fantasy Award for Life Achievement, in recognition of his influence on the genre.

2003

The documentary *Painting with Fire* celebrates Frazetta's life and career.

2010

Following another stroke, Frazetta passes away on 10th May, aged 82.

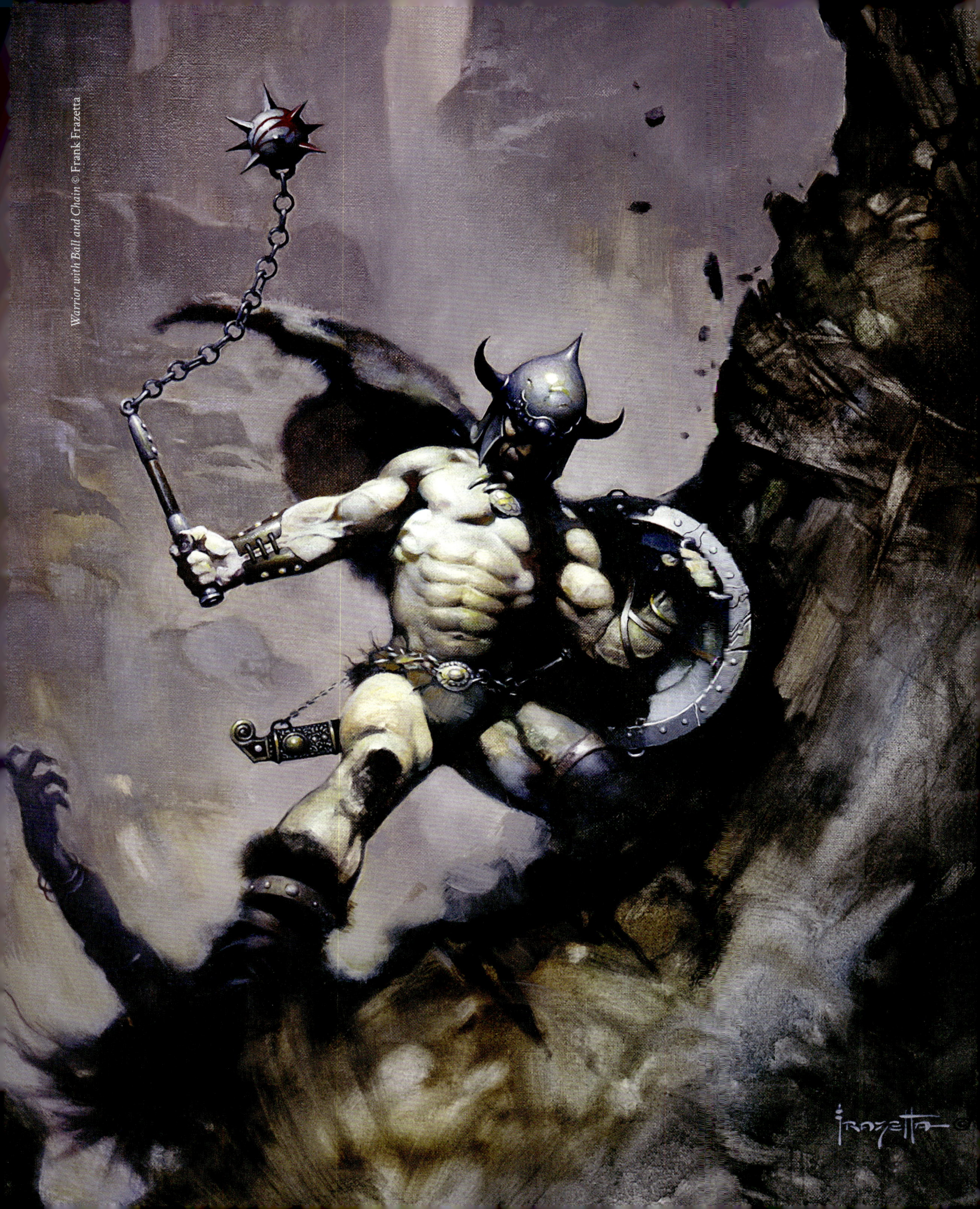

Warrior with Ball and Chain © Frank Frazetta

'Who sees like that?'

by Robert Rodriguez

Frank Frazetta was the most successful and influential science-fiction and fantasy artist of all time, and has been a major influence on generations of artists, writers, and filmmakers, including me. He was like a rock star to me growing up. He was the Jimmy Page of fantasy artists. By the age of eleven, I was cutting out pages from the mid-1970s Ballantine books of Frank's art and putting them on my walls.

My dream was, of course, to work with him someday. I never thought it would happen. I started as an artist, but then got into movie-making, and after a few films I got to live my dream. I loved Frazetta's movie posters, like *The Gauntlet* and *Fire and Ice*, so I commissioned a poster for my film *From Dusk Till Dawn*. We became friends through that project.

To meet him and work with him was an honour, but to get to know him and be his friend was a gift. I got to see firsthand his love for fantasy, for creativity, and for his family. I found it enormously influential to see how his art inspired his children and grandchildren, who are all creatives in their own right.

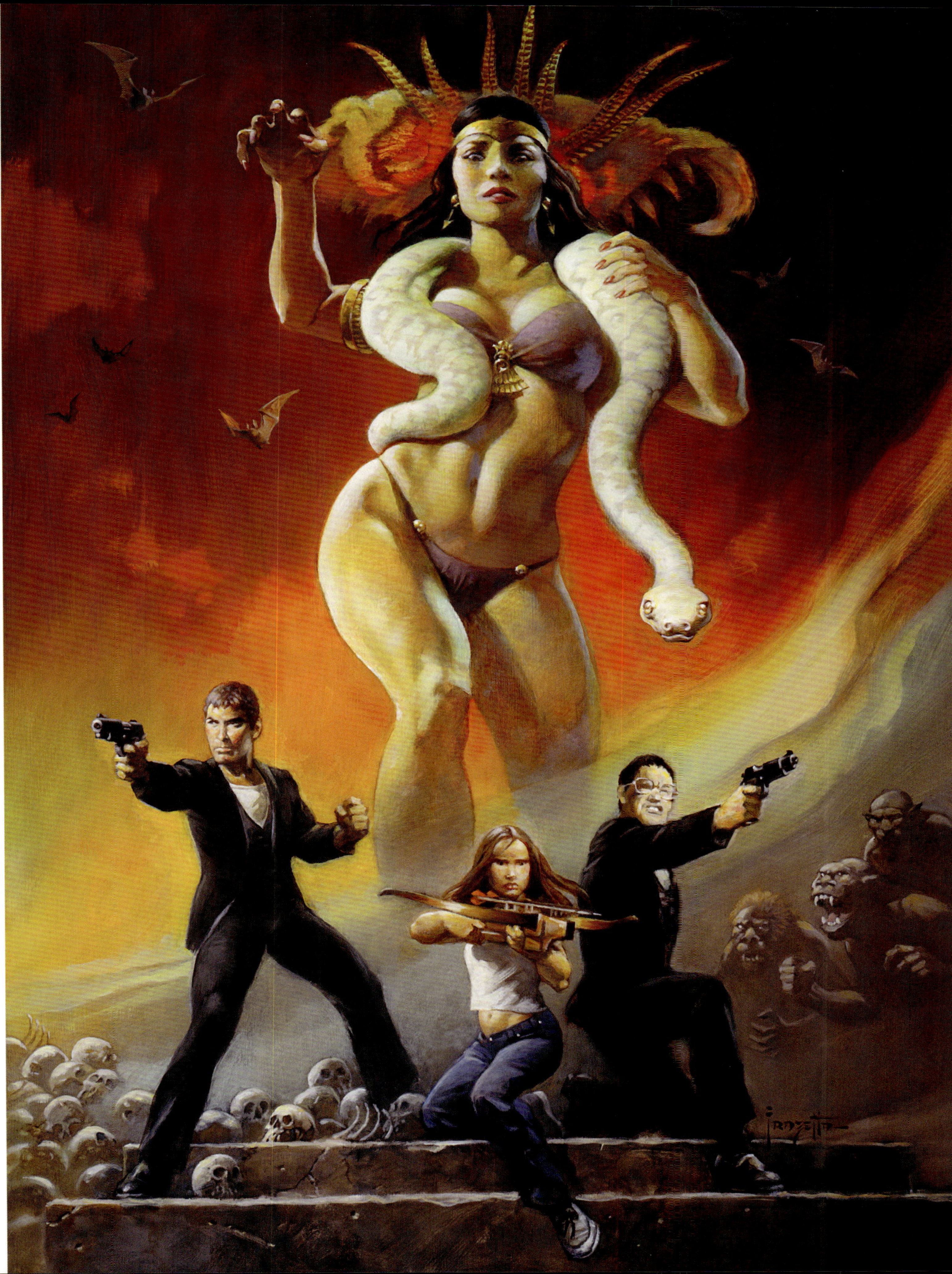

From Dusk Till Dawn © Frank Frazetta

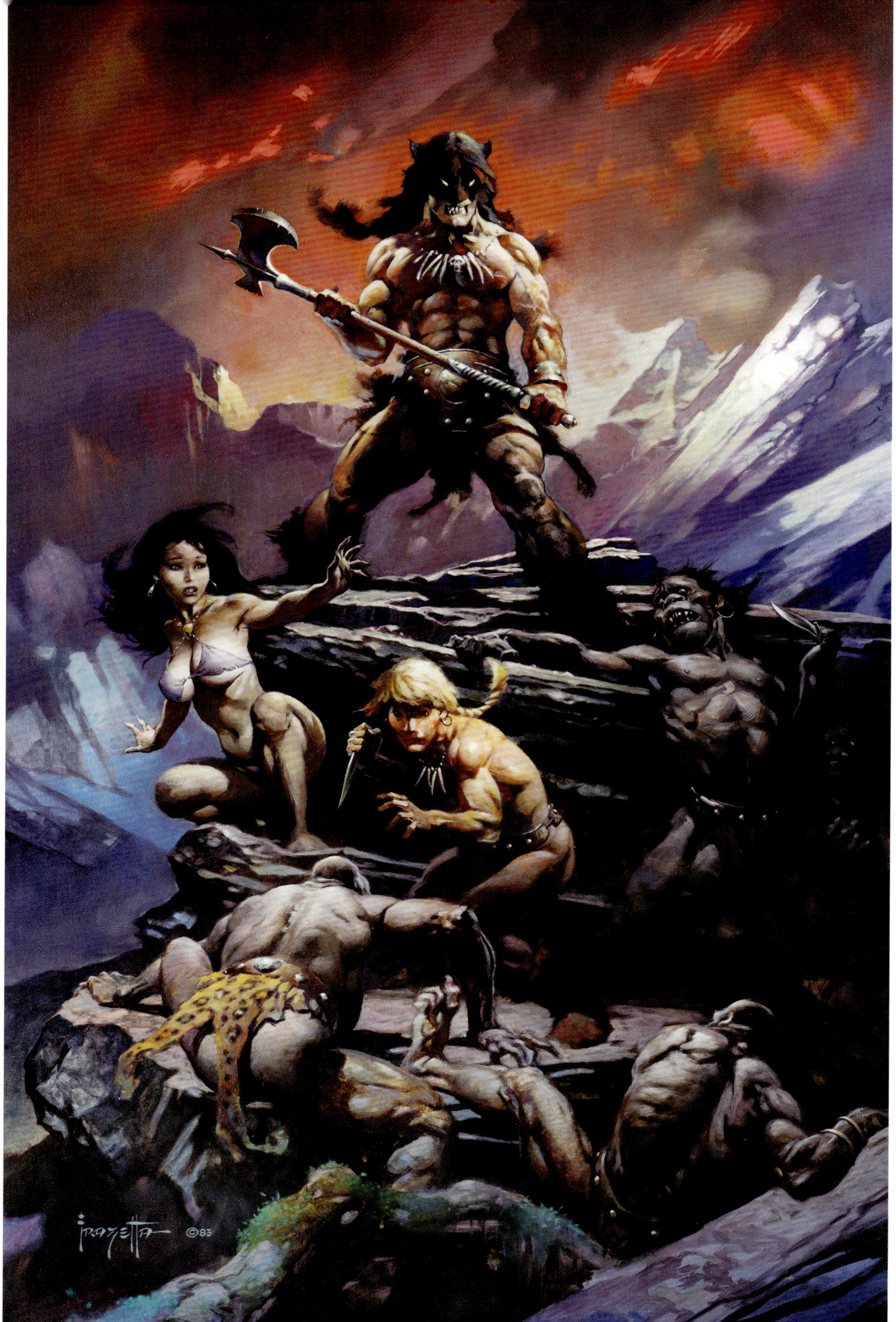

Fire and Ice © Frank Frazetta

He inspired me on so many levels. When he first showed me his museum I couldn't believe how many of his all-time classic originals were in it. And to have him talk about each one? I was truly living my dream – a dream I saw others live when I got to show them the Frazetta art I had collected over the years or that were donated by the family for a handful of pop-up gallery installations.

I saw some of the world's best artists gaze with utmost humility at the sight of Frank's originals, and talk in great reverence of what his art meant to them. People like James Cameron, Guillermo del Toro, Jon Favreau, George Miller, and Frank Miller, who upon seeing the originals said, 'The thing about Frazetta... is that he knew what dreams were.' Jim Cameron, completely in awe, was eyeing the lighting on *Death Dealer II* and said, 'Who sees like that? I can't see like that, can you?'

Frank created the looks for what have become iconic characters, such as Conan the Barbarian, Tarzan, John Carter of Mars, and the Frazetta original – Death Dealer. In the 1960s, *Conan* paperbacks would fly off the shelves, mainly because of the cover art he made.

As an artist, Frazetta created a reality with undeniable power, often at the height of action, and introduced us to an unprecedented universe of characters, creatures, and landscapes.

His work lives on, not just through his paintings, but in the countless number of artists that have been astounded by his work, and inspired to create works of their own.

The man, the myth, the legend. Frazetta became as iconic, revered, and mythical as any of his many creations. ❖

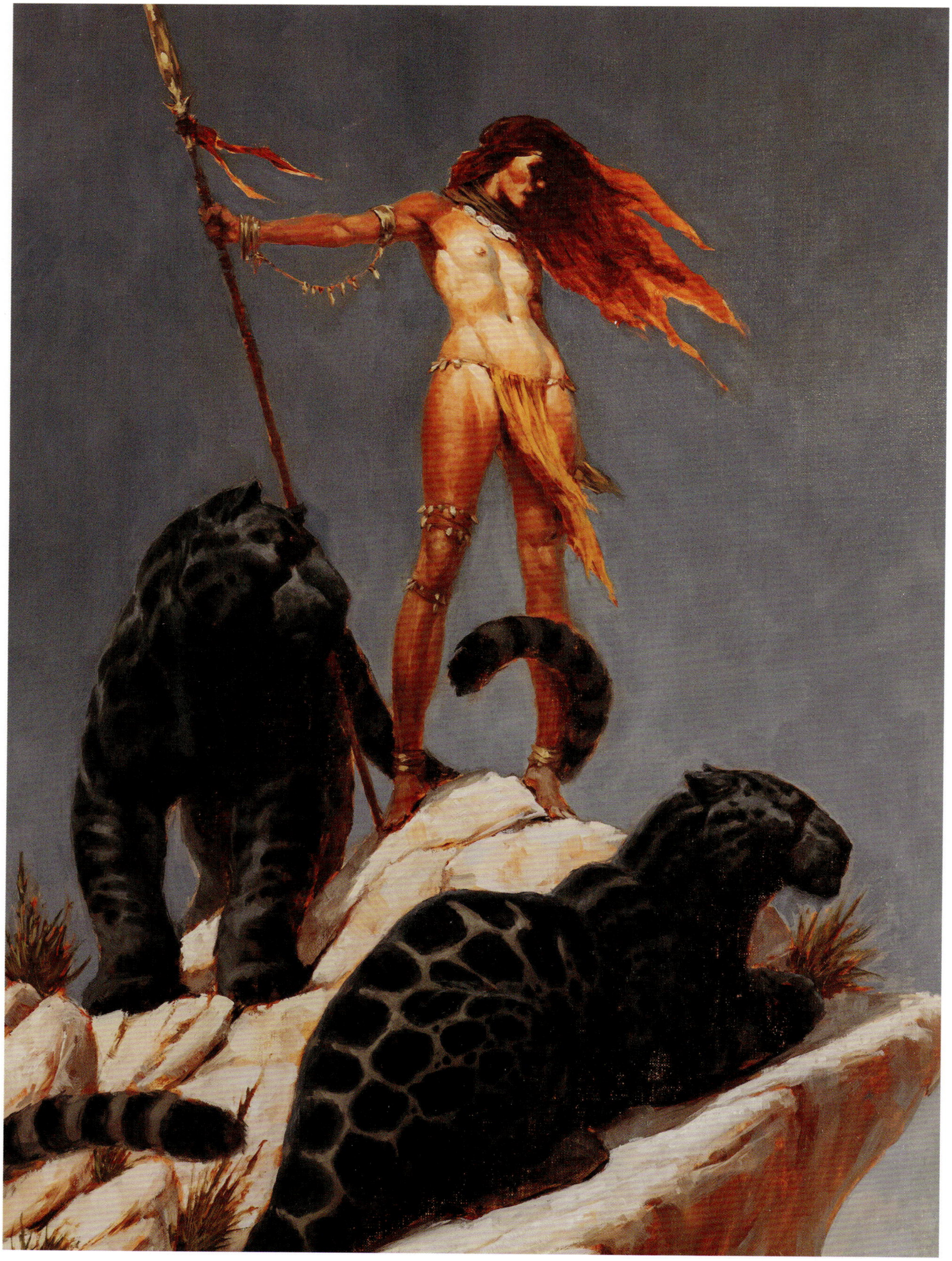

Final image © Daniel Landerman

The Nomads

by Daniel Landerman

Creating *The Nomads*

What do I love about Frazetta's art? Strong, primal warriors and strong, primal animals. I always loved drawing animals but Frazetta took them to a new level for me. The warriors and the creatures were one unit; they were equal and they respected each other. He also had a way of using oil paint as if it were watercolour, which was his preferred medium, and I always loved that. The range of opacity in his paintings allowed Frazetta to achieve great textures in a short amount of time. With this assignment, as you will see, I instantly thought, *'Warrior woman and big cats. Giant big cats! And oil paints!'* What can I say, I'm a cat guy! The challenge, always, is to paint them in a way that doesn't feel trite or out of place – to paint this primal fantasy world with some kind of credibility.

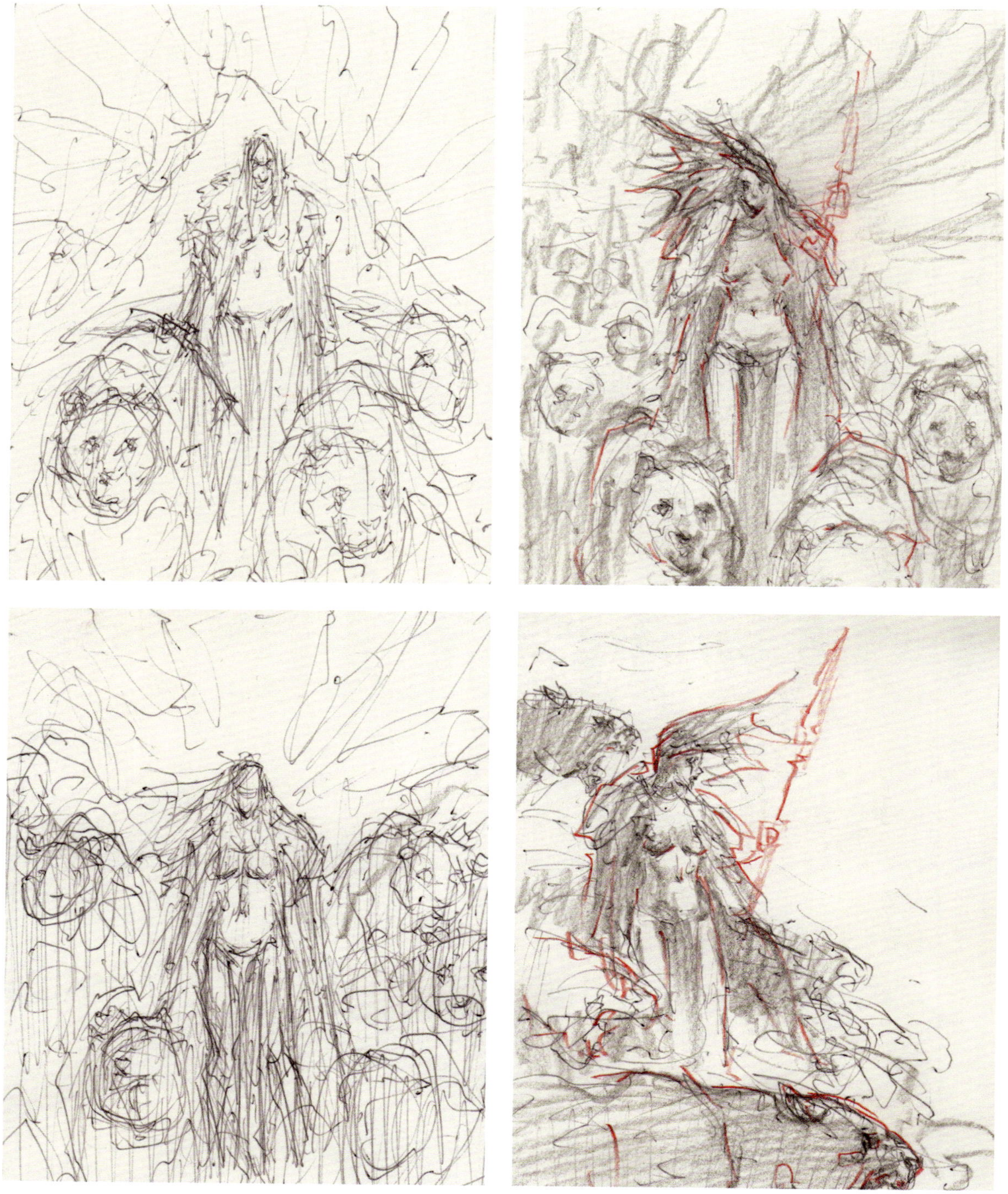

Ink and coloured-pencil thumbnails on an A5 Moleskine and A4 paper

01 Thumbnail sketches

My first step is always thumbnails, or at least very small sketches. Each is about A6-sized – small enough to not get caught up in tiny details, but big enough that I can get specific in some areas. I think about the mood I am trying to convey. What sort of composition might support that mood or narrative? I always use calligraphy ink for this step, as I can achieve a great organic feel by adding a little water, and the textures can do a lot of heavy lifting for me. The first few sketches here are just ballpoint pen and pencil, because those tools were close to hand, but I soon pull out my fountain pen, fill a cup with water, and grab my Winsor & Newton Series 7 #2 brush to use instead. I shade a bit afterwards with a Col-Erase Rose pencil, just because I like that look.

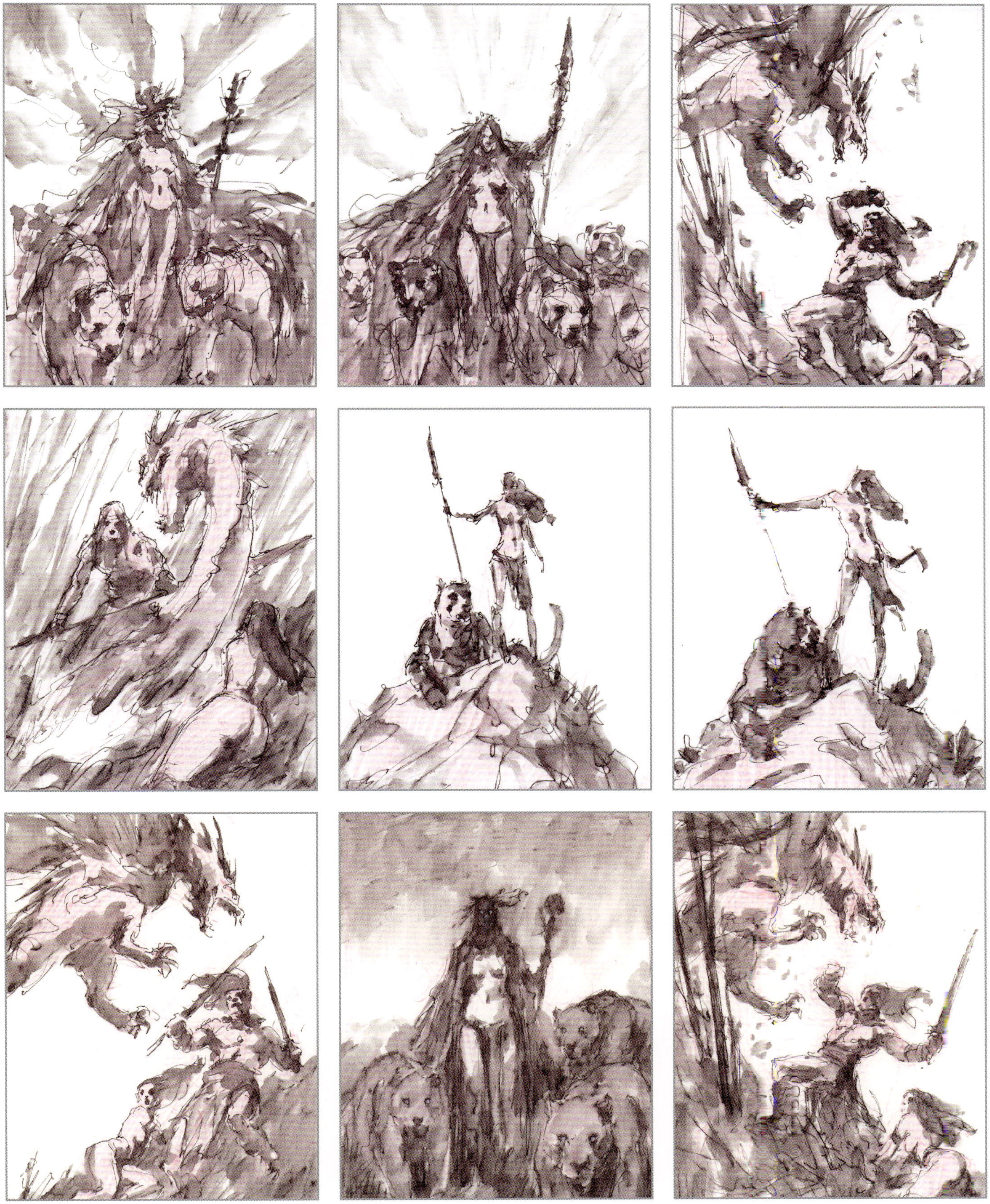

02 Composition sketches

As I begin to refine ideas, I like to be able to push and pull shapes and fine-tune compositions, so an erasable medium is a good way to go. I have a couple of ideas to run with, oscillating between a 'beast, warrior, damsel' story and a 'nomad woman, big cat' story. It's quite obvious which option I am leaning towards, but it's always good to explore options. One thing Frazetta excelled at was iconic compositions. Simple, striking, and powerful. In roughs ***b*** and ***c***, I toy with something a little 'quieter', which I often love doing, but as soon as ***f*** appears, I am sold on the potential of that gesture.

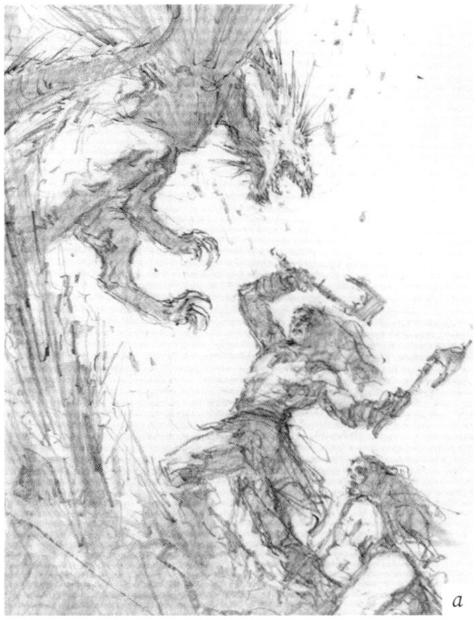

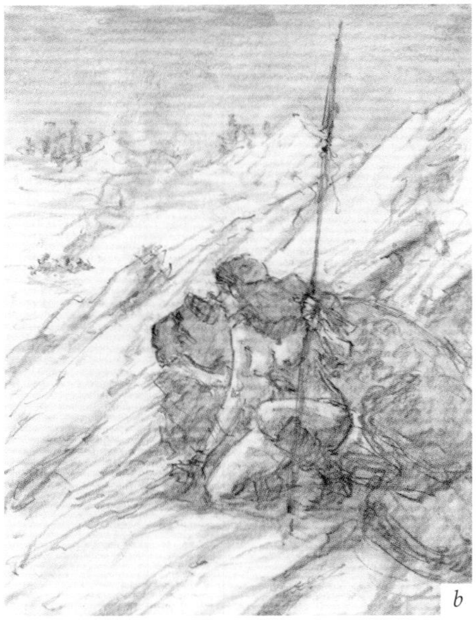

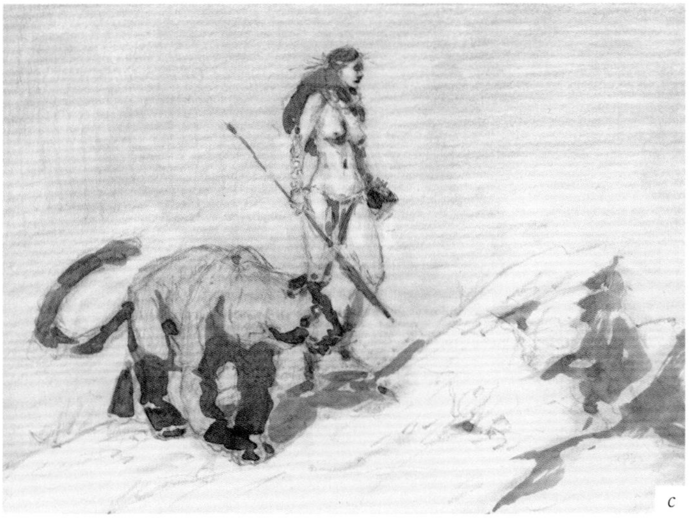

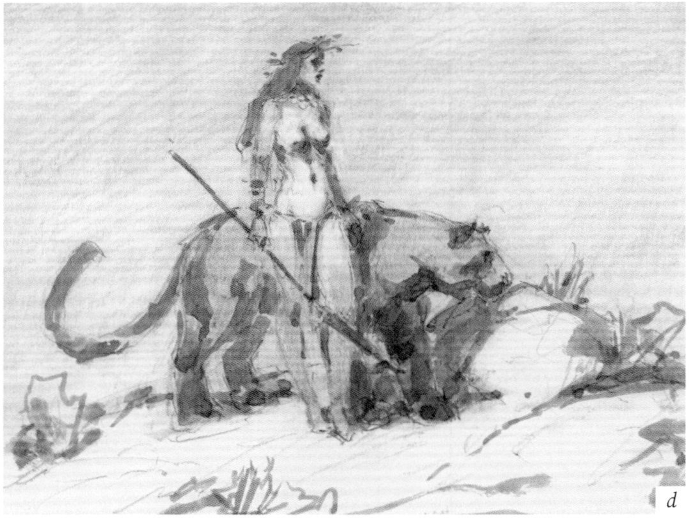

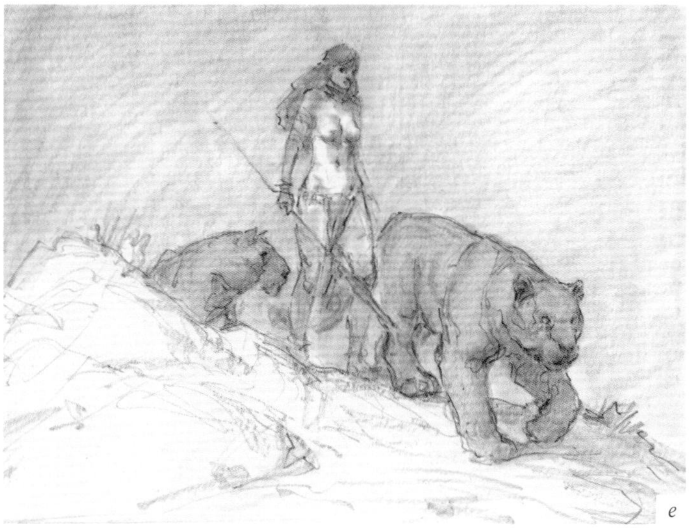

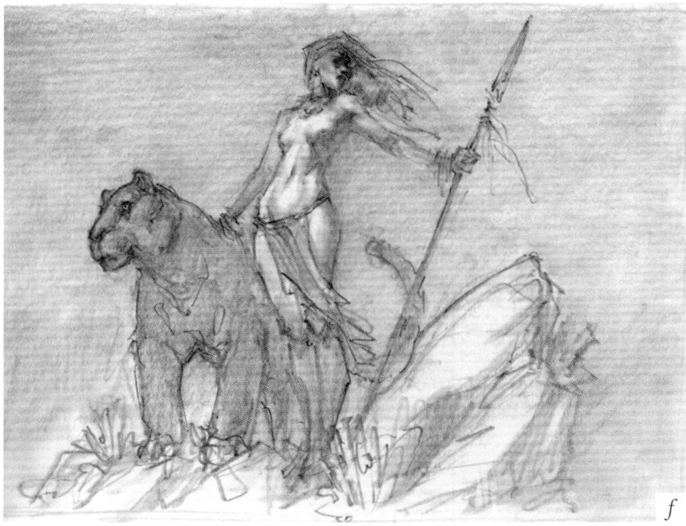

Roughly sketching on an A4 Moleskine using graphite or graphite with ink wash

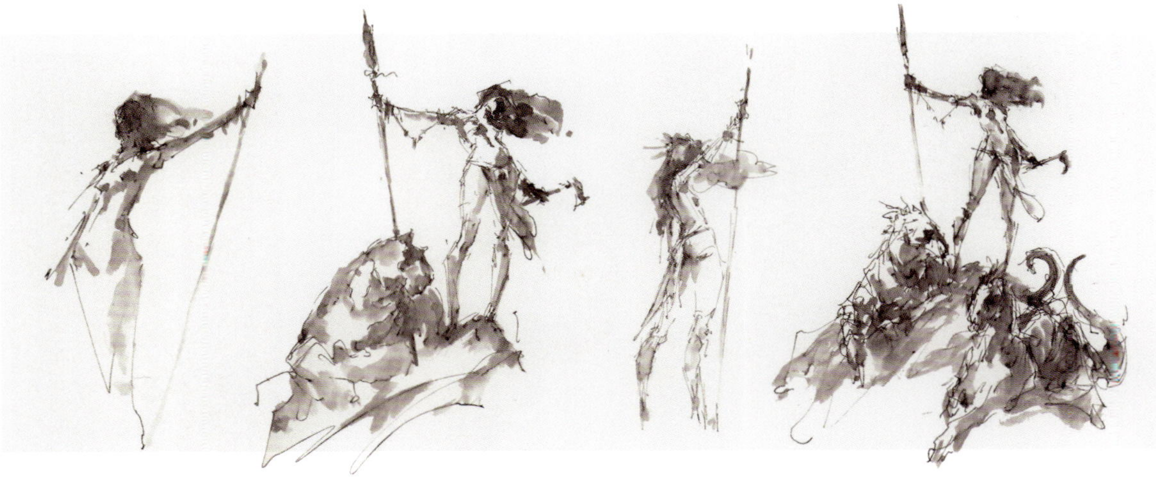

I even try introducing some dragons, which I decide against using!

03 Character gestures

In rough *f* I could already 'see' the colour palette and value grouping I want to use for the final. Artists such as Frank Frazetta, Jeffrey Catherine Jones, and Phil Hale often push the skin tone of a character's lighter torso and darker appendages far apart, more than is realistic if we think about it for too long, but the effect is visually powerful and appealing. But first, I need to figure out this gesture. I just want to get the right 'vibe' for the character and I realize that a vertical composition would work best.

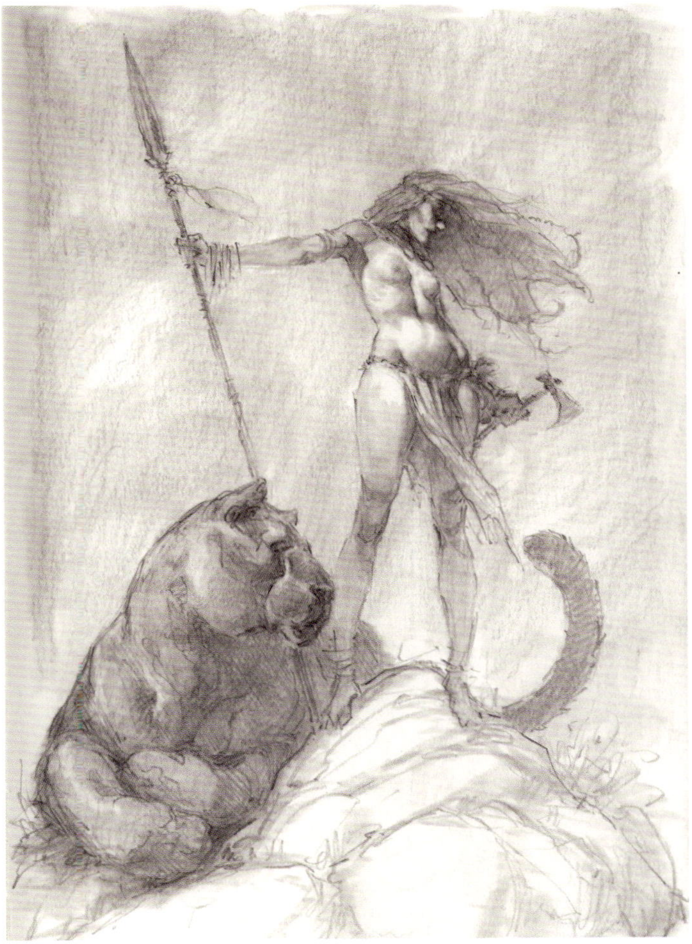

04 Base sketch

When making my larger base sketch, I consider more closely the mood I want from the poses of my nomad and her feline companion. I begin to think about the value structure as well as what sort of reference I might want to use. I based the cat on a black jaguar, so I look around online until I find a reference that has the type of bulk I am looking for, and something close to the angle I want as well. Reference doesn't need to be perfect; when drawing from reference, it is often better to push and change your interpretation a bit, especially if you are not working from your own photography.

Making a full-size sketch with the help of reference

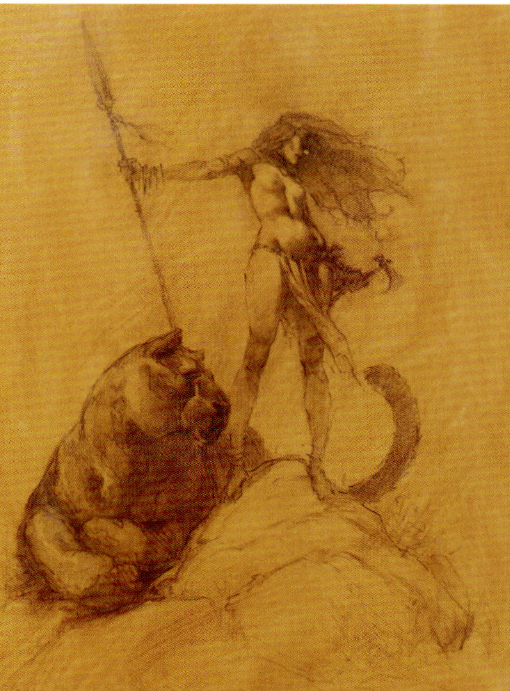

05 Base tone

Knowing that the final painting will be larger, ultimately 56 × 76 cm, I scan in my sketch and adjust it digitally to give the figures more breathing room. I want a sense of open air around them. I am now ready to start figuring out the colours, which I prefer to do in the same medium as the final painting, or at least something similar. In this case, I plan to use oil paints for most of it. I print out my sketch on heavyweight paper, 28 × 43 cm in size, add a layer of clear gesso on it, and then tone the entire page with a Transparent Yellow Iron Oxide oil paint. Even if I don't plan to use this colour in my final palette, I always make sure to cover up the white canvas as quickly as possible, whether I am working on a traditional or digital painting. I prefer working up and down in value from a midtone.

Adding an oil-paint wash of Transparent Yellow Iron Oxide over clear gesso

06 Limited palette

As I mentioned in step 03, I knew what my colour palette would be when I drew the last rough in step 02. I prefer working in a limited palette as it creates nearly automatic harmony in the final image without a struggle. I rely mostly on shifting value and saturation to give the impression of colour. For this traditional painting, I opt for Transparent Oxide-Red Lake, Indian Yellow, Titanium Zinc White, and Payne's Grey. Here you can see the range of colour I can achieve with this limited palette and how all the colours work very well together. If I were working digitally, I would start with an earthy monochrome painting and then nudge colour into it by barely moving the Hue slider.

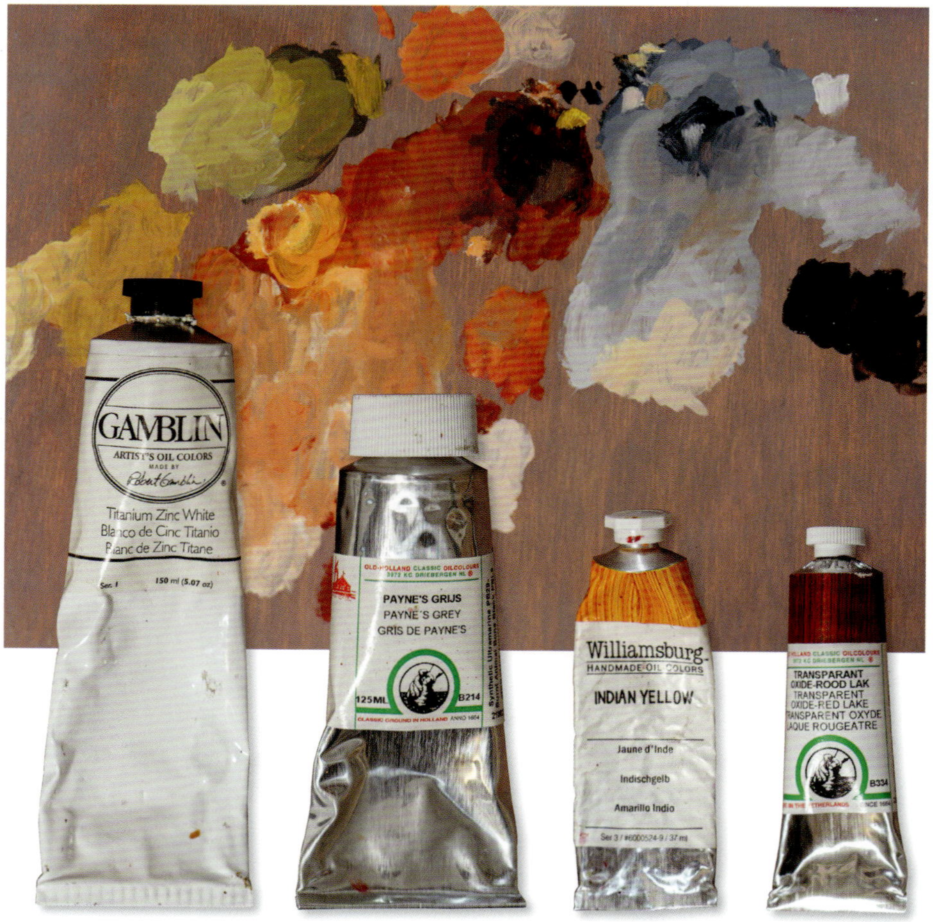

When using a limited palette, I restrict the saturation to one of the colours (in this case, Indian Yellow)

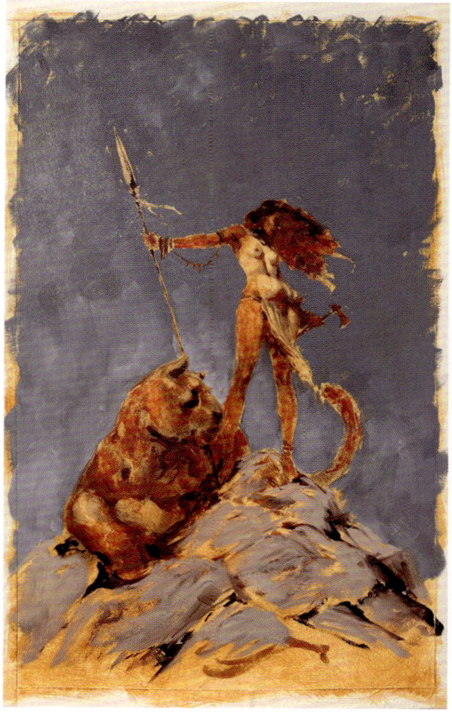

07 Blocking in colours

Now I start to block in colours. This test version is about a quarter of the final size; it could be smaller, but there are details I want to figure out, so I opt for slightly larger. You can see how blue the Payne's Grey looks when mixed with white and placed next to something as warm as the Oxide-Red. The next thing I do is place my darkest and lightest values, which helps establish a clear value range to work within. Not every image needs to go to pure black or white and bracketing my values helps create a more believable sense of light.

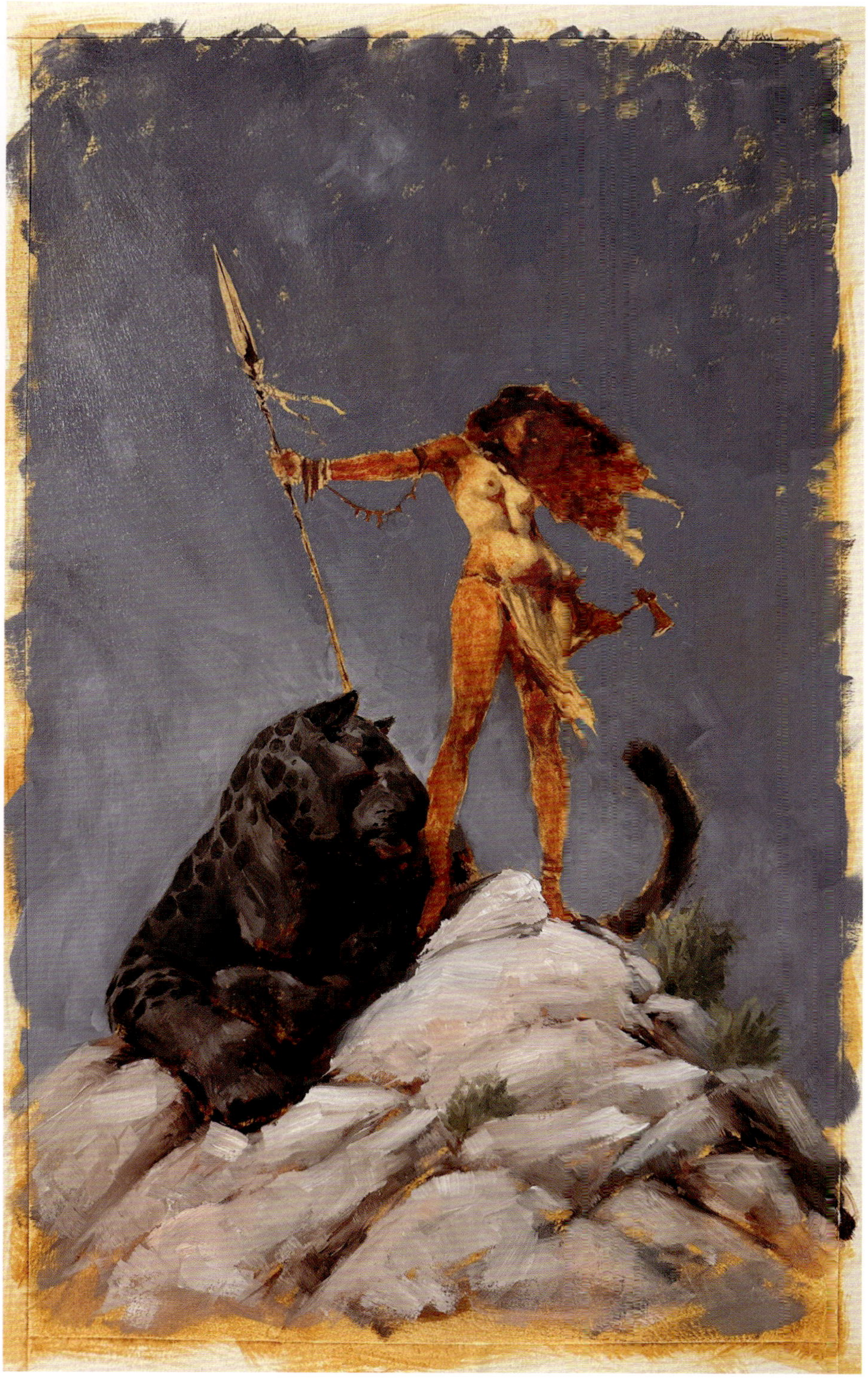

Considering first the value structure and then how the colour palette might support that structure

08 Chosen palette

This colour rough takes three to four hours of work, so I now have a strong composition and colour scheme without having sunk a lot of time into it. Some edges have been softened and pushed back using 'simultaneous contrast' (the effect of two colours side by side with the same value, but different hues or saturation), while other edges are carved out strongly for a pleasing graphic treatment. Some of these elements will make it through to my final version, while some may still change a little. The main goal here is to make sure I have the values and colours worked out. However, true to form, I am already wondering, 'What if I just did *this*...?'

09 What if...?

So, what if this character had *two* giant cats? While the rocks are technically an element, I would rather have three living elements, as the viewer will really be looking at the character and creatures. I return to my sketchbook to see if I like the idea, and decide that I do. I like the feeling and potential for narrative that the two cats lend, though I change their poses. This sketch just confirms that I am on the right track. Three elements are better than two!

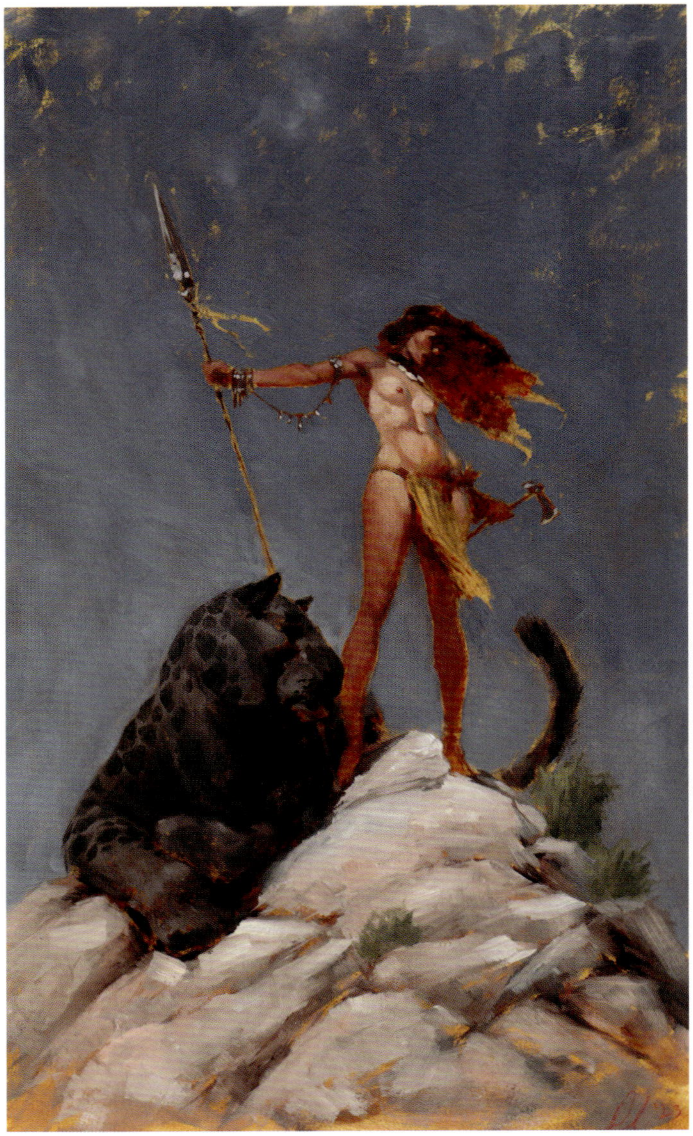

The final colour draft, painted with oils on 28 × 43 cm paper

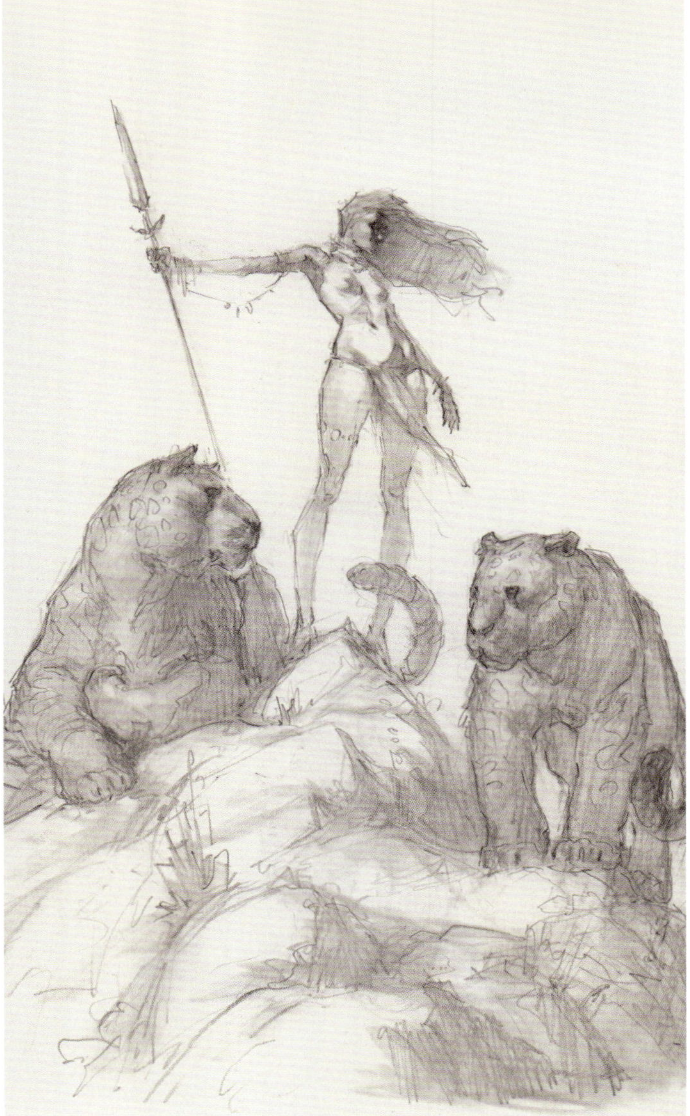

Making a quick revised sketch in my A4 Moleskine sketchbook

10 Digital fine-tuning

Knowing I want to add another cat, I scan in my colour sketch and bring it into Procreate. All I need to do is colour-pick and paint the new elements. I want to create the feeling that the characters are high up, so I decide to cut away at the rocks, losing the plants in the process. I also adjust the ratio to properly match the final 56 × 76 cm canvas and fine-tune the composition accordingly. Now I have all the poses and colour information I need to jump into the final piece – the hardest parts have all been figured out and I can just have fun painting. If the final was digital, I would just increase the resolution and start painting, but in this case, I'll return to a physical medium.

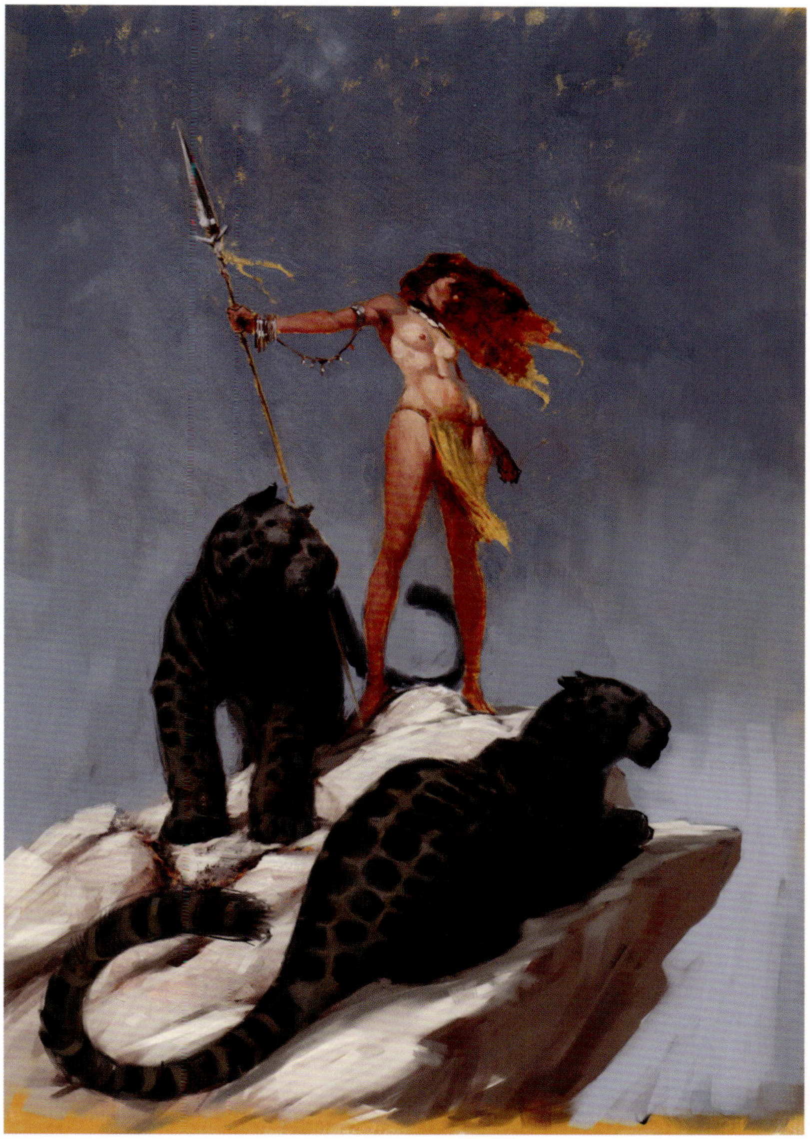

Revising the composition by editing the oil painting in Procreate

11 Projecting the image

To begin creating the final painting, I need to transfer the composition to a linen panel. I do this with a 1080p projector. I simply project the digital sketch onto my panel, set the size to what I want, and then trace the projection with pencil. I often make slight tweaks along the way. For example, once I see the image at full scale, I decide to scale the characters down slightly to give them more breathing room in the composition.

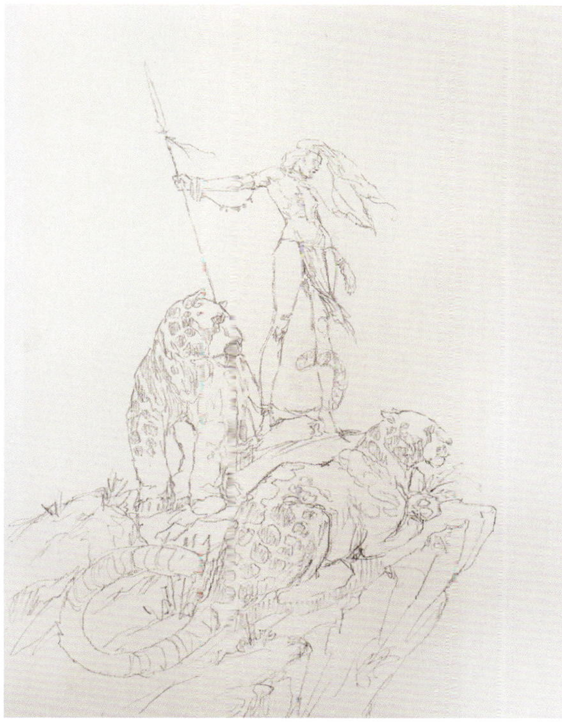

Transferring the image to a linen panel using a projector

12 New base tone

In step 05, I used Transparent Yellow Iron Oxide to tone down the white paper. As I am not using Yellow Iron Oxide in the rest of my palette, I stick to my four colours, using Transparent Oxide-Red Lake as a base tone instead. I always let some of my underpainting show through in the final, and I know I want that warm red peeking out in places. Here you can also see that I am second-guessing the undercut of the rock!

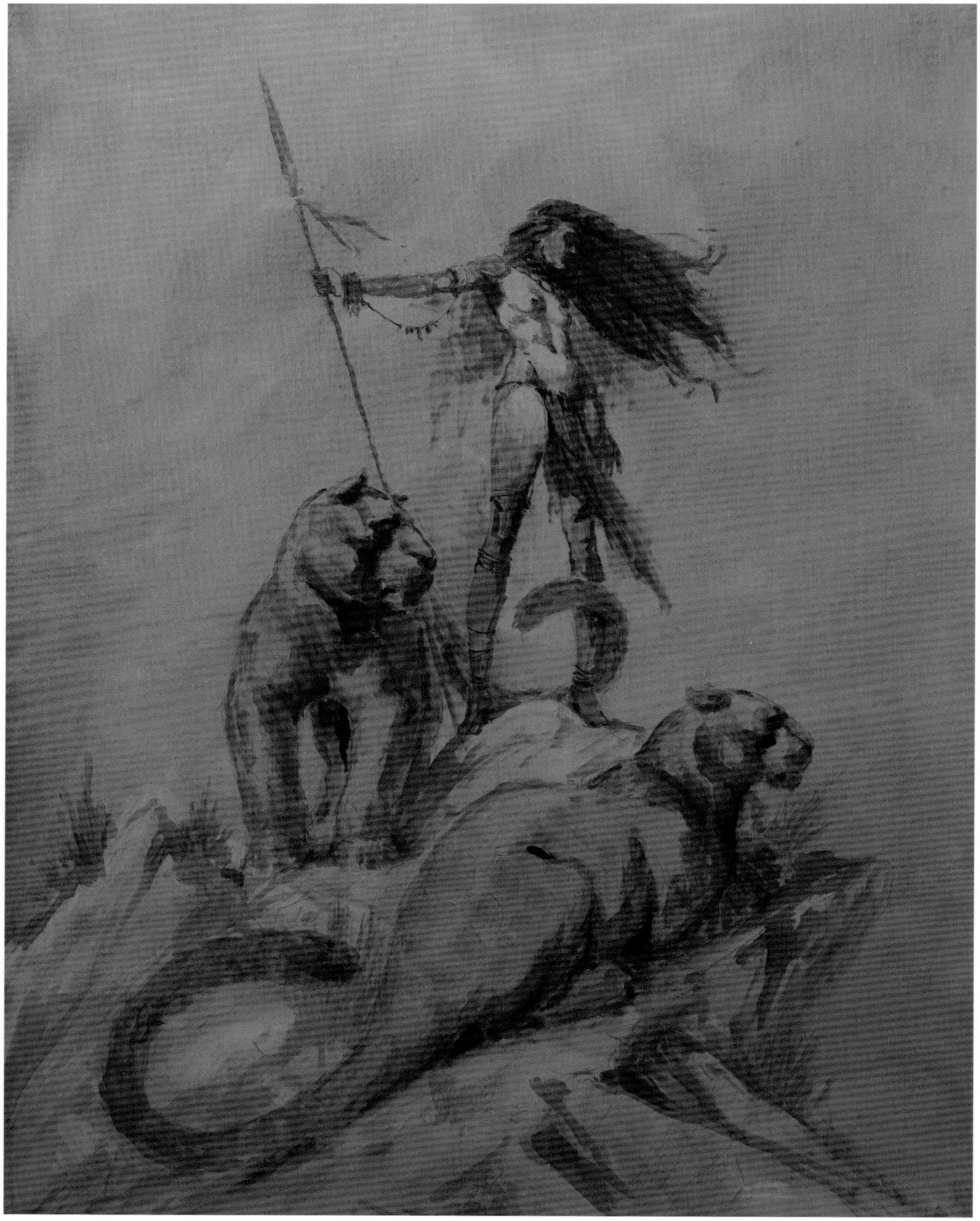

Painting washes of Transparent Oxide-Red Lake on a linen panel

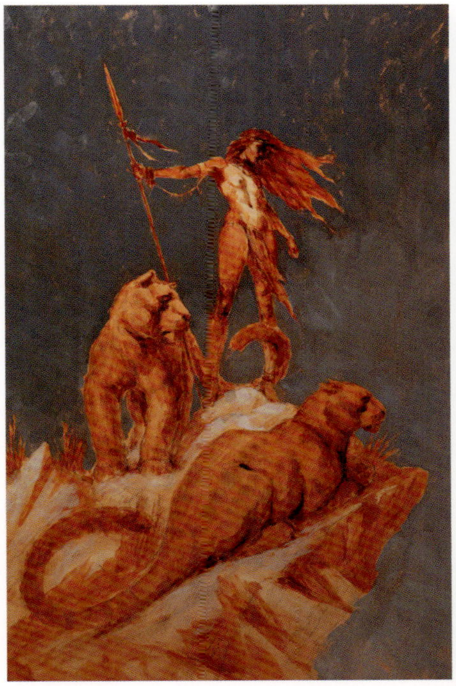
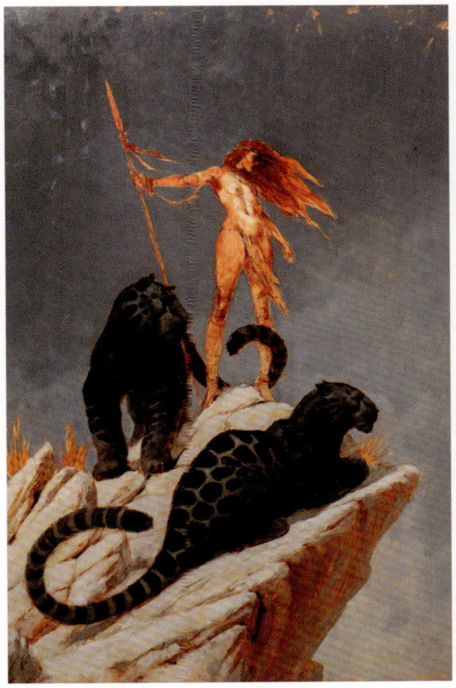
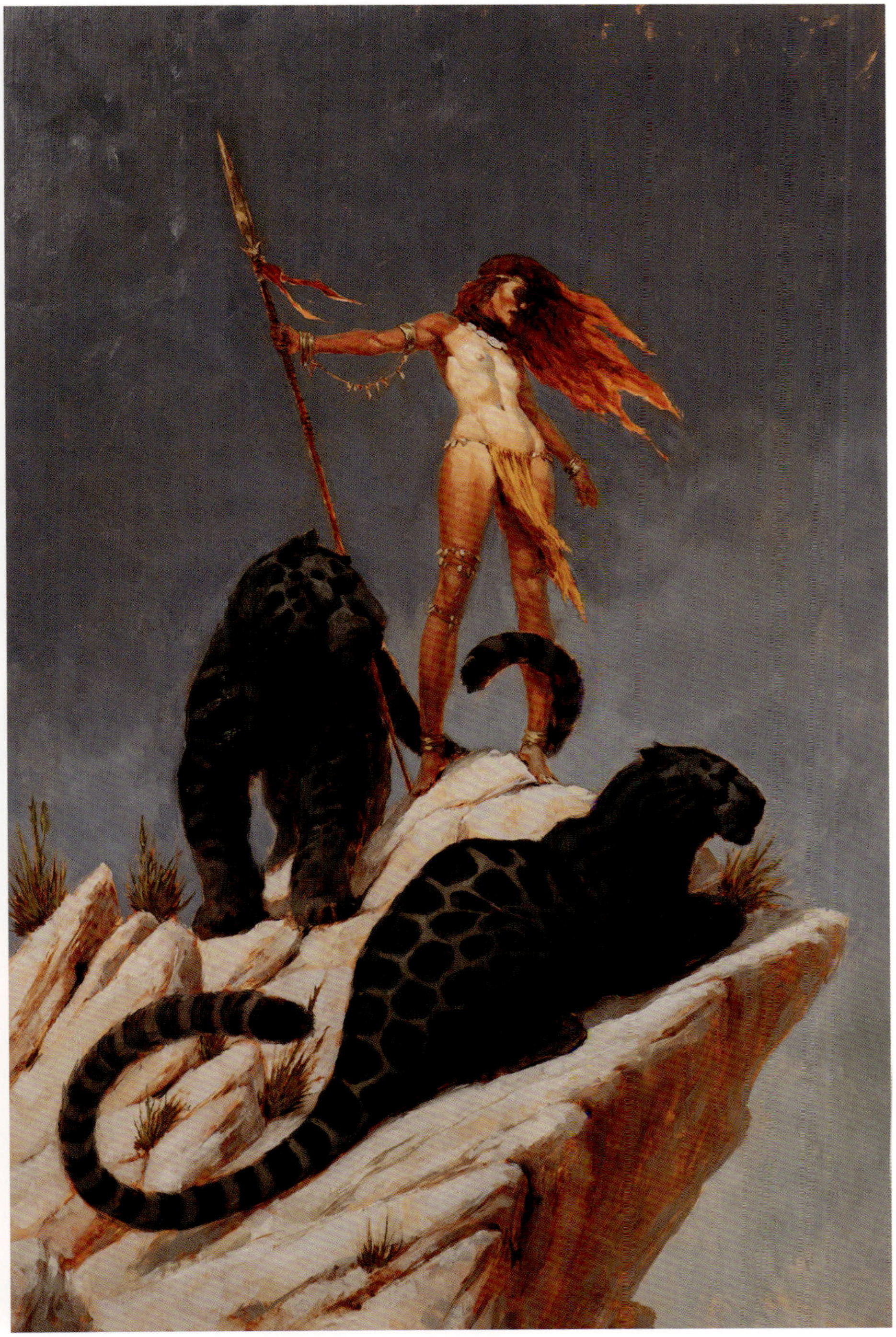

13 Painting process

Thankfully I veto my second-guess of the rock shape, but I do make one mistake here due to my impatience. In step 05, I waited for the yellow wash to dry, but this time I don't wait long enough and the Oxide-Red mixes with the Payne's Grey in the sky. I end up having to do another pass once the sky has dried a bit, to make it as blue-feeling as it can be. Like with step 07, I block in the sky first, followed by the lightest and darkest values. I also bring back the bushes that were lost in step 10, as I feel the image desperately needs those greens. At the end of this step, I decide that the painting is finished – I had ordered a custom frame and couldn't wait to see it all together!

The full limited palette on display: Transparent Oxide-Red Lake, Indian Yellow, Titanium Zinc White, and Payne's Grey

Discovering Frazetta

I had seen Frazetta's work often as a child without knowing who he was. I would go into the music store and see Molly Hatchet album covers hanging on the wall; I was fascinated with *Death Dealer I*, but it hung above the door beyond my reach.

It wasn't until I was seventeen or eighteen (the late 1990s) when I was in a bookstore perusing the art section that I found the Frazetta art book *ICON* by Arnie and Cathy Fenner. It had a compelling cover and some beautiful pencil drawings, as well as pen-and-ink art that made my head spin. When I reached the gallery section and saw the close-up of *Egyptian Queen*, I was mesmerized. At the time, spending thirty-five dollars on a book was a big deal for me, but I couldn't get *Egyptian Queen* out of my head. I looked through the whole book multiple times and connected the dots between the album covers I had spied as a kid and this amazing artist named Frank Frazetta.

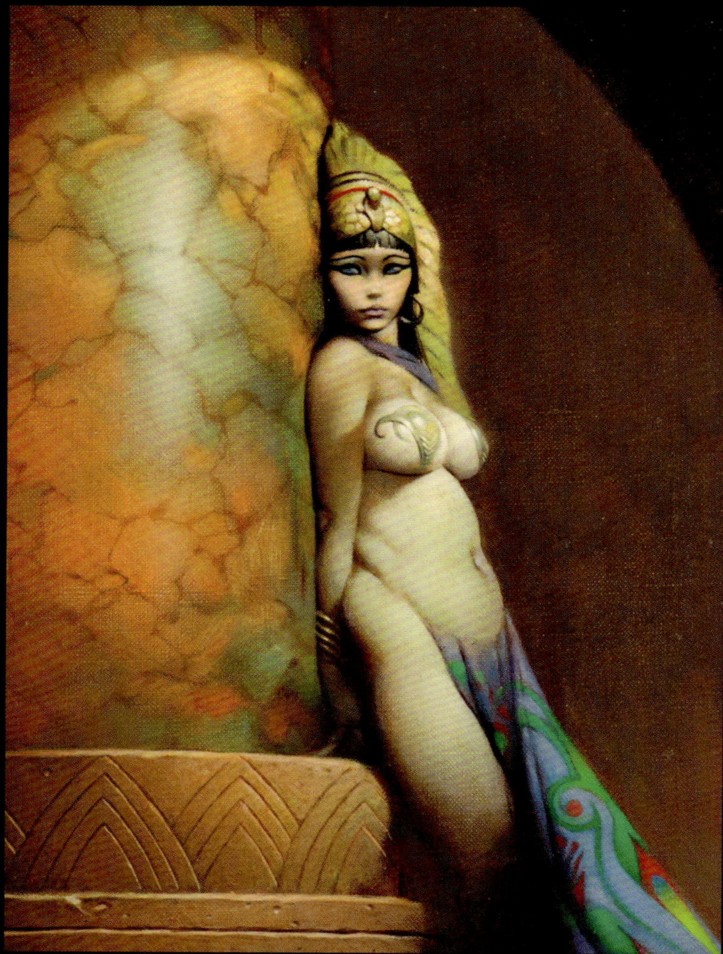

Egyptian Queen © Frank Frazetta

I think I spent another couple of days debating the purchase but ultimately felt I didn't have a choice. He seemed to be an artist who was doing what I wanted to do: painting and drawing worlds that I wanted to create in, and doing it all with a very serious respect for the craft. He did not think fantasy and sci-fi art was silly. He loved it and lived it.

Finding Frazetta changed my life because he changed how I considered and approached art. Frazetta made me want to create 'fantasy fine art', too. Now I ask myself what a Cornwell-Frazetta or a Waterhouse-Frazetta might look like and I try to paint that.

For image in full, turn to page 197

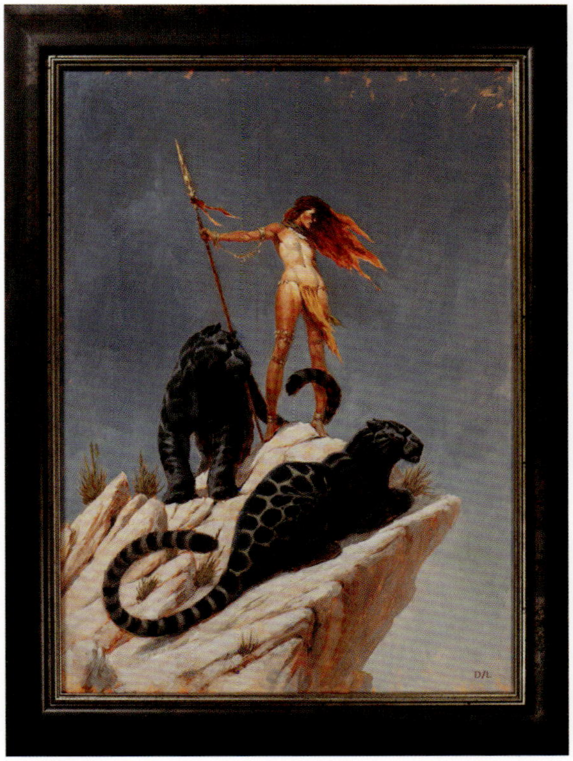

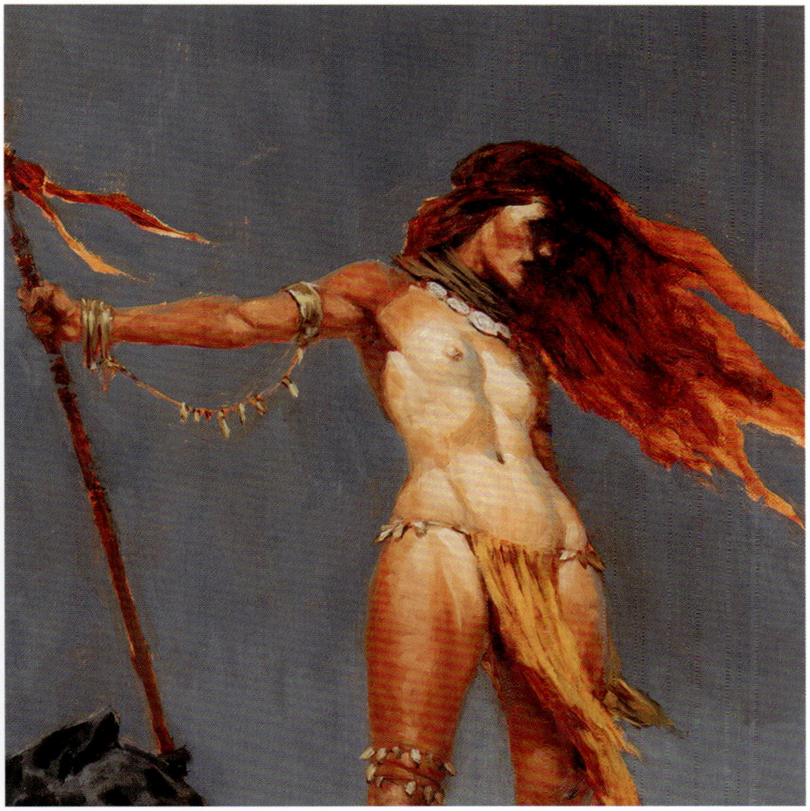

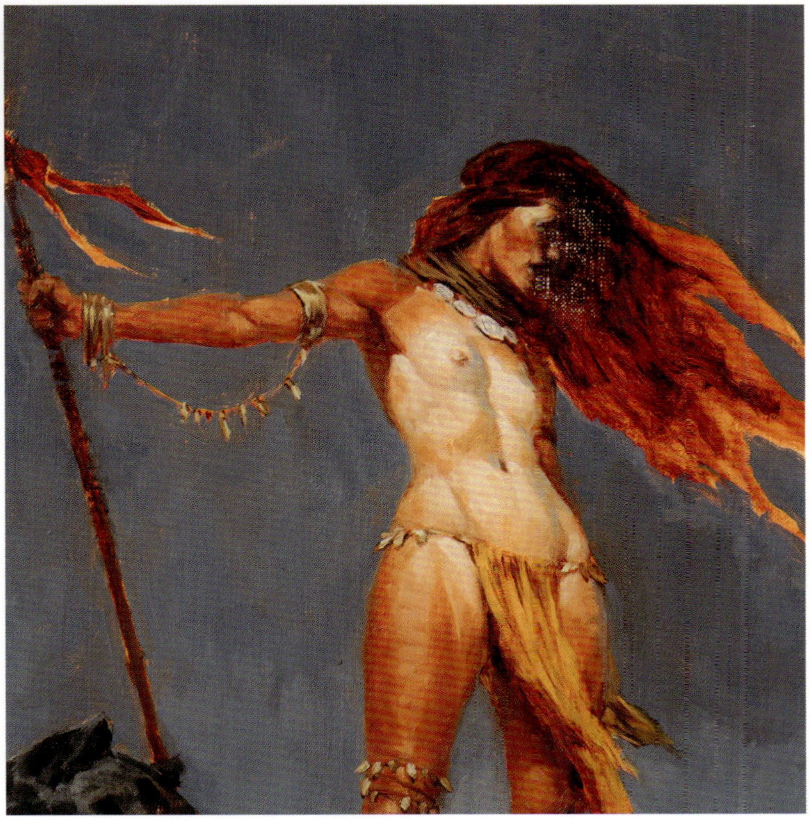

It's never too late to make corrections – even if the painting is already framed!

14 What if, again...

'*What if I just did...*' strikes again. The nomad's back arm is bothering me and I need to push her head forward a little in value. I want the cats to have more colour variation as well. All of this needs to be painted in physically, as I can't just nudge things or use Liquify like I might for a digital piece. I make those changes, sign the painting... and then notice that some of the shadows are a little too dark and opaque. I prefer to have more 'air' in my shadows. Luckily, this is nothing a little sandpaper cannot fix. I simply rub the shadows around her face and on the cats with sandpaper and paint light washes over them again.

15 The framed final

Now the image is *really* done. I like the colour play and the range of values. I am happy with the feeling of the light and the composition, and how the frame complements the palette. Presentation is always worth pondering, whether it is a digital or physical image. Frames are the last element you should take into account, as there's a finality to them. You may choose no frame, which should be a very deliberate choice. Digitally, the choice might be as simple as a flat white or black frame. Either way, the frame is something that will encapsulate the image in its own world, like a window through which we are glimpsing the story. It's well worth considering.

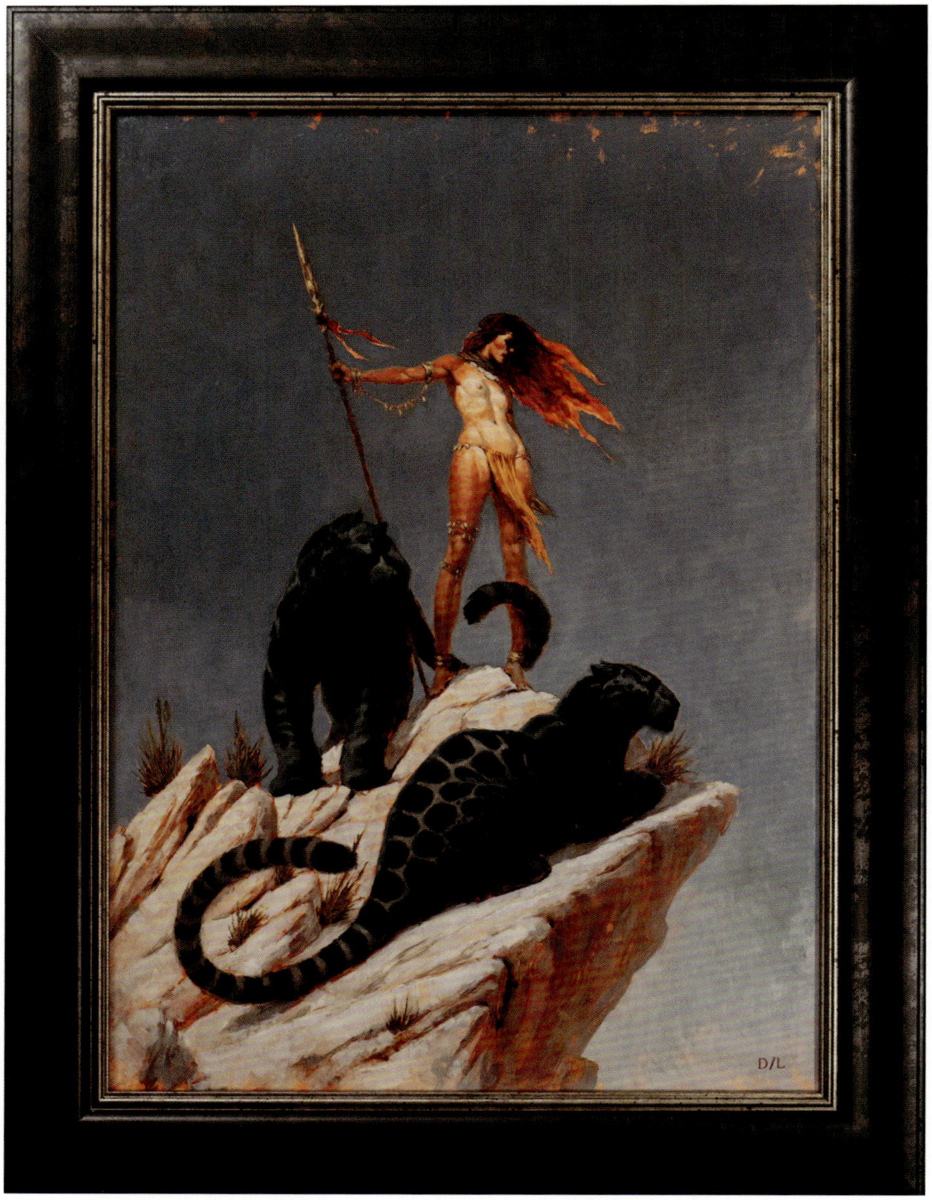

The final painting is 56 × 76 cm, made with oils on RayMar L64C linen ACM panel

Conclusion

Frazetta was so adept at capturing a sense of wild wonder, and I hope I did the grandmaster of fantasy art justice in some small way. My goal here was to give a sense of time and place – I wanted to capture a feeling that something happened before this moment and something is going to happen after, and encourage the viewer to create that narrative for themselves.

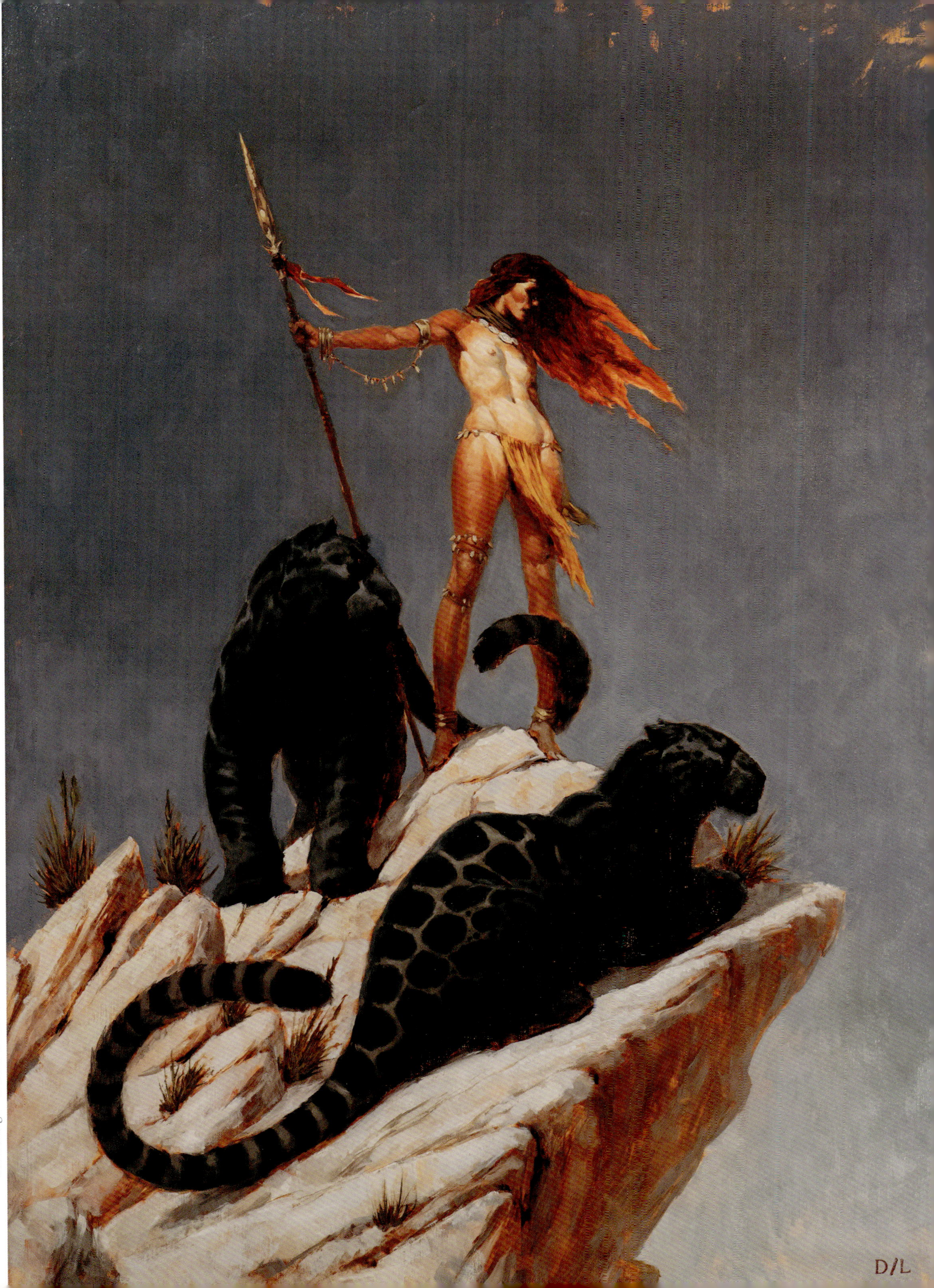
D/L

Gallery

by Daniel Landerman

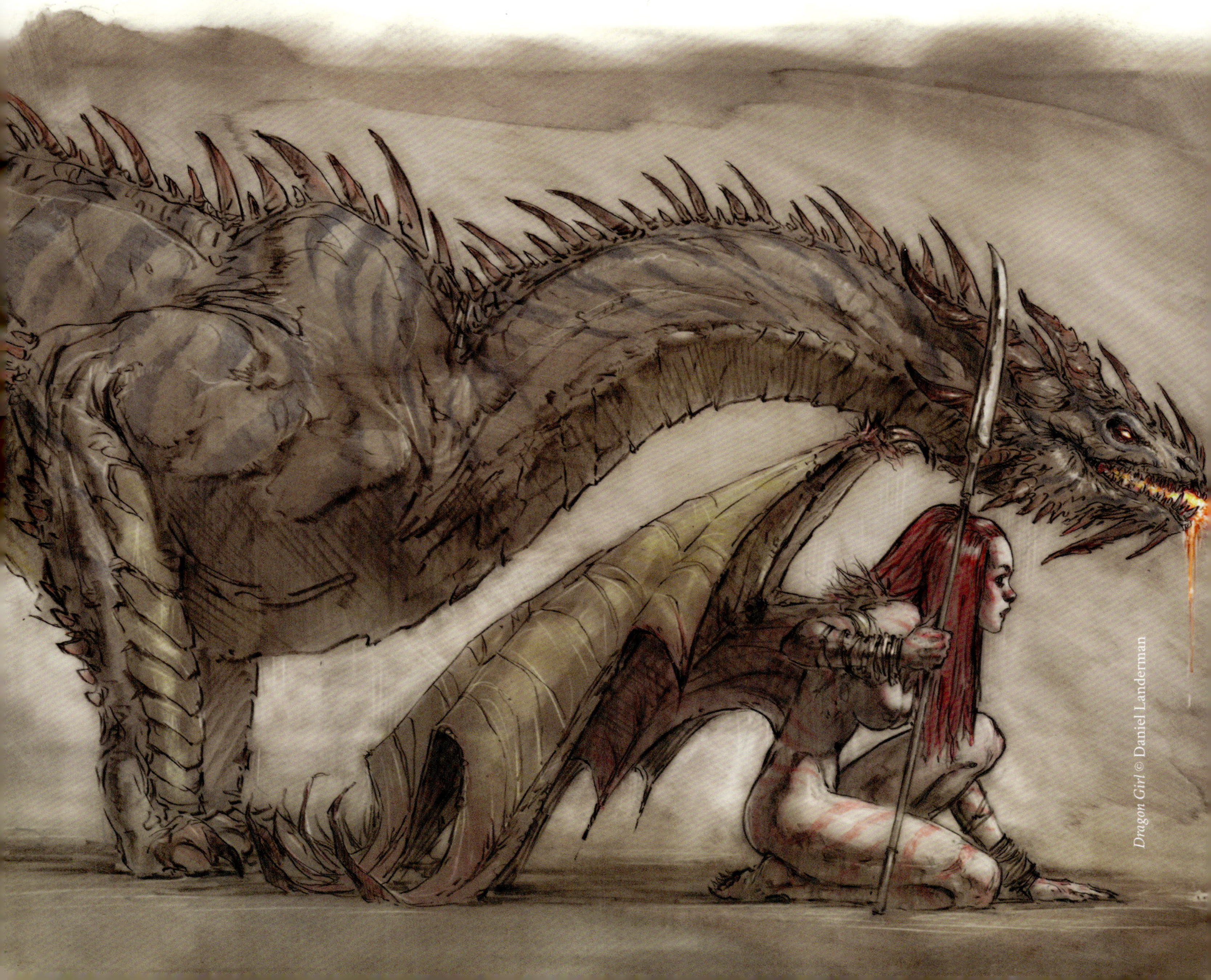

Dragon Girl © Daniel Landerman

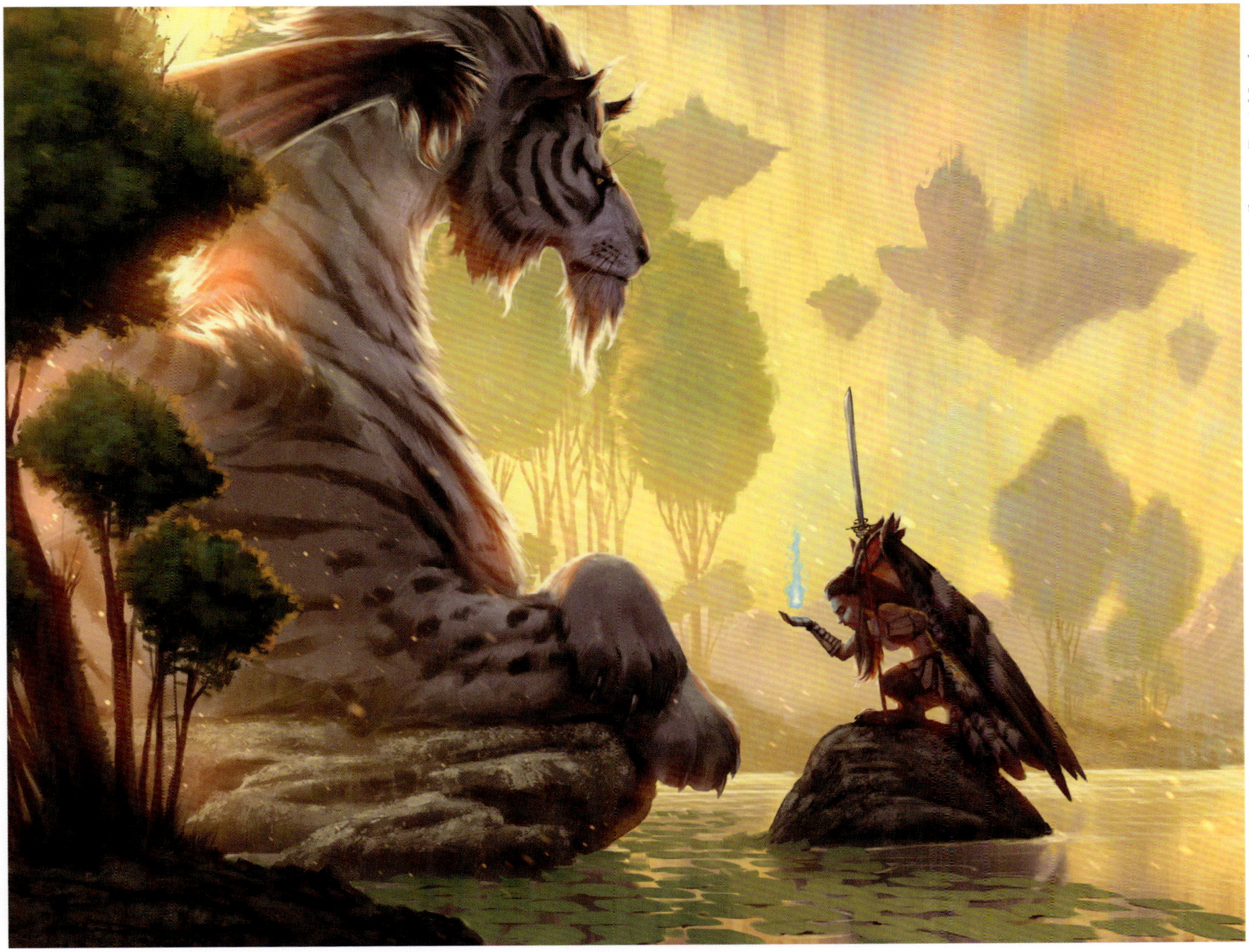

The Offering © Daniel Landerman

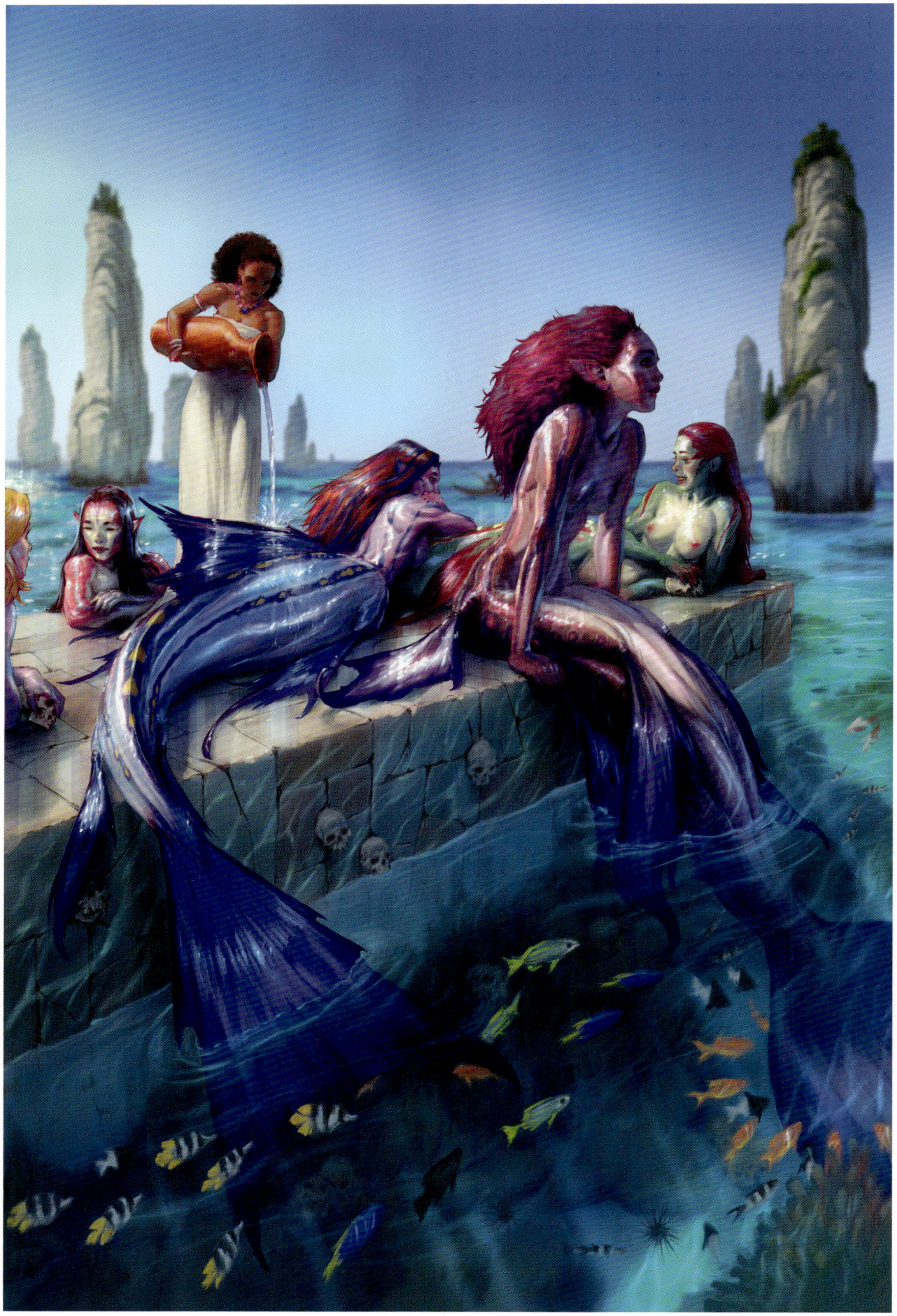

Azure Gardens © Daniel Landerman

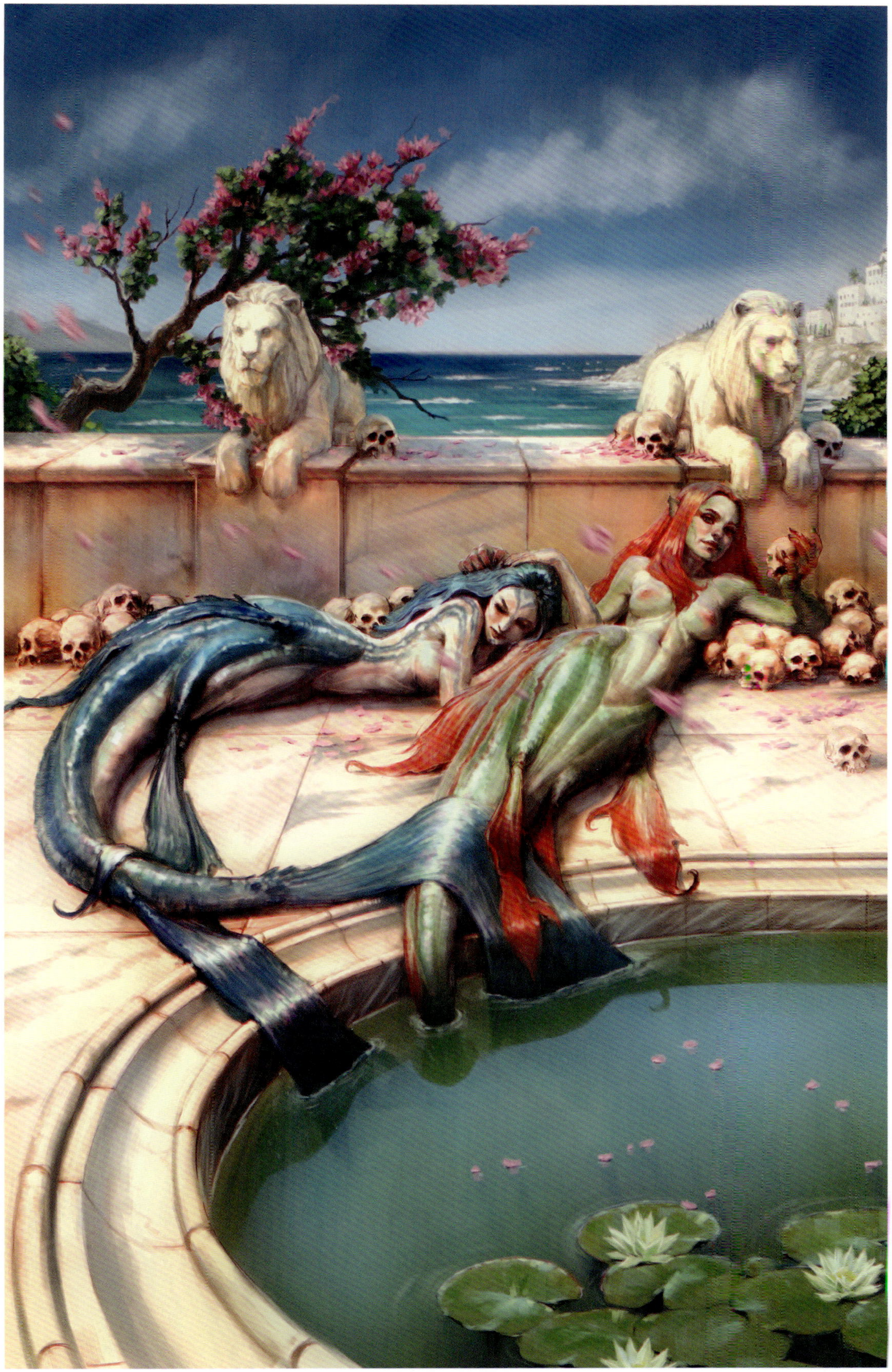

Maiden Isles © Daniel Landerman

Final image © Anato Finnstark

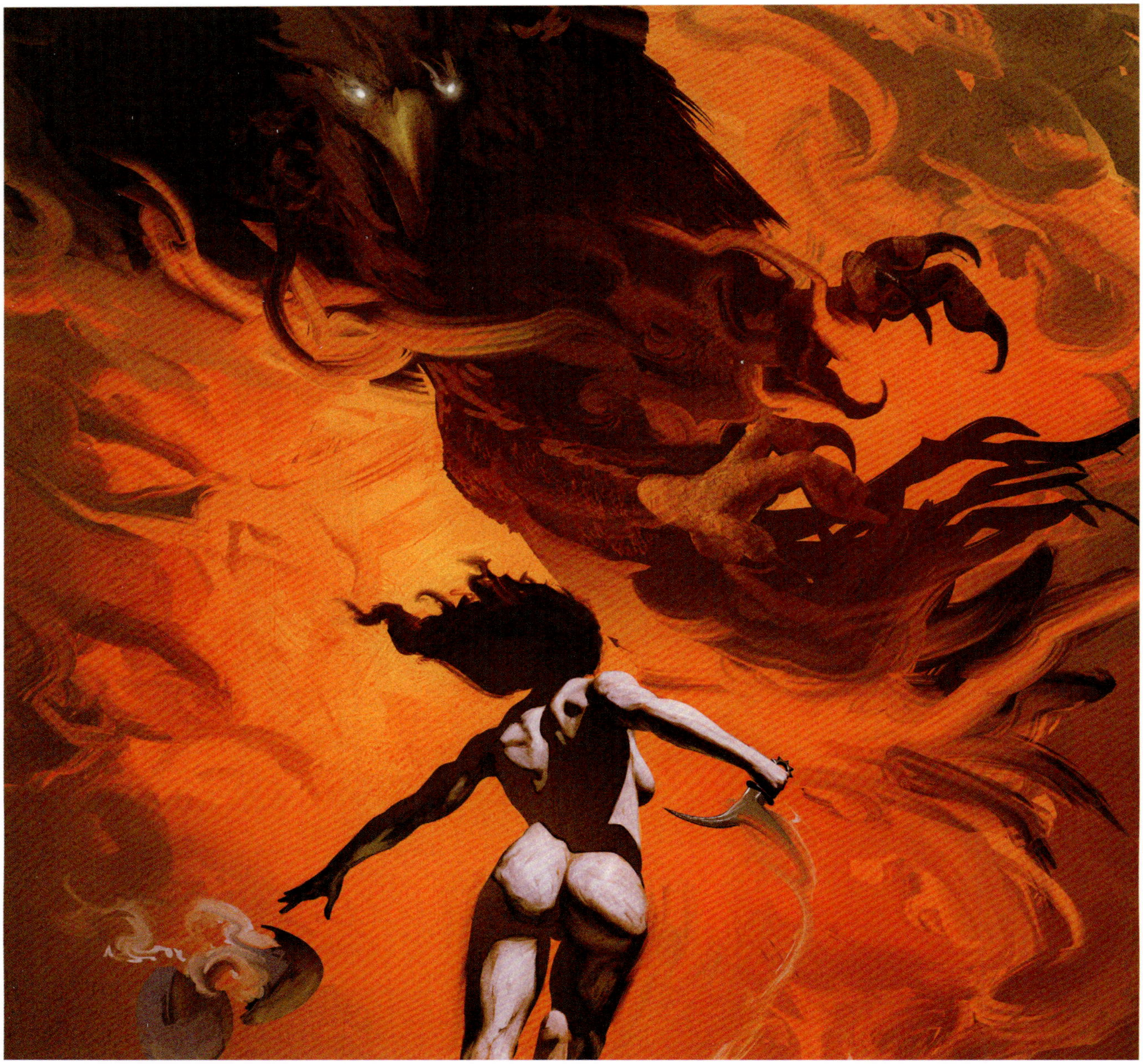

by Anato Finnstark

Momen

Creating *Momentum*

Frank Frazetta is like a muse permanently perched on my shoulder. He instils a lot of humility in me because I know the weight of his influence has been major for countless artists around the world and across the years. I know I'm not the only one to be inspired by his work, which pushes me to take this influence with a lot of reflection. It would be easy to succumb to the temptation of just emulating his work, without really understanding the value his influence has on my art. I don't want my work to just be 'sub-Frazetta', so I try to take his creations as a source of inspiration and symbolic motivation, and not as a model to follow. It would be easy to get lost in the vision of such a great artist. Styles are built with experience and regular practice; Frazetta had his own experience and way of working, and his art is the result, just as I have my own way of working and living.

What I like about Frazetta's work above all is his way of being direct in his art. I never knew him personally, but his art transmits something 'uncompromising'. His characters have fantastical bodies; their movements are at the limit of muscle rupture; they are alive and we can feel how much he liked to put them in extreme positions throughout his epic scenes. Through his paintings, we can feel his love of human anatomy, flesh, and muscle.

tum

In this project, I will try to capture a theme that Frank Frazetta knew how to do best: the moment before the impact. It's something I particularly like, because the suggestion of an event to come is sometimes much more evocative than the event itself. This is what I want to convey in this illustration, and why it is called *Momentum*. My goal is to capture the instant before the action resolves – the evocative power of 'something to come' that leaves room for the imagination and allows the viewer to decide what outcome will follow. Who will win this duel? Is this fight already lost? If so, for whom does the death knell sound?

01 General composition

It is important to determine where you want to place your main elements, in a very simple way, using simple geometric shapes. This allows you to have an early idea of the image's balance. Here I have chosen an hourglass-shaped composition to make a strong, symmetrical visual impact, but you will see later that this was not the wisest choice!

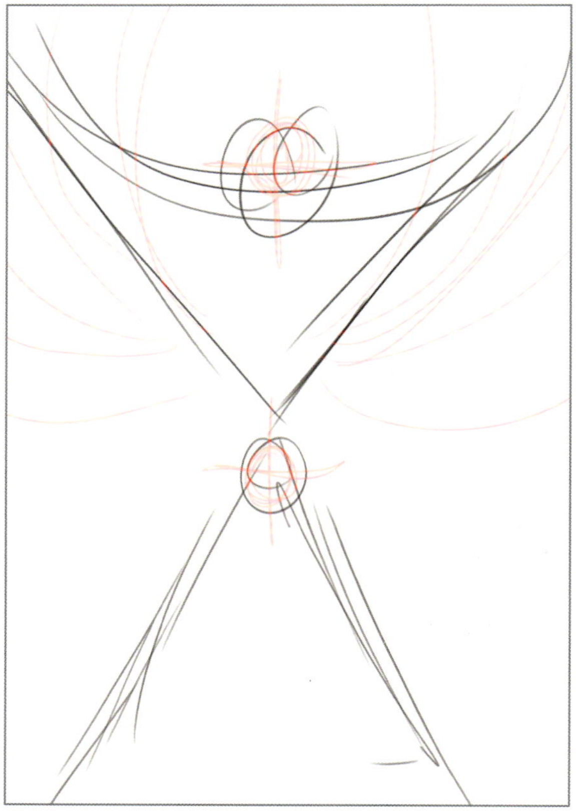

Sketching a very rough, simple plan for the composition

02 Simple sketch

I usually make a simple sketch to lay a few lines down before the next step, or sometimes I start directly in value, but it is very rare that I push a sketch to a detailed level. The red lines here indicate the movement of the woman in the foreground – it is a useful visual landmark so I do not lose sight of the dynamism I want from the scene.

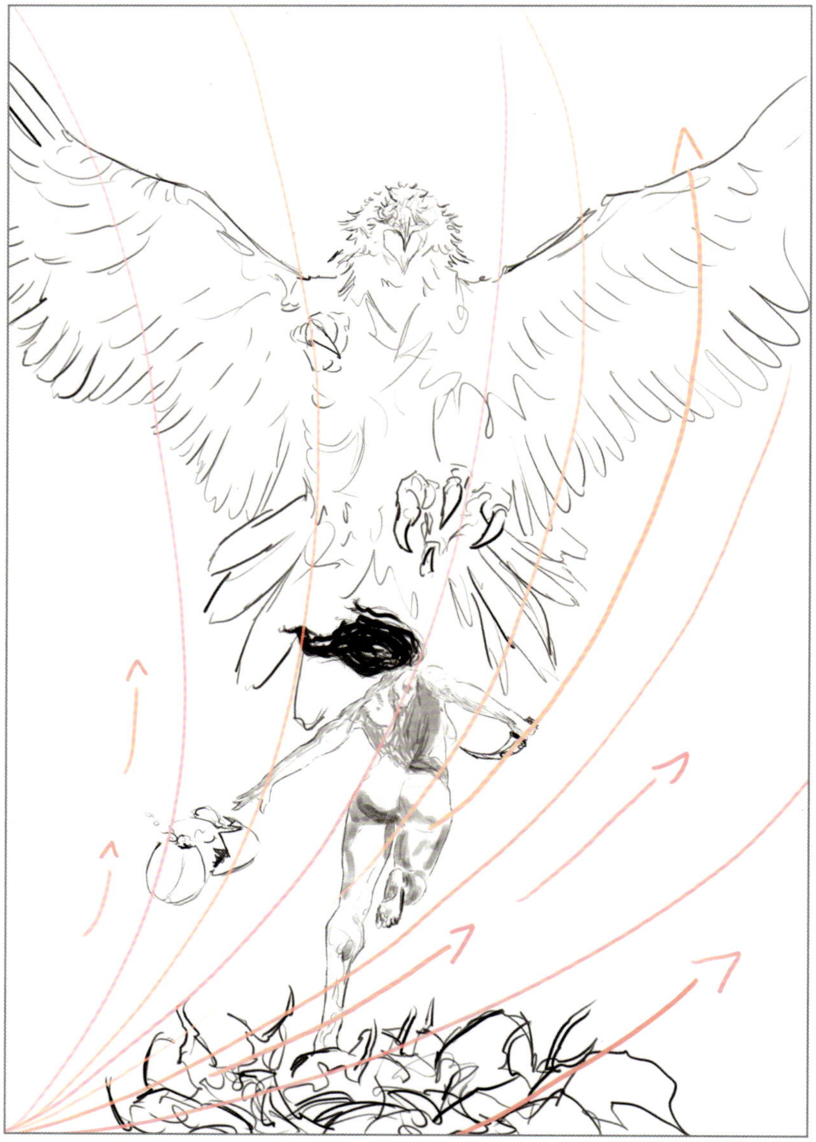

Loosely sketching the two main figures and the image's general flow

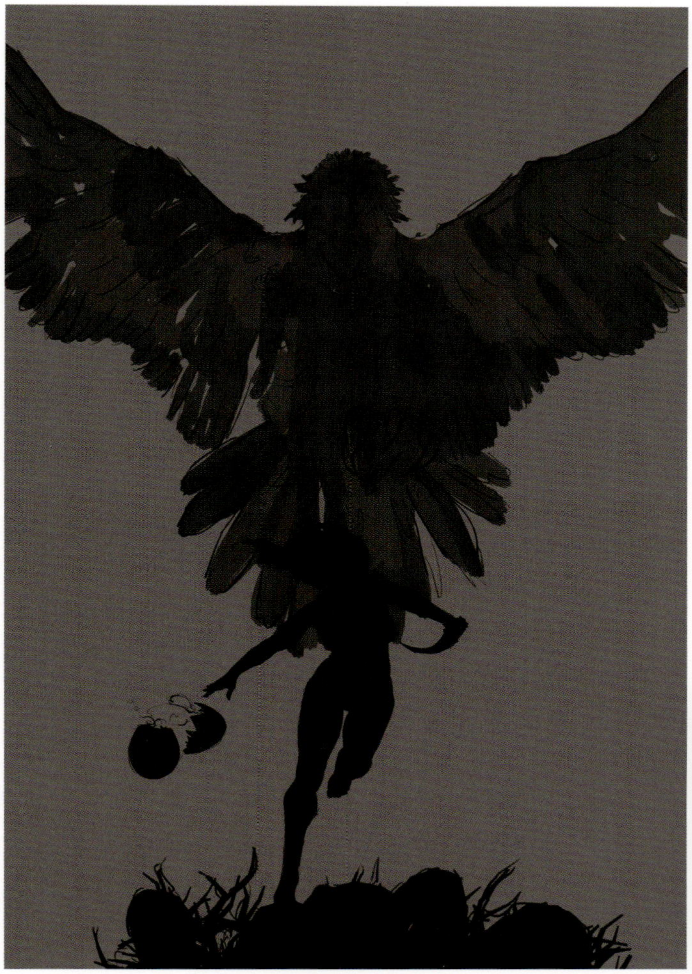

Adding initial greyscale values to the composition

03 Silhouettes

Next I fill out the silhouettes with simple grey values. Blocking out the dark values anchors the subjects in the image and helps me understand their placement in the composition. The woman and eagle's nest are closer to the viewer, therefore darker and more distinct, while the huge eagle is a medium grey, further back in the composition but still creating an imposing silhouette.

04 Background light

I define a background light source in order to clarify the silhouettes and give them more impact. Dynamic, random brushstrokes give substance and movement to the background; they will be revised and refined as more colour and lighting is added to the image.

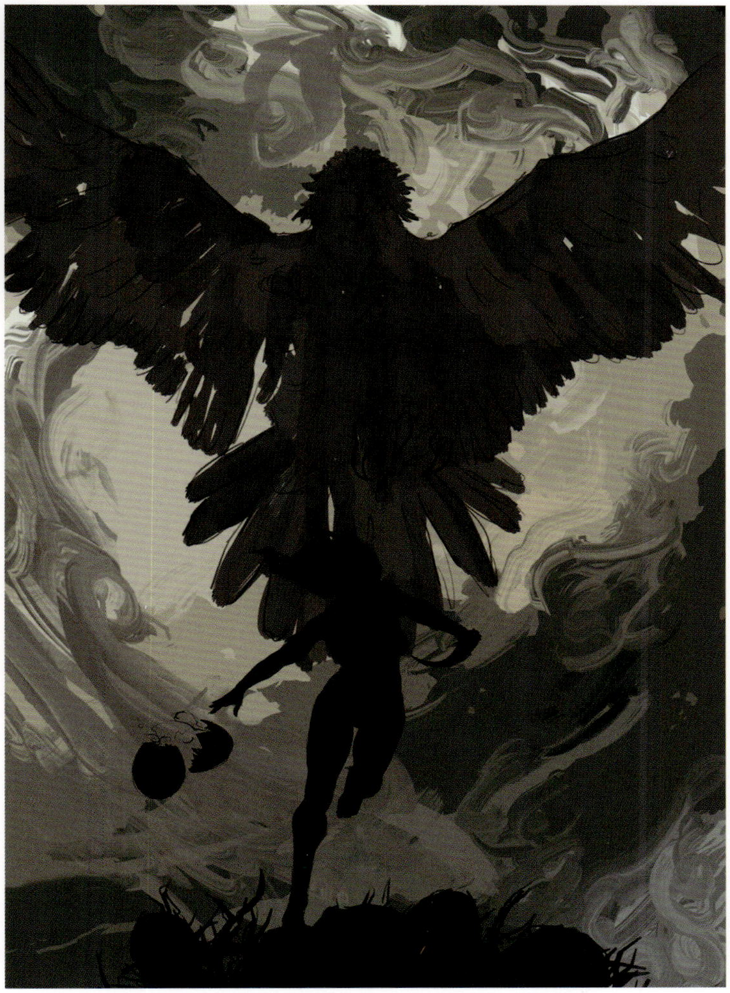

Painting in a loose, abstract background light source

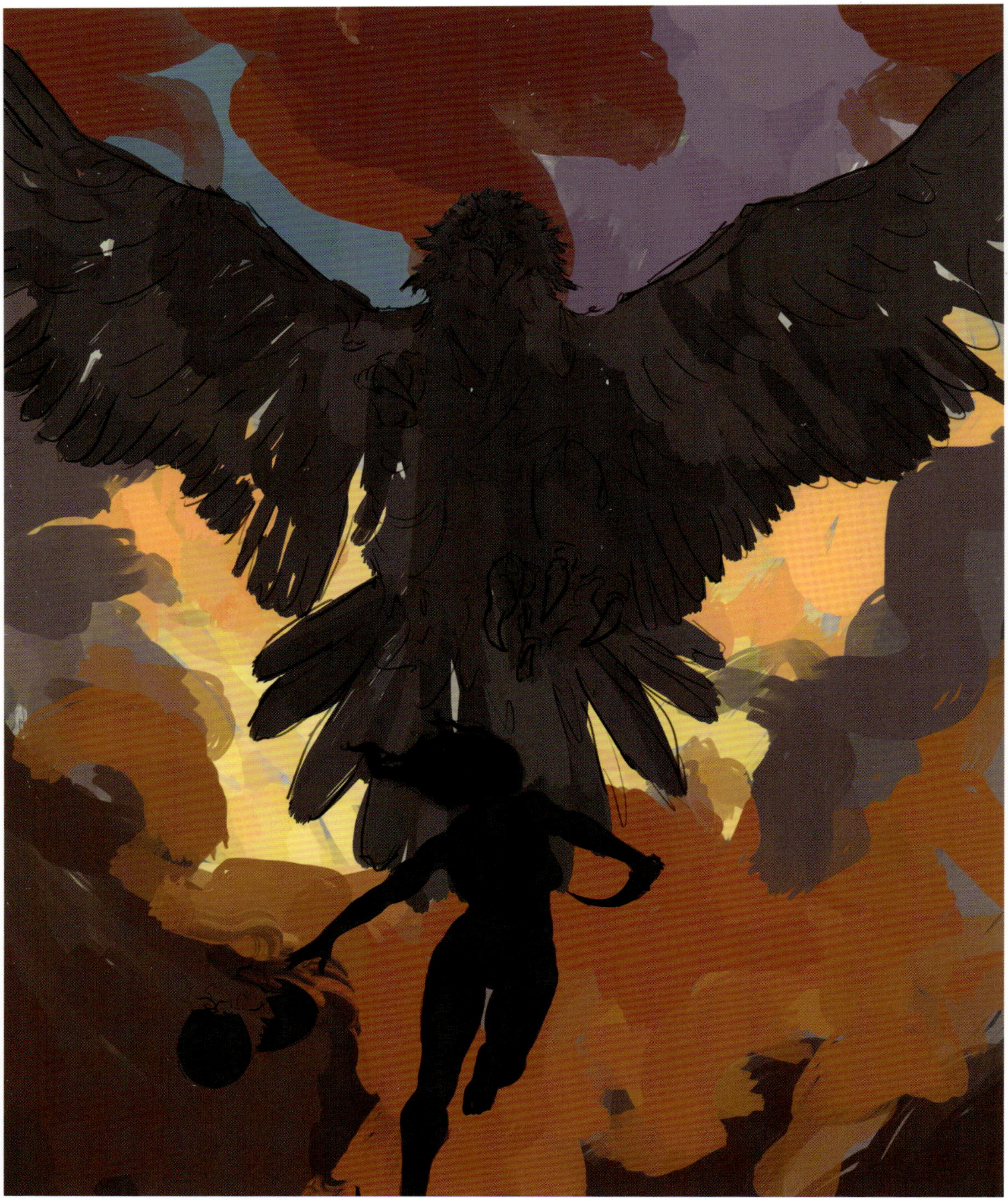

Introducing some colours that are not necessarily the final palette

05 Background colours

At this stage the colours are not defined and do not necessarily need to be. I usually switch very quickly to colours because I am more comfortable with them than greys. I drop a new layer behind the characters and lay down a warm palette of colours, roughly following my greyscale plan for the background lighting.

Tanar of Pellucidar © Frank Frazetta

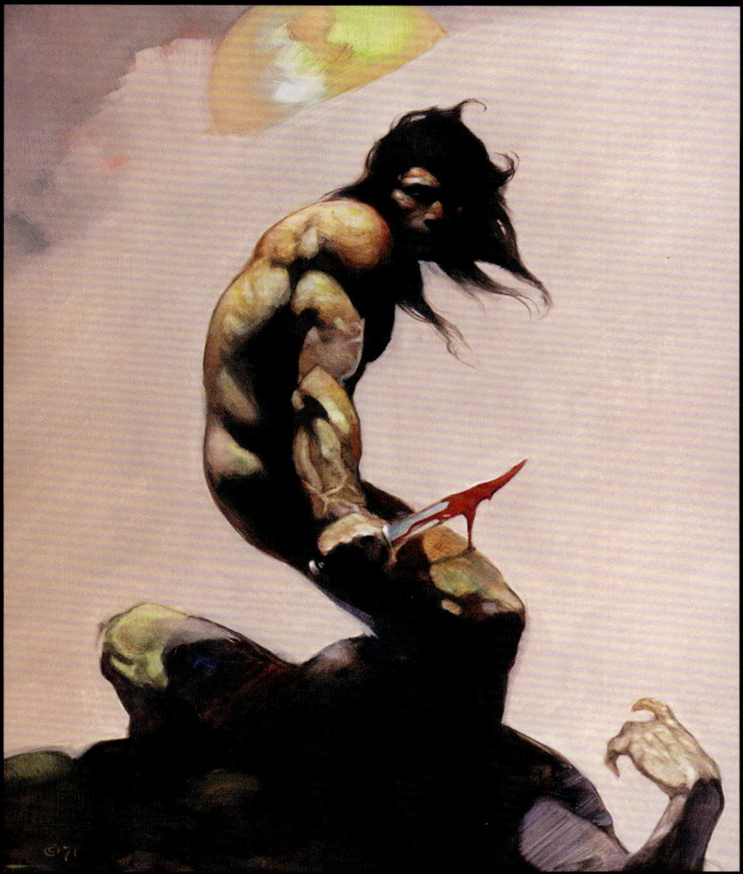

Discovering Frazetta

The first time I saw Frank Frazetta's art, I think I was a teenager. A friend had a little *Death Dealer* lithograph hanging above his desk and I was immediately captivated by the dark power that this character evoked. I think that image alone sums up the iconography of dark-fantasy art.

Another of my favourites is *Tanar of Pellucidar* because it represents what I like most about Frazetta's work: a sense of composition achieved with few elements. That quality is something that I really like, because it's always more difficult to make something beautiful with less – there is no room for error. This illustration perfectly represents the genius in simplicity.

That simplicity is one of the things that influences my art the most. The way in which Frazetta possessed the art of suggesting, without showing everything, is something I find tremendously elegant.

For image in full, turn to page 239

06 Silhouettes

I apply a gradient, starting from the top of the eagle's head, so that its head and upper wings are darker than the lower half of its body. This slight but important change makes the eagle stand out from the background without blending with the main character's values, so each part of the painting is placed in a plane of its own.

I mirror the painting constantly as I work, as it helps me keep control of the whole creation and avoid any unwelcome surprises. It is absolutely crucial to know if an illustration is working correctly at all levels (anatomy, value, light, colours, and so on) and mirroring is invaluable for that.

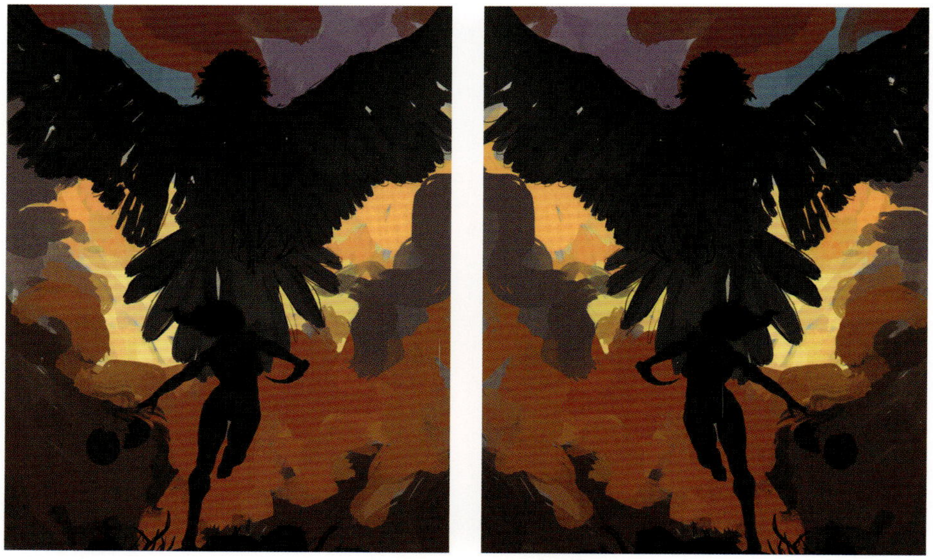

Reinforcing the eagle with a gradient and flipping the canvas to check for errors

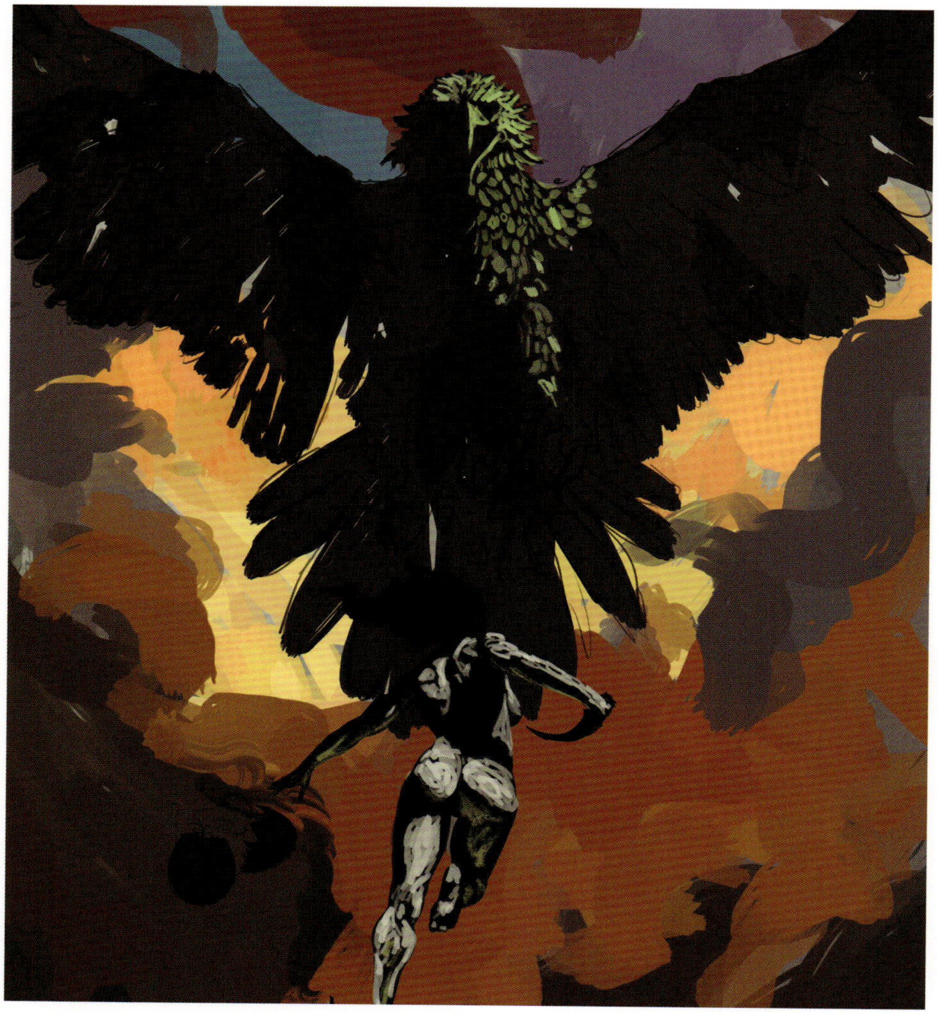

Beginning to build up the characters' forms and details

07 First details

At this stage I like to add the first high-contrast values, giving the image a strong visual direction. I start to accentuate some details on the eagle, and define the secondary light coming from the ground to give more impact to the woman's silhouette. It's this foreground light source that illuminates her muscles and gives tension to her pose.

08 Maintaining contrast

As the eagle is in the background, it's important that it does not detract from the foreground character. After roughly painting all its interior details, I block over the eagle with very dark values; this homogenizes its silhouette and pushes it further into the background. I really like to separate an image's detail levels this way.

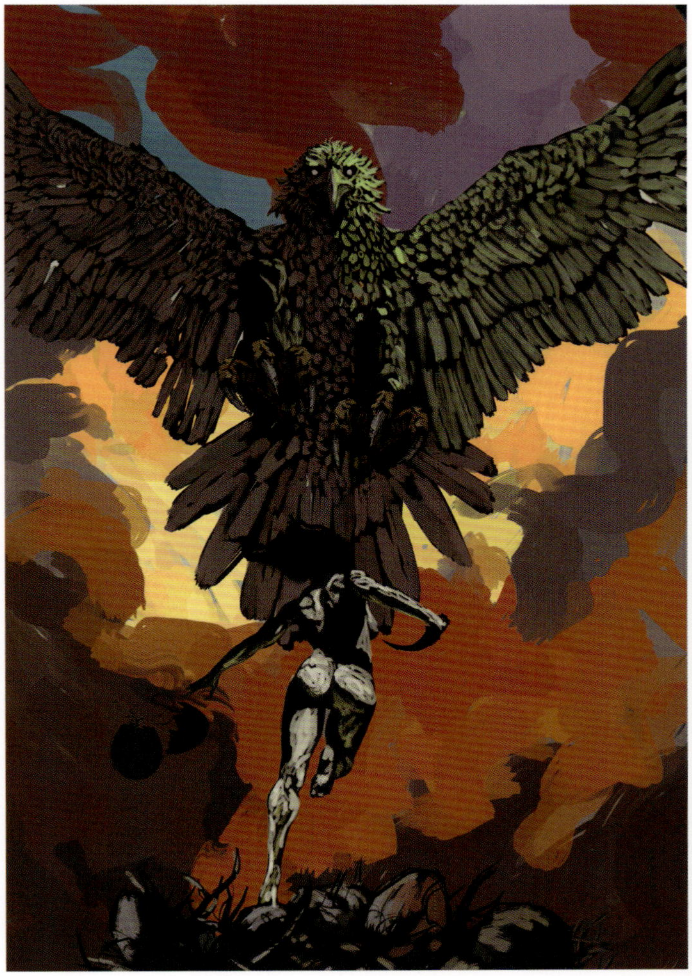

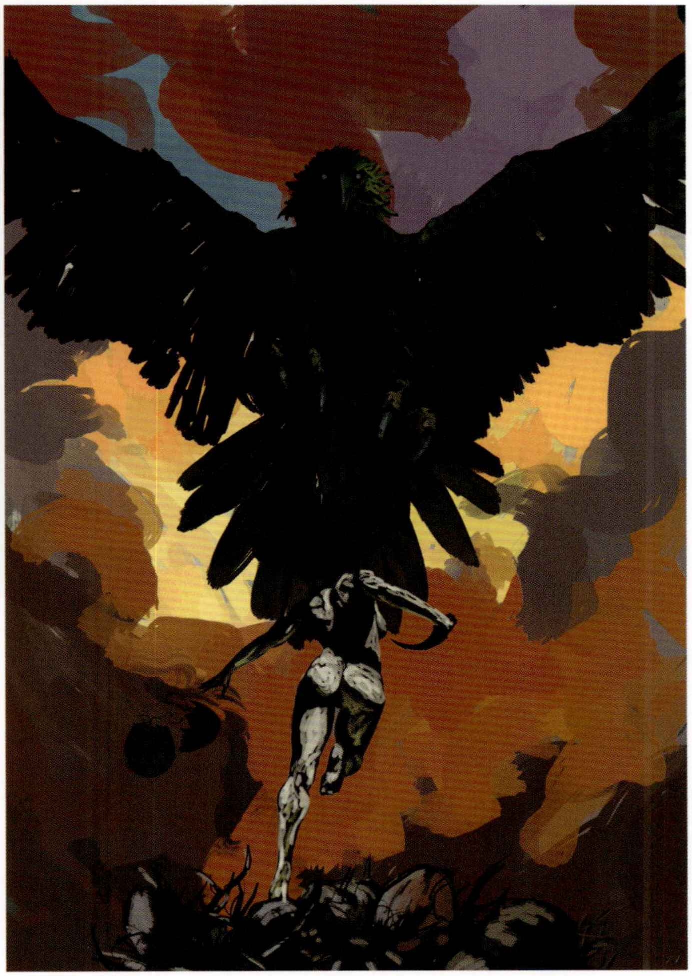

Pushing the painted eagle into the background again by darkening it

09 Blending the background

I mix the background using the Smudge tool, which allows me to blend the colours and create a feeling reminiscent of oils. It is important to keep control of the values and to separate the key focal areas. This is something I review constantly. For example, at this stage the woman's hair has become too close in value to the eagle, so her silhouette is getting lost.

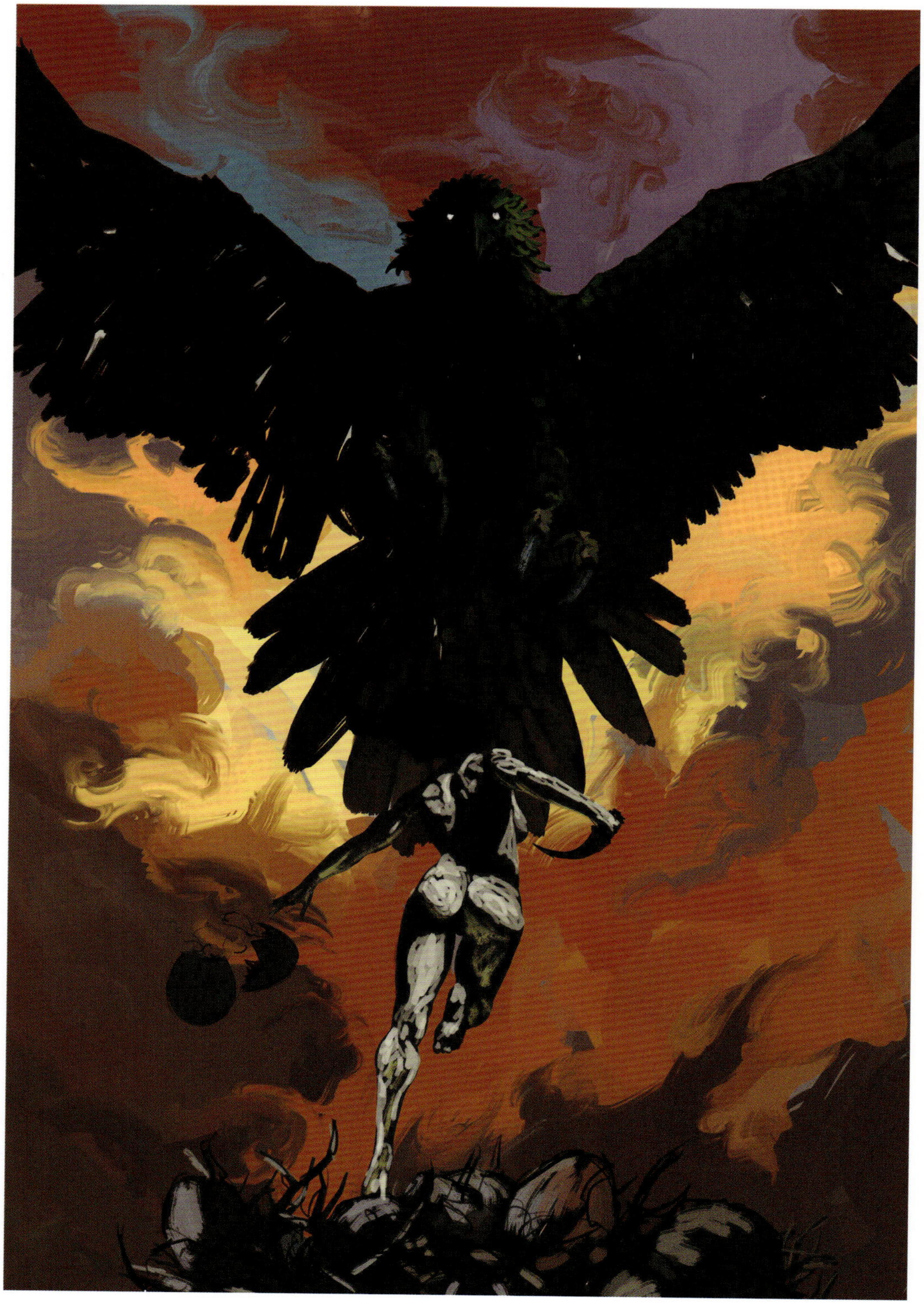

Blending the background colours while evaluating the image's clarity

10 Light gradient

I apply a diffuse light in the centre of the image to accentuate the focal points and place the characters in a more organic environment. To ensure the foreground character still pops enough, I darken her silhouette and give her more solid shadows. Then I carefully work on her values, ensuring her skin is smooth and blended, painting over the base of colours and lighting I have already applied. It is important to spend time on this step, as the character is in the foreground and must give life to the whole painting.

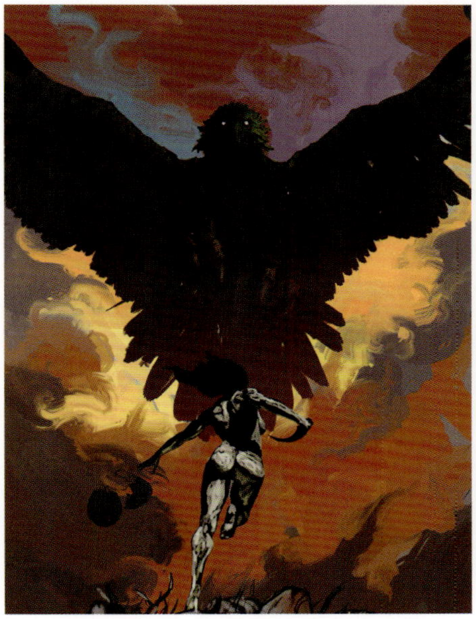

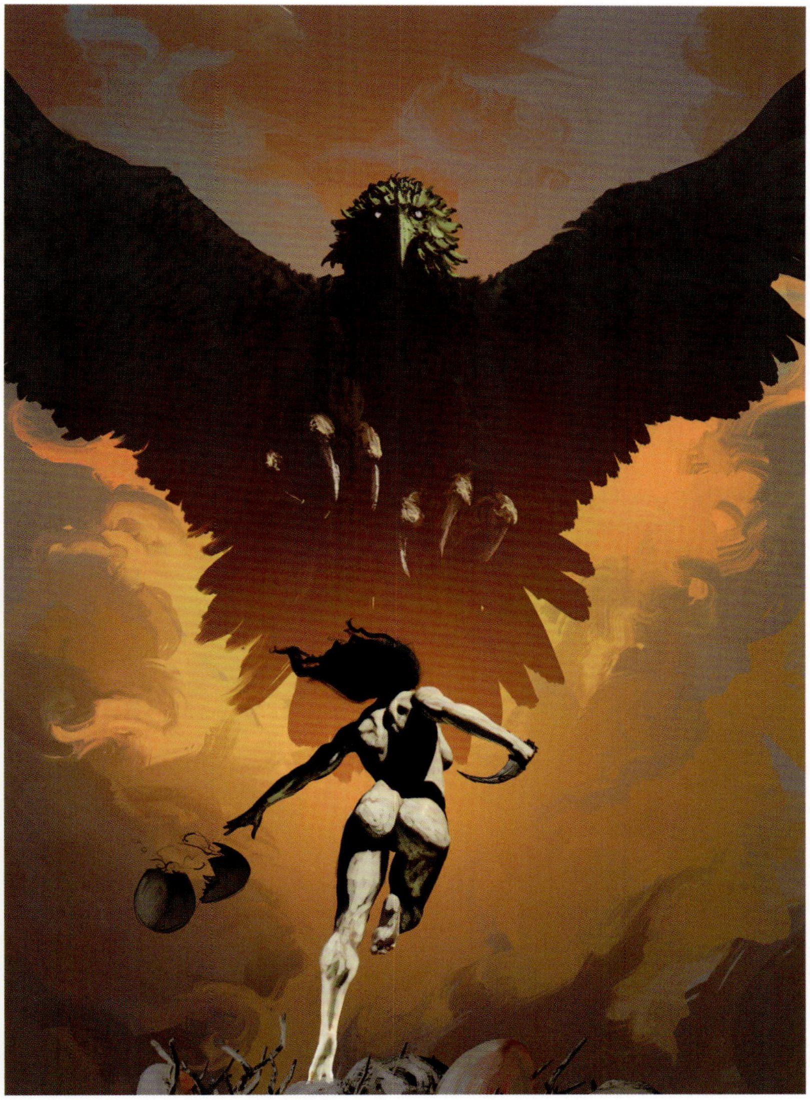

Separating the two characters with a gradient of warm light

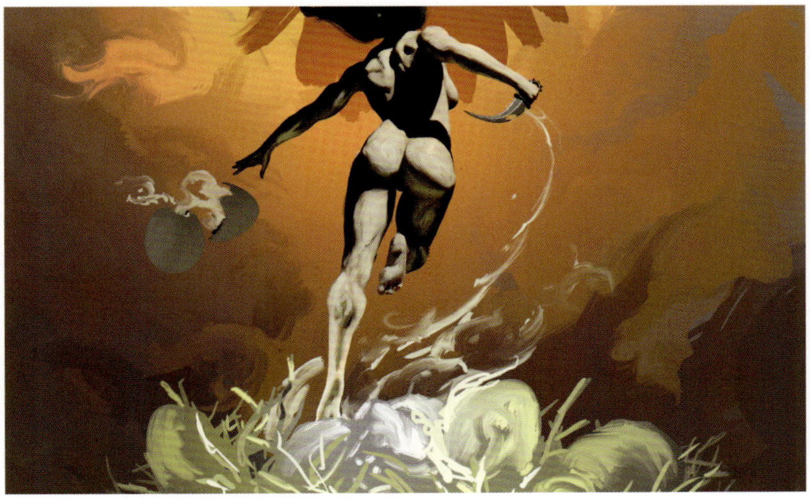

11 Foreground rendering

At this stage you will have noticed that the female character has evolved a lot. I solidify her body structure, refine the dramatic shadow shapes, and begin to paint the nest of eagle eggs. Frazetta had a way of blending his characters and environment elements together; it's common in his work to see characters whose feet become one with the ground, blocked in by shadow in a way that makes the whole image feel extremely organic (like the example overleaf). That is the effect I aim for here as I detail the foreground nest and light the character's lower body.

Painting the nest and refining the main character

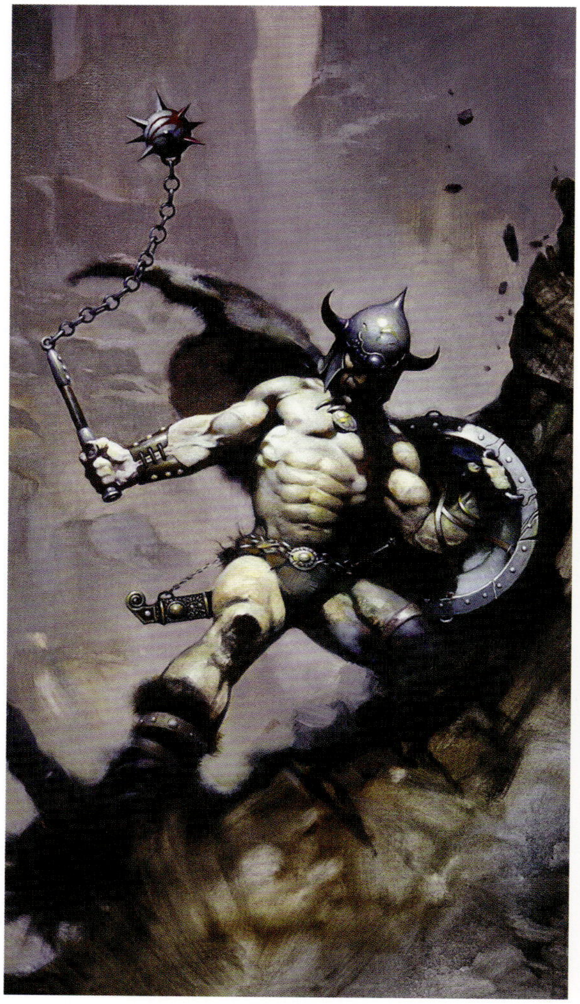

Warrior with Ball and Chain © Frank Frazetta

In many of Frazetta's pieces, the character merges into the ground

▶▶ *For image in full, turn to page 17*

12 Radical change

I decide to make a radical change in the composition, as the eagle's posture and silhouette lack dynamism. It can be tedious to revise such an important part from scratch, but if it's for the good of your image, it is worth going through with it. I sketch out a new silhouette and pose for the eagle, this time swooping into the scene in a way that flows better with the main character and the sense of direction I had originally planned.

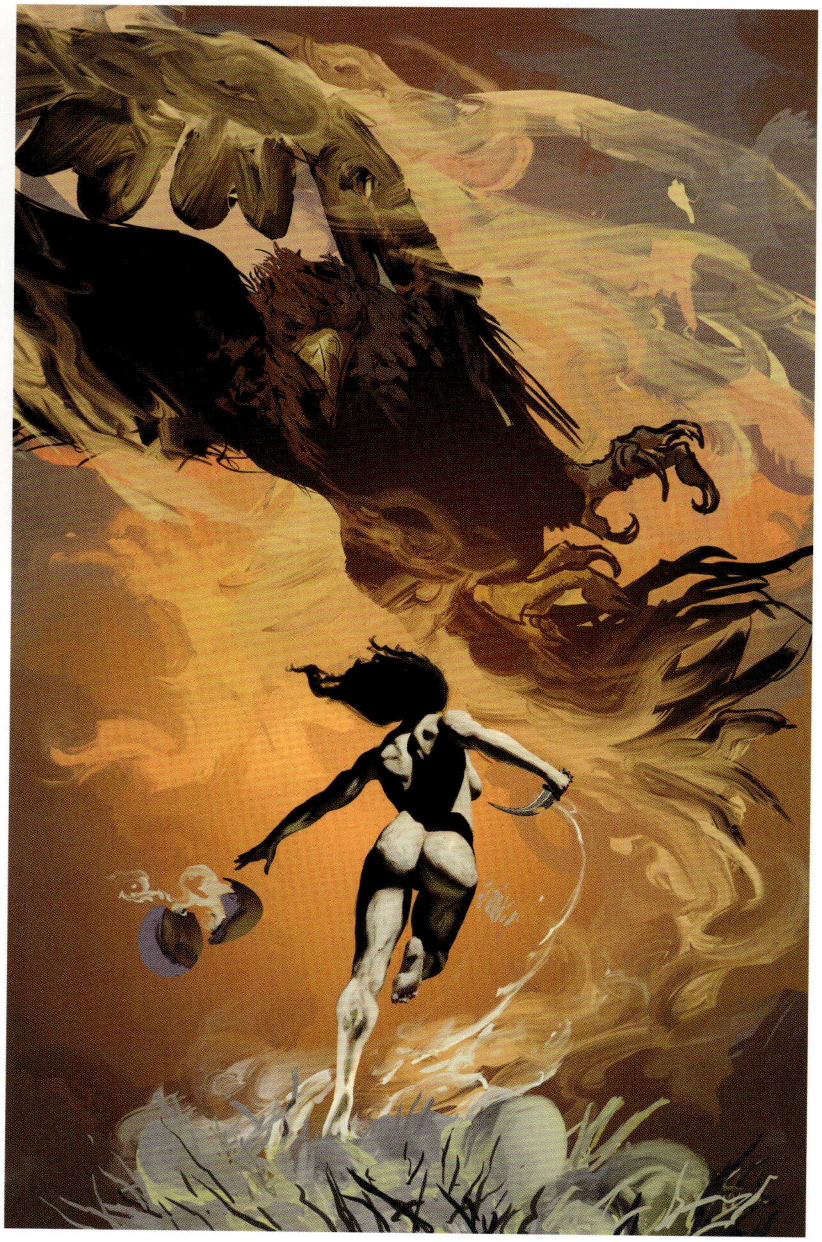

Revising the composition to make it more action-packed and less static

13 Colour adjustments

As I continue building up and refining the new eagle, I also adjust the image's colours. I choose to accentuate the reds and oranges to give the scene a more aggressive mood. Coupled with the loose, painterly brushstrokes, the effect is much more fiery and forceful than before.

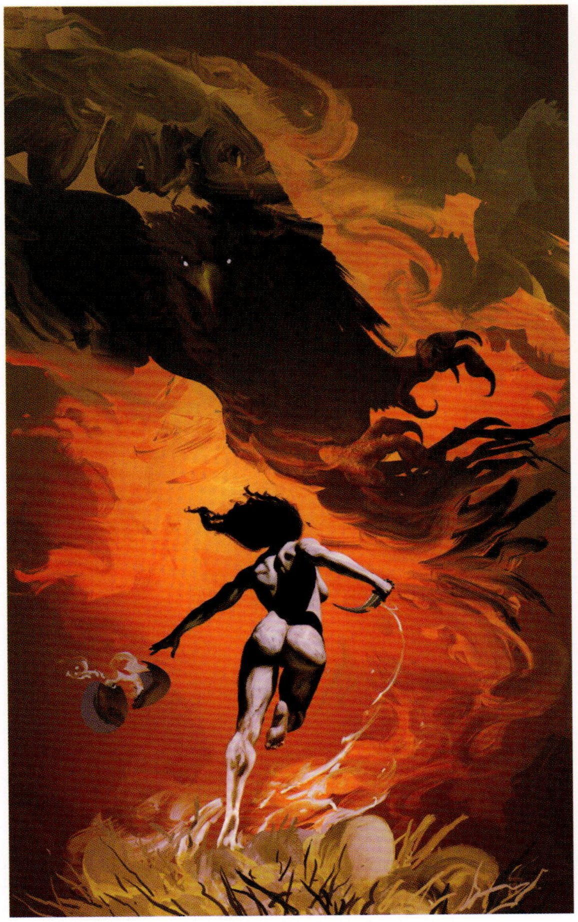

Boosting the warm palette, emphasizing the oranges and reds

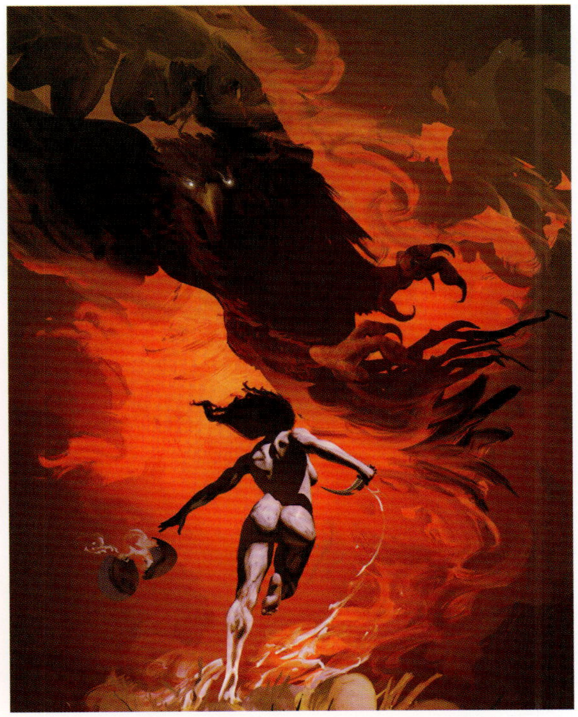

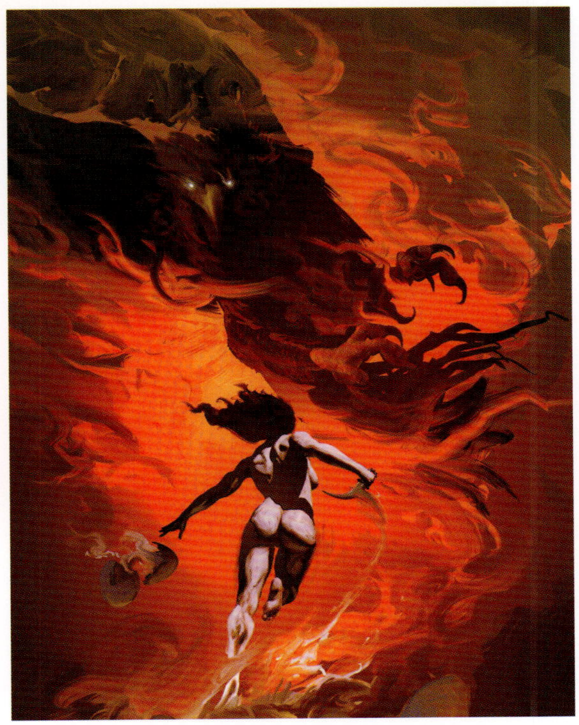

Blending and brushstrokes emphasize the scene's flow and action

14 Final blending

I blend some of the elements into the environment, almost as if the two characters are moving and taking the scenery with them. This gives more dynamism and power to the whole painting. I simplify the eagle's nest, so that the twigs and branches are not distracting the viewer from the action. I add a yellowish secondary light that bounces up from the foreground and into the shadowed areas of the female character, making her look more three-dimensional and immersed in her environment.

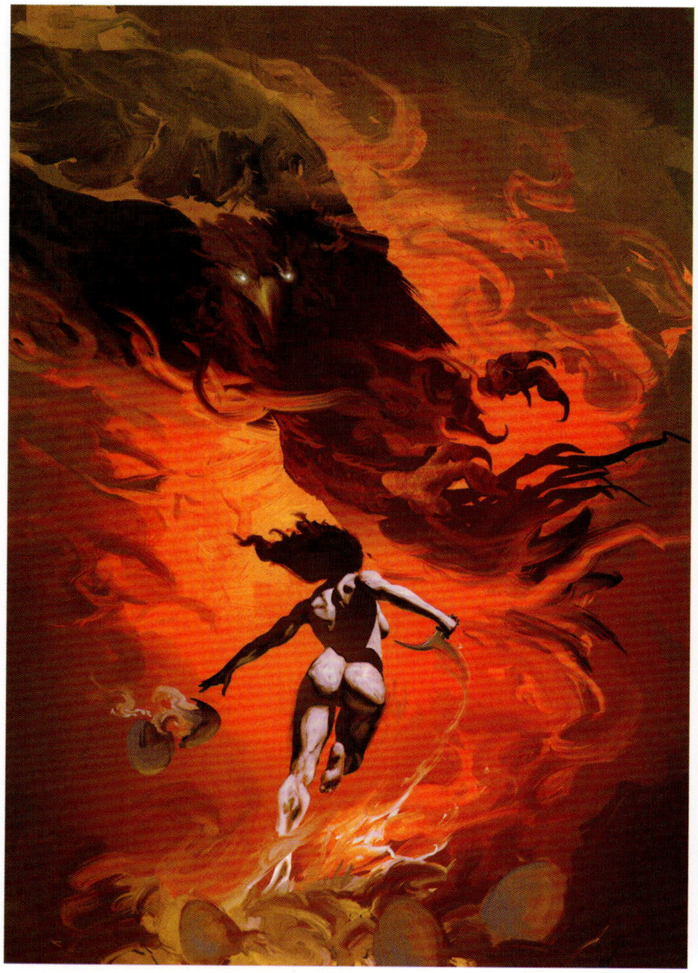

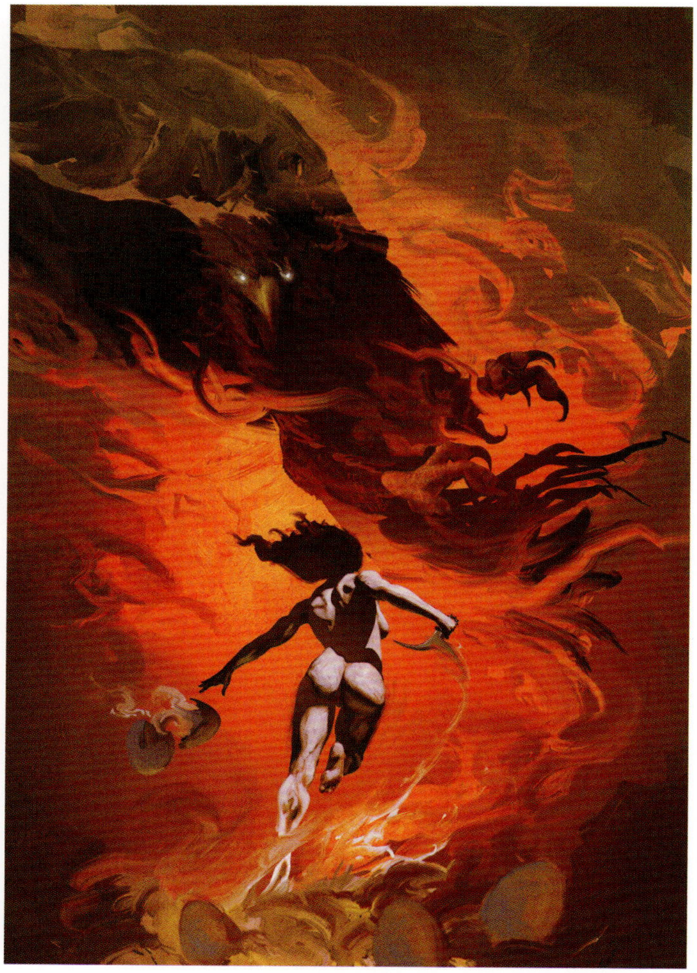

Applying a couple of final digital adjustments to complete the image

15 Final effects

The painting is now basically complete, but a few small digital adjustments can be made to enhance its final presentation. Overlaying a brushstroke pattern enriches the image's painterly look, followed by a slight film grain for a touch of cinematic retro texture. I keep these effects subtle to emphasize the loose, organic quality of the painting and not overwhelm it.

Conclusion

This illustration was a real pleasure to make, as it allowed me to immerse myself in the work of Frank Frazetta and capture the essence of what makes his work a timeless source of inspiration to me – paying tribute to his work while remaining myself. I know that Frazetta, like many other artists I admire, are all distilled in my art, and it's impossible to completely detach from these influences – and that's not a bad thing, because nothing is born from the void. So, thank you, Mr Frazetta, *de tout mon coeur*.

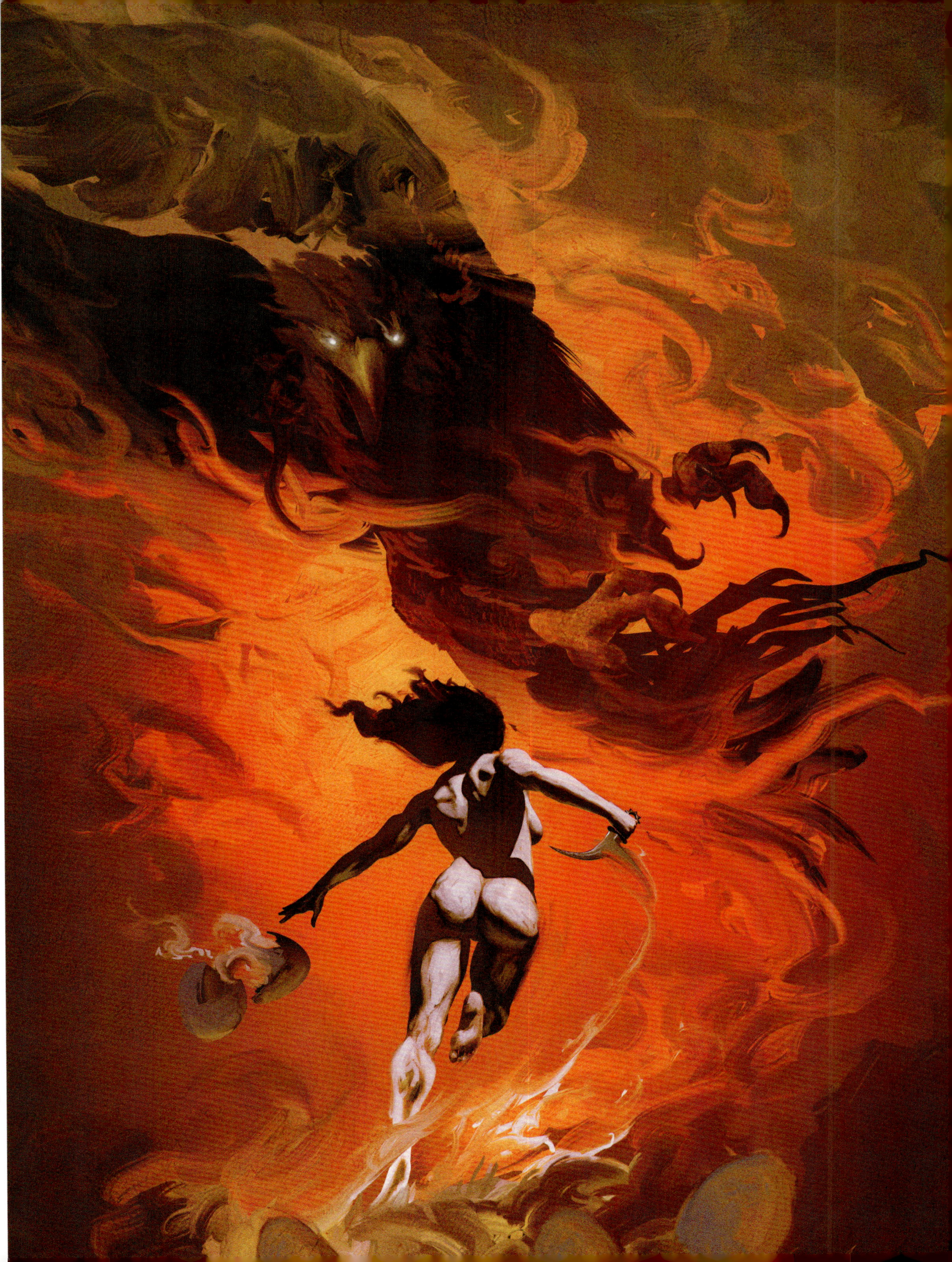

Final image © Anato Finnstark

Gallery

by Anato Finnstark

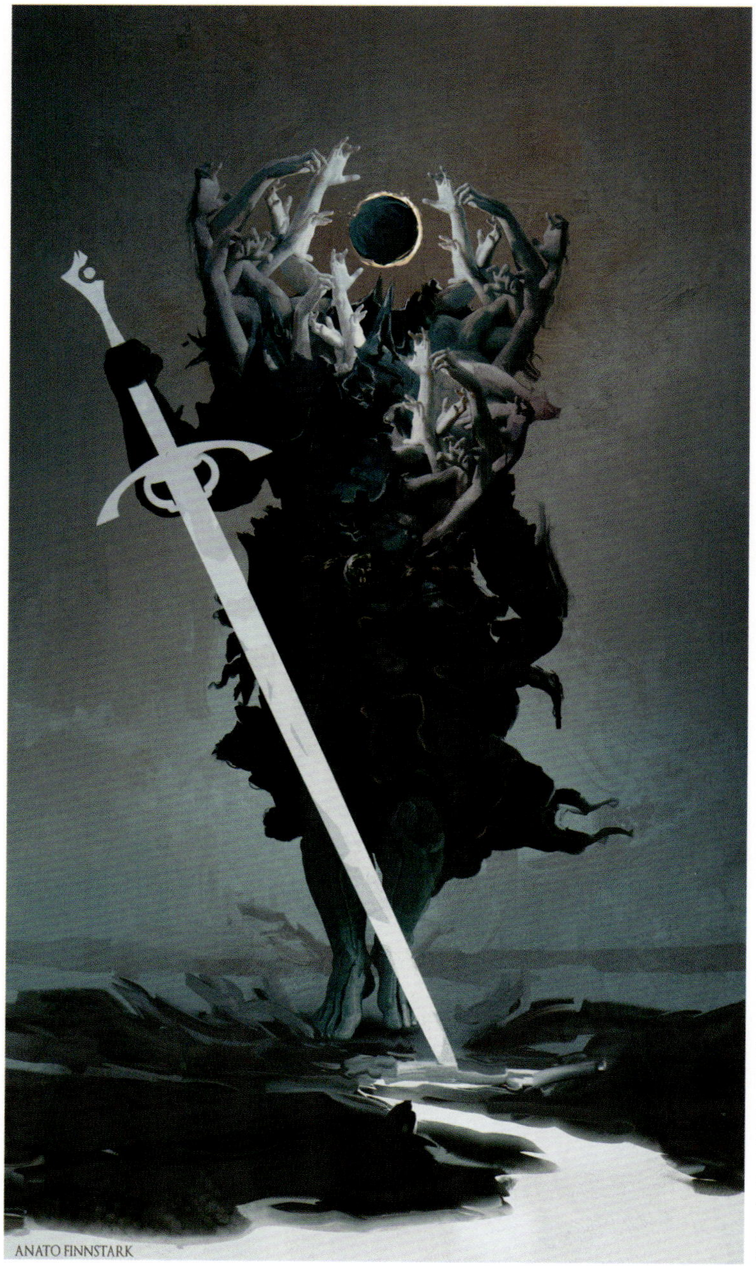

Eclipse's Herald © Anato Finnstark

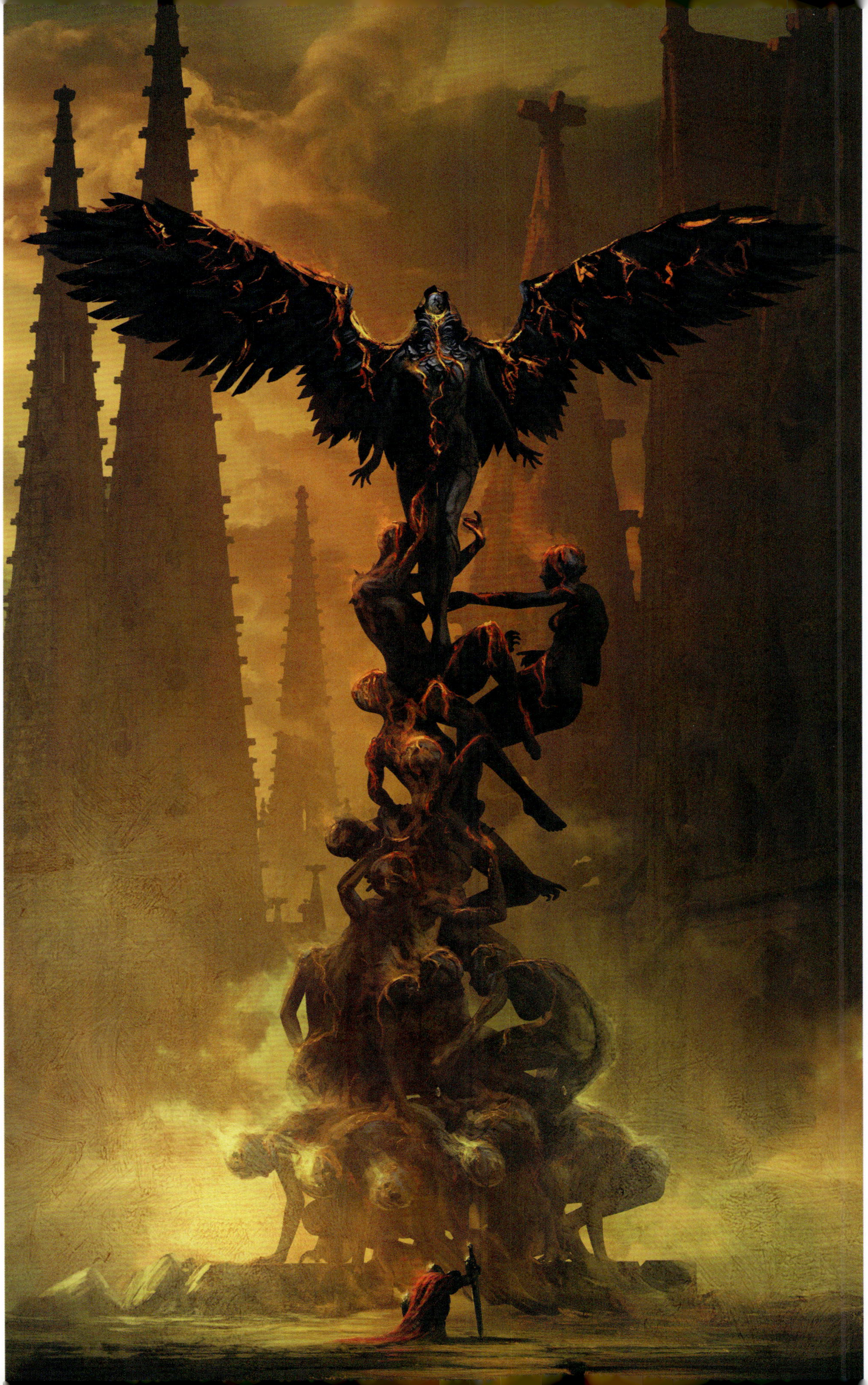

Oath to the Fallen © Anato Finnstark

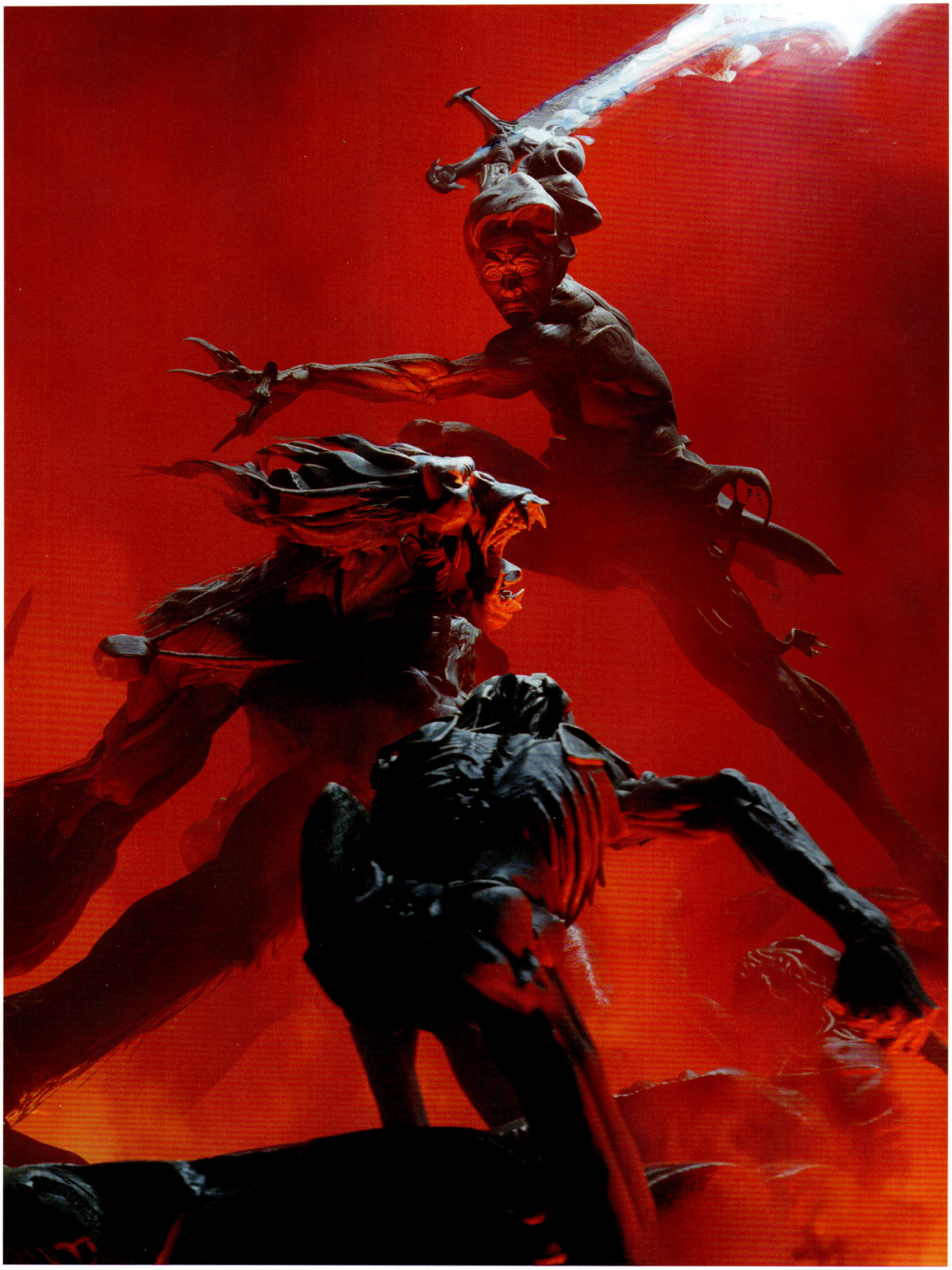

Final image © Jama Jurabaev

Goliath

by Jama Jurabaev

Creating *Goliath*

One of the main feelings I want to achieve in this tribute is a sense of energy. It's something you can clearly see in Frazetta's work – he captured frozen moments in time, still full of dynamism, where you could almost see the characters or creatures move.

I have been in love with Frazetta's work since I was a little kid. I took a different career path and forgot about my passion for art for quite some time, but in my mid-twenties I took a U-turn and decided to get back to what made me happy and excited when I was a child. That was when I rediscovered Frazetta's art. This time around, I wanted to know more about him and his career. I remember spending hours and hours studying the lighting and atmosphere in his paintings.

I have a few of his art books on my shelf, which I go through now and then to recharge my creative batteries. They remind me of how great he was as an artist and that his legacy will live forever through the millions of artists he inspired. I have learned a lot from Frazetta's work and want to show that here.

01 Virtual-reality sketch

Getting that 'Frazetta' level of energy is tough and is something I personally struggle with in my own work. I've managed to learn how to capture energy in my quick sketches, but I often feel that the more time I spend on a piece, the less dynamic it gets! So, most of the time, I constantly go back and forth to bring the energy back.

In the past, I would have made a few rough sketches to put my basic idea on a canvas, but this time around I want to push myself. I start straight away in 3D. I think virtual-reality (VR) sculpting is the best way to make quick 'sketches' in 3D, so I start this sculpture in Gravity Sketch.

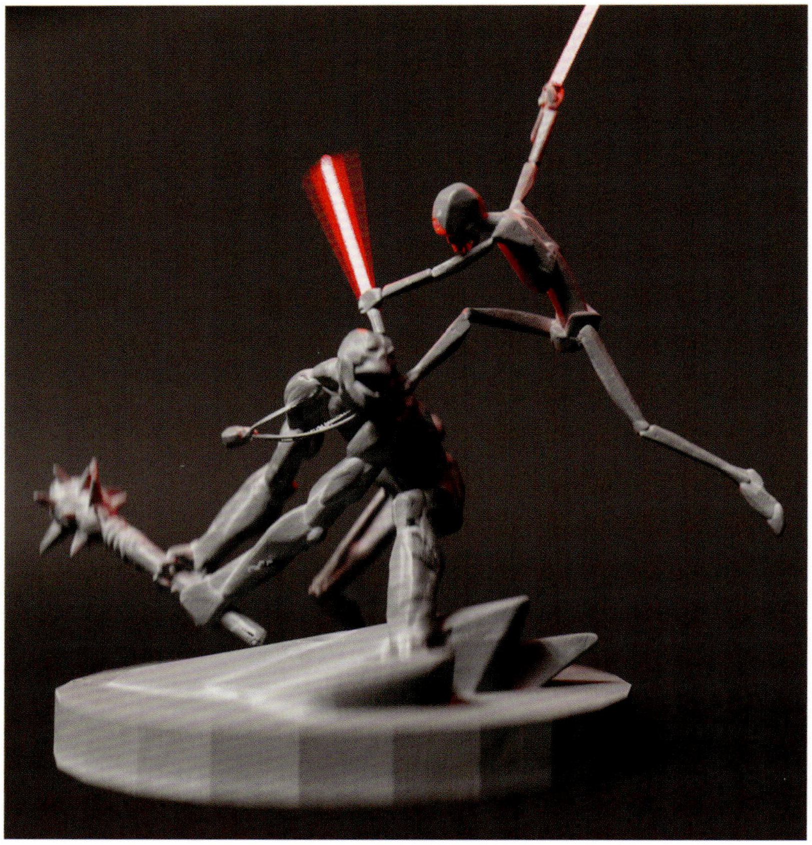

This stage is less about the design and more about movement and energy

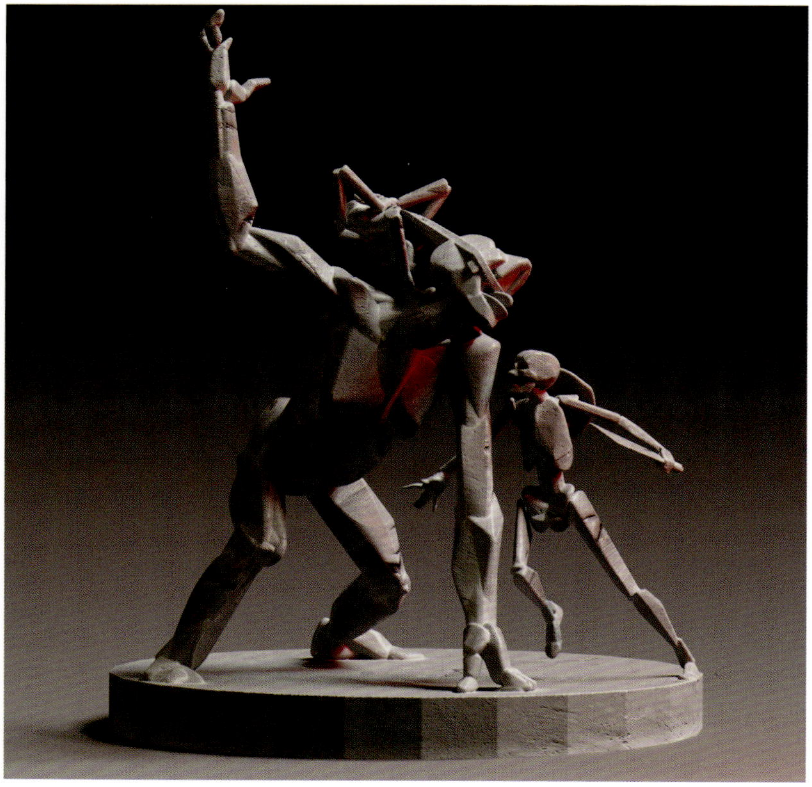

02 A second idea

I continue exploring ideas with another sketch. Sometimes I have a very solid idea in mind before I start a piece, but for these sketches I just go with the flow. I have a vague idea of some sort of battle – a 'David and Goliath' story, with a warrior going up against a formidable enemy. I absolutely love how you can see these motifs in Frazetta's art, and I want to recreate that sensation in my tribute.

Like with the first sketch, I focus purely on movement and action, saving the details for later

03 Dramatic potential

I'm now more or less decided on my first idea, because I like the potential to introduce glowing elements that will form strong focal points in the composition. One of many reasons I love working in 3D is having the ability to rotate and see the sculpture from different angles. With 2D art – which, don't get me wrong, is challenging as well – you are setting up only one specific angle. Once you add another dimension, there are so many possibilities to consider, and you are trying to make the piece look good from multiple angles. It's very challenging but rewarding at the same time.

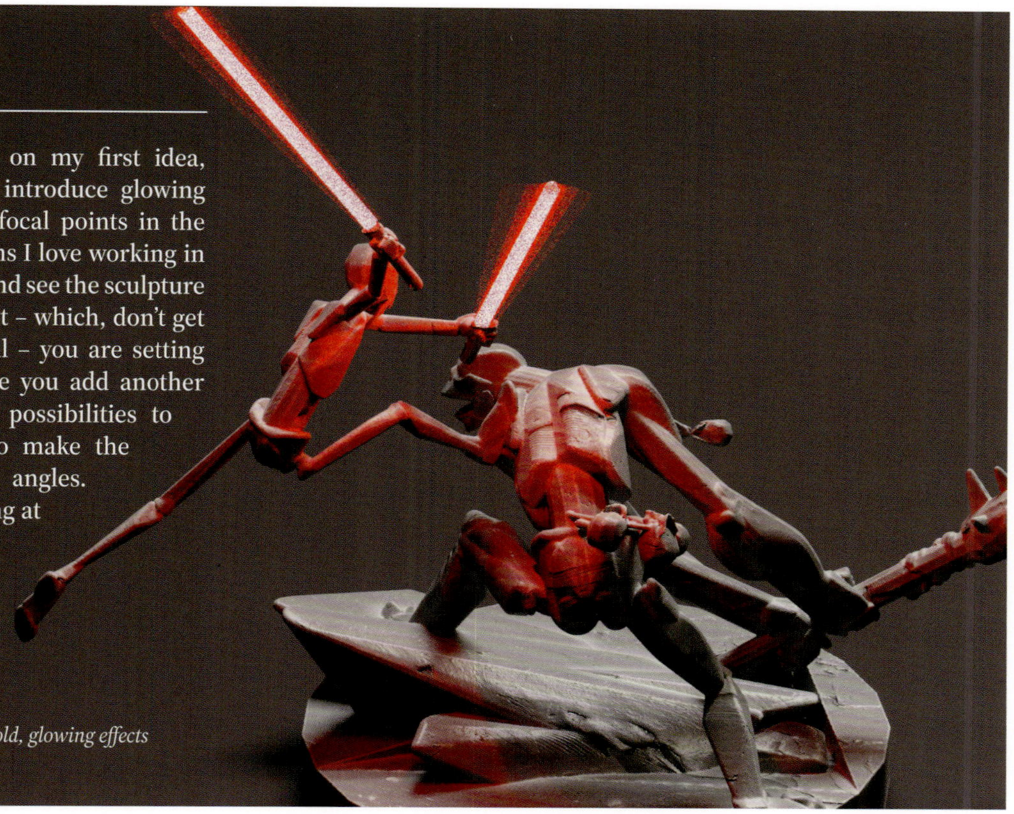

My first idea offers great cpportunities for bold, glowing effects

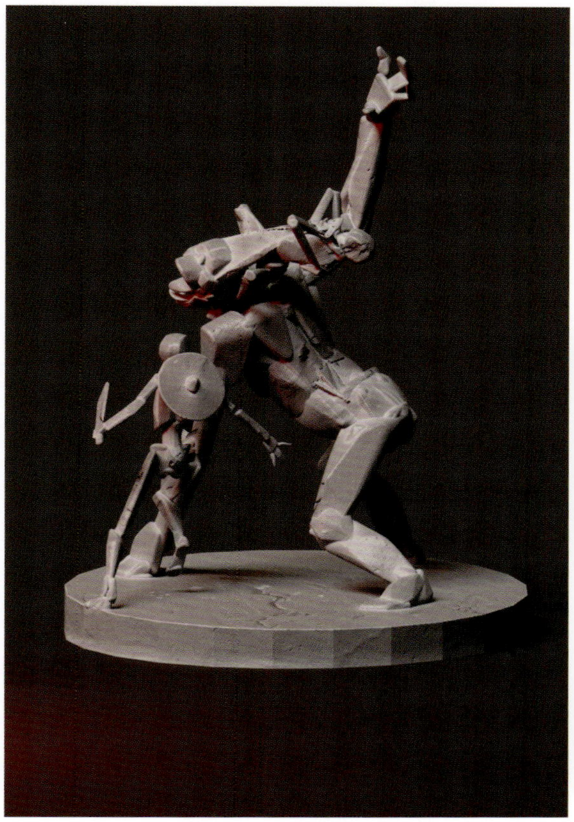

04 Comparing ideas

Having these sketches in 3D feels almost like having real clay models on my table. I rotate them around, taking notes of areas I can improve and amend. Comparing them side by side confirms that I'm leaning towards my first concept, though I could bring in some secondary characters from the other. Since I have all the elements in 3D, I can simply strip some off one sketch and reuse them in another.

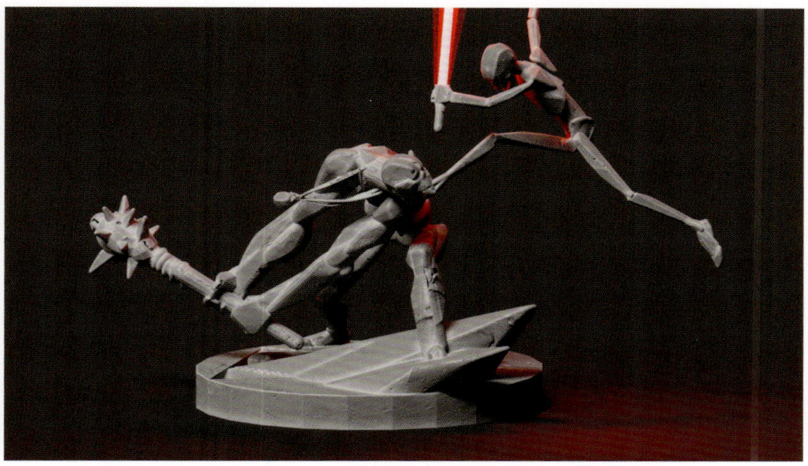

I usually make two or three sketches that I can mix and match together if needed

05 Stick figures

The forms I've used to describe the anatomy and proportions are very simple so far. This is done on purpose, as I always try to stick with a simple rule: gesture, then volume, then details. In a way, it's like playing with a stickman. I start simply to get a strong gesture, then introduce additional volumes, and after that add a pass of detail. It sounds easy, but it requires a lot of practice. It's very challenging to make quick, dynamic sketches in 3D, but it's something I practise on a regular basis to help me retain the energy and movement in my work.

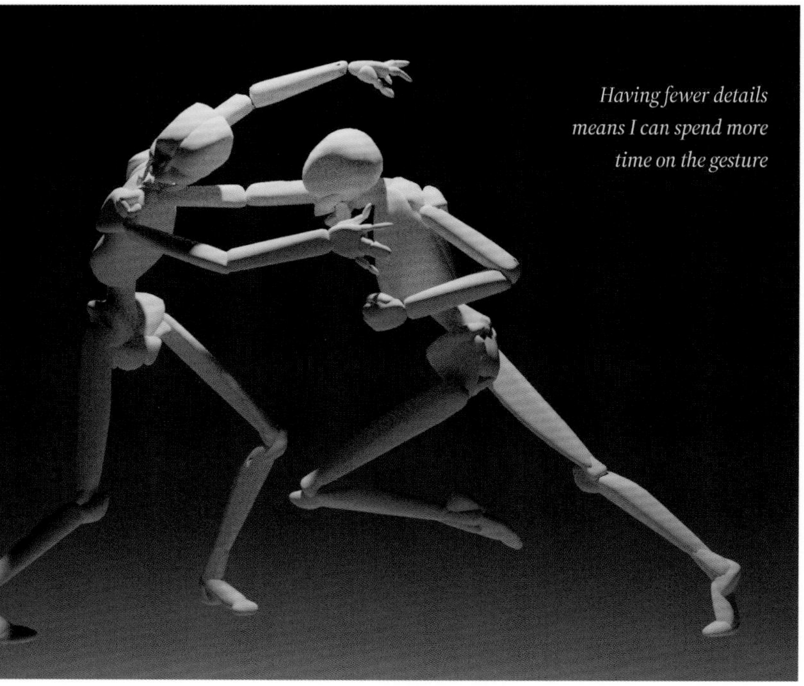

Having fewer details means I can spend more time on the gesture

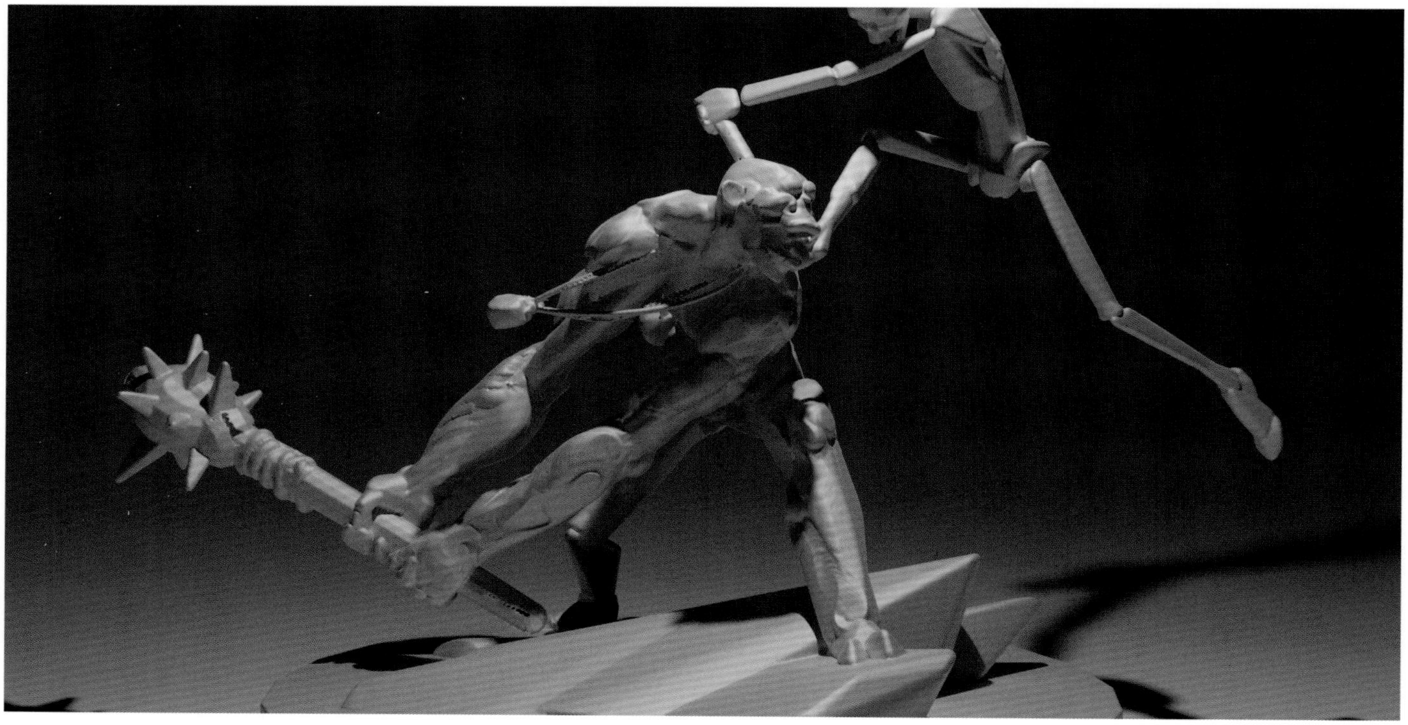

06 Initial volume

Now it's time to start introducing some volume. I do most of my sculpting in 3DCoat as it reminds me of the way I draw in 2D, and it offers both 'voxel sculpting' and 'surface sculpting' tools. Voxel sculpting tools allow me to 'draw' with geometry in 3D space. I love having some of these 3D brushstrokes visible in my final sculptures – it's part of retaining that initial energy of my gesture sketches.

I still have lots to do, but I now have a solid base for the sculpture

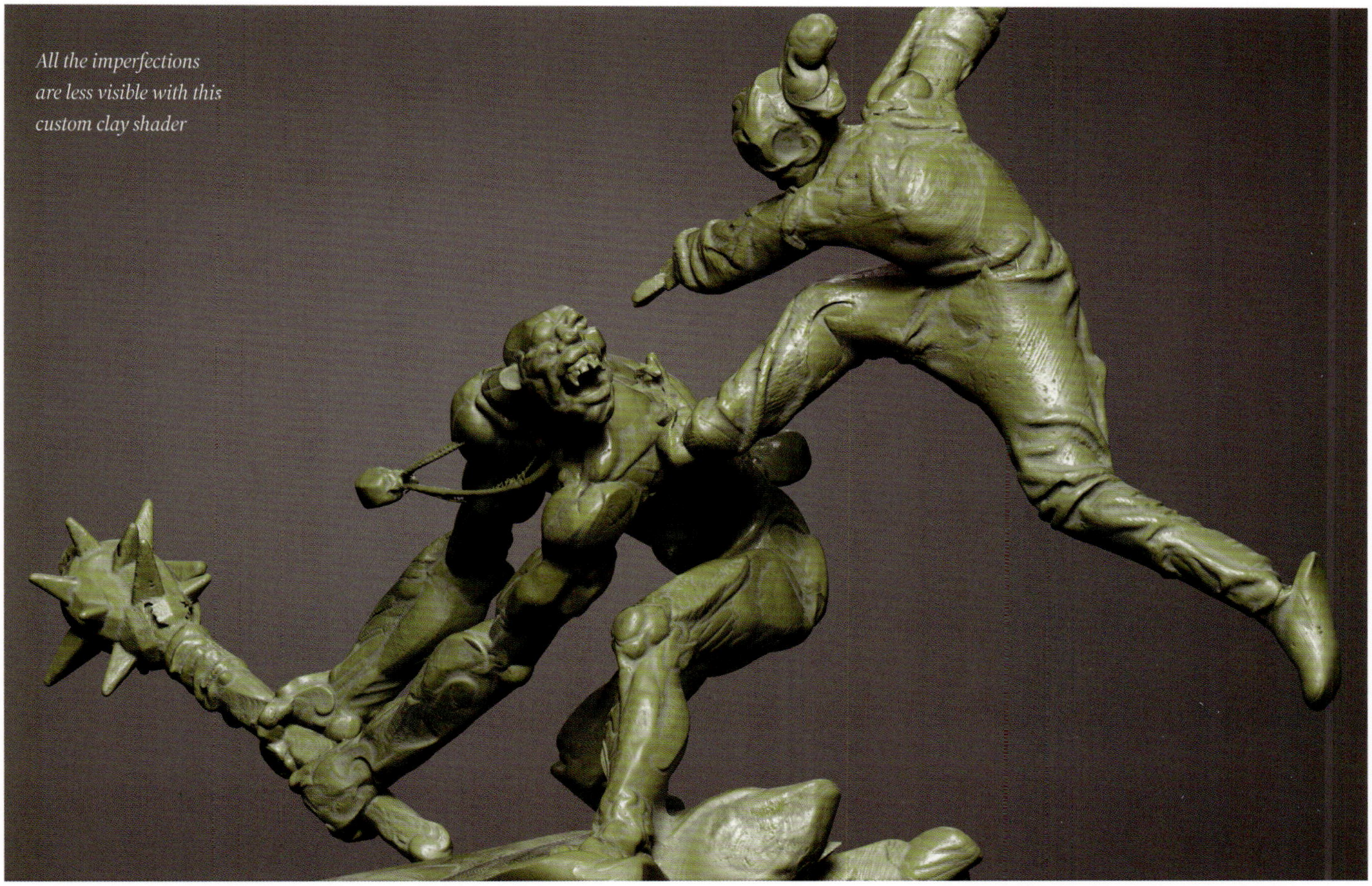

All the imperfections are less visible with this custom clay shader

07 Clay shader

While adding volumes in 3DCoat, I apply a clay shader that I have custom-made. This is a purposeful choice, as the shader helps me focus on the bigger picture, rather than zooming in and focusing on details. I use this approach frequently in my professional work, so I don't get distracted by people offering feedback on the look and rendering of the sculpt. Anyone looking at this clay shader will know the sculpt is just a work in progress, which keeps me focused on dynamism.

To show how shaders can strongly affect how a sculpt is perceived, on the right is an example of the same sculpt with both a clay and a metallic shader. It feels completely different in artistic look and finish. For this specific project, I will stick with the clay shader to the end, but the possibilities in 3D are endless.

The 3DCoat team liked my shader so much, they included it in their official release – you can find it in the 'Jama' folder in 3DCoat's shaders panel!

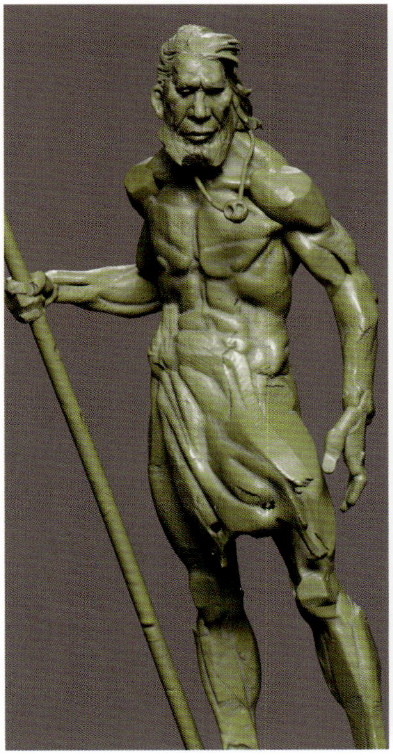

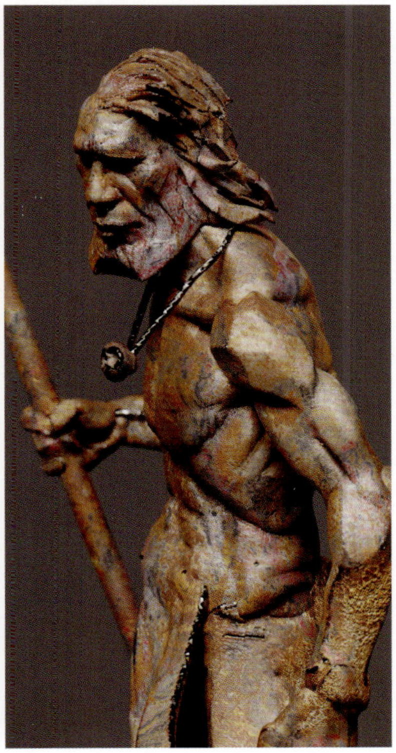

Discovering Frazetta

I was born in the Soviet Union, where we sadly weren't exposed to much Western culture and entertainment. My dad was a member of a central library in our city, and I used to ask him to borrow books for me. I had no clue what I wanted to read, as there was no one around to ask, so I usually went for the books that had cool covers.

That is how I discovered Frazetta's art. I don't think I even knew his name at the time, but what struck me most was that his art looked surreal and fantastic but very real at the same time. I still remember the books and images I used to look at.

Years later, when I rediscovered art and became an artist myself, I immediately knew whenever I saw Frazetta's work. It always had this element of mystery and movement, which has definitely played a significant role in my own work. These days I have a better understanding of the gigantic talent and sheer amount of hard work behind his art, which makes me appreciate it even more.

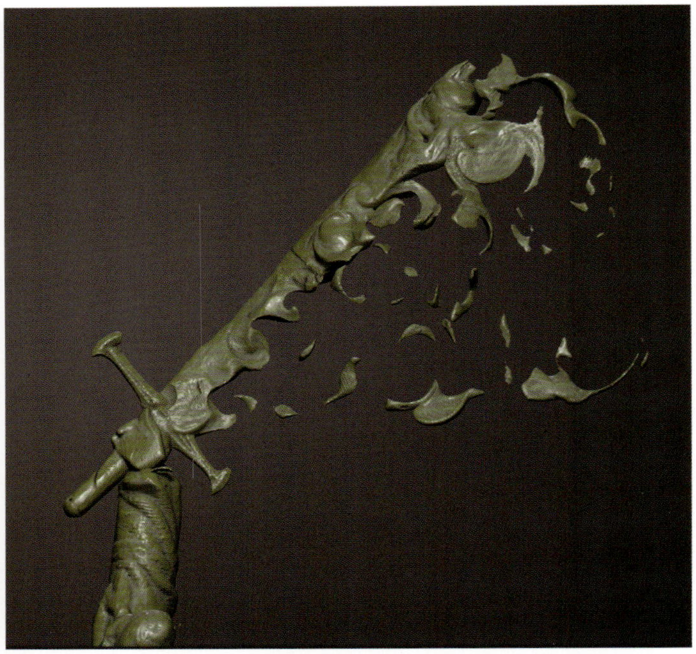

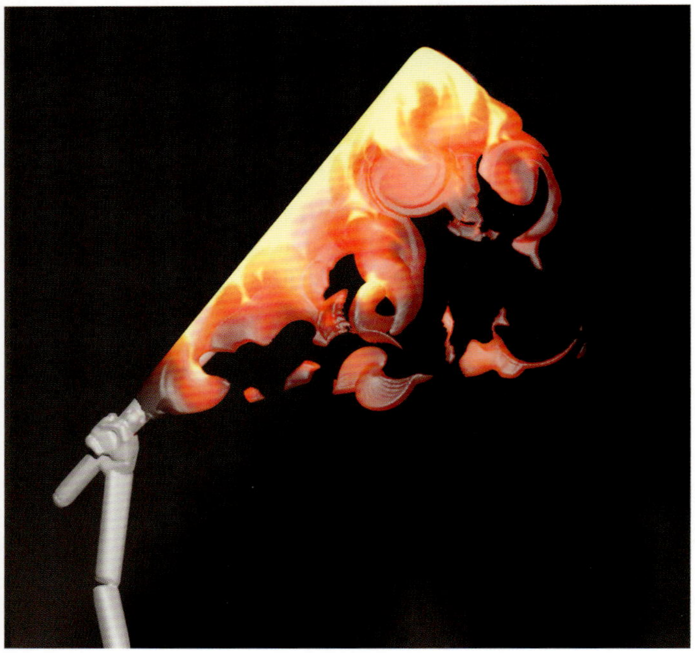

08 Fiery sword

As I'm refining the sculpture, I carry out a test for a flaming sword effect. For the sculpted element, I give the sword and fire a swirly, stylized look. For the rendering, which I test in Blender, I initially go for a typical orange flame, but this could easily change to a more fantastical colour later.

Sculpting the flaming sword in 3DCoat and making a test render in Blender

09 Additional enemies

In step 04, I mentioned that I wanted to add some extra background characters from the other sketch. I explore those now. I know I want to have multiple enemies, so I make a modular figure of an undead character, which I can easily duplicate and pose. I love how 3DCoat allows you to carve into your sculpture, almost like real clay – it's perfect for modelling these zombies.

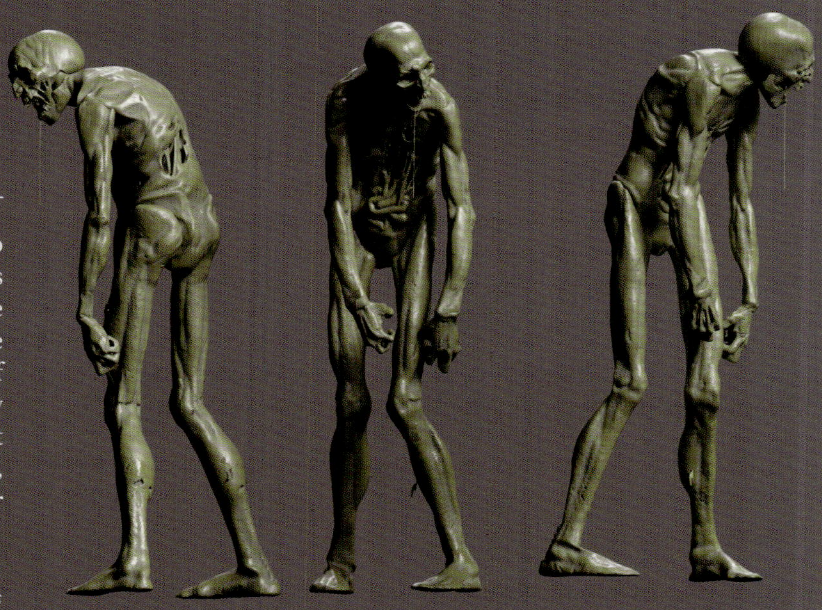

Modelling and duplicating the extra enemy characters

10 Building up the scene

Now everything starts to come together. Based on my initial strong sketch idea, I begin to incorporate the additional characters and refine details here and there. The first detail pass is done, but there are still many more to go.

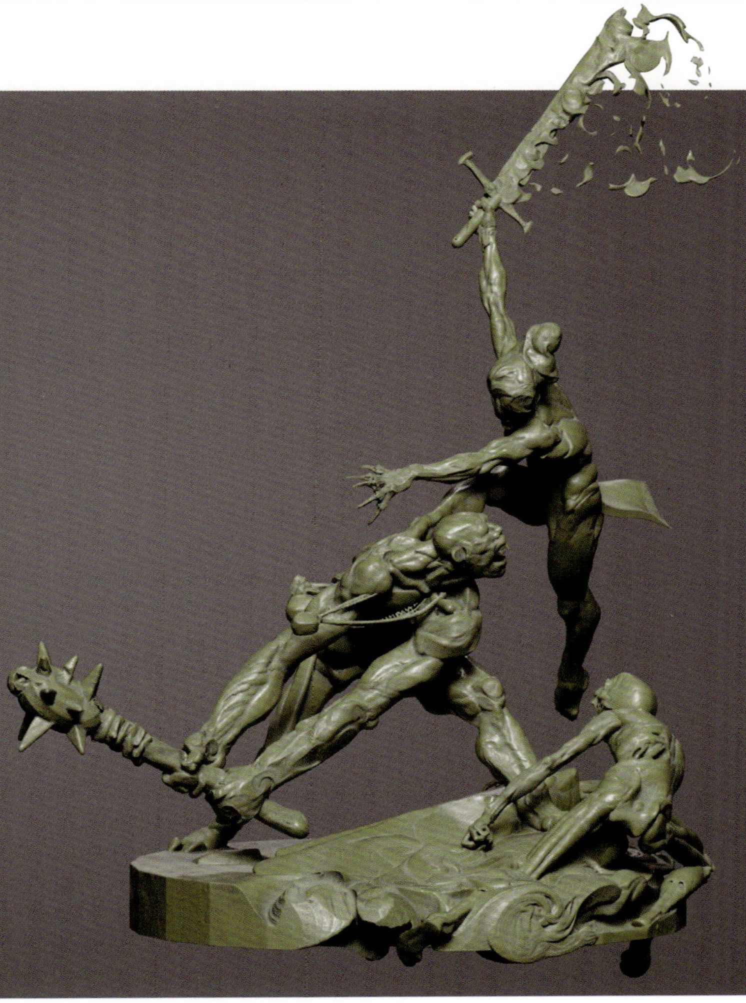

I begin to add more detail and more characters to build up the scene

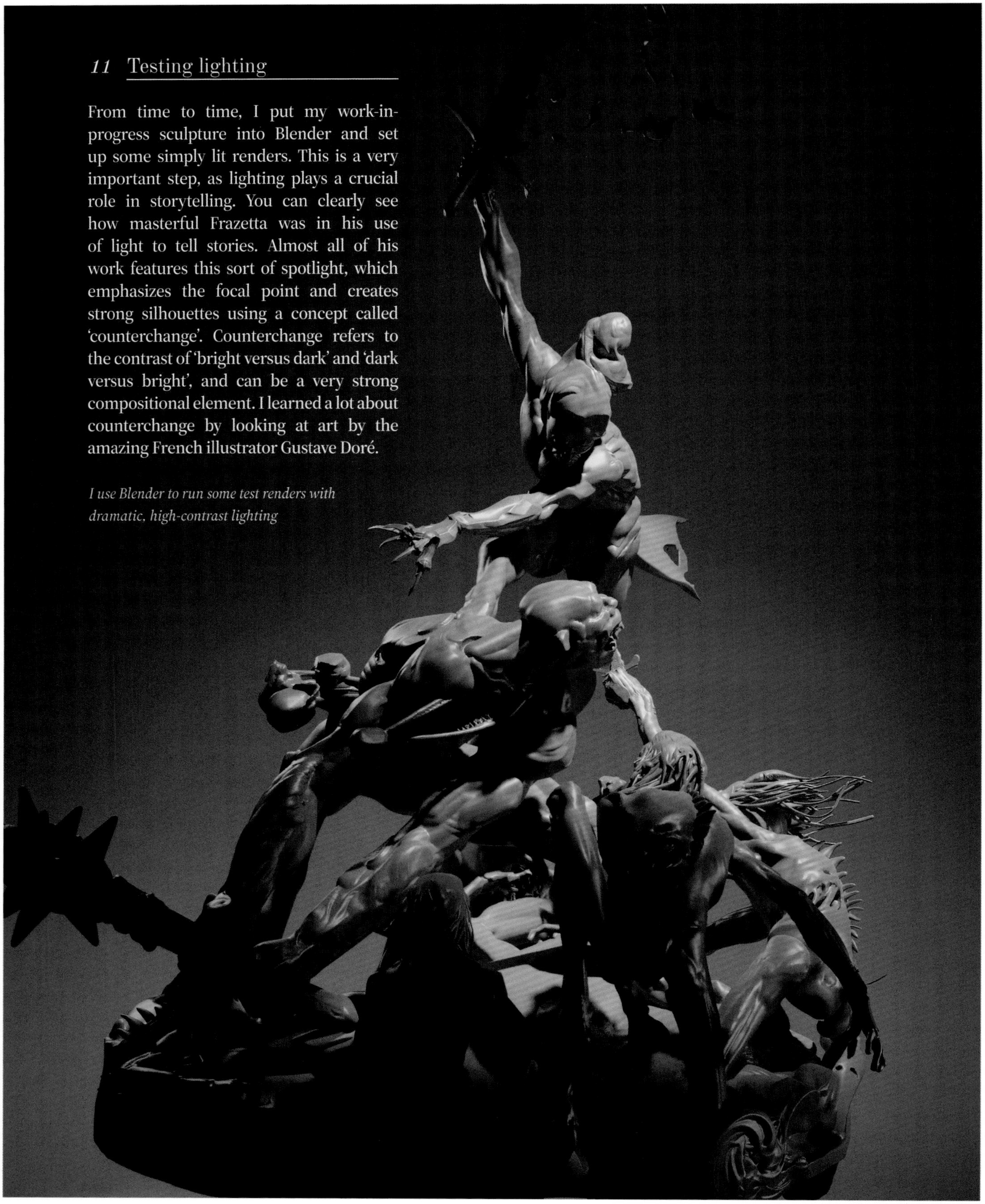

11 Testing lighting

From time to time, I put my work-in-progress sculpture into Blender and set up some simply lit renders. This is a very important step, as lighting plays a crucial role in storytelling. You can clearly see how masterful Frazetta was in his use of light to tell stories. Almost all of his work features this sort of spotlight, which emphasizes the focal point and creates strong silhouettes using a concept called 'counterchange'. Counterchange refers to the contrast of 'bright versus dark' and 'dark versus bright', and can be a very strong compositional element. I learned a lot about counterchange by looking at art by the amazing French illustrator Gustave Doré.

I use Blender to run some test renders with dramatic, high-contrast lighting

12 The finished sculpt

This is how my completed sculpture looks. I decided to change the head design of the 'Goliath' character, making it more ape-like. I love how Frazetta used animal creatures in his paintings, giving them humanoid bodies and posture, and I wanted to have some of that in my sculpture. Note how some areas are refined while others are left very loose. This is done on purpose, as I come from a background in 2D art and wanted to simulate the effect of sharp versus soft edges: sharper towards the focal point and softer as we move away from it. You can observe the same effect in all of Frazetta's paintings.

The finished sculpture, ready for lighting and final composition

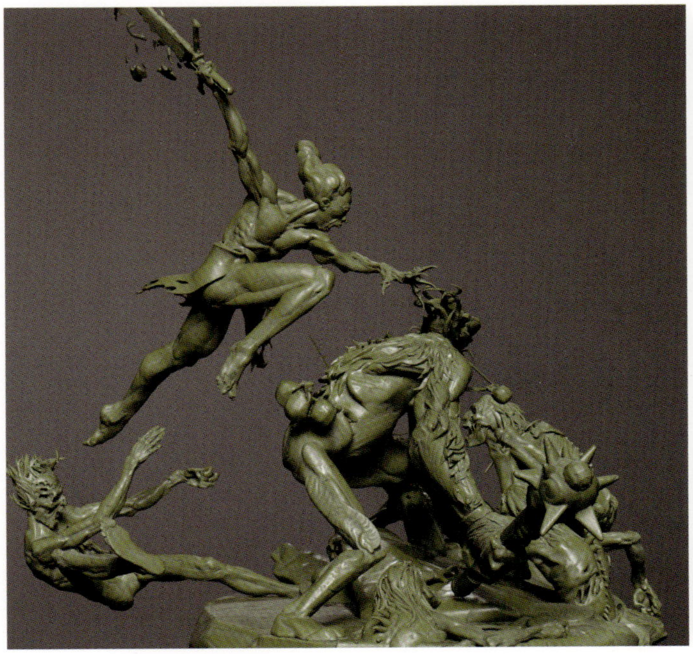

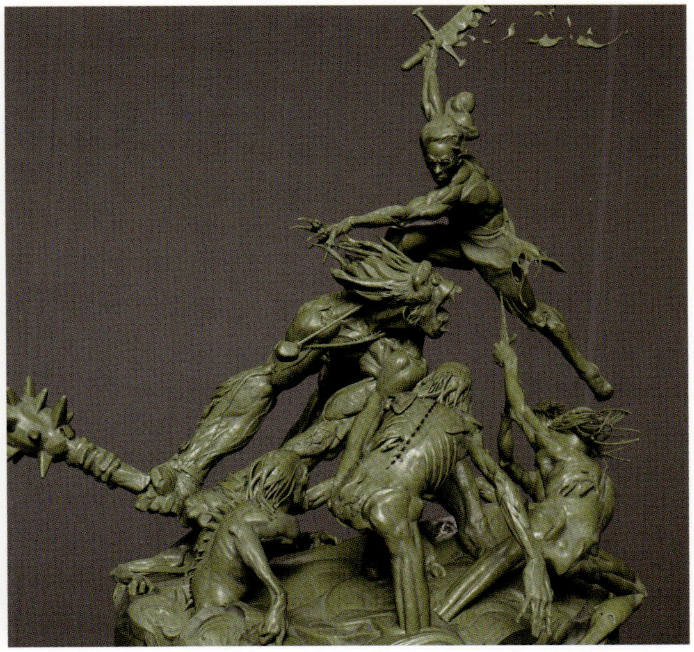

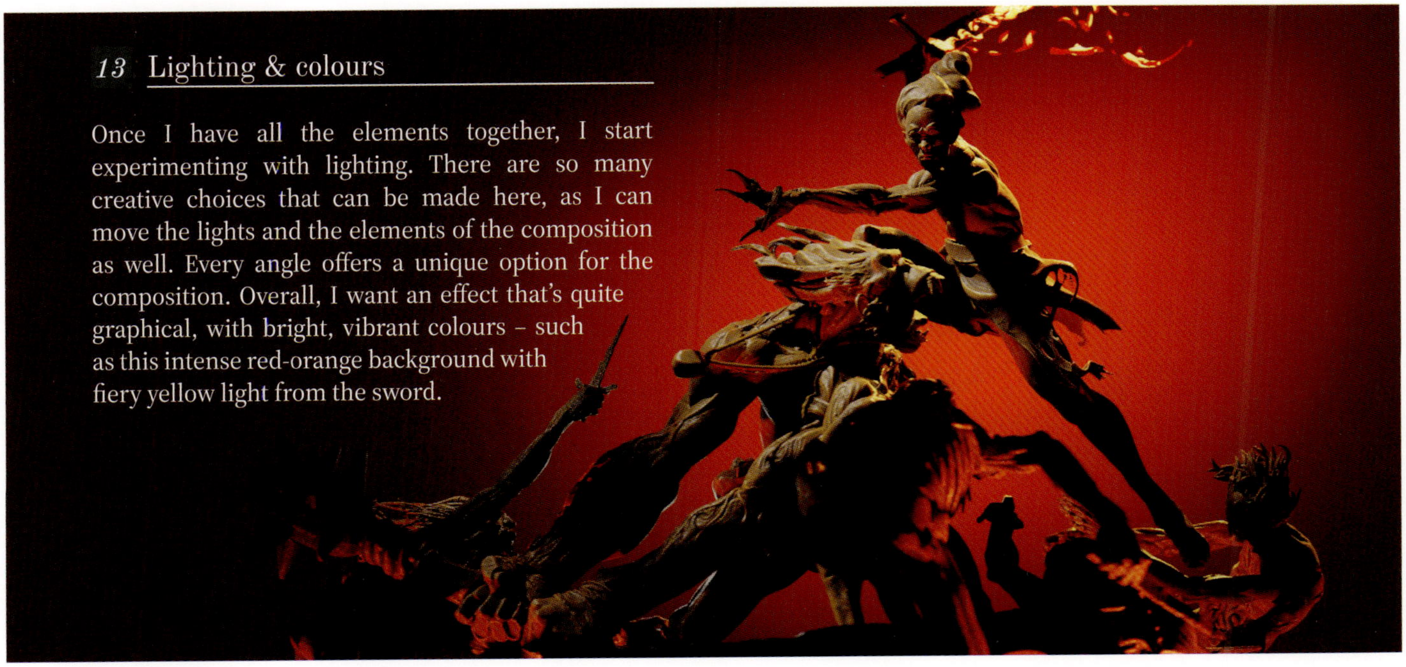

13 Lighting & colours

Once I have all the elements together, I start experimenting with lighting. There are so many creative choices that can be made here, as I can move the lights and the elements of the composition as well. Every angle offers a unique option for the composition. Overall, I want an effect that's quite graphical, with bright, vibrant colours – such as this intense red-orange background with fiery yellow light from the sword.

I try to achieve the spotlight effect you often see in Frazetta's work

14 Testing more ideas

Another great advantage of working in 3D is that I can try different ideas just by repositioning my characters. For example, I can flip the main character to see a new version of the same story. I can even explore pose changes, such as lifting the character's leg to create a different dramatic movement.

Exploring some variations of the composition

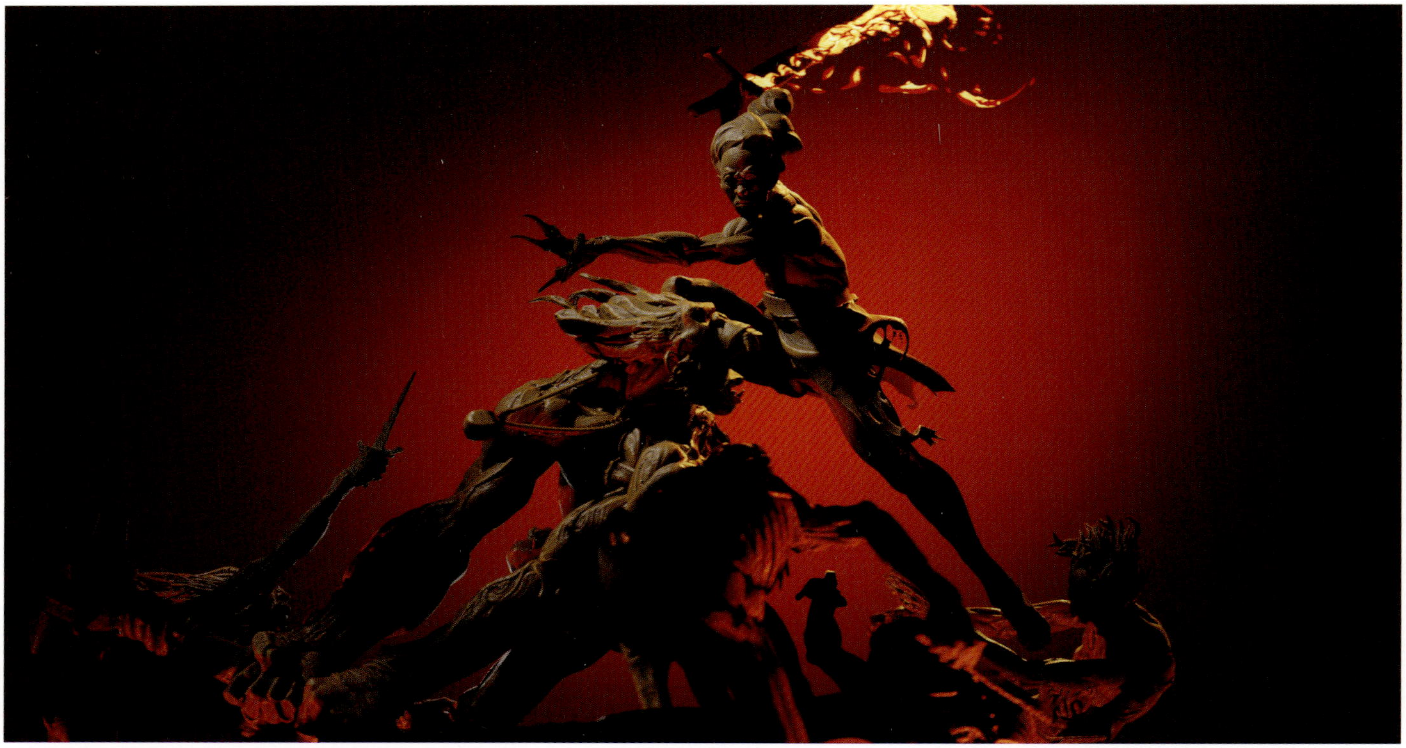

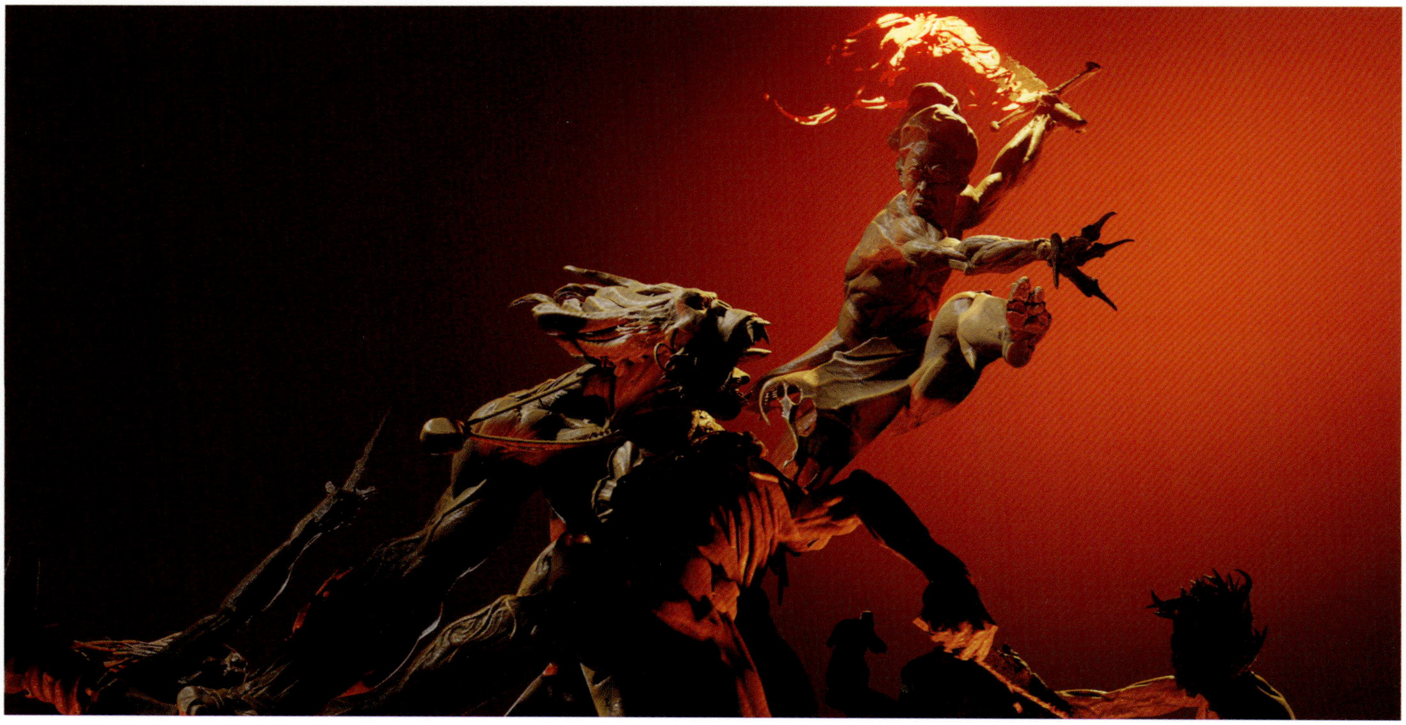

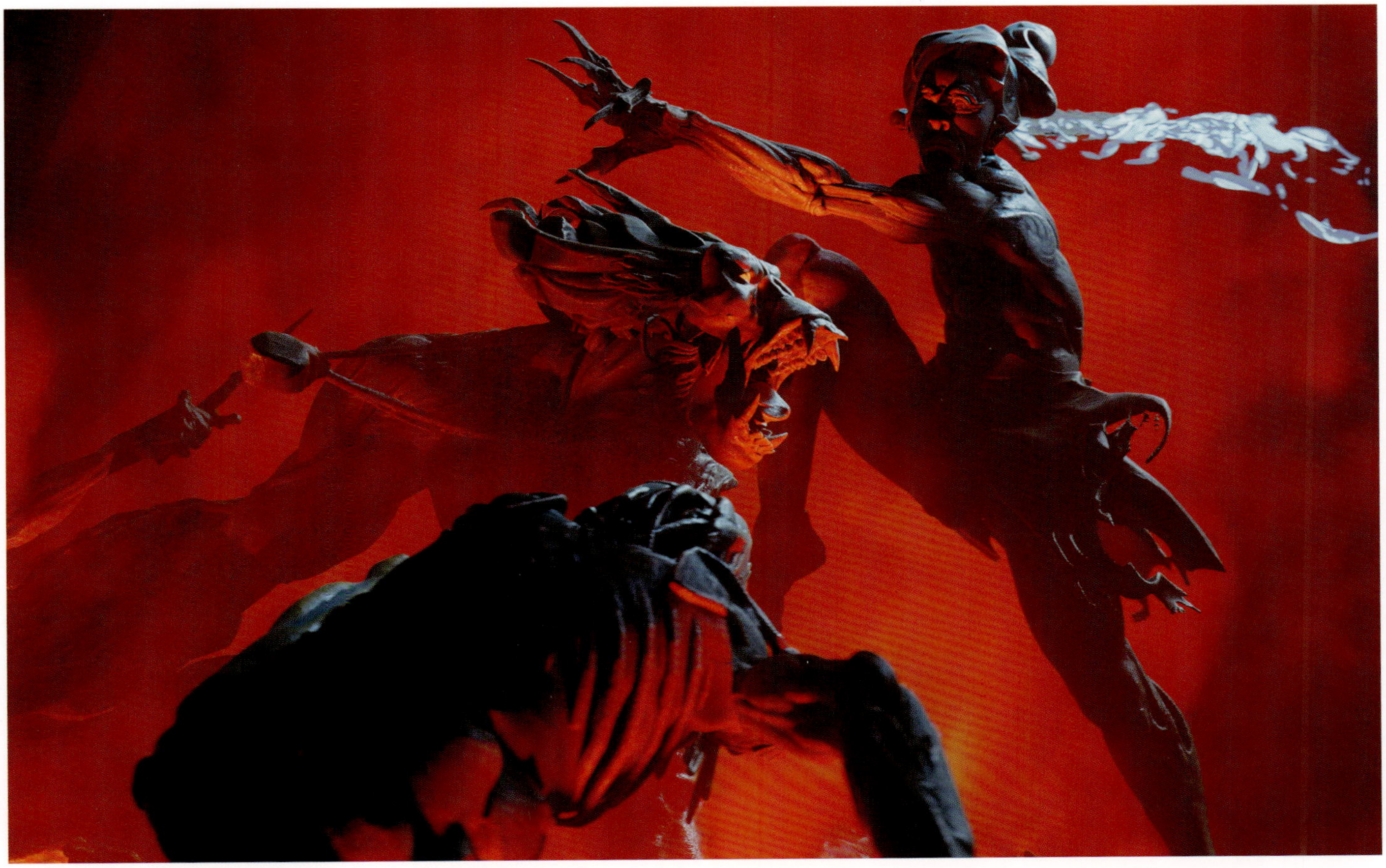

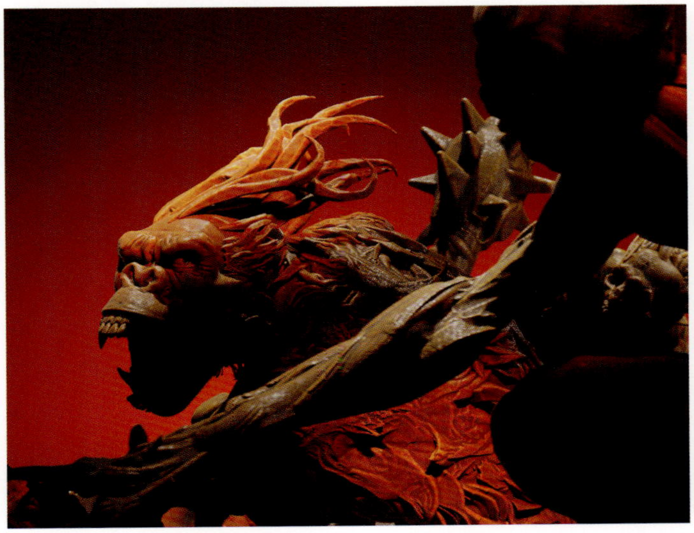

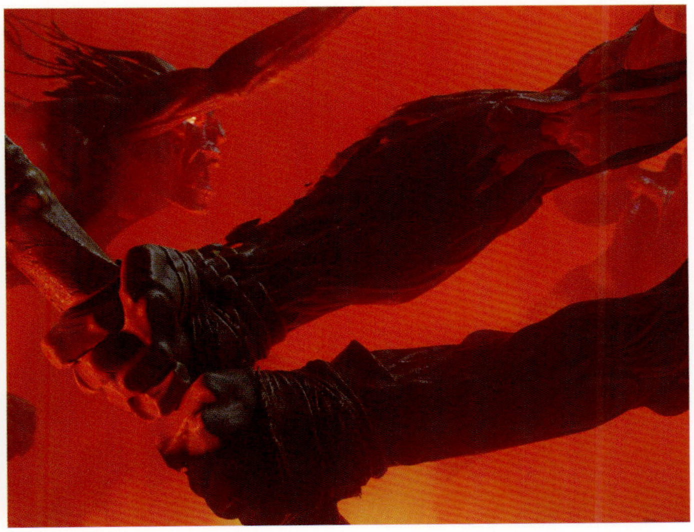

15 The final render

It's difficult to stop here, as there are so many different angles I could still explore. Here are some final renders and a few close-ups of the finished scene. I introduce some smoke elements to make the image more atmospheric and suggest at more of the environment.

Changing the sword's flame to a pale, magical blue creates a strong complementary contrast with the rest of the colour palette. For the very last, main version pictured overleaf, I make some minor adjustments in Photoshop – mainly colour correction and refining some areas that still felt a bit flat.

Making the final renders and adding some refinements with Photoshop

Conclusion

I really enjoyed working on this tribute. It reminded me, once again, of what a skilful and visionary artist Frank Frazetta was. Working on this project has made me a better artist, as I learned new things and expanded my visual library – I feel lucky to be able to study and be inspired by Frazetta's art.

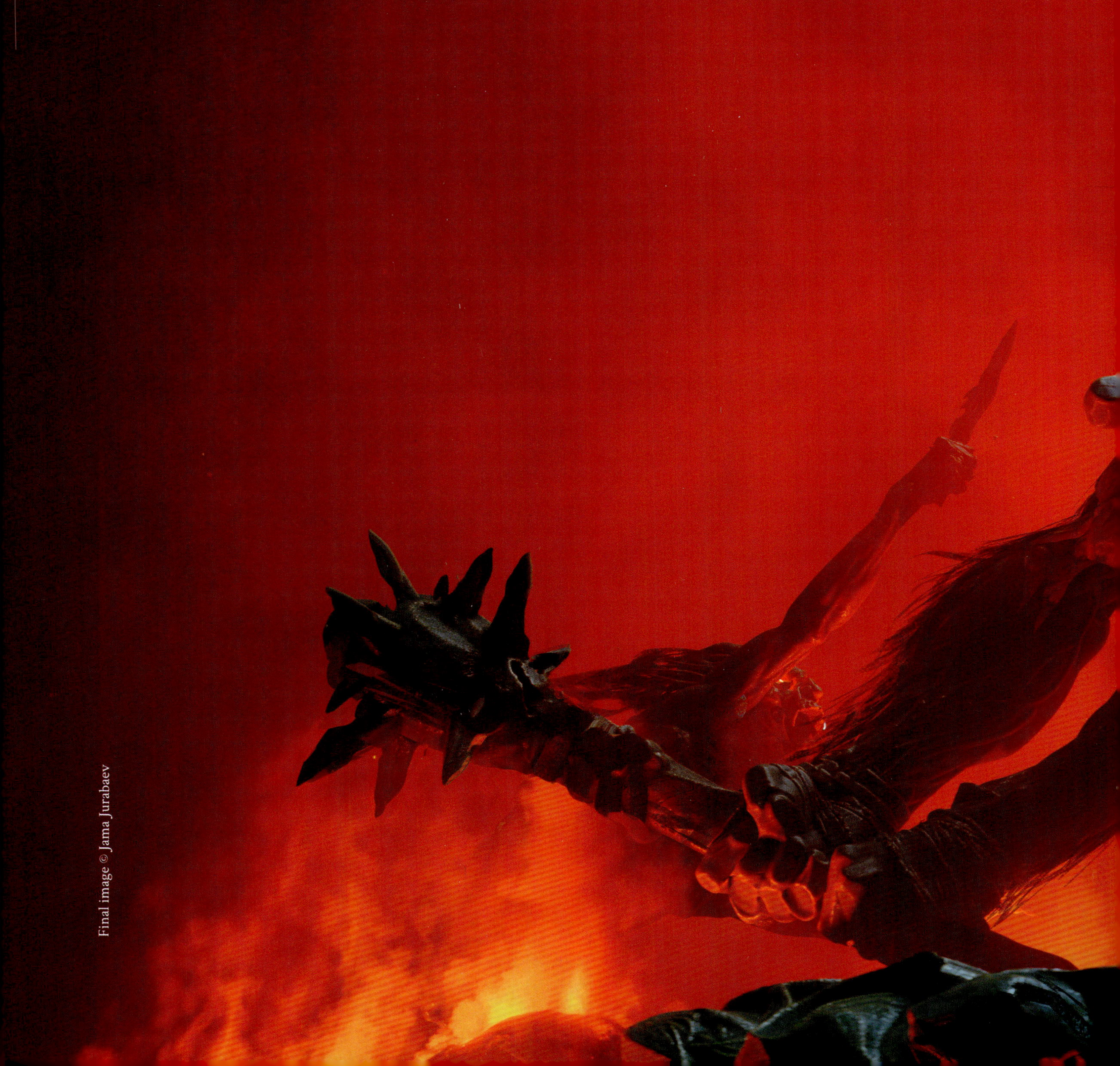

Final image © Jama Jurabaev

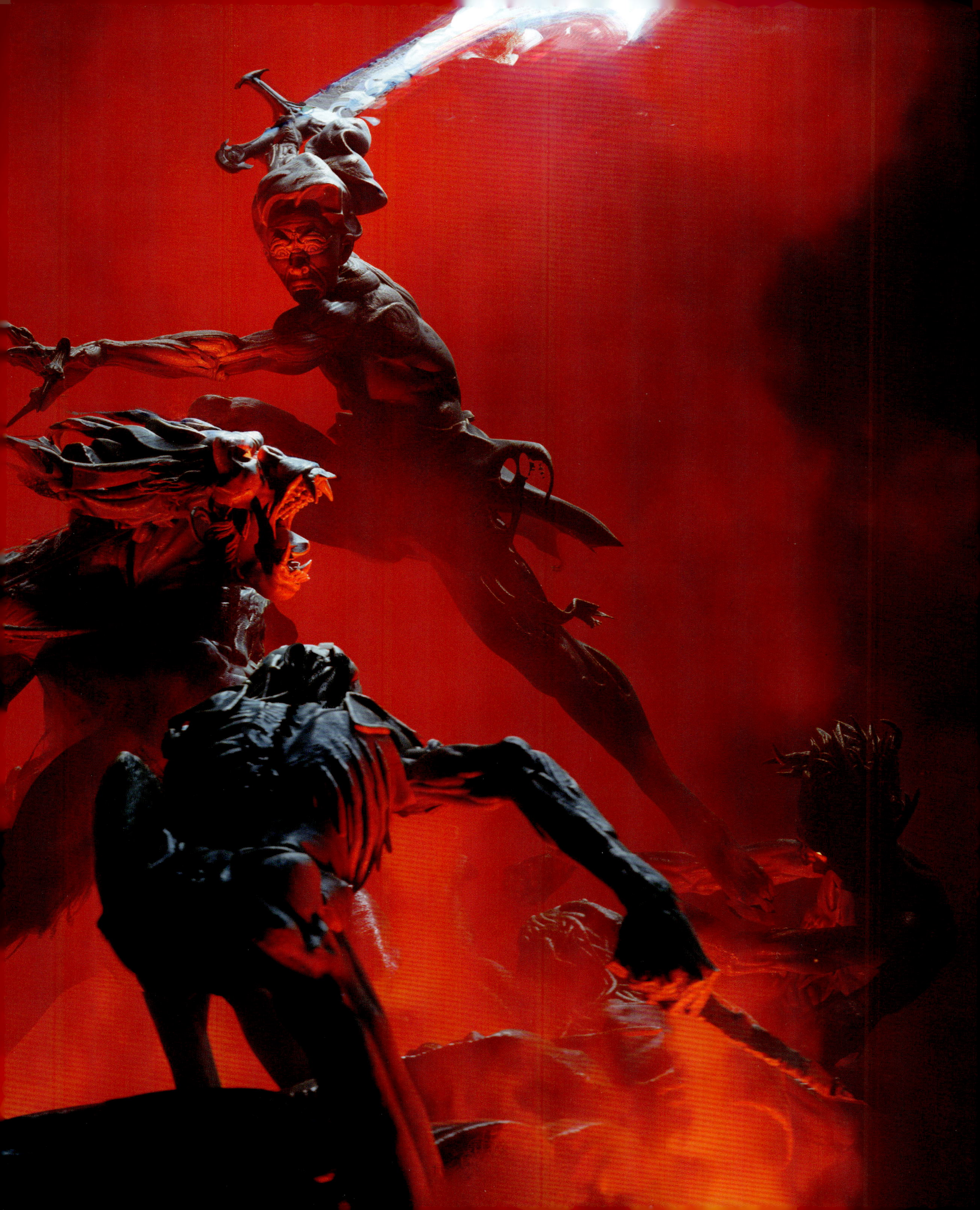

Gallery

by Jama Jurabaev

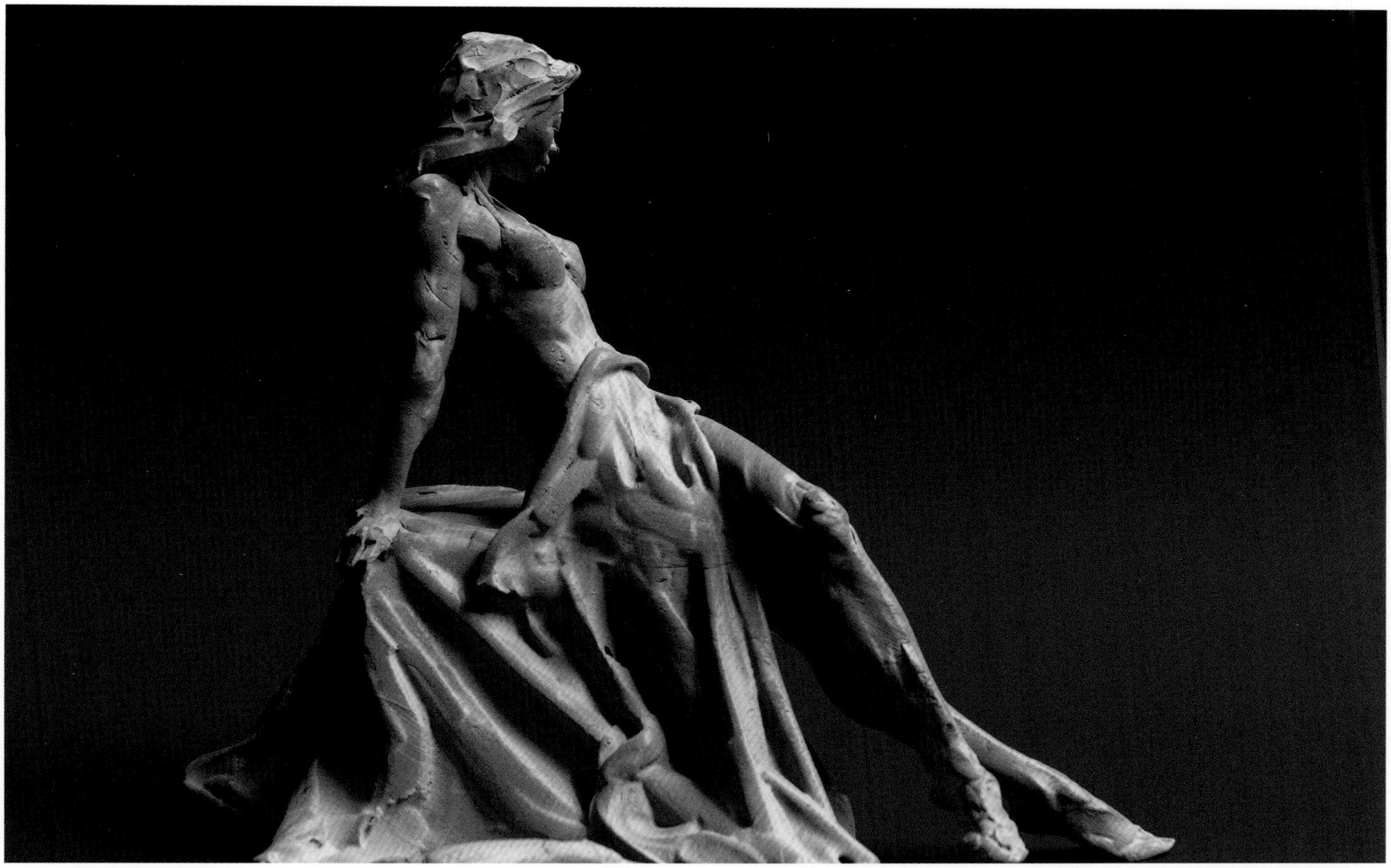

Digital clay sculpts © Jama Jurabaev

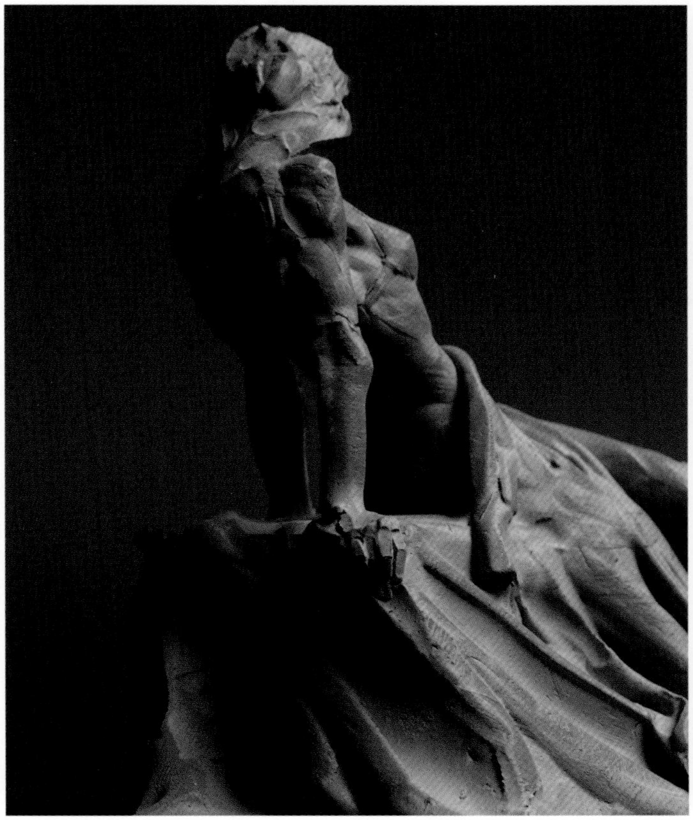

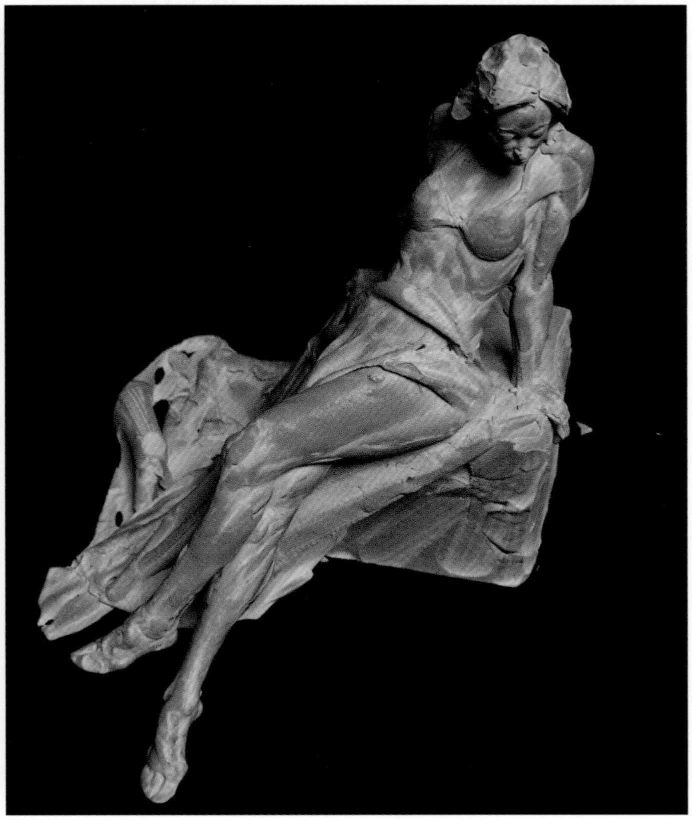

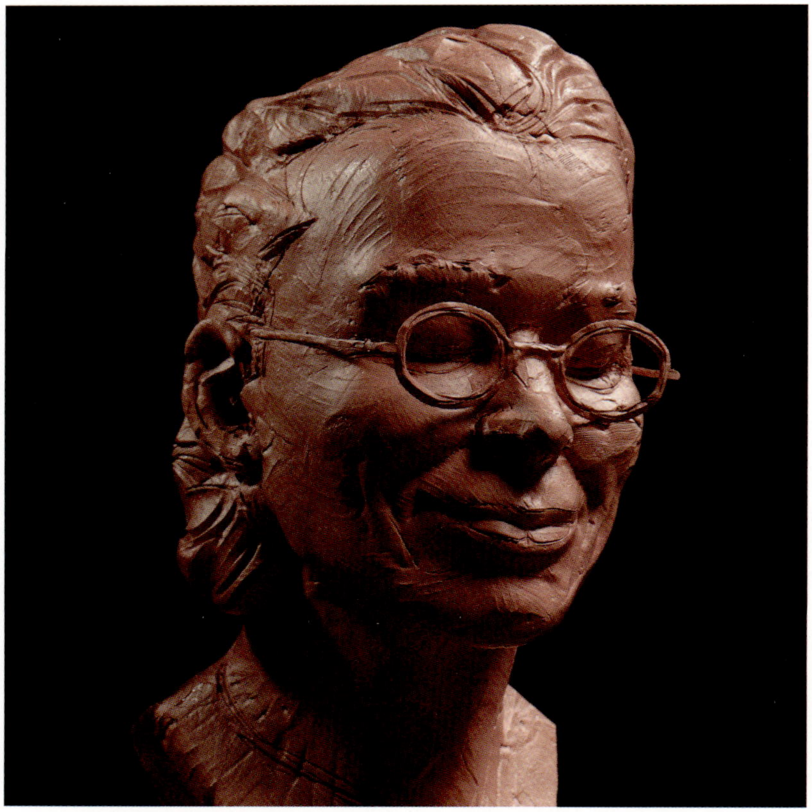

Character sculpt © Jama Jurabaev

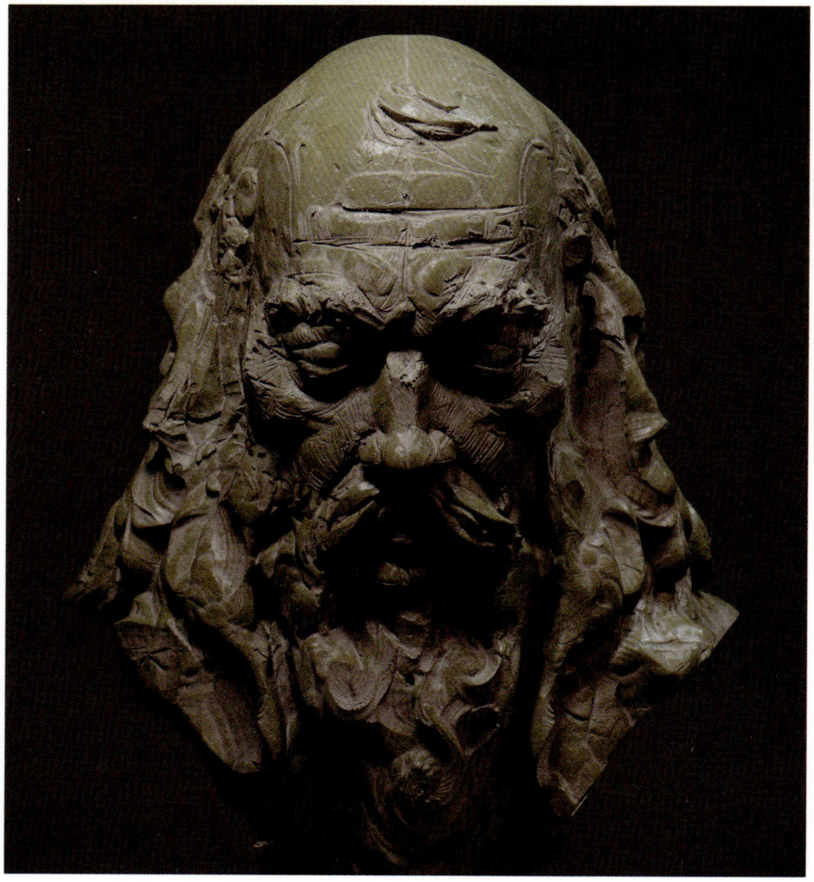

Character sculpt © Jama Jurabaev

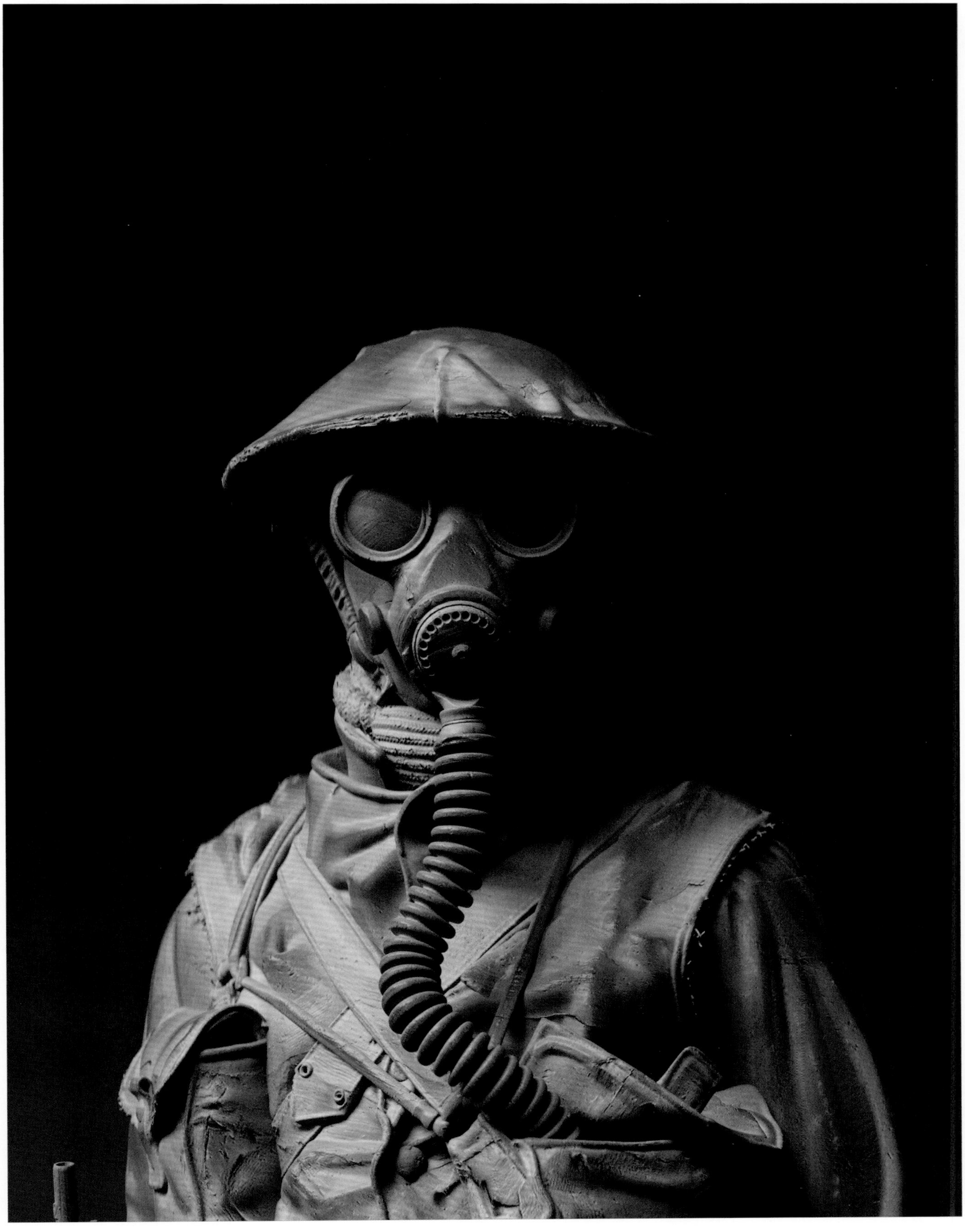

Character sculpt © Jama Jurabaev

In Conversation With:

The Shiflett Brothers

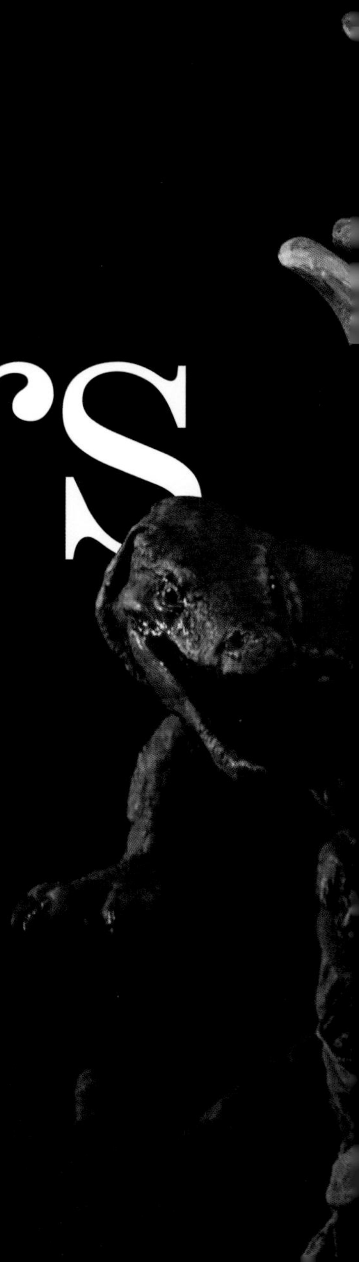

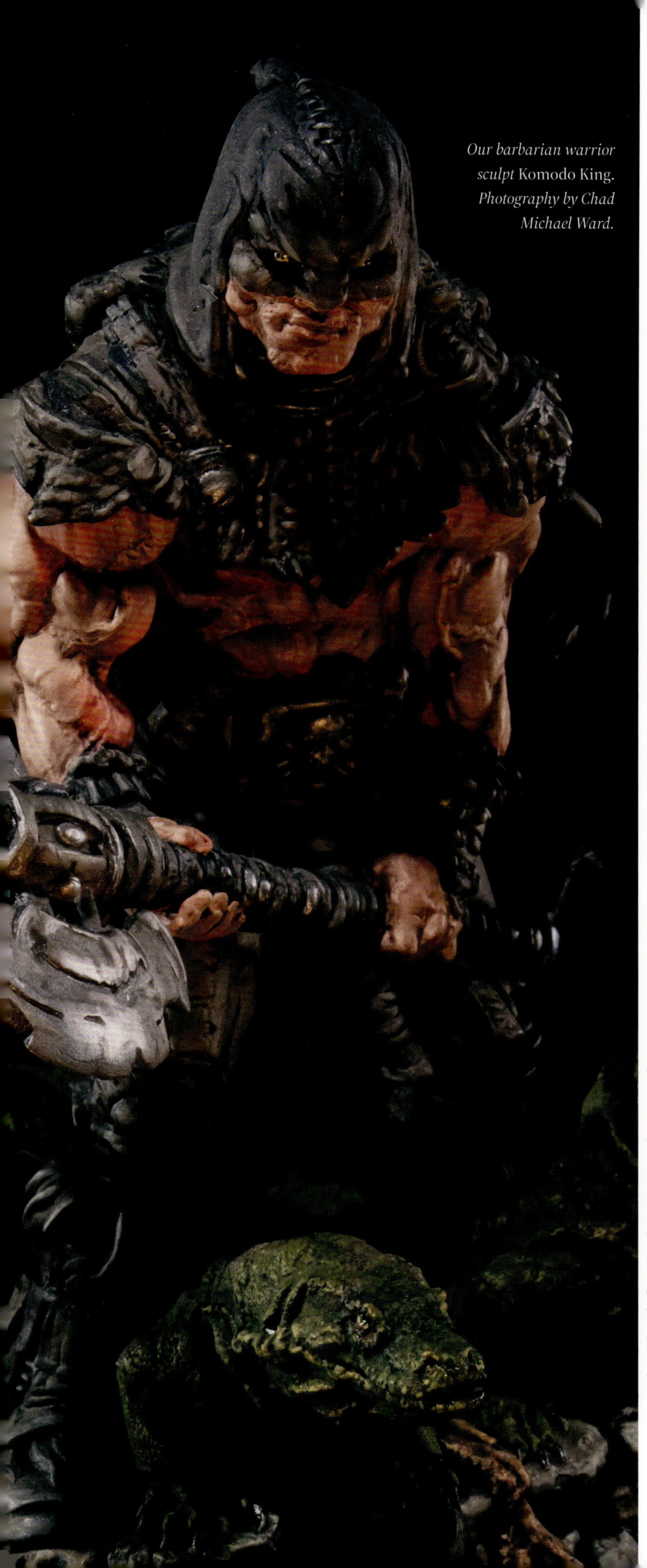

Our barbarian warrior sculpt Komodo King. *Photography by Chad Michael Ward.*

For those who don't know, please introduce yourselves. How did you both start out in art and where has your career path brought you?

Brandon: My brother Jarrod and I started sculpting traditionally, in clay, way back in the early 1990s. We were inspired by the comic books we were reading at the time, as well as fantasy artists and illustrators from the 1960s, 1970s, and 1980s. We started out doing a lot of commercial work for Marvel Comics and many other clients, but these days much of what we sculpt is our own characters, telling our own stories.

Jarrod: We are fanboys who became industry sculptors. While we have a great respect for digital work, we have always remained traditional sculptors because we need that tangible feeling of clay between our fingers.

Besides Frank Frazetta, who or what are your big creative influences or the cornerstones of your taste in art and media?

B: We have always been in love with the work of the legendary French comics illustrator Mœbius. Much of his work expanded our minds and our imaginations, just as Frazetta's paintings did.

J: We were also really affected by the art of Jeffrey Catherine Jones, a contemporary of Frazetta's for at least part of his career. As comic-book readers during the 1980s and 1990s, the work of comic-book artist Bill Sienkiewicz made a big impression on us, as well as that of British comics icon Simon Bisley. Many, many other comic artists influenced us, including Steve Rude, Mark Texeira, and the great Mike Mignola. It may seem strange that all of our early influences were artists who worked in two dimensions instead of three, but they were definitely the artists who defined what was cool for us. We just tried to translate that coolness into clay.

Which Frazetta images first grabbed you? What did you think about his work?

J: I suspect many artists would say the *Conan* book covers – and of course those blew our minds as well – but even before we encountered those, and at a very young age, we happened upon the cover for Molly Hatchet's 1979 album *Flirtin' With Disaster*, which featured Frazetta's painting *Dark Kingdom*. We were too young, I think, to even really understand it as fantasy art, but it must have opened up new pathways in our brains and we never looked back. That image is still as powerful today as it was the first time we saw it.

Moon Maid © Frank Frazetta

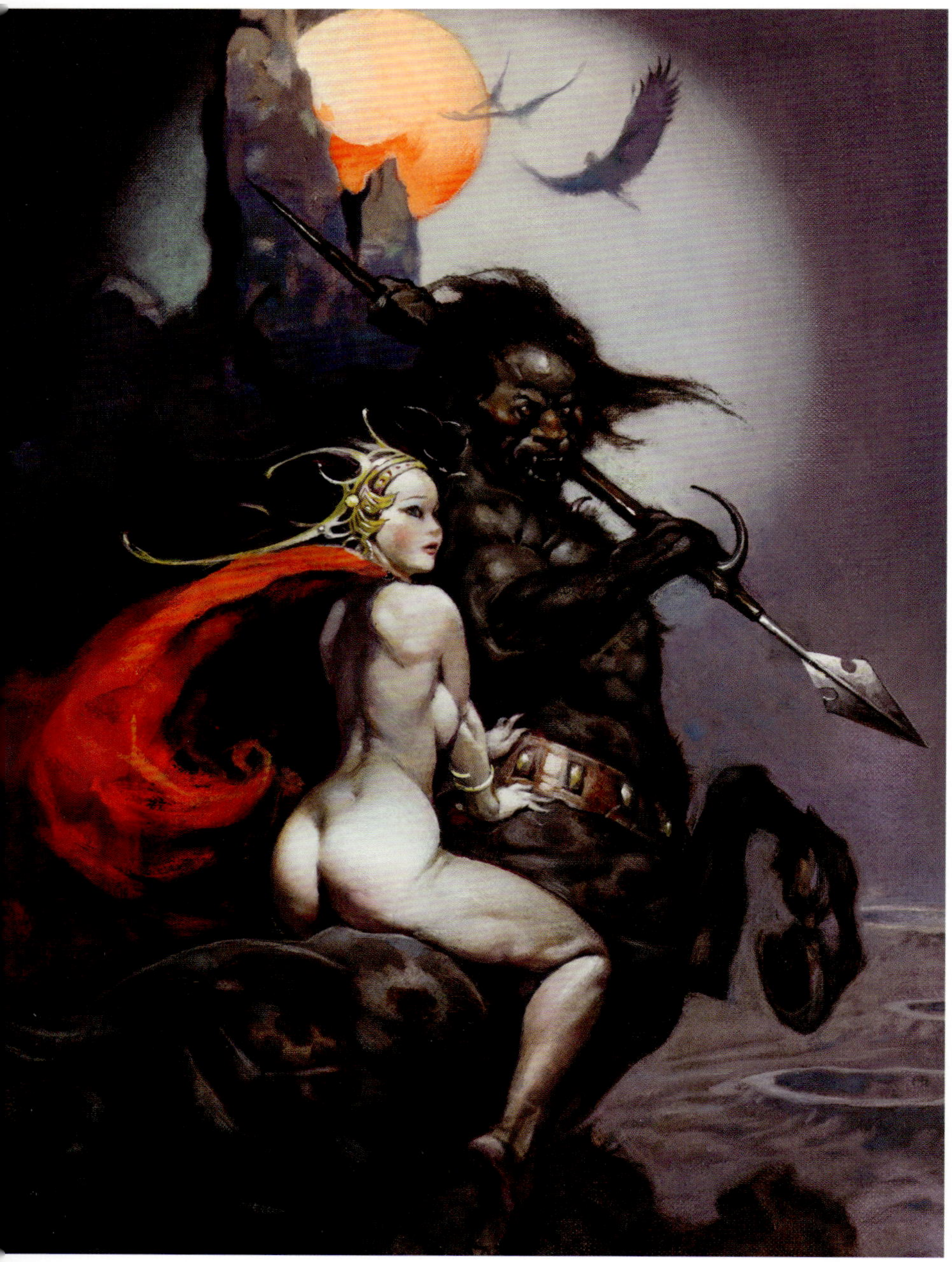

▸▸ *For image in full, turn to page 240*

What kind of imagery comes vividly to mind when you think of his work?

B: Barbarians and maidens and dinosaurs and rocket ships and ray guns and monsters!

What are your favourite Frazetta pieces?

B: I have always loved *Moon Maid*. I just think the balance and composition of the piece are impeccable. It's absolutely gorgeous. I was lucky enough to see the original painting in person once at Robert Rodriguez's pop-up gallery in Austin and the colours just dazzled! It was a really special moment for me.

J: The most meaningful piece to me is the *Dark Kingdom* painting, as we mentioned before, that we first saw as the cover of a Molly Hatchet album. The character's presence, I think, striding forward, is still one of the most dramatic images in the history of fantasy art.

What has your relationship with Frazetta's work been like over time? How has he influenced you?

B: Well, first and foremost, we are obviously huge fans of his loose, raw painting style and that has had a *massive* impact on our own work, even though we aren't using paint, but instead translating that feeling into clay. We try to get that organic, painterly feeling into every piece we create.

J: And there is a power and dynamism that he achieves that we have tried to study and figure out how to translate into three-dimensional poses. There is also this idea of what we call 'The Frazetta Triangle', which is a design and composition technique that one sees over and over in Frazetta's work. It has to do with having a wide base, compositionally speaking, leading upwards to a tip, or one spot at the top, creating a triangle effect. It's a design idea that can completely transfer over to sculpture. It's classic, it's pleasing to the eye, and it always works.

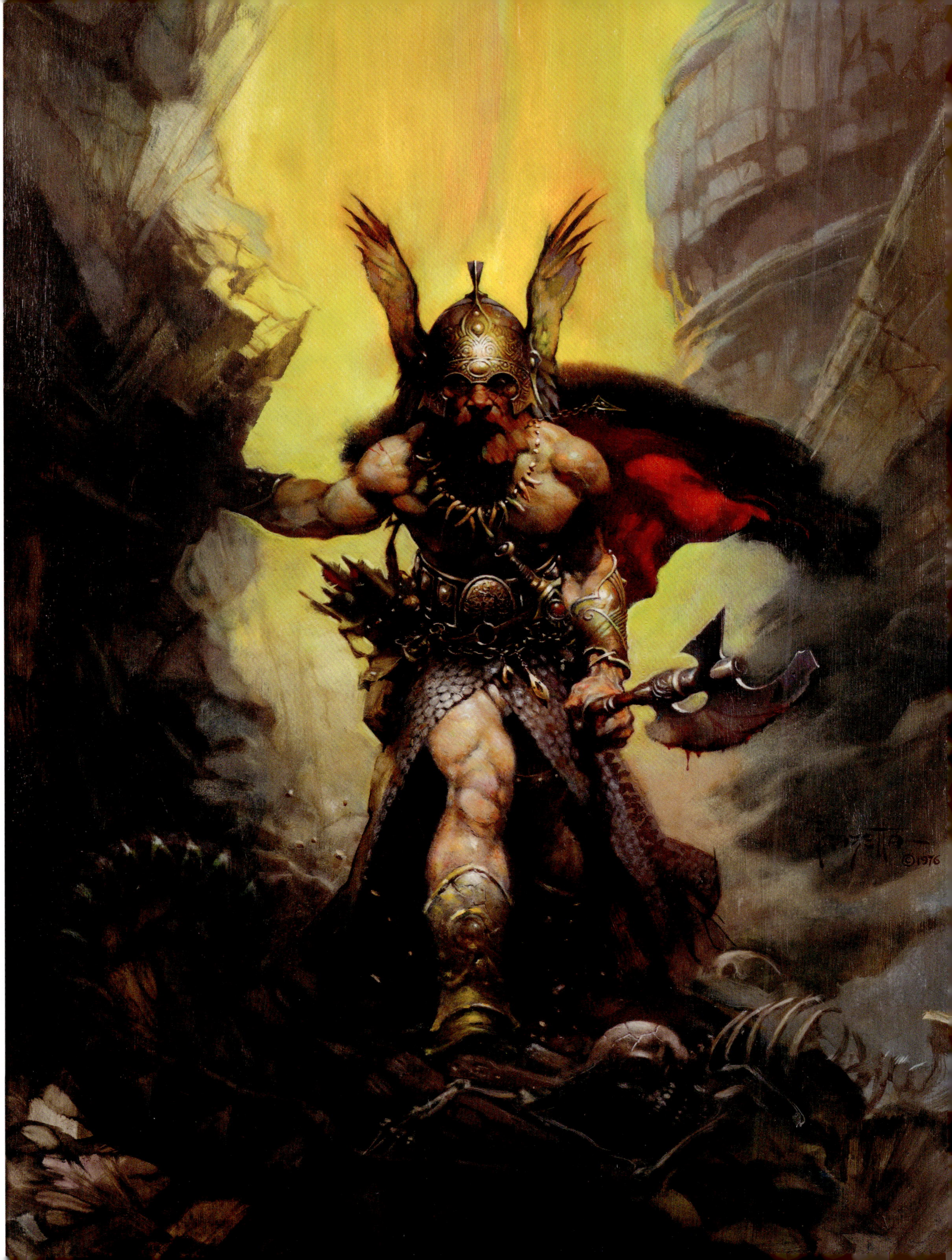

Dark Kingdom © Frank Frazetta

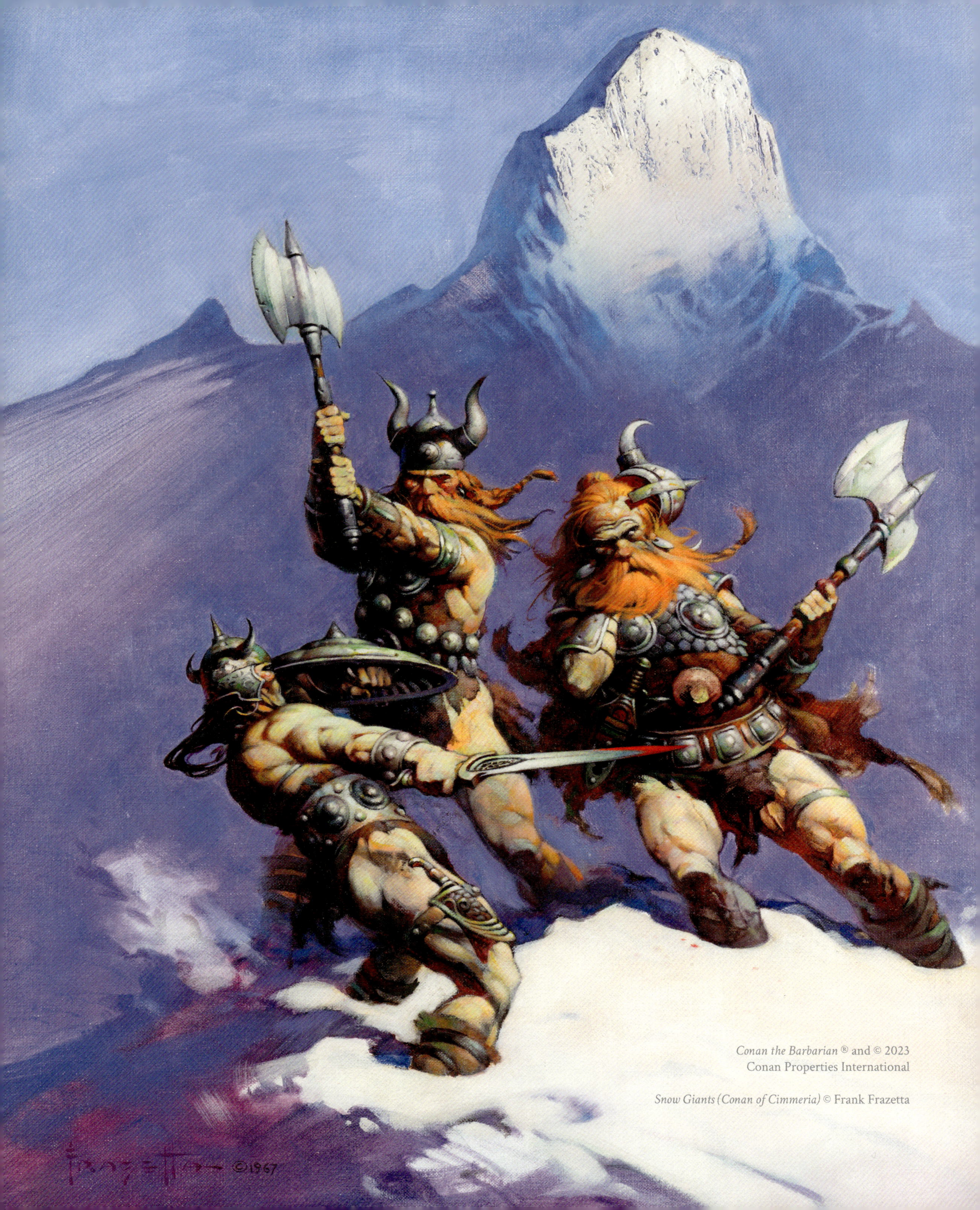

What are some favourite personal or professional projects where you've consciously drawn on that Frazetta influence?

J: Oh wow, there are so many. We created a resin kit and a bronze piece called *Komodo King* (see page 77), which is a masked barbarian with an axe standing among three Komodo dragons. People sometimes ask us, 'Is this from a Frazetta painting?' Well, it's not, but it so could be! And that's the point of it – it's a little homage to the master.

B: Yes, we love homages. We've never been the kinds of artists who hide our influences or try to pretend that it's all some kind of mystical, innate design skill at work. We, all of us working artists in this genre, stand on the shoulders of giants – and the giant among the giants is Frank Frazetta.

What are some of the joys and challenges of translating a Frazetta concept into a three-dimensional medium?

B: One of the joys can definitely be if you are lucky enough to capture one of those ineffable qualities of his work, like the power or the dynamism. I don't think these things are captured on a purely technical level, either... I think that there is some heart and love involved.

J: Frazetta painted the aspects of the characters that were important to him: the arms holding the axe for instance, or the forward leg – the things he felt were most important to the overall piece. But if there is an unimportant leg that is in the background, it can often just fade away or turn to blackness in the painting. Trying to figure out how Frazetta *would* have painted – or even sculpted – that leg can be daunting. This goes for the backs of characters as well. You can do as much research as you like, but in the end, on some pieces, you are simply forced to make up some design work in what is your best 'Frazetta Style'. You are basically guessing how the master would have handled it. It's downright intimidating!

Where do you see his legacy when you look around today?

B: Oh, everywhere! Obviously, book covers. But also comic books, feature films, video games, board games, advertising – and yes, even Shiflett Brothers statues.

J: And on the sides of totally kickass vans! ❖

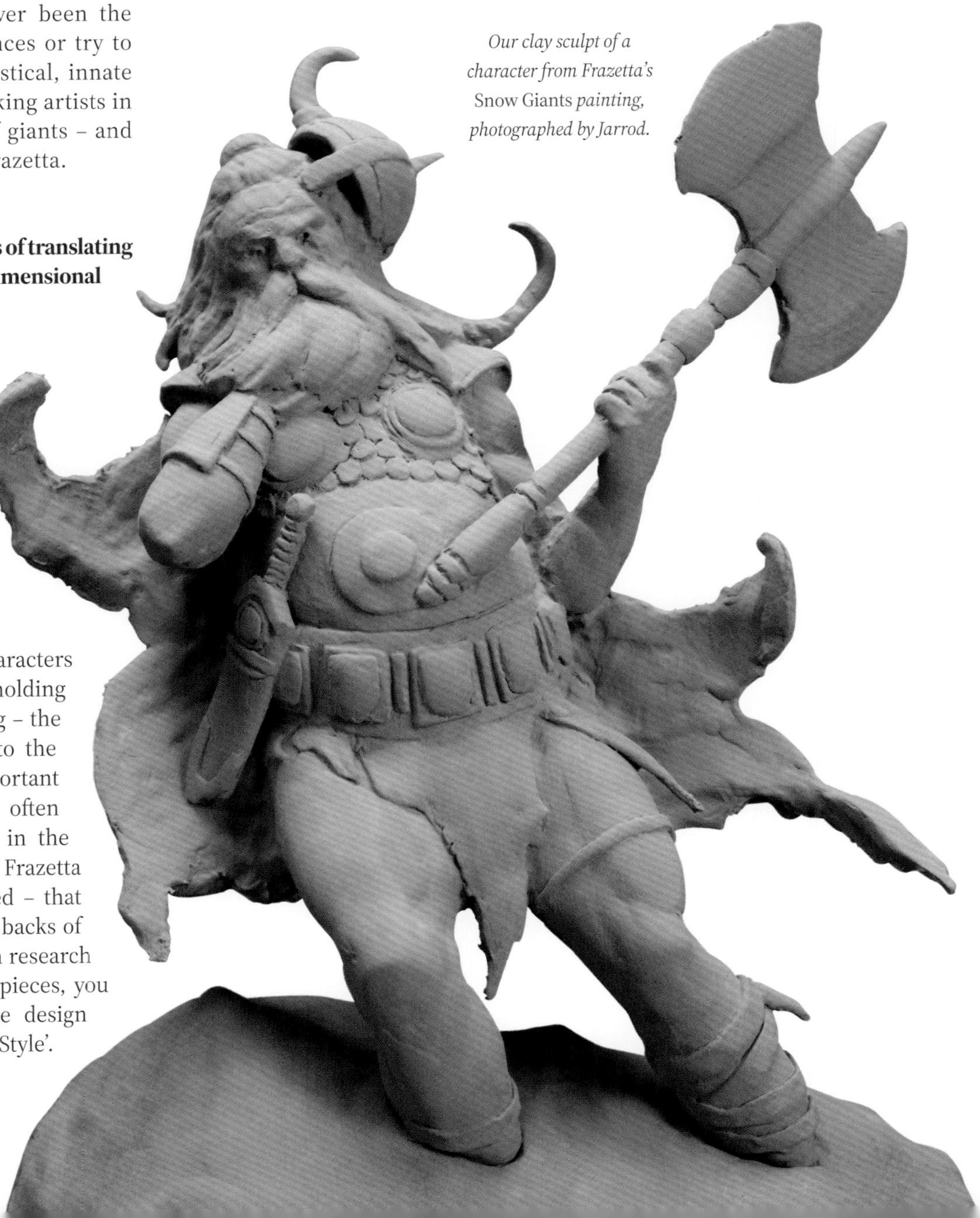

Our clay sculpt of a character from Frazetta's Snow Giants *painting, photographed by Jarrod.*

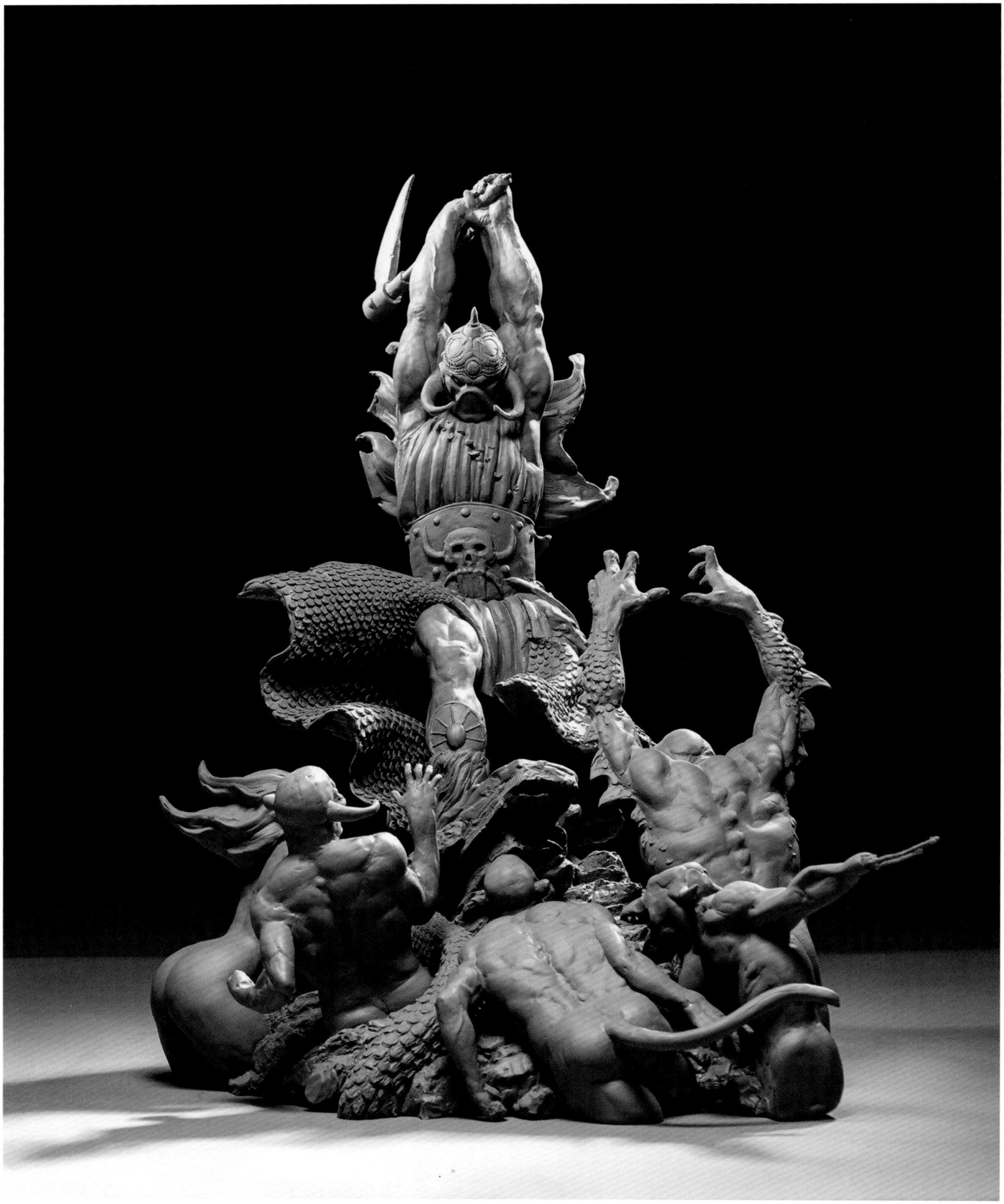

Our version of Death Dealer II, *sculpted for Frazetta Girls. Photography by Matt Mrozek.*

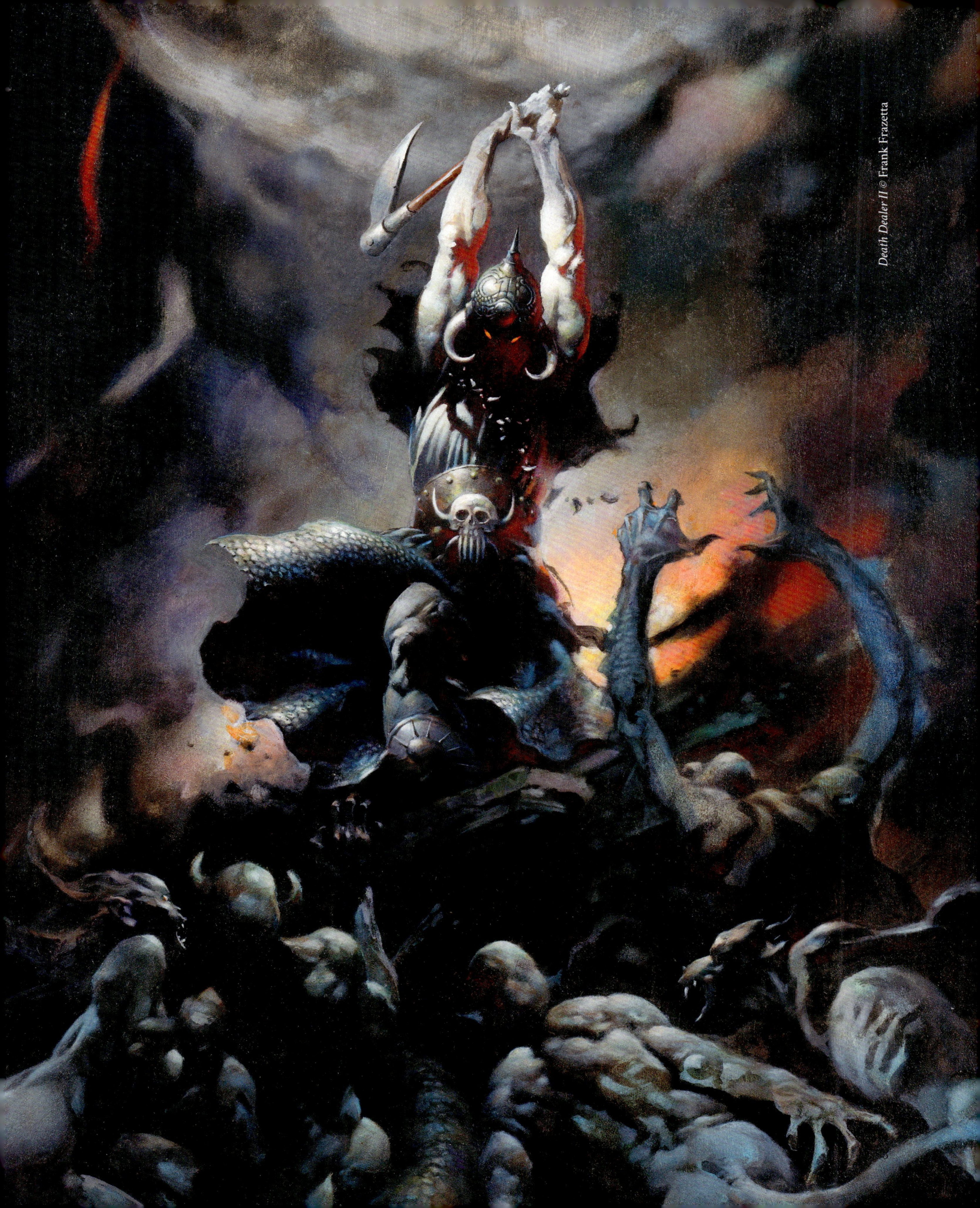

Death Dealer II © Frank Frazetta

The

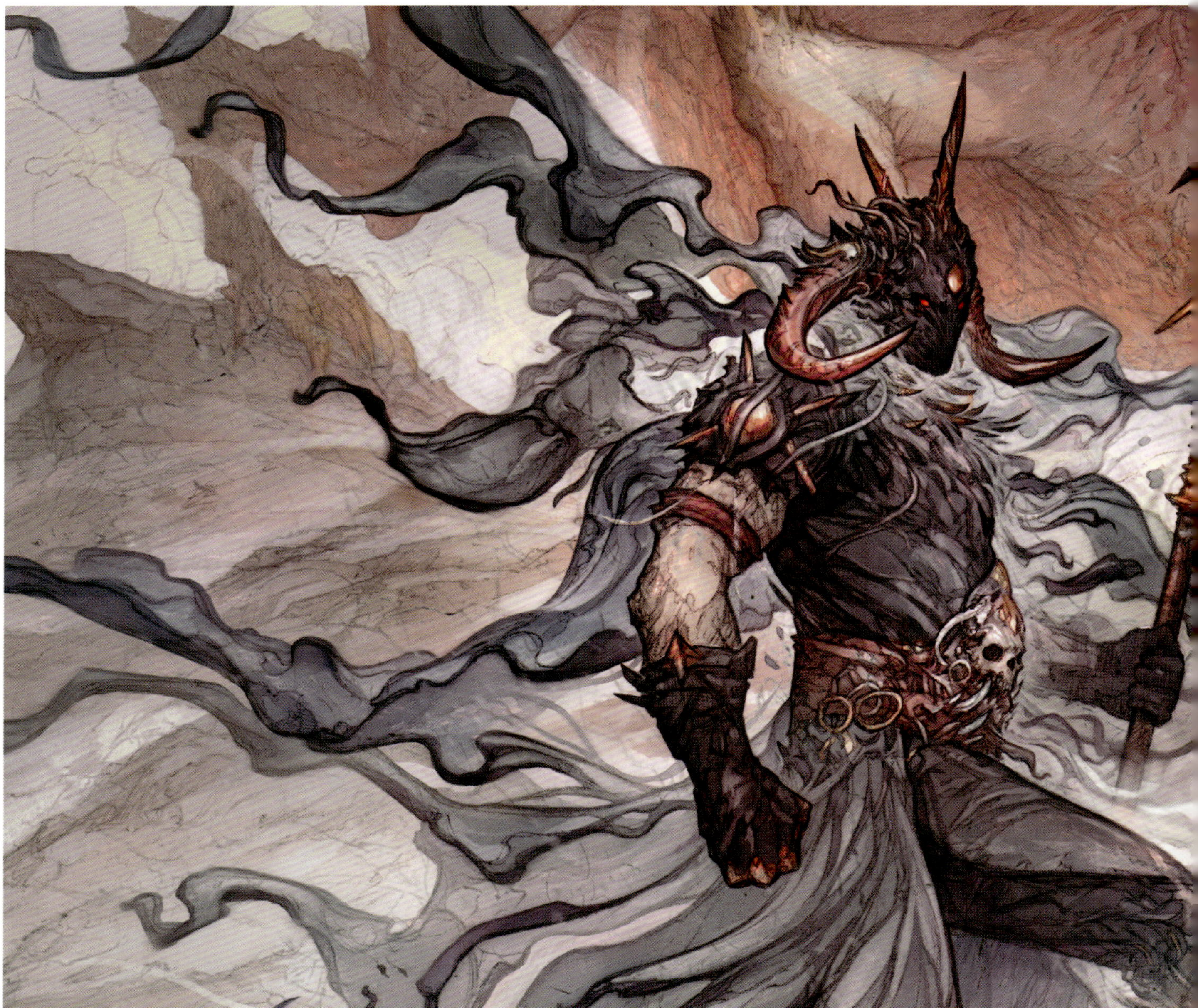

Final image © Dibujante Nocturno (Fran Garcés)

Warrior

by Dibujante Nocturno (Fran Garcés)

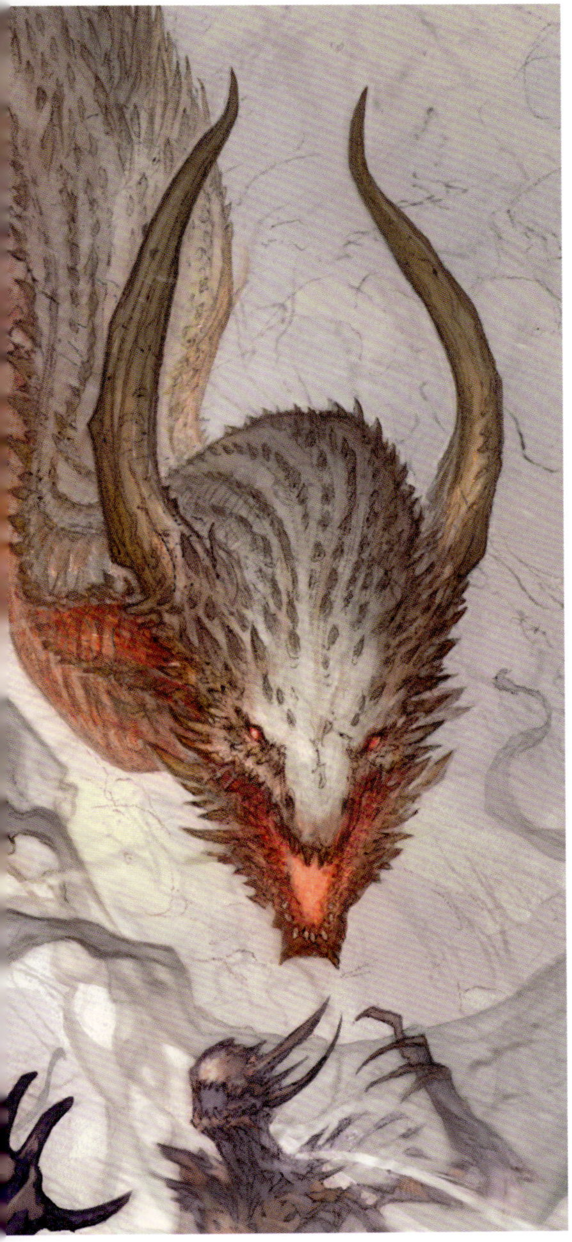

Creating *The Warrior*

Finding Frazetta's work was like discovering a path; it provided me with an artistic direction to follow and a goal to aim for. I thought, 'I want to be able to paint like that!' The strength of his paintings has influenced me considerably, to the point that I always look for that in my art. I fell in love with *Death Dealer I* due to its strength, darkness, and the power it conveys. The brushstrokes in Frazetta's artwork flow like a beautiful storm, creating epic atmospheres. While I cannot recreate a Frazetta masterpiece, I hope to be able to capture something of that darkness and elegance in my artwork.

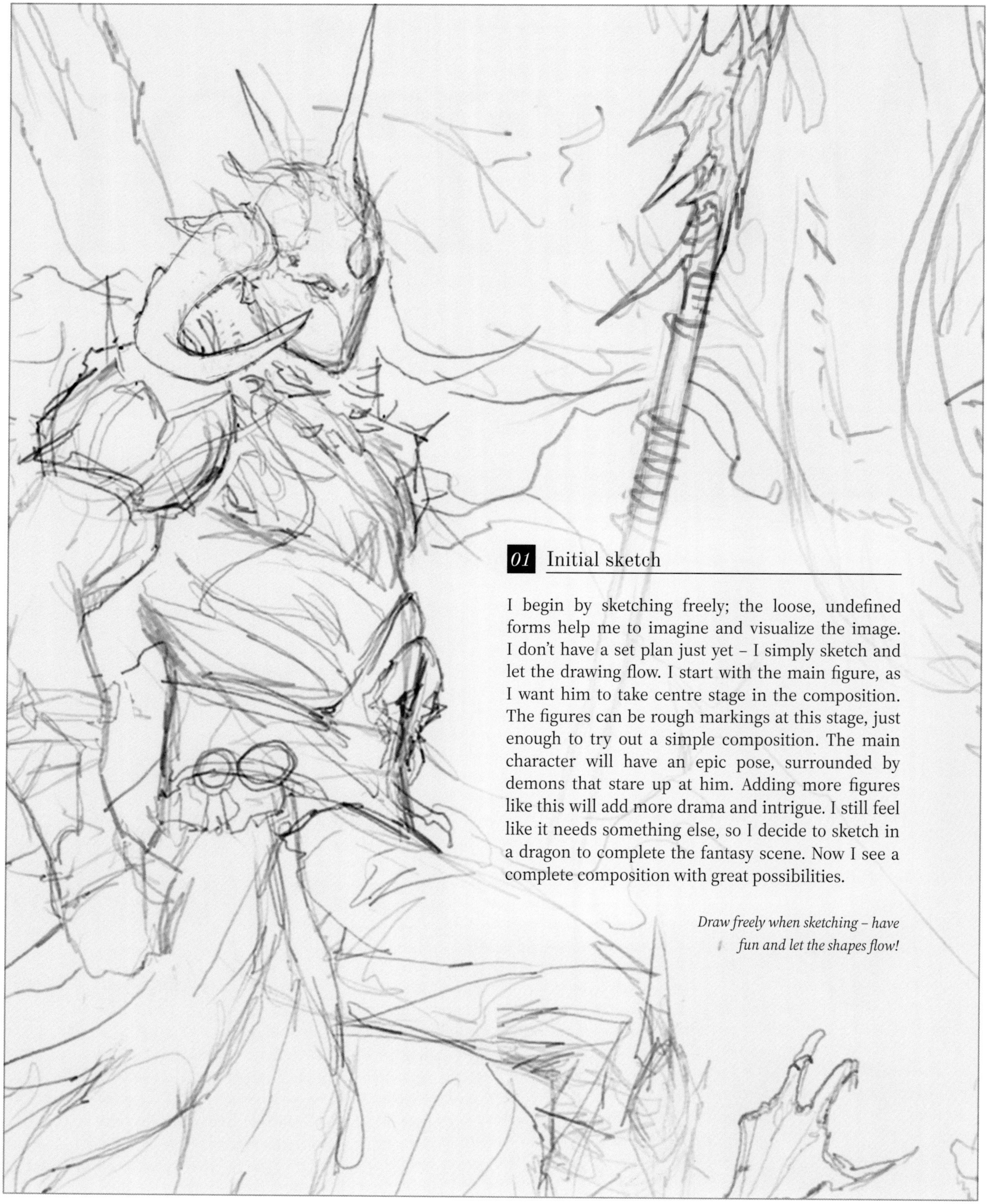

01 Initial sketch

I begin by sketching freely; the loose, undefined forms help me to imagine and visualize the image. I don't have a set plan just yet – I simply sketch and let the drawing flow. I start with the main figure, as I want him to take centre stage in the composition. The figures can be rough markings at this stage, just enough to try out a simple composition. The main character will have an epic pose, surrounded by demons that stare up at him. Adding more figures like this will add more drama and intrigue. I still feel like it needs something else, so I decide to sketch in a dragon to complete the fantasy scene. Now I see a complete composition with great possibilities.

Draw freely when sketching – have fun and let the shapes flow!

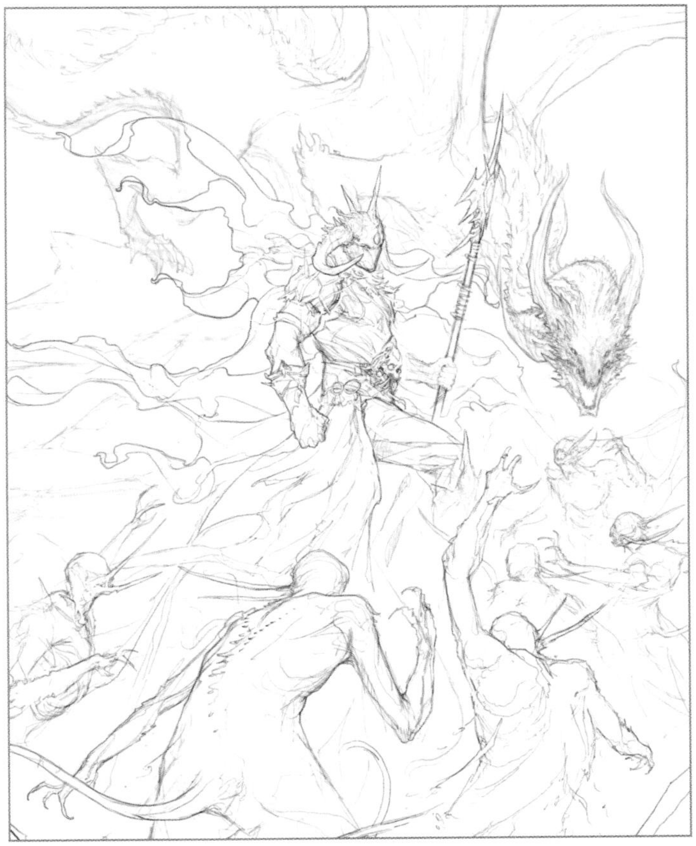

Making the lines dynamic to communicate the character's epic nature

02 Dynamic lines

Once I have the composition and central figure down on paper – the rough sketch, without detail – I add dynamism using lines that flow, like the warrior's cape. To create a cape for him that is pure fantasy, I experiment with various types of fabric until I find one that best conveys his magic, power, and strength. Good line work is something I really value and want to be the driving force of this image.

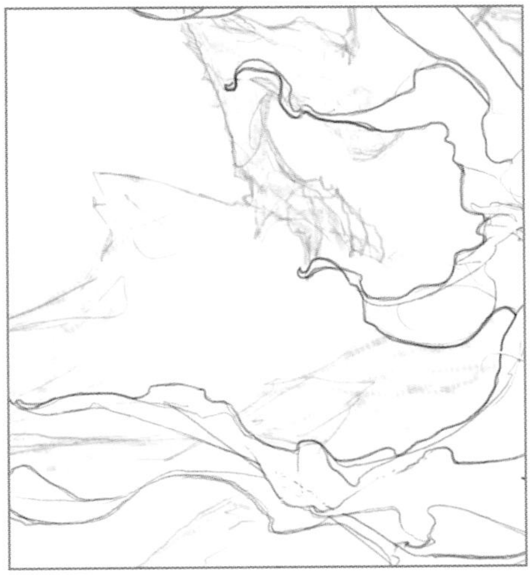

03 Defining the sketch

I begin to define and add a certain level of detail to the drawing. The loose-lined characters now possess some definition, though they are still very sketchy. Similarly, I start to define the main character's armour, drawing the details of his belt and helmet – now he is beginning to look real. This process must advance gradually; allow yourself time to reflect and let the drawing tell you what the next step is.

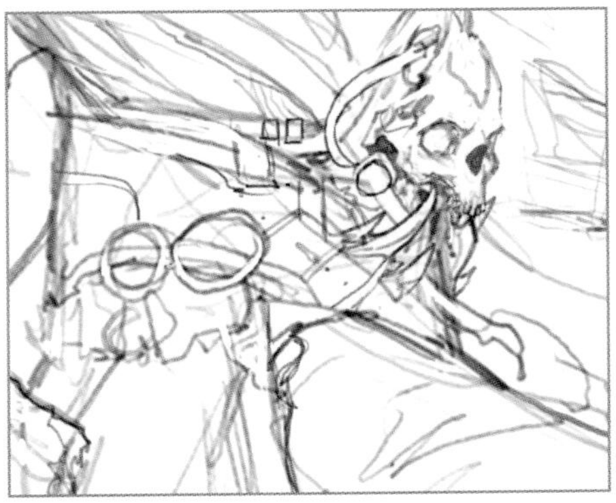

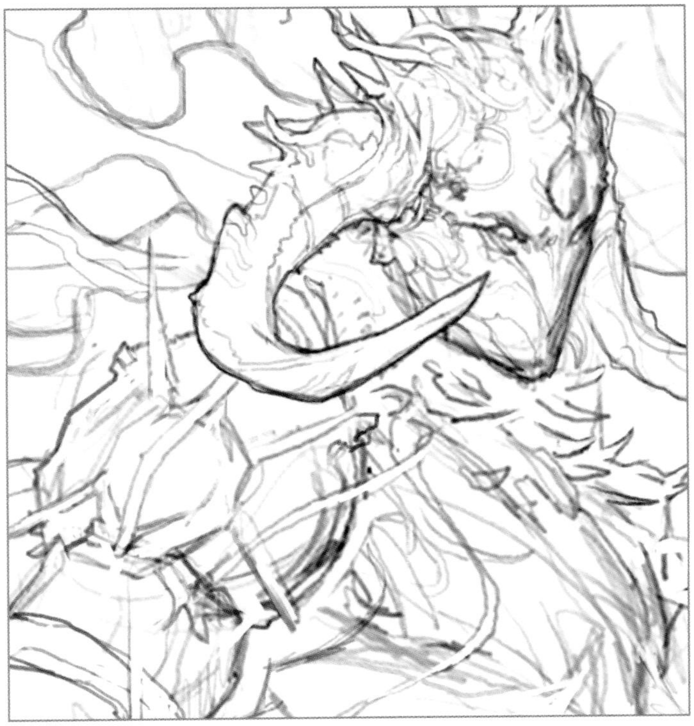

Defining the sketch with more detail, giving life to the drawing

04 Line work

It's important to me that my line work is prominent in the final artwork, so I dedicate a lot of time to this part. Drawing with a pen, I use a light table to transfer the composition onto good paper in A3 format. The size of the drawing is important, as it must be big enough to allow for the amount of detail I want to include for the main character. If it were smaller, it would be difficult to detail with the pen and I would not be able to achieve the level of finish I'm aiming for.

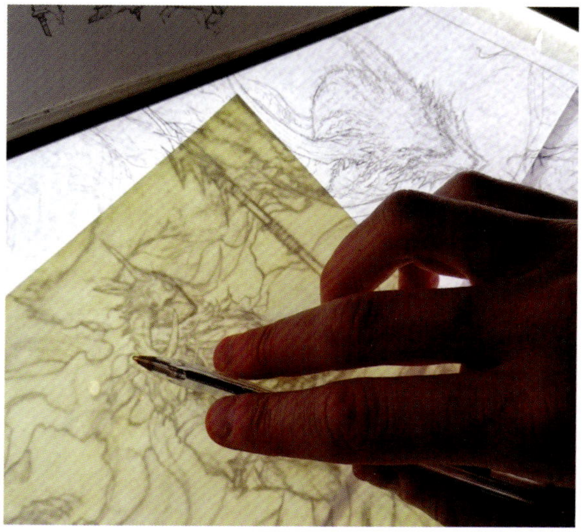

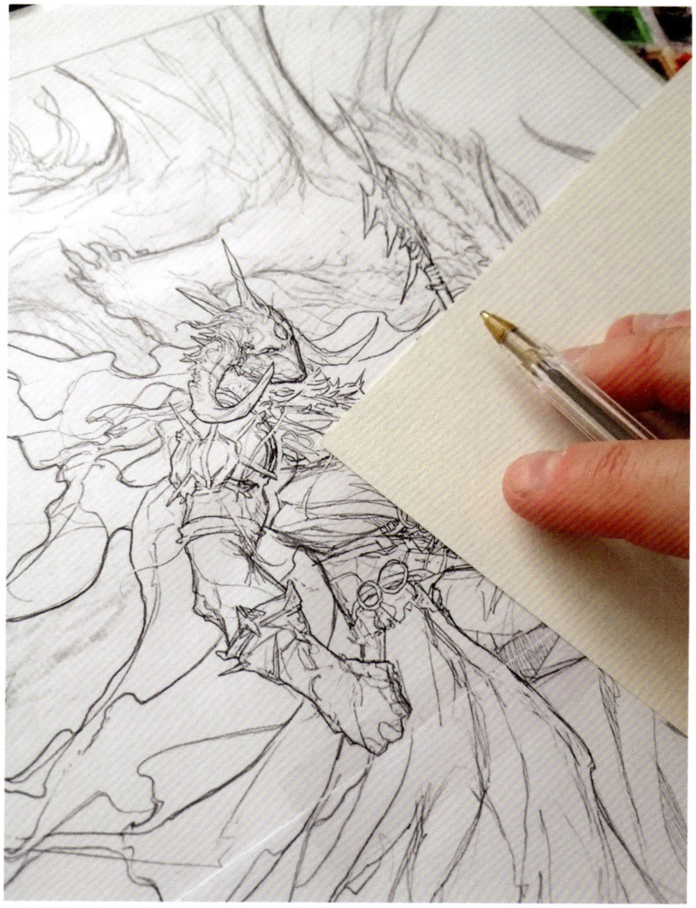

Transferring the drawing onto good A3 paper with ballpoint pen

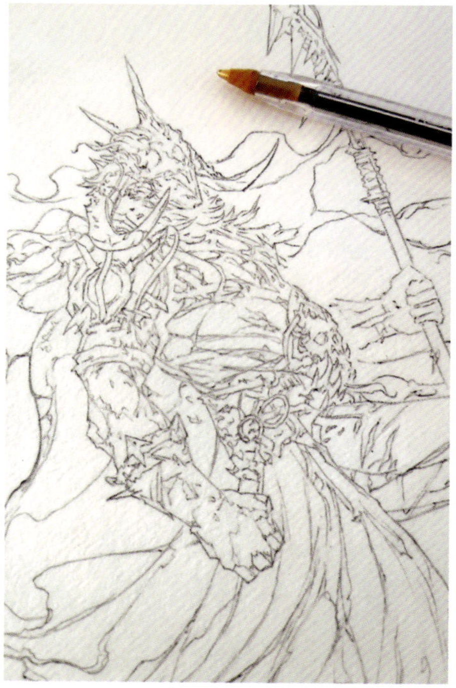

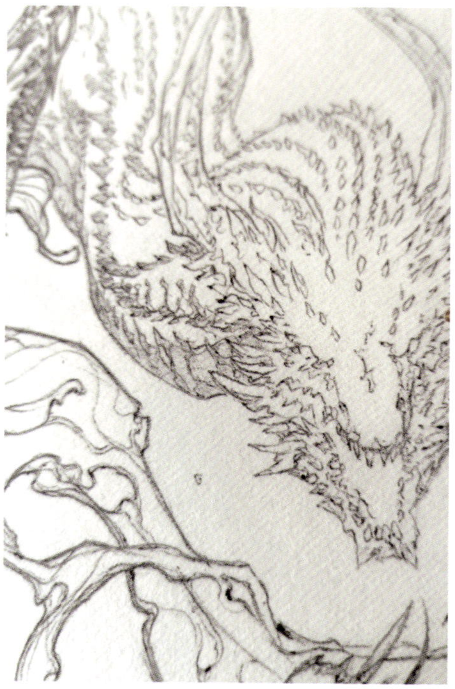

05 Texture & shapes

While drawing the image using pen, I lightly improvise the texture. I create a kind of map of lines that will later allow me to add detail and little by little reinforce the definitive lines. I draw in a very organic way and try to flow with the forms of the subject. In this way I can generate a base rich in texture and possibilities, upon which I can craft the definitive result.

Gently and loosely using pen to create textures and shapes – this will form a map to guide me through the detailing process

06 Building up the lines

This hand-drawn process is very important to me. I feel great fulfilment watching as the drawing evolves little by little. Gradually I draw over the lines that form the silhouettes. I do this in layers, going over the image numerous times. I use light hatching for the shading, as it's very soft-looking and creates a delicate result. Modulating the opacity is crucial to achieve depth and to make some elements stand out more than others; for example, compare how I shaded the warrior's foreground fist with the other.

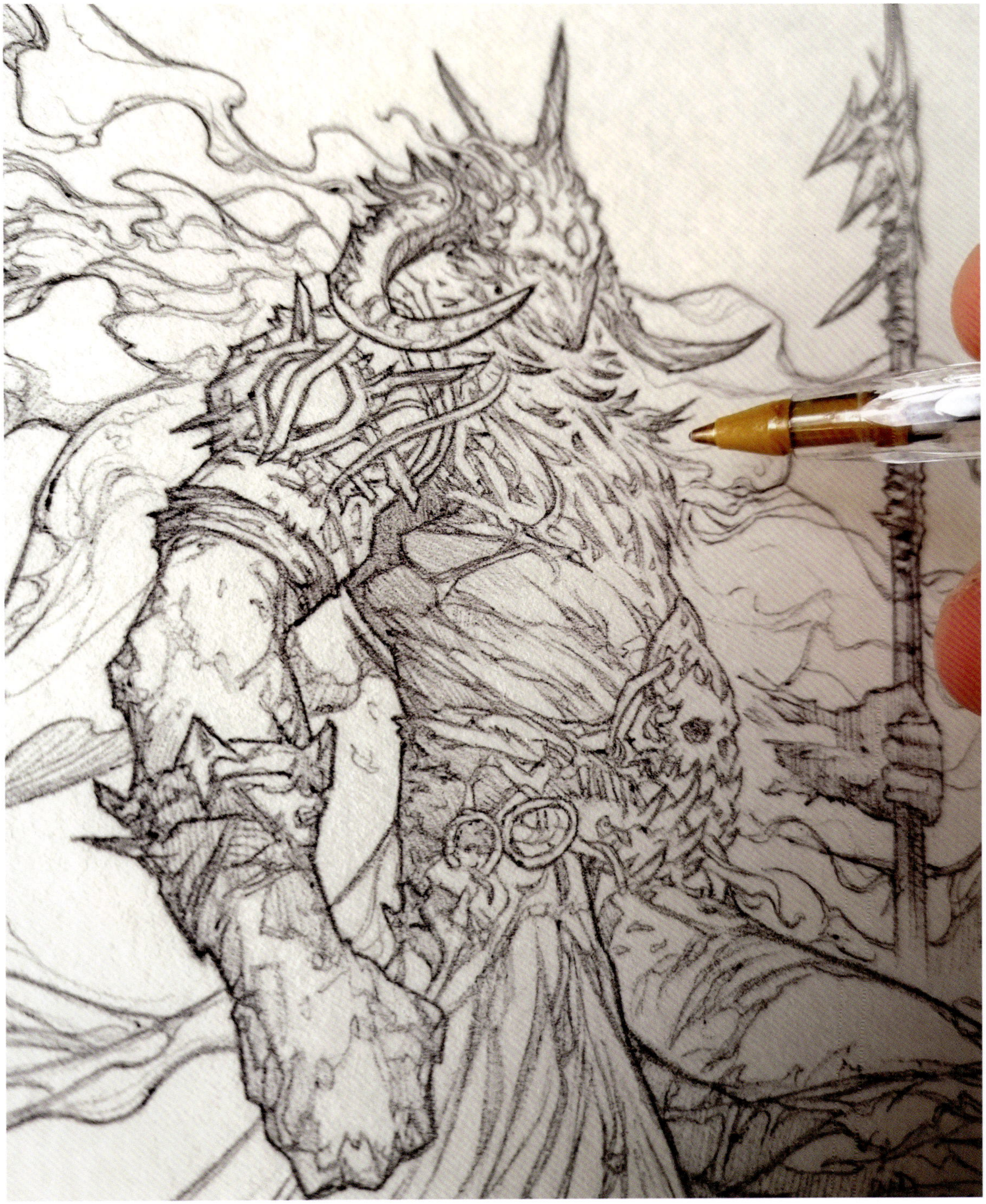

Reinforcing the lines little by little, stroke by stroke – shading with soft hatching, you can see the beautiful evolution of the drawing

07 Allowing space

The art of the line is like a dance between the pen and the hand. I aim to draw with ease and delicacy, exercising patience as I work to make the different planes stand out, giving space to the figures to ensure they read clearly. For example, the lines of the creatures do not touch each other, and if they do, there is a difference in opacity between them. Despite the amount of detail, I try to allow the various elements room to breathe and to cement their place in the drawing.

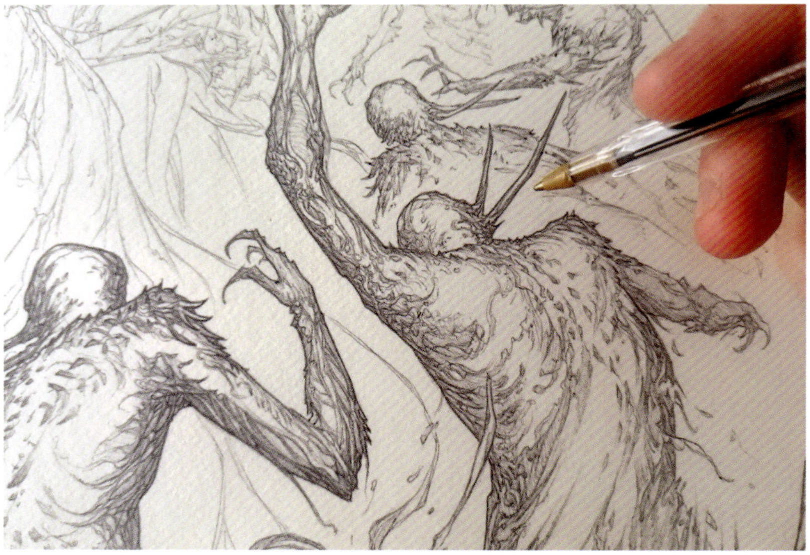

Each figure needs its space – take care to ensure the line work is precise, especially where elements overlap

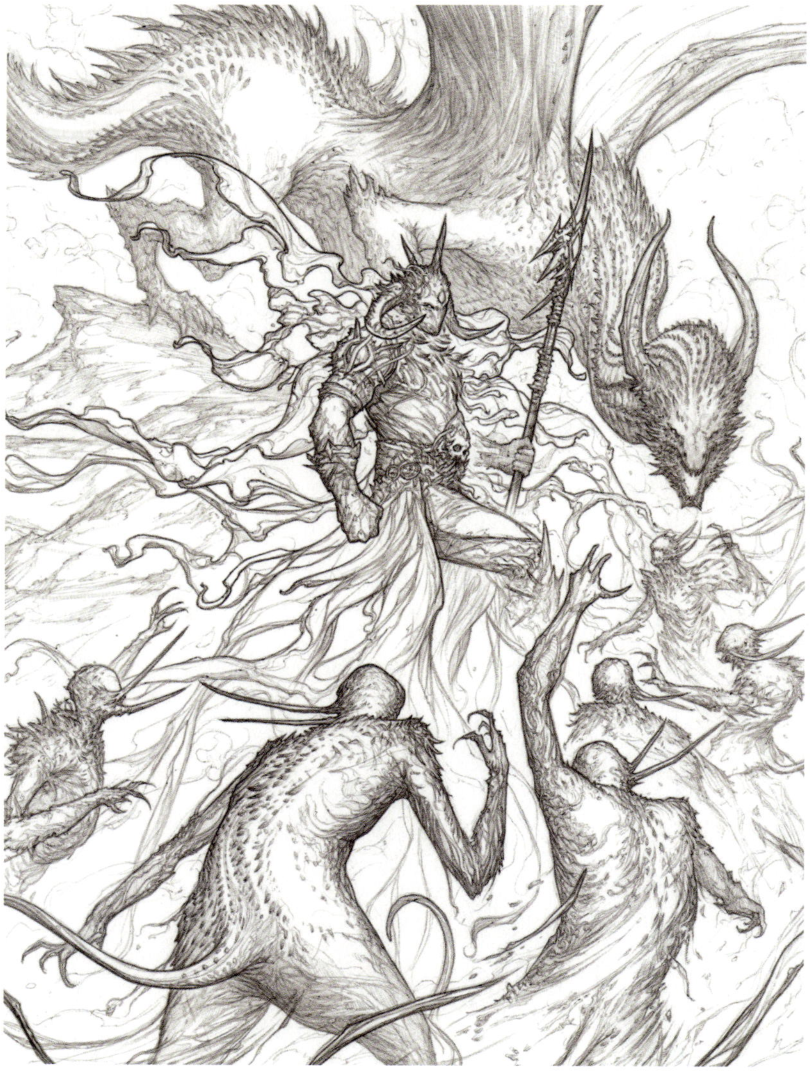

08 Finished line work

Working with a traditional medium and workflow can be time-consuming, but the texture I can create with pen and the beauty of the grain of the paper are certainly worth it. I feel a sense of accomplishment when I see the completed drawing and once scanned into the computer, it looks even more beautiful. I'm excited to add colour in the next step, while still respecting the line work rather than hiding it.

The result of craftsmanship, the texture of the pen, and the grain of the paper is a beautiful combination

Discovering Frazetta

I remember perfectly when I discovered Frank Frazetta's work. My first mentor lent me a Frazetta art book, which was also the first art book I'd ever held in my hands. I was just starting out drawing and didn't know anything about art, but I found it utterly spectacular. I liked everything about Frazetta's artwork and am still a huge fan today. Discovering fantasy art was a turning point in my life, an explosion that changed everything. Inside Frazetta's book I found the most impressive character I had ever seen; one that is still a great inspiration for me today. *Death Dealer I* is perhaps his most famous piece and therefore the most 'obvious' inspiration for a tribute piece, but for me, it's more than that – this artwork has been too important for me.

It is incredible to look back and see how great artists and their works can influence us and lead us down a certain path. I always admired Frazetta's power in his painting; a loose, organic brushstroke with strength and contrast could at the same time possess great definition and elegance. I valued, and continue to treasure, being able to see his sketches as well as his paintings. I am a lover of the sketchbook and believe that the sketch is an invitation the artist extends to us, encouraging us to imagine and ultimately complete the story.

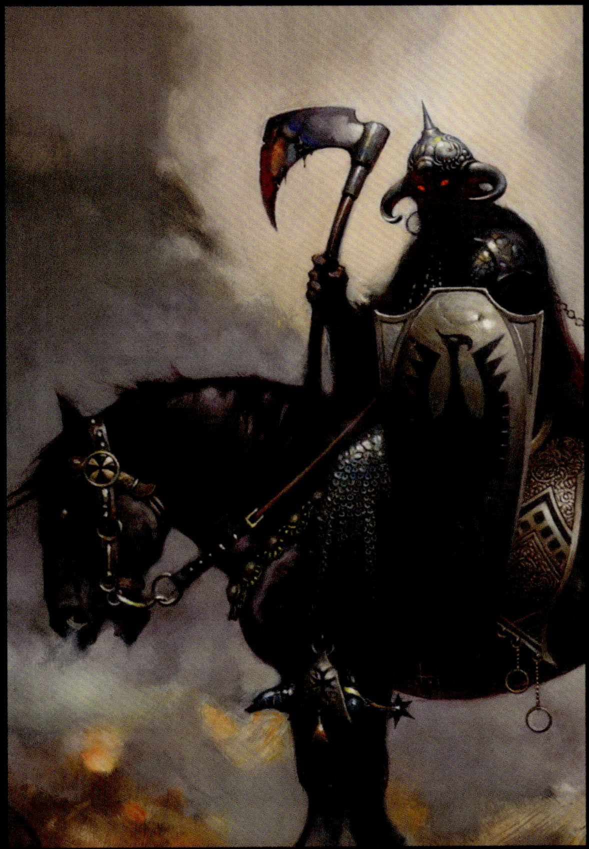

Death Dealer I © Frank Frazetta

▸▸ *For image in full, turn to page 15*

09 Cool base colours

Now I can start to colour! I like to establish a base using medium tones without much saturation. As with the line work, I work in layers, taking care to respect the drawing and ensure it remains visible. I want to create a Frazetta-inspired balance of elegance, delicacy, and strength. When choosing colours, I see what I think will work well with the theme and mood of the piece. Cool tones seem perfect for these characters.

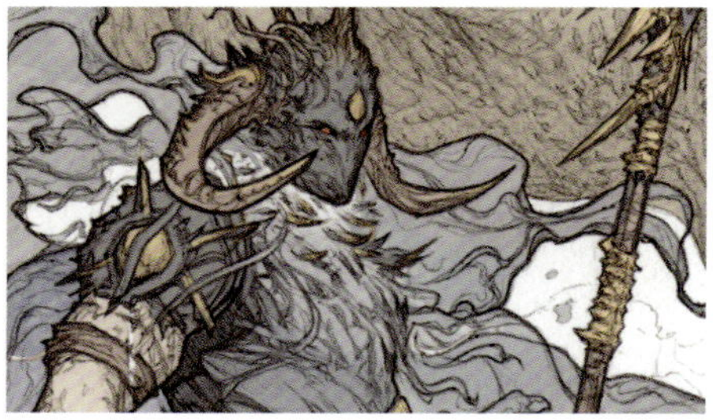

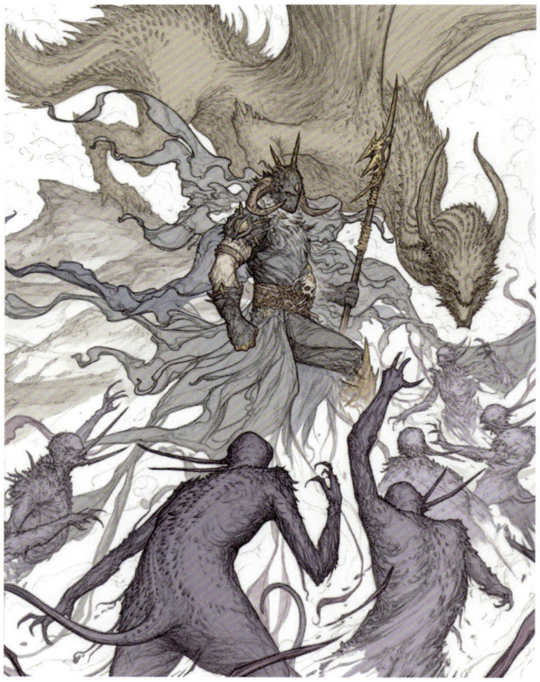

Applying a colour base of midtones and soft colours, taking care not to cover the line work in the process

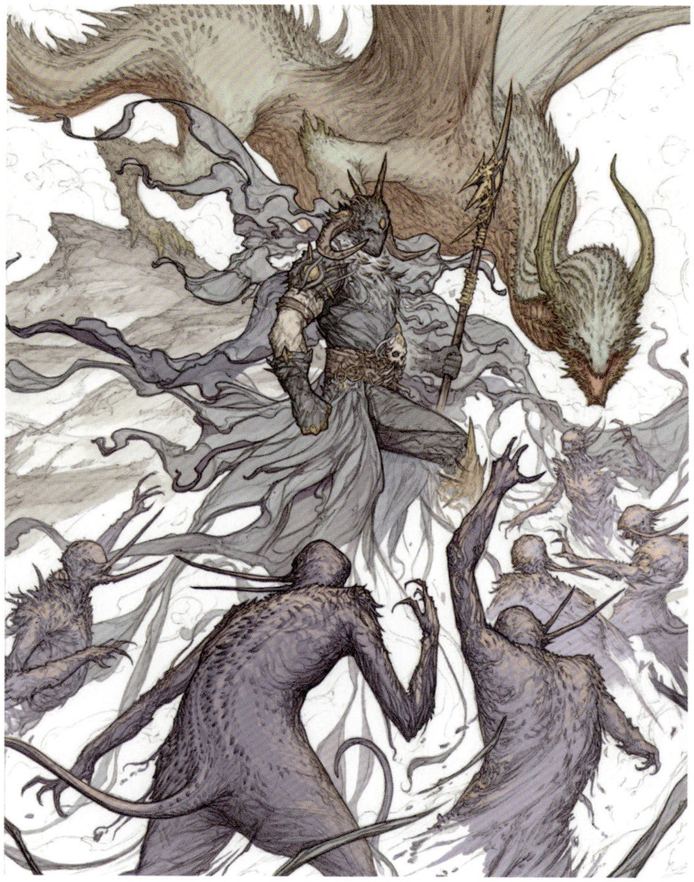

10 Light & shadow

With the base colours complete, I now want to add more lighting information – a layer of shading and a layer of light to create volume and give life to the scene. It's beautiful to see how the light-green illumination and red-toned shadows awaken the dragon! Seeing such progress is very exciting when you're painting.

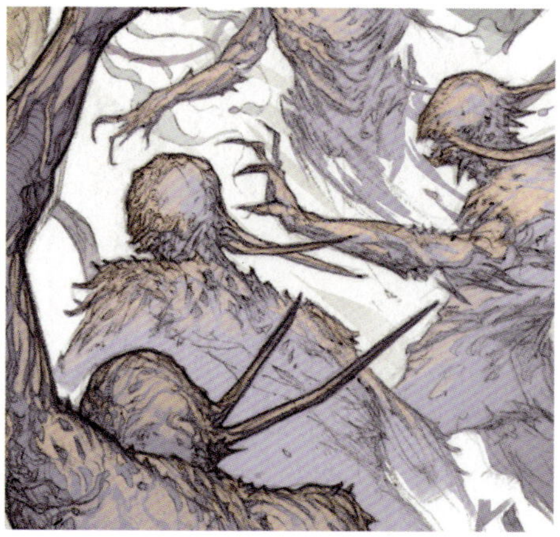

Add the first layer of shadows and lights to the figures to give them volume

11 Atmospheric mist

The next step is to give the scene an atmosphere that places the characters in a more concrete setting. I softly paint the background with warmer tones, which contrasts against the cool-toned characters and makes them stand out. Using a very pale tone, similar to the background, I paint light layers of mist between the elements and layers of cloth to separate them from one another, to make sure the piece reads clearly. Adding mist between the dragon and the main character creates more separation and depth between them. The word 'enveloping' defines well what I'm looking to create with the mist at this point.

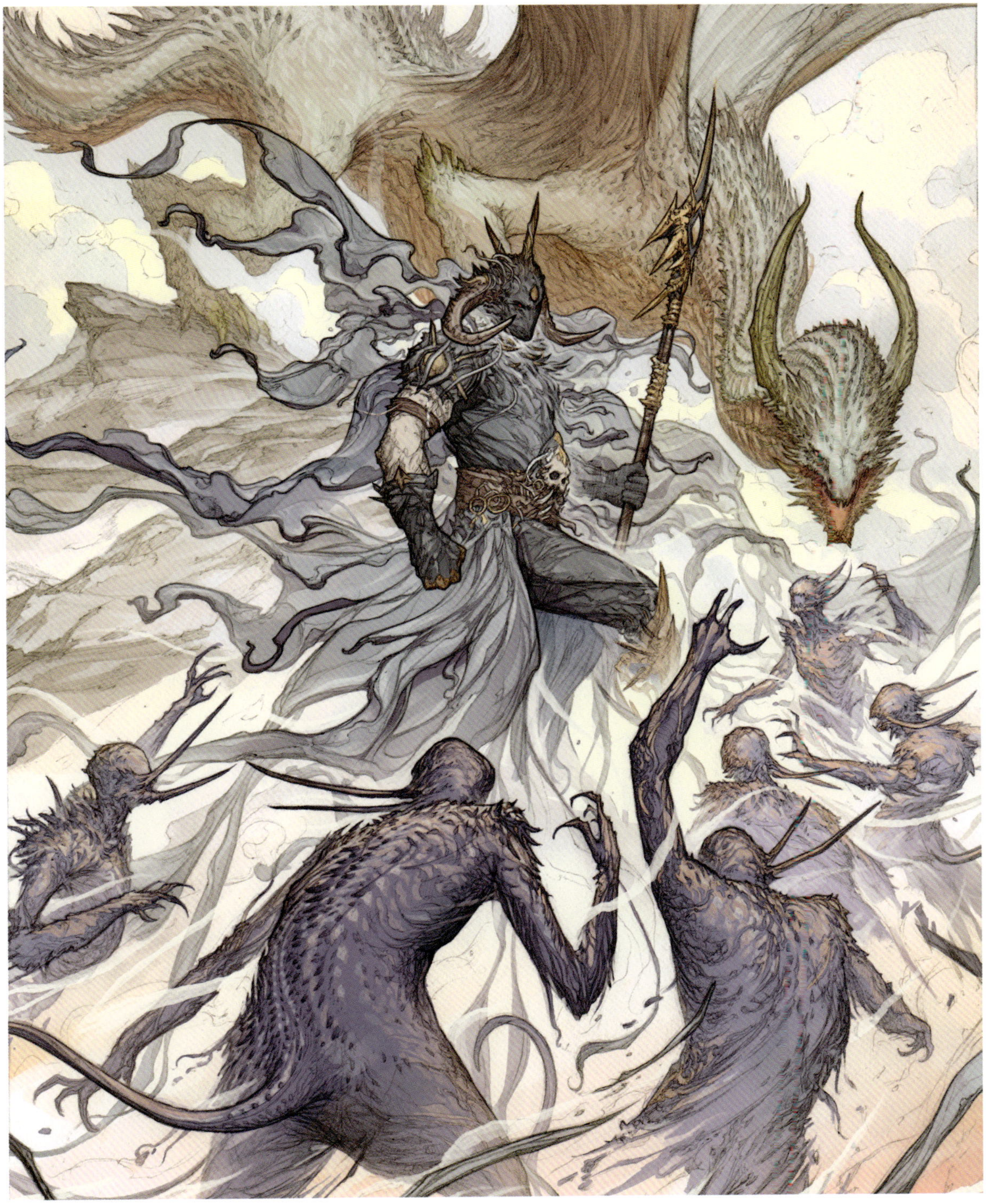

Giving the scene an atmosphere of its own and an ambience that envelops and places all the characters in a real environment

12 Darkness & hierarchy

Once I'm happy that I have placed all of the figures solidly in their environment, the next step is to instil the scene with some Frazetta-like darkness. I do this by applying a layer of dense colour to each figure, extracting the main points of light in each element. This also helps to achieve a clearer level of hierarchy between the figures, highlighting some over others based on contrast between light and dark tones. It seems an abrupt change, but it maintains the same delicate, soft line that I carry through the whole process.

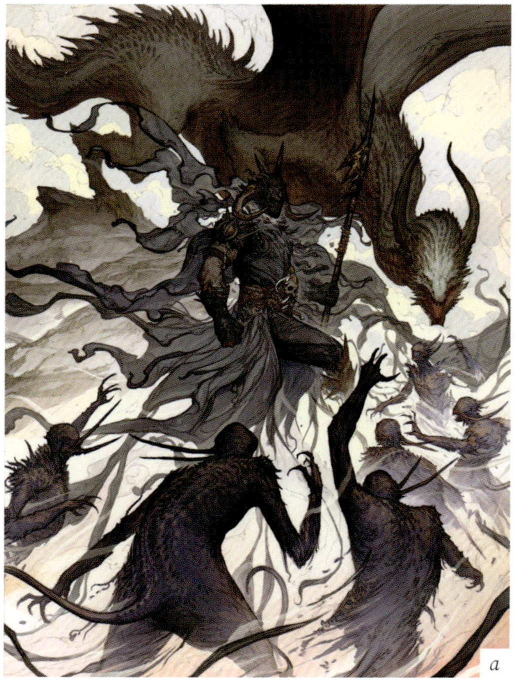
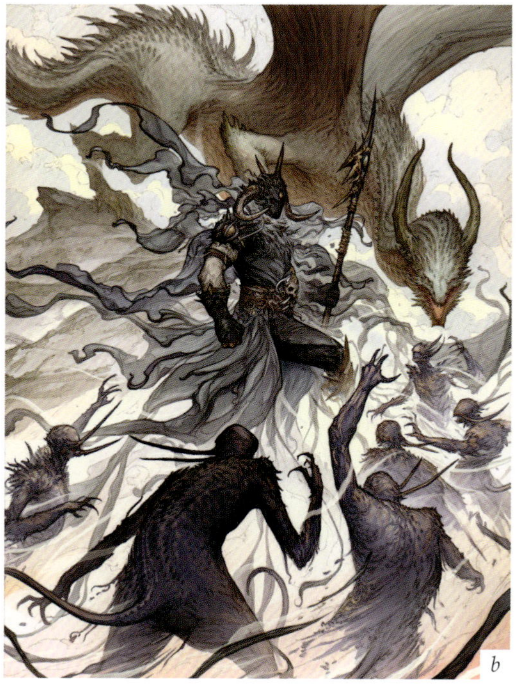
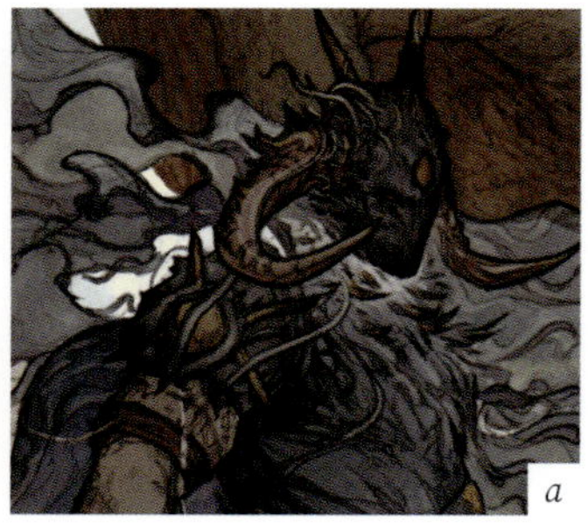
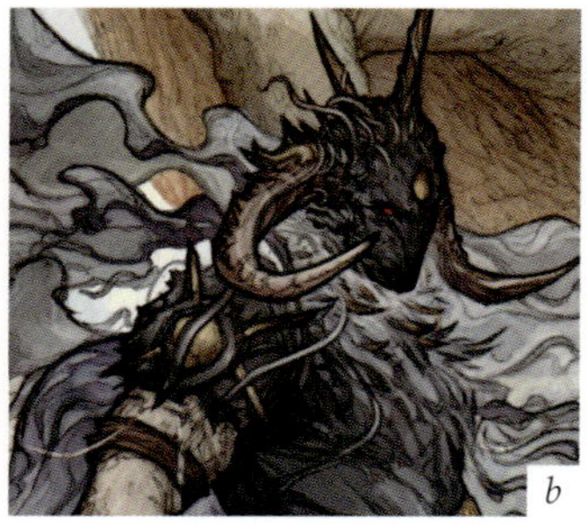

Darkening the figures (a), making the more important elements stand out (b)

13 Focal points

For the whole scene, I follow the same process as with the figures. Using a warmer tone, I darken the whole image slightly, just enough to be able to erase and establish lighter areas on the main warrior character, the main demons, and the dragon's head. This will direct the viewer's attention to those focal points, while also helping to create a pleasing harmony across the whole scene.

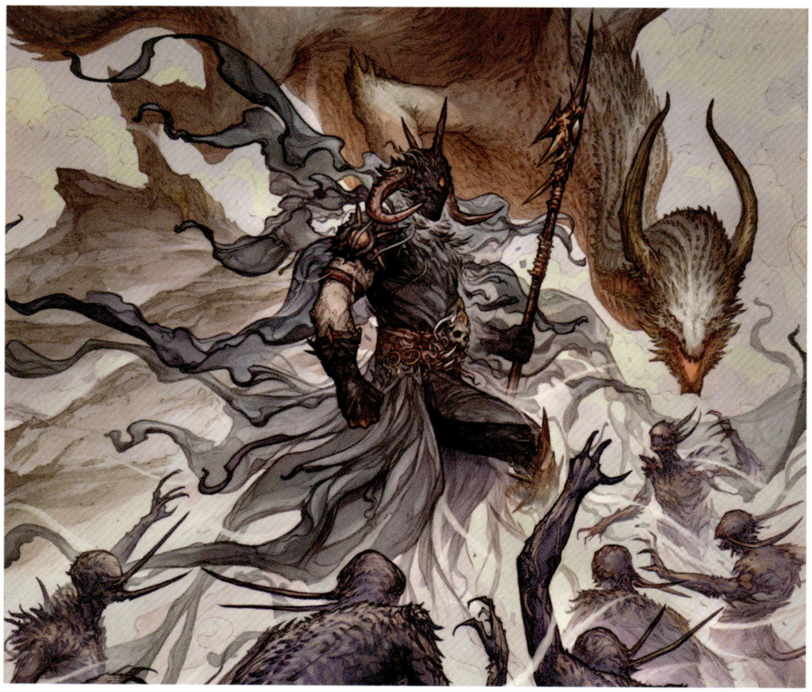

Adding a warm, dark glaze across the whole scene, leaving the warrior protagonist and other focal points more illuminated

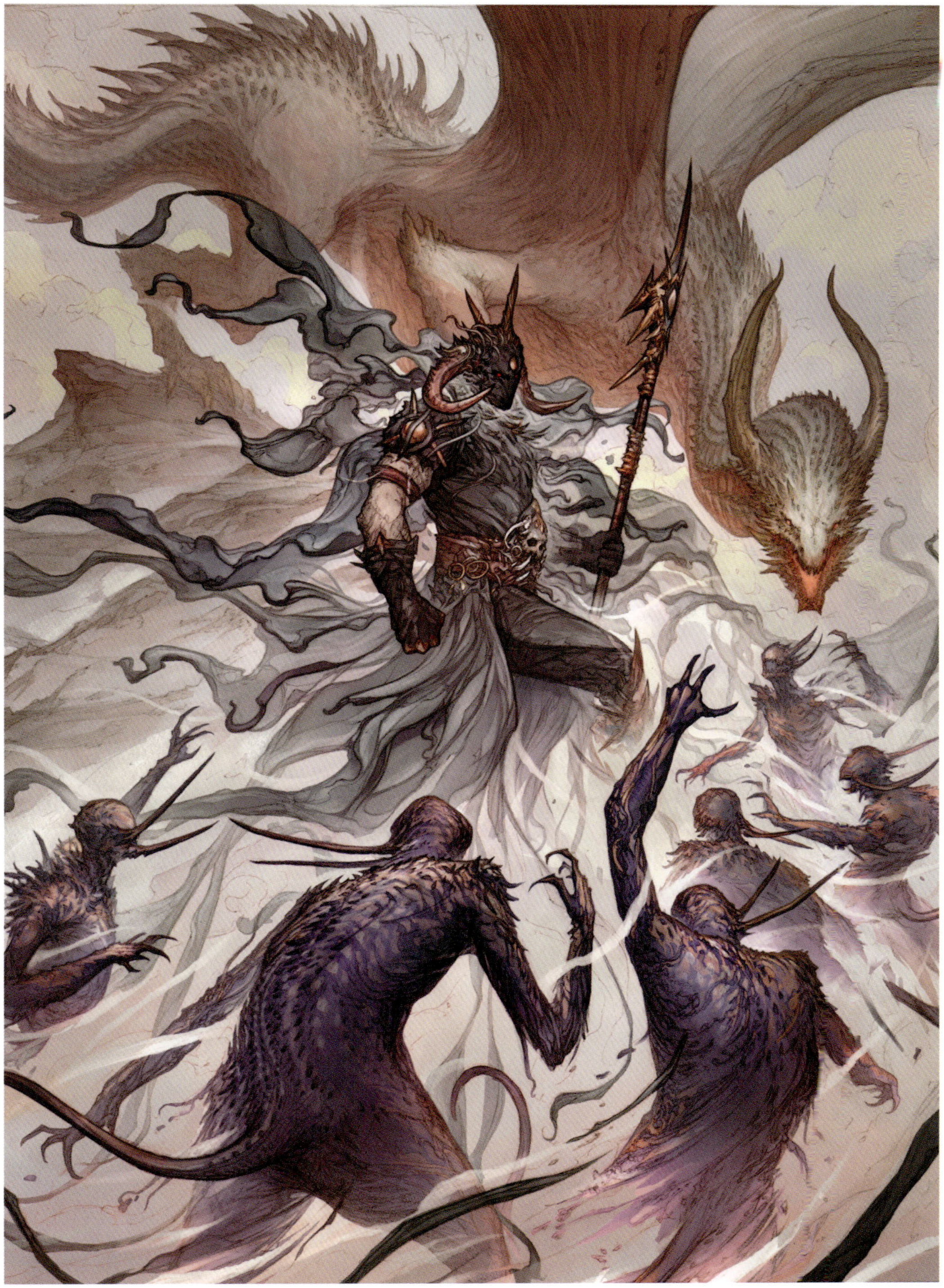

Lighten the image with a lighter glaze, except for the warrior to ensure his darkness stands out

14 Lightening

I use a slightly violet glaze to lighten the image, which once again helps me to harmonize the whole scene. I leave part of the warrior and his cloak unlightened to ensure that he stands out from the rest of the image as a darker, more contrasting element. I do the same with the demons in the foreground, which creates a sense of depth. The lighter tone of the dragon shows that it's in the distant background, making the separation between the dragon and warrior even more evident. Next, I refine the silhouette lines of the characters, giving the illustration definition and elegance.

15 Final refinements

Saturation is a great resource for establishing focus, but I like to use it with care and moderation. I apply a little on the warrior to make him stand out and ensure the viewer recognizes him as the main character and focal point of the image. I love adding moving particles, as they give dynamism to a scene. I also like to add some extra pen textures; for this I use a piece of one of my sketches, applied in some areas at low opacity. This adds the feel of a traditional brushstroke, which I like to recreate in a digital piece. Taking a step back, I always discover things to correct, such as elements that need more space and tangents that I overlooked. Once these are corrected, the illustration is finished.

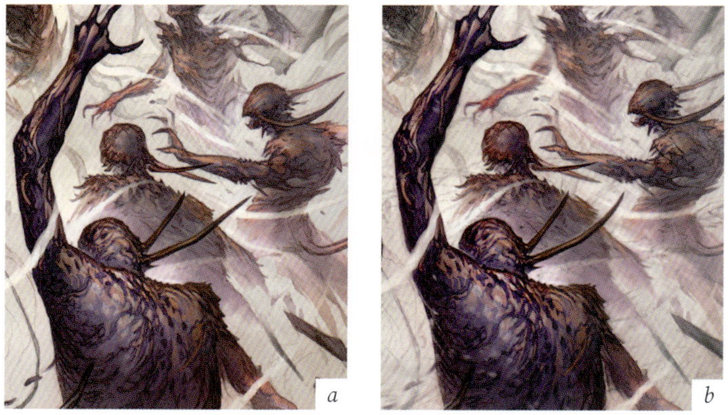

Before (a) and after (b) experimenting with saturation, dynamism, and pen textures for the final corrections

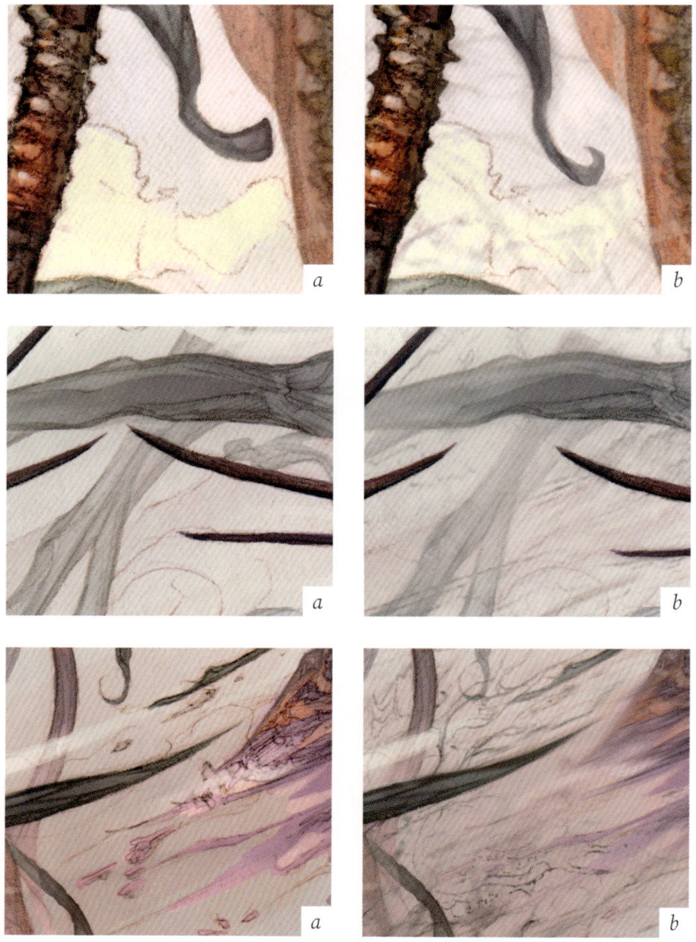

Conclusion

It's always satisfying to see the final piece after hours of work. I have achieved my aim of creating a mixed-media piece that still has the feel of traditional artwork. I always say that the most important thing is to enjoy the process, to put love into each step, and to remember that art is an end in itself. Frazetta has inspired me throughout my life as an artist; the search for the elegant, epic, and darkly beautiful in my work is something I owe to the legacy that he left behind, and I am very grateful for that. It has been a real joy to be able to honour him with this project.

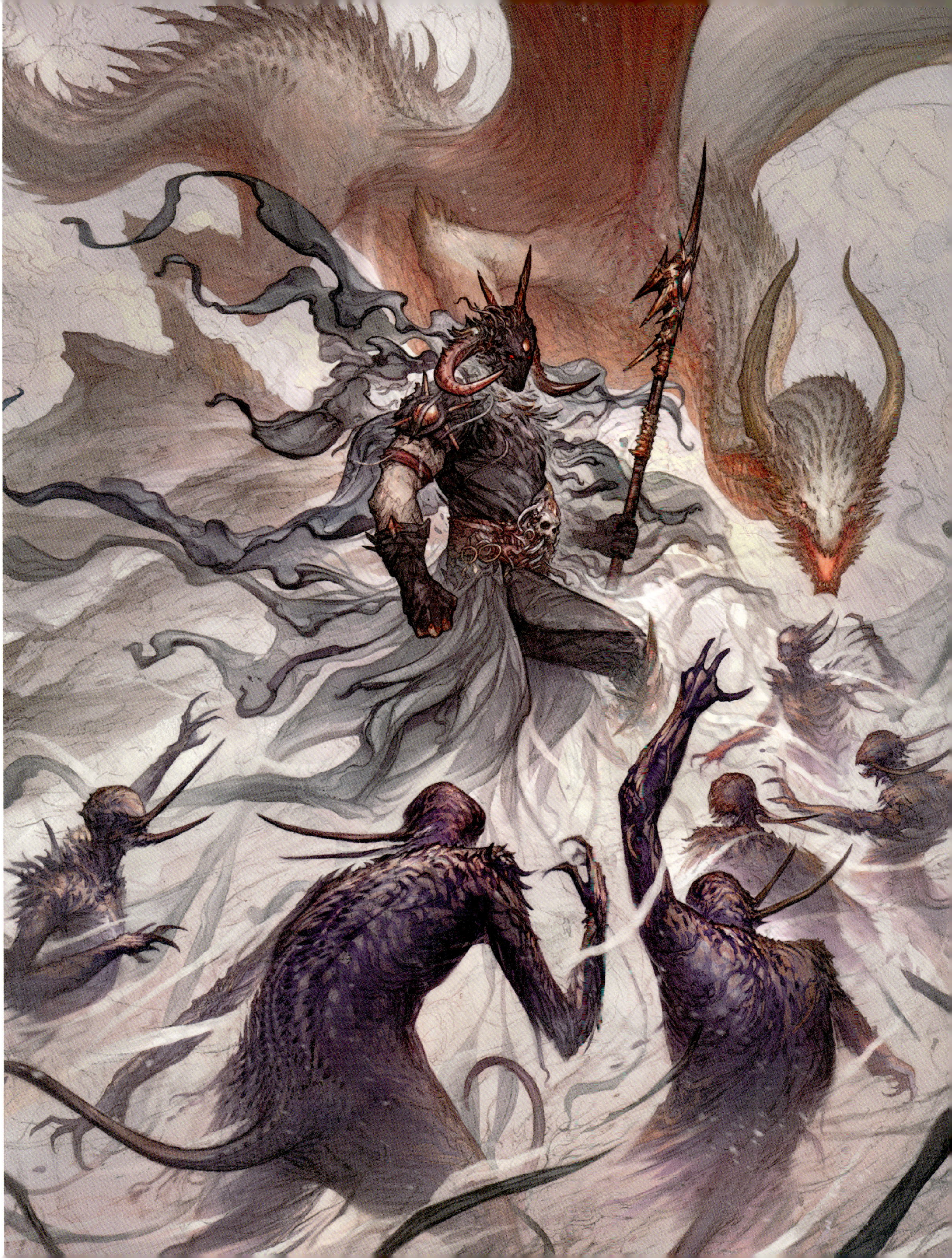

Final image © Dibujante Nocturno (Fran Garcés)

Depth © Dibujante Nocturno (Fran Garcés)

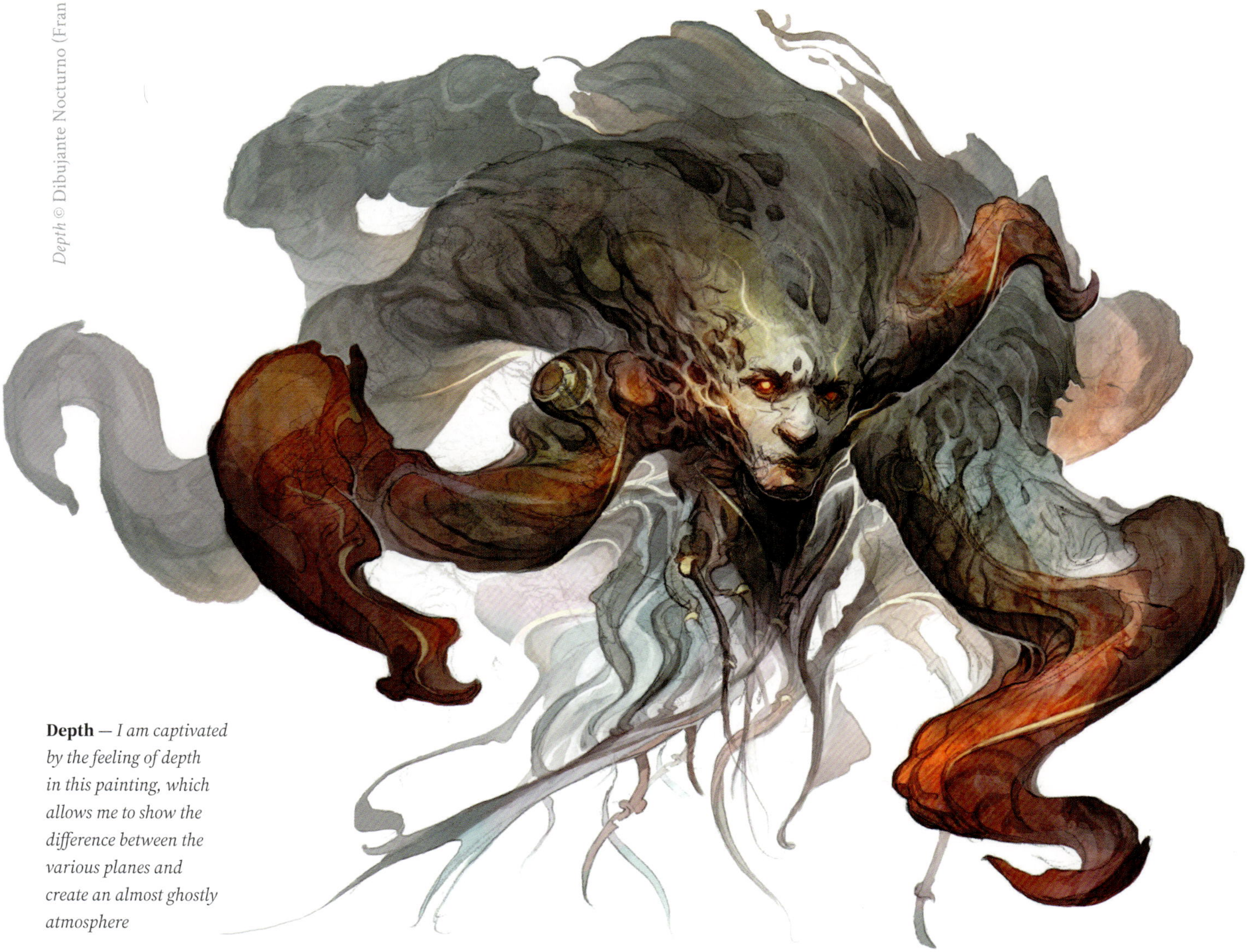

Depth — *I am captivated by the feeling of depth in this painting, which allows me to show the difference between the various planes and create an almost ghostly atmosphere*

Gallery

by Dibujante Nocturno (Fran Garcés)

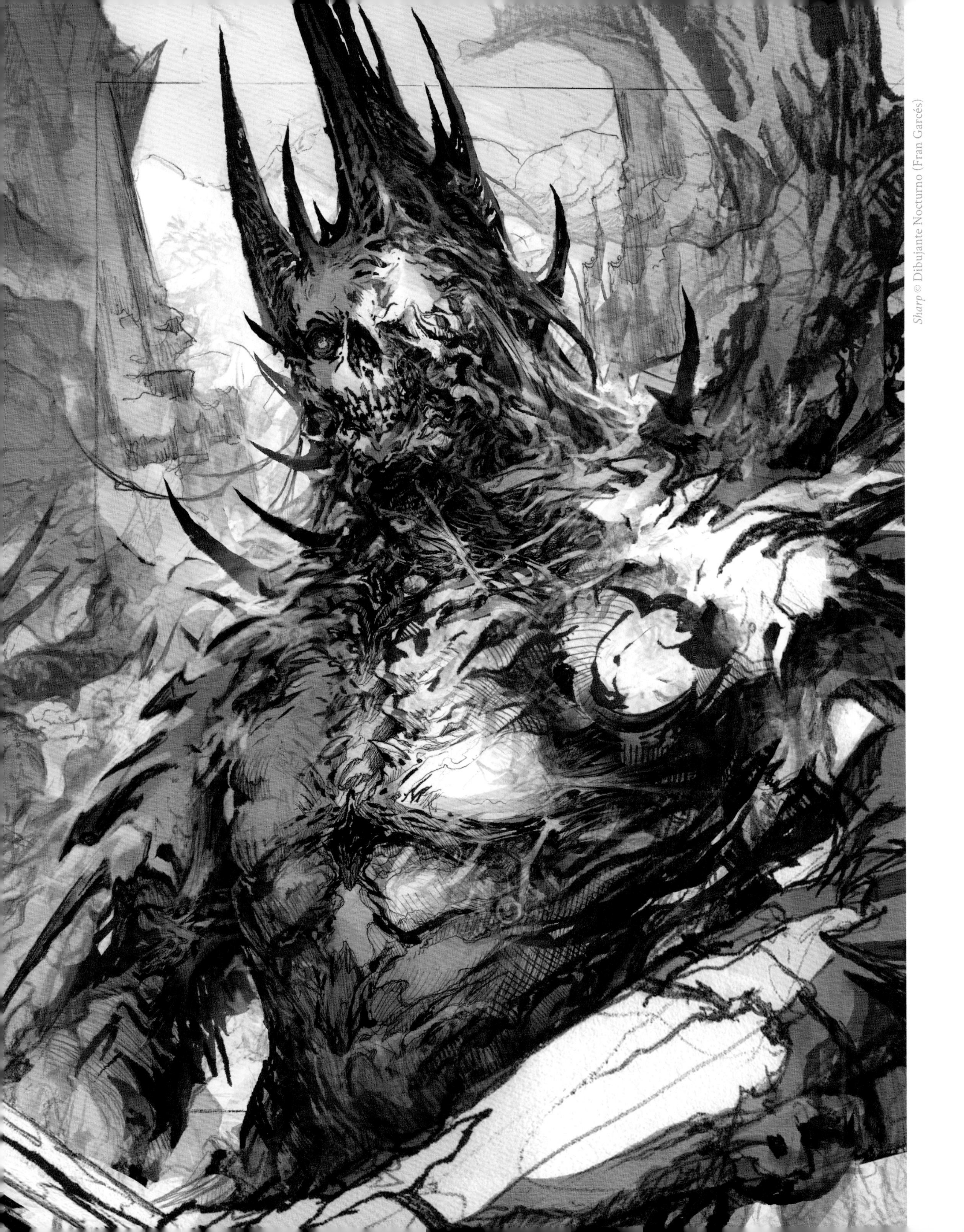

Sharp © Dibujante Nocturno (Fran Garcés)

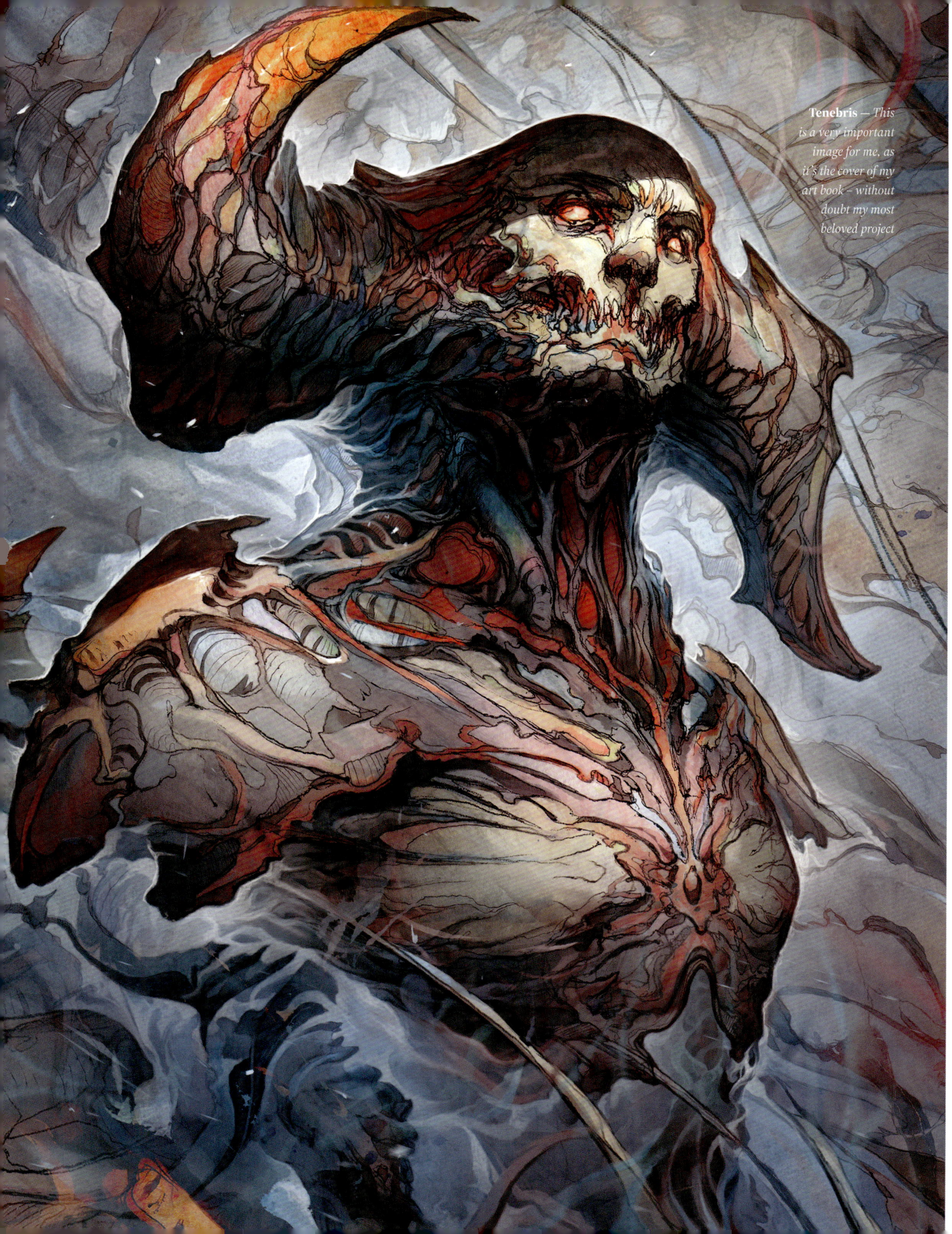

Tenebris – *This is a very important image for me, as it's the cover of my art book – without doubt my most beloved project*

Tenebris © Dibujante Nocturno (Fran Garcés)

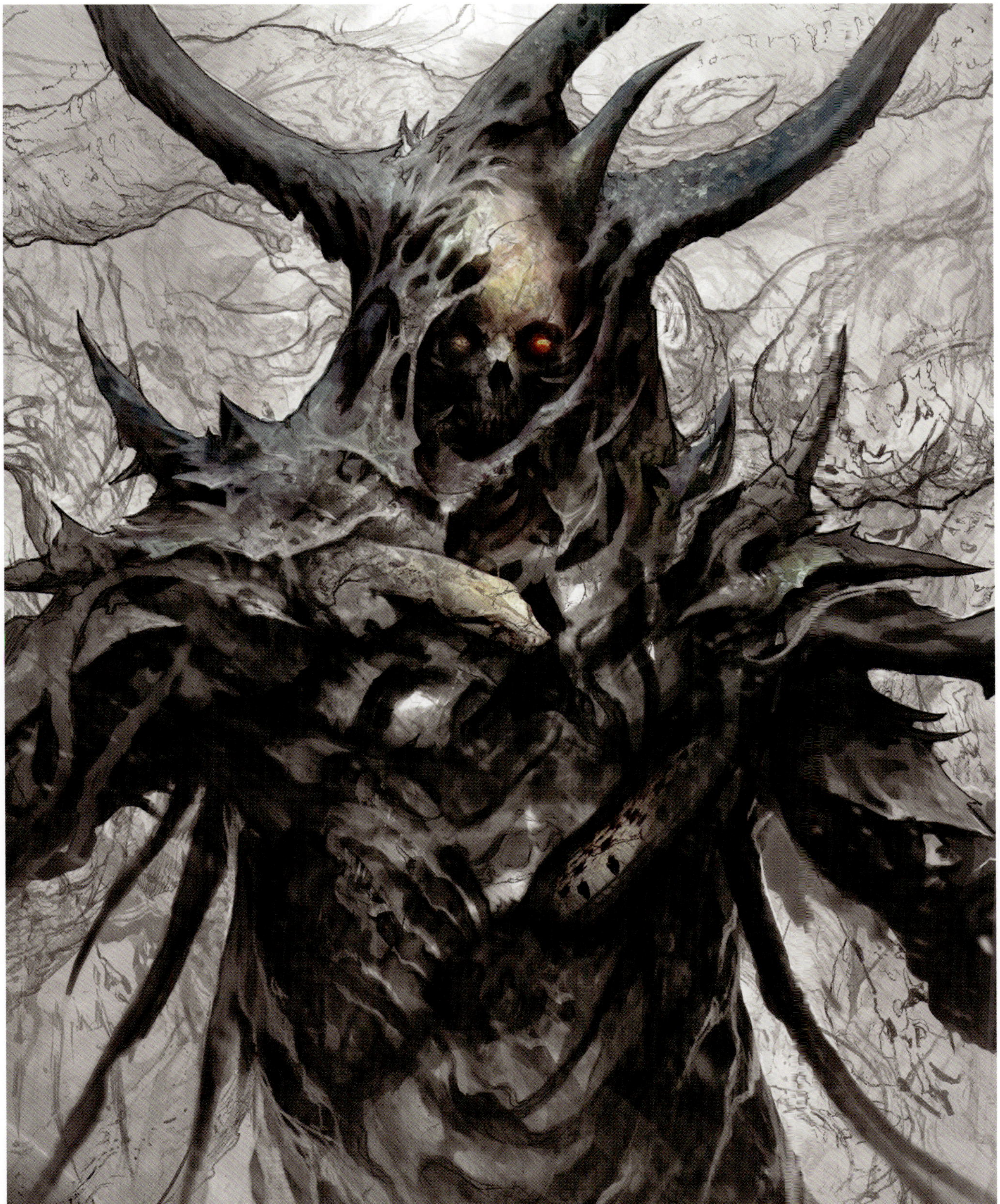

Asphyxia – *Representing a slight hint of life in something visually dead is a concept that I'm passionate about in fantasy art. For example, eyes that glow where there should be nothing, or a body that moves when there is clearly no life.*

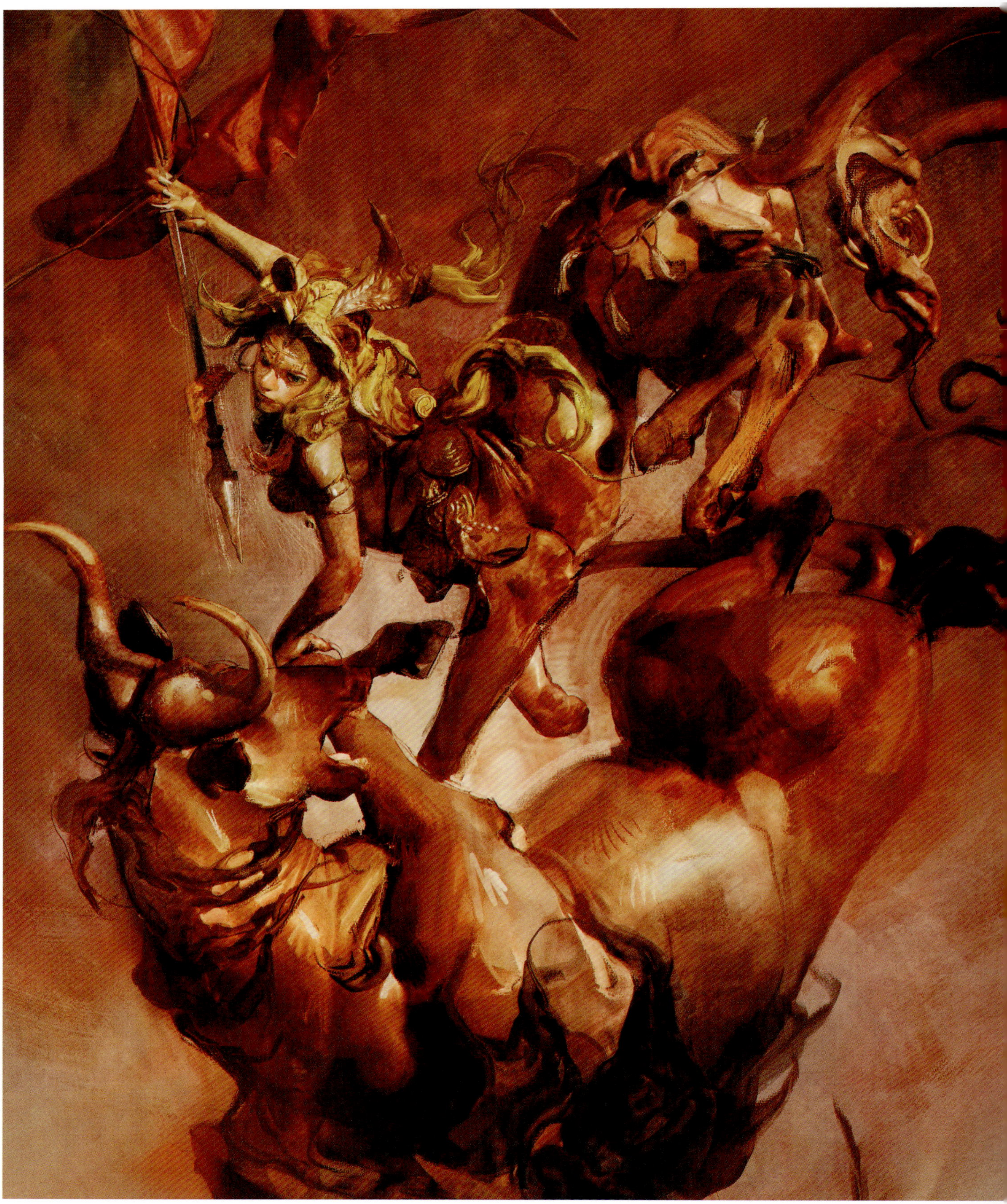

Final image © Entei Ryu

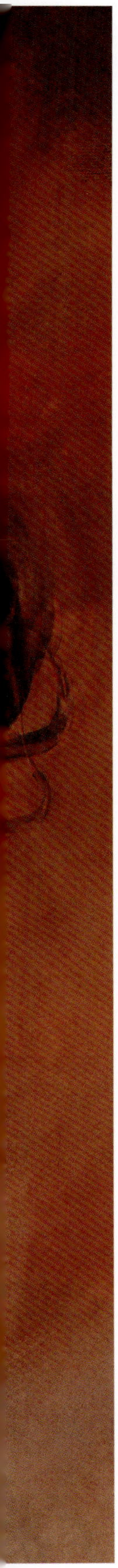

Killing Angel

by Entei Ryu

Creating *Killing Angel*

I want to infuse a part of Frazetta's style into my own sculpture series. The *Chimera* series is a collection of digital 3D sculptures with half-human, half-animal characters set in a fantasy world. For each piece, I merge a new animal with certain cultural decorative styles that I want to explore. For example, a mermaid in a dark, Gothic style, a Chinese-inspired bird-girl, or a drake woman in a Viking style. For this piece, I want to create a lioness character that incorporates the wild, powerful, primal style of Frazetta's work.

01 Initial sketch

In this small initial thumbnail, I establish a dynamic scene where a female warrior with a lion's body leaps from the sky, pouncing on the wild buffalo that is her prey. This scene could work well for the powerful energy that I want to capture. Big cats were a common theme in Frazetta's work, so the idea fits well here.

Making a quick, tiny sketch of my initial idea

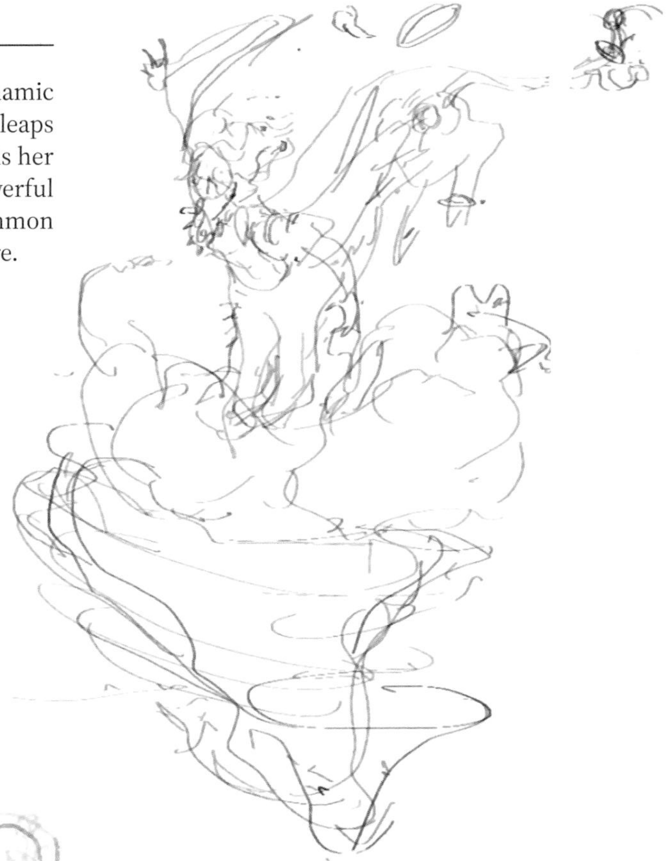

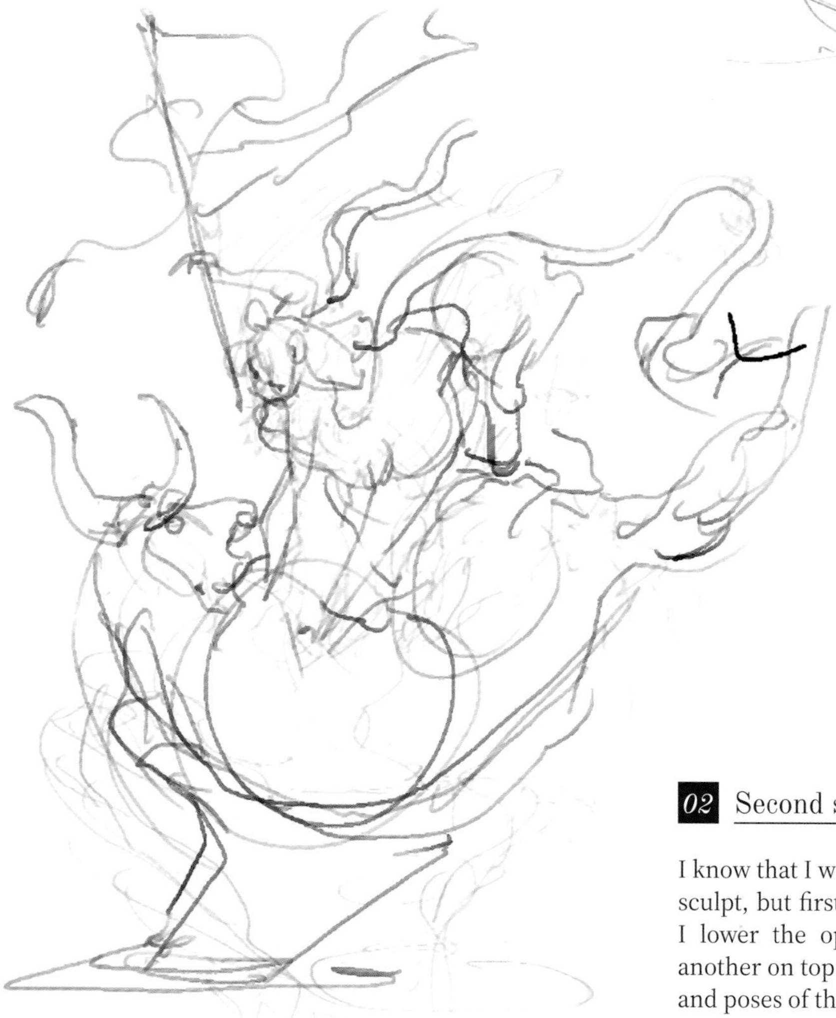

02 Second sketch

I know that I will be creating this piece as a digital 3D sculpt, but first I will plan out the sketch more fully. I lower the opacity of the first sketch and make another on top of it, more clearly defining the figures and poses of the hunter and the falling buffalo.

A second pass of sketching to define the concept

03 Detailed sketch

This shaded sketch is a modification of the previous one. I actually make this after starting the 3D sculpting process, just as a visual aid before I get too far. I focus on adjusting the overall dynamic curves, making the contours more fluid. A simple background makes the figures and negative space easier to see as I work.

Another sketch to help keep the 3D sculpting process on track

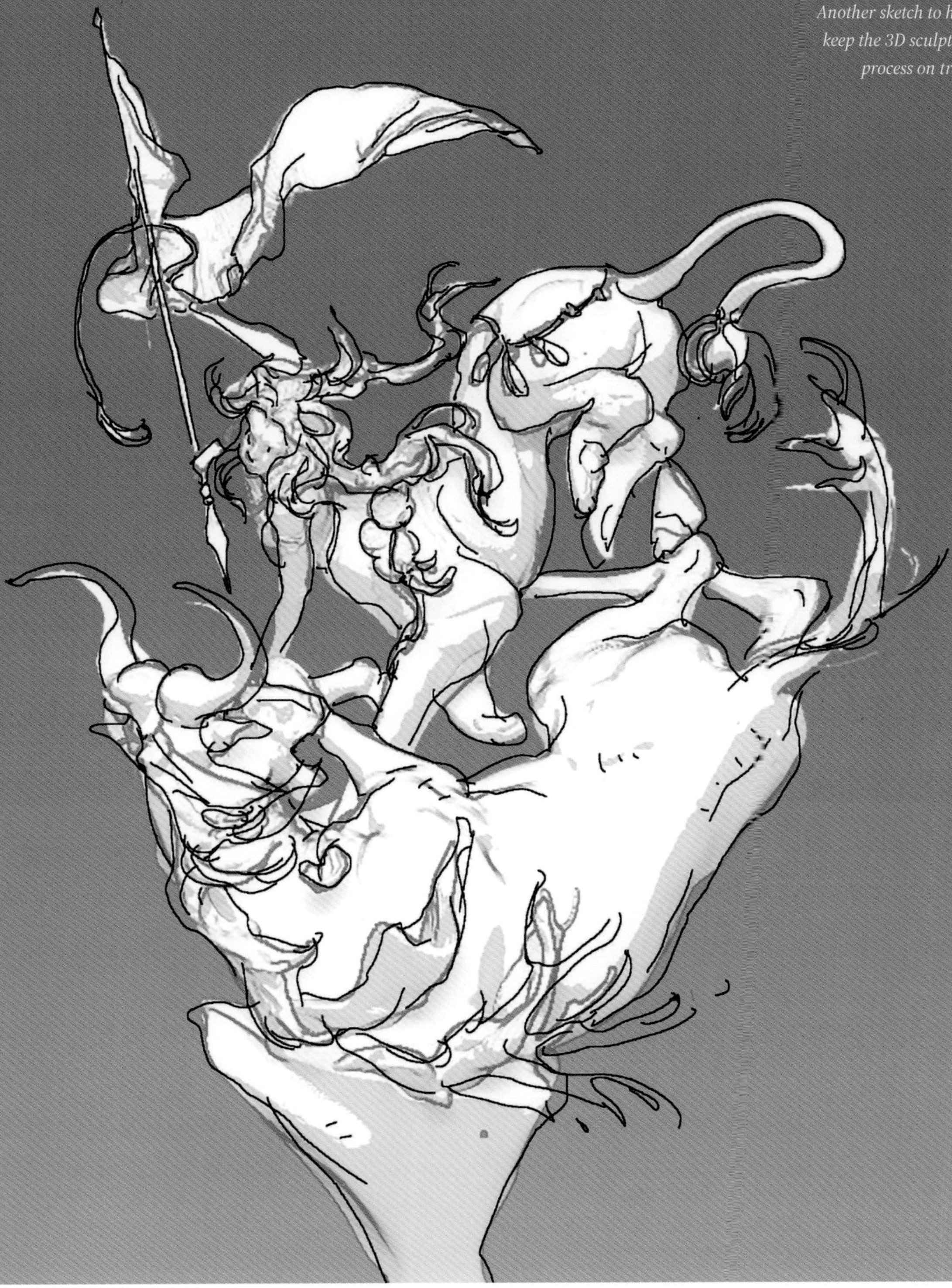

04 The lioness

First, I focus on modelling the half-human, half-lion female character. I emphasize a strong upper body with slight muscular definition, similar to the female figures in Frazetta's works. The exaggerated, dramatic pose tightens and stretches certain muscles, creating a sense of dynamic beauty within these details. I also pay attention to the leonine half of her anatomy, accentuating the muscular lines to convey the character's strength and vitality.

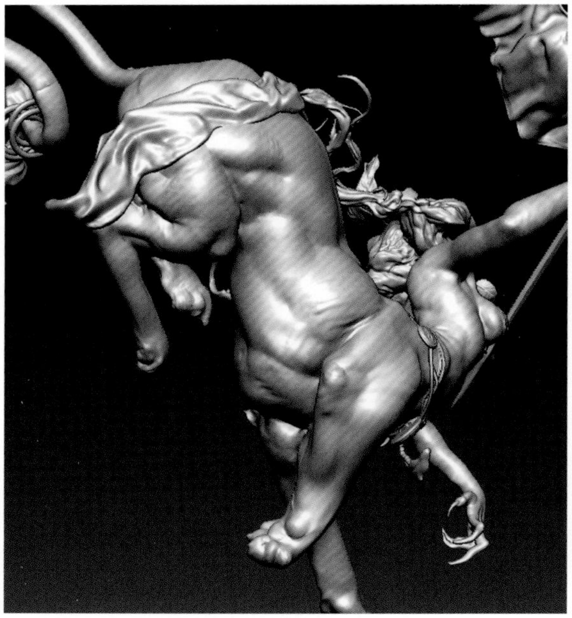

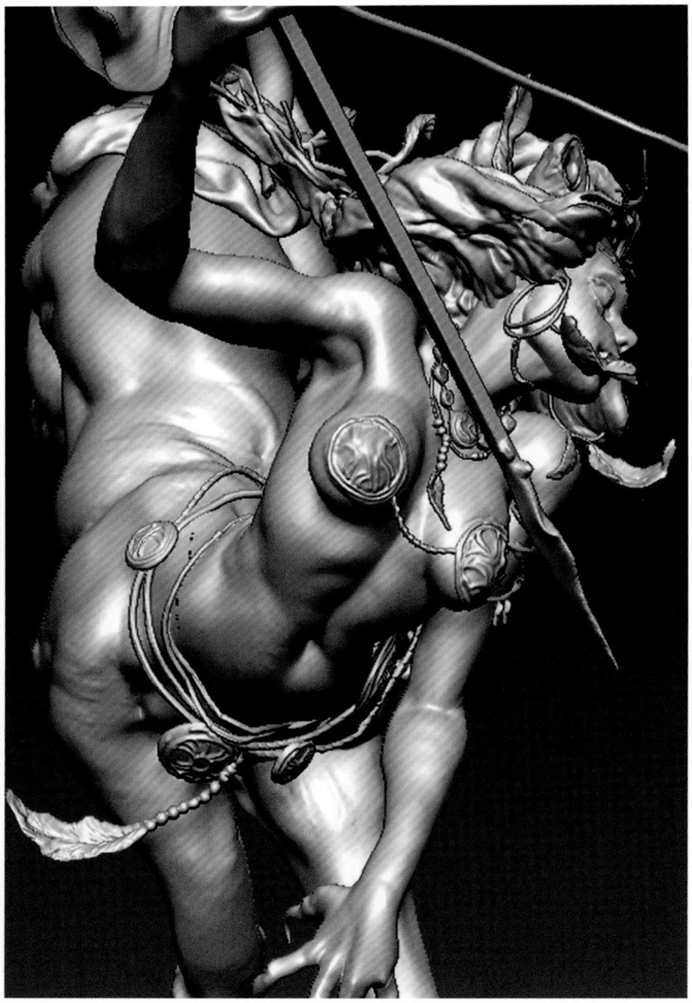

Sculpting the female warrior character

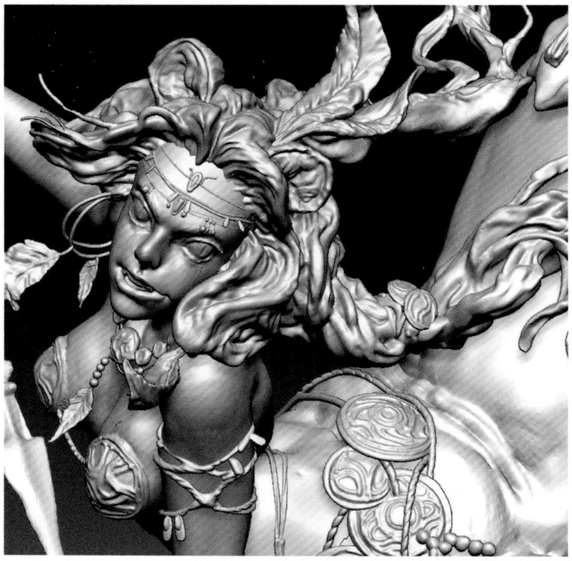

Attention to detail will give the character personality

05 Character details

Although the character's hands are a woman's hands, they have beast-like claws, which serve as another weapon for attacking prey. In terms of portraying her face, she has cat-like pupils, sharp teeth, and lion's ears, all of which represent her wild nature. Feathers, ropes, and metal adornments give her some cultural attributes, aiming to capture the look of beautiful tribal decorations.

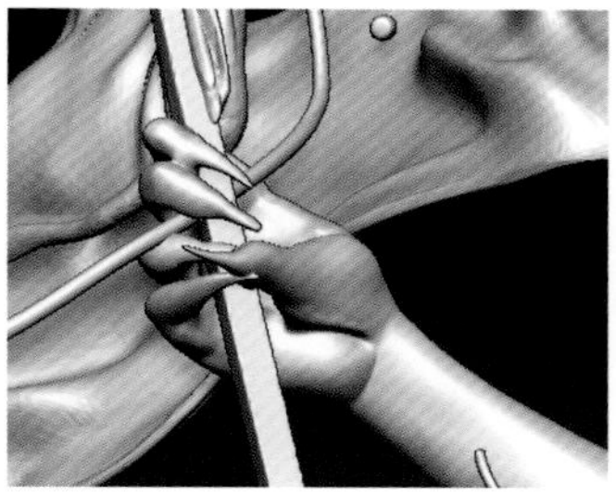

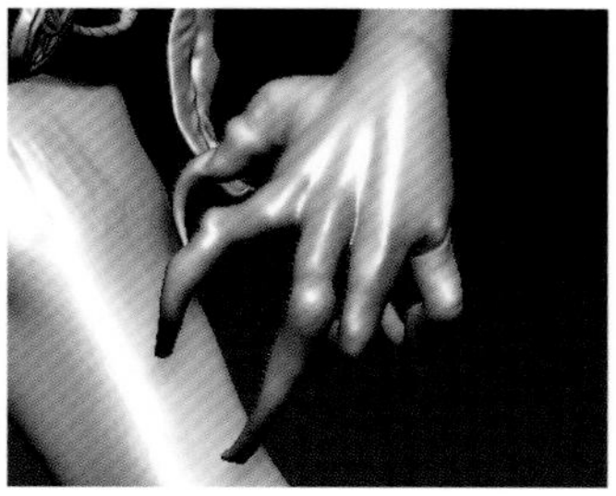

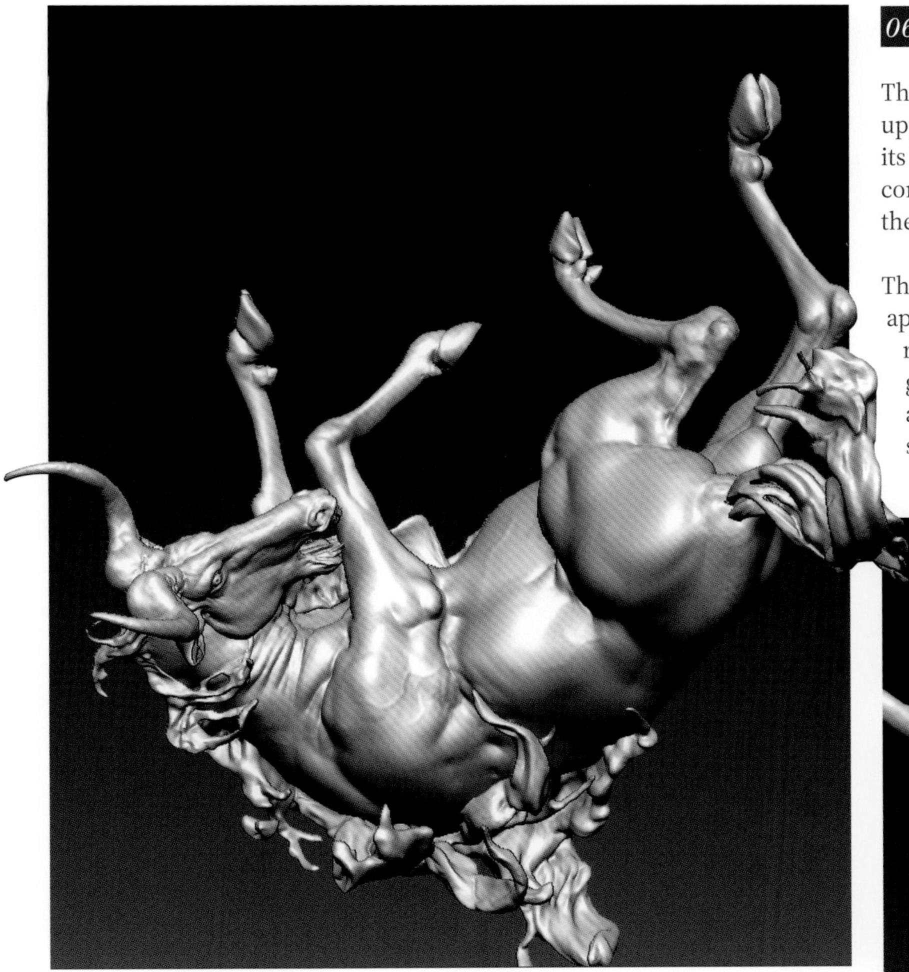

06 The buffalo

The fallen buffalo's centre of gravity is focused in its upper body, which is pressed against the ground while its hind legs are flung upwards. I choose this unstable composition to create a strong flow of energy between the two characters' forms.

The buffalo's head is turned to face the lioness hunter approaching it, displaying a look of fear. I study reference photos to capture the detail of the exposed gums, which create an expression of extreme horror and loss of control. The tension lines on its neck show its instinctual struggle in the face of a crisis.

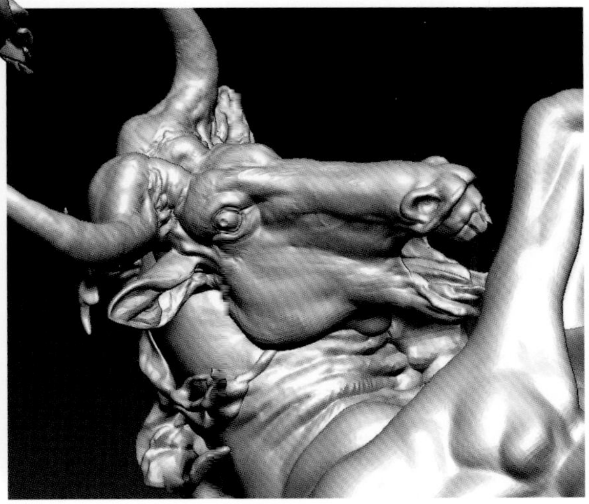

The buffalo's anatomy and expression are key to the drama of this scene

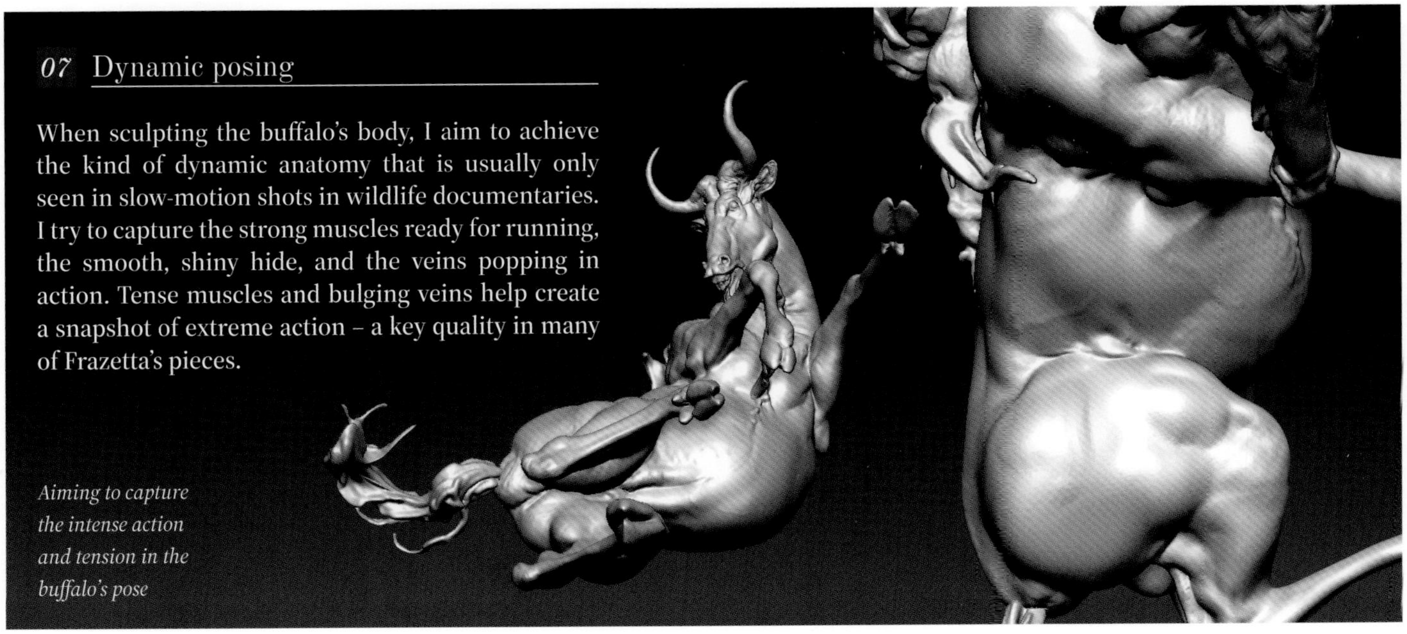

07 Dynamic posing

When sculpting the buffalo's body, I aim to achieve the kind of dynamic anatomy that is usually only seen in slow-motion shots in wildlife documentaries. I try to capture the strong muscles ready for running, the smooth, shiny hide, and the veins popping in action. Tense muscles and bulging veins help create a snapshot of extreme action – a key quality in many of Frazetta's pieces.

Aiming to capture the intense action and tension in the buffalo's pose

Discovering Frazetta

As an artist who loves fantasy themes, the master artist Frank Frazetta really inspired me in the early stages of my career. When I think of his work, the first thing that comes to mind is the vibrant fantasy worlds he made, with classical colour palettes and compositions, powerful human figures, and dangerous wild animals.

These were the elements that inspired me the most and therefore, when creating this artwork in tribute to Frazetta, I am trying to incorporate all of these favourite aspects.

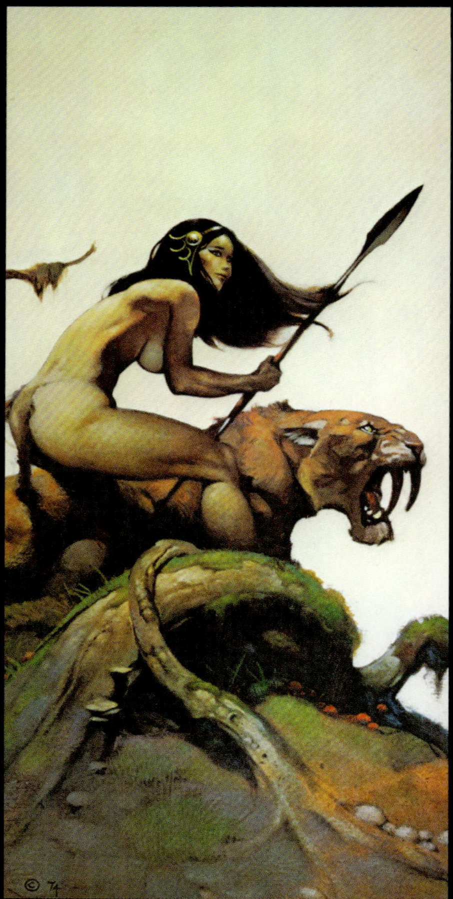

Savage Pellucidar © Frank Frazetta

▸▸ *For image in full, turn to page 3*

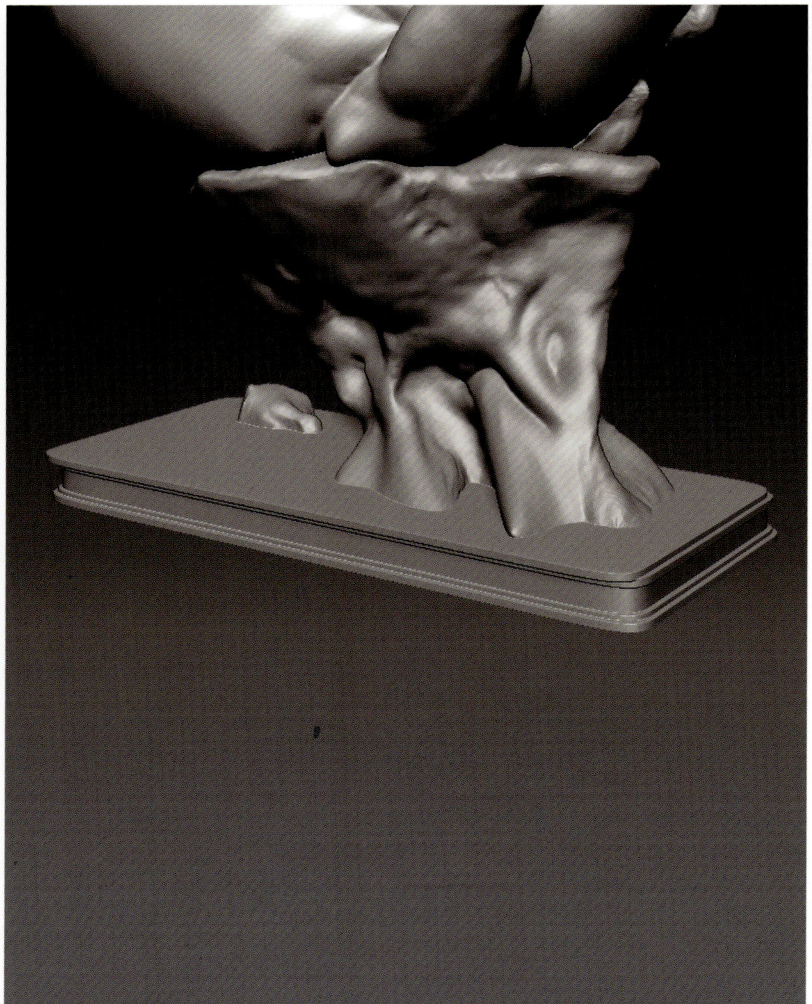

08 The sculpture's base

For the base of the design, I simply place a rock that complements the overall composition. I don't need to provide a detailed explanation of the scene; I want to leave room for the viewer to imagine the environment, as Frazetta often did in his paintings. The two figures are almost suspended in space – a perfect way to capture this dramatic moment.

A very simple base will keep the focus on the characters

09 Exploring angles

While a painting typically requires only one main perspective, a sculpture needs to be appreciated from various angles in a three-dimensional space. However, I will also be creating a digital painting from this sculpt, so I approach each angle with a painterly mindset, imagining how it would look composed on a canvas. I want the sculpt to work well in both two and three dimensions.

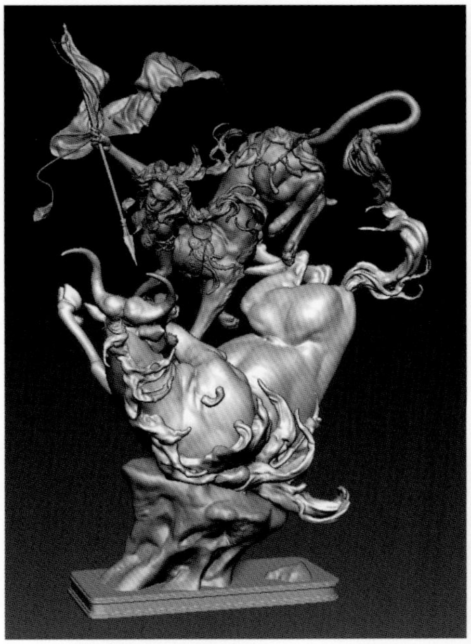

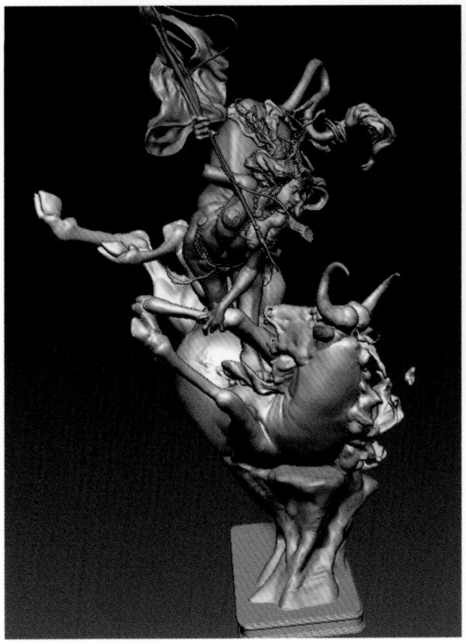

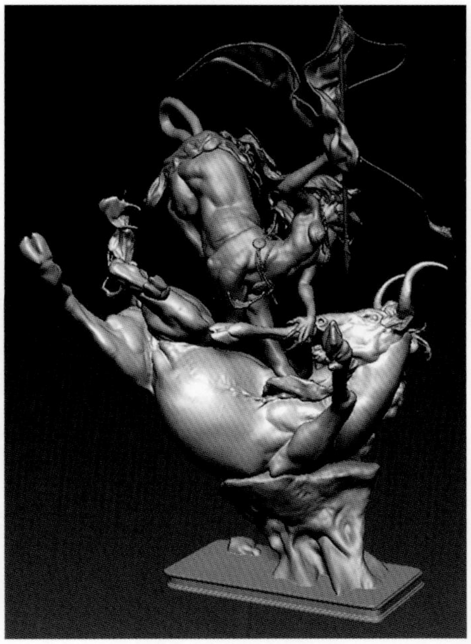

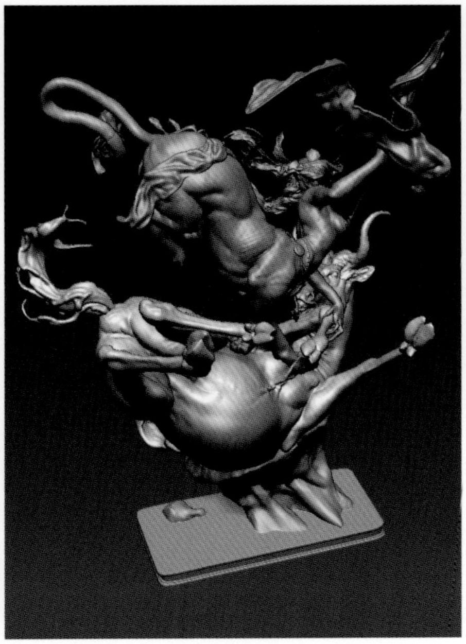

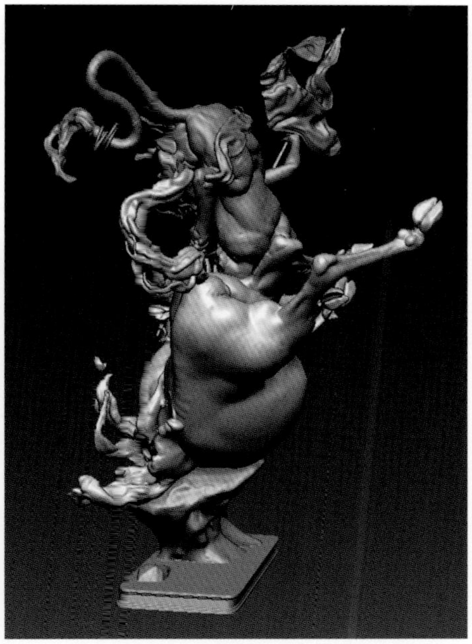

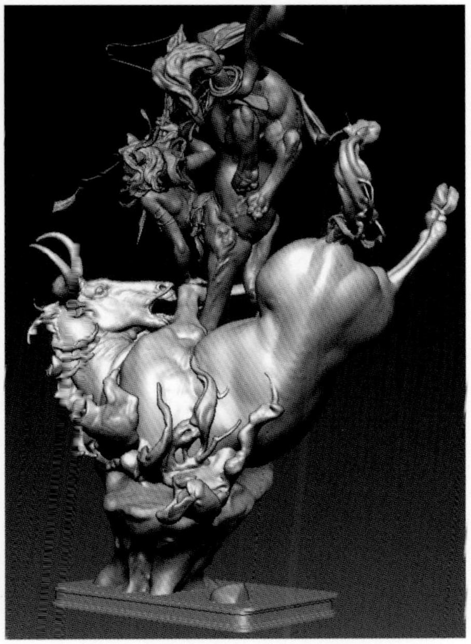

Refining the sculpture from all angles

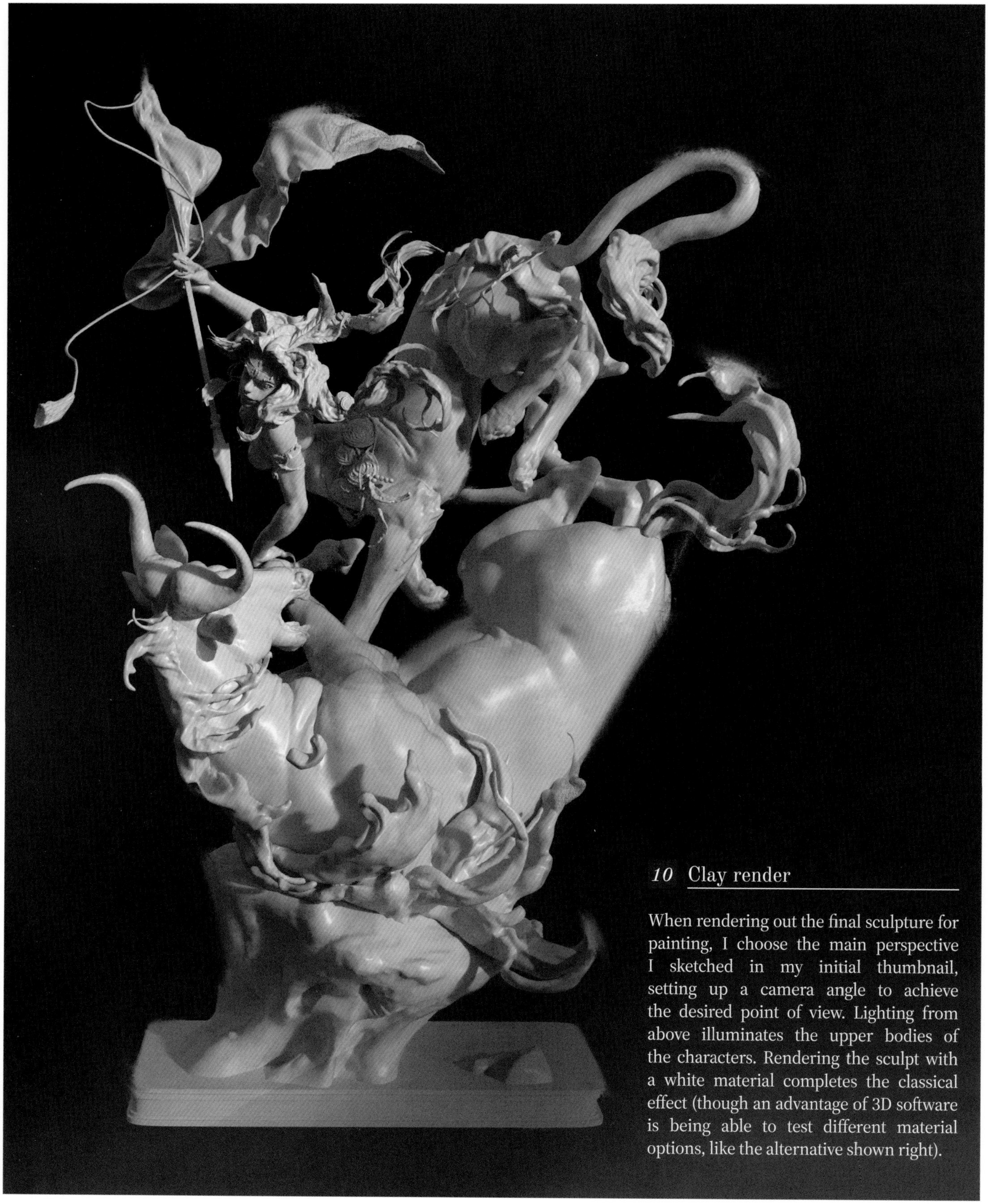

10 Clay render

When rendering out the final sculpture for painting, I choose the main perspective I sketched in my initial thumbnail, setting up a camera angle to achieve the desired point of view. Lighting from above illuminates the upper bodies of the characters. Rendering the sculpt with a white material completes the classical effect (though an advantage of 3D software is being able to test different material options, like the alternative shown right).

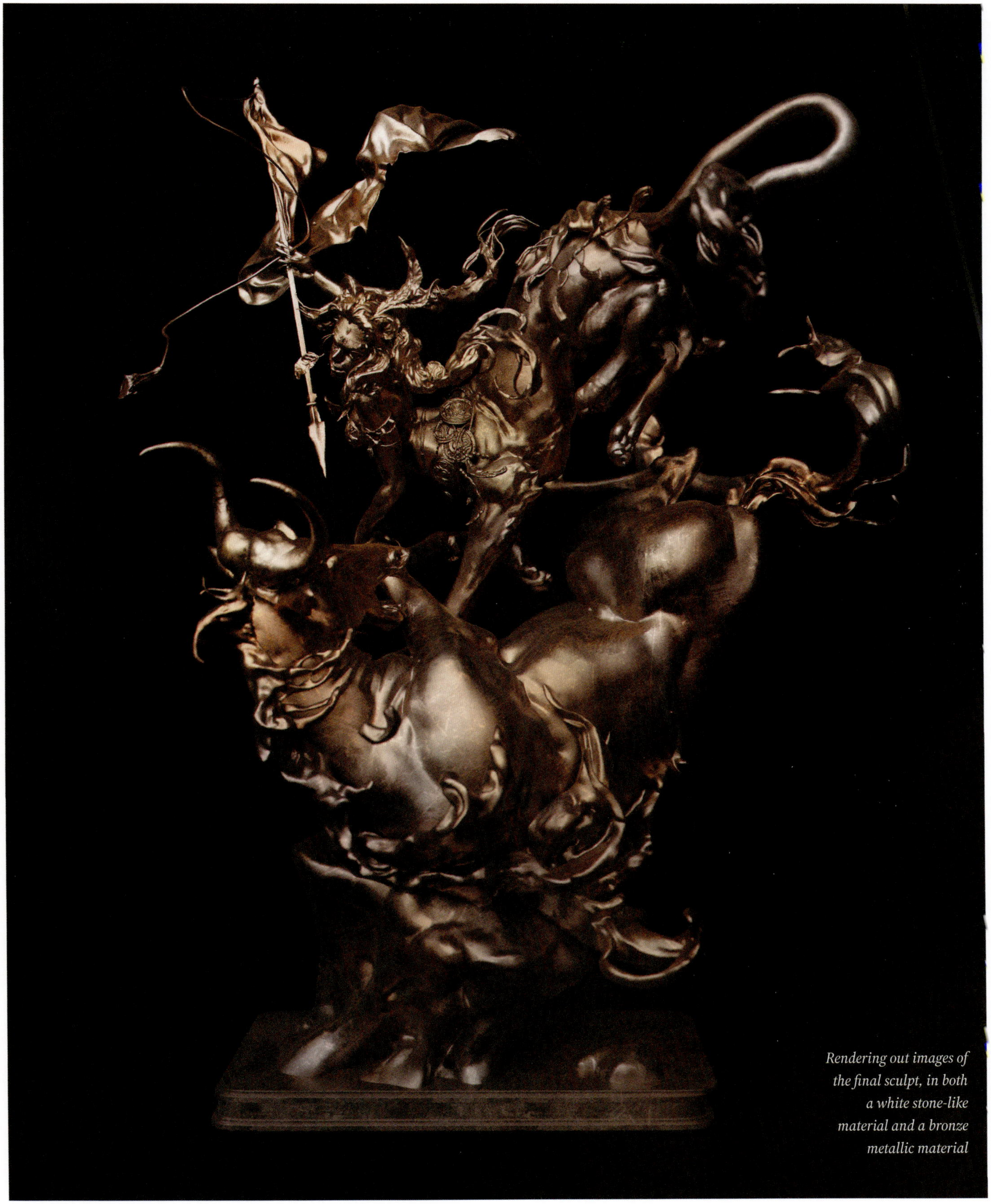

Rendering out images of the final sculpt, in both a white stone-like material and a bronze metallic material

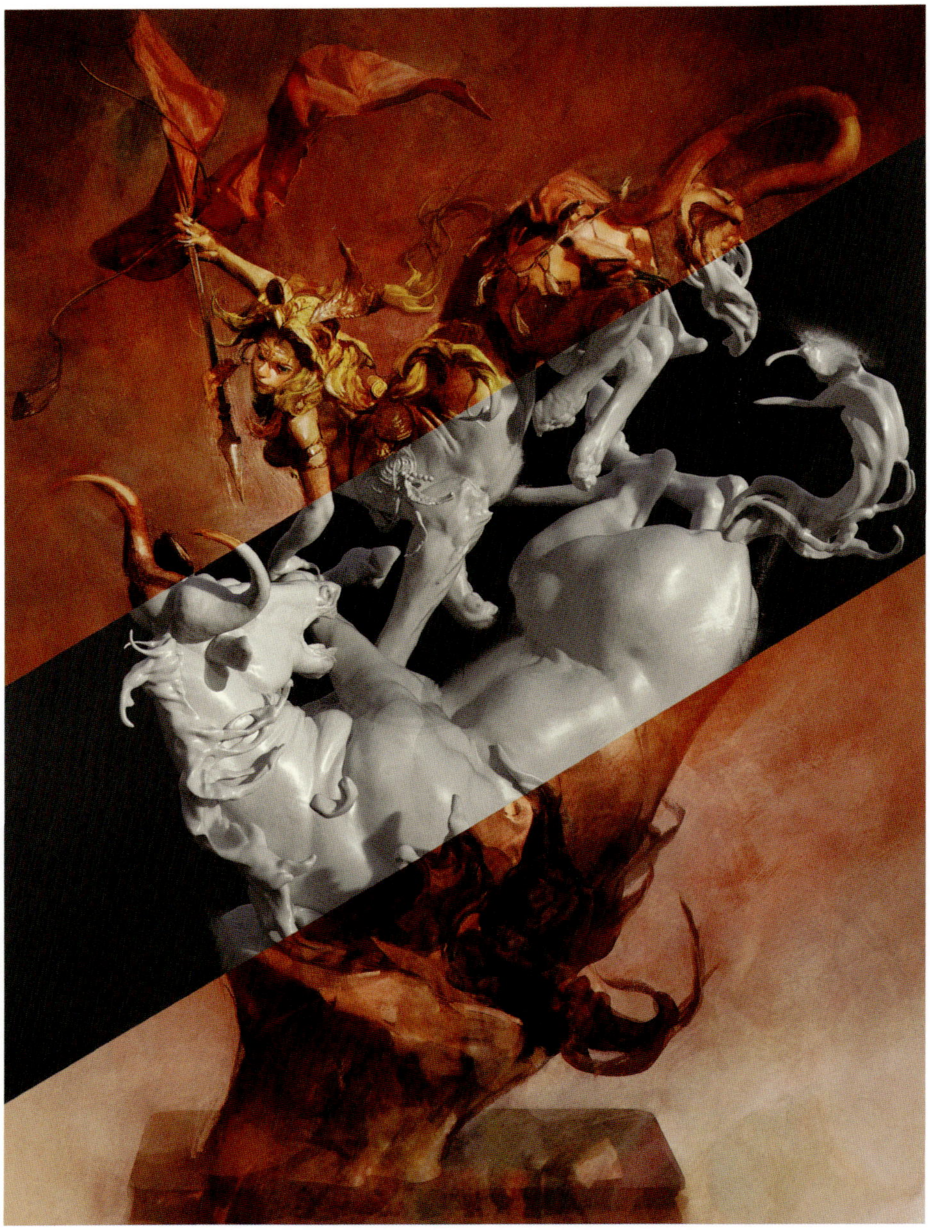

11 Paintover

I bring the rendered image into Adobe Photoshop and use brushes to adjust the shapes, composition, and relationship between light and shadow. I keep the colour palette simple and classical-looking, with warm red, gold, and bronze hues and loose, painterly strokes. I use my brushstrokes to emphasize the highlights and textures of the animal and character, enhancing the flow of fur and air.

Comparison of the 'clay sculpt' and paintover versions

Conclusion

The final completed image showcases a classical colour scheme and composition, with warm tones exuding vitality and dynamism, depicting a dangerous hunting scene. A burst of light background value emphasizes the point of impact between predator and prey. These aspects all combine to recreate the sense of awe that Frazetta's fantasy worlds have evoked in me.

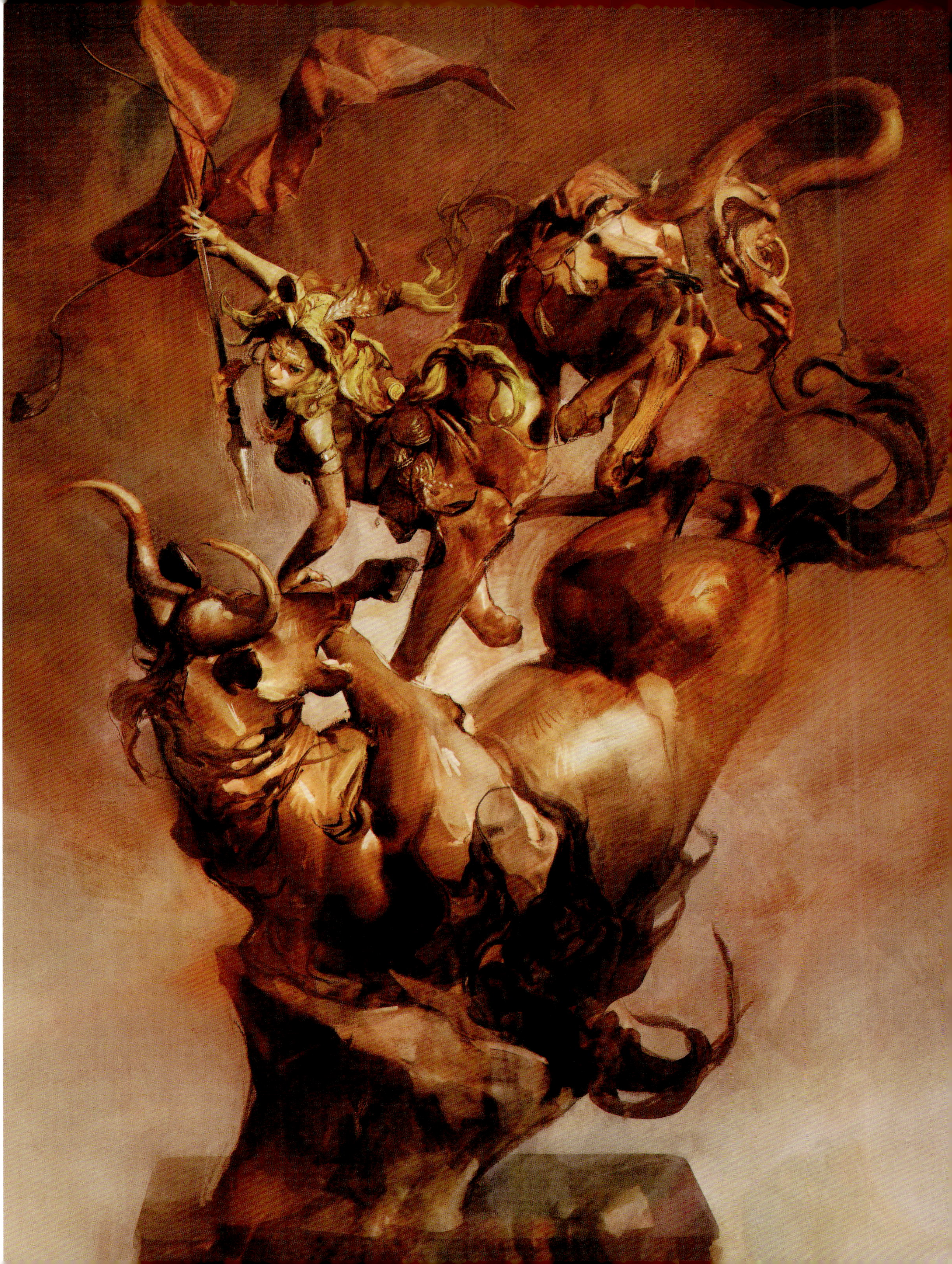

Final image © Entei Ryu

Gallery

by Entei Ryu

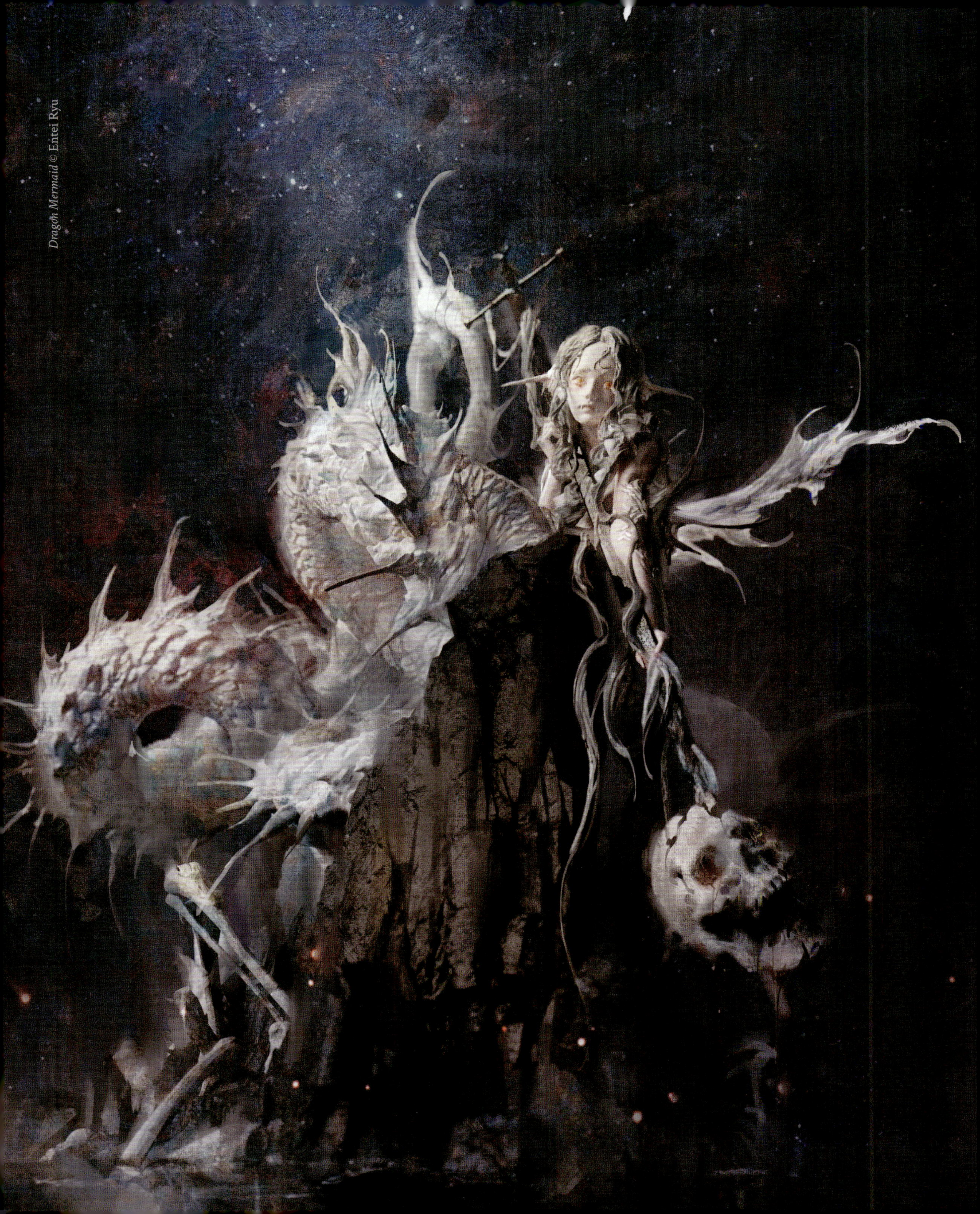

Dragon Mermaid © Entei Ryu

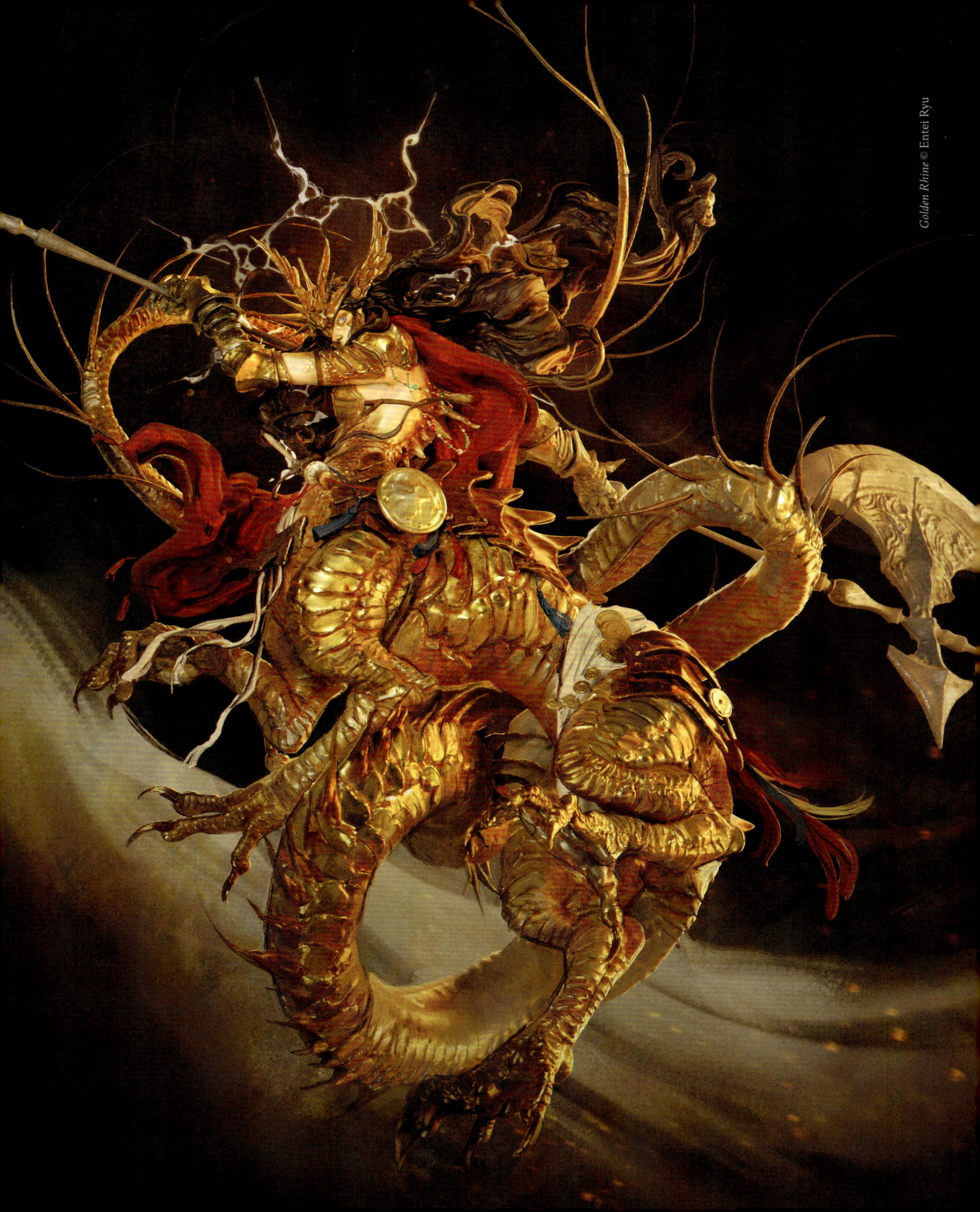

Golden Rhine © Entei Ryu

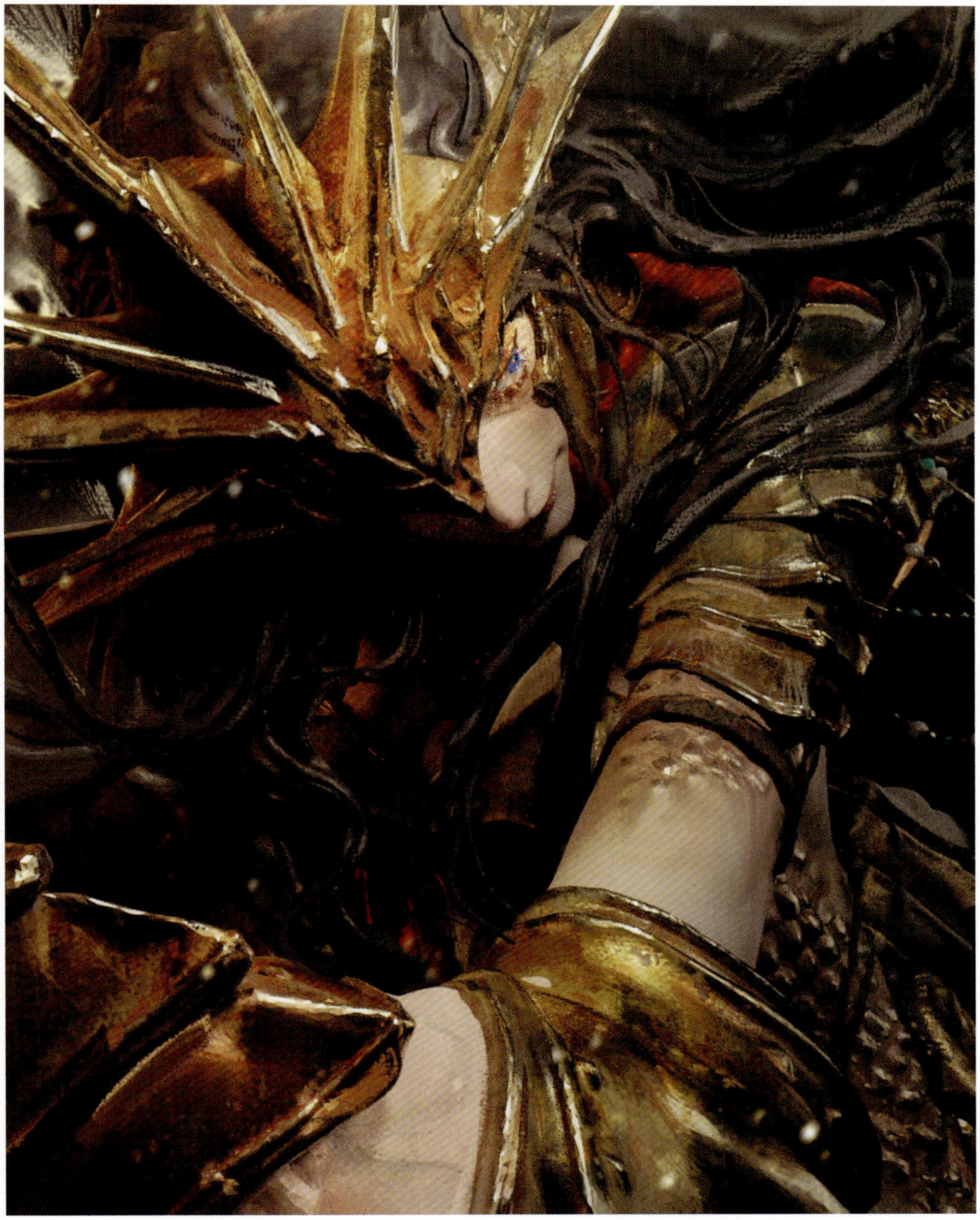

Golden Rhine © Entei Ryu

In Conversation With:

Rafael Grassetti

Hello, Rafael. Please introduce yourself – how did you start out in art and where has your career path taken you?

I've been an artist working in the entertainment industry for the past twenty years. I started as a traditional sculptor and quickly migrated to digital sculpting when the 3D software ZBrush came out. I have been working for the collectible and game industry for a long time and had the opportunity to contribute to many incredible titles; most recently, I was the art director for the new *God of War* series for the PlayStation, being responsible for designing and creating the iconic characters for the franchise.

Besides Frank Frazetta, who or what are your big creative influences or the cornerstones of your taste in art and media?

I am a product of so many different artists including Frazetta. To bring up some from that same time, my favourites include Boris Vallejo, Michael Whelan, H.R. Giger, and Jeff Easley. I also learned so much from traditional sculptors like Rick Baker, Steve Wang, and so many others.

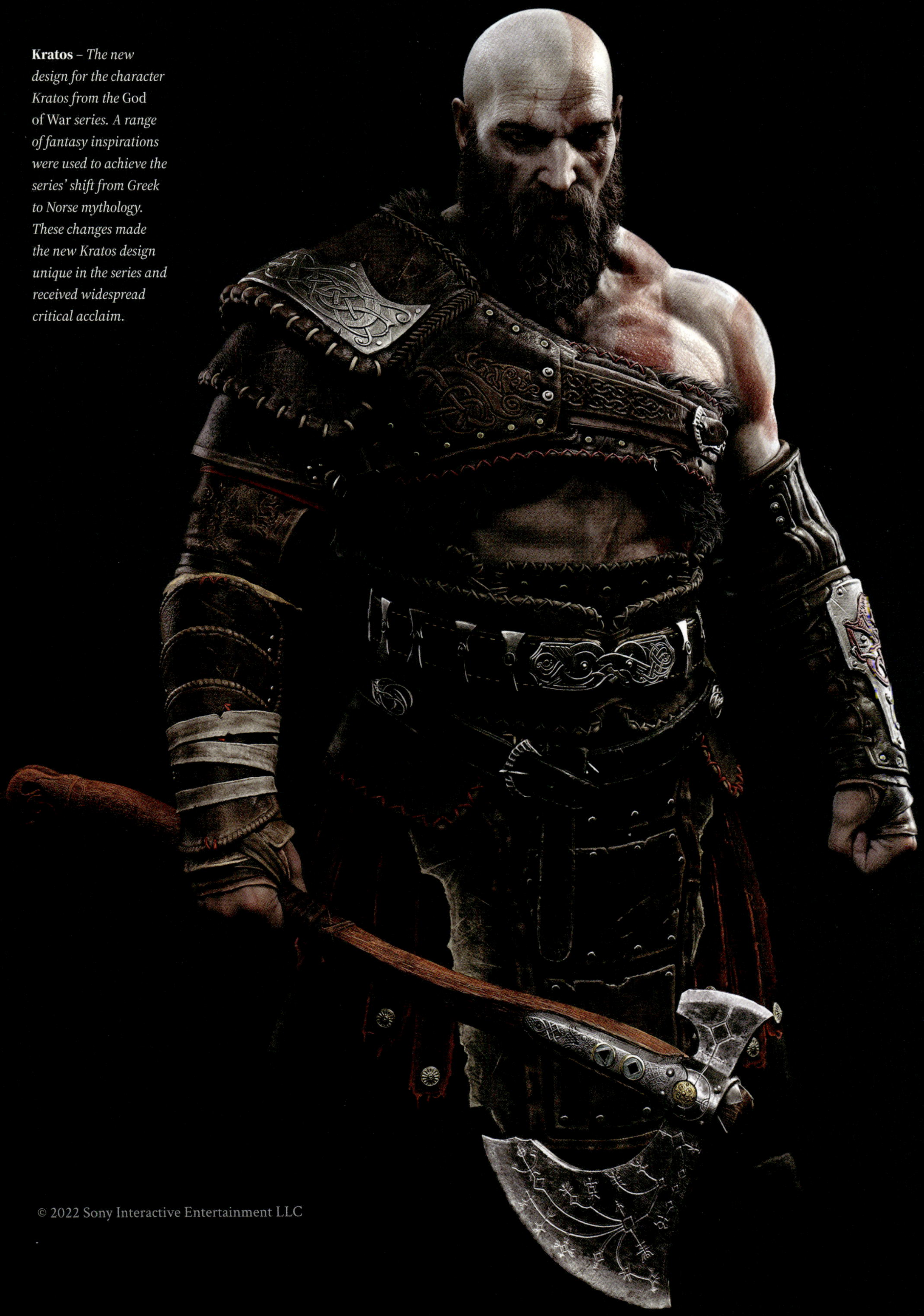

Kratos – *The new design for the character Kratos from the* God of War *series. A range of fantasy inspirations were used to achieve the series' shift from Greek to Norse mythology. These changes made the new Kratos design unique in the series and received widespread critical acclaim.*

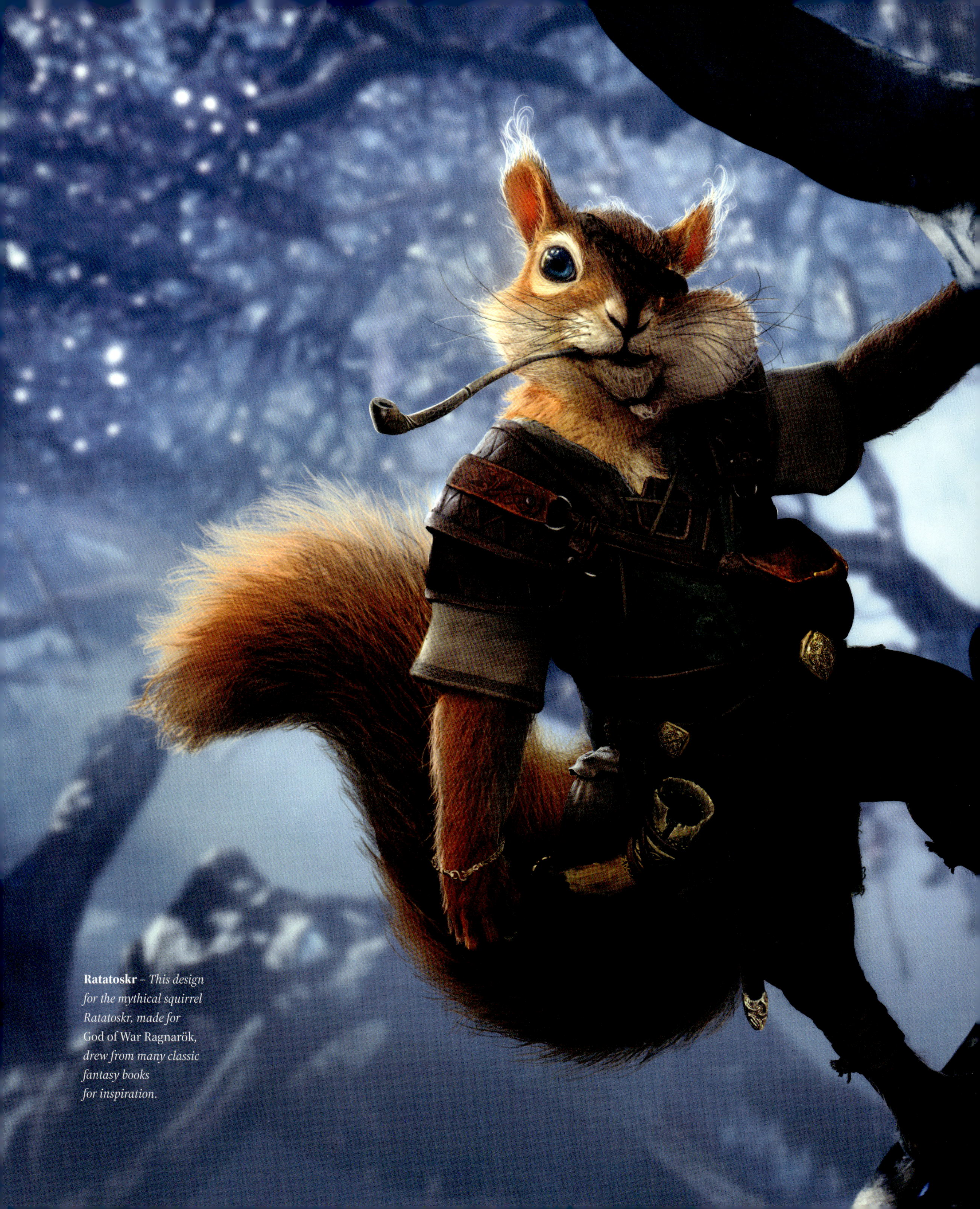

Ratatoskr – *This design for the mythical squirrel Ratatoskr, made for* God of War Ragnarök, *drew from many classic fantasy books for inspiration.*

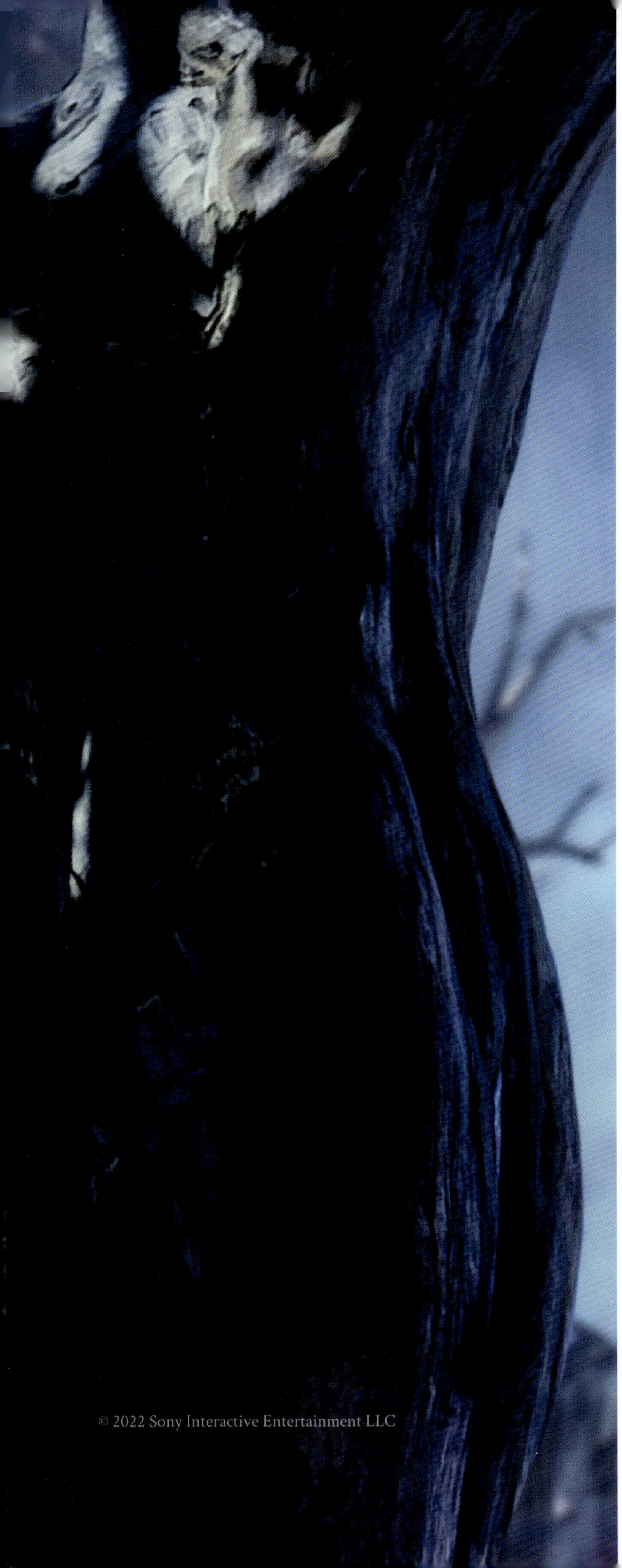

When and how did you first discover Frazetta's artwork? What did you think of it?

I don't have an exact memory of when I discovered Frank Frazetta, but I remember seeing his work without knowing who he was. Once I started to get more involved in traditional sculpting and found myself always going back to those same images, it made me stop and study more about the artist. His work was always striking and extremely inspiring when I was starting out. To this day, I look back on those images and still get inspired by them to start something new and improve my art.

What kind of imagery comes vividly to mind when you think of his work?

I think of the *Conan the Barbarian* illustrations. Frazetta helped define the popular image of the iconic character. The dynamic action in his paintings, and the ability he had to capture the raw energy and power of Conan in battle, are defining features of his work.

Do you have a favourite Frazetta piece?

The Death Dealer character is perhaps my favourite creation. The ominous, helmeted warrior atop a horse has become an enduring symbol of dark fantasy. The character is instantly recognizable due to his striking visual design and you can see his design influence in a lot of different media. I love the paintings where he looks menacing, riding a horse.

What has your relationship with Frazetta's work been like over time? How has he influenced you as an artist?

When I was studying sculpture, Frazetta was always among my references. The way he portrayed his characters' anatomy is both realistic and idealized, and he had a talent for rendering the human form in a way that highlights the things you need to learn while sculpting. Over the years I also learned to appreciate his compositions, the dynamic action in his paintings, the emotional depth of the work, and his use of colour and light. All of these things helped me become a better artist while studying his work and trying to replicate many of his techniques.

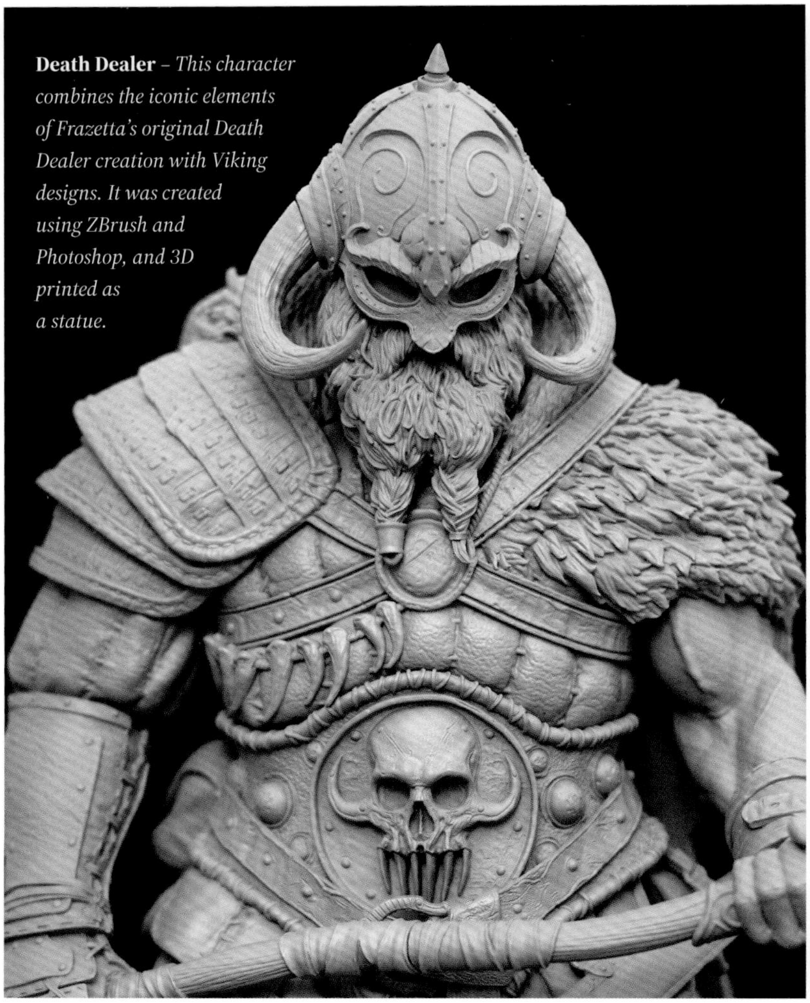

Death Dealer – *This character combines the iconic elements of Frazetta's original Death Dealer creation with Viking designs. It was created using ZBrush and Photoshop, and 3D printed as a statue.*

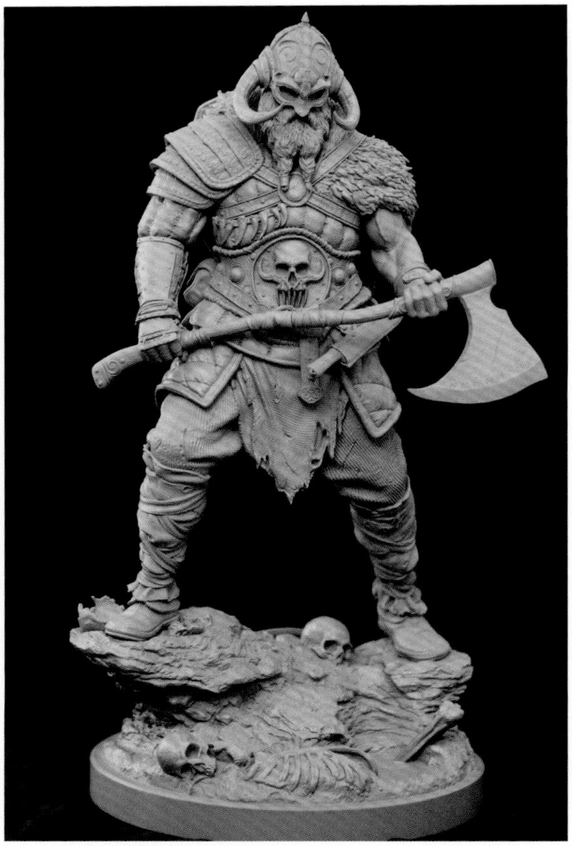

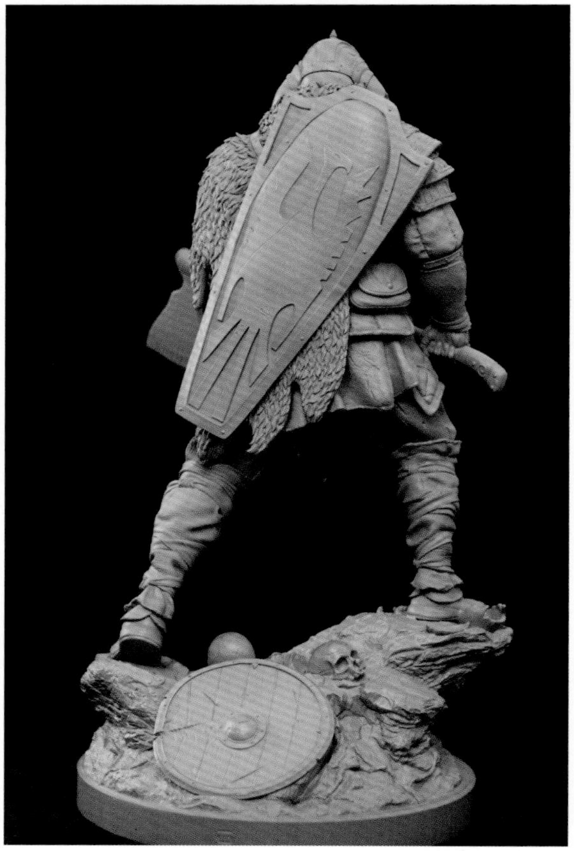

What are some favourite personal or professional projects where you've consciously drawn on that Frazetta influence?

You can see Frazetta inspiration in many of my works, including *God of War Ragnarök*. As an art director on the project I was always pushing for a more classical look, trying to find inspiration to bring us closer to that 'fantasy book' feeling we get from 1980s movies, which were heavily influenced by Frazetta's works. The Viking *Death Dealer* statue I created in 2022 is a direct homage to the artist, mixing his Death Dealer design with Viking elements to create a unique interpretation of the character.

Where do you see his legacy when you look around today?

Frazetta's distinctive style and approach to fantasy art continue to inspire contemporary fantasy artists and illustrators – I think many artists draw inspiration from his use of dynamic compositions, vivid colours, and powerful character designs in their own work. The influence of Frazetta's artwork can also be seen in video games, especially in the designs of characters, monsters, and fantasy landscapes. Games set in medieval or fantastical settings often exhibit visual elements reminiscent of Frazetta's work, as you can see in my *God of War* examples here. ❖

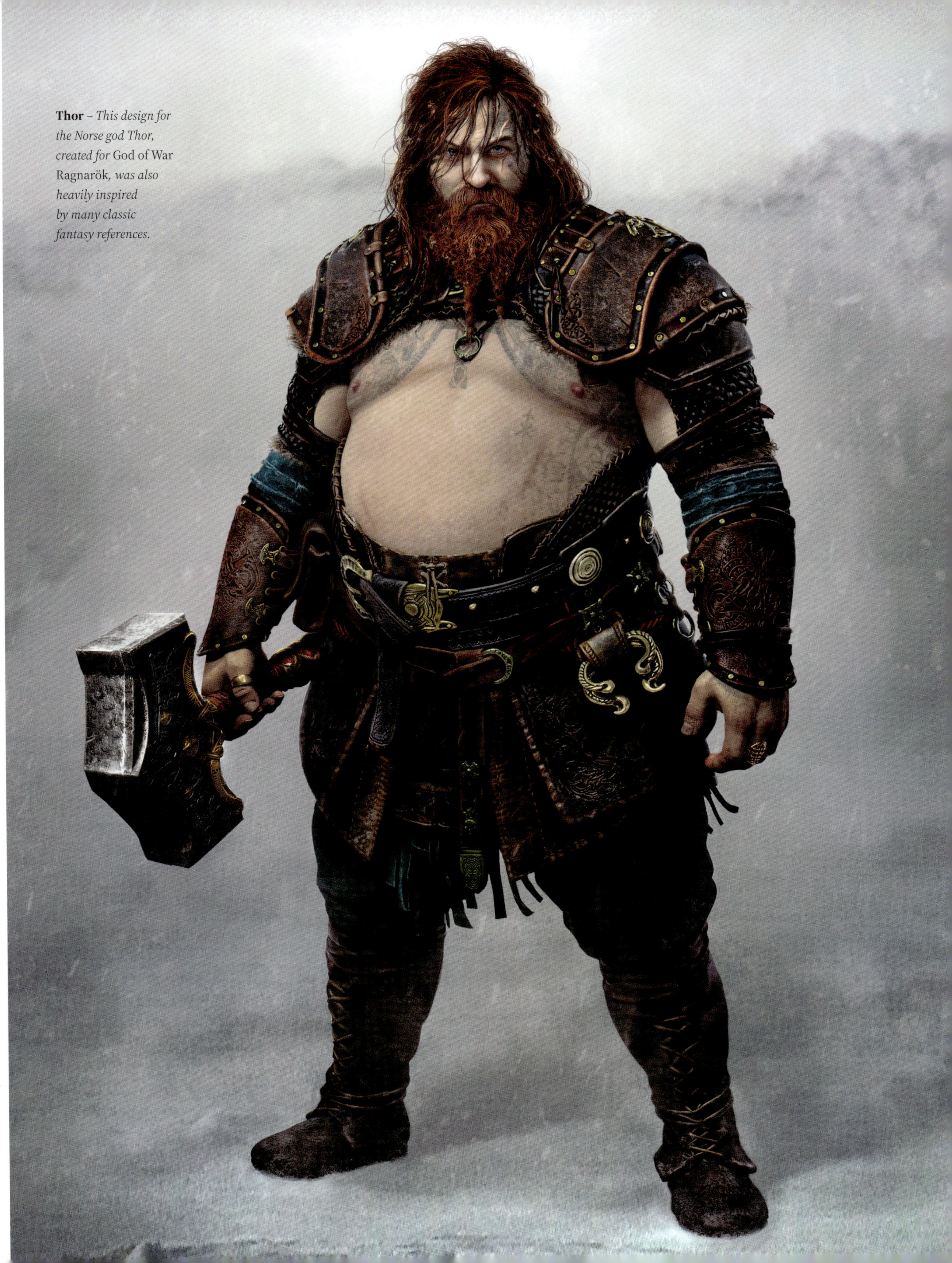

Thor – *This design for the Norse god Thor, created for* God of War Ragnarök, *was also heavily inspired by many classic fantasy references.*

The Sur

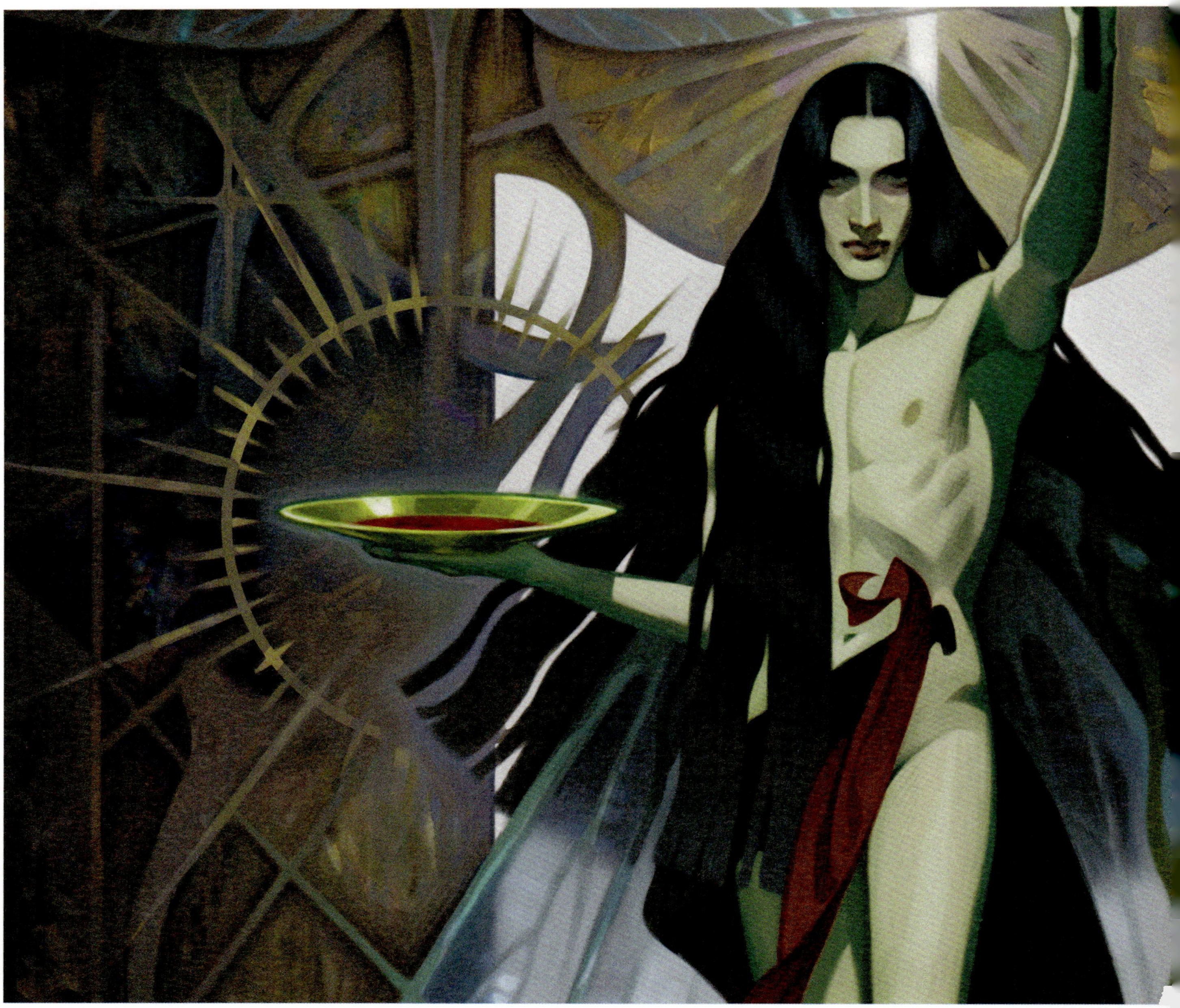

Final image © Valentina Remenar

moning

by Valentina Remenar

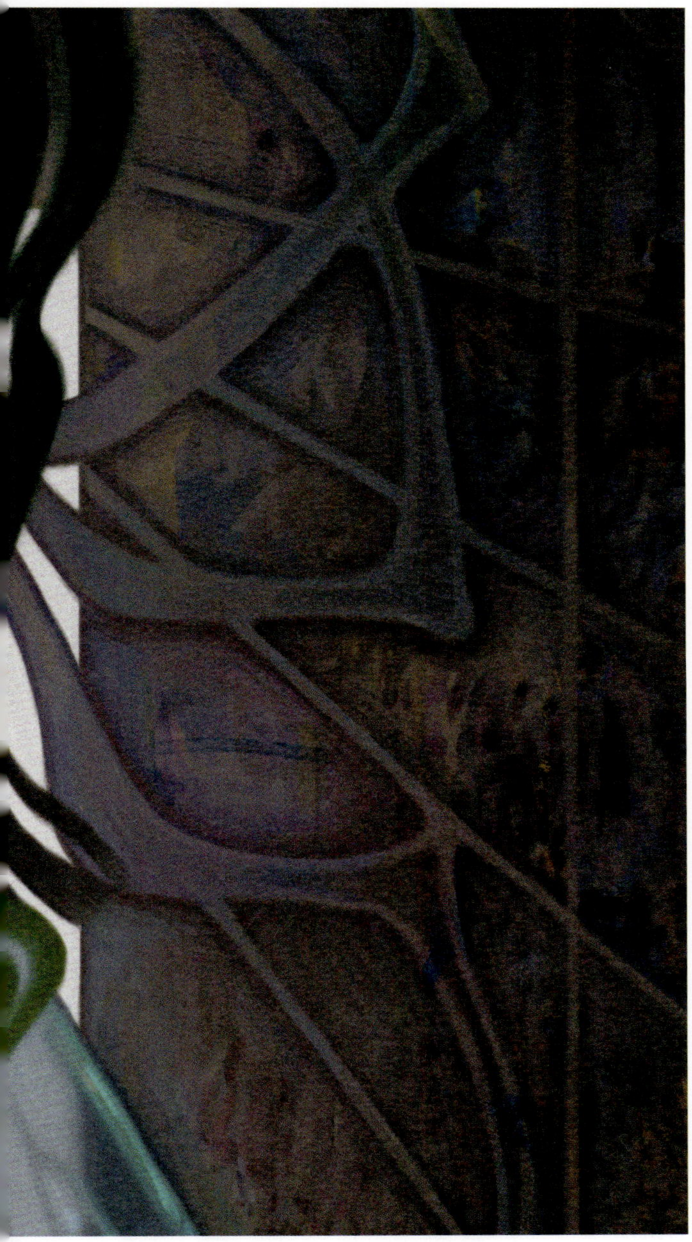

Creating *The Summoning*

Frank Frazetta's mastery of light, texture, values, composition, and storytelling is what inspires me the most. These are the aspects of his work I want to pay tribute to in my painting. My art in general is often inspired by tarot and many pagan aspects; I want to explore that with this painting and capture a concept that is darker, but not depressing, and is still colourful. The main themes will be summoning and ritualism; the viewer may think these have negative connotations, but the summoner character will be bathed in bright light to symbolize his positivity in the painting.

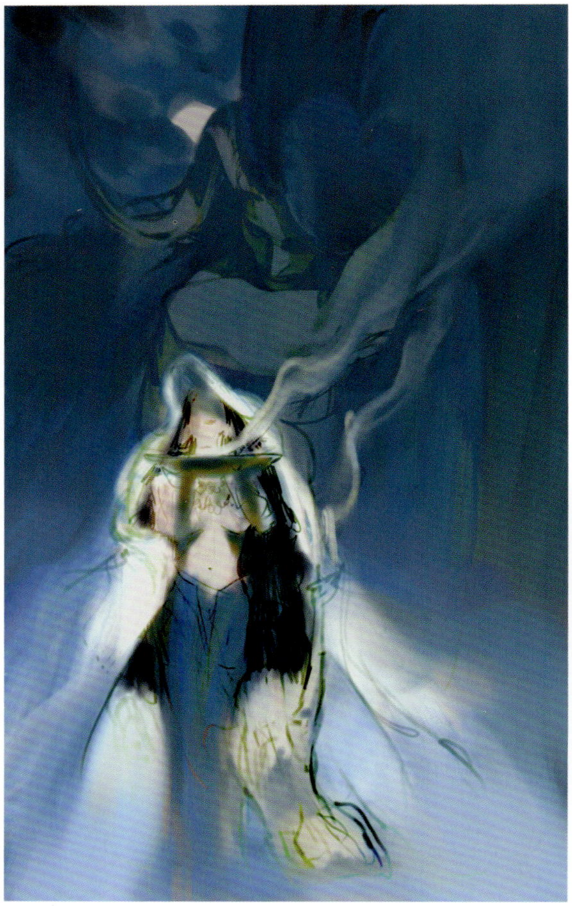

The rough first draft of my idea for The Summoning

01 First sketch

Since Frazetta mostly painted women, my first concept is of a woman protagonist performing a summoning ritual. In this first concept, I want to make the woman the focal point in the light; meanwhile, in the dark, a masculine demon lurks in the shadows. For the symbolism, my focus is on the contrast between light and dark, with the ritual taking place at night – a time where bad things are mostly said to happen. The mood feels right but I am not quite happy with the idea yet.

02 Second sketch

For this second version, I go with a male character instead, as masculine figures are my speciality and comfort zone. This change alone makes me much happier with the painting. This time I try to include more storytelling aspects; while the core symbolism remains the same, I make some changes to those aspects as well, such as the inclusion of the goat to represent the devil being summoned. The man holds a moon-shaped sickle towards the night sky. At his feet burns a bonfire to represent his ritualistic summoning – fire representing destruction, transformation, and creation.

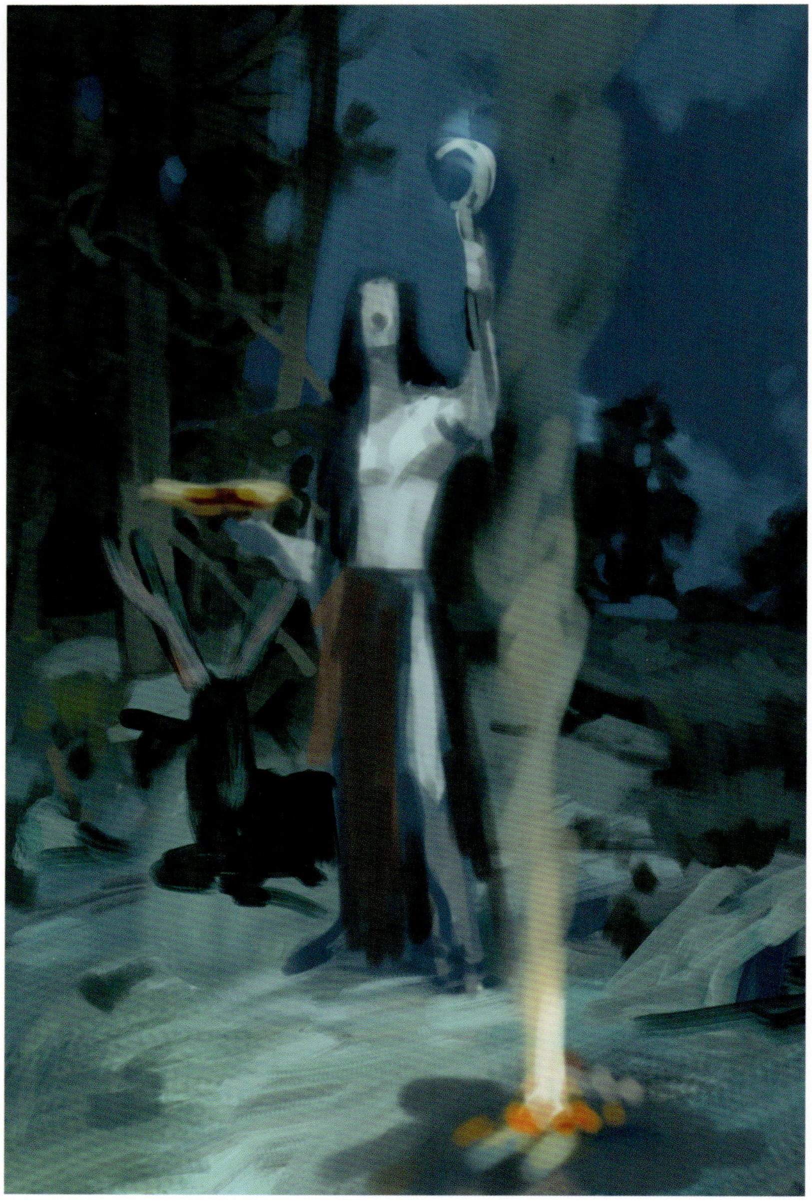

My second concept sketch takes a different approach

03 Line drawing

After the rough sketch is done, the next important step is to make a detailed sketch. Refining the sketch will help me to quickly add colour and shading to the painting, without needing to fix or redraw the character in the later stages due to anatomical inaccuracies or similar issues. This greatly increases the speed of my painting process. I focus on making the anatomy as accurate as possible, as well as designing the clothes, so that I'll be able to accurately place the colours.

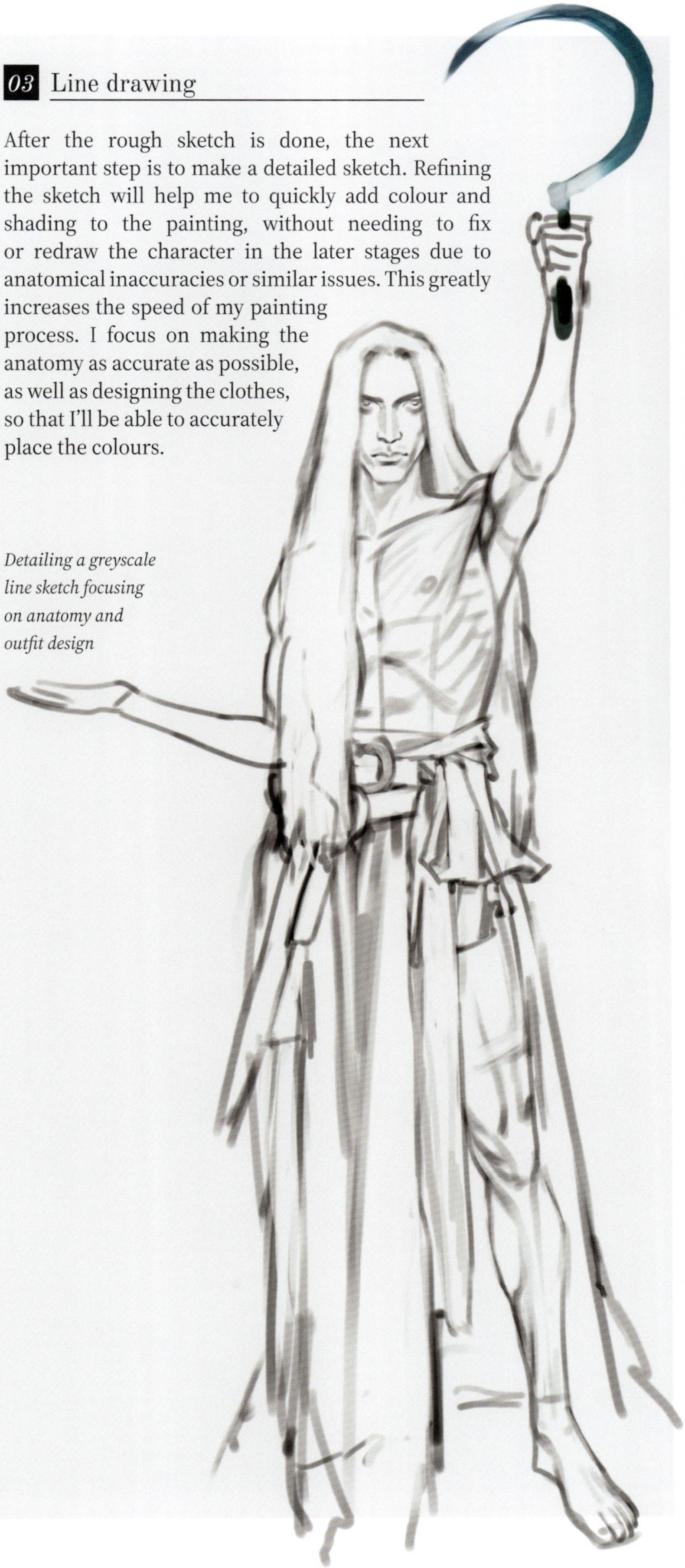

Detailing a greyscale line sketch focusing on anatomy and outfit design

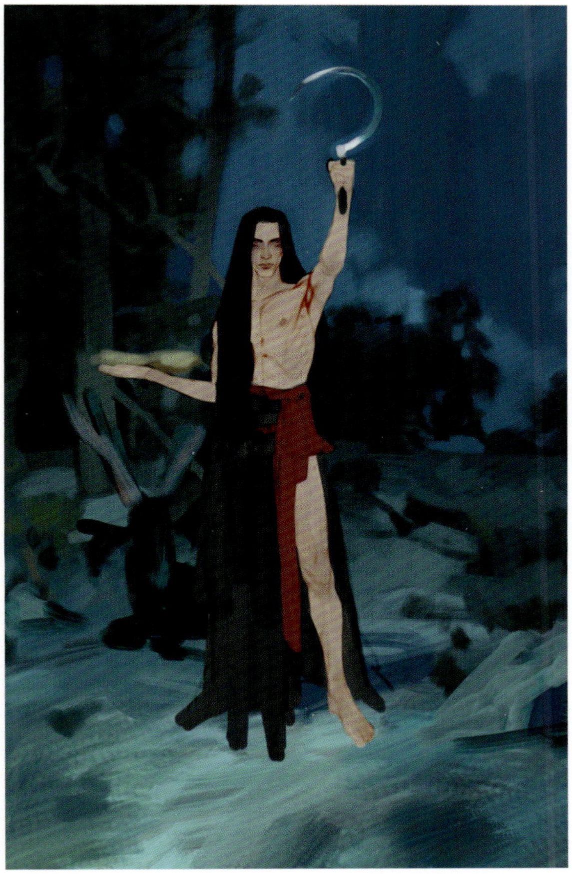

Setting the sketch layer to Colour Burn mode and painting base colours below it

04 Base colours

After I finish the detailed sketch, I merge all the character sketch layers with a white background, and I change its blending mode to Color Burn. I convert the layer to a Smart Object and apply a Hue/Saturation adjustment onto the layer itself, tinting the sketch towards a warmer tone. Using Photoshop's Smart Object option, instead of normal layer, helps me to make adjustments and tweak effects applied to that layer at any stage of the process.

Below this sketch layer I add the flat base colours. The line art of the sketch, as it's in Color Burn mode, becomes vividly colourized as I paint under it. The colours that I pick for the base are always the ones true to the character's skin tone and outfit, without any ambience, lighting, or other effects applied. This allows me to put the character into any environment and stay true to their actual colour palette, without overthinking how specific colours would behave under a certain light.

05 Cool ambience

With the flat colours in place, I can start adding some ambience. Below the sketch layer and above the flat-colour layer, I add two layers; one in Linear Light mode and another one in Vivid Light mode. I use the Paint Bucket tool to fill these layers with cooler tones that fit the night scene I'm trying to achieve. The resulting effect gives the character a much more blue-green, nocturnal tone.

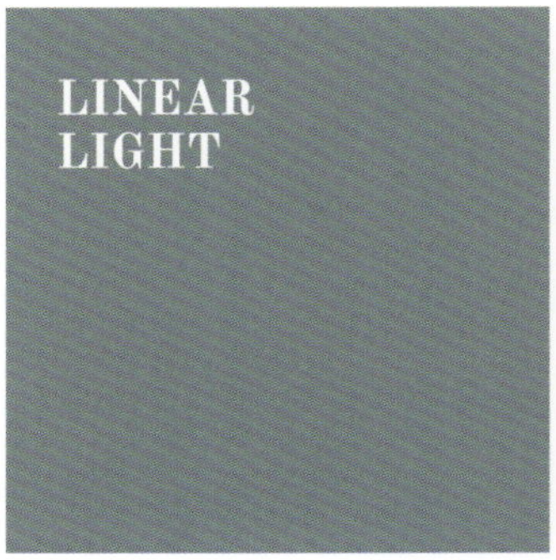

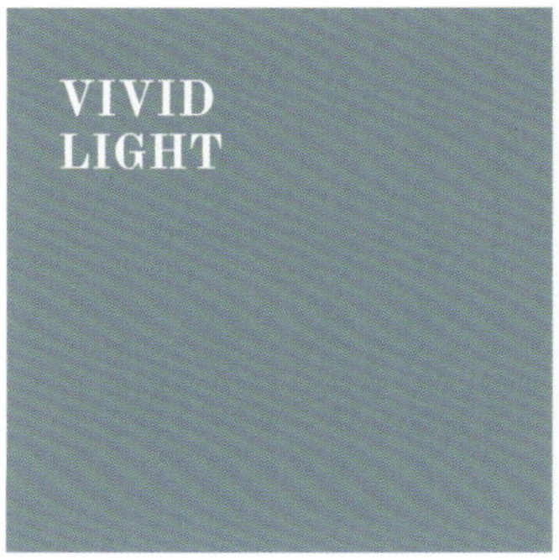

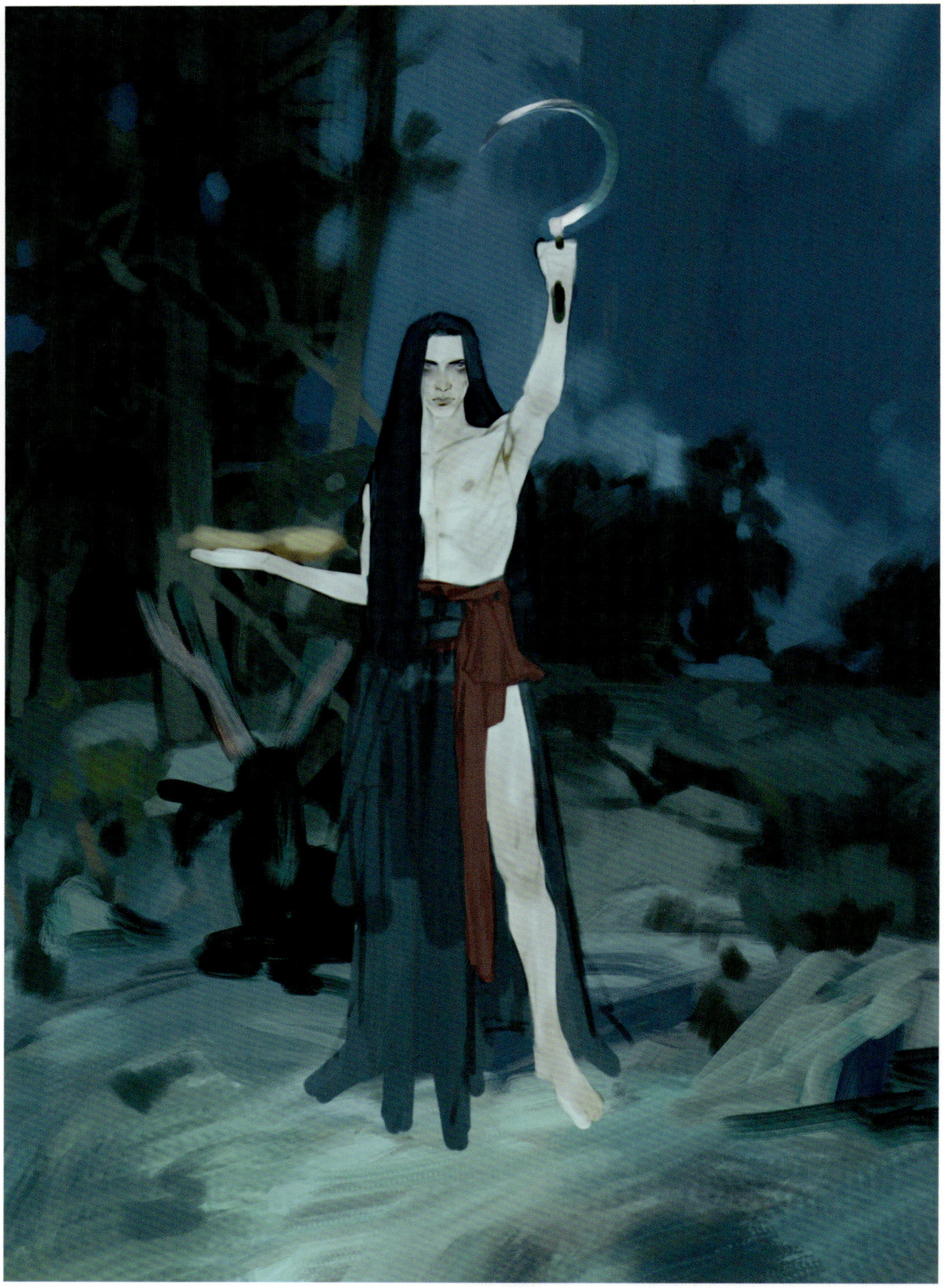

Using Vivid Light and Linear Light to create an ambience that fits the night scene

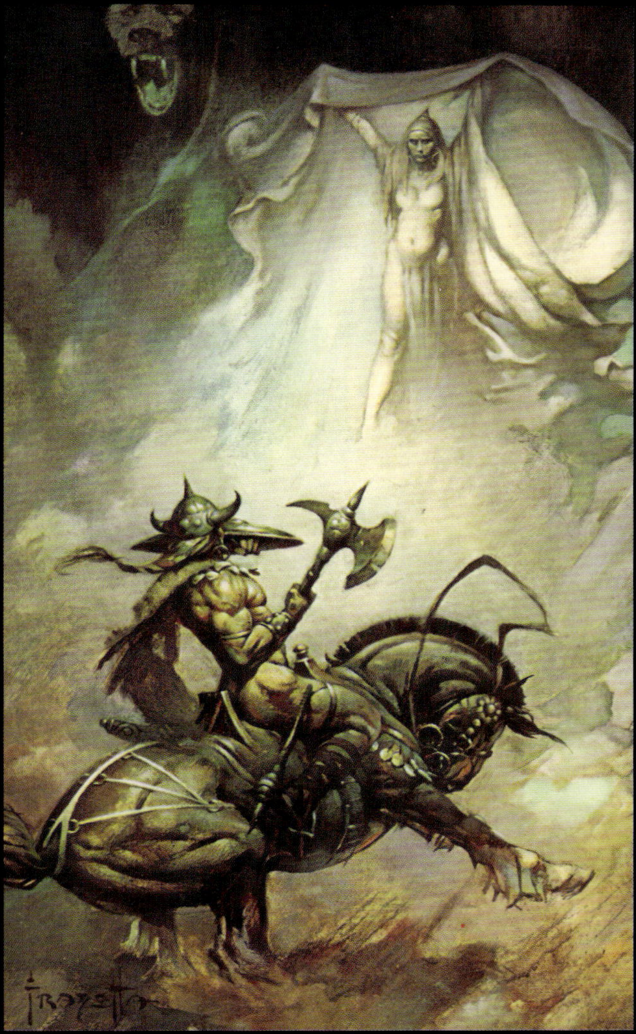

The Apparition © Frank Frazetta

Discovering Frazetta

I discovered Frazetta's work while browsing online. I don't remember which of his paintings I saw first, but some personal favourites include *The Apparition* and *At the Earth's Core* (see on page 236). One of the aspects of his work that resonated with me was his mastery of lighting, combined with strong shadows that made the silhouettes and figures of his paintings pop. I love how his paintings are often a mix of dark and mysterious themes, and how he combined storytelling with surreal elements. His ability to simplify and his incredible surreal backgrounds are always inspiring to me.

In my own artwork, I am mainly inspired by his use of light, texture, and surreal themes, as well as how he creates focal points in his paintings through masterful use of values. I appreciate the way he subtly tells a story through composition, posing, and the characters in general. Using *The Apparition* as an example, you can see how the horse has come to an abrupt stop, and that the character is looking upwards in surprise at the apparition. Through composition alone, Frank Frazetta guides the viewer's eye firstly to the main character, whose gaze we naturally follow to the feminine apparition, followed closely by the dark and bestial figures around her. It's like the viewer is experiencing the story, the moment, that the main foreground character is going through.

▸▸ *For image in full, turn to page 235*

06 Light source

Now I can focus on the light and light source. For this piece I want to have a single light source that will create strong shadows that emphasize the character's muscular body, as well as create a dark, mysterious vibe, similar to what Frank Frazetta did so masterfully in each of his paintings. I decide to have the light source coming from above, as both a nod to Frank's choices in lighting and to create those long, dark shadows. For the shadows, I make a new Hard Light layer above the sketch and flat-colour layers and paint them there.

Creating a light source that adds both depth and mood through the use of long shadows

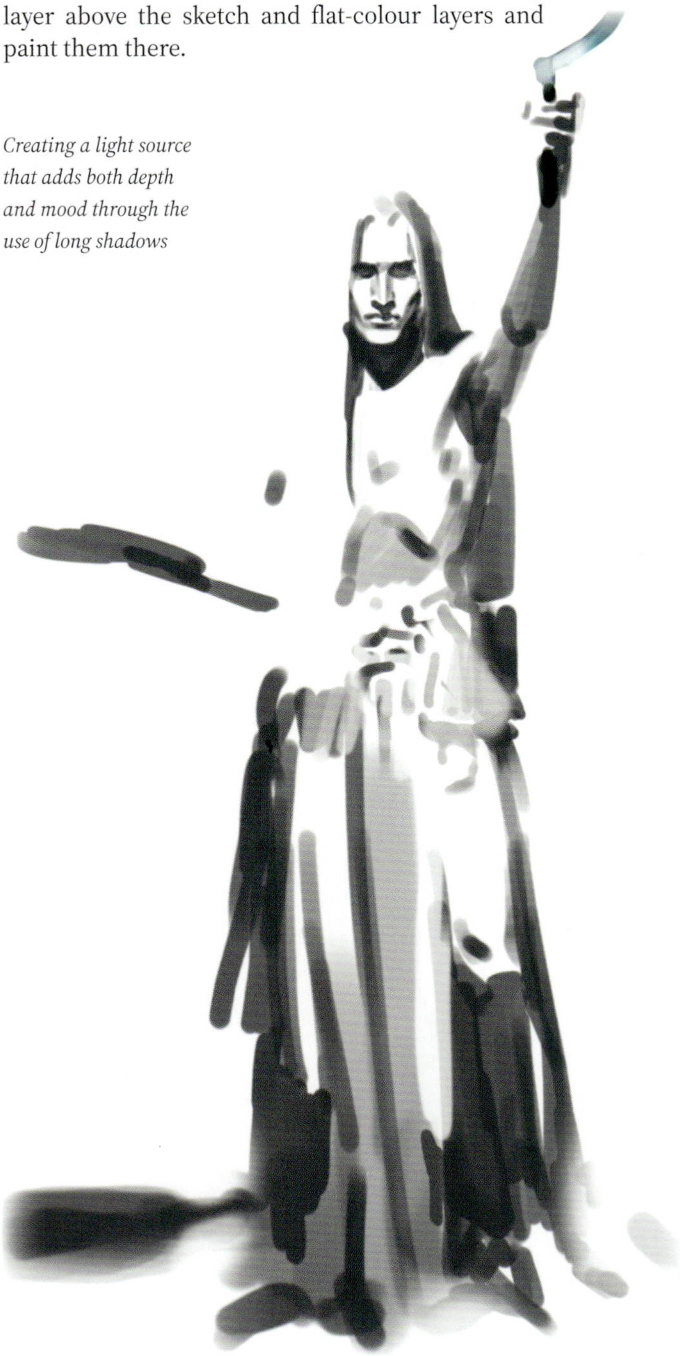

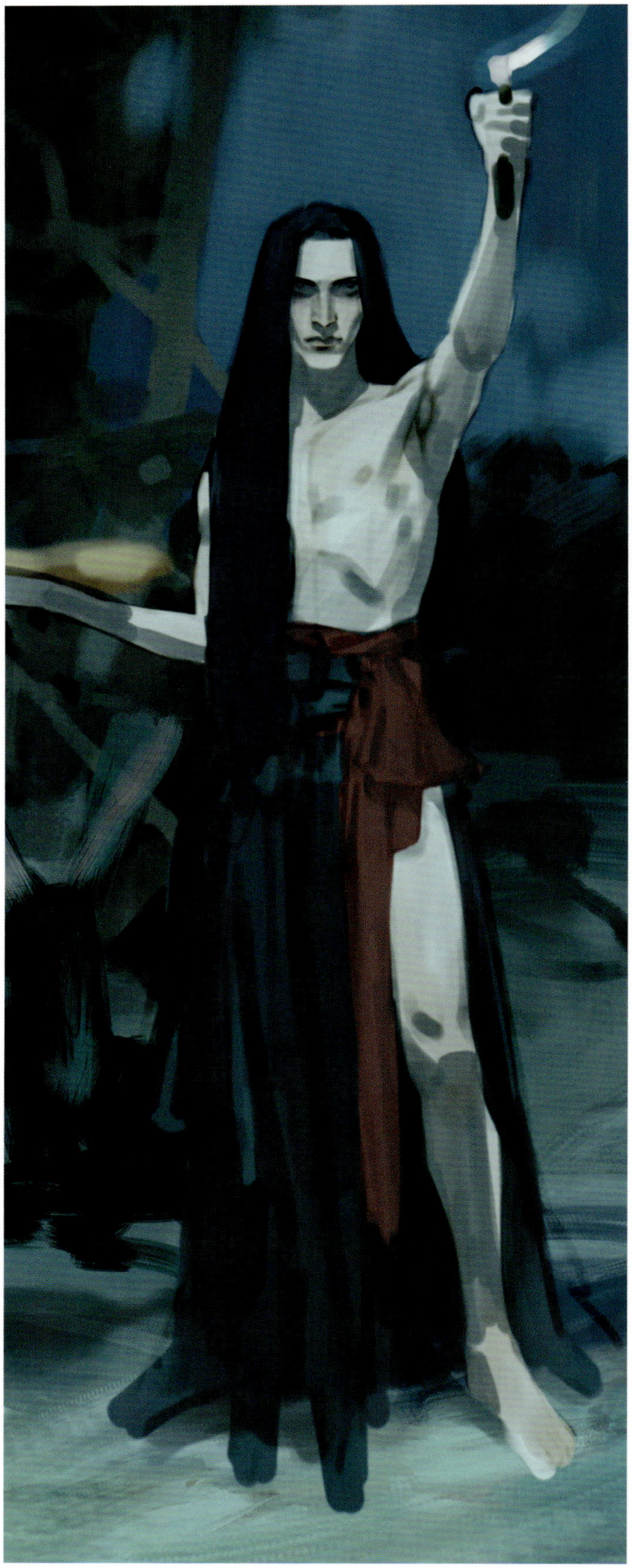

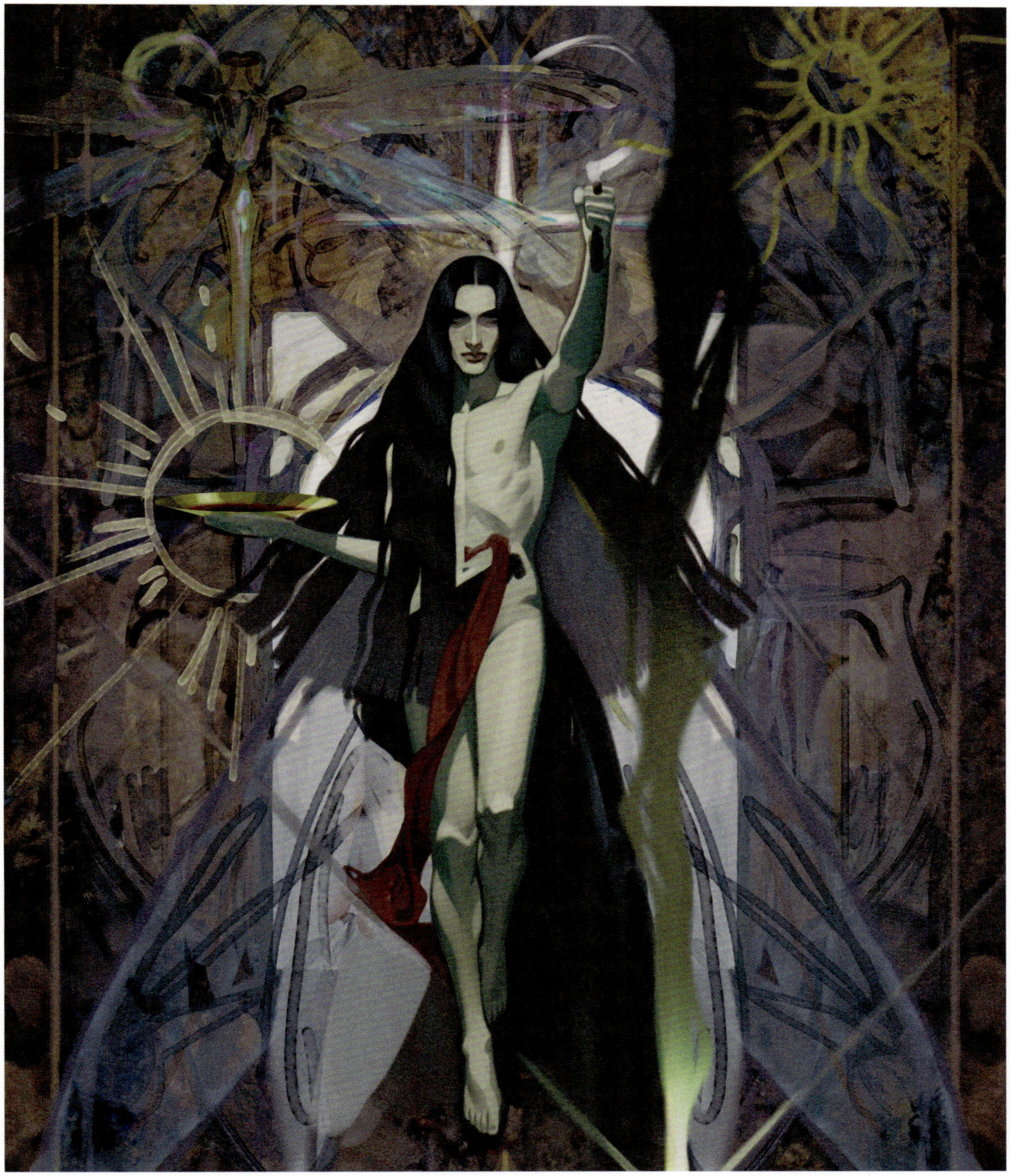

Making a major change in the painting process, with further tweaks and inclusions of symbolism and inspiration

07 Changing approach

In this step, the entire painting process changes. I decide to change the background, as well as a lot of the figure, as I want to use more direct inspiration from Frazetta's art. His use of textures and surreal qualities is one of my biggest inspiration points, so I decide to make the texture feel more like a traditional painting, and to include more surrealistic elements in both the character and the environment. I decide to include elements of insects, such as the spider background and the character's fly-inspired wings, because insects are often seen as a symbol of death and evil. Drawing upon my tarot inspiration, I likewise include the sun to contrast the moon-like sickle, playing upon the symbolism of light and darkness or good and evil.

08 Triangular composition

Even though I don't move the character, I try to change the composition slightly, so that it isn't made with only straight vertical and horizontal lines. A triangular composition will give the impression of being less static and will help me to achieve a focal point; the diagonals meet on the character's face, which helps the viewer to focus on that area. For secondary focal point, I include a white rectangular shape in the centre, which makes the silhouette of the character pop out, thus amplifying his importance.

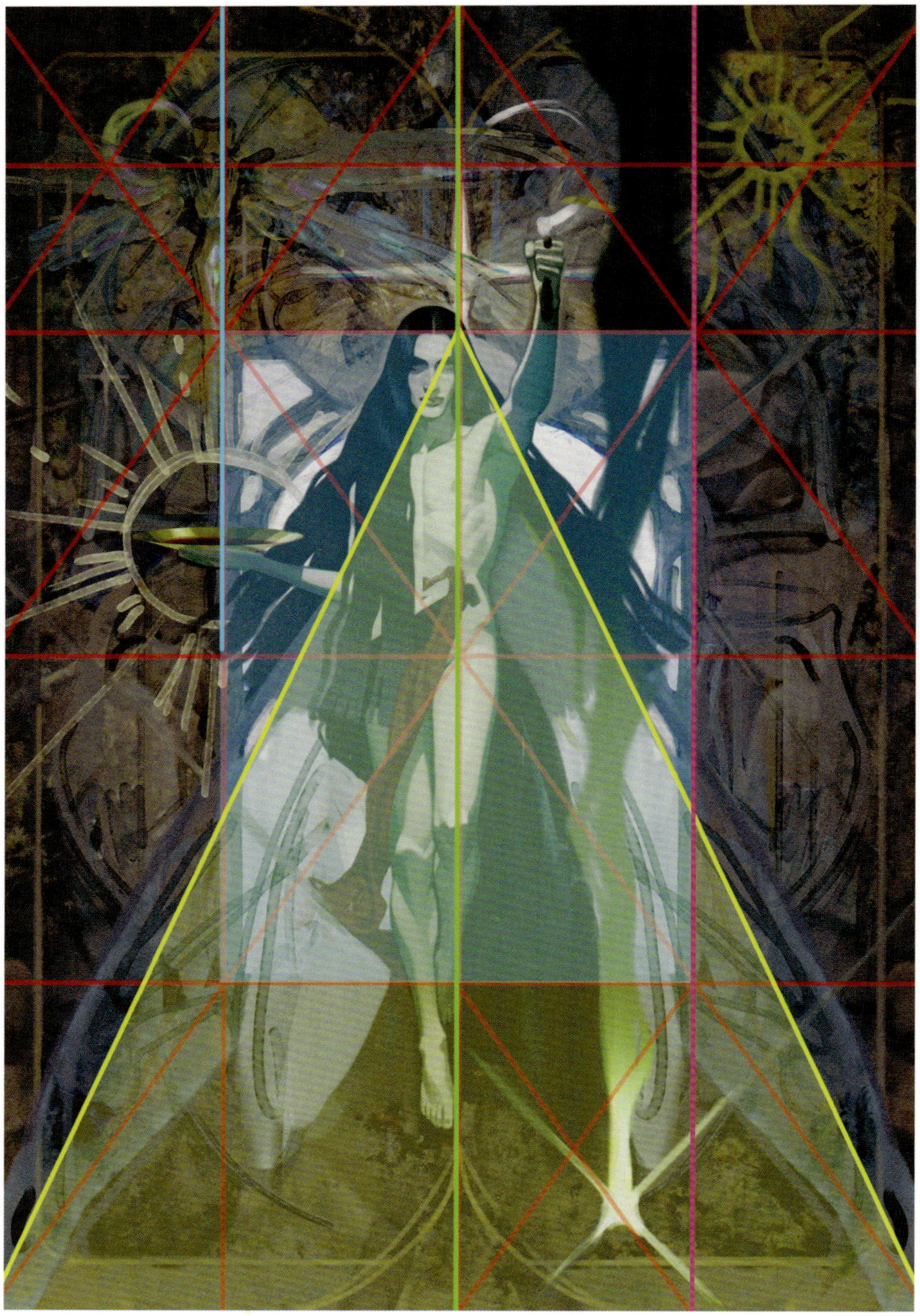

Making use of a triangular composition, commonly found in Frazetta's paintings, to emphasize the focus on the character

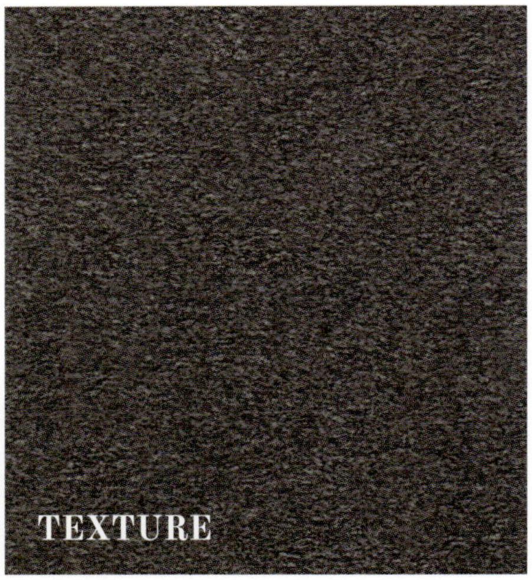

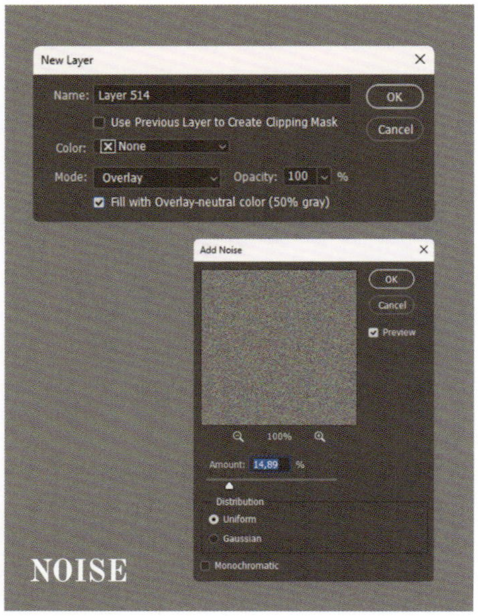

Adding texture to create the illusion of a traditional painting with a digital illustration

09 Adding texture

I have always been inspired by the textures of Frank Frazetta's work. I want to capture that feeling here and make my digital work seem like a traditional painting. First, I add a paper-like photo texture courtesy of Yuri Shwedoff (yurishwedoff.gumroad.com). I duplicate it twice, change the blending modes to Luminosity and Lighten for each, and set them to a very low opacity for both. To add even more texture, I create a Smart Object layer with a 50% grey colour, apply Noise to it, and finally change its blending mode to Hard Light.

10 Painting the wings

I want the wings to be a bigger part of the painting, but I don't want to make them too detailed or the viewer might get distracted. I decide not to include patterns or to complicate the wing design. Instead, I decide to make the wings appear translucent, so that the light spreads softly through them. The softness of the wings' shape and shading creates contrast with the harsh angles and lines in the background. I shade the wings without the veins first; only after the base is properly shaded do I start adding veins and reflected light.

Starting work on the character's wings, taking steps to ensure they don't distract from the character himself

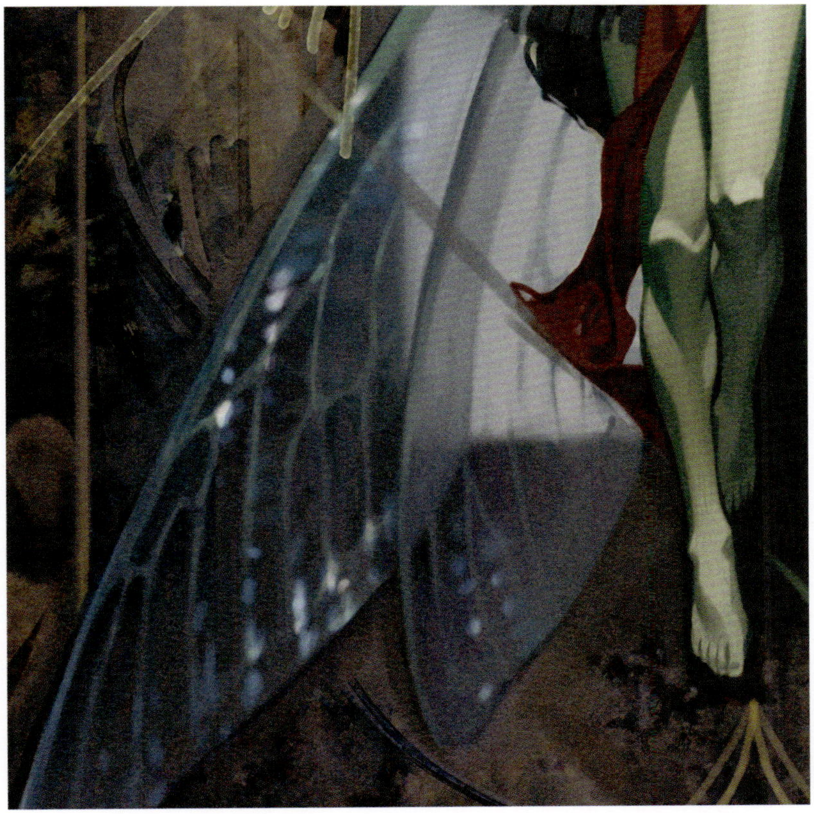

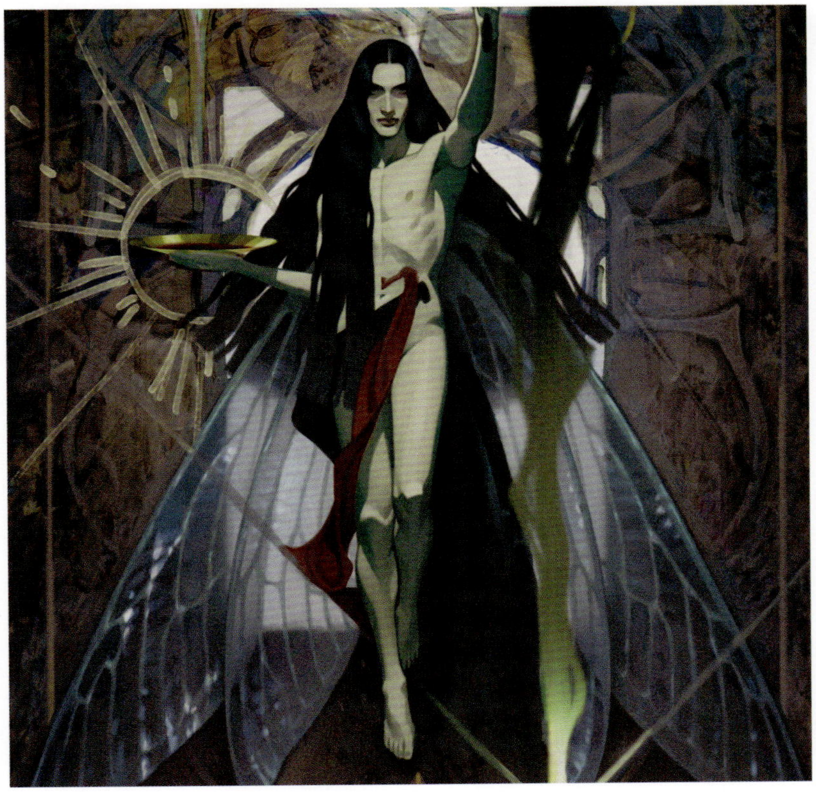

Finishing the wing base and refining the textures using textured and watercolour brushes

11 Wing details

I finish detailing both wings by adding some final veins and reflections, then shift my attention to the background. The rough base, which I painted with mixer brushes, is perfect for adding rough texture and colouring. However, I want the texture to be slightly more detailed and less chaotic. I start refining the details with textured brushes, such as watercolour brushes and impressionistic brushes. Any additional details or shading is painted with many smaller hatched lines, which helps me preserve the texture underneath and creates a pencil-drawn look.

12 Frame & background

I try to soften the shading in the background so there aren't too many rough lines. I keep the lighter colours closer to the centre, where the character is, while I keep the darker colours around the edges. I also decide to keep the golden frame in a darker colour, so it blends with the background and doesn't stand out too much. The geometric shapes included in the background help to emphasize the focal point – the lines meet in a star shape that stands slightly above the character's face, which is where I want the viewer's eye to focus first. The whole effect of the background and framing brings to mind a tarot card, another big source of inspiration.

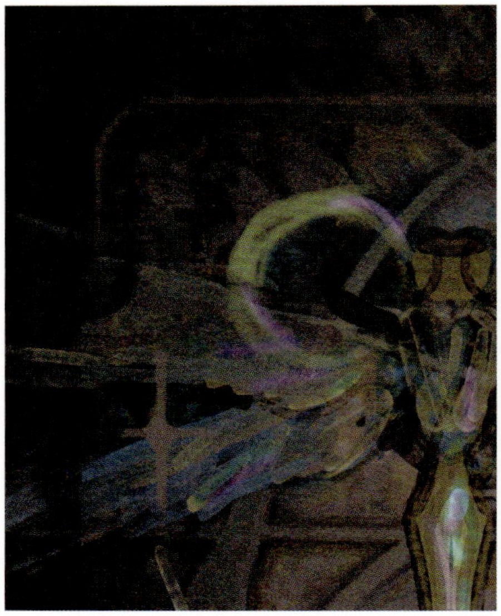

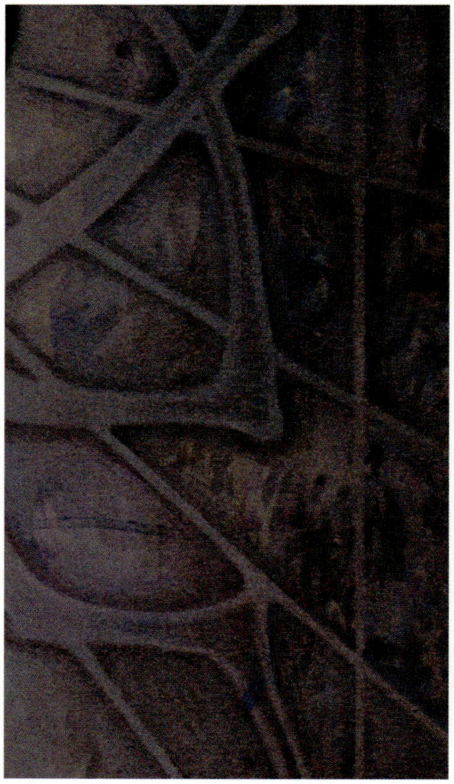

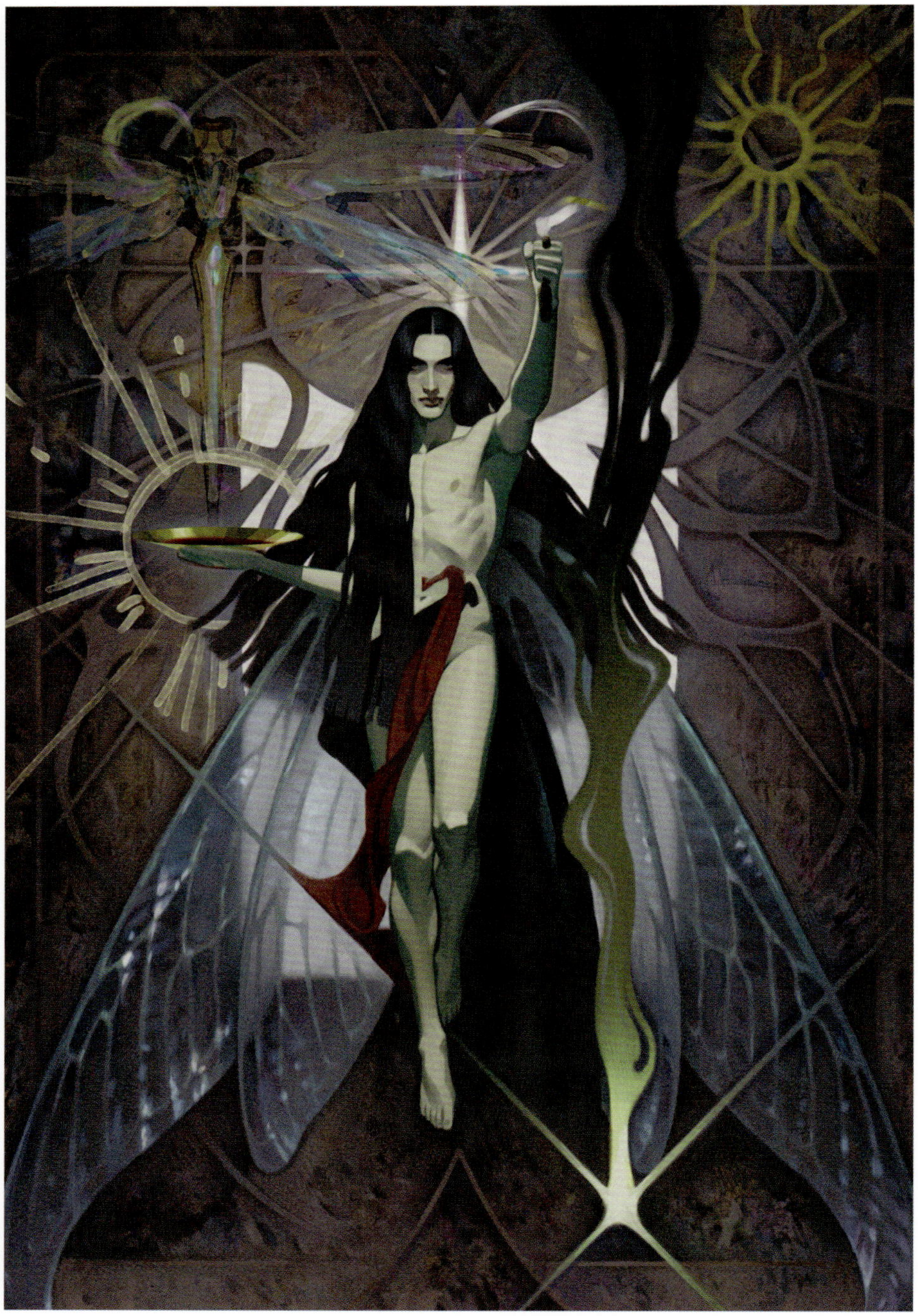

Working on the background and making use of geometric shapes to emphasize the focal point

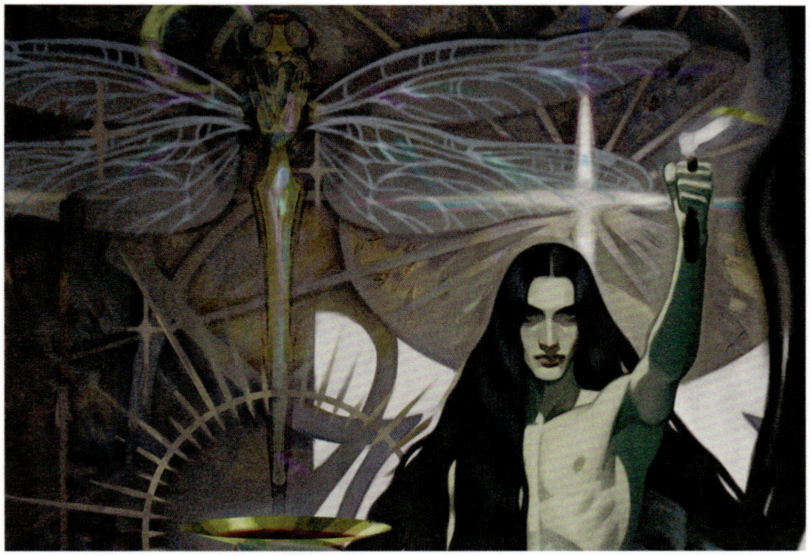

13 The dragonfly

Next I start working on the dragonfly, starting with the wings. I paint the wings in a similar way to how I painted the character. First I paint the wings without the veins, keeping the main wings translucent. On a separate layer, I add the veins, using a mix of blues, pinks, and magenta in Color Dodge mode to bring out the iridescence. At this stage, I also begin work on the circular aura you see shimmering around the golden plate. For this I use the Ellipse tool to create the circle, then create one line that is duplicated and rotated multiple times to form the rays of light.

Painting the dragonfly wings and the golden aura

14 Polishing details

I finish up the dragonfly's wings by shading the veins properly and making sure the left side of the dragonfly is darker to fit the lighting correctly. While using Photoshop's Symmetry option can be very useful for a base, I don't want my final result to feel too symmetrical, so I make sure to disable it before completing the wings. I also use Color Dodge to add the shiny white light reflections on top of the wings, giving them a shimmery look.

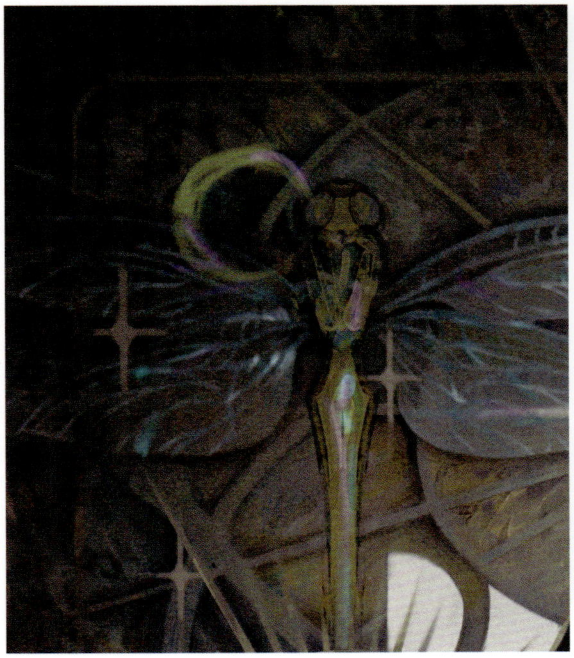

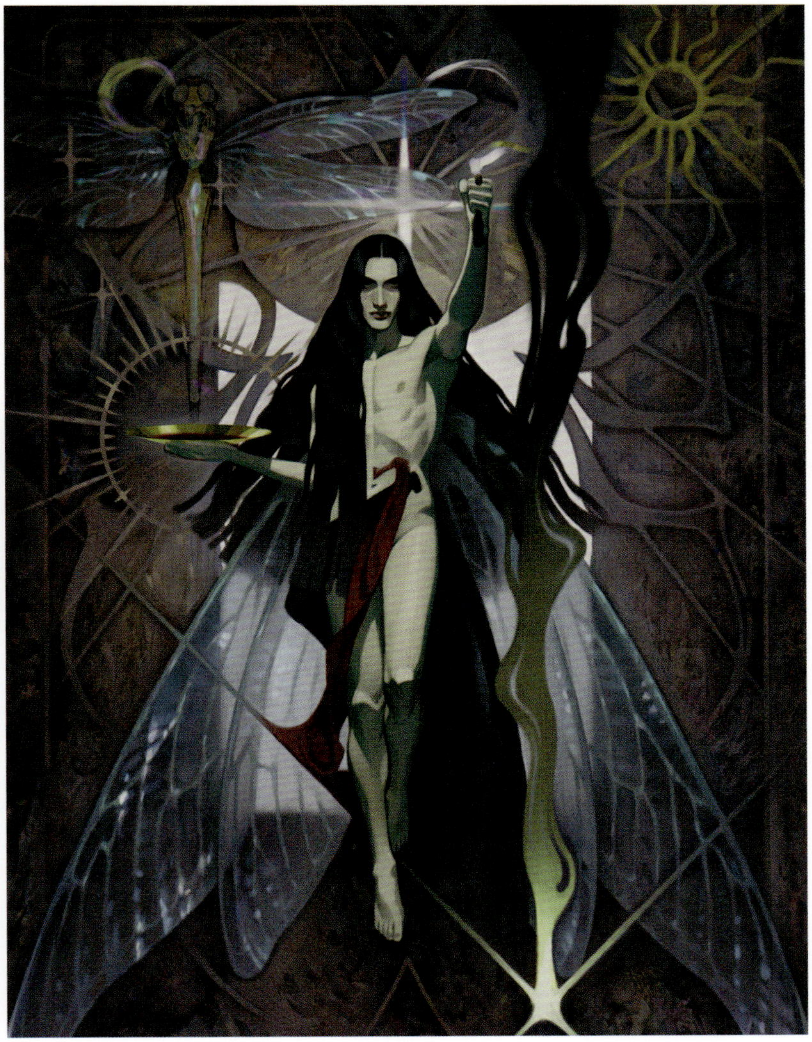

Adding final touches to the dragonfly, including shading, lighting, and refining details

15 Finishing touches

Here I make the final steps to completing the painting: finishing all the details on the dragonfly, finalizing the golden plate and the blood inside it, and adding some other finishing touches to the character, such as the fabric behind him and the sickle in his hand. The way I paint the sun is identical to how I made the aura circle around the plate. As a final touch to the whole painting, I adjust the Vibrance and Exposure options to make the colours richer and add more contrast.

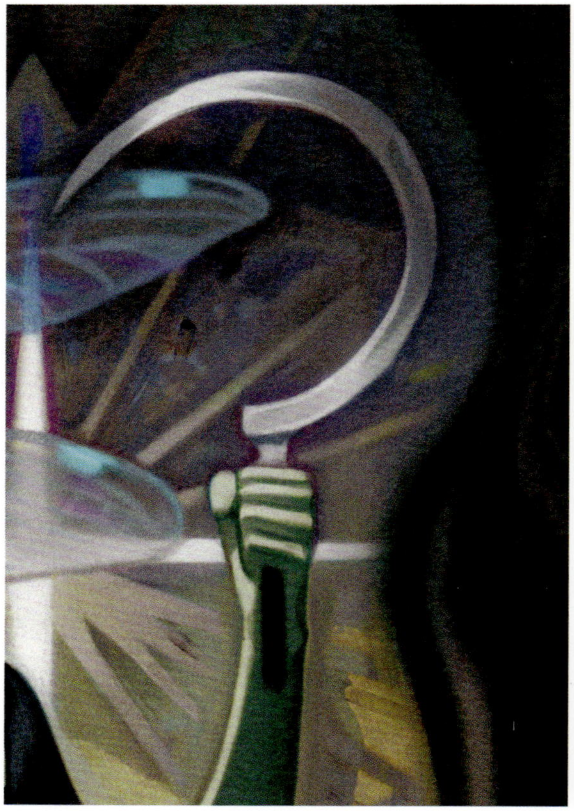

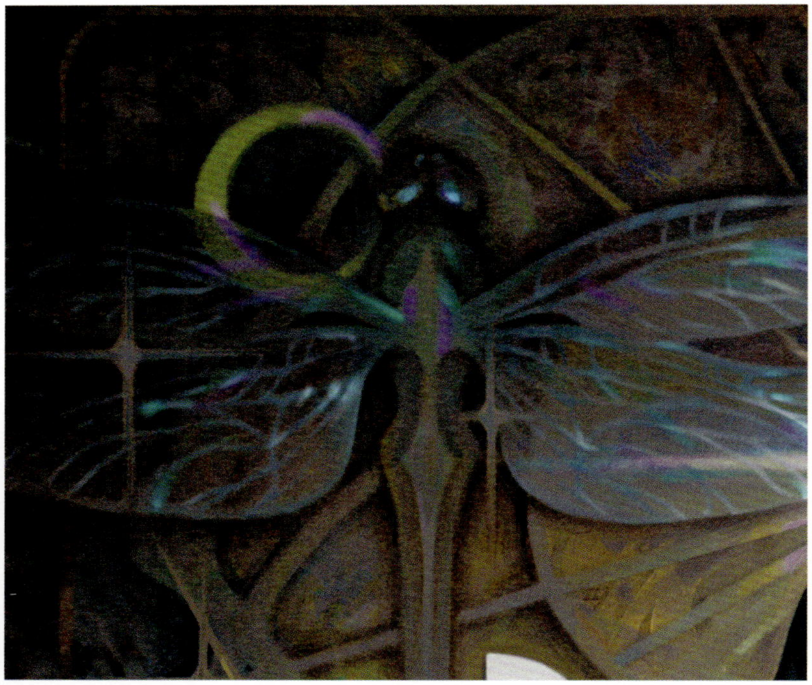

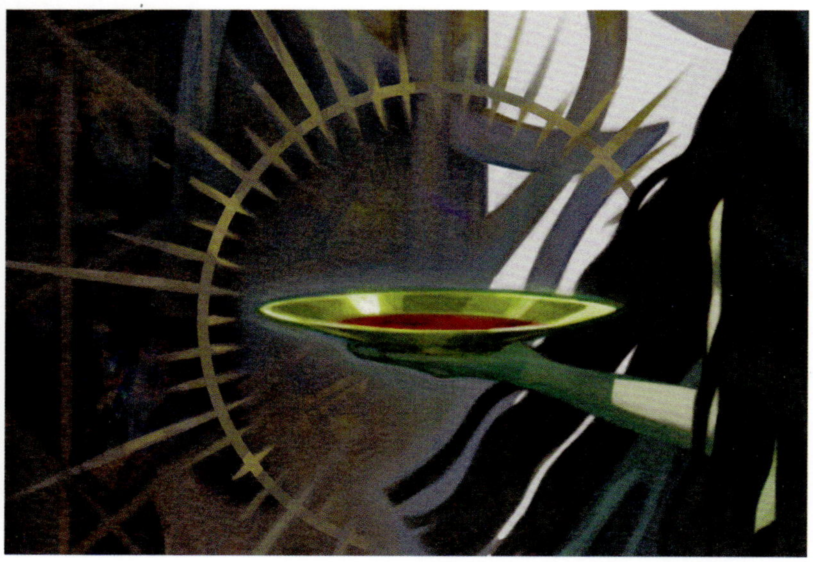

Final touches, completing details, and finalizing colours

Conclusion

The final piece achieves what I wanted: portraying the balance between light and dark, and being colourful without being too vibrant. I wanted to capture that Frazetta feel of a traditional painting with dark, surreal fantasy themes, aiming to keep true to that while using digital tools. Although my process can be chaotic, I want to encourage you to have a fearless mentality – don't be afraid to change something if you think it will work better.

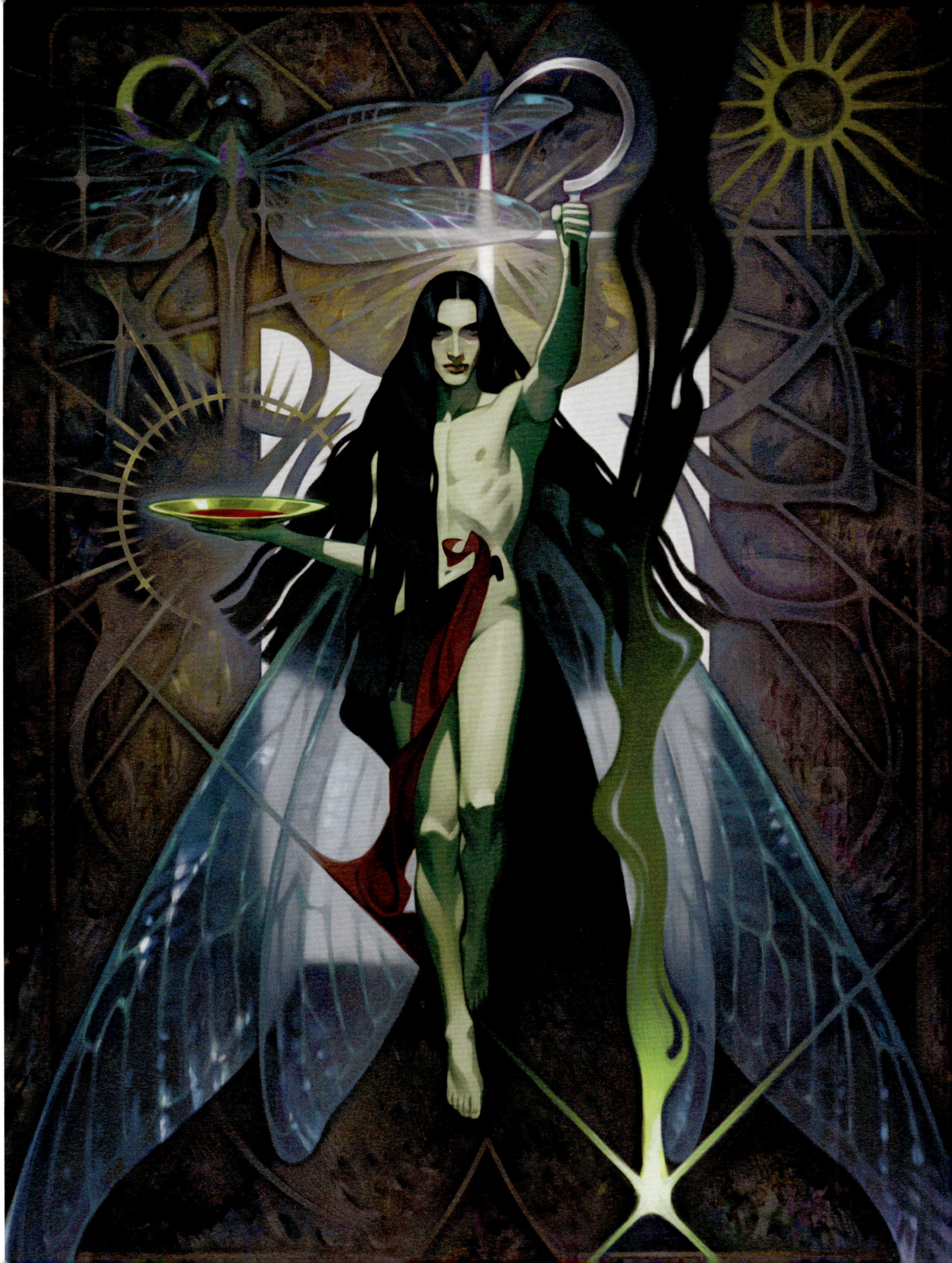

Gallery

by Valentina Remenar

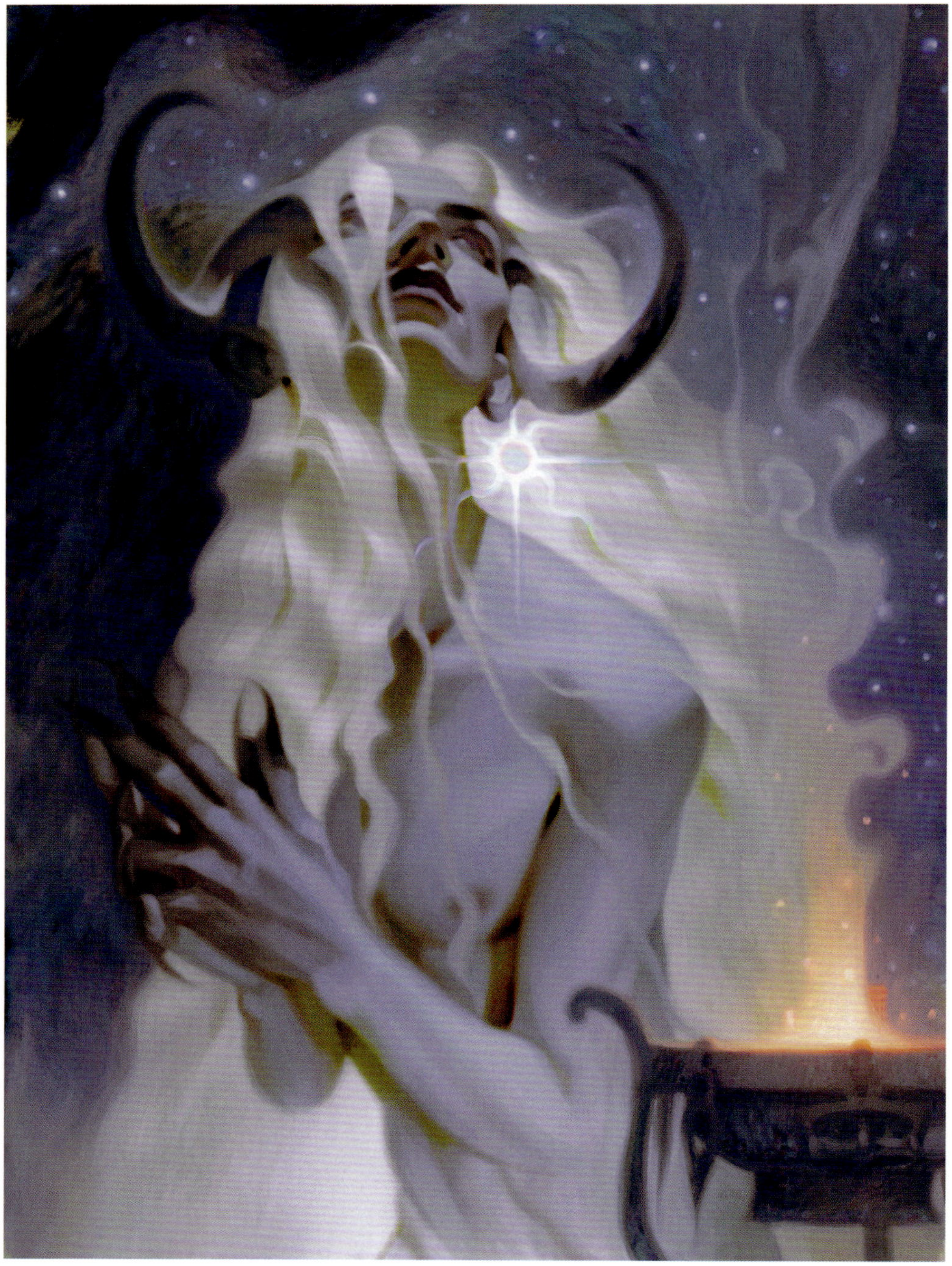

Aries © Valentina Remenar

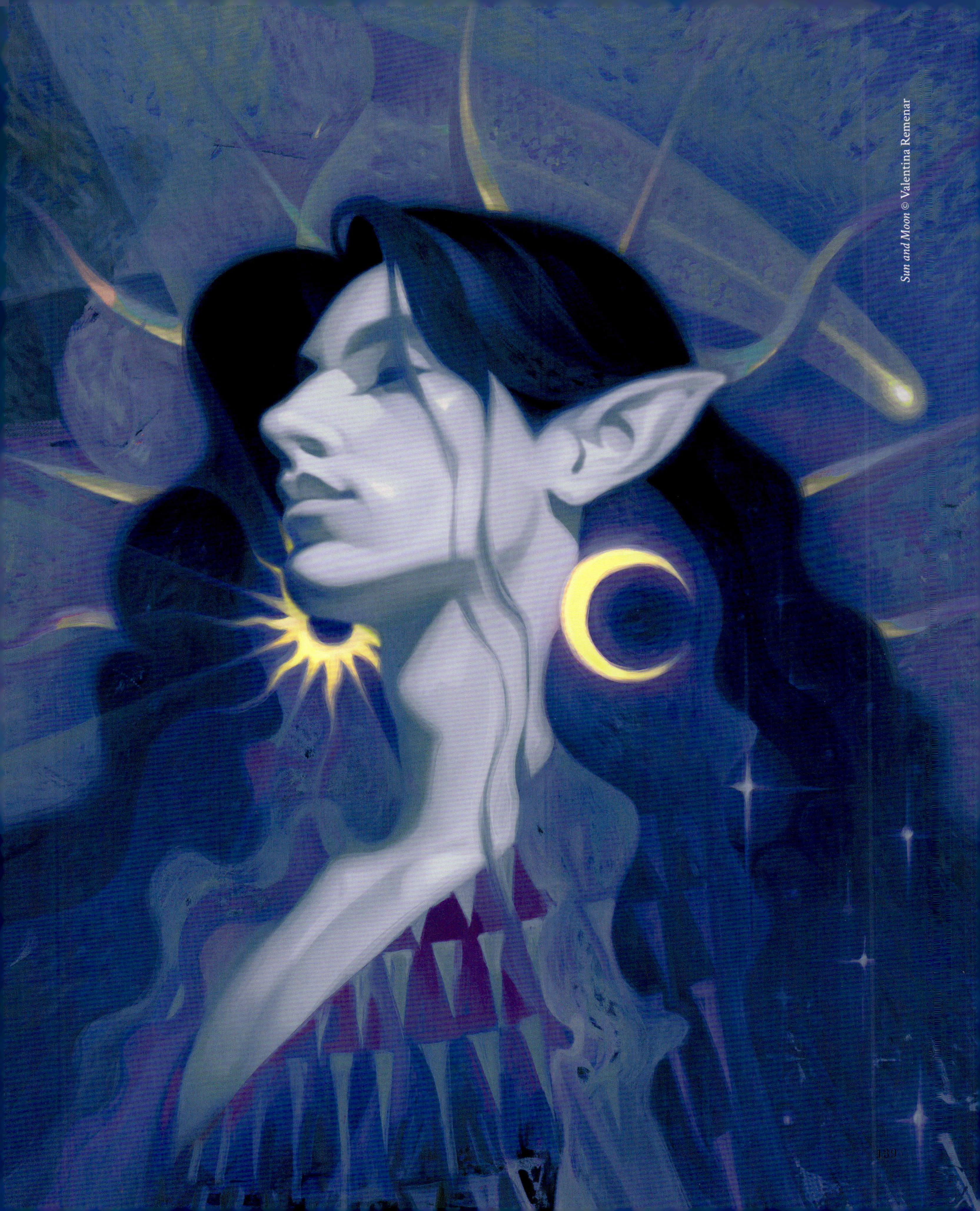

Sun and Moon © Valentina Remenar

The Sun Knight © Valentina Remenar

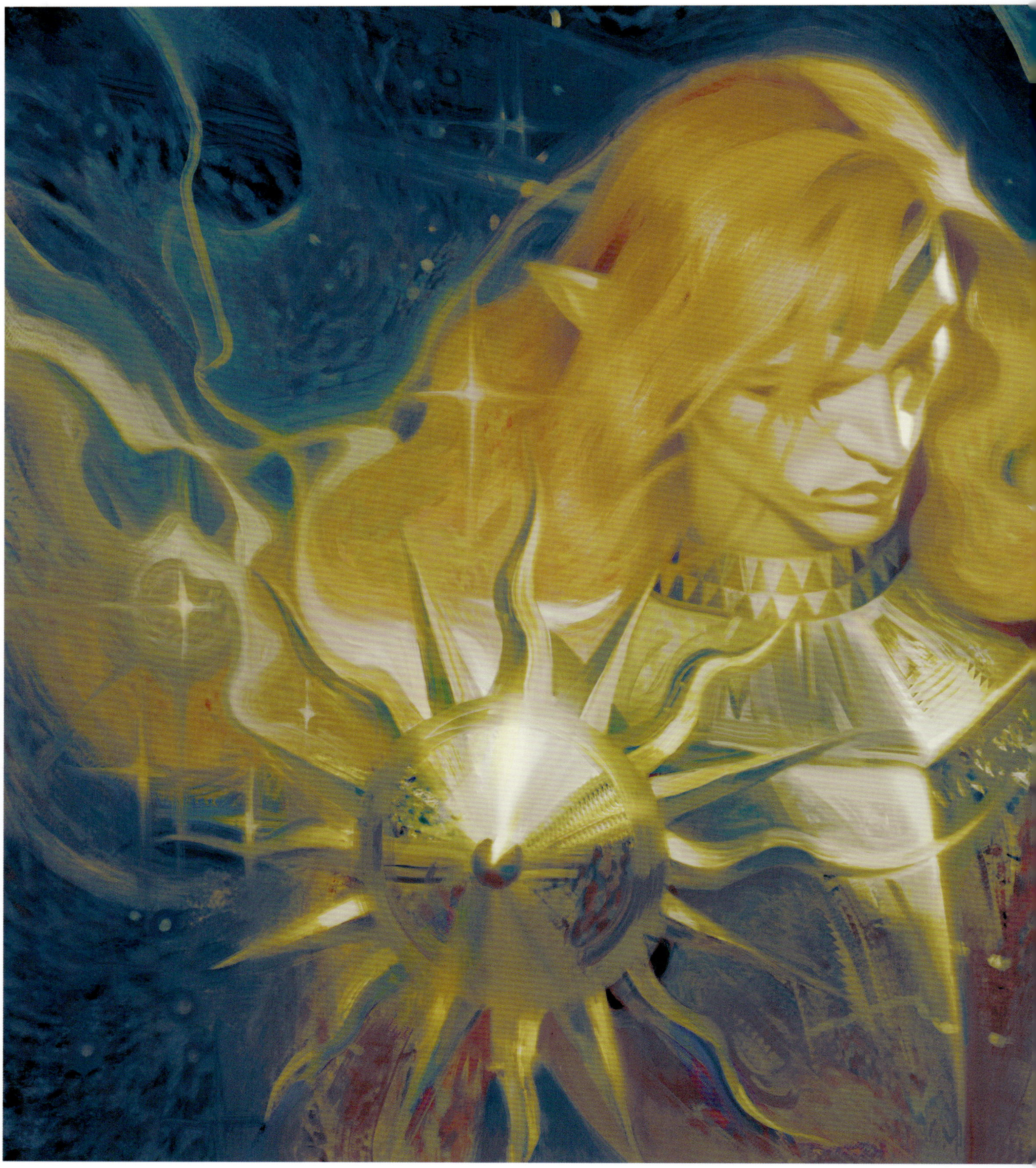

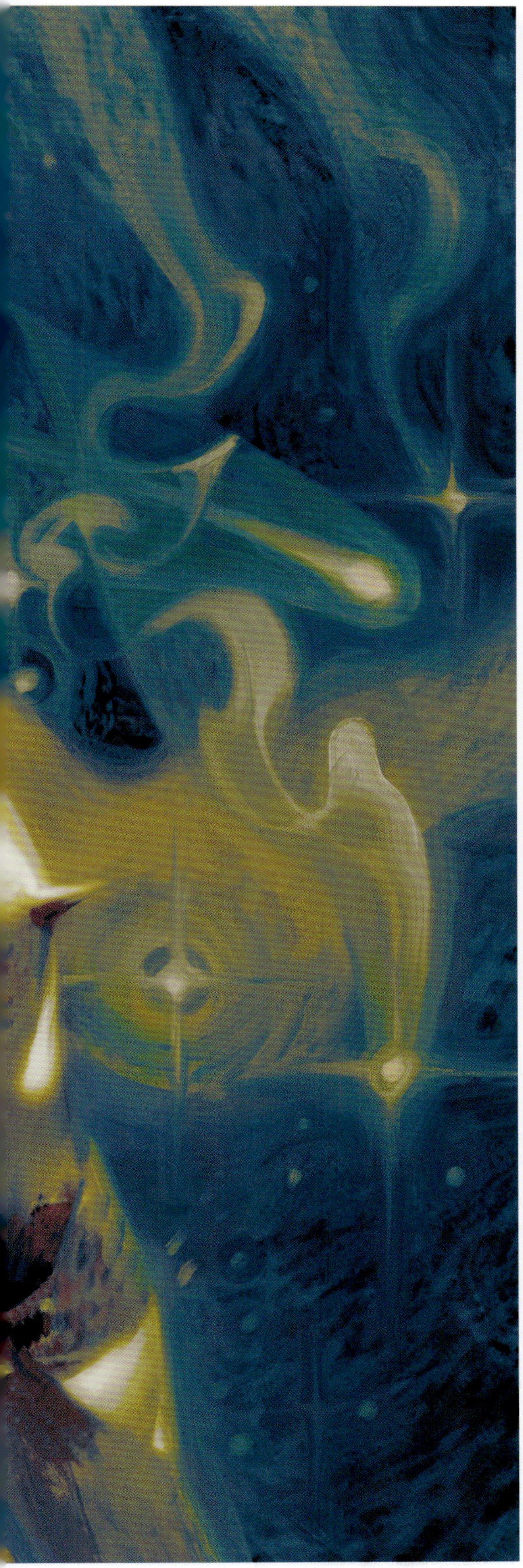

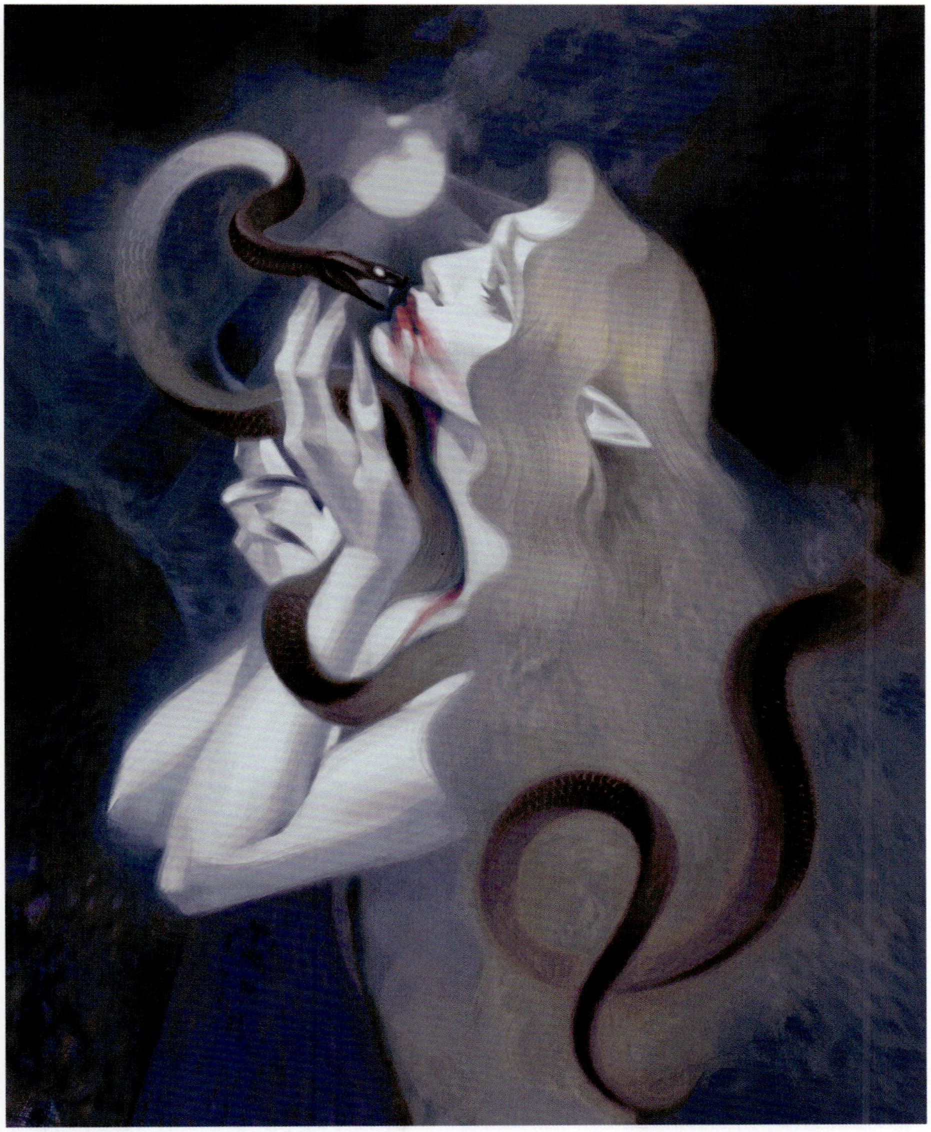

Temptation © Valentina Remenar

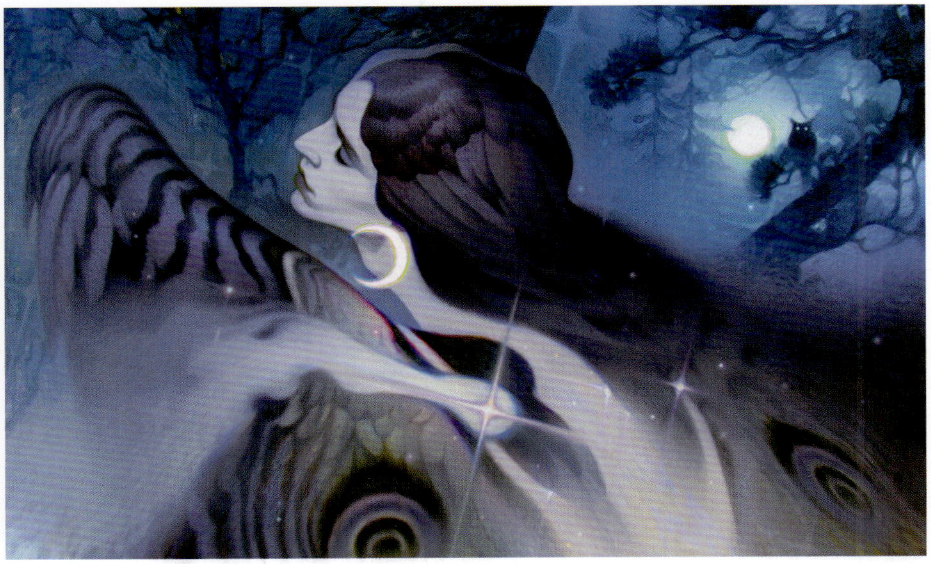

Harpy © Valentina Remenar

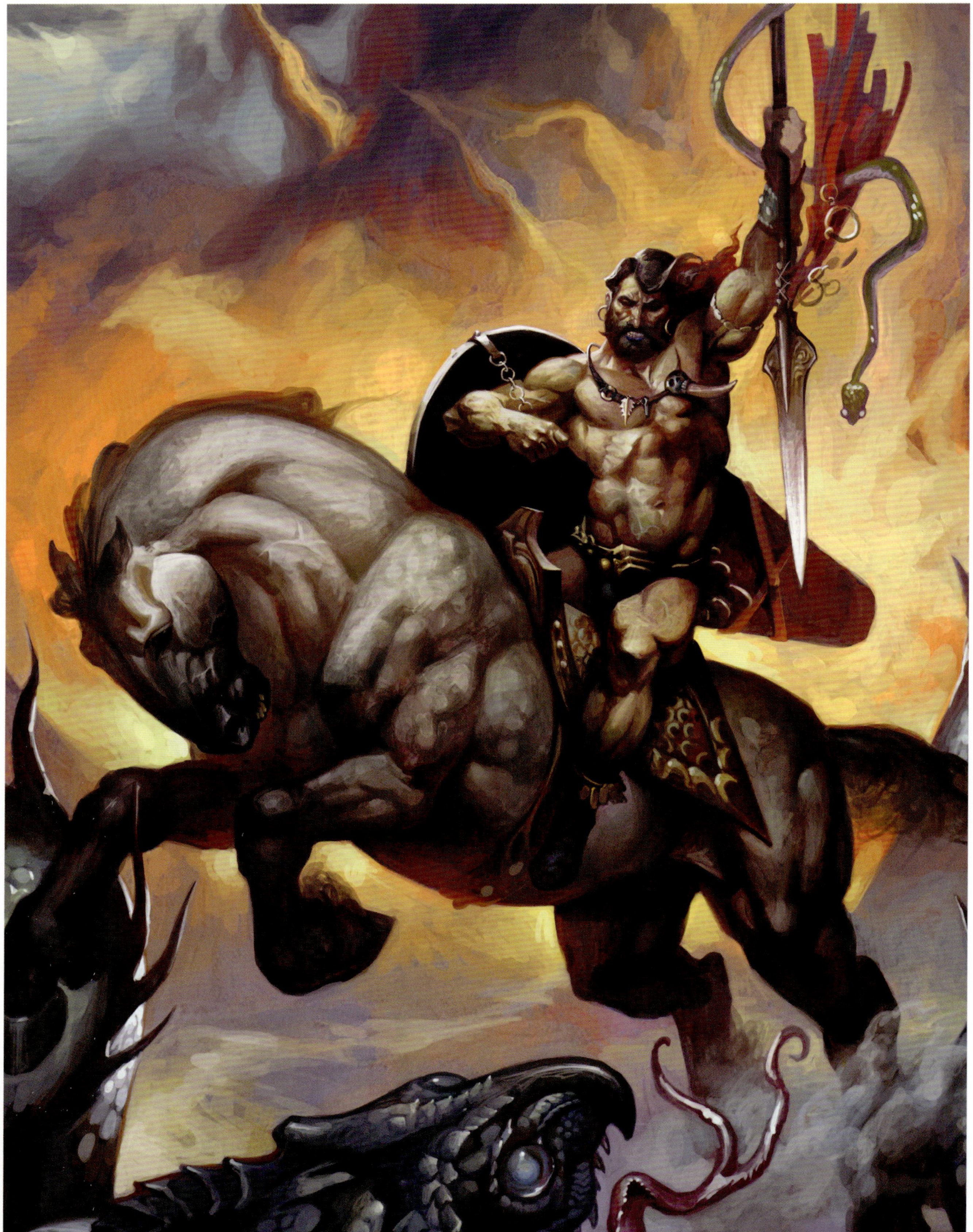

Final image © Gustavo Pelissari

Saint George

by Gustavo Pelissari

Creating *Saint George*

I admire very much how Frazetta gave life to barbarian characters and this is a theme I like to explore. I also appreciate how Frazetta drew his horses. For this painting, my goal is to pay homage to the imagery Frazetta created in this genre, so I have decided to combine these two themes into a barbarian interpretation of Saint George and the Dragon. I will be looking mainly at Frazetta's ability to design light and shadow, as well as his inspiring use of colour.

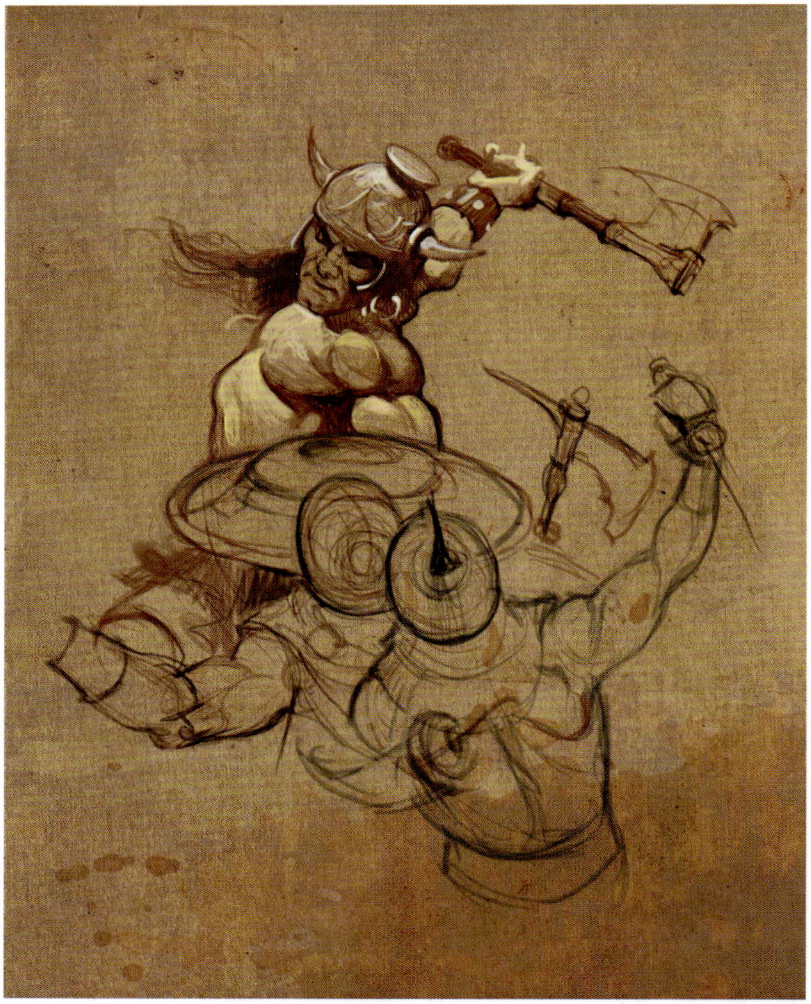

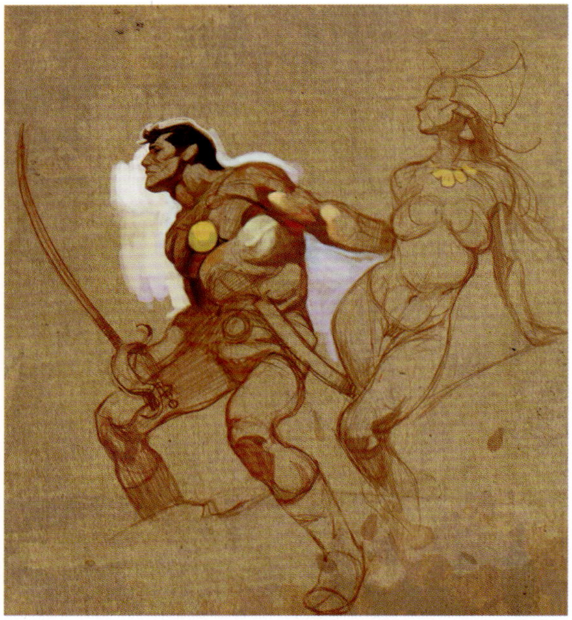

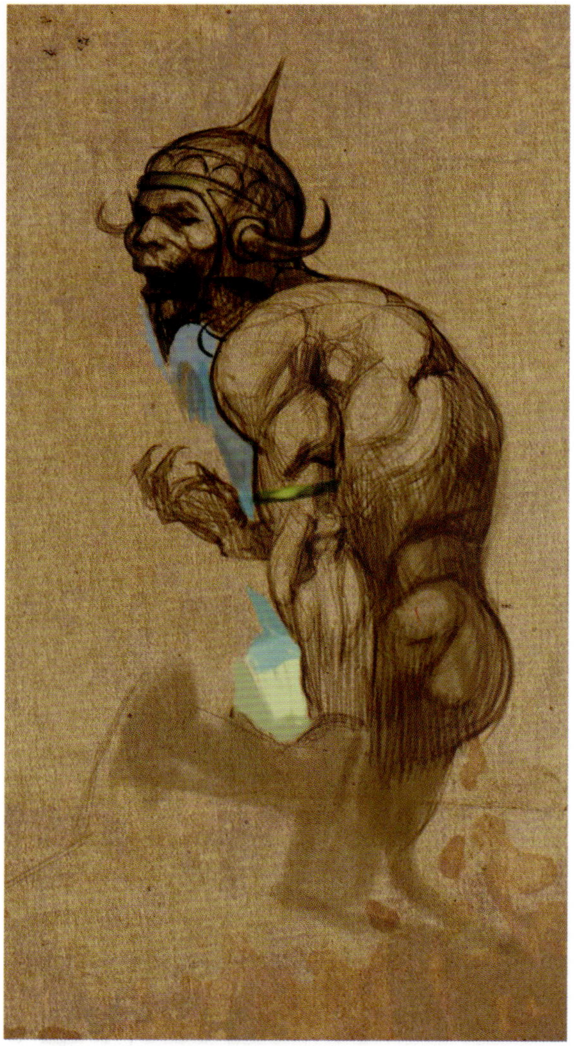

Studies after the work of the master

01 Studies

Before I jump into the creation process, I take time to study some Frazetta pieces I hadn't before. While my goal here is to channel his energy on a thematic level, I also need to pay special attention to his shape language and how he painted human figures. After doing these studies, I also make some other test drawings just to see how much I have learned from using Frazetta as a reference.

02 Thumbnails

I first explore a few different ideas that relate in some way to the Frazetta 'universe'. This exploratory beginning phase is very pleasant to me – the potential wonder hidden in the next thumbnail makes me want to keep exploring for hours! However, I eventually settle for the option depicting a powerful rider and dragon-like creature, which reminds me of Saint George's legendary encounter.

Thumbnails exploring different possibilities for the painting

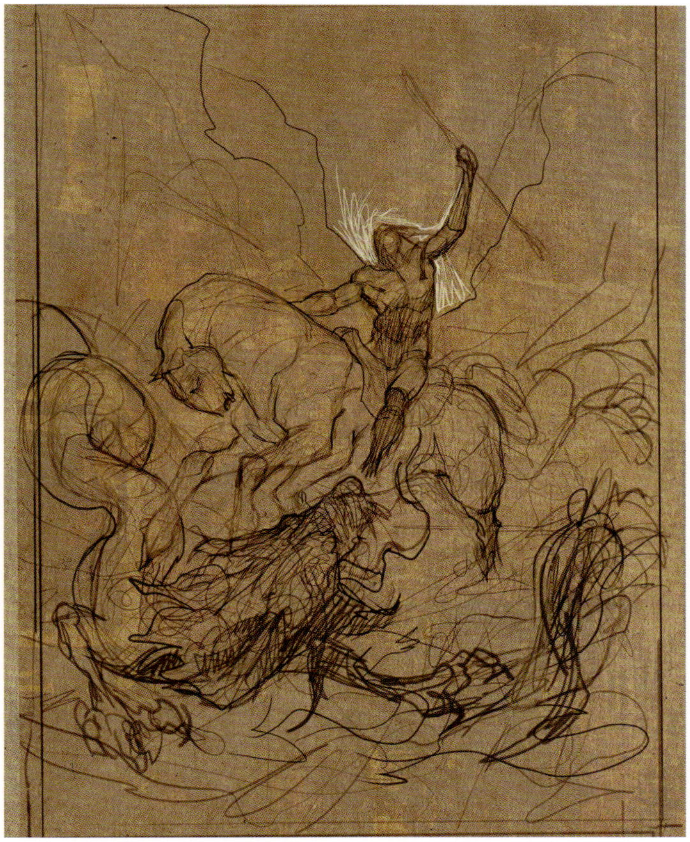

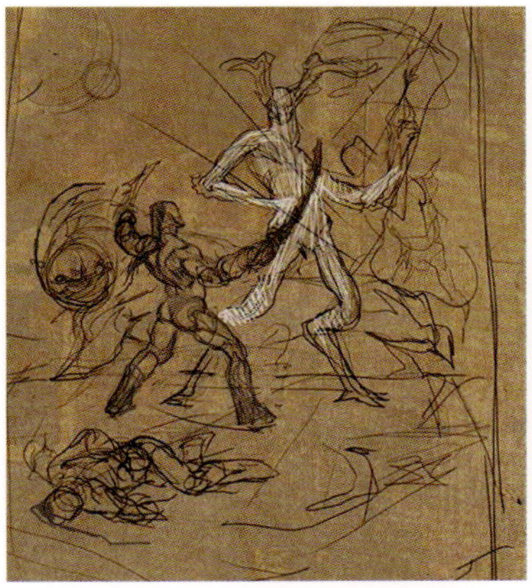

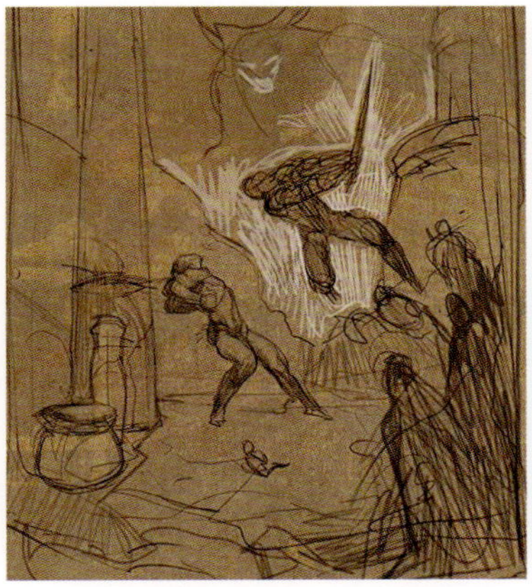

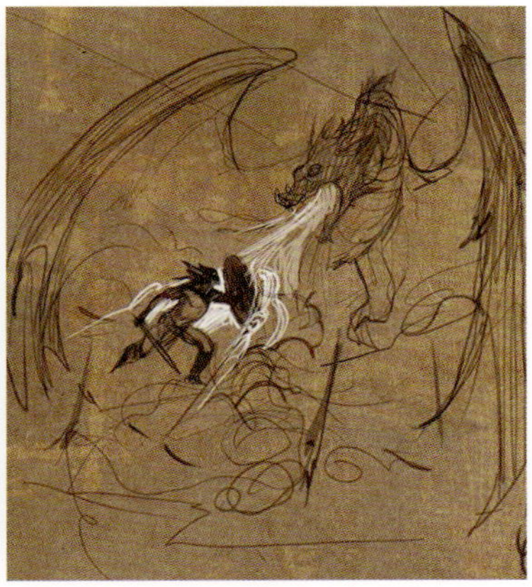

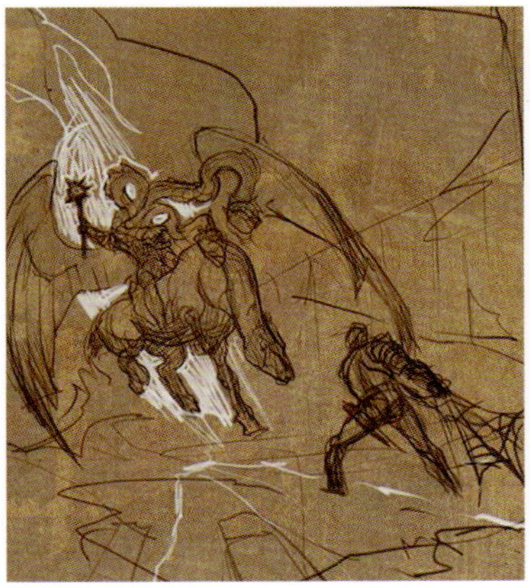

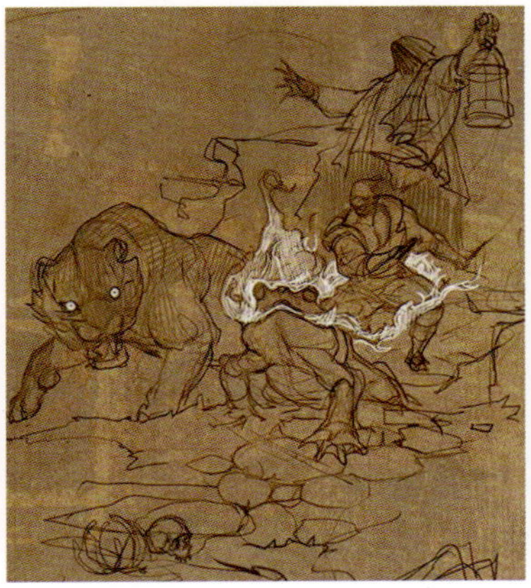

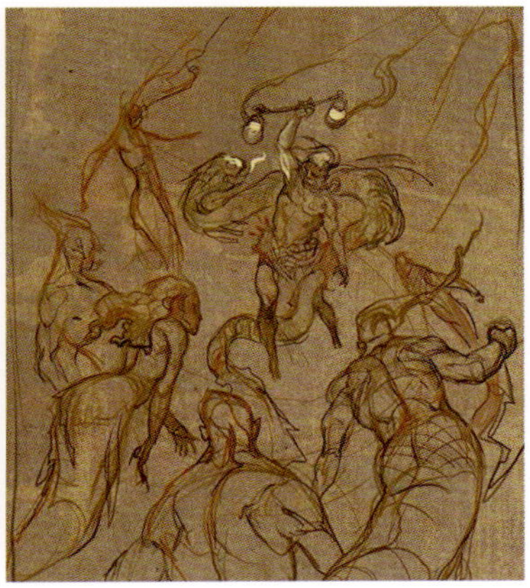

03 Horse explorations

Once the thumbnail is decided, I start to separate the subjects of the illustration in order to design each concept one at a time. The first one I tackle is the horse. It has been a while since I last ventured into drawing and painting horses, so I start by making several studies using different references. My initial idea is to make the horse a six-legged one, like Sleipnir from Norse myth, so these studies explore that direction.

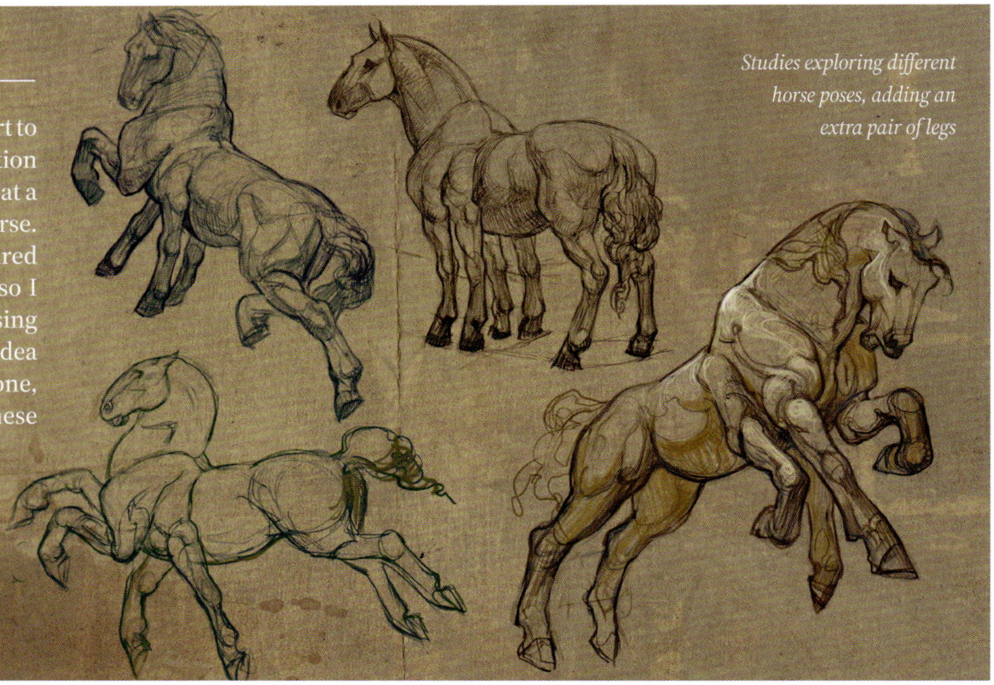

Studies exploring different horse poses, adding an extra pair of legs

04 Saint George

Next I start exploring Saint George's character. I intend to give him a different depiction than usual, without full armour and with a less Western look to his facial features and weaponry. The lack of armour will allow me the freedom to explore the anatomy, which is something I admire in Frazetta's work. I sketch some silhouette and portrait explorations, where I start to define not just the figure but also an initial design for his weapons. To finish, I make a more robust drawing to define the final look of the character, while still leaving some scope for honing the design in the rendering stages.

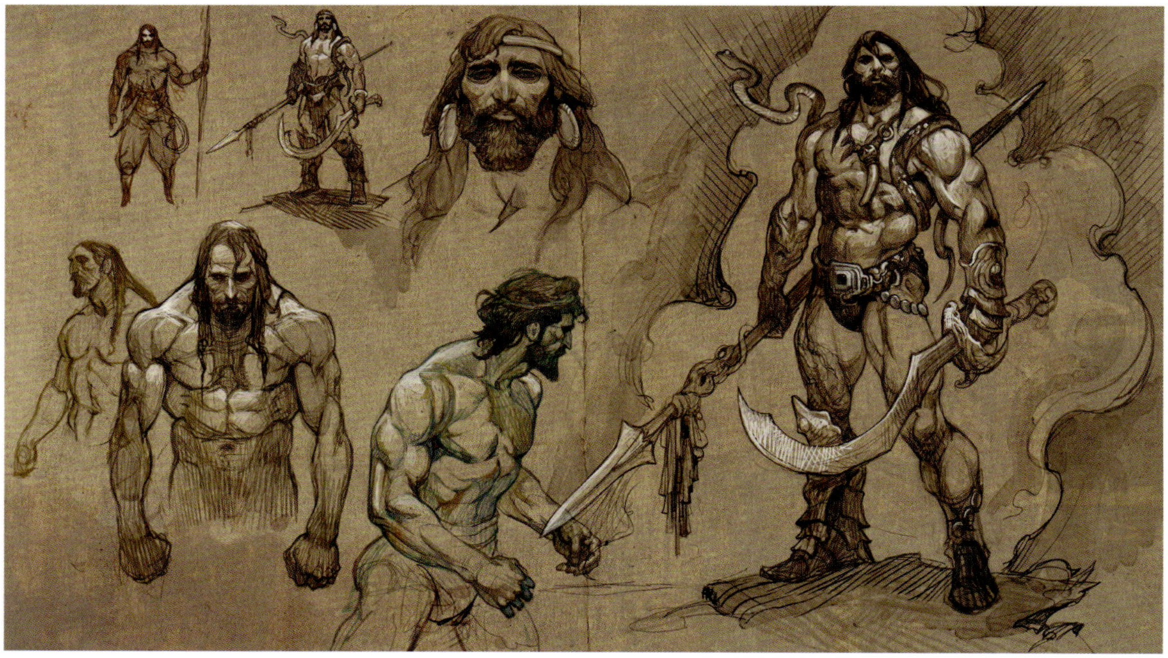

Design exploration and final concept for the main character

05 Dragon exploration

The last element remaining is the dragon. In the thumbnail in step 02, I was aiming for a long, snake-like dragon with a Chinese influence in its design. However, when I start looking for reference, I find some of Gustave Doré's illustrations and fall in love with his representations of dragons. I like how fresh those designs still look and decide to create my own version. I explore a tiger-dragon hybrid that could be a great homage to Frazetta's felines, but in the end I go for a more classic reptilian look. I also realize that giving the horse six legs puts too much information near the dragon's head, so I abandon that idea.

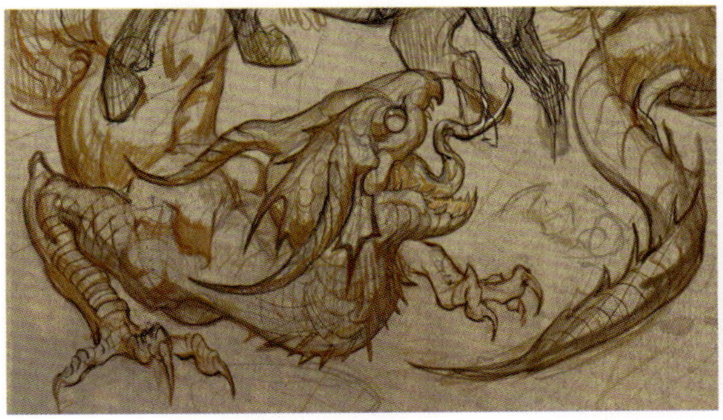

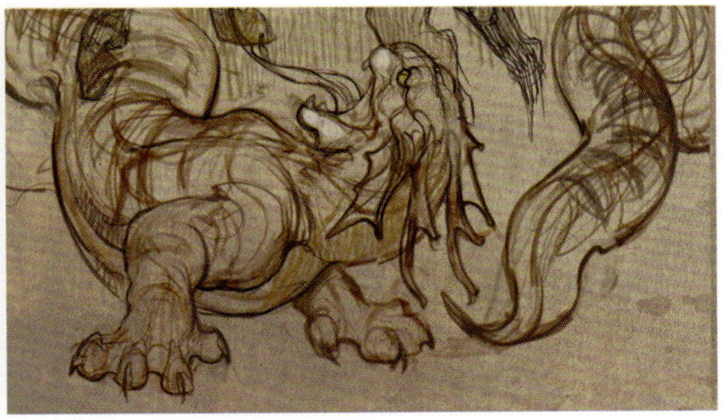

Design explorations for the dragon

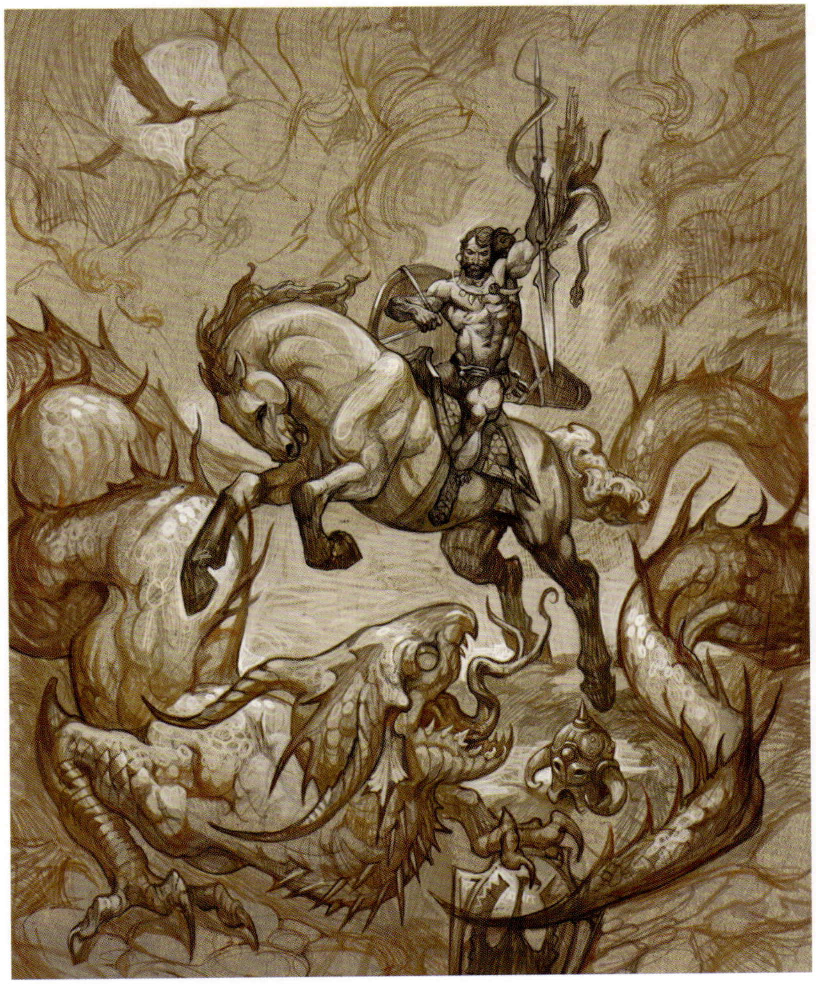

Preparatory drawing before I start painting

06 Tight drawing

One step I pay heavy attention to is the drawing. A well-developed drawing gives me the confidence to start painting with fewer doubts. I use a toned background with an old paper texture, which gives me the warmth that digital media often lacks. I focus on creating a solid design for the shapes of shadow and light; I try to create depth by using more contrast for the main subjects and foreground. I also add some 'Easter eggs' referencing Frazetta's work, such as the Death Dealer's helmet and shield and the flying vultures!

07 Colour composition

Before I dive into the painting, I make a rough colour composition using some of Frazetta's artwork (such as *Death Dealer VI* and *Jongor Fights Back*) as inspiration for a dramatic palette. I also refer to the work of the illustrator Petar Meseldžija (for example, *The Giants Are Coming*), which helps bring me to a colour scheme that I like. My idea is to work with a cool general palette, with a fire lit in the background, creating a centre of pure warmth and giving a clear silhouette to the rider. I work over the drawing on a small scale, which helps me pay attention to the general reading of the image without getting into the finer details.

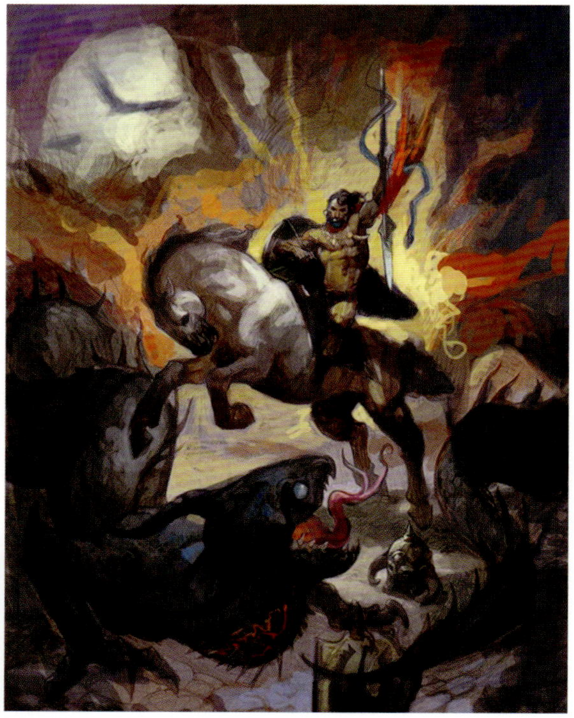

Colour exploration before starting to paint

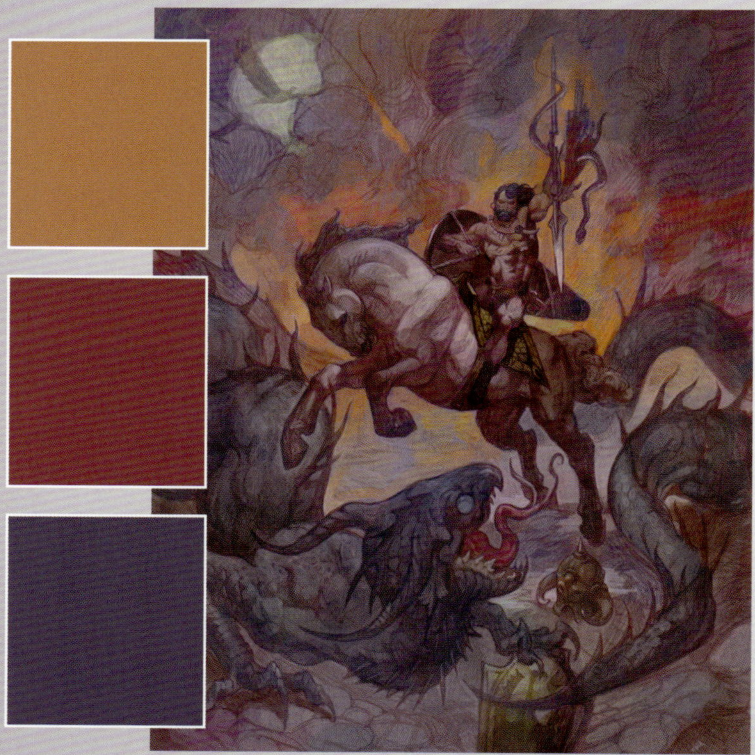

08 Semi-opaque layers

I now feel confident enough to start the final painting. In all of my digital work, I try to emulate traditional media in the way I paint. I think the best way to do this is to limit the digital tools to only the basics, such as layers and brushes. My approach is to begin the painting with semi-opaque layers. This way my drawing is preserved as the brushwork starts to build up colours and textures. I aim to create abstraction and texture in each inch of the painting.

Applying the first layer of translucent colour

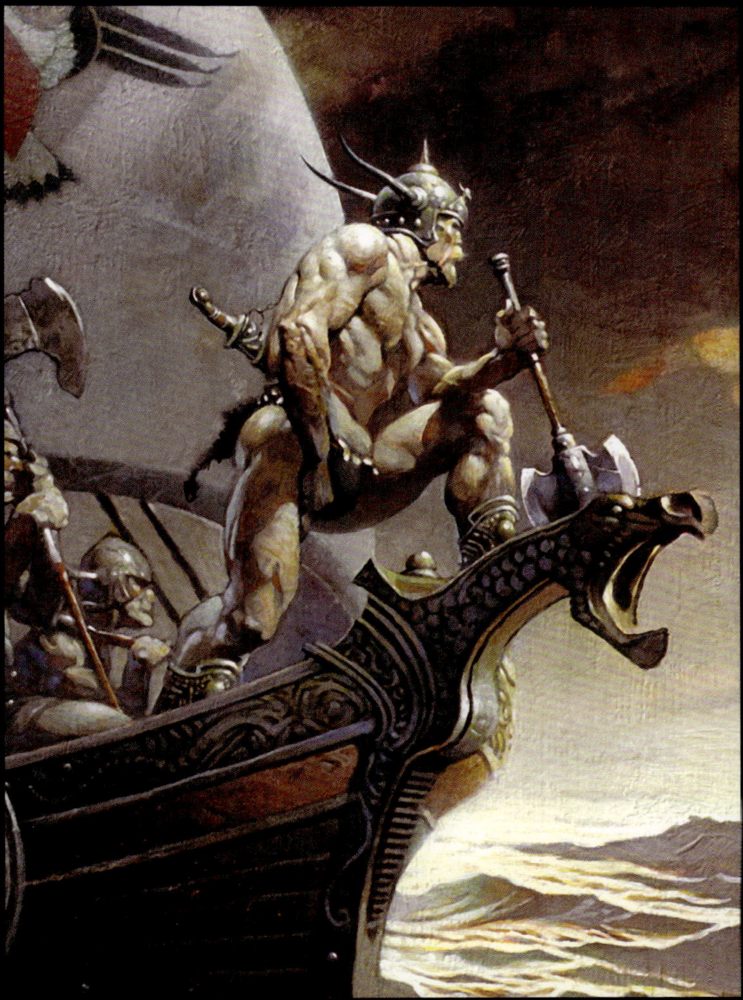

Kane on the Golden Sea © Frank Frazetta

Discovering Frazetta

I discovered Frazetta's work through a figure-drawing teacher in 2008 while I was studying at university. He saw me drawing chunkier figures and imagined that I was going to like how Frazetta handled anatomy and gesture. Oh boy, he was right! The first time I saw a Frazetta painting, I was in complete awe – not just at his human figures, but all the drama, action, composition, colours, and his drawing capabilities.

I love the spontaneity of his works, although, at the same time, he was truly a master of meticulously designing the shapes of shadow and light. To this day, I look up to his work for motivation and inspiration in every possible way. I feel like I have studied with the man himself because, on some level, I reproduce his work on a daily basis. Every reproduction is a lesson learned. I also appreciate all the influence his work has had on artists such as Jeffrey Catherine Jones and Simon Bisley. To me, he is the father of 'sword-and-sorcery' art.

It's difficult to choose only one favourite Frazetta piece – all his Conan works are epic, not to mention the savage way he portrayed Tarzan or his fantastic sci-fi pieces of John Carter of Mars. But there's one that especially stands out to me. *Kane on the Golden Sea* invites me to be on that ship, looking to the horizon for the next adventure. As an art teacher, I keep introducing Frazetta's work to my students hoping that they fall in love as I did years ago.

▸▸ *For image in full, turn to page 242*

09 Centre of interest

My painting process follows the principle of flowing from transparent to opaque colour. This way the saturation occurs mainly in the shadows and midtones, leaving the unsaturated colours in the lights. This is something I have absorbed from Frazetta's paintings. I slowly build up the translucent layers as if they are glazes of paint, focusing first on the centre of interest and spreading out as I progress. This strategy helps me to evenly detail the other parts once I have established the main character.

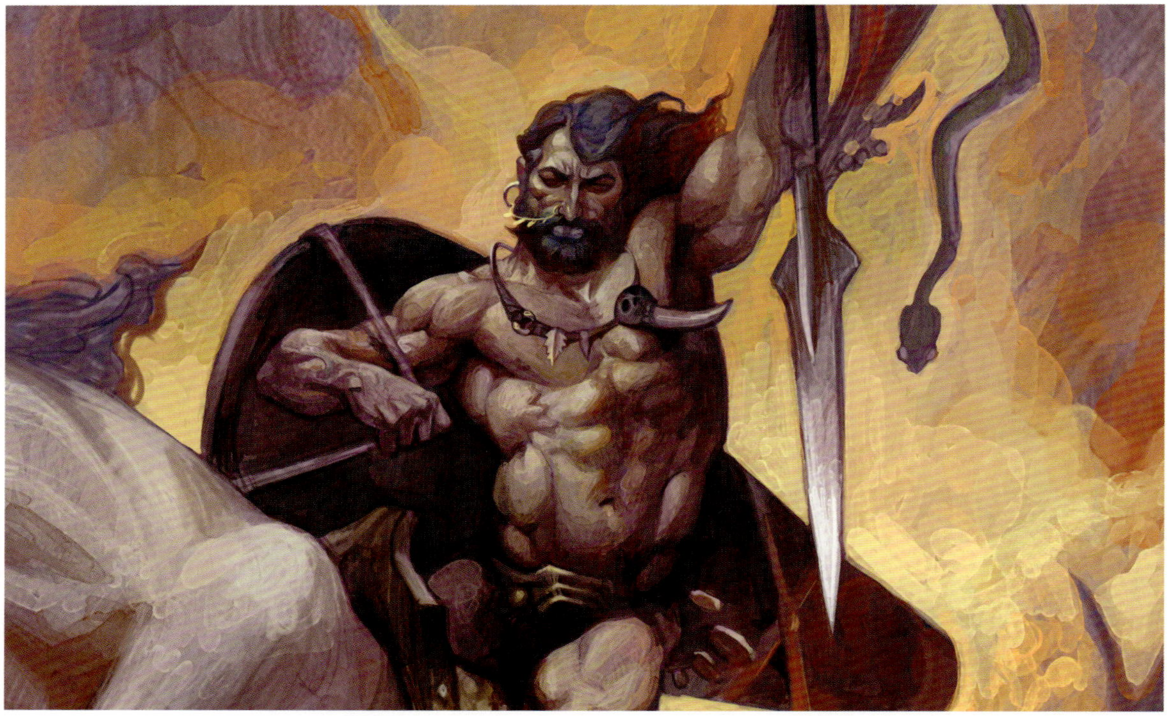

Adding the first layer of translucent colours to the character

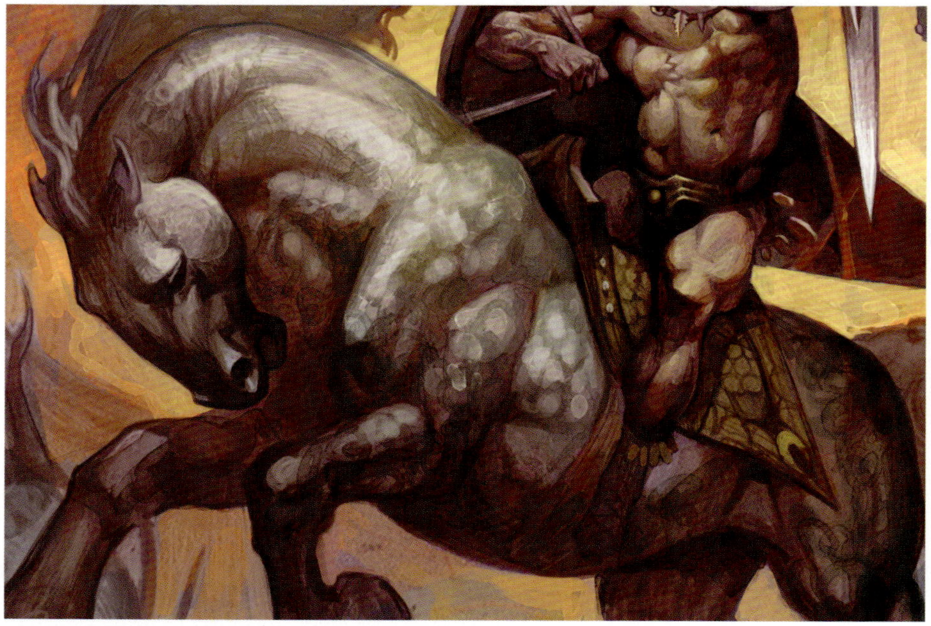

The horse's coat is painted with a few different techniques

10 The horse's coat

I don't like to keep my concepts closed off while I am painting – I like to leave some room for improvisation and new ideas. Here I come up with varied solutions for the horse's coat that I didn't intend in the first place. The fact that the horse is not pure white gives it a rougher association in the image's mood and narrative, which is something desirable to me. At this stage, I am still building up gradually with translucent colours and layers.

11 The horse's head & neck

One very common thing for me is to rebuild parts of the image during the painting process. Even when I am happy with the drawing stage, I often start to reconsider my decisions when I start adding more values and colours and the shapes begin to change. I think this represents a maturation in the artist's perception of the painting and should be embraced. For example, I realize I am not satisfied with the horse's head and neck, so I find new references and rebuild all of it.

Repainting the head and neck of the horse

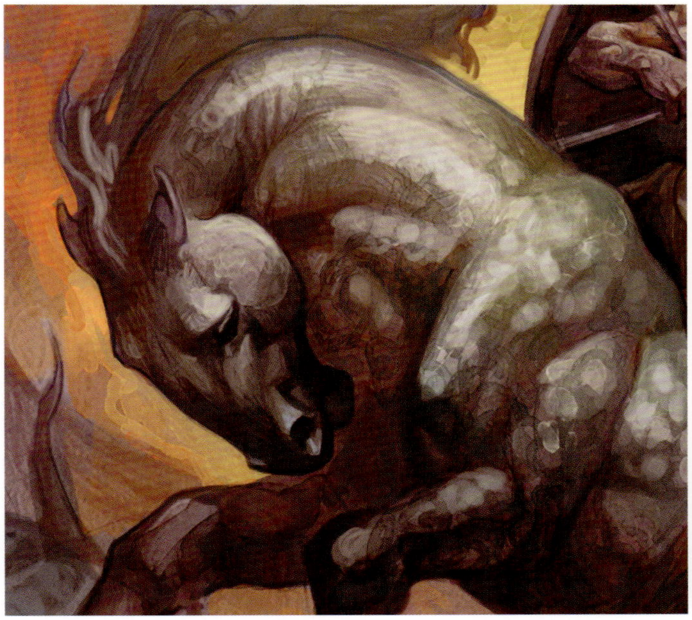

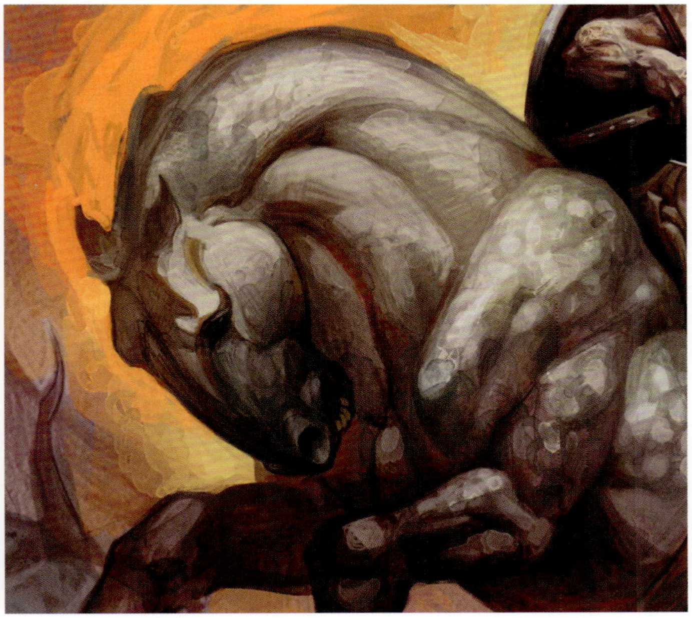

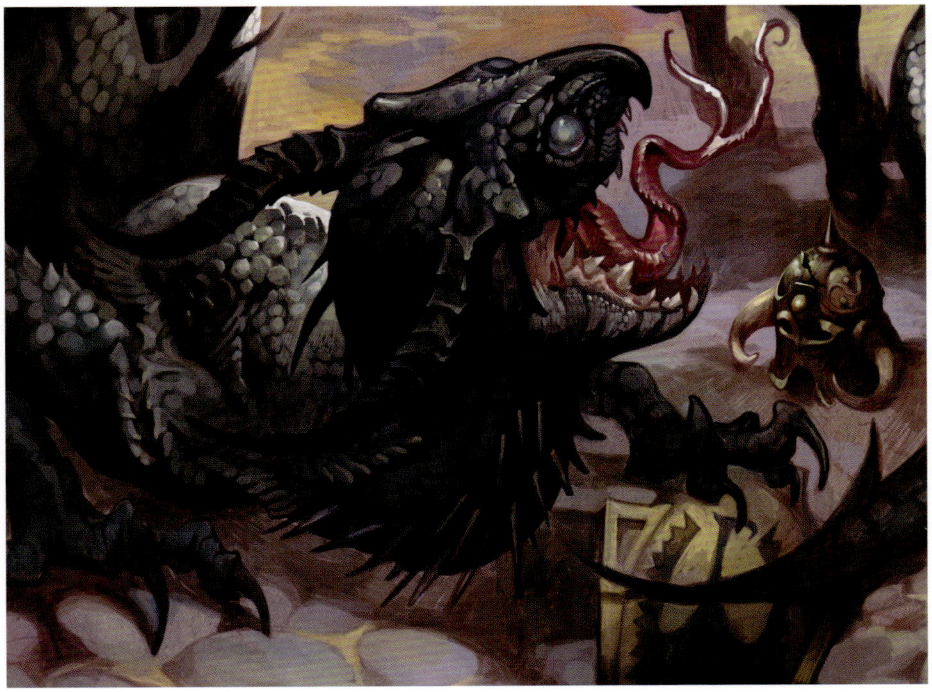

Painting and detailing the dragon

12 The dragon

The next challenge to tackle is the dragon. Although I have painted dragons before, I'm not as familiar with the subject as I could be. I know I want to create the feeling of intricate scale-work with a simple shape design for the dragon's head and body. I think this is a good way to give contrast. I rely on Frazetta's work for inspiration on how to approach this, looking at his paintings with snakes and lizards. I also look for references in Justin Gerard's work – he is a master of the craft.

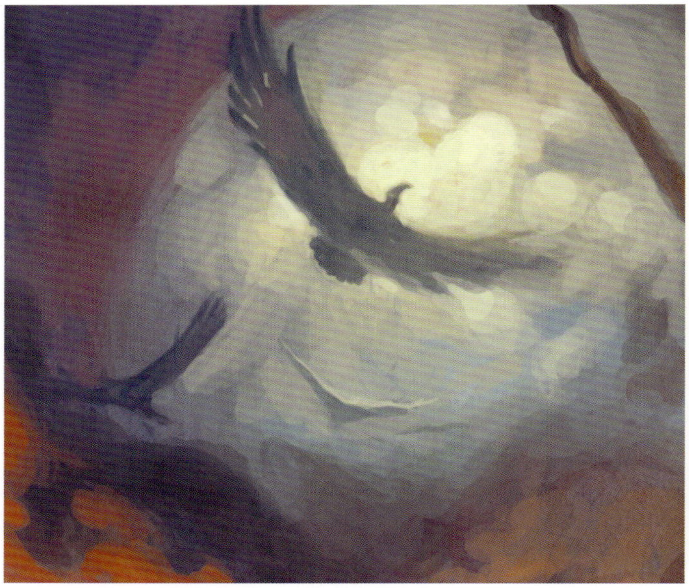

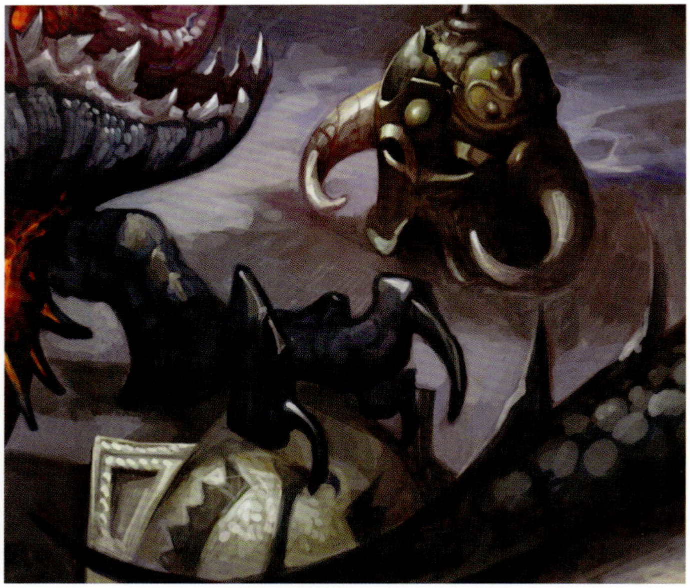

13 Finishing touches

To finish off the image, I work on the background and the Easter eggs in the foreground. I aim to give the background enough attention to support the main subjects without competing for attention or looking over-painted. This is another thing I love about the work of Frank Frazetta – if you look closely at high-resolution images or prints of his paintings, you can sometimes see the translucent early layers and even some drawing present, mainly in the background and secondary elements, while the centre of interest is more rendered. For me, this is another quality that gives a painting life.

Focusing on painting the background and extra details in the foreground

Conclusion

While I was writing the tutorial I was constantly looking at my work and wanting to paint over some parts, change the colour palette, or add more details to the character. Maybe someday in the future, I will repaint it from the ground up, which is something Frazetta did on many occasions. Our perception and ability keeps evolving with time, and it's natural to want the results of our efforts to reflect this. However, I finish the painting satisfied, knowing I have done my best to pay homage to this great artist who has inspired me so much, for such a long time.

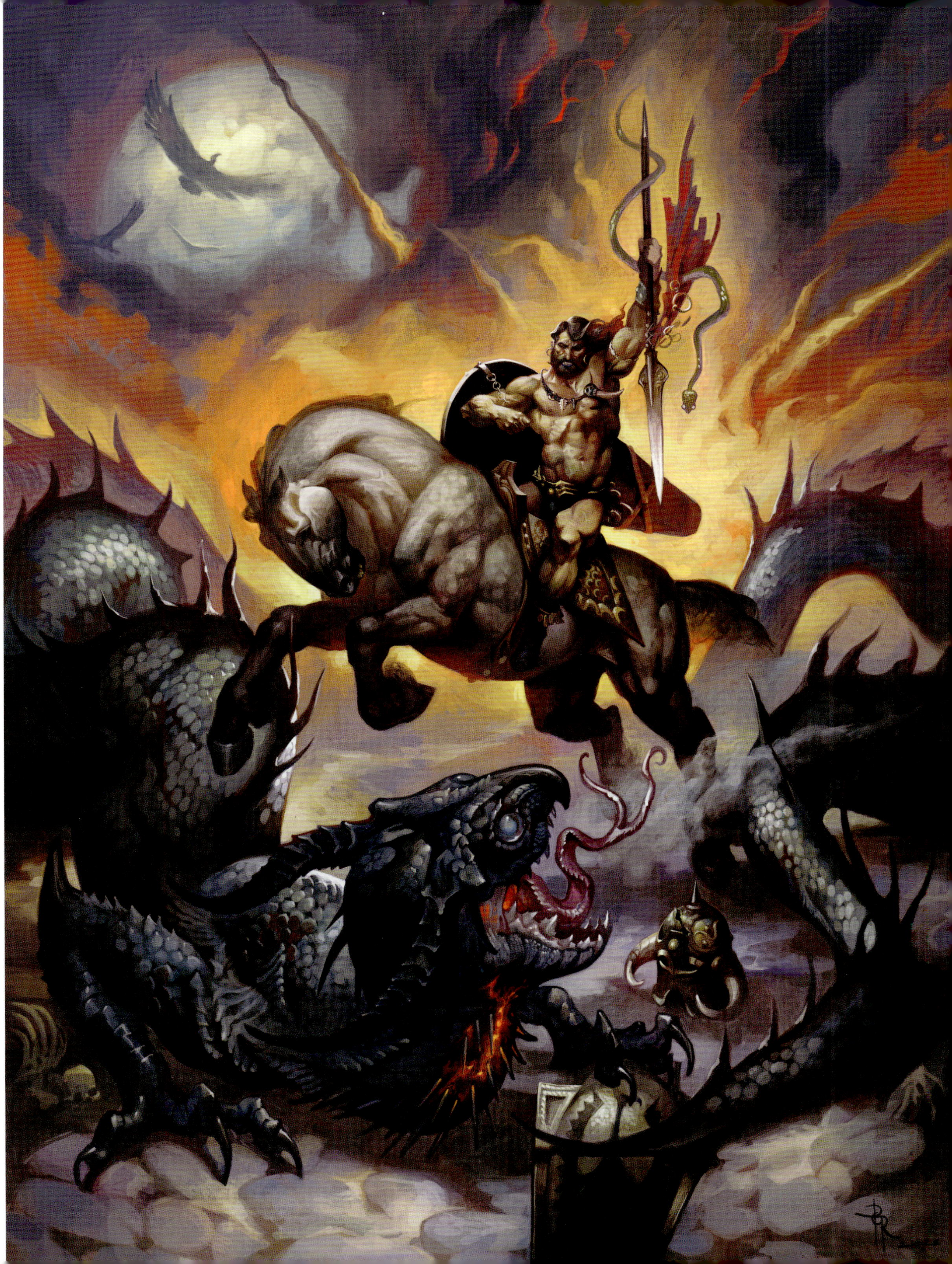

Final image © Gustavo Pelissari

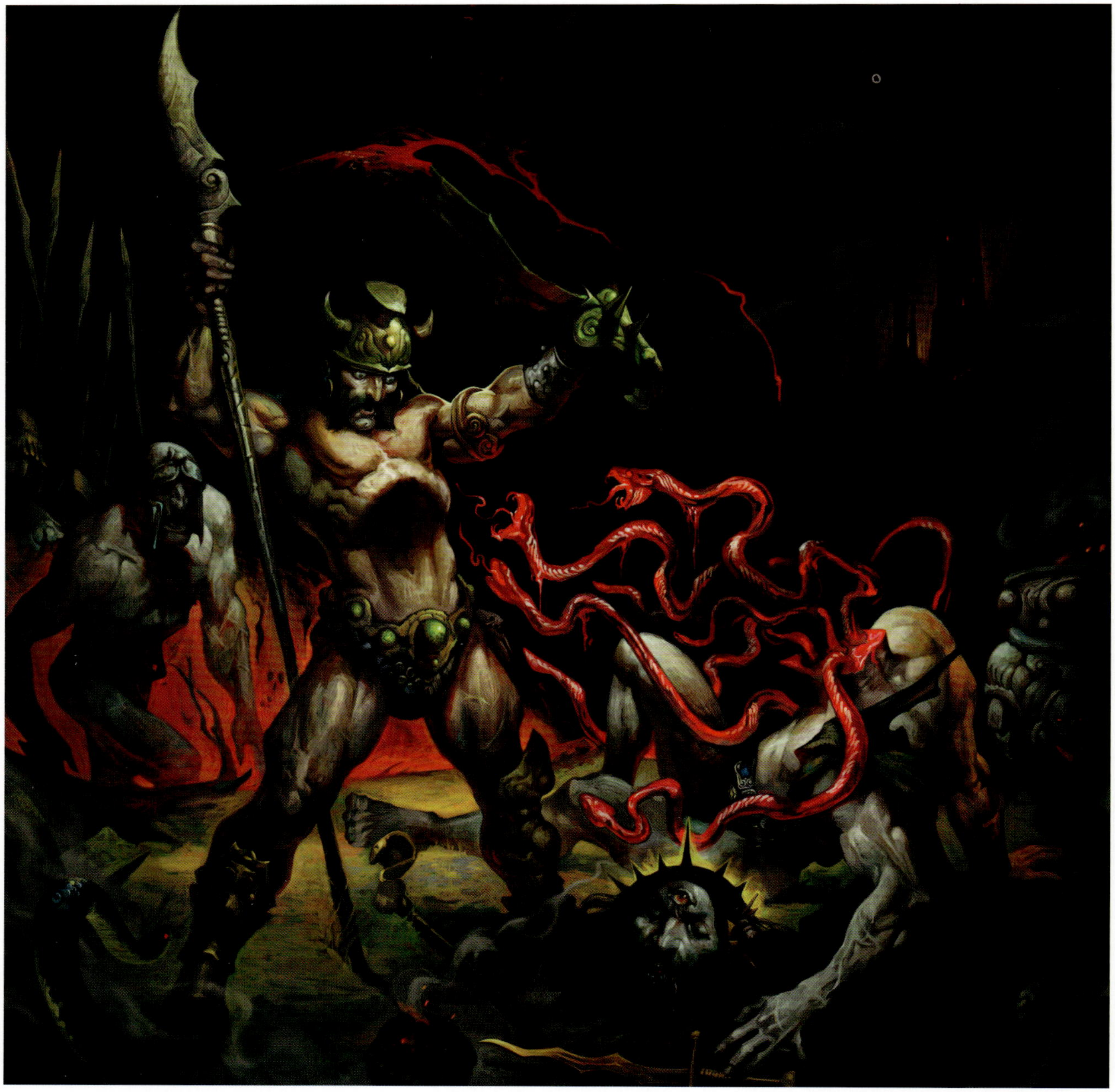

The Way of Steel © Gustavo Pelissari. Created for the album *O Caminho do Aço* by Riffcoven (riffcoven.bandcamp.com)

Gallery

by Gustavo Pelissari

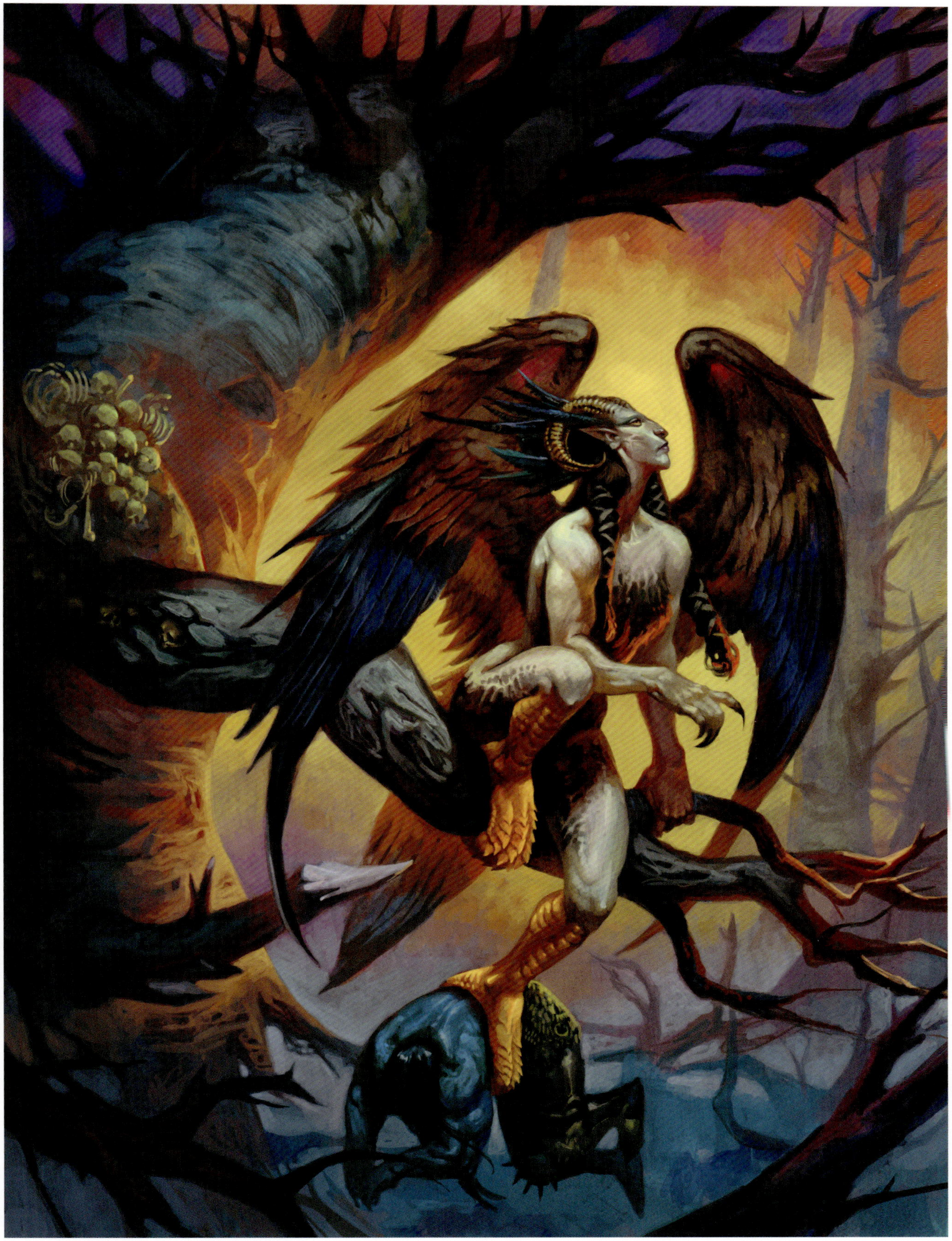

Hunter and Prey © Gustavo Pelissari. Created for the cover of *ARCADIA* magazine by MCDM Productions (shop.mcdmproductions.com)

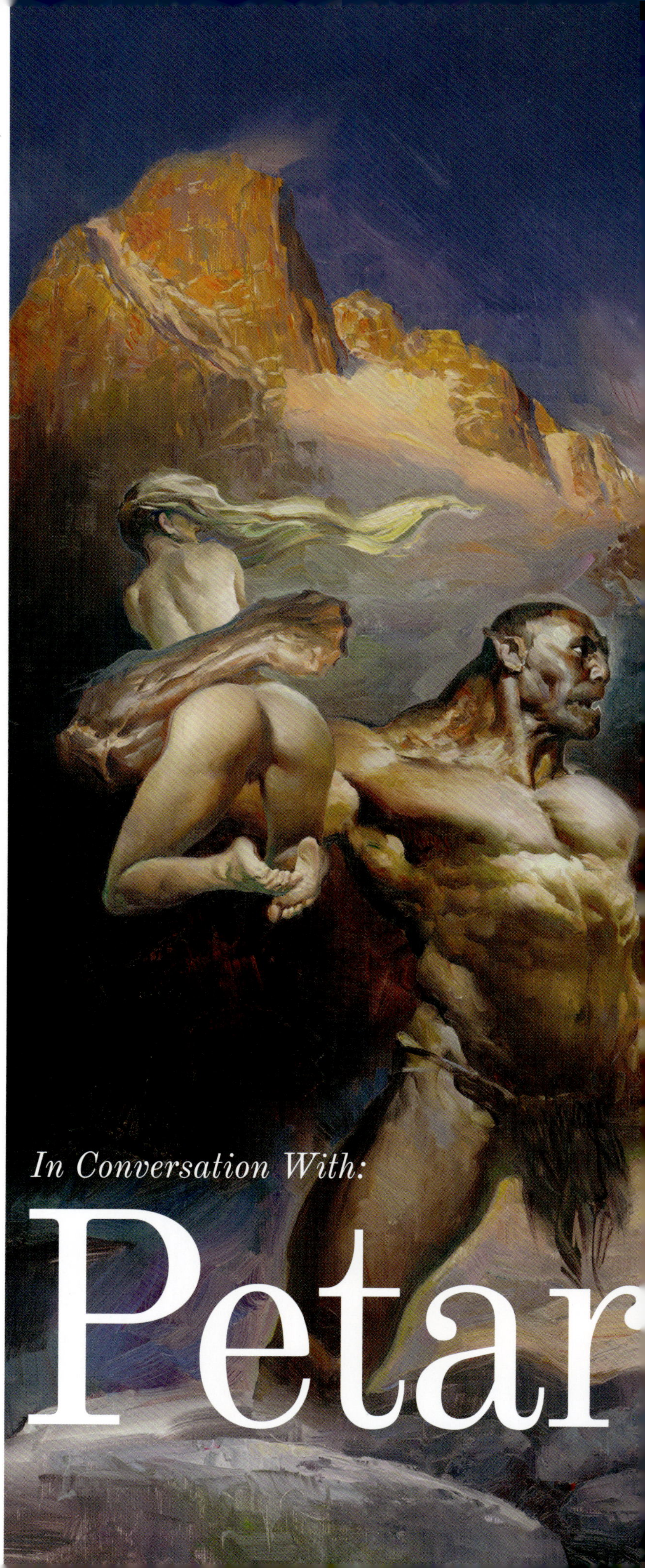

The Beast © Petar Meseldžija

The Beast *(2020) – 100 × 70 cm, oil on canvas. A painting unintentionally reminiscent of one of Frazetta's less-known works.*

In Conversation With:

Petar

Hello, Petar. How did you start out in art and where has your career path taken you?

Petar: I began my artistic career in 1981 by publishing my first comic strip 'Krampi' in *Stripoteka*, one of the best-known comic magazines in what was then Yugoslavia. This was followed by a series of short stories, and the work on the European version of *Tarzan*. From the mid-1980s I studied at the Art Academy of my native city of Novi Sad, and in 1991 I moved to the Netherlands, where I still live to this day. Soon after I left Serbia, I stopped doing comics and switched to illustration and painting instead. Since then, I have worked on posters, illustrated books, and painted book covers. There are various book collections of my work, from sketches and drawings to art books such as *The Legend of Steel Bashaw*, *The Book of Giants*, *Prince Marko and the Dragon*, and my latest book *Archetype – The Art of Petar Meseldžija*.

What sort of imagery and themes are you generally drawn to?

For as long as I can remember, I have been drawn to the phenomena of colours and pictures, and the most fascinating of all visual materials was the world of the fantastic. Later, as I grew older and more self-conscious, I realized why the realm of the fantastic was so attractive to me – it offered my imagination a way to run wild and to break through the conventional limitations of the social and cultural background of my surroundings. The urge for freedom of expression and the discovery of my own unique path gradually crystallized in my mind, proving to be one of the most dominant aspects of my personality and my artistic endeavours.

My interests within the field of fantasy art have shifted through time. From general fantasy, it slowly evolved towards legends and fairy tales, eventually arriving at the more fundamental or mythological common ground it all springs from: the hidden world of archetypes and metaphors, the archetypes of the Hero and the Wise Old Man/Woman being the most important ones for me. They grabbed my heart and soul and never left it. The 'water' from this deep source has been quenching my thirst, sustaining and guiding me and my expression as an artist ever since.

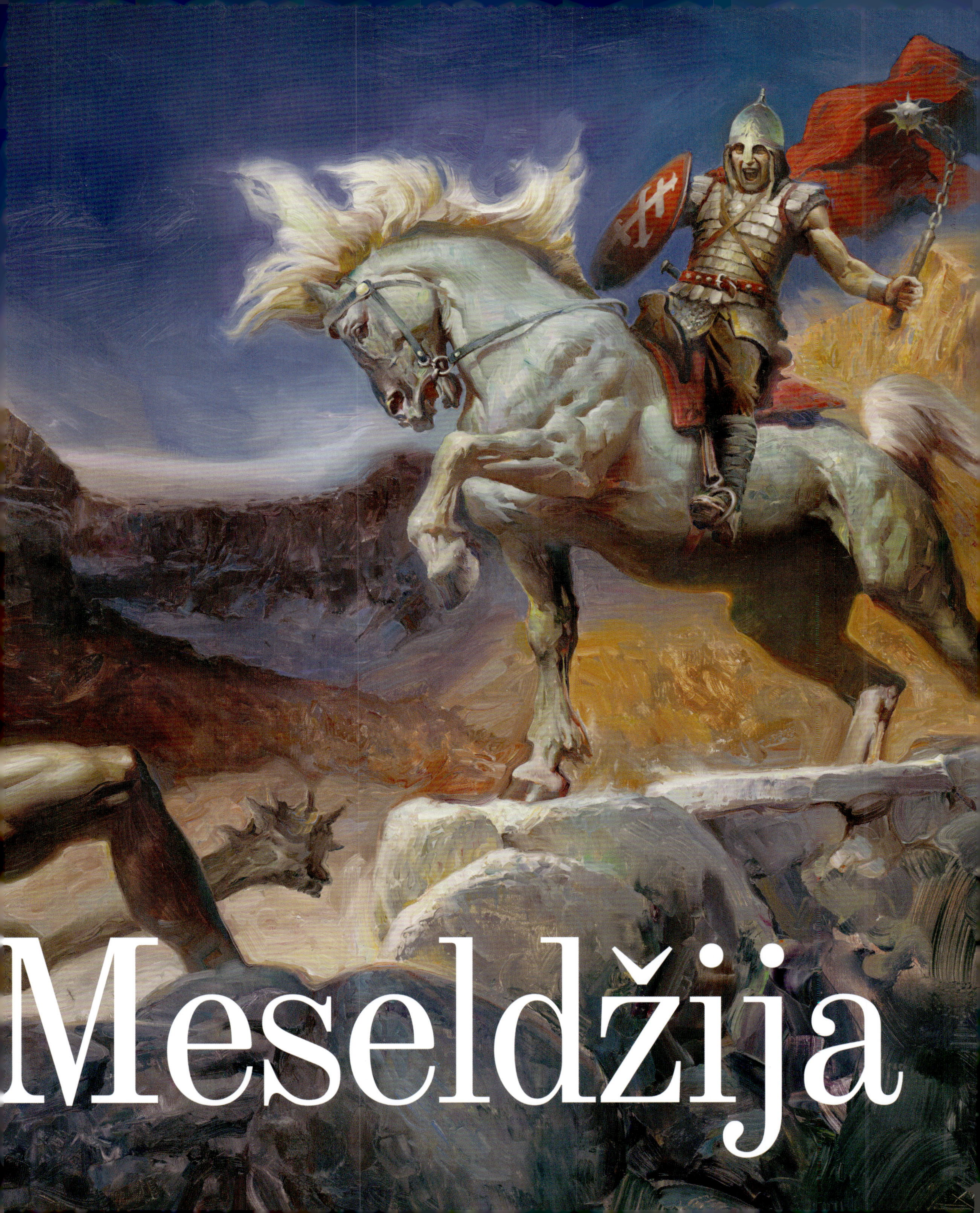

Meseldžija

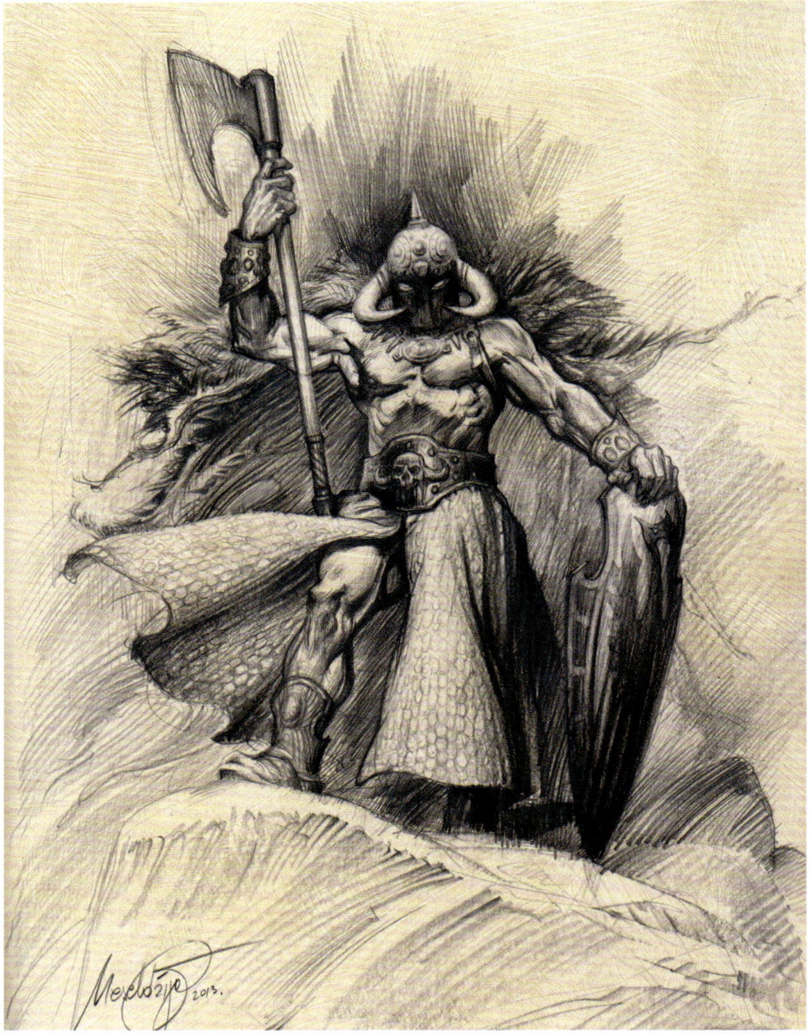

Preliminary drawing 2 © Petar Meseldžija

Preliminary drawing 2 – *Graphite pencils on paper. A drawing inspired by Frazetta's Death Dealer that was later used as the preliminary study for* Homage to Frazetta 2.

When and how did you first discover Frazetta's artwork? What did you think of it?

At the beginning of the 1980s, while still very much into drawing comics, I came across Frazetta's illustrations for the first time. Like virtually all of my fellow comic artists, I was deeply impressed by Frazetta's supreme art, his superior drawing skills, and his ability to capture the essence of dynamic movement. The wonderfully evocative worlds he created with his brush have made a lasting impression on me. In the ensuing years, his work became a guiding light in the early stages of my artistic development, and he remains one my favourite artists to this day.

What are your favourite aspects of his work and how has he influenced you as an artist?

As far as I am concerned, one of the most important aspects of Frazetta's art is its ability to communicate deeper layers of content and meaning. For instance, when you see Frazetta's art for the first time, presuming that you have an inclination towards the fantastic and Frazetta's subject matters in particular, you are usually blown away without knowing why. Now, that is a proper way to face great art. Great art surpasses the level of rational comprehension and touches a deeper ground in our psyche, a level that you can only access intuitively or emotionally. It's a domain of archetypes, like I mentioned before – the primordial images situated in the collective unconscious, that make up the foundation of one's individual and collective life and behaviour.

Frazetta's images point to the primal urges that still exist at a deeper level of the human psyche. They reveal that our fundamental nature, or the 'beast' in us, although covered up with relatively thin layers of civilized development, is still very much alive and potent. To use Friedrich Nietzsche's terminology, Frazetta's art speaks to that 'Dionysian' aspect of our being – our instinctive, unpredictable nature characterized by irrationality, passion, and chaos – as opposed to our 'Apollonian' side that represents a world of reason, logic, and order that protects us from our primal instincts.

Our often spontaneous and intense reaction to his images is a testimony to the existence, the vitality, and the necessity for acknowledging this deeper aspect of our human nature. It's as if his art is trying to say that a civilized human being does not mean an individual who has been cleansed and liberated from his primal, animal nature. Such a person cannot exist. It's all about integrating all aspects of who we are by bringing them into the light of awareness.

Do you have any particular favourite Frazetta pieces or Frazetta-related media?

I have many favourites among Frazetta's paintings, but the first *Death Dealer* painting is the most iconic and the ultimate Frazetta for me. It is the pinnacle of his art and legacy – the ultimate artwork of the grand master that sums up his unique artistic vision and proves his genius. This is an artistic creation that cannot be surpassed. It is timeless because, within the confines of the style and the genre, it vividly communicates the essence of one of the most gripping archetypes – that of Thanatos, the death drive, the instinct for destruction.

Homage to Frazetta 2 *(2018) – 50 × 40 cm, oil on wooden board. My second Frazetta homage, and last interpretation of the Death Dealer, done as a private commission.*

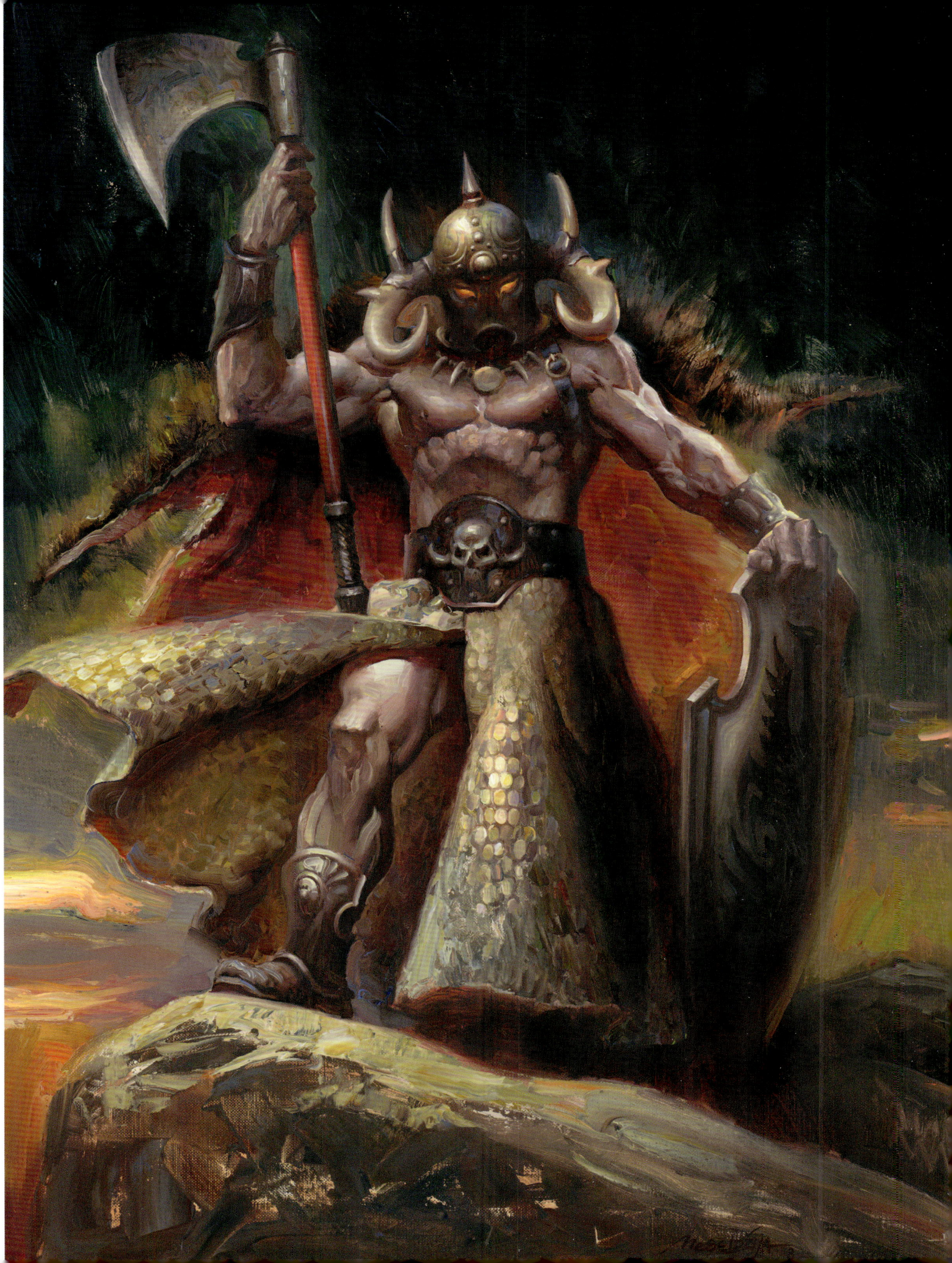

Homage to Frazetta 2 © Petar Meseldžija

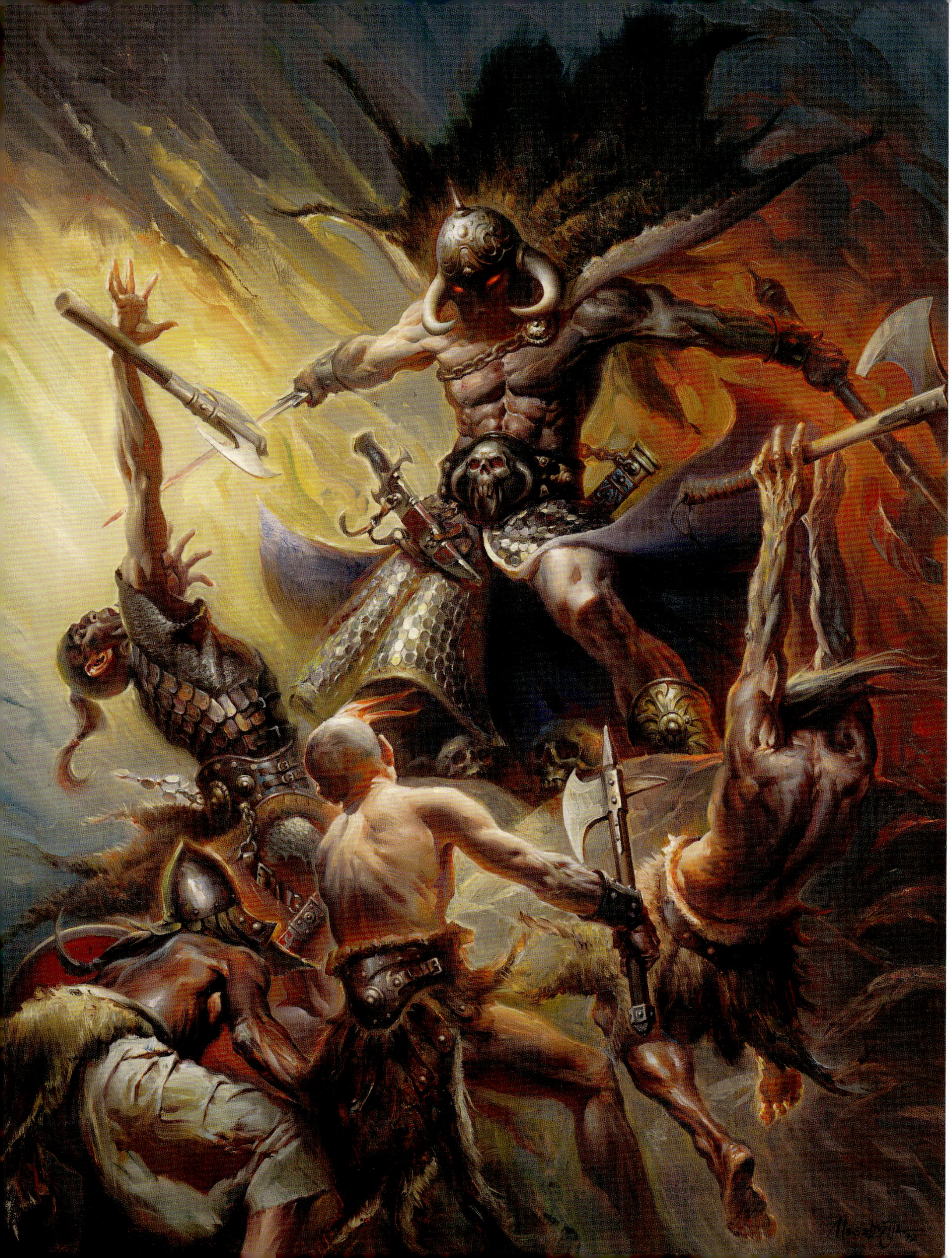

Homage to Frazetta 1 © Petar Meseldžija

Homage to Frazetta 1
(2012) – 72 × 55 cm, oil on wooden board. This is my first 'tribute to Frazetta' painting. It was painted as a private commission for an American art collector.

Like Frazetta himself, you use a range of analogue tools, but are especially recognized for your oils. What is it about oils that resonates with you?

Although I used to draw a lot in the past, I actually never saw myself primarily as a draughtsman, but rather as a painter. Likewise, I tried my hand at all traditional mediums, but oil paint always had the strongest appeal to me. It felt like the most magical, most inspiring medium for depicting or interpreting our existing reality and creating new ones.

Technically speaking, oil painting is in a way a summing-up of all other painting techniques. After truly mastering oil painting, you can master all other painting techniques more easily. Almost all that is to be found and done with traditional mediums is potentially in oil paint, if you are able to unravel it. For me, it is the vibrancy and disobedience of oil paint, as well as the complexity of the technique itself, that keep me animated and inspired. Besides, having a strong inclination towards classic art – many of my early role models and inspirations were classic painters – I naturally tended to follow in their 'oily' footsteps!

Could you talk a little more about the creation of one of your Frazetta homages – what you wanted to capture, and any challenges you encountered on the way?

When painting a Frazetta homage, I don't have a specific plan for the technical aspects of his art that I might want to capture. As one of my most important 'mentors', he is a part of my artistic profile; I seem to have internalized his work to an extent that some of its qualities have simply merged with my own sensibility and vision. This allows me to work intuitively, with no trouble invoking his style.

Together with a number of other artists, Frazetta played an important role in forming 'Meseldžija the fantasy artist'. After all, we all stand on the shoulders of those who came before us. However, I am not Frazetta, nor is my work a copy of his art. So, while working on the painting *Homage to Frazetta 1*, my intention wasn't to make a copy, but rather to pay homage to the master by projecting his famous character into my world, and letting it go through the prism of my own vision.

The essence of my interpretation has been correctly expressed by a friend of mine, and a fellow artist who, upon seeing the painting, commented: 'Ah, you are on their side as well!' Another spot-on remark I heard from another person was: 'This is perhaps the lightest Death Dealer painting I have ever seen, but still the darkest Death Dealer, because it appears to me that *he* is the bad guy!'

Back then, it seemed to me that Frazetta's *Death Dealer* paintings, when approached from a straightforward perspective, reflected a rather black-and-white approach to the relationship between good and evil, although it was never very clear to me how a bringer of death could be seen as a representative of good. What I didn't realize at that time was that on a deeper, archetypal level, he is neither good nor evil, being a symbolic representation of Thanatos, the death instinct. The fact that his foes are often depicted as demonic creatures – as if they are a symbolic manifestation of the Jungian 'shadow', or the primal urges – who are bound to be slain and destroyed, made me interpret the subject matter of these paintings and the relationship between the characters rather superficially.

Following that logic, I tried to 'correct' the situation by bringing in certain shades of 'grey', creating a scene where the line between the good and the bad is rather blurred. The Death Dealer's foes are apparently not demonic creatures in my painting, but rather regular barbaric warriors who, for whatever reason, fight against the menacing character of the Death Dealer. It is not clear who's attacking who, or whose 'side' one is supposed to choose, in terms of good versus evil. I think this was the most important aspect of my interpretation of the Death Dealer.

Where do you see Frazetta's legacy when you look around at fantasy art and popular culture today?

While fantasy art, as a genre of the 'fantastic', will always have a somewhat limited reach within the wider (global) cultural landscape – and Frazetta was an artist primarily working in this field, whose work was a product of American society, its culture and development – Frazetta's art possesses many evocative, universal qualities, like beauty, vitality, and the ability to communicate ancient, archetypal phenomena. As far as fantasy art is concerned, I compare Frazetta to Michelangelo. In terms of his level of technical mastery; the intensity, power, and grace of his art; his undeniable genius; and the impact of his legacy on other artists and the development of the fantasy art genre, they are equals in my experience. ❖

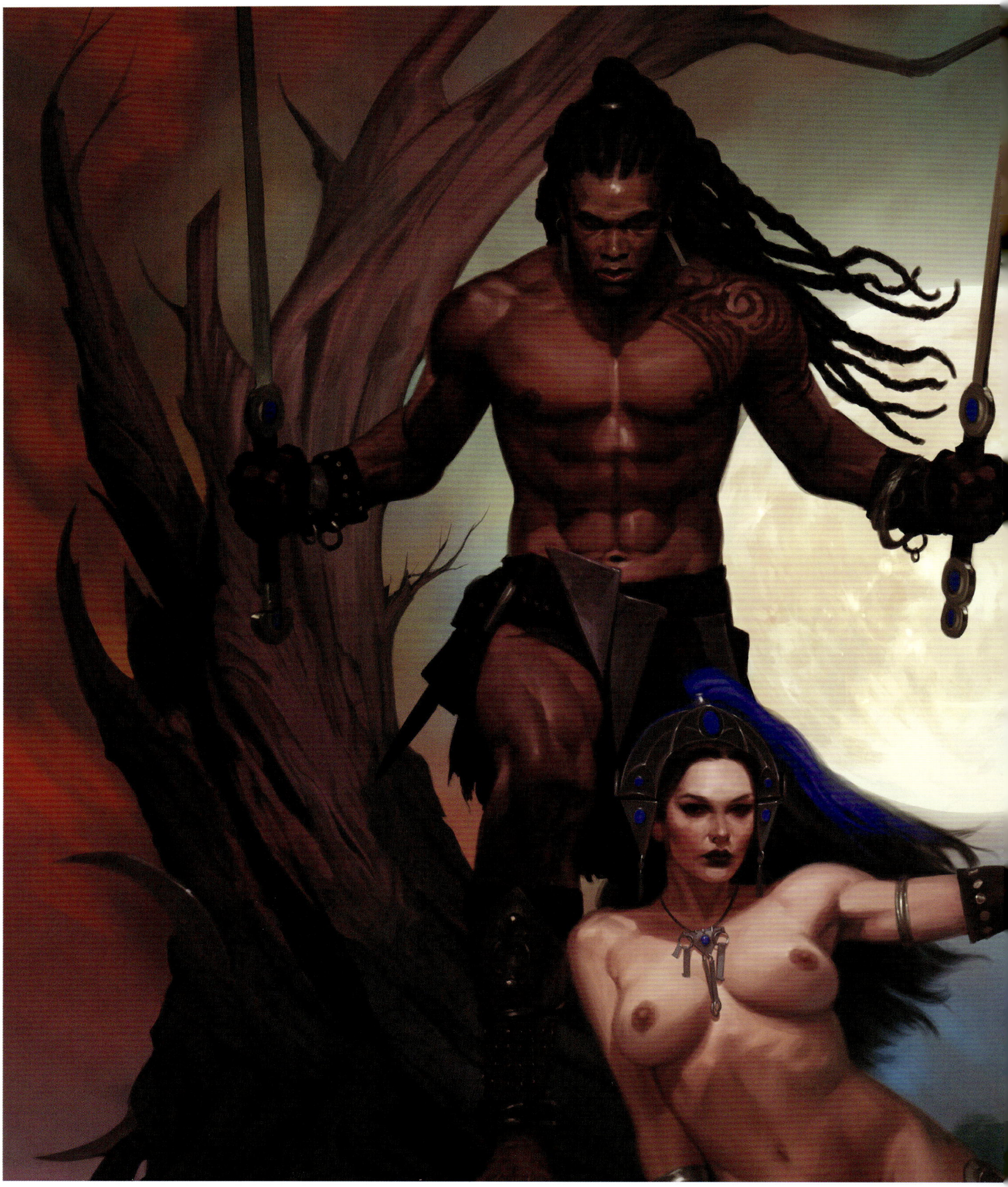

Final image © Jodie Muir

Full Moon

by Jodie Muir

Creating *Full Moon*

Frazetta's design sensibility in the arrangement and composition of an image has been hugely influential in my own work. It has taught me to be selective in the elements I want to highlight or push back to create illustrations that grab the eye. His work is not afraid to be an illustration; he embraces the nature of a two-dimensional image and totally exploits it. The other aspect of his work I would love to pay homage to is the feeling of power it radiates. I want to capture that in my own artwork, as it's such a defining characteristic of his work in my mind.

01 Rough sketch

I begin by roughing a quick sketch without the aid of any reference, just to capture the general energy that I want the image to carry across from Frazetta's work. I connect the two figures at different heights to form one large, dynamic diagonal across the page. I use a tree as a framing device to further enforce the composition around the moon.

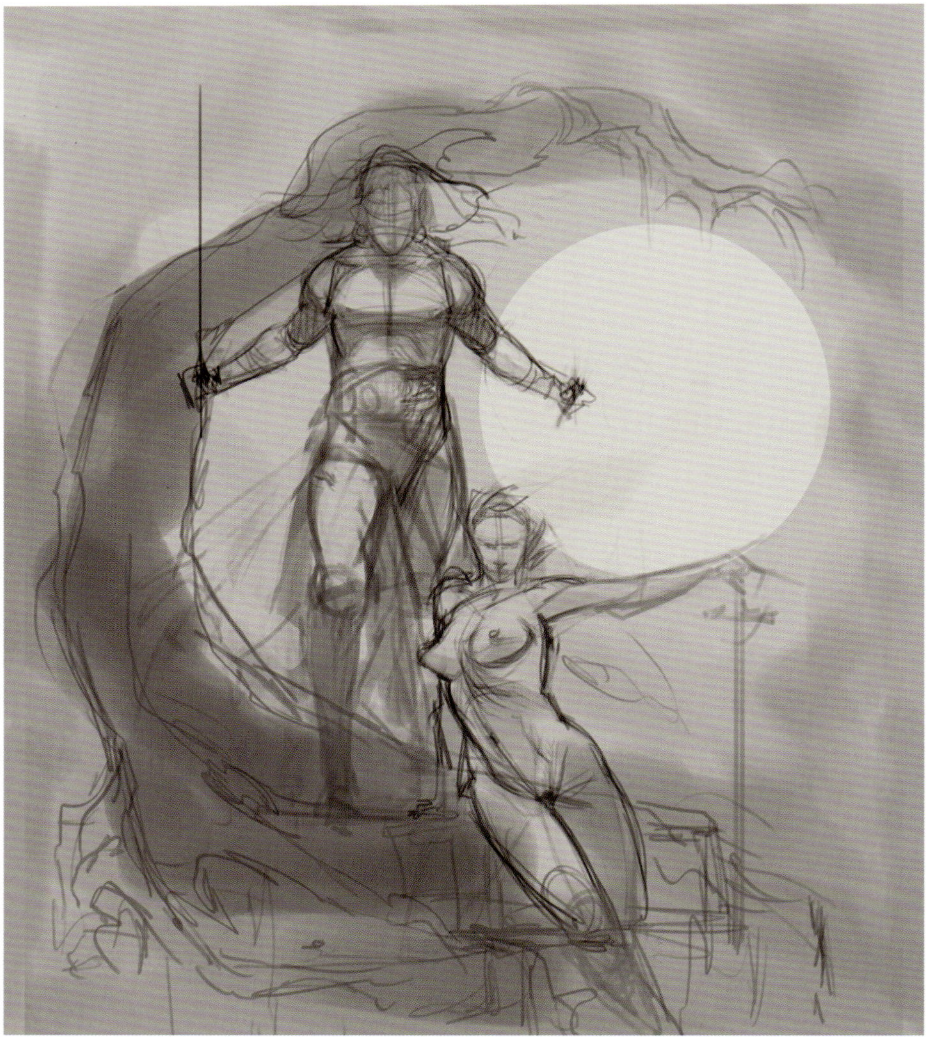

Initial layout and composition sketch to capture the general direction of the piece

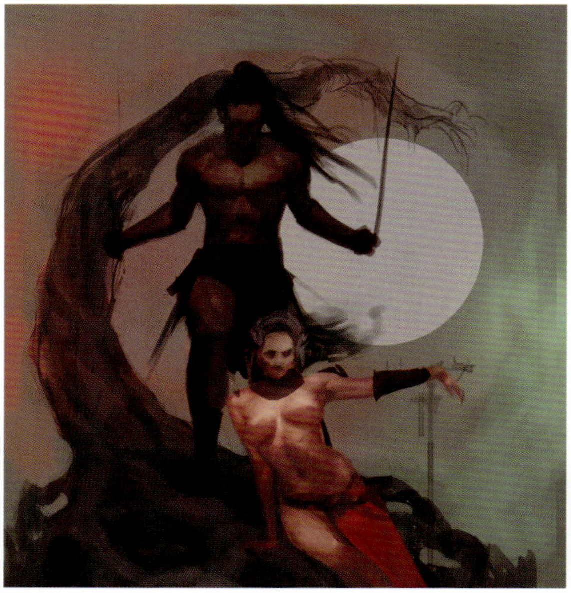

Laying down the big shapes and passages of colour

02 Value & colour

After the initial sketch, I start mapping out the large value and colour masses to better see where the image is heading. I really want to capture that feeling of power so palpable in Frazetta's work, so I use a lot of red to intensify the mood. To balance this out, I introduce some green to conflict with it and to complement the purple undertone I began with. A lot of Frazetta's colour palettes are fearless, big, and bold, which I lean into here.

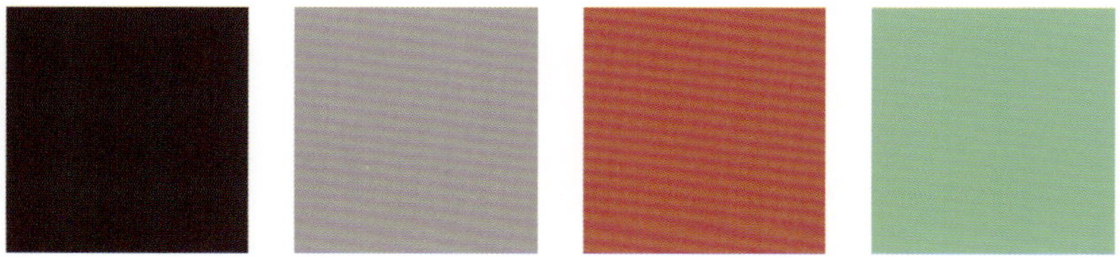

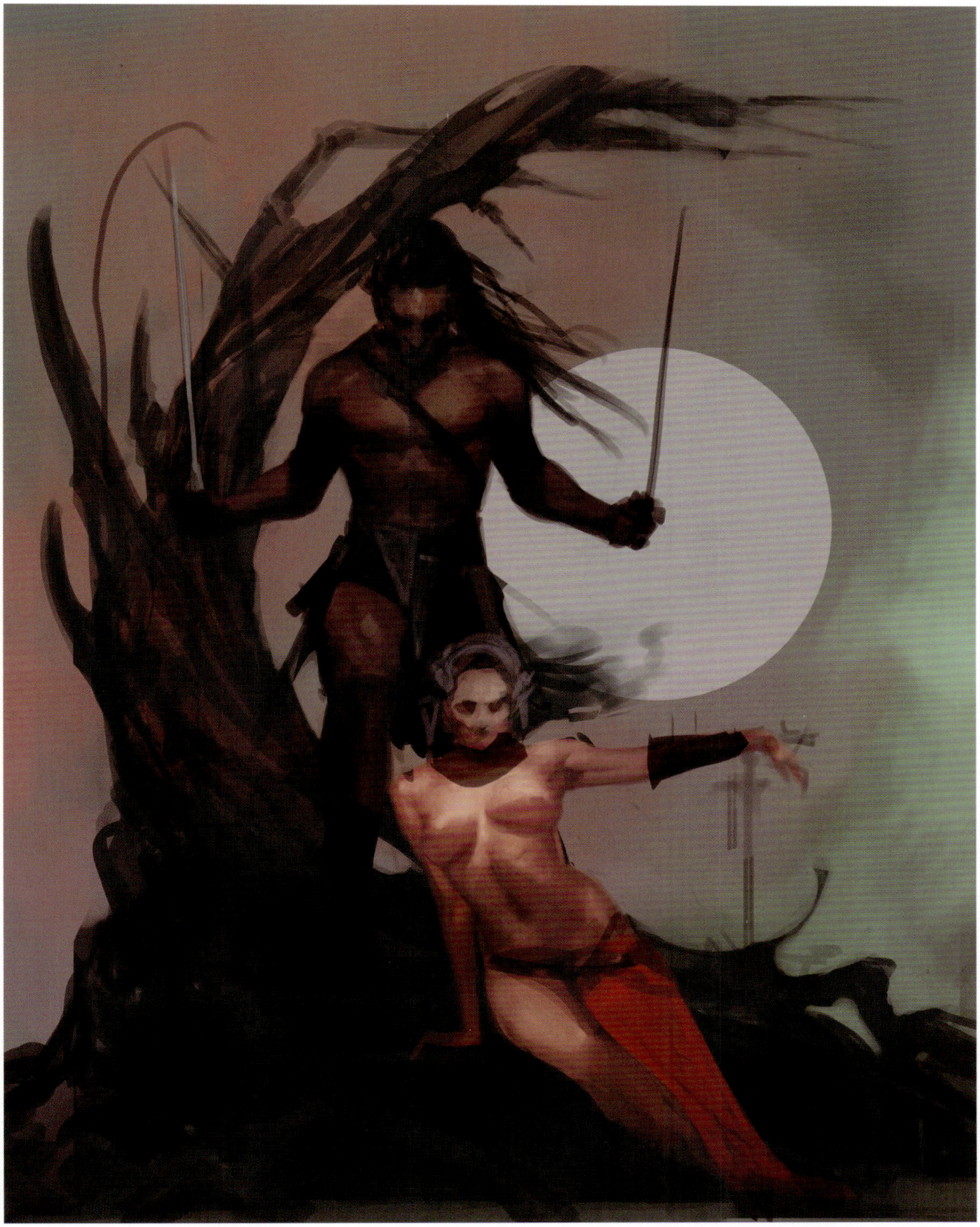

Slightly adjusting the composition to find the right balance

03 Composition & balance

Upon review, I feel I've lost some of the scale and proportion that I had in the initial sketch, so I adjust accordingly. Balance is key for good composition, as demonstrated by Frazetta, so I'm mindful to maintain that throughout. I also start to build up the form of the tree in an exaggerated manner. Everything in Frazetta's paintings has its own sense of character and the tree will be no exception here.

04 Colour & visual language

Now the composition is working better, it's time to give the colours more energy, as they are looking a little washed out. I introduce a lively blue to add some interest to the background and shift the moon's hue towards a warmer yellow. I also add a couple of diagonal elements at the base of the tree to strengthen the aggressive visual language.

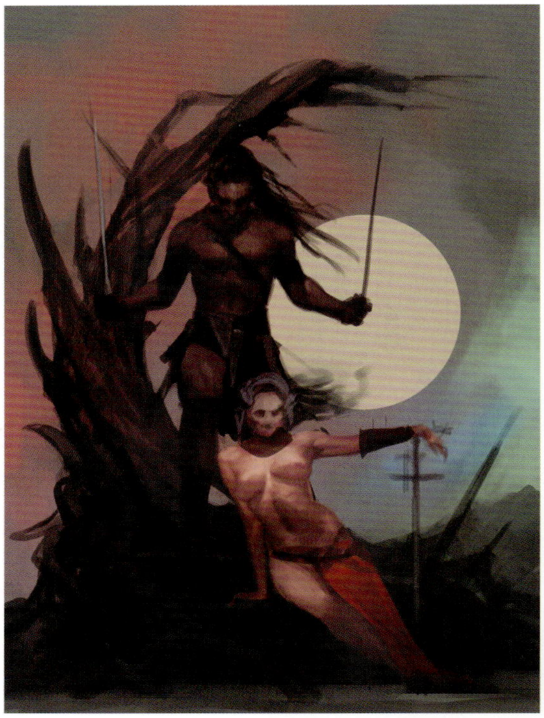

Adding more vibrancy to the overall palette for greater impact

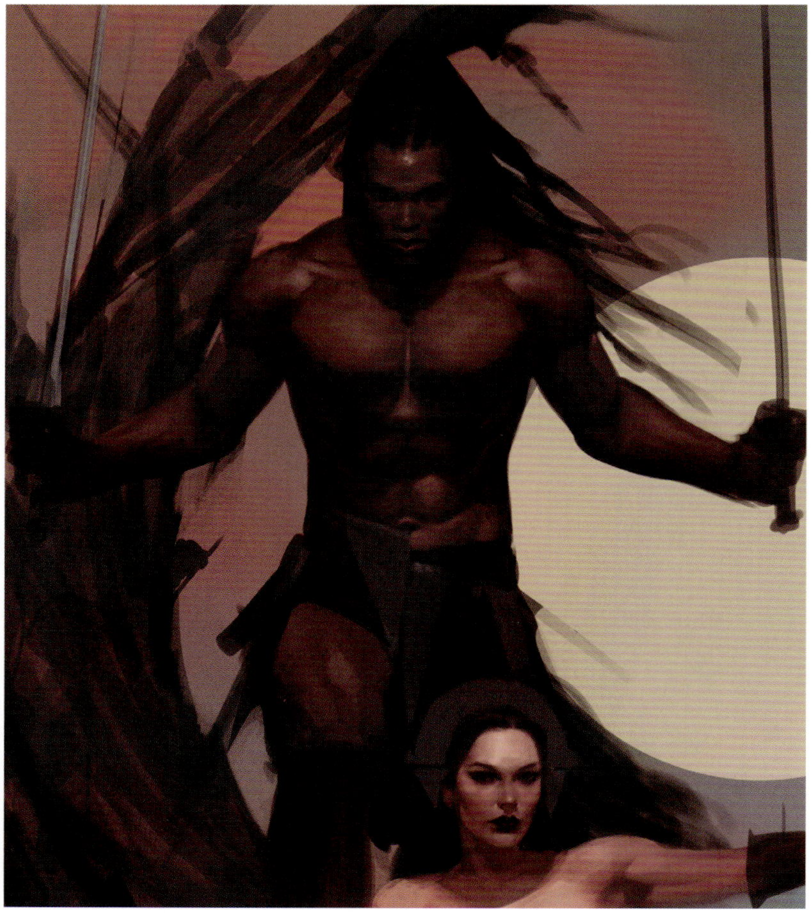

05 Pose & expression

Now the large elements of the piece are working together, it's time to make a more considered pass over the two figures, focusing mostly on the male warrior first. At this point in the process, I firm up the likenesses and take a closer look at the anatomy. I want the poses and faces to possess the same kind of fierce attitude that can be found throughout Frazetta's character work; a kind of 'don't mess with me' intensity.

Taking a closer look at the figures' poses and expressions

06 The female figure

I take a closer look at the female figure next. Frazetta's women are feminine and dangerous. They are a magnificent mix of reality and fantasy. He did not airbrush out too many imperfections in the way a lot of modern fantasy and media does. In fact he idealizes, enhances, and celebrates the fuller figure. It's an element of his work I really love and want to try and incorporate into this piece.

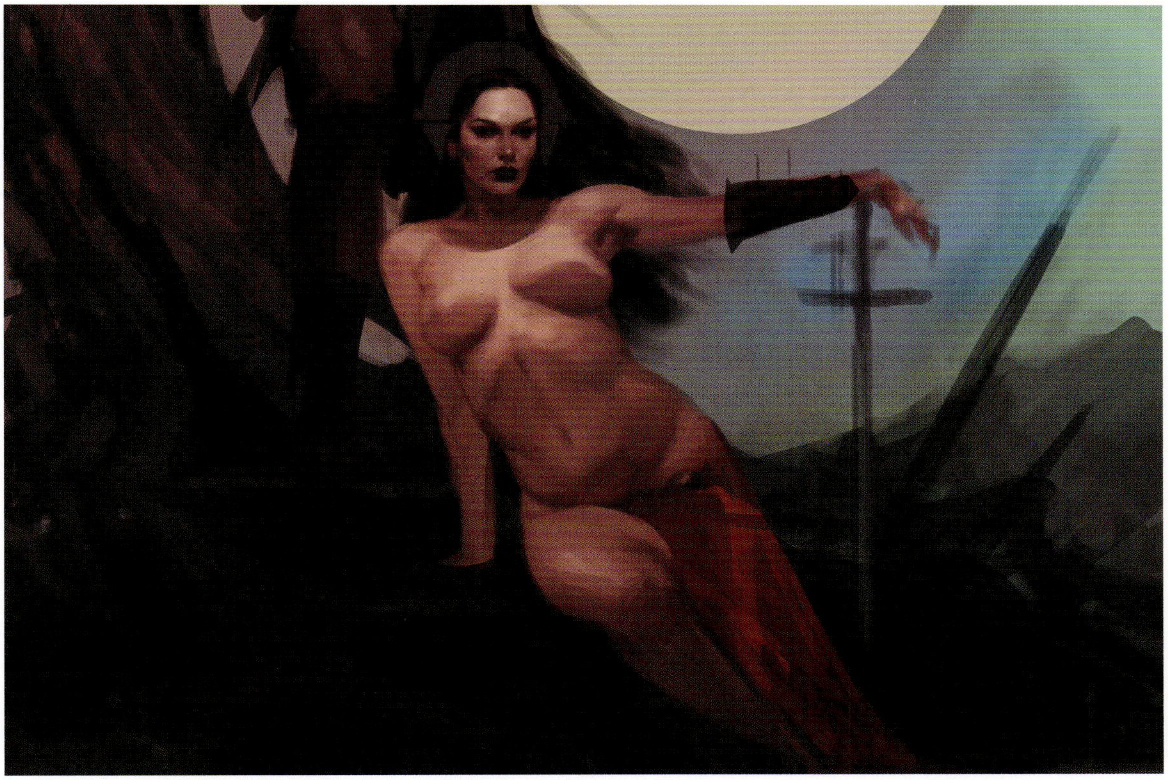

Developing the anatomy of the female figure

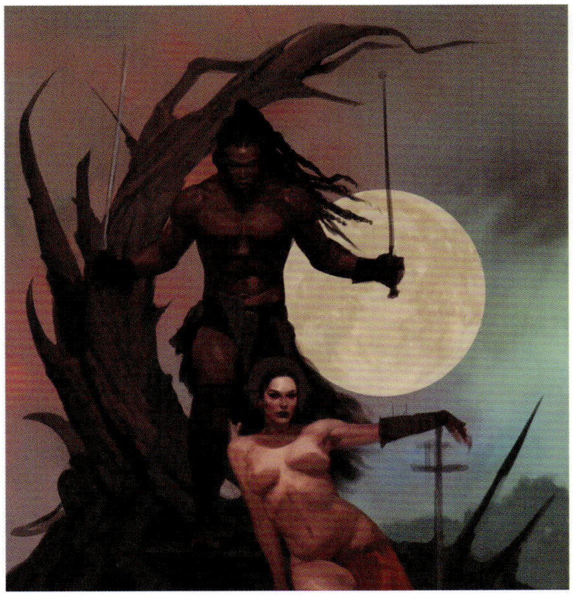

07 Background elements

After going over the two figures with a second pass, I take another look at the background. I work on the tree and moon some more; I want to really push and twist the personality of the tree further to give it a creepy, gnarled, and eerie appearance. It should be just a few steps beyond what might naturally occur, to add to the sense of drama.

Working on the background a little more to create personality and mood

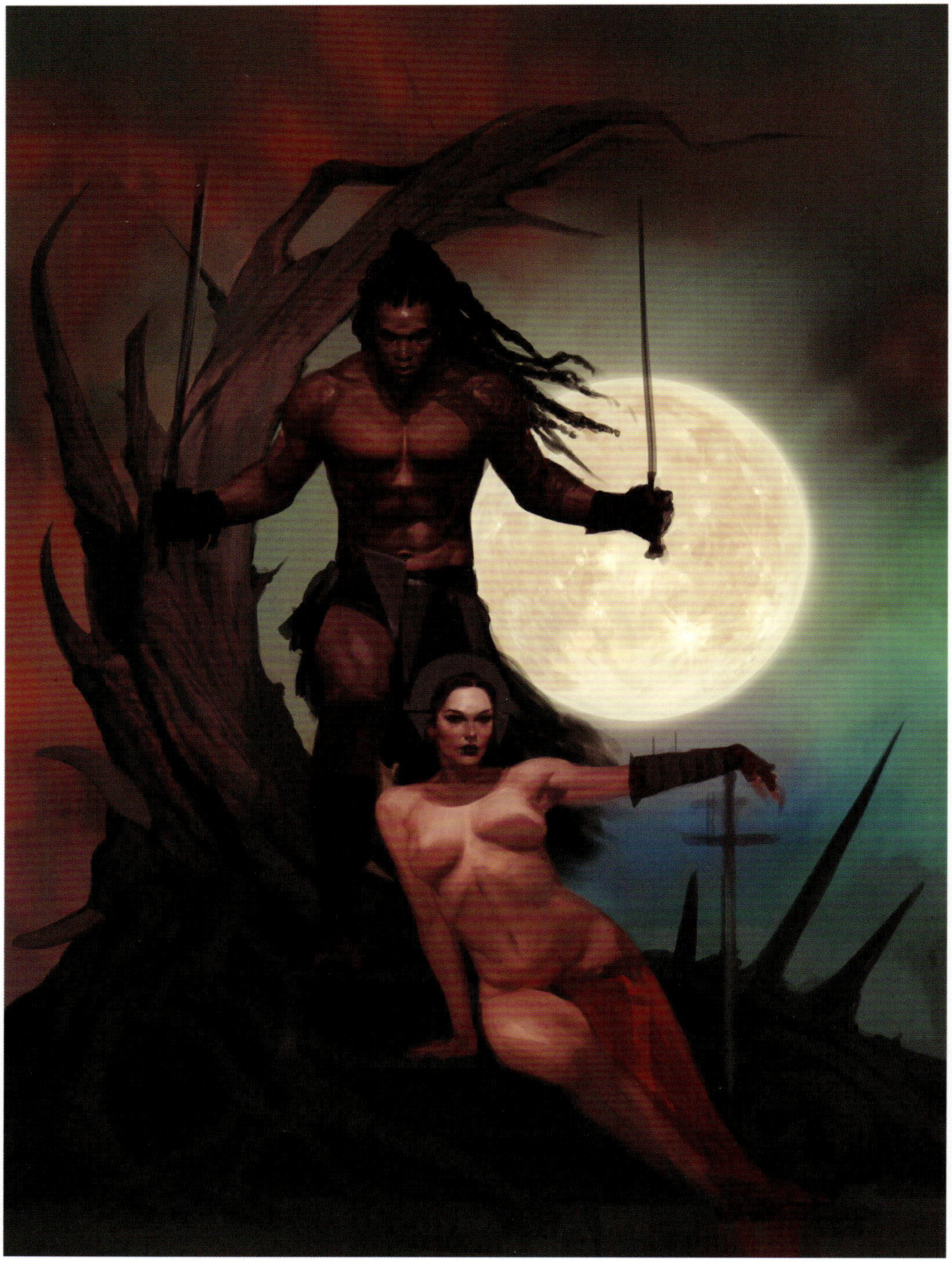

Shifting the values of the sky to create a more dramatic mood

08 Mood & energy

The background still looks a little washed out for the mood I am trying to create. The painting should encapsulate the power seen in Frazetta's paintings; I want it to be bold yet still quite brooding, so I adjust the values of the background to achieve more of that energy. I also start to map out the lower portion of the tree, adding a skull for good measure.

09 Separate forms

The tone of the male warrior and the tree behind him appear a little too similar, so I decide to increase the highlight of the tree to ensure the shape of the figure remains readable. Frazetta's silhouettes are always very clear and legible, and I don't want to lose that. Next, I move into the enhancement stage and add a little bombast to the red clouds in the sky.

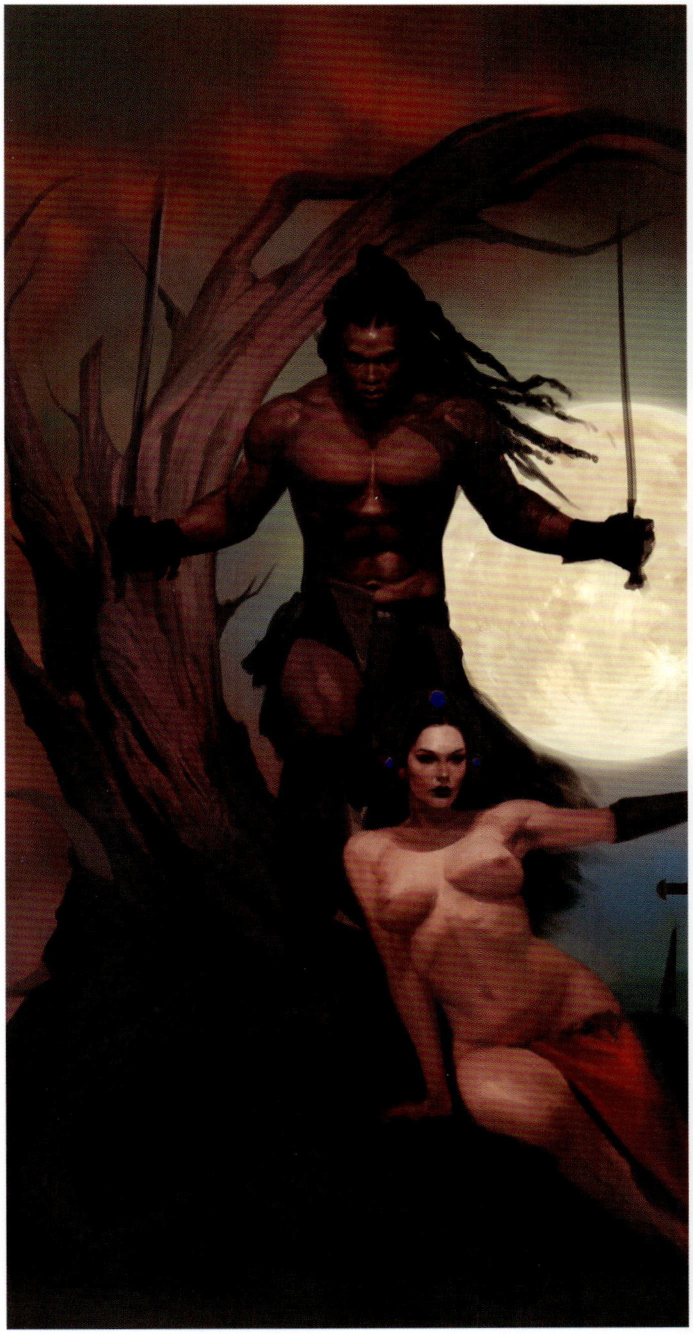

Using light to separate the forms where they appear slightly too close in tone

Discovering Frazetta

I don't think I'm alone in having fallen in love with Frank Frazetta's work the moment I saw it. It's hard not to when his illustrations are commanding, powerful, and incredibly seductive all at the same time. The first piece I came across was an illustration of Conan on a book cover. At the time, I hadn't really seen fantasy represented like that before; it was a little darker, intimidating, and awesome. Frazetta painted Conan as this foreboding and kind of mysterious mass, with the whole world beneath his sword. A challenge to the viewer, almost. The image was arresting and engaging, but also pared down and simplified with a serious sense of design and intent.

The men and the women in Frazetta's work are fantastically beautiful, sculpted, and posed. The exaggeration and celebration of form in his subjects, human or otherwise, only serves to enhance the feeling of otherworldliness. His sense of composition and the way he navigates colour is masterful and restrained in all the right places. Everything feels deeply considered and arranged for maximum visual impact. Simply put, it grabs you, and I don't think it ever lets you go. What I admire most about Frazetta's work is the way it makes you feel. His paintings really do emit a sense of power. There is an attitude, confidence, and strength throughout his work that I find incredibly inspiring. It's effortlessly cool and has a dark beauty that I've been mesmerized by ever since.

10 Rendering & detail

Once I have covered the main elements of the illustration, I begin to move into the rendering stage. This is when I pick out the fun details in the piece, such as the jewellery, headdress, the male figure's hair, and hands. It's never too late to fix mistakes, so I make a slight anatomy correction to the female figure at this point too. I try to avoid staying overly attached to any element of a painting.

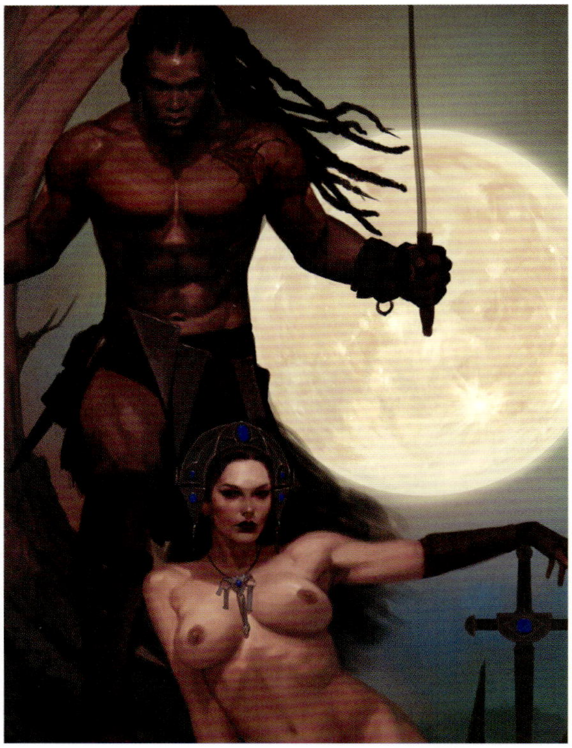

Now that everything is in place, it's time to start looking at the detailing

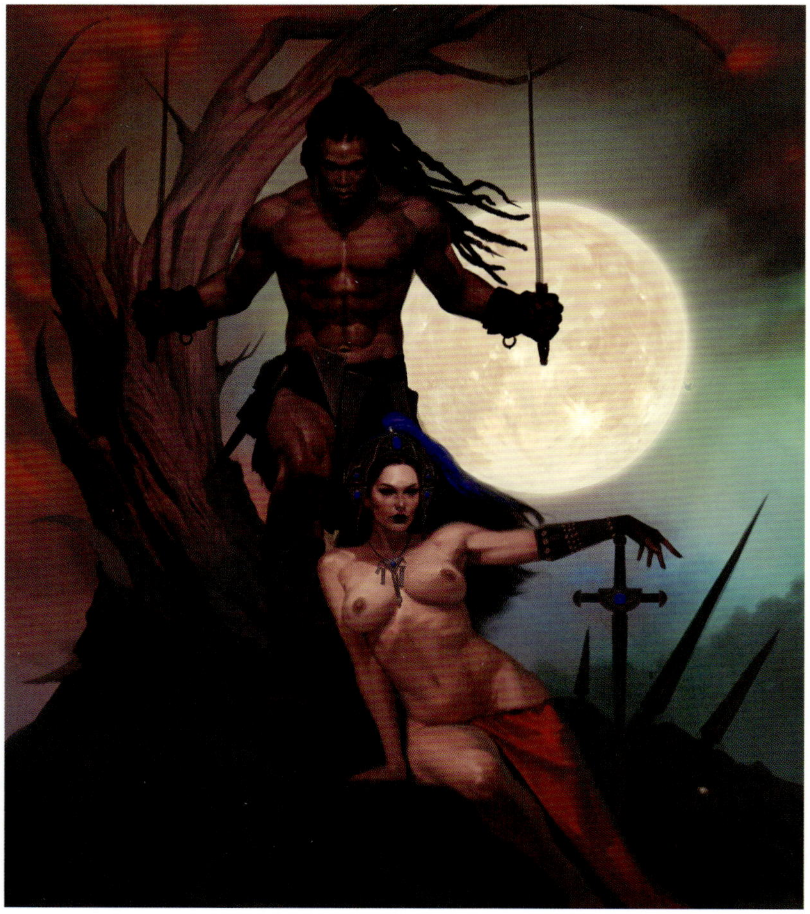

11 Balancing the lighting

Overall, I feel the illustration is starting to get a little too dark at the back. It needs some brighter passages to prevent the foreground elements and the background from merging. As I brighten the sky, I darken the foreground a little too. I also add a blue streak to the headpiece of the female character to break up the line of the figures a little better.

Frazetta wasn't afraid to 'lose' an edge in a painting; no interpretation he made was too literal. Therefore, I plan to shadow out much of the base of the tree to give an intentionally concealed or even purposefully incomplete look to the piece.

Balancing the lighting to separate the foreground and the background

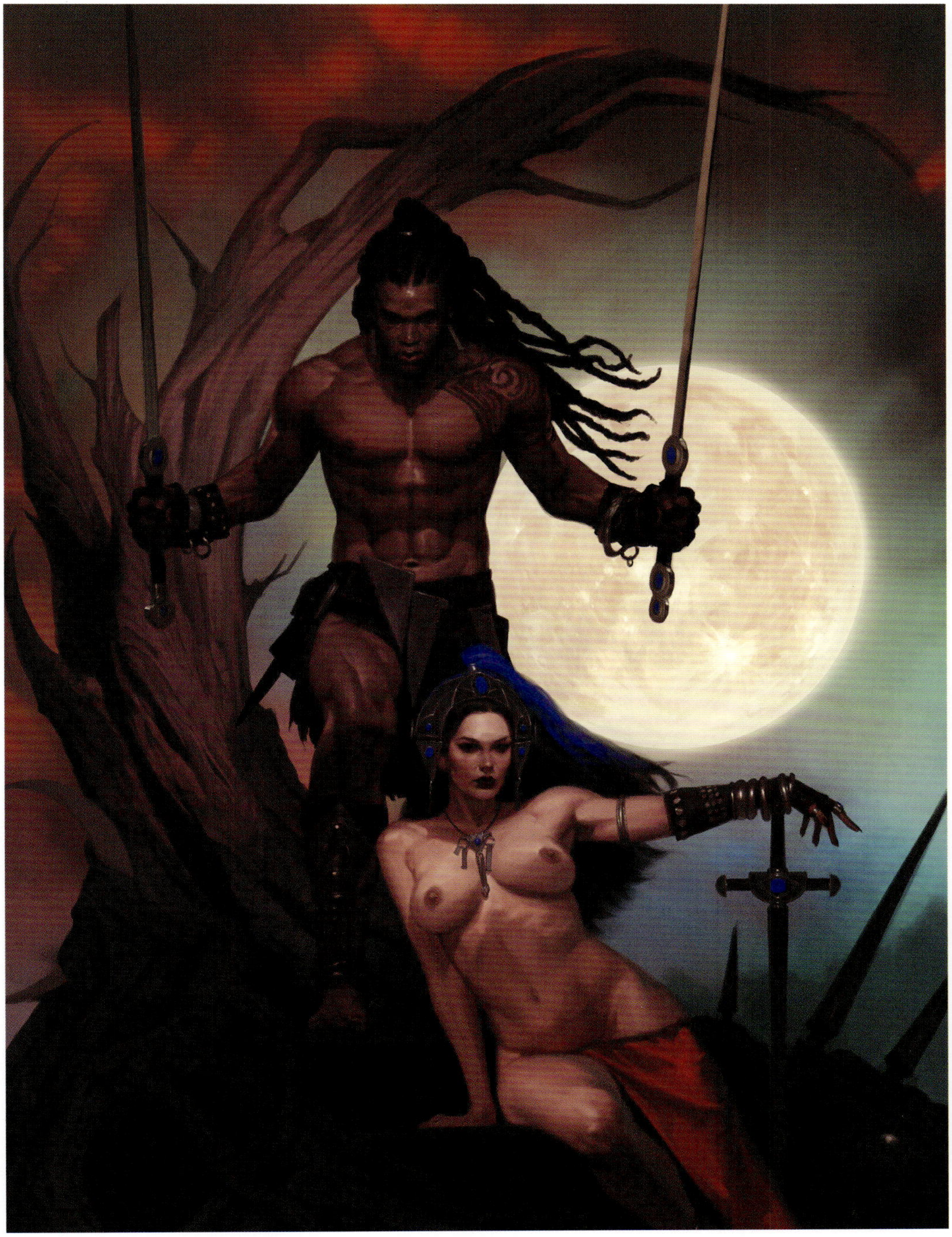

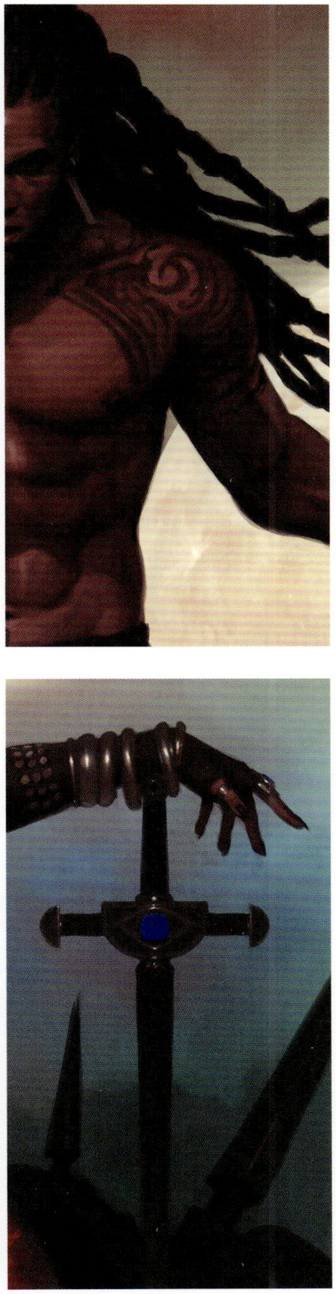

Adding finishing touches to the figures and their decoration

12 Embellishments

Now the painting is almost finished, it's time to start adding the final touches and embellishments. I love the ornamentation of retro fantasy and Frazetta's artwork was some of the best. It was never too much nor too fussy. I try to maintain a coherent style between the male and female counterparts to avoid elements becoming too visually noisy.

13 Brightness adjustments

To finish the painting, I drop in a hard shadow at the bottom to create the 'edgeless' feeling often seen in Frazetta's illustrations. I also work a little further into the clouds to add some more energy, aggression, and flow to the composition. Adding a few brightness tweaks here and there to both the moon and the characters helps to finish off the piece.

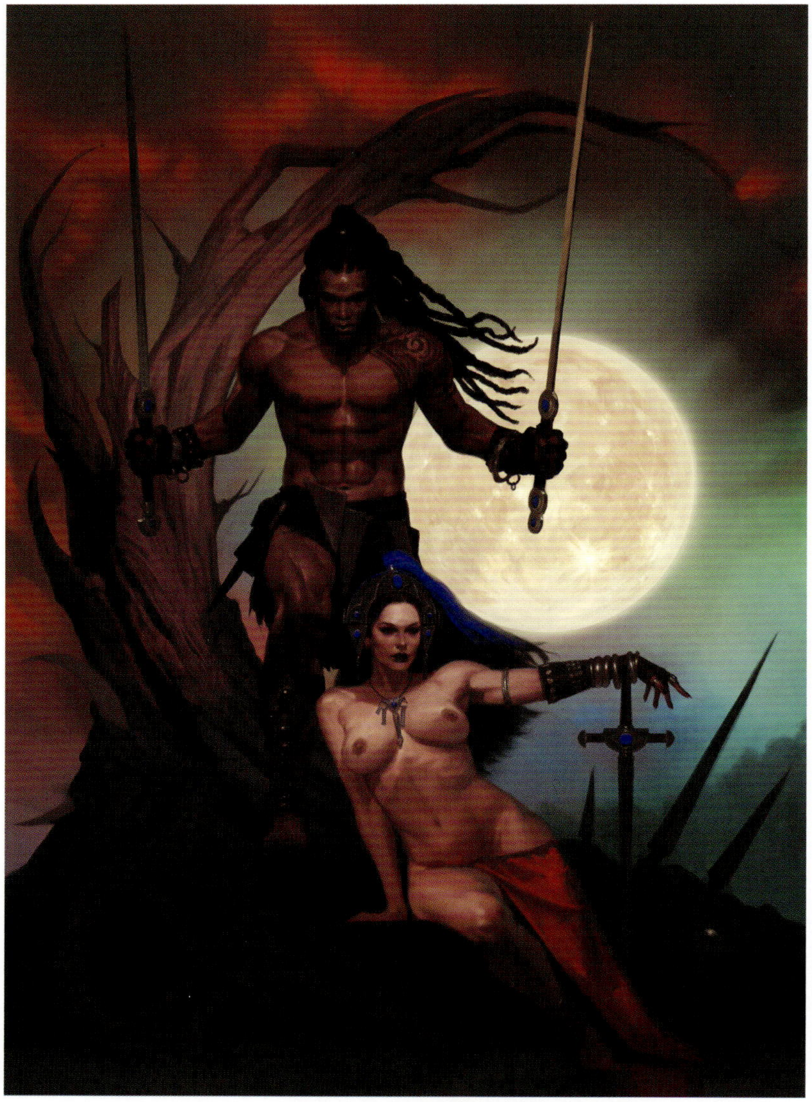

Adding some splashes of light and dark to take the illustration to its final iteration

Conclusion

I hope I have managed to capture some of that Frazetta magic in my painting! He is, of course, impossible to imitate in that way, but I hope some of the dark, powerful mystery that his work evokes shines through in this piece. It was a joy to explore just how masterful and fearless he really was at arranging an illustration.

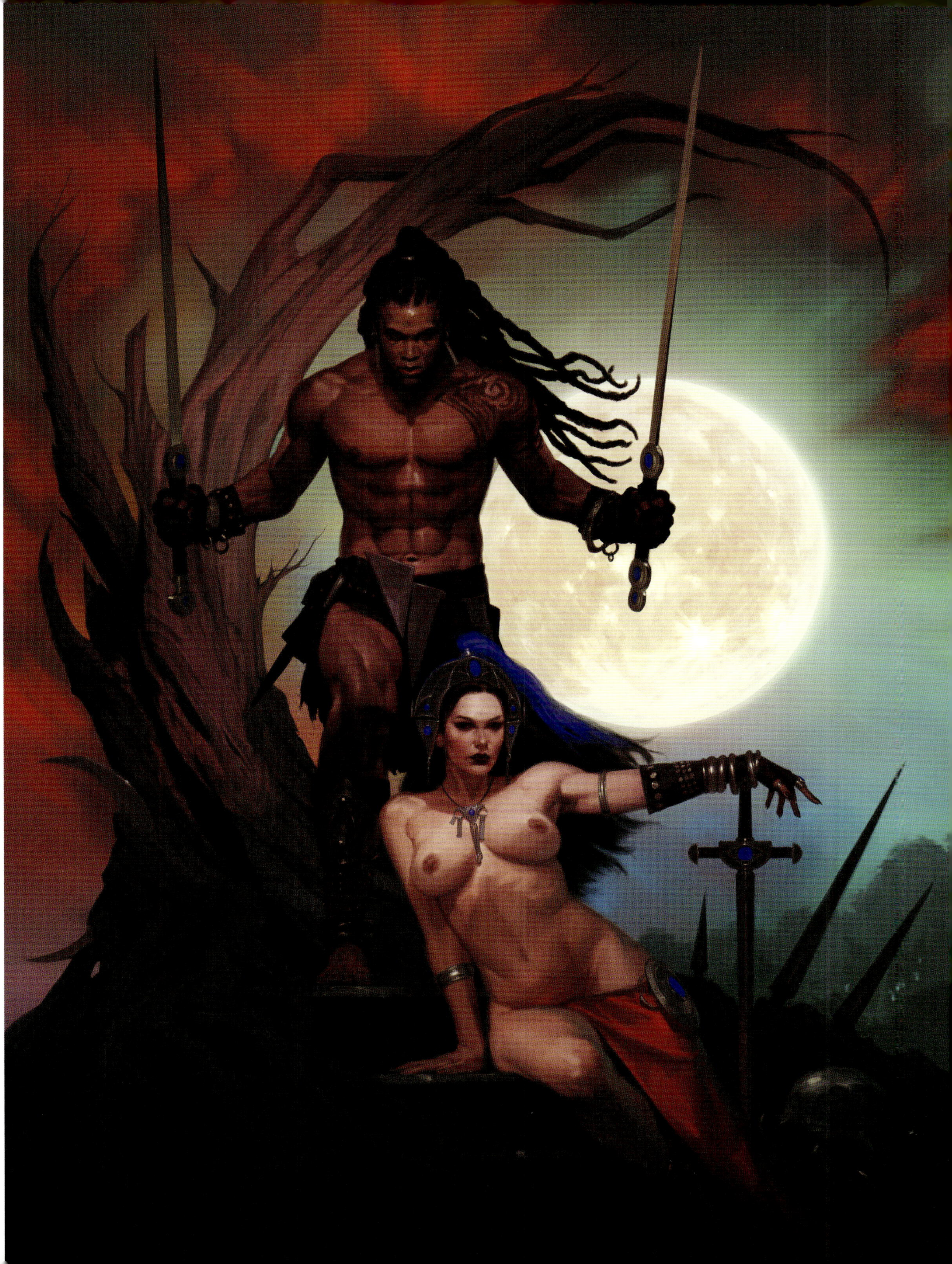

Final image © Jodie Muir

Gallery

by Jodie Muir

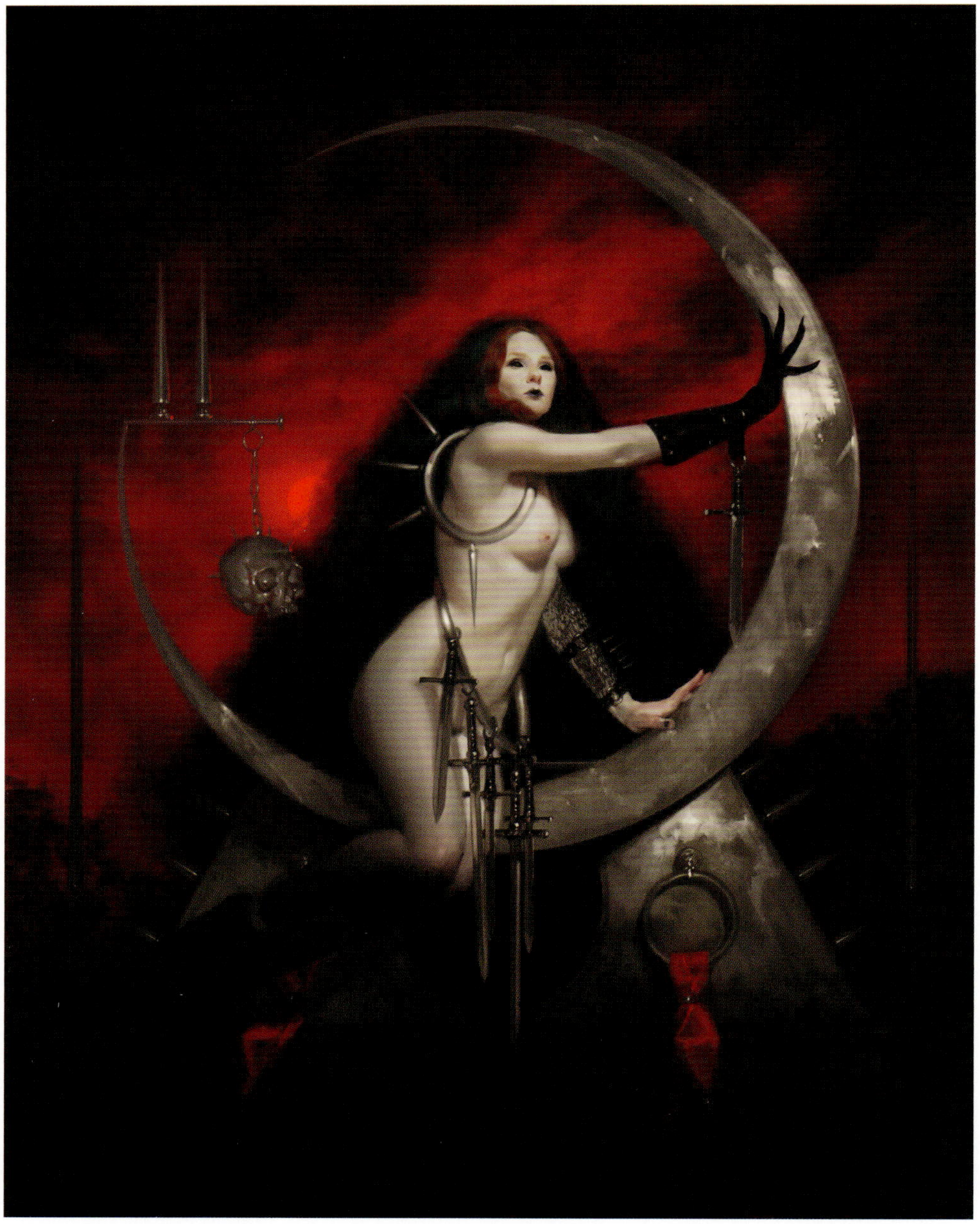

Metal © Jodie Muir

Metal — *One of my favourite personal pieces – a celebration of all things metal!*

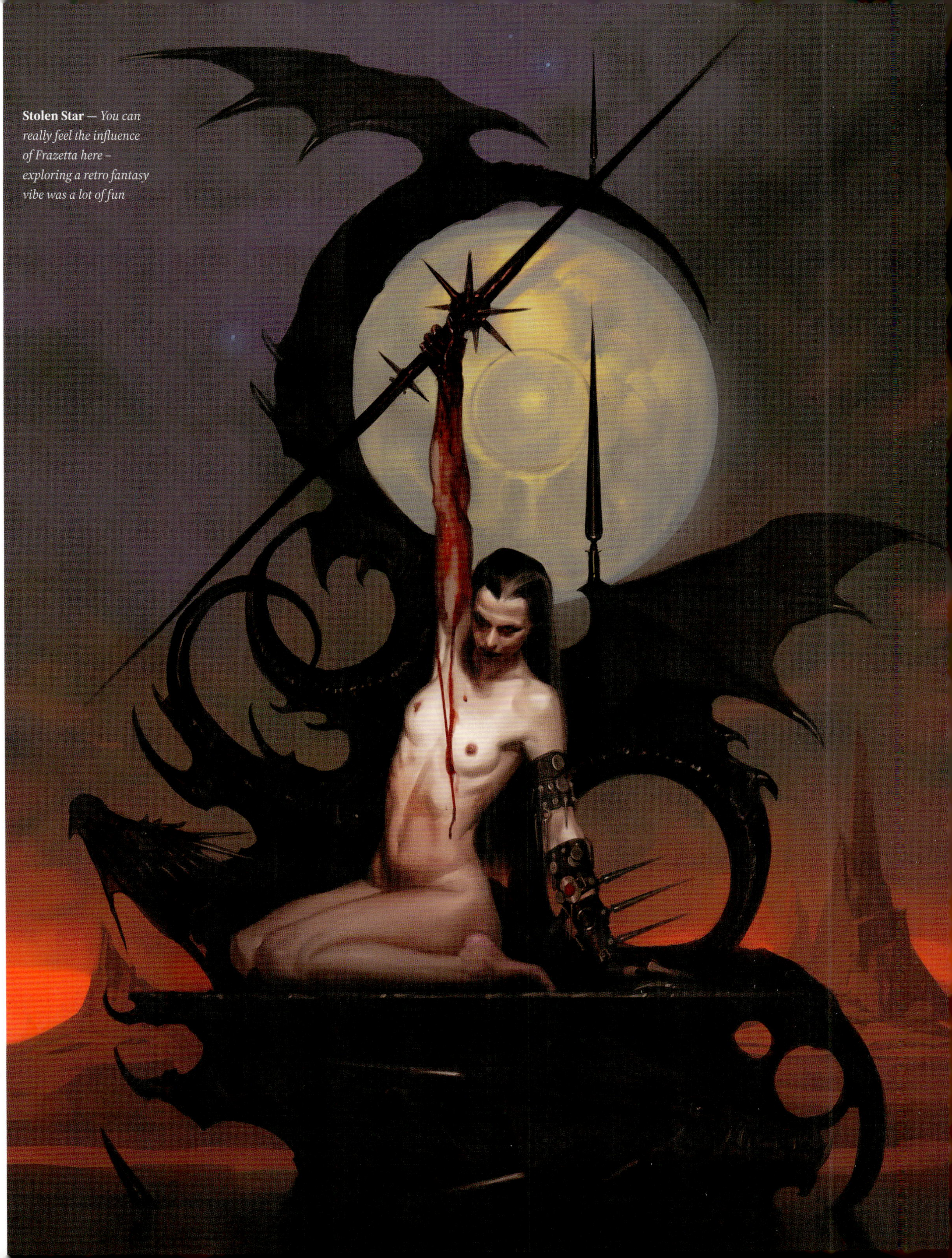

Stolen Star — *You can really feel the influence of Frazetta here – exploring a retro fantasy vibe was a lot of fun*

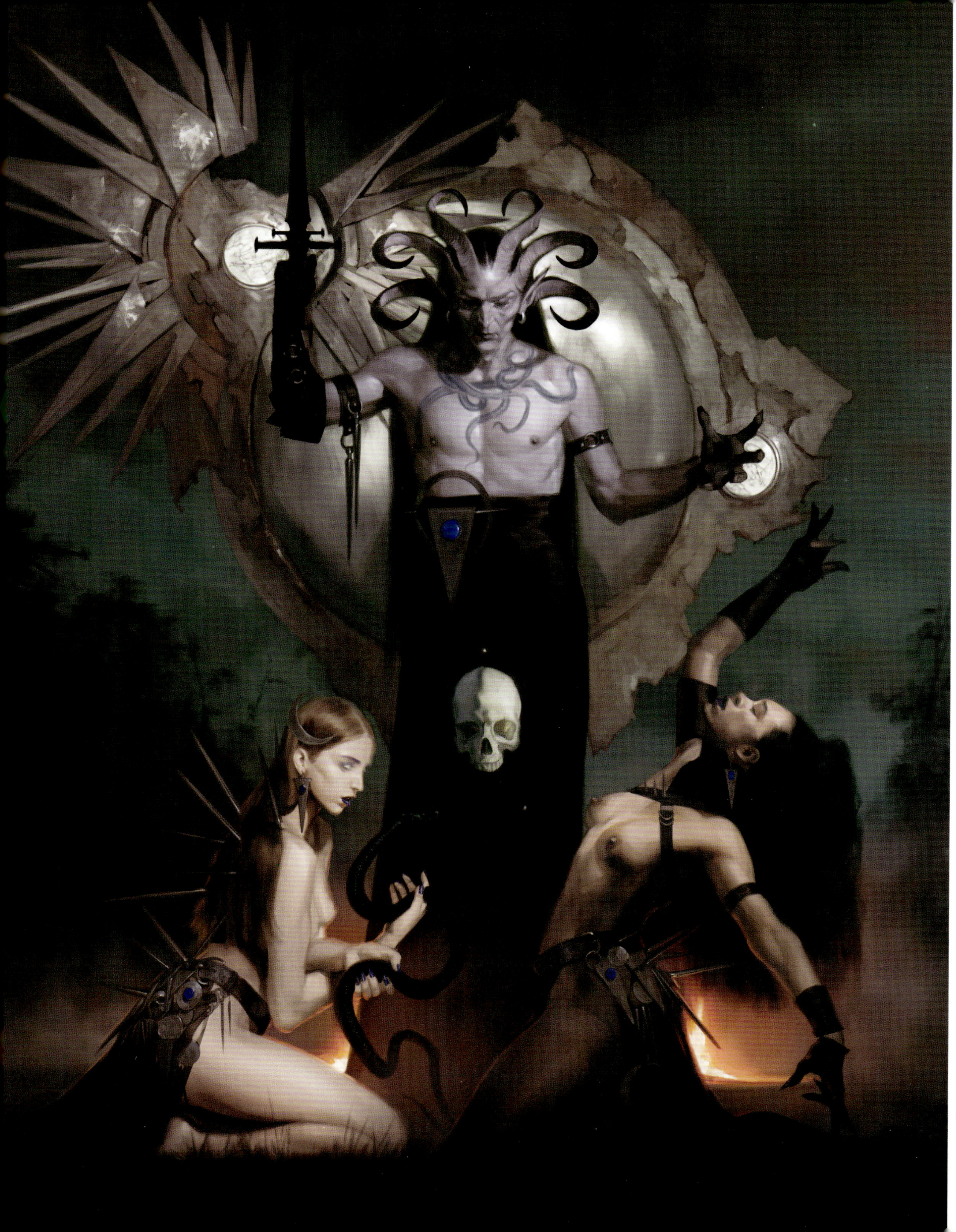

The Ritual © Jodie Muir

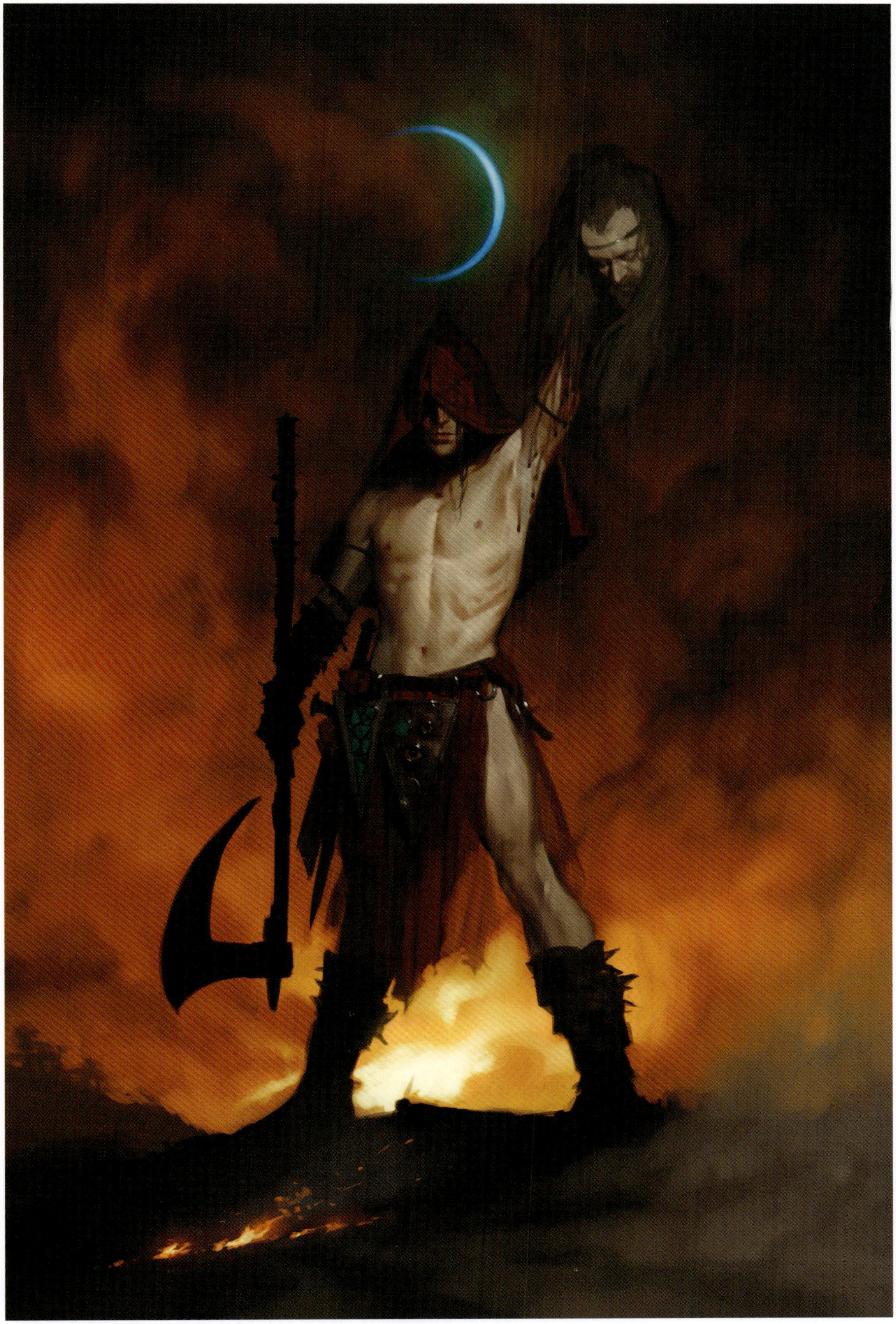

Executioner © Jodie Muir

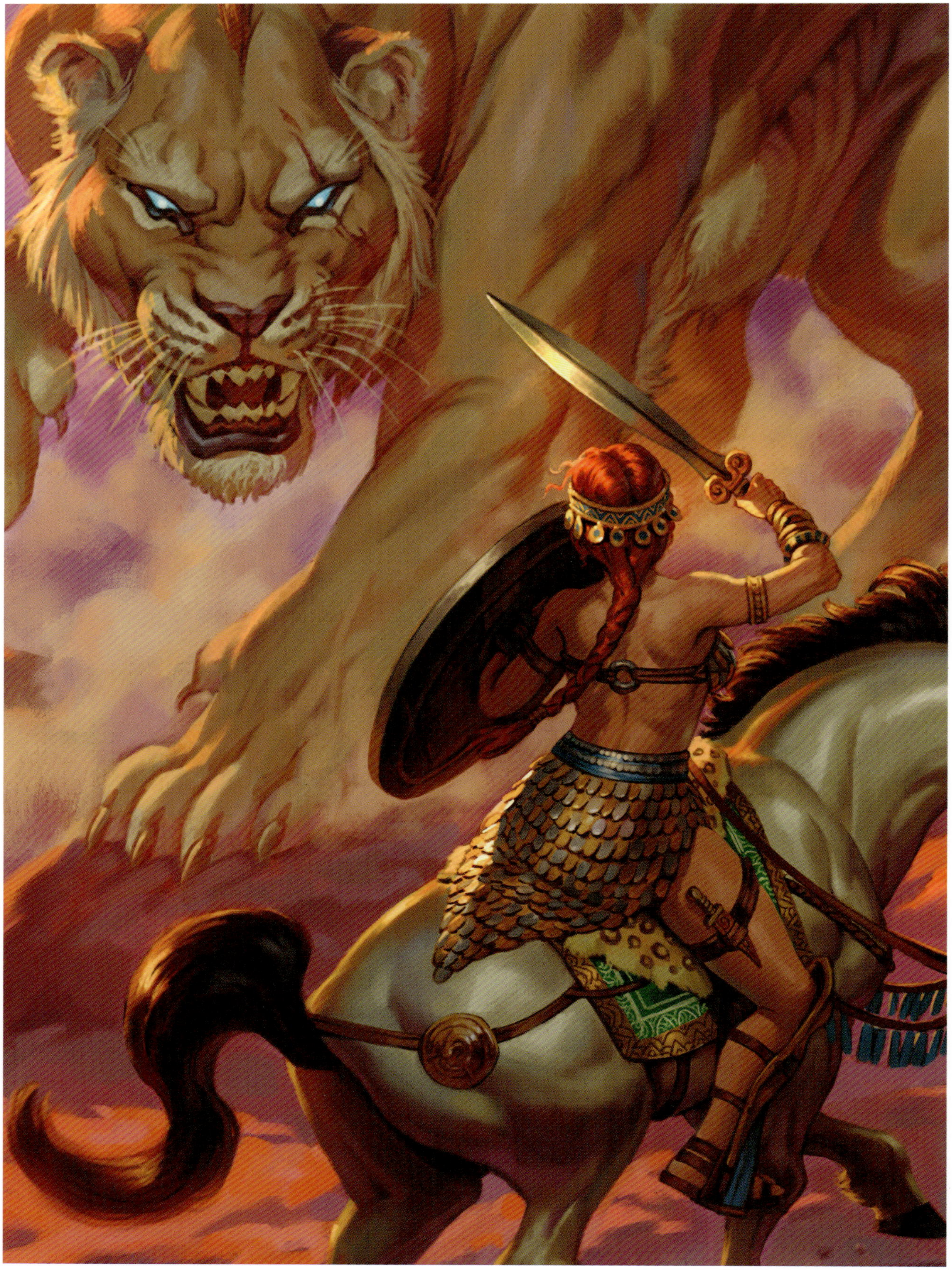

Final image © Hazem Ameen

The Manticore Fight

by Hazem Ameen

Creating *The Manticore Fight*

Frazetta's unrelenting prowess in depicting characters, whether in a dynamic pose of action or an imposing stance in worlds beyond our own, has always inspired many. But the reason he is able to convey all of this is his mastery of composition and the graphic design of the various elements within said composition. His paintings are simultaneously vividly real and an abstract exercise in designing shapes. This makes sense – the human eye is prone to all sorts of illusions and tricks as we soak in the shapes of the world around us before our brain is able to comprehend them. His mythic subject matter meets in the middle with brilliant composition and that is what I will be trying to pay tribute to here.

01 Thumbnails

I make three quick and loose thumbnail sketches to figure out what picture I will be investing my time in. 'Quick and loose' is the key here – there's no use worrying about anatomy, perspective, or the finer details of light and colour yet. What I have chosen to focus on is composition and gesture, which will be what define any piece at the end.

Options ***a*** and ***c*** are more reminiscent of Frazetta's play with shapes of light and dark, but ***b*** is action-driven, and the dynamism of his art is also something I have always admired. I will go with option ***b*** and attempt to illustrate this fierce redhead and her loyal steed taking on the savage manticore.

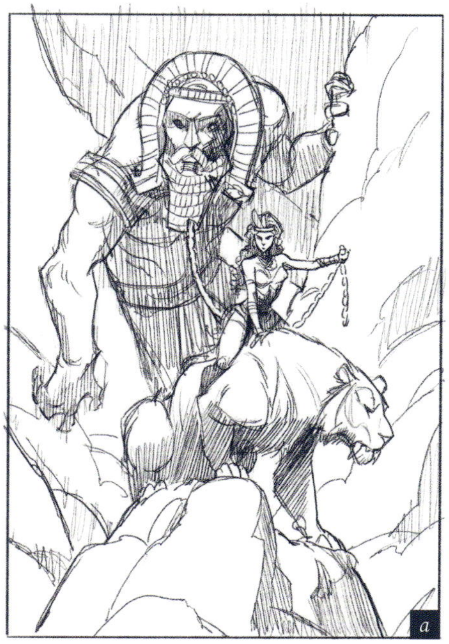

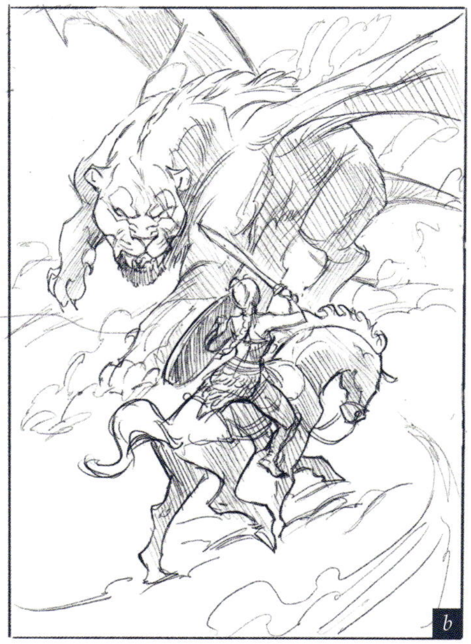

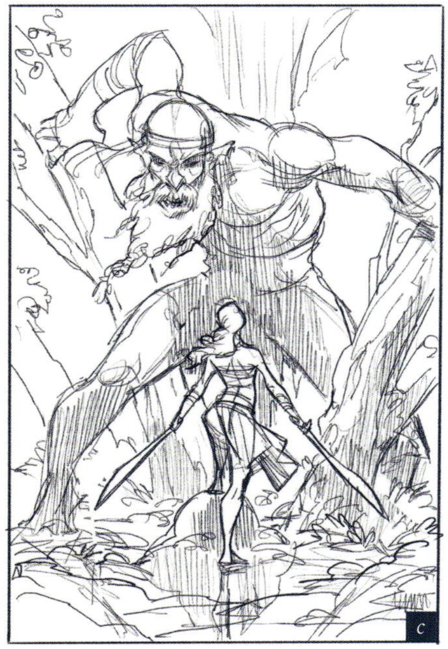

Rough thumbnail sketches of my initial ideas

02 Colour options

I am not sure where to go with the piece in the realm of colour, so I paint two very rough colour layouts on top of the thumbnail sketch. The first one seems interesting, with a chilly and spooky atmosphere, but it's not quite right for this painting. The second one emits the feeling of epic adventure, battling a beast atop a rocky outcrop in the setting sun, and that is what I will go with.

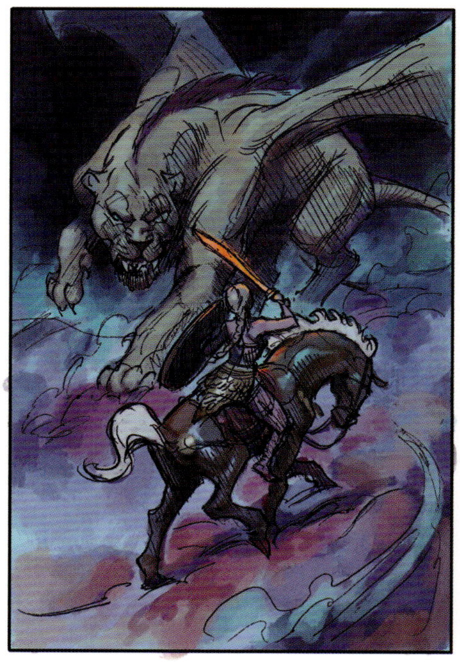

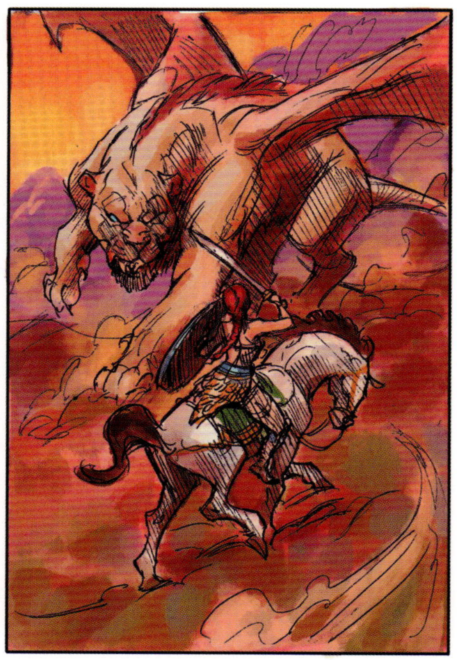

Two colour options: a nocturnal and a sunset version

03 Studies

Frazetta would boast of never using references, so his mastery could only have come from visual observation and practice. I will settle for studying and practising everything before leaping onto the canvas, like sharpening an axe before chopping a tree. Gestures, anatomy, materials – never shy away from studying what you don't know.

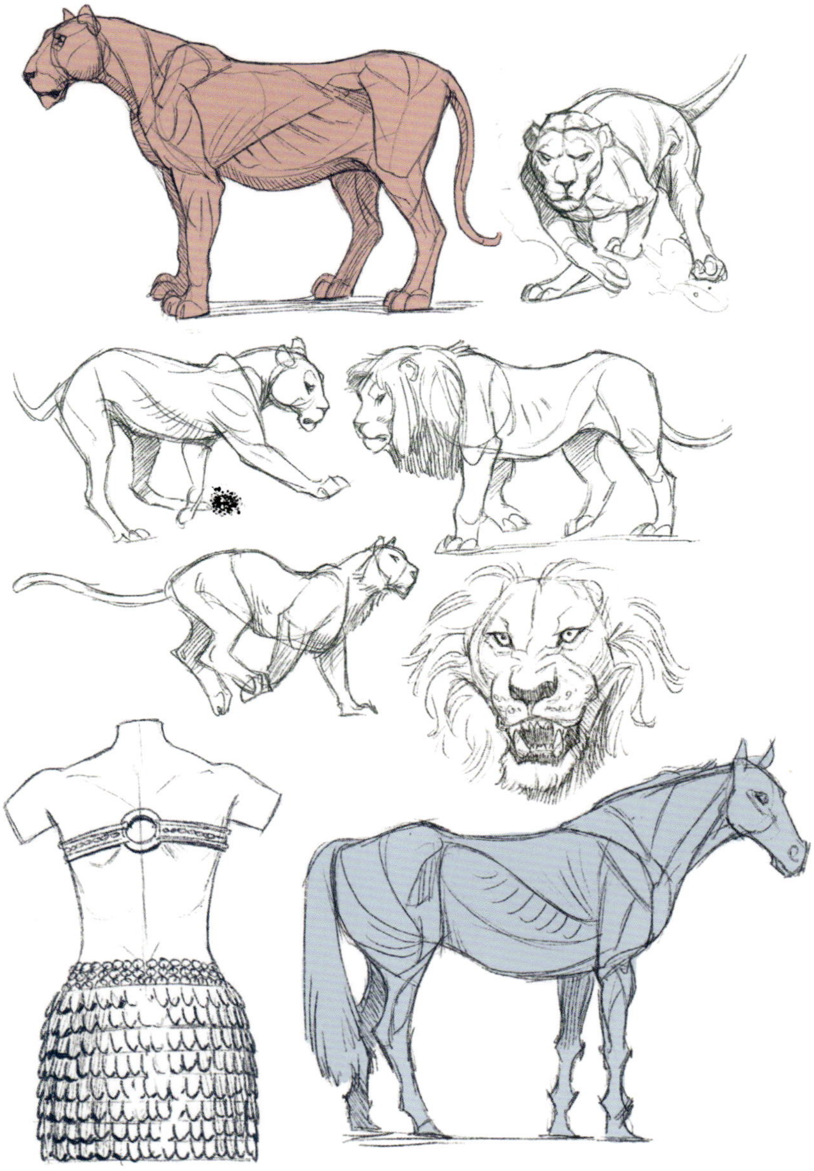

Studying elements that will help me execute the image

04 Building the structure

It's easy to get lost in the abstract nature of the colours and shapes and forget that under every Frazetta piece there is a great understanding of form. Form and structure are the bedrock of a painting and no amount of rendering can mask a poor skeleton underneath. As I approach the line art stage, I will have the underlying structures and anatomy of the subjects in mind.

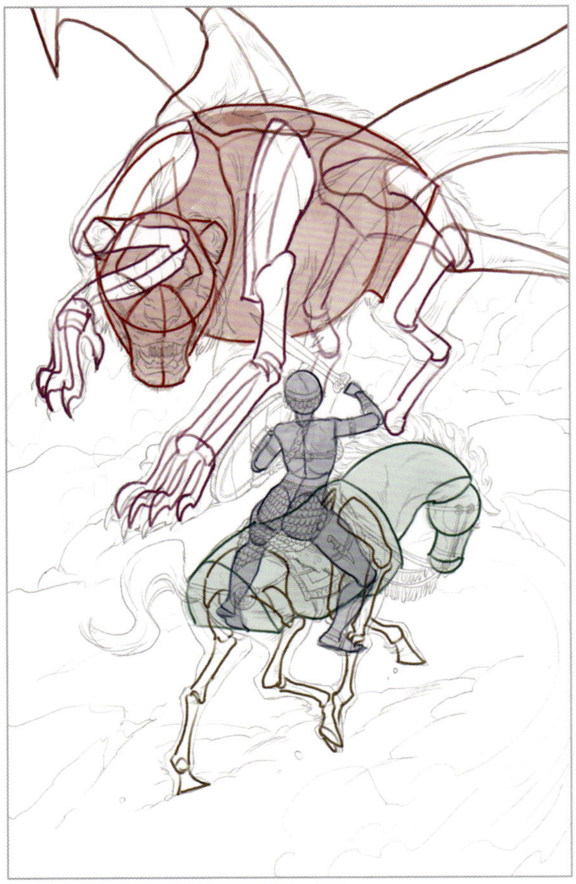

A well-structured line drawing will help make a successful painting

05 Line art

While I am proceeding with line art for this particular image, this stage of the process is very much image-specific. Some images work better with line and others with colour and form; if you are going to create a line drawing, make sure it will serve the painting to come. The line art is not the end product and must work with the process ahead, not fight with it.

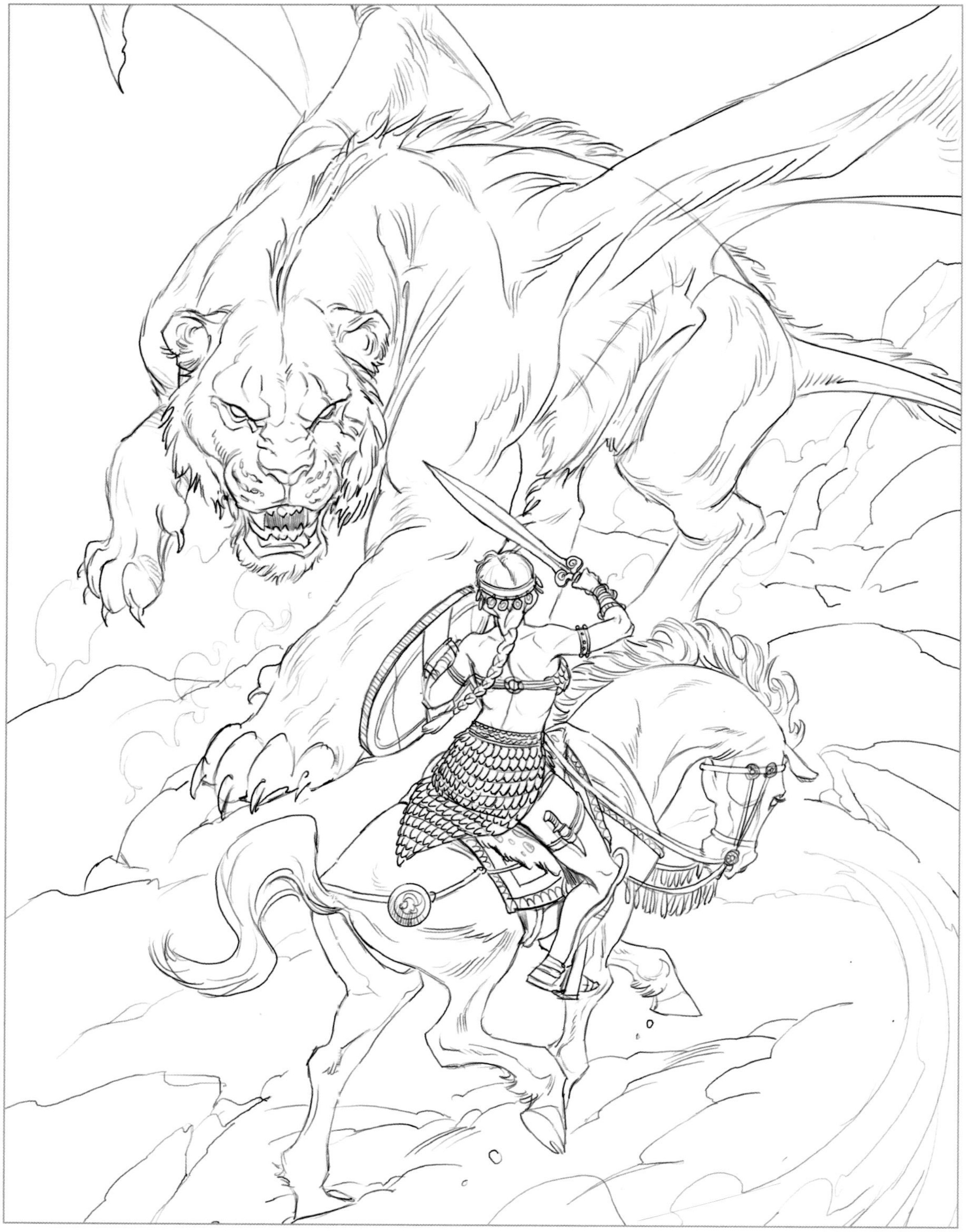

The completed line drawing that will serve as a base for painting

06 Colour flats

Next I lay down the mostly flat hues that will help me build upon the colours further. Remember, none of this is set in stone, as you will see later. Pulling, pushing, and changing a painting like a sculpture is a part of every piece; like how Frazetta's happy accidents with oil paints can help with the process, the same can be true of digital art.

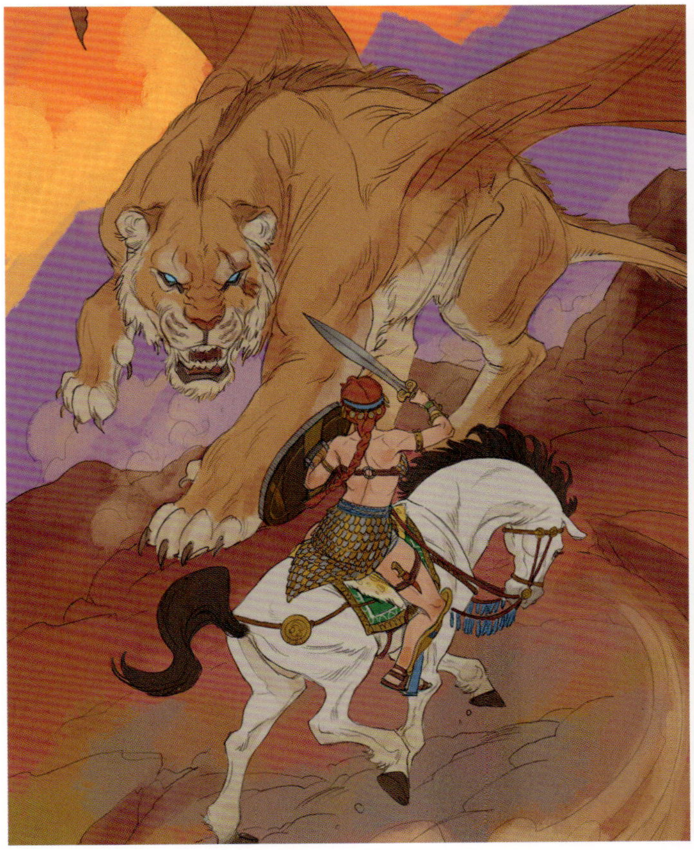

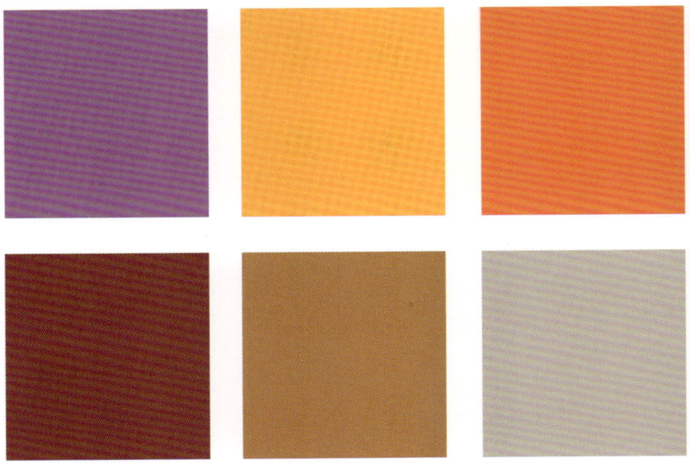

Adding the scene's base colours below the line art

Egyptian Queen © Frank Frazetta

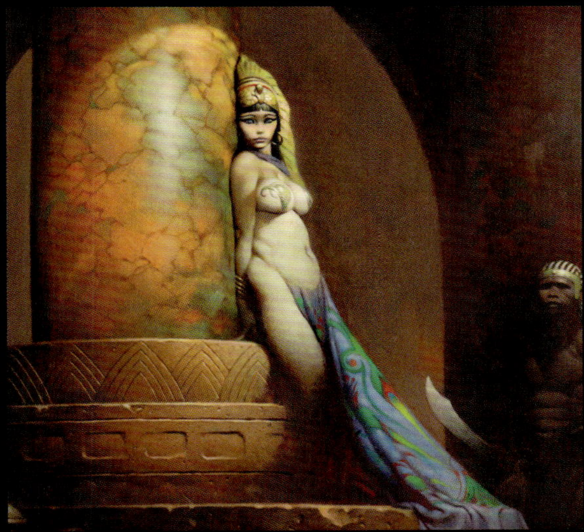

▸▸ *For image in full, turn to page 197*

Discovering Frazetta

I actually don't remember a single moment when I 'discovered' Frazetta's work, because his art always felt like it lingered behind all of fantasy art in general. It peeks through every artist that tries to delve into sword-and-sandal mythic fiction. In a way, that is a testament to the might and influence a great visionary like Frank Frazetta had on an entire field, where his stamp can be found even in places where you wouldn't expect it. His command of the graphic shapes that characterize comic-book art, and his merging of that with the world of classical painting, produced something so vibrant – ethereal yet grounded and realized – that many of us still chase after it to this very day.

It's always difficult to choose one piece from a gallery of brilliance, but if I had to, I'd settle on *Egyptian Queen*. The sensual nature of the queen as she rests on the almost tangible rendered marble, surrounded by the fierceness of the guard and the leopard, is all enveloped in a beautiful angular composition. The most important thing about any painting is how it makes you feel; Frazetta's art always manages to transport us to another world, while still imparting familiar feelings of adventure, triumph, and in this case, a mesmerizing tension.

07 Shadows

From here I add one of the many elements Frazetta played with: shadows. Not only do light and dark help accentuate the form, but they also act as a key part of the composition. The manticore, the warrior's sword, and the horse all form an 'S' shape that trails the viewer's eye through the piece.

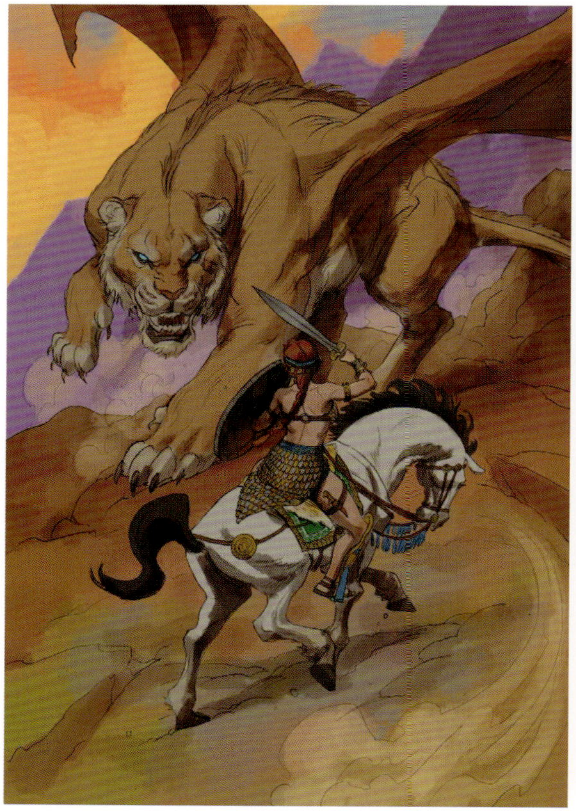

Roughly blocking out the shadow shapes

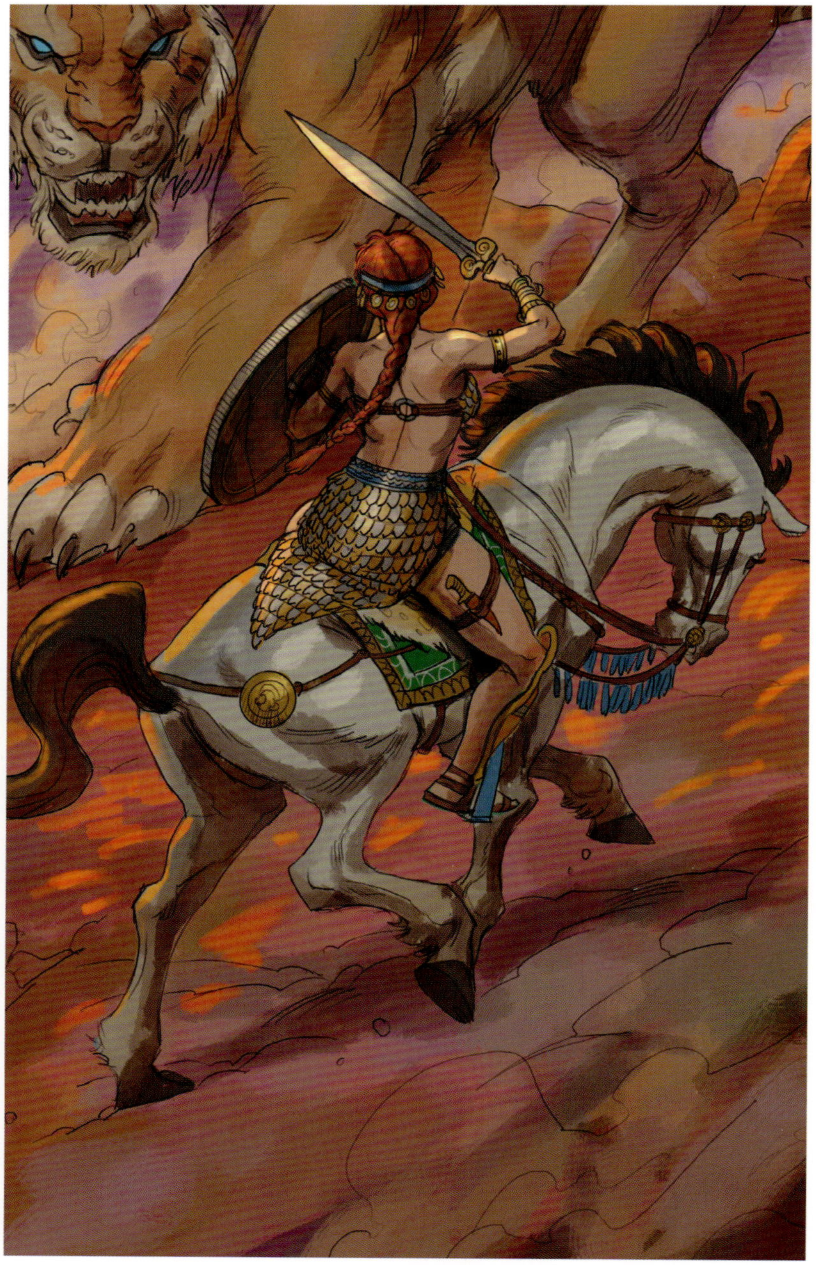

Adding more lighting and improving compositional elements

08 Lighting

The more you try to define any painting, the more the various amorphous marks you may have made earlier will need refining and explaining. Here I choose to replace the gust of wind near the horsewoman and incorporate its design into the rock itself. The mountains behind have to help the composition, not hinder it, so I adjust their shape to direct focus towards the characters. The orange rim light helps accentuate the characters and give the piece a cinematic flair.

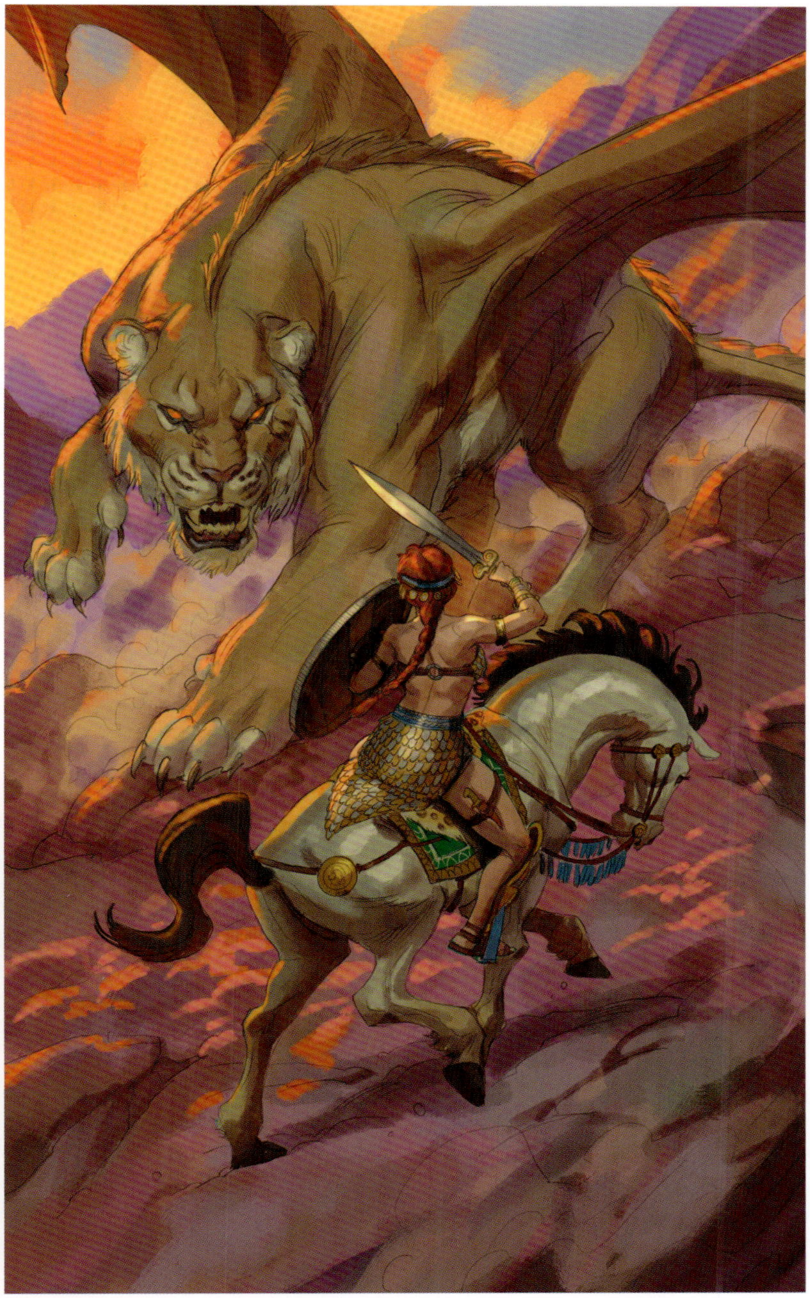

Gradually building up and refining the colours and forms

09 Rendering colour

Letting colours bleed into the objects around them, in ways they wouldn't necessarily in real life, helps give a dreamlike and fantastical nature to a painting's world. Hints of complementary colours, such as a touch of purple in the ochre under the manticore's wing, can help elevate the vibrancy of a painting.

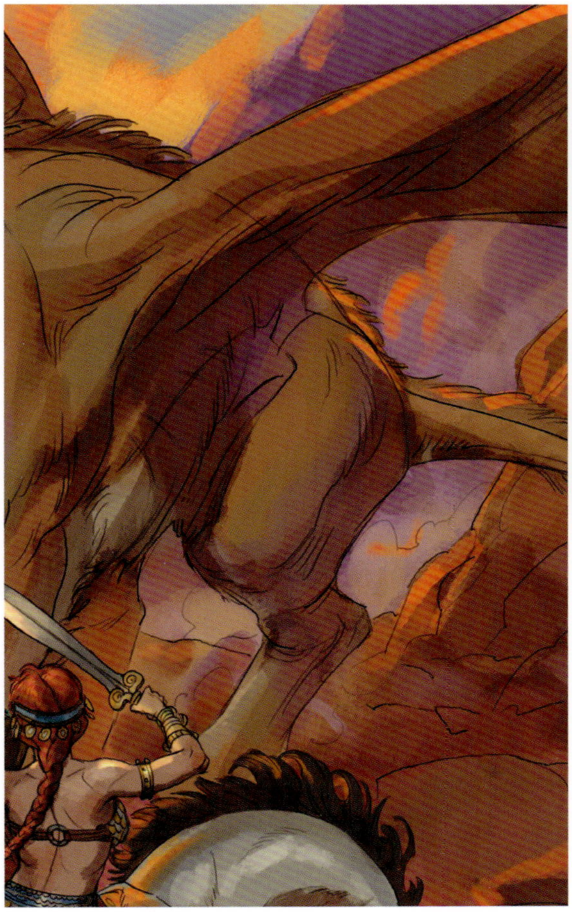

A heightened sense of colour and light can create a fantasy mood

10 First render pass

In my first stage of rendering, I add some variation of hue and gradually mould the image with further brushstrokes. I reduce the opacity of the line art, as I want the final piece to grow independent of it, like a butterfly leaving behind its cocoon. I consider changing the manticore's eyes to a golden glow, to be more in line with the warm sunset hues of the rest of the piece, but I'm not fully decided on it.

11 The manticore's head

Before I can be free of the line art, I will use it to its fullest potential. All of the marks I made earlier, detailing the manticore's lion head, help me flesh out the form with light, ambient shadows, and darker shadows. As I'm rendering, I realize that blue eyes create a stronger contrast, which I think is important.

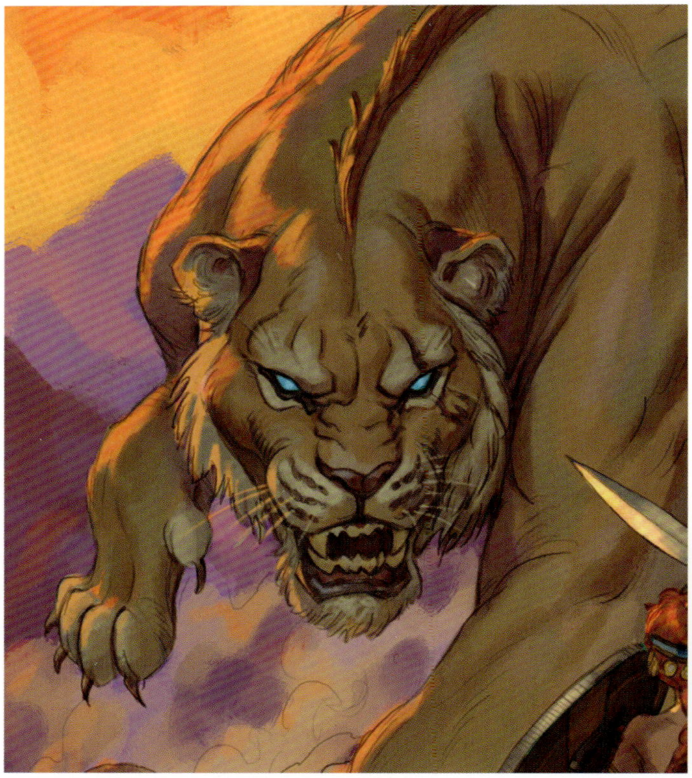

Using the line art as a guide to deepen the manticore's lighting and detail

12 Going lineless

For me, one of the benefits of this line-drawing method is the ability to maintain the dynamism of the characters' forms. This can be done with shapes and hues, of course, but trying your best to not let your figures stiffen is a key part of rendering. As I conceal the line art, I aim to keep the same level of fluidity and energy in the figures' anatomy and gestures.

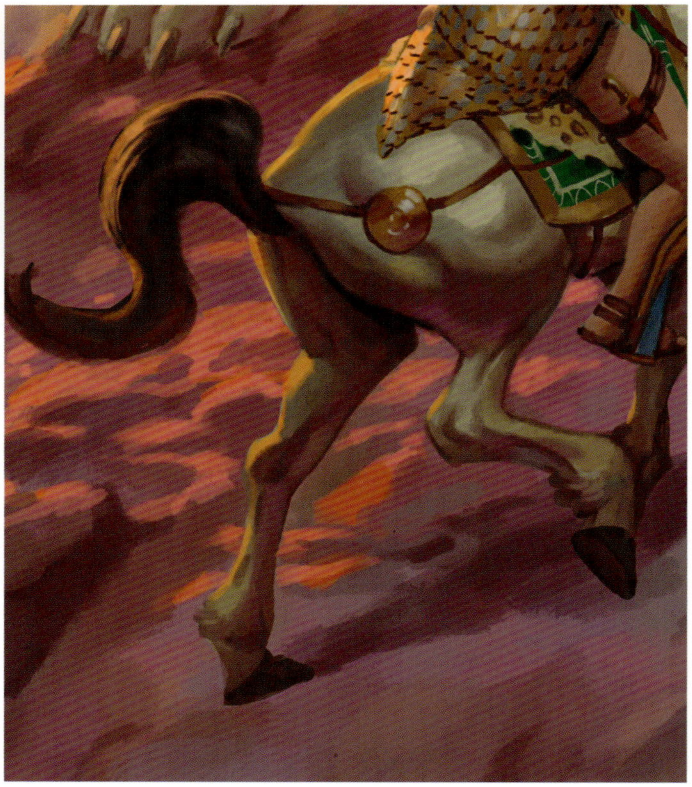

Gradually painting over the line art

13 Before refinement

Free of their line art, my heroine and beast may finally battle it out! All the final pieces of the painting are already there – they just need to be finely hammered out. These final stages of rendering are usually what take up most of the time in pieces like this, but the results will be worth it.

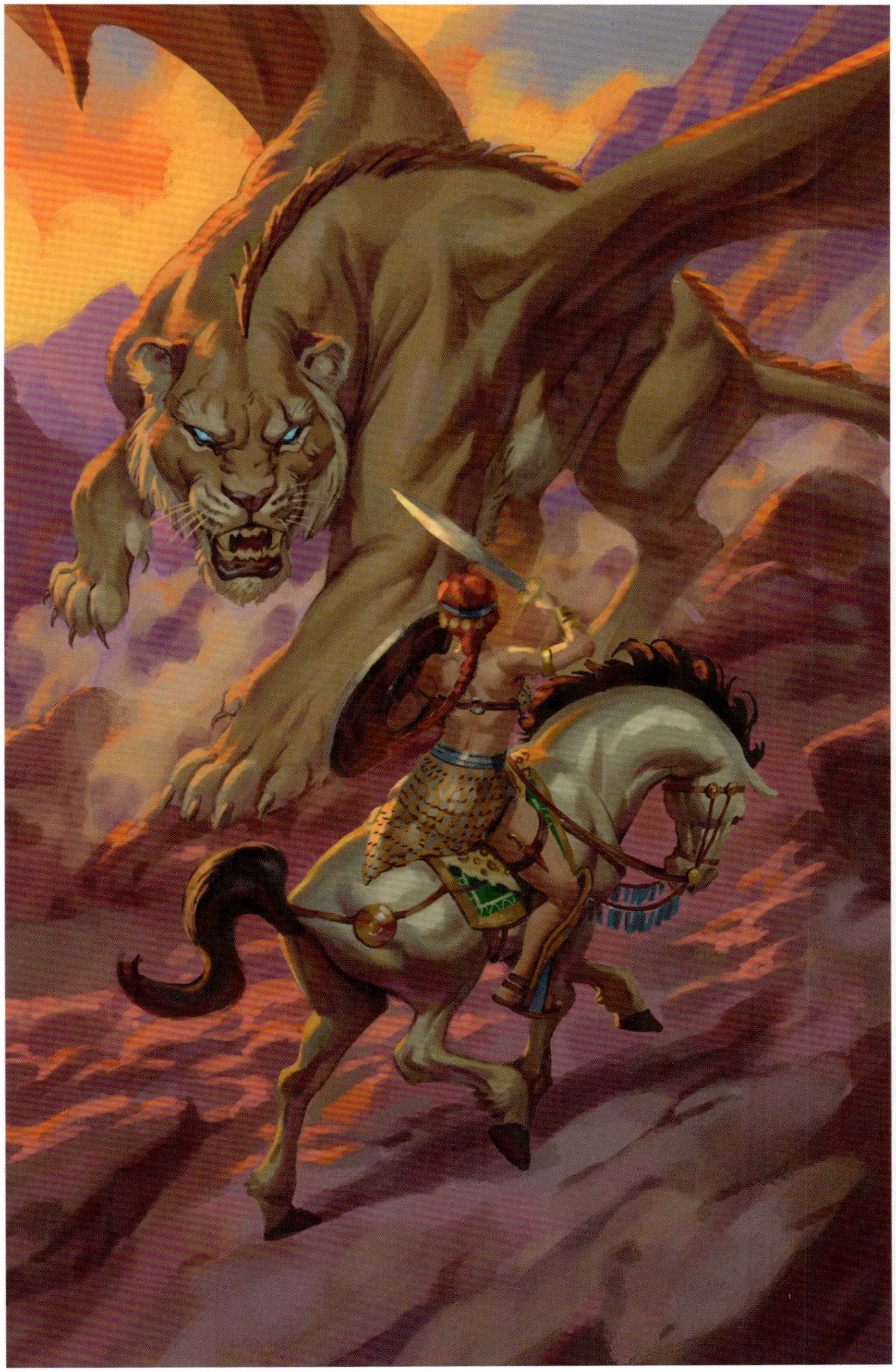

The painting is almost fully rendered, ready for the final polish

14 Rendering materials

Rendering different materials often comes down to simplifying the visual information rather than aping it. Varying the levels of detail is also crucial; our eyes tend to focus on one thing a time, and the parts of the image that aren't as important should not be as detailed as the parts that are. This is how you signal to the viewer where to look, and is a quality you will notice in so many of Frazetta's works.

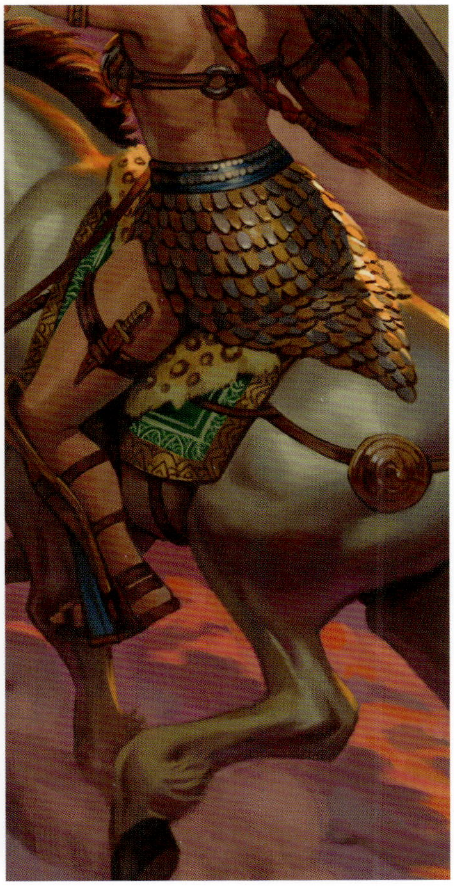

Refining materials, keeping focal points in mind

15 Final polish

I darken the foreground and warrior with her horse to give them a stronger shadow in the sunlight, and push the manticore back in values with reflected orange light, adding to the distance and dusty atmosphere. With some final flourishes, playing with the colours and level of detail, *The Manticore Fight* is finished. The result is a picture that, I hope, alludes to the daring spirit of sword-and-sorcery that Frazetta exuded so effortlessly in all of his paintings.

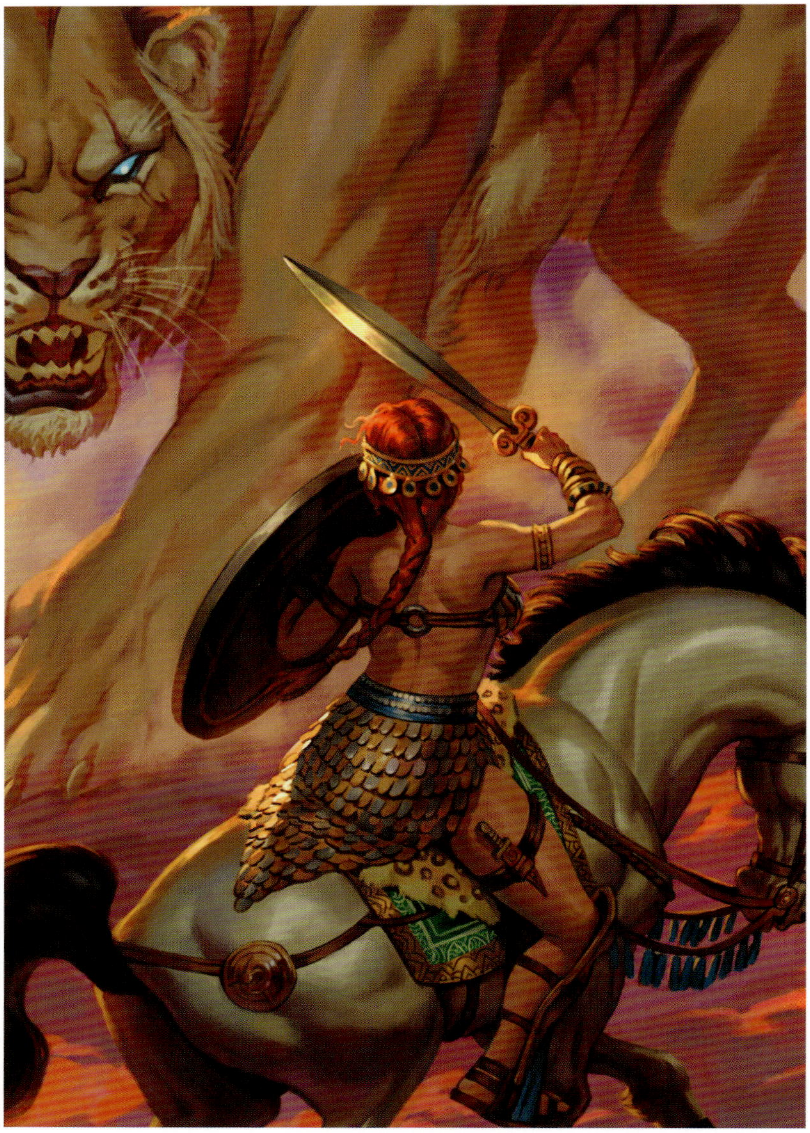

Making final refinements and tweaks to colour and value

Conclusion

My final piece achieves what I set out to do, though it's tempting to keep tweaking and revising it. Not being fully satisfied with your own work and wanting to push it further is a sentiment I'm sure the master himself could relate to – a man who never tired of adding to his paintings years after they were 'finished'! I hope anyone who reads this feels inspired to take hold of what they find fascinating about Frazetta's art and try to incorporate it into their own process. His work may already live on through the annals of fantasy art, but taking the time to scrutinize his art yourself may yield unique fruits that you didn't expect.

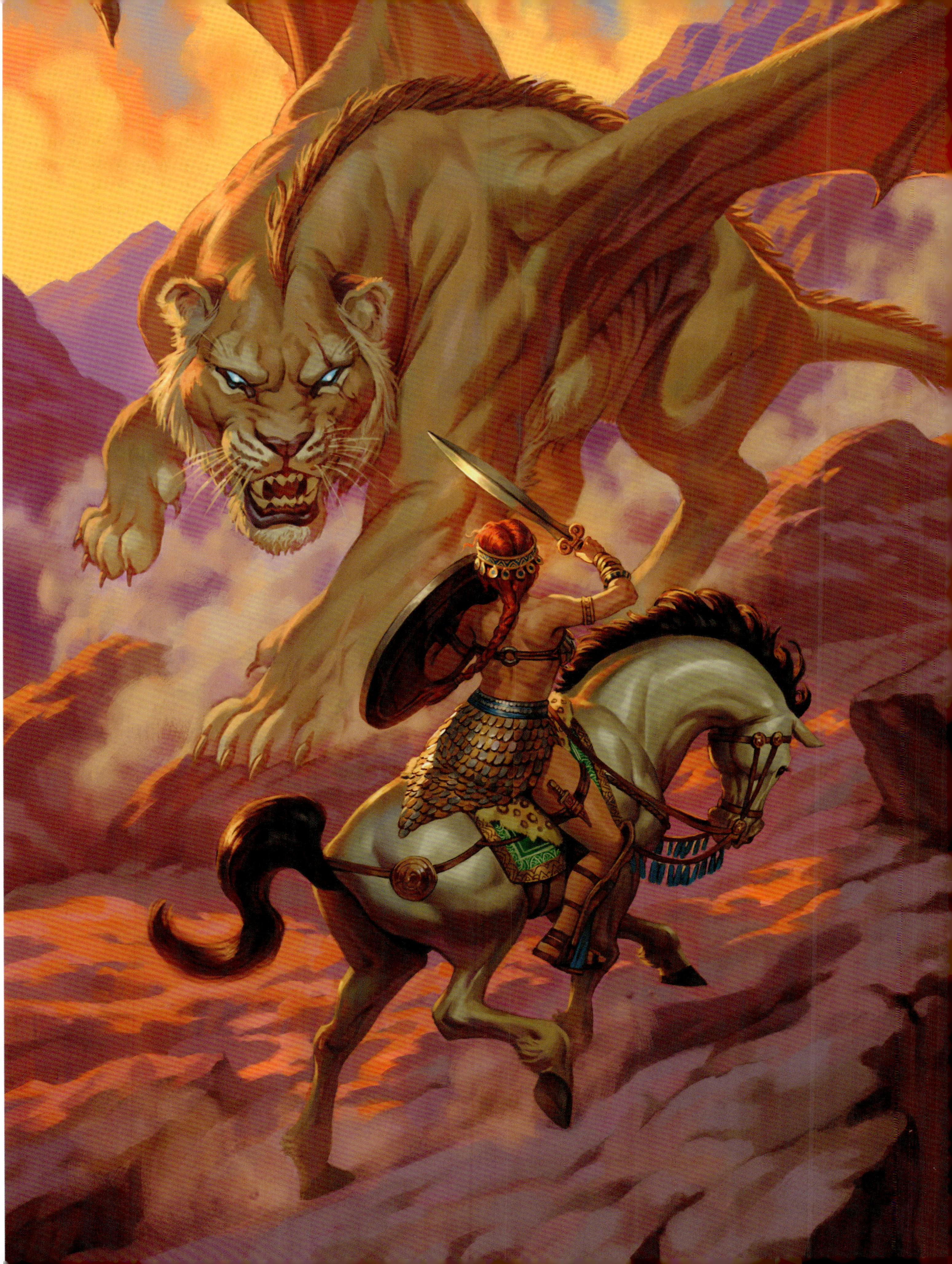

Final image © Hazem Ameen

Gallery

by Hazem Ameen

Apedemak © Hazem Ameen

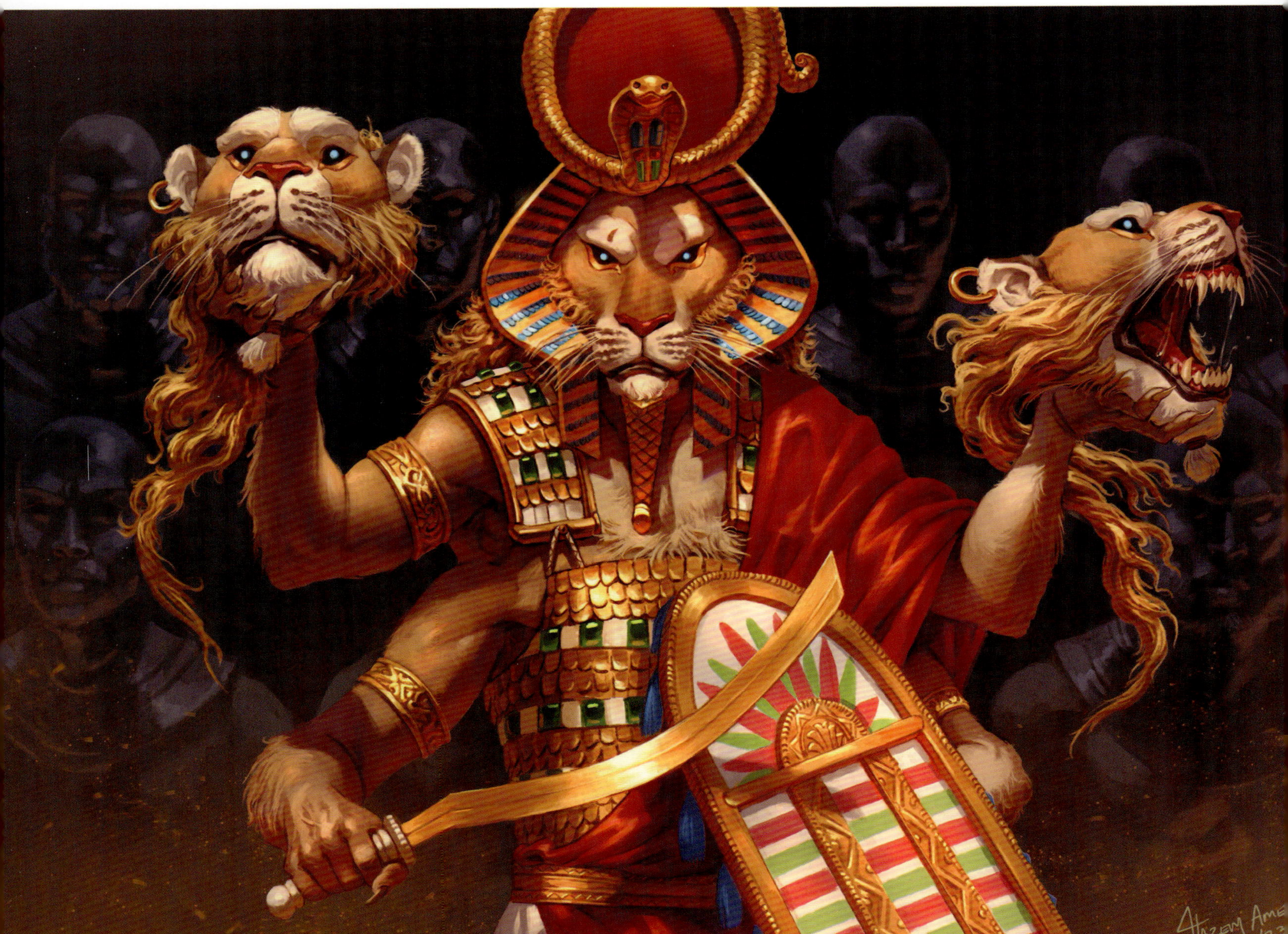

Apedemak — *The Nubian war-god Apedemak is said to have three heads, each counselling their own strategies and ferocity in battle. His devotees stand firm behind him, ready to fight when their god says the word; the background of standing men also serves as a cool contrast to the very warm-hued character.*

Al Manat — *Al Manat, the Arabian goddess of fate, sits with her pride in a secluded cave. She writes the fates of kings and beggars alike with blood as her pets feel cared for around her. The two light sources play an important role here, the skewed sunlight entering the cave and the cooler light from above glazing the statues and figures, providing a sharp contrast.*

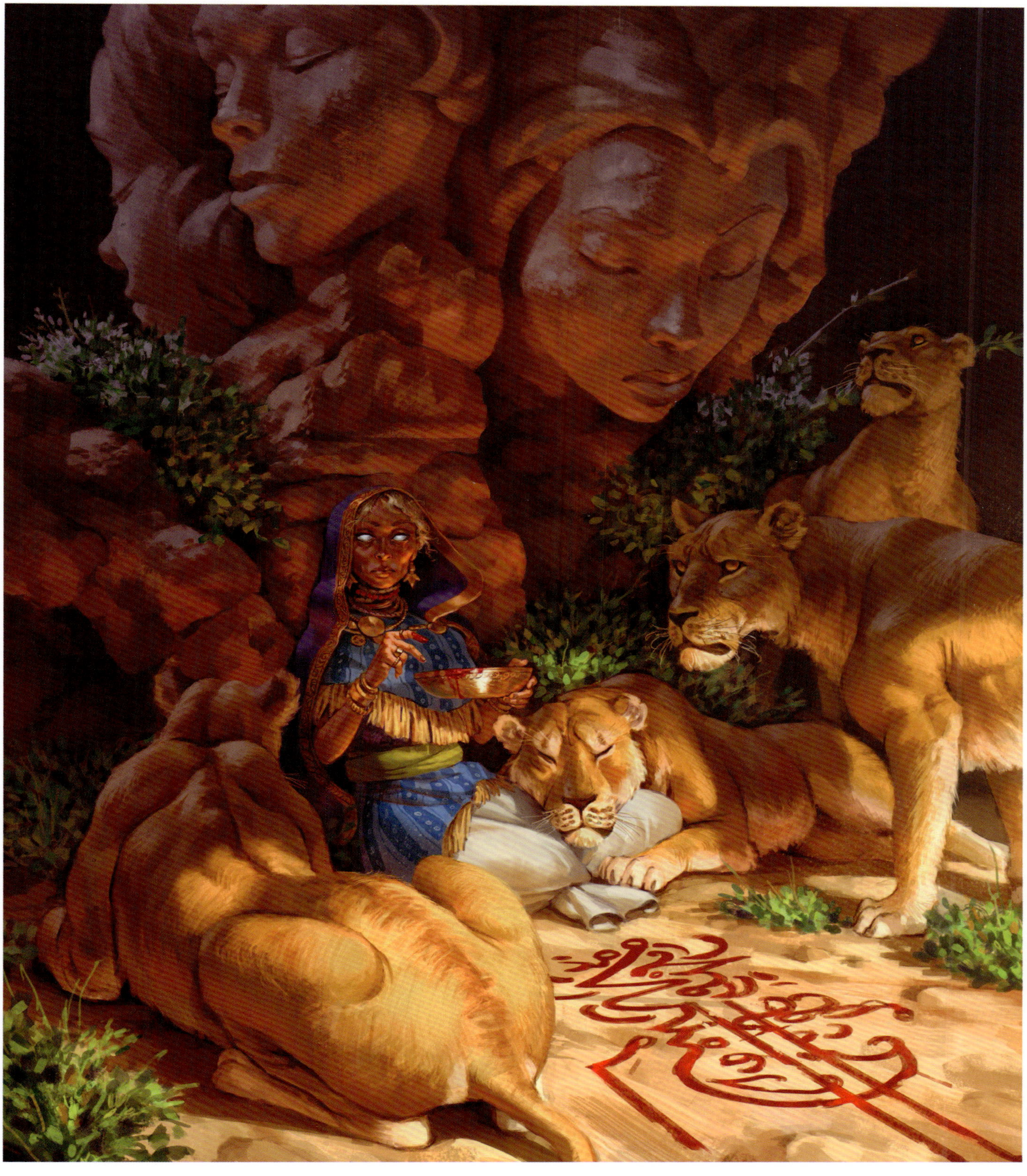

Al Manat © Hazem Ameen

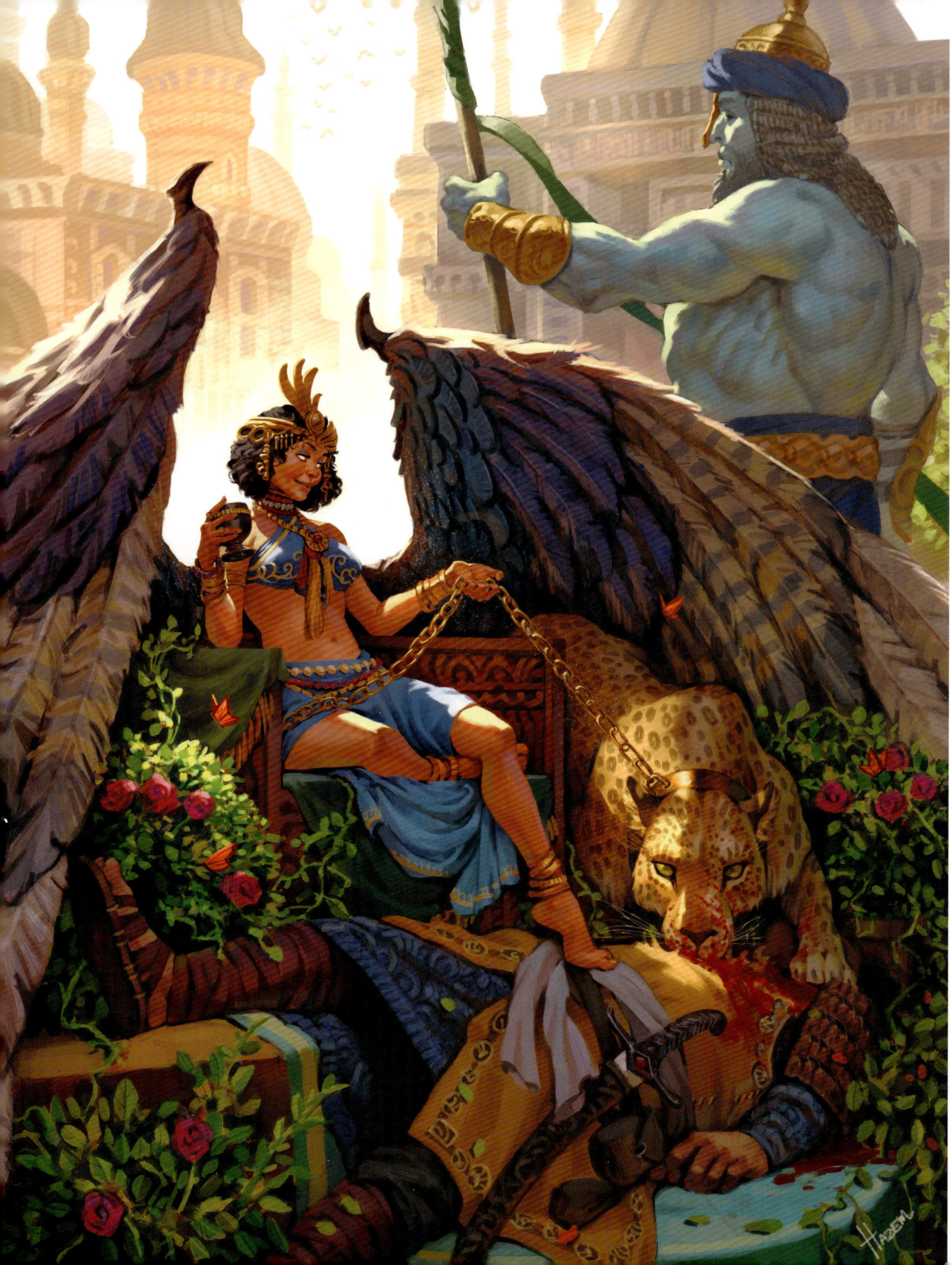

Al Uzza © Hazem Ameen

Al Laat © Hazem Ameen

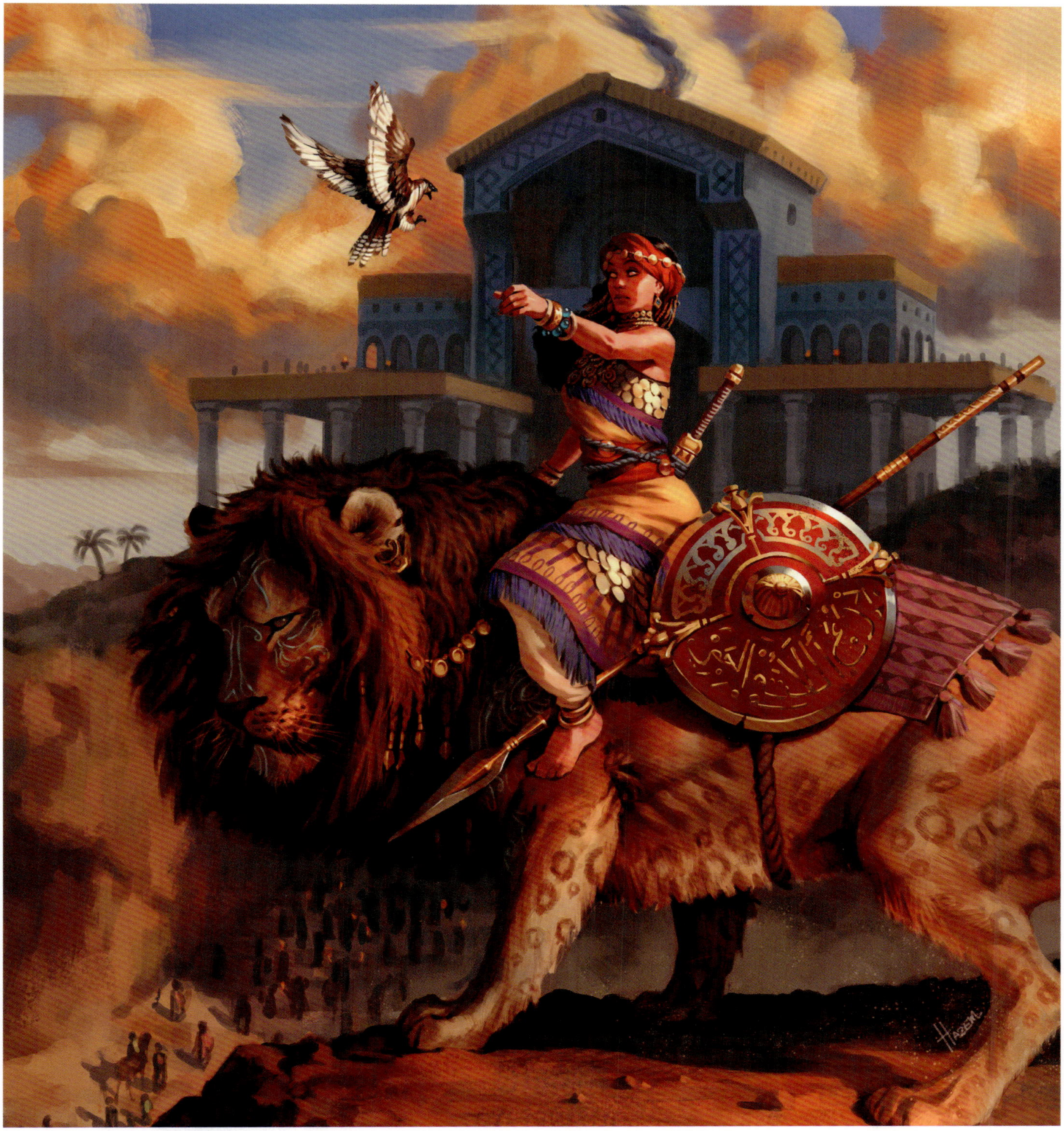

Al Uzza — *The Arabian goddess of love and war, Al Uzza, sits on her winged throne, as her leopard devours an unruly and disrespectful mortal. The guardian behind her looms large with his spear in the heavenly city. The triangular composition helps frame the focus on the piece; the way the back light illuminates the leopard and figure is a key part of the piece.*

Al Laat — *The Arabian goddess of wisdom and strategy, Al Laat, stands vigilant atop a red rock, overseeing the pilgrims making their way to her temple. The cool hue of the temple lets the warm figure stand out; the angular composition from the smoke rising above to the position of the spear informs the viewer where to rest their eye.*

In Conversation With:

Fernanda Suarez

Hello, Fernanda. Can you tell us a bit about yourself and your career in art?

Fernanda: I am an artist from Chile and I have been painting and drawing for as long as I can remember. Art has always been my biggest passion. I studied Fine Arts at university, but when I was about to finish my degree, I discovered digital art and never looked back. Throughout my career I have worked on various projects such as board games, illustrations, book covers, classes, and private commissions. At the moment, my focus is on character design, book covers, and personal projects.

When and how did you first discover Frazetta's artwork? What did you think of it?

I discovered his work around the time I was in university. I came across one of his pieces online and it left such an impression on me – I thought his work was captivating. I admire the way he worked with composition and made his images so dynamic. His use of colour was wonderful, especially the way he mixed warm and cool tones so gracefully. When I think of Frazetta, I think of fantastic scenarios with lots of movement, with a powerful presence of human anatomy and a feeling of adventure.

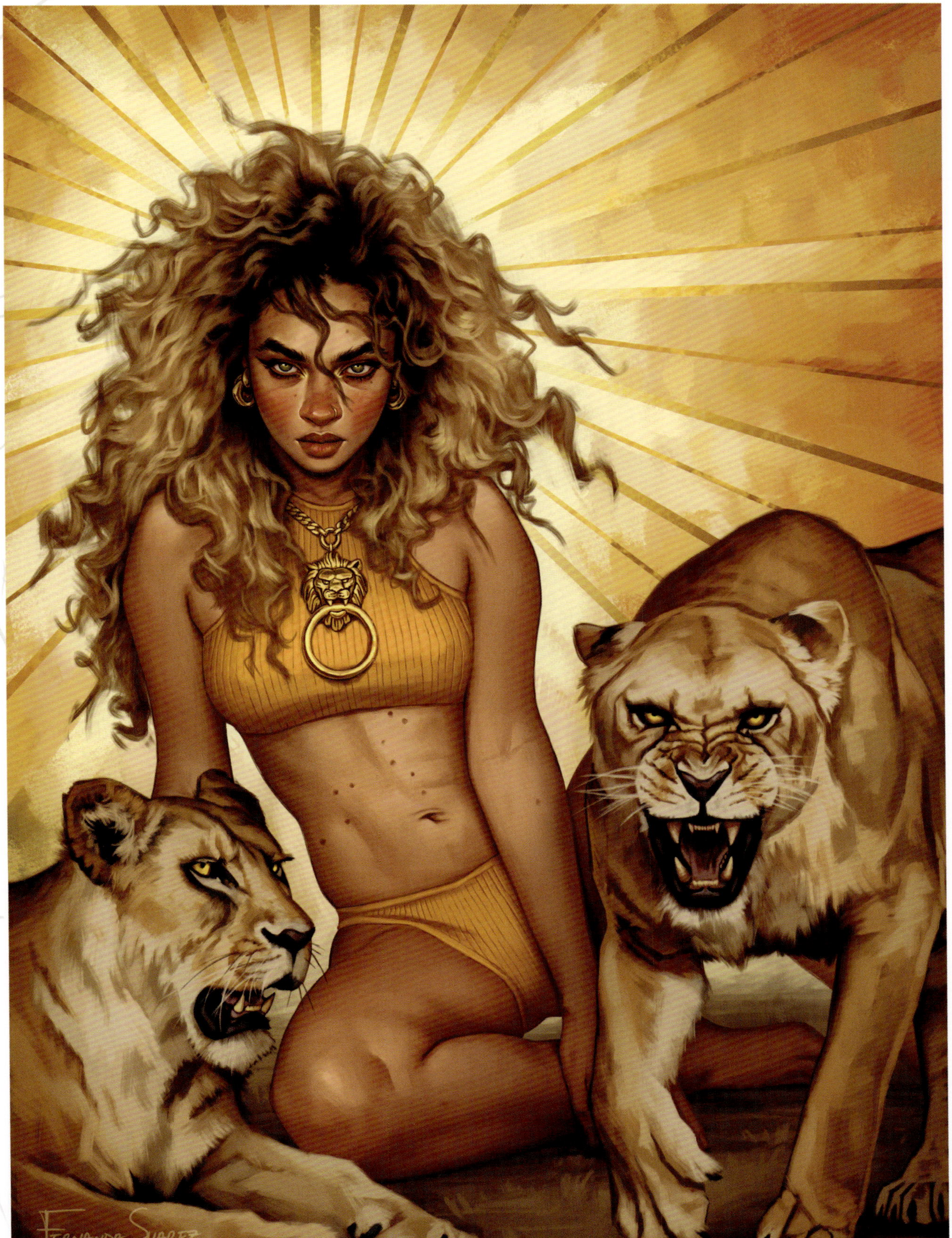

Leo © Fernando Suarez

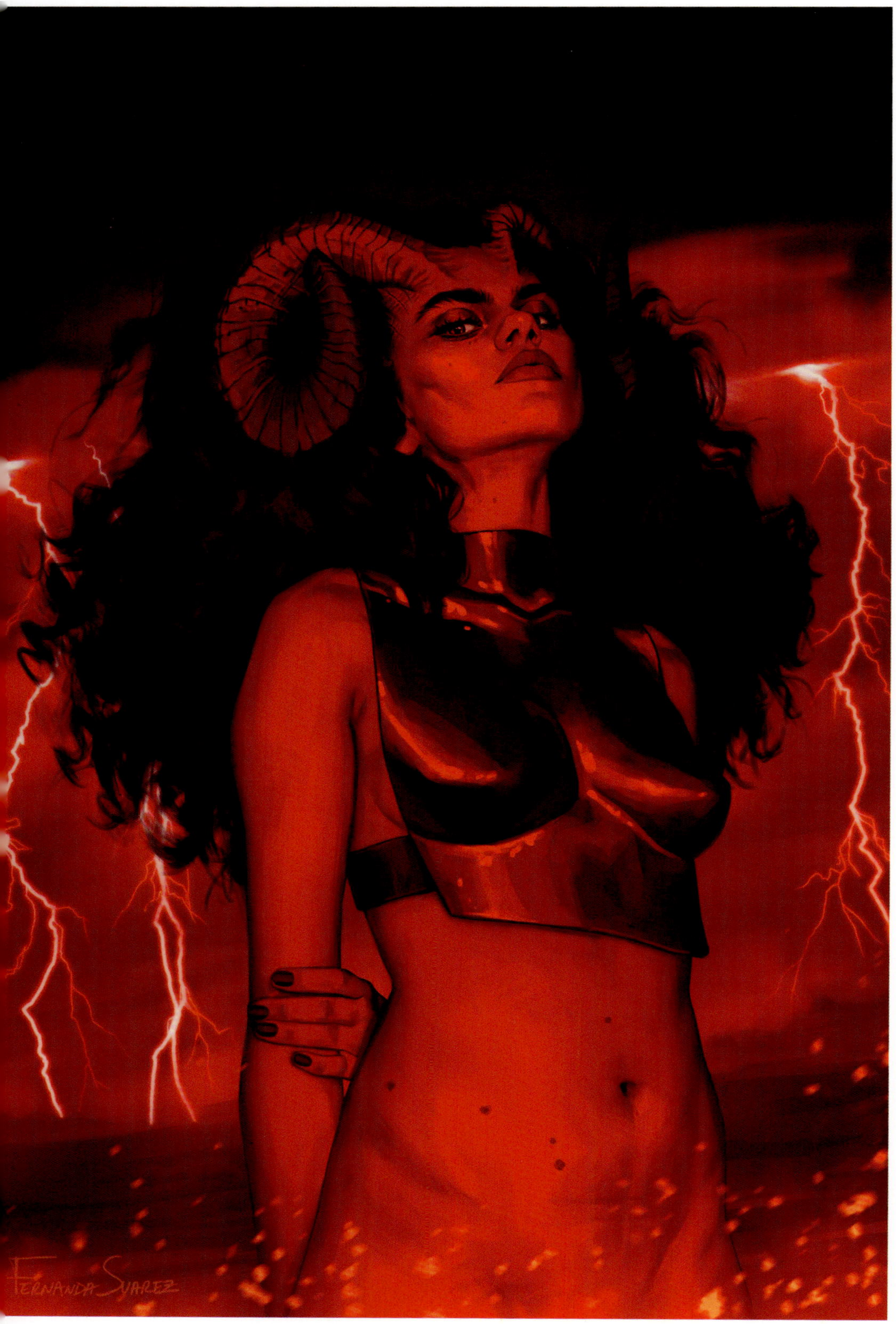

Aries © Fernanda Suarez

Who are your favourite artists, and how does Frazetta fit among your influences?

I think my taste in art has been heavily influenced by traditional art, since that is my background. One of the artists that has inspired me is John Singer Sargent. He is just a master of his craft; the way he captured people in his portraits is truly wonderful. I always look at his work for colour and value guidance. Another inspiration is João Ruas. His work is so captivating and I love its dark themes; I admire the way he can create such a cohesive body of work. I never forget one of his pieces after looking at it.

Frazetta has definitely been a source of inspiration and guidance for my own art journey. One thing that I try to take from his work, when I look at it, is to remind myself to work on things for which I truly feel passion, and to not restrict myself to only 'realistic' scenarios. Sometimes I have an idea and instantly tell myself that it wouldn't work, but looking at his art reminds me to have freedom in my creativity and in the subjects I can imagine and paint. He also inspires me to try to tell stories with my painting – something he did so masterfully.

Do you have a favourite Frazetta piece?

One of my favourites of his pieces is *Red Planet*. I feel captivated looking at it. The imagery he gives us forms a million different stories in my mind. The painting has an eerie, haunting quality that I love. The ominous red planet and the characters' anatomy make for a perfect piece for me. Another of my all-time favourites is *Egyptian Queen* – I love the mood and atmosphere of the scene; how the use of dynamic lighting spotlights the column and then lets you wander around the piece, discovering the rest of it. It leaves you intrigued and wondering what's about to happen next.

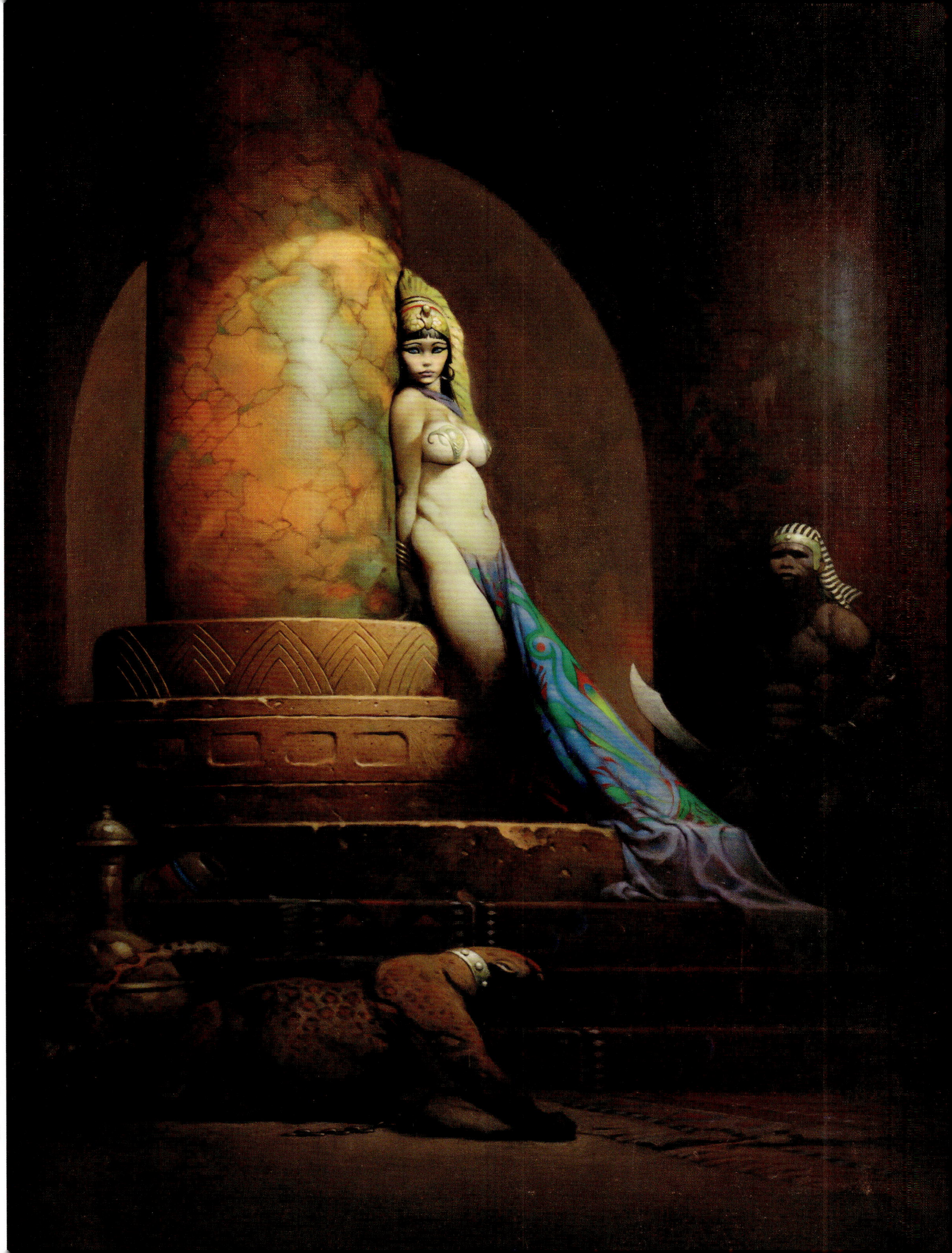

Egyptian Queen © Frank Frazetta

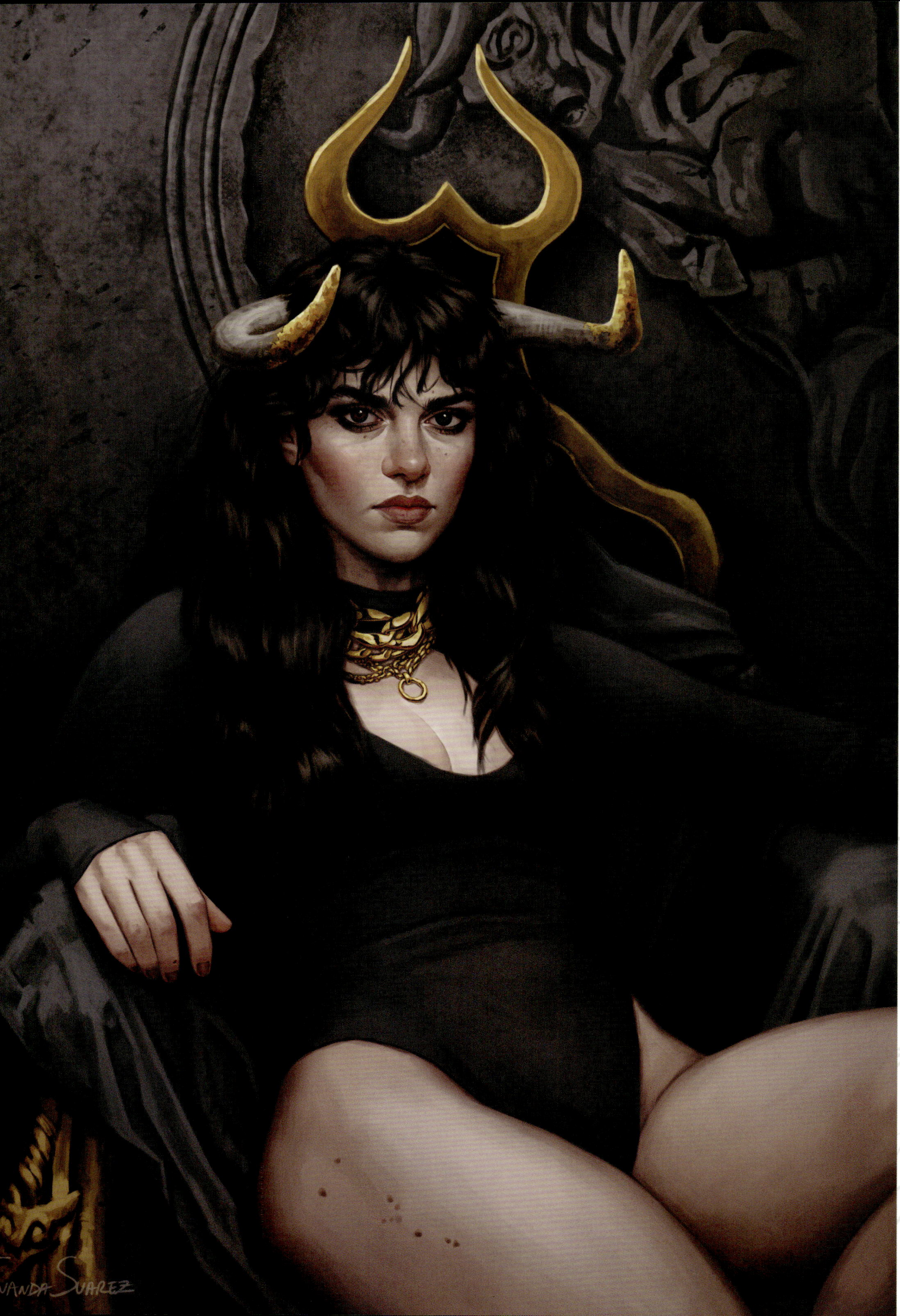

Taurus © Fernanda Suarez

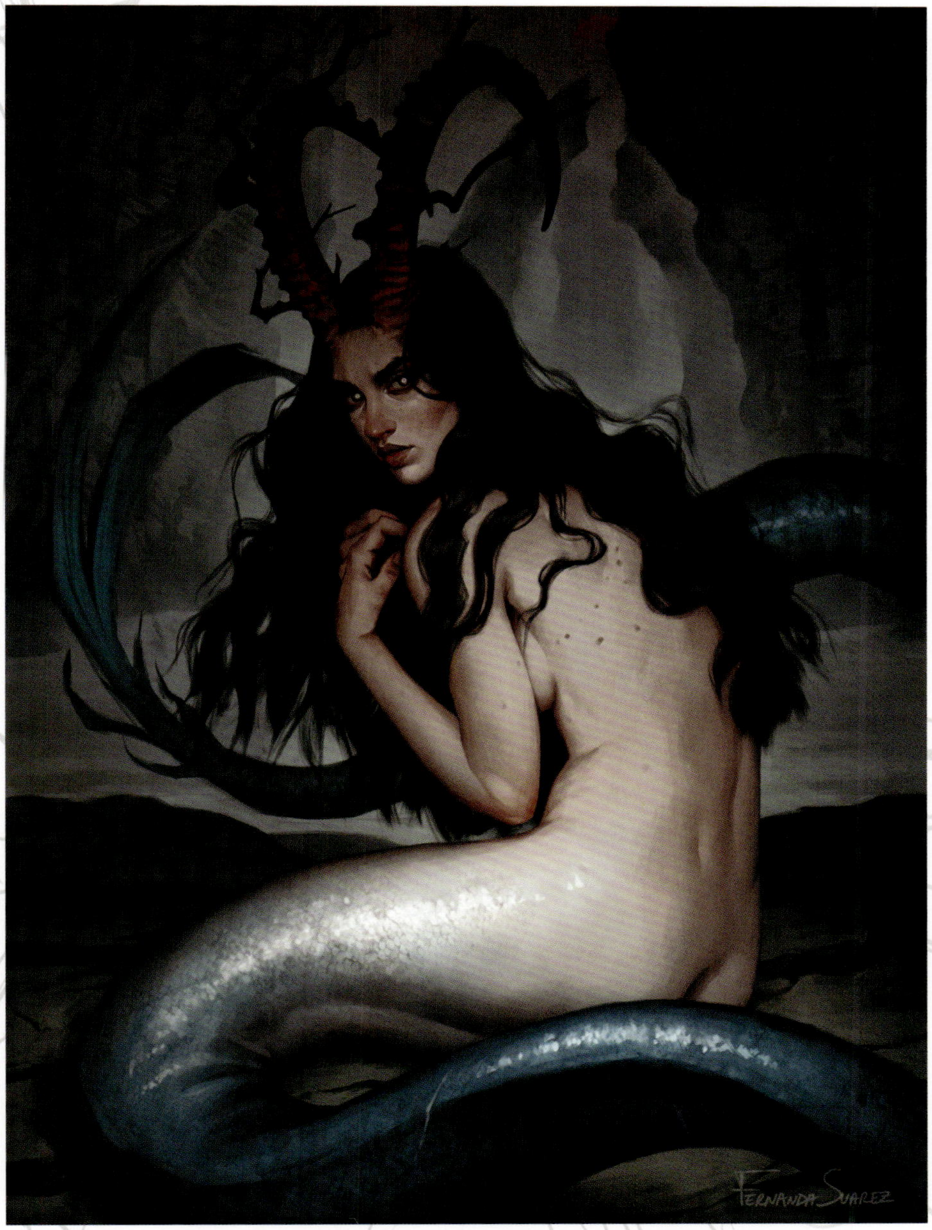

Capricorn © Fernanda Suarez

Could you tell us more about a project where you've consciously drawn on Frazetta as an inspiration?

He was one of the inspirations for my *Zodiac* series, from which you can see some examples here. The series depicts each Zodiac sign as they would appear as beings in the modern world, showcasing each sign's strength and weakness. I really wanted to bring that 'fantastic' feeling, combining fantasy and reality, using bright vivid colours, and showing strong female characters with a powerful presence – all things that I admire in Frazetta's work.

Where do you see his legacy when you look around at fantasy art today?

Frazetta has been a true influence in the world of science-fiction and fantasy art – I don't think anyone who is interested in those themes has not been affected by him somehow. The way he told fantastic stories through his paintings, gave us captivating characters and narratives, and blended different genres to create something new and exciting... I don't think pop culture would be the same without his work. ❖

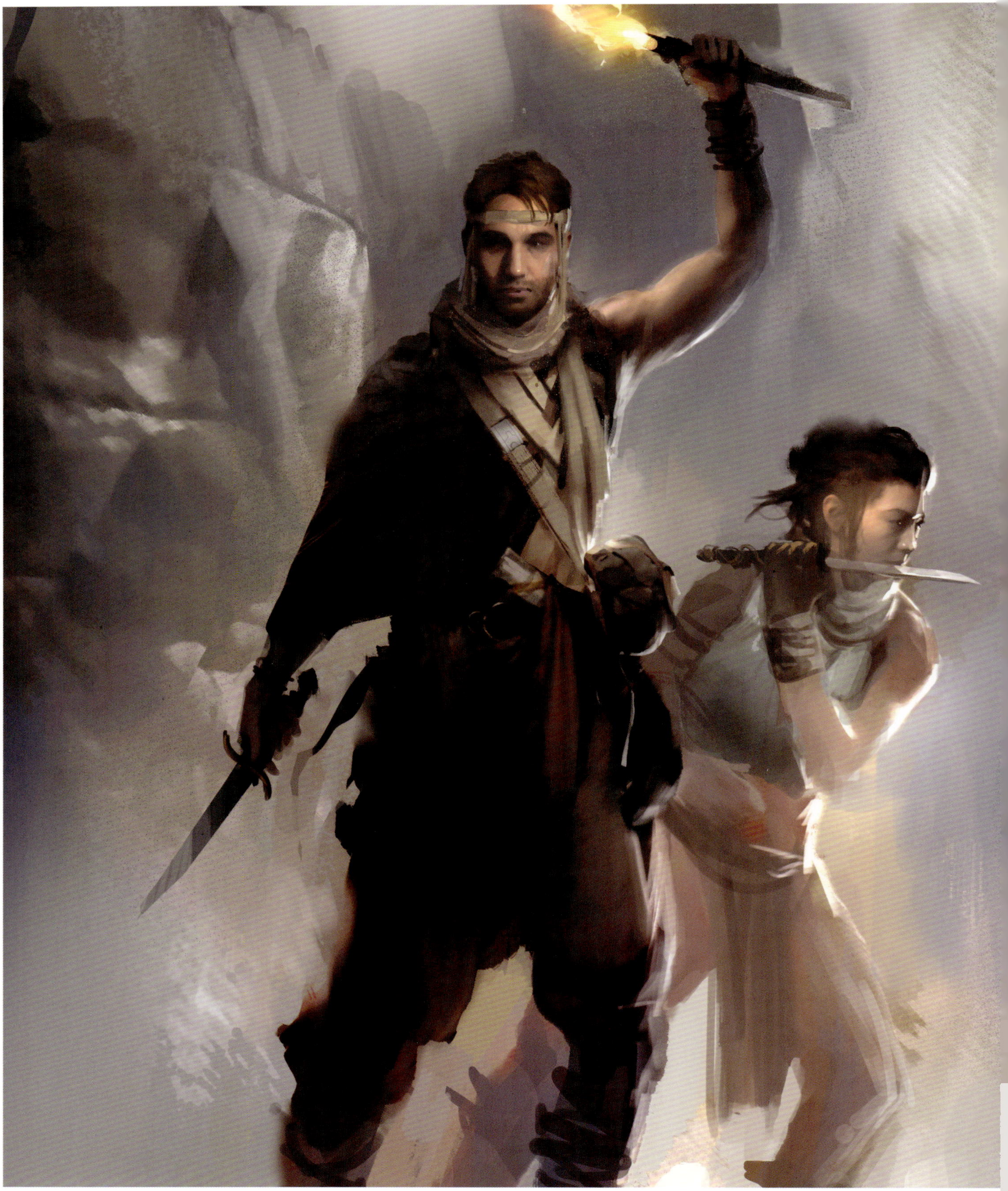

Final image © Dom Lay

Journey to the East

by Dom Lay

Creating *Journey to the East*

In this artwork, I aim to infuse Frazetta's techniques into my lighting and framing, as those are the main elements that really draw me to his work. I will make an adventure scene, as part of my personal project *Journey to the East*, illustrating a heroic composition with my two main characters.

Discovering Frazetta

When I first discovered Frank Frazetta's work during my time in art school, I was impressed by his ability to convey storytelling in such a simple yet complex manner. One of his series that caught my eye was his illustrations of John Carter of Mars, which combine science fiction and fantasy to craft an otherworldly genre. Much of this inspires my own work, where I blend those same genres together to create something that pushes beyond solely fantasy or sci-fi.

The compositions Frazetta created are so dynamic and beautiful, using strong light and shadow to guide the viewer's eye around the canvas. His vertical-format compositions are what stand out the most to me because of how much storytelling he was able to convey with limited elements. He managed to depict dominant yet elegant poses, especially where he used triadic compositions. Scenes where he only used one to two characters are still captivating on an emotional level, with fluid gestures and a strong sense of anatomy.

He was able to blend a surrealistic factor with realism, taking the viewer to different imaginary locations while still remaining grounded in reality. He was the pioneer of early concept art and epic illustration. His work was ahead of its time and his influence will be felt by many modern artists, both digital and traditional, for many years to come.

For image in full, turn to page 241

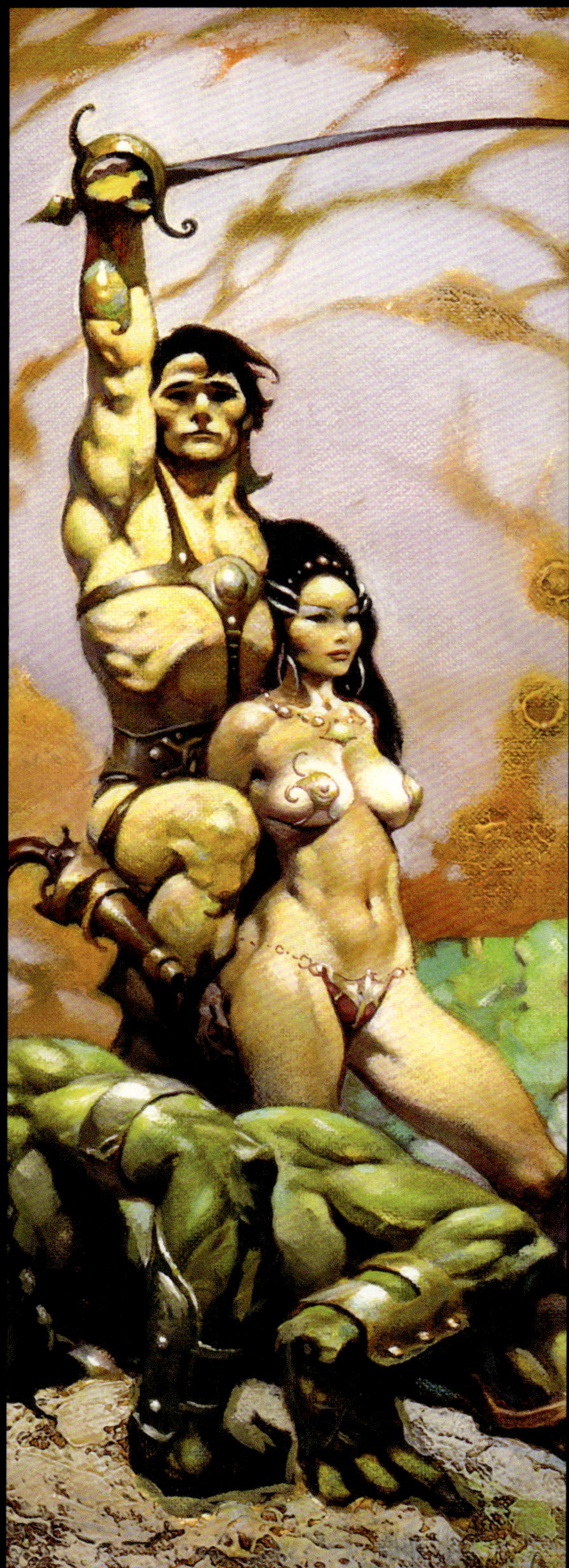

Princess of Mars © Frank Frazetta

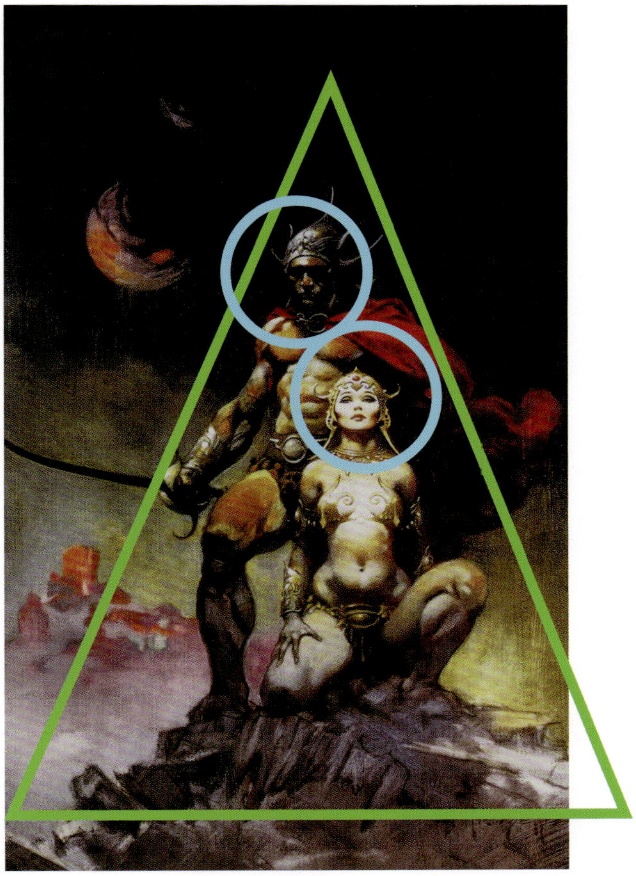

Mastermind of Mars © Frank Frazetta

An example of Frazetta's classic triangle compositions

01 Analysing reference

Before diving into my own illustration, I first study Frazetta's approach to composition, lighting, posing, value, colour, and mood. This is an important step to make sure I can recreate some of the elements he frequently uses. Frazetta had a very specific way of framing his characters that made them epic in their demeanour, with striking triangular formations that I try to analyse below. I consider having my main character stand tall and imposing, while having my secondary character a bit more crouched behind him. This play on size and shape variation will help break the tangent of characters being the same size.

▸▸ *For image in full, turn to page 237*

02 Initial sketch

I then draw out a line sketch to see how the overall composition could look. I am not focused on making everything look one-hundred percent accurate, just on giving myself an overall idea of what elements should be in each part of the canvas. This helps me to figure out how close or how far the characters should stand next to each other, as well as the arrangement of background objects.

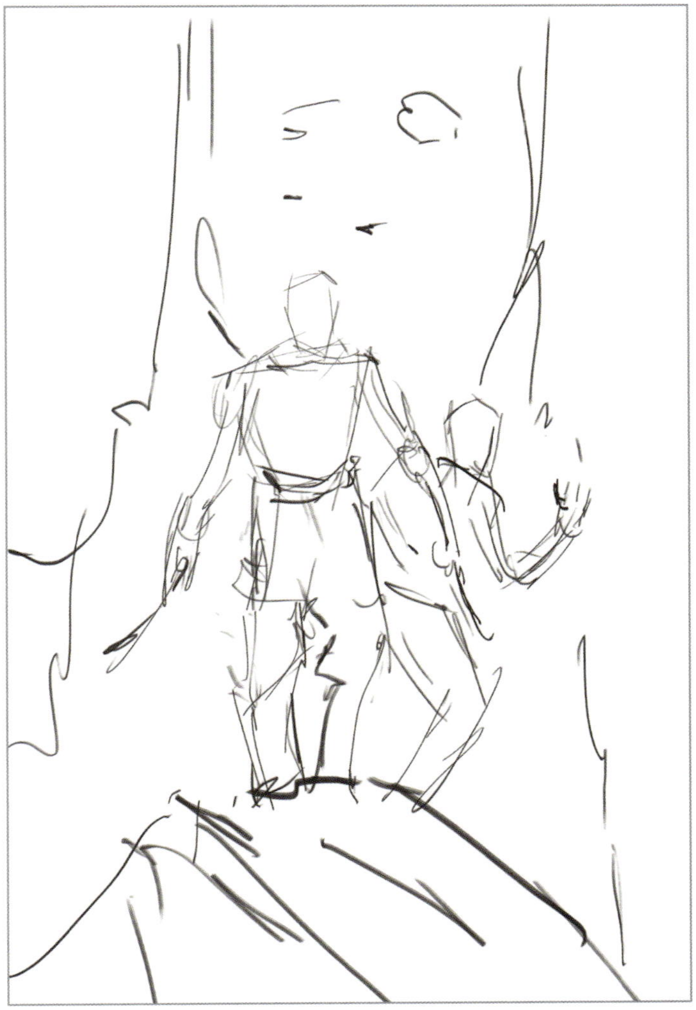

A drawing is the blueprint for any image; we can easily map out our composition

03 Rough values

Now I want to block in a very rough value draft with distinct shape language. Planning the value structure and silhouettes of the characters will make the colouring stage much easier, as strong values will give intensity to the temperature of the colours applied later. In this step I can also figure out the light source and its direction much more easily. Frazetta had a very distinctive way of lighting his subject matter from above, which I want to replicate in my own way.

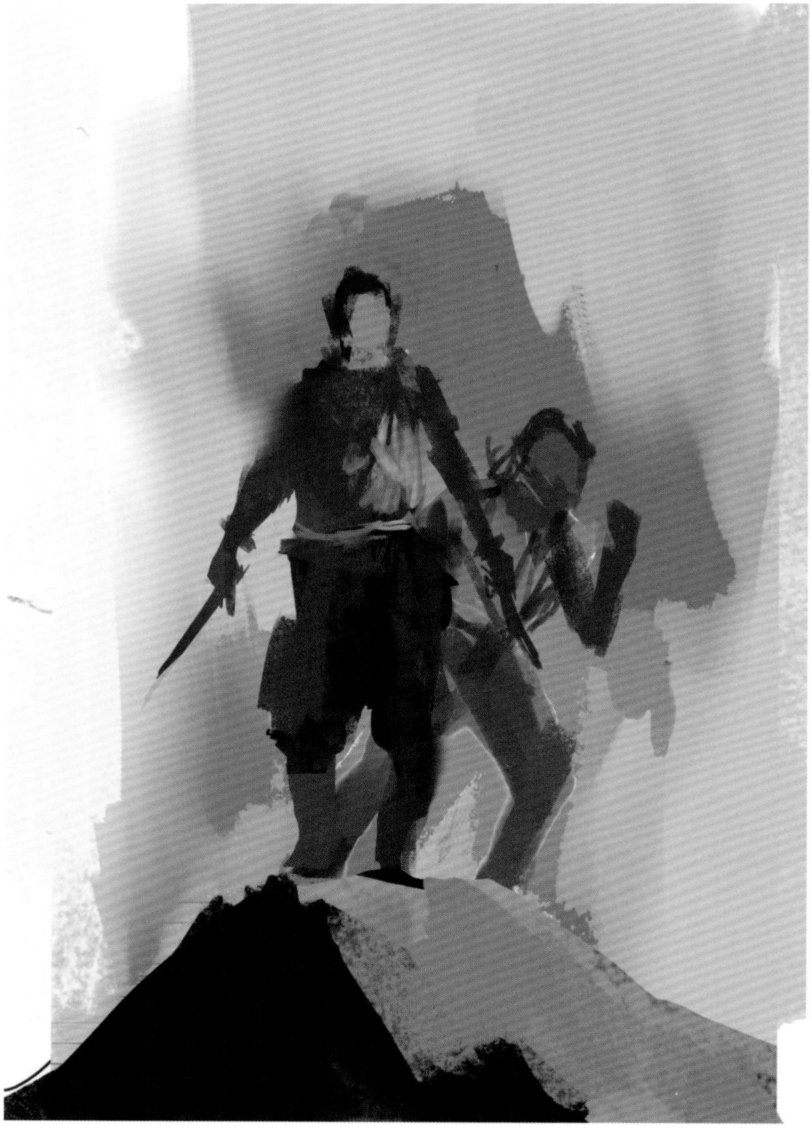

Blocking out the big shapes first before diving into any small details

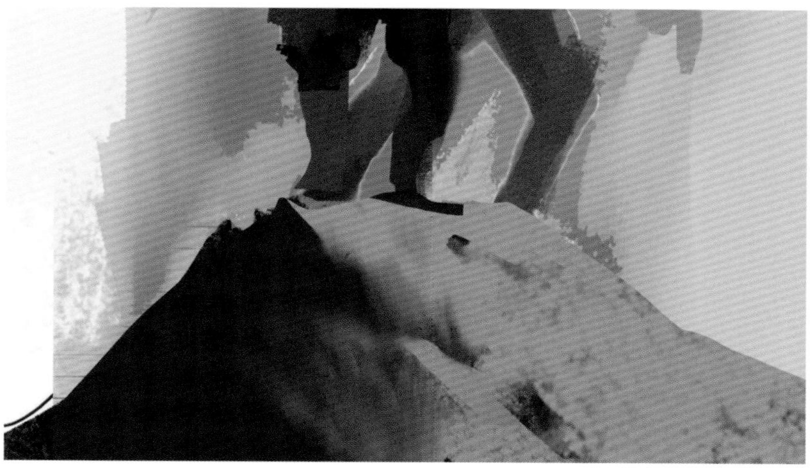

04 Adding a base

Next I add a little more detail to the rock on which the characters are standing. In many of Frazetta's compositions, his characters are mounted on a raised base to bring out their imposing stance. I think this is a very simple way to balance and stage a character in the middle of the composition and achieve that triangular 'A-frame' shape. I can later add more details to this base if I need to support the theme of the piece.

Giving the characters something to stand on emphasizes the vertical composition

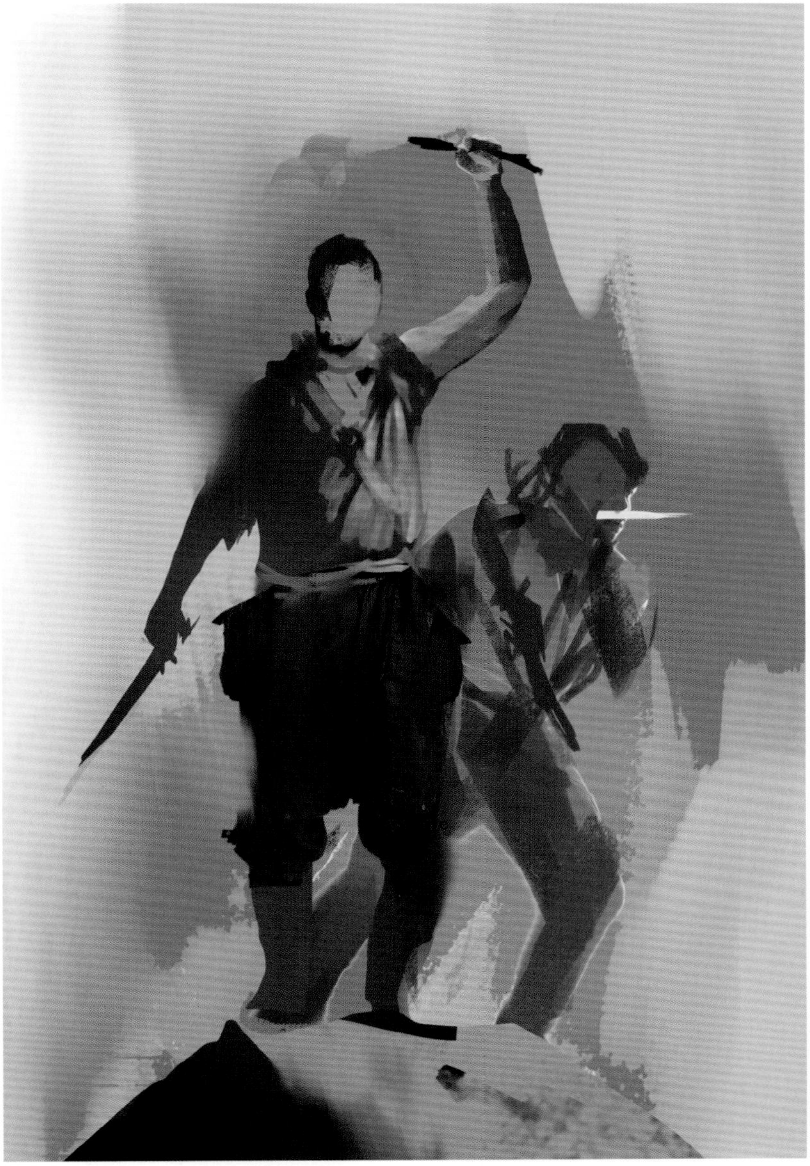

05 Changing poses

I decide to change the posing of the characters a bit, especially the character in front, to make them more heroic. I want to place the main character's arm above his head, holding a torch, to accentuate the dominant triangular composition. As for the character behind him, I want her to be holding a dagger pointing out to the right, moving the viewer's eye in a triangle by 'connecting the dots' with the main character's dagger and torch.

You can change characters' poses at any point if their gesture looks unnatural

06 Background statues

I now want to place more focus on the theming and cultural aesthetics of the piece, which is focused on adventure. Adding some background elements will help to push this story more; as I am working digitally, I can use resources such as 3D models and my own photography and artwork. Perhaps these characters are treasure hunters or tomb raiders who have arrived at a temple of some sort. From here we now know the context of what is happening. At this stage the statue faces are conflicting in detail with the characters, so in order to maintain focus on the characters I will fade the statues into the background later.

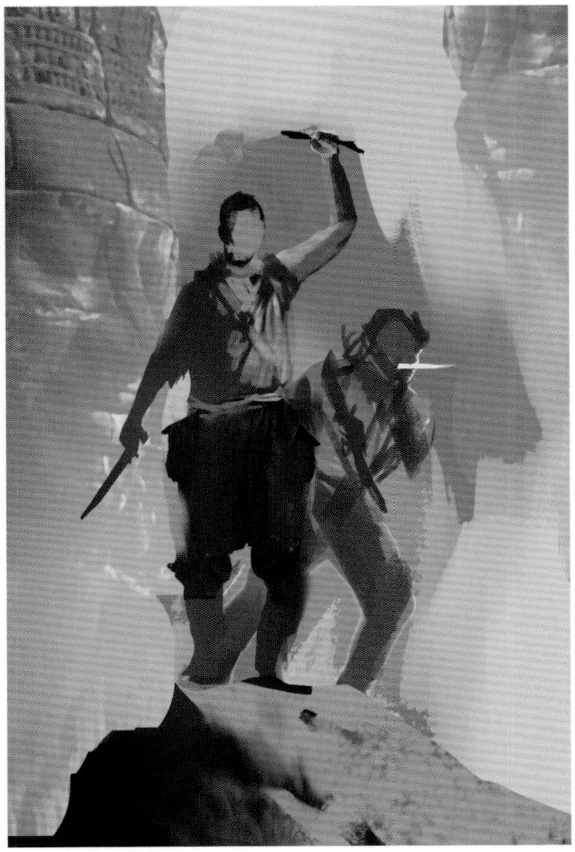

Adding something in the background of any character illustration gives it more narrative

Photoscan of Angkor Wat, Cambodia, by awrench on Sketchfab.

Strong greyscale values make colouring easier, as you can more easily determine how bright or dark a colour should be

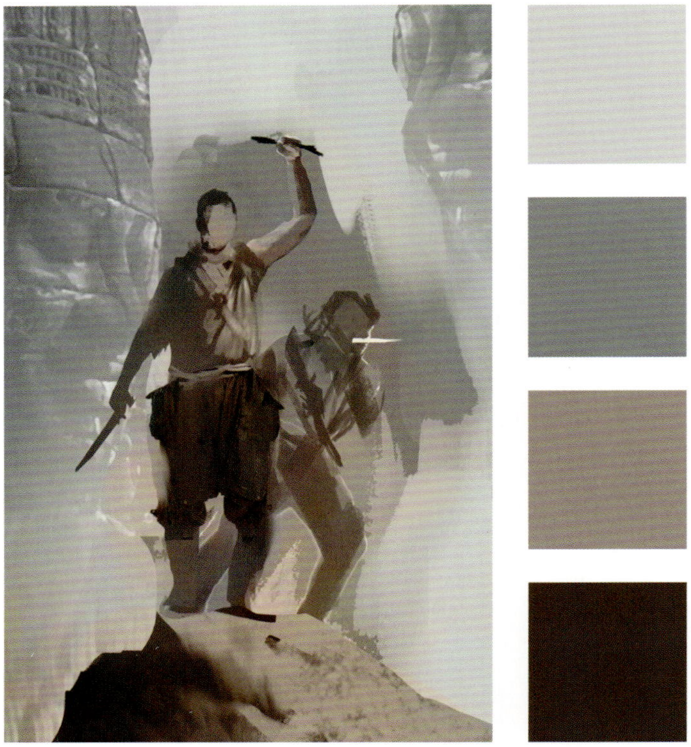

07 Incorporating colour

Now that the greyscale sketch is fairly fleshed out, I can throw on a very quick wash of colour. The greyscale base helps me determine which areas I want to be warm or cool in colour temperature. To create tonal contrast, I want the background to be cooler than the foreground. The main hero will be lit by the torch he is carrying, so having a warmer palette in the foreground is a perfect fit.

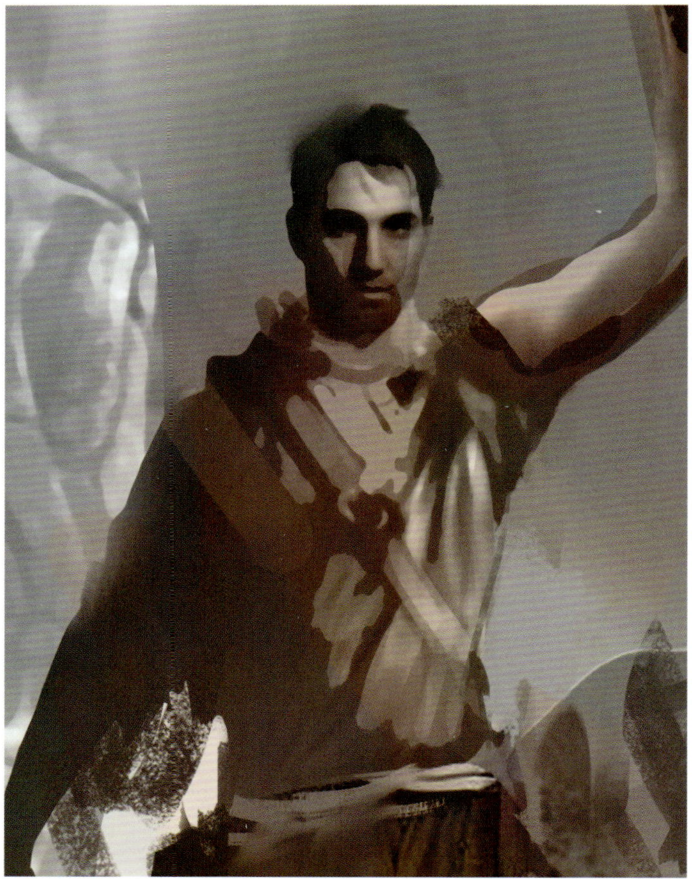

08 Giving life to the characters

At this stage, I want to add a bit of personality to the main character. For now I add a placeholder face in order to see what sort of facial expression and emotion he might have. With Frazetta's approach, he liked to have his characters' faces lit with strong light versus dark. I do my best to replicate the same effect here, but it may change later in the piece. In any character illustration, painting or drawing a proportionally correct face helps immensely in making the character feel real-world and believable.

As humans, we can easily connect to a person's face in any painting

09 Detailing the clothing

The main character's clothing needs more aesthetic development to indicate that he is an adventurer. I add some more drapery and belt tassels to his upper body. I focus more detail around his face and torso area, while the lower part of his body receives much less detail; this helps the viewer to focus more on the relevant areas of the character. I also begin to define the flame emerging from the torch he's holding, which will bring in a stronger light source from above his head.

Context is important when illustrating characters; asking questions while designing is caring about our piece

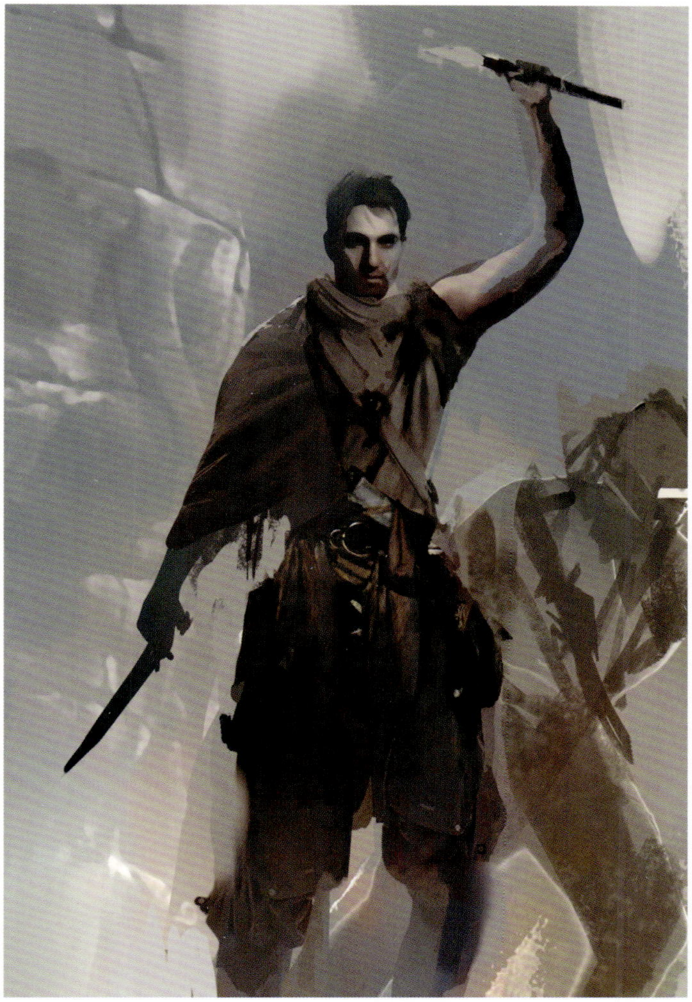

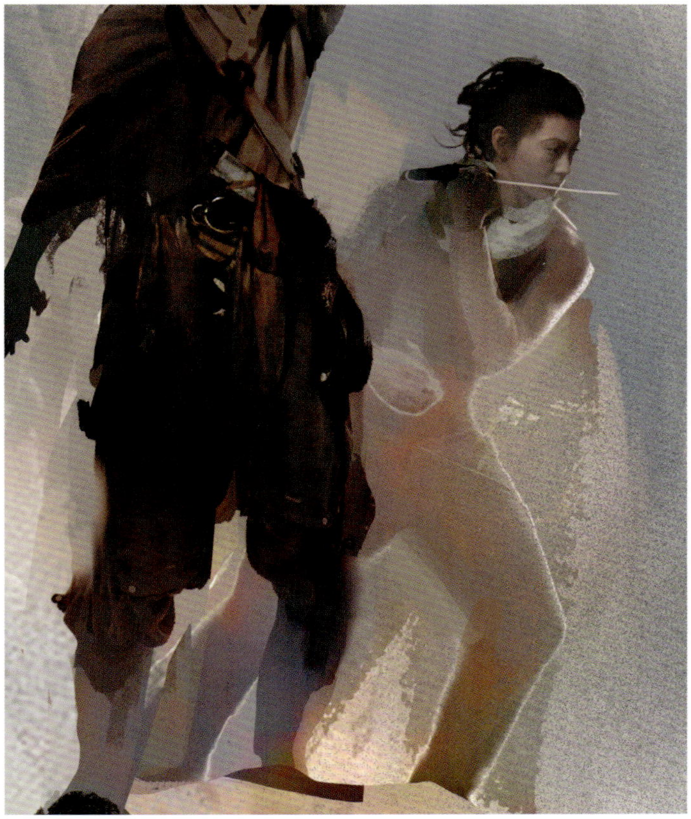

10 The second character

I now begin defining the image's secondary character, starting a rendition of the facial features and exploring what she could look like. Perhaps she is the main character's companion on his quest to find a lost treasure. I want her expression to be more serious, as this indicates in the narrative that she is protecting and watching his back, ready to strike at any enemies they come across. The secondary focal point will be on her face, so the rest of the details are pushed further back to bring more emphasis there.

Singular characters can be great on their own, but supporting characters give more storytelling ideas

11 Adjusting hues & rim light

I now have the structure and foundation of the characters, but the lighting is looking quite flat. I decide to include some rim lighting against the right side of the characters. Having that strong, distinct light adds so much to the midtone values, allowing me a greater range of values to play with. It also indicates where the main natural light source is coming from and helps to make the scene really pop off the canvas. Building on the blue hue, I introduce a more reddish tone to the values to create some warmth.

Rim light can be used to pop out the edges of a silhouette for more readability

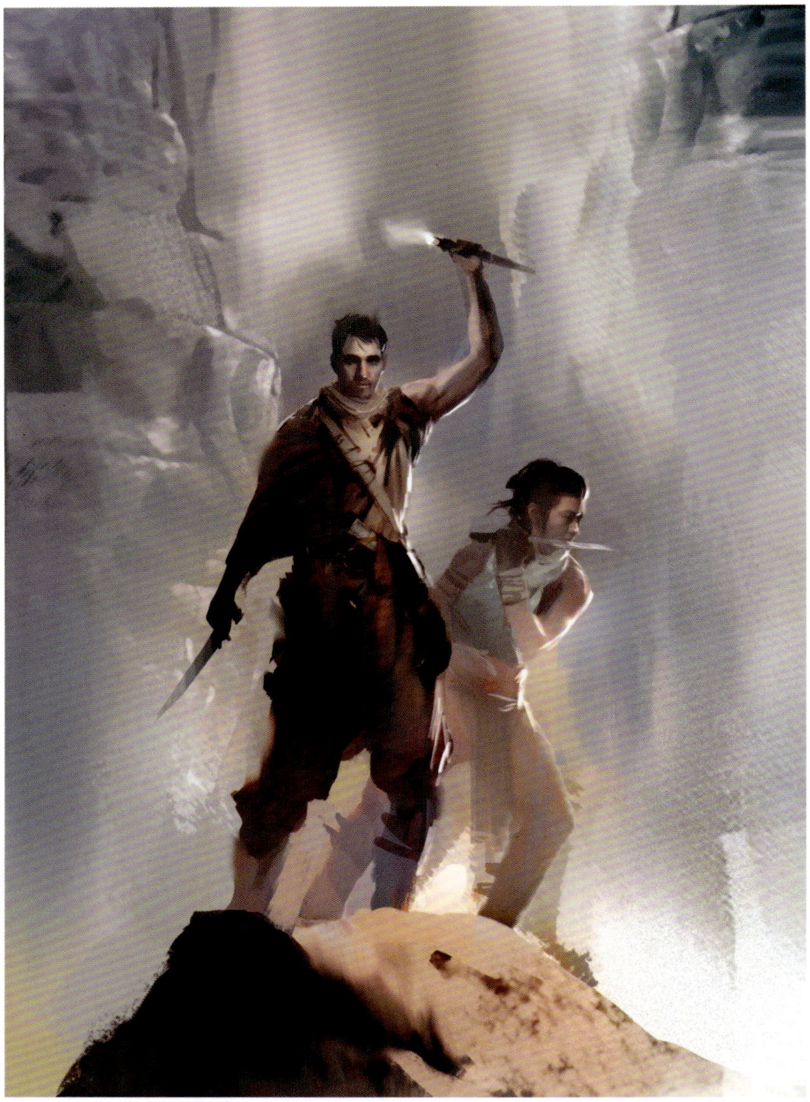

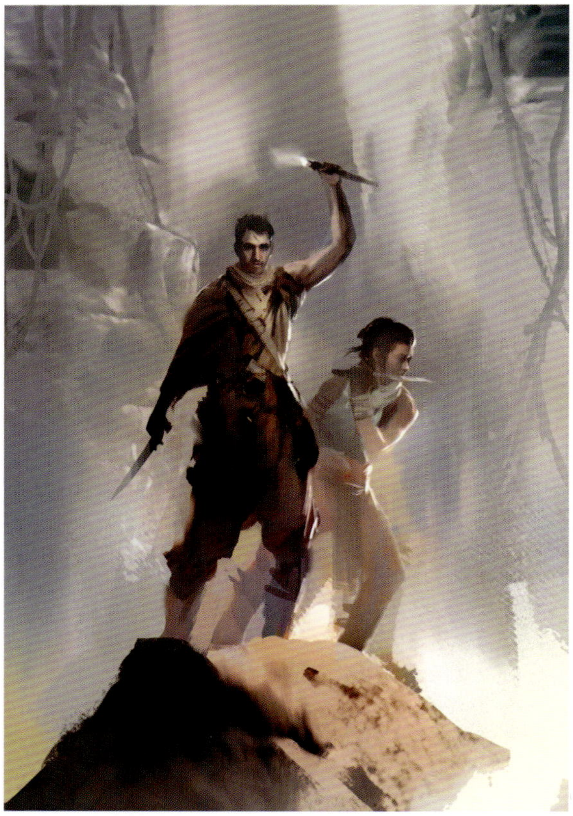

Using a limited palette, we can still achieve a powerful, convincing image with three tones

12 Adding smaller details

I begin adding secondary details to the background, such as the vines. This is a very small detail but it adds a lot to the piece by indicating where the story is set – now the characters are clearly in a jungle of some kind. It is always a good idea to have a hierarchy of big, medium, and small shapes to balance out the image, but they should be built up in that order. I adjust the overall hue again, adding a subtle yellowish tone so that the image is not just red and blue. This third tone helps to mesh the rest of the palette together.

13 Adjusting contrast & lighting

I bring down the contrast a little by slightly darkening the background, which allows the characters to really pop out of the image. In Frazetta's work, he regularly used a strong dynamic push between dark and light. I am drawing on that for this piece, but I will not go as intense in contrast, since I want to maintain a level of realism to the lighting. I also rework the main character's face into a much more believable, realistic one that matches the direction of the torchlight.

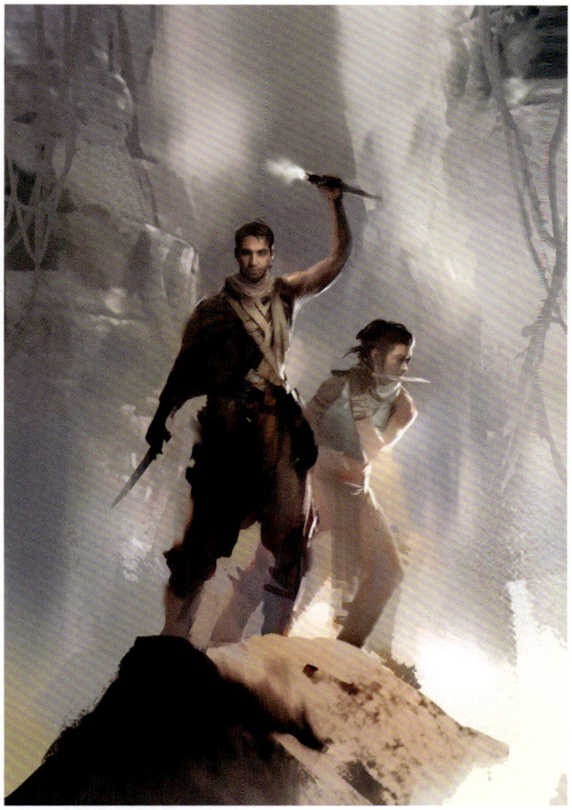

Having a bit of contrast helps the values read much more clearly

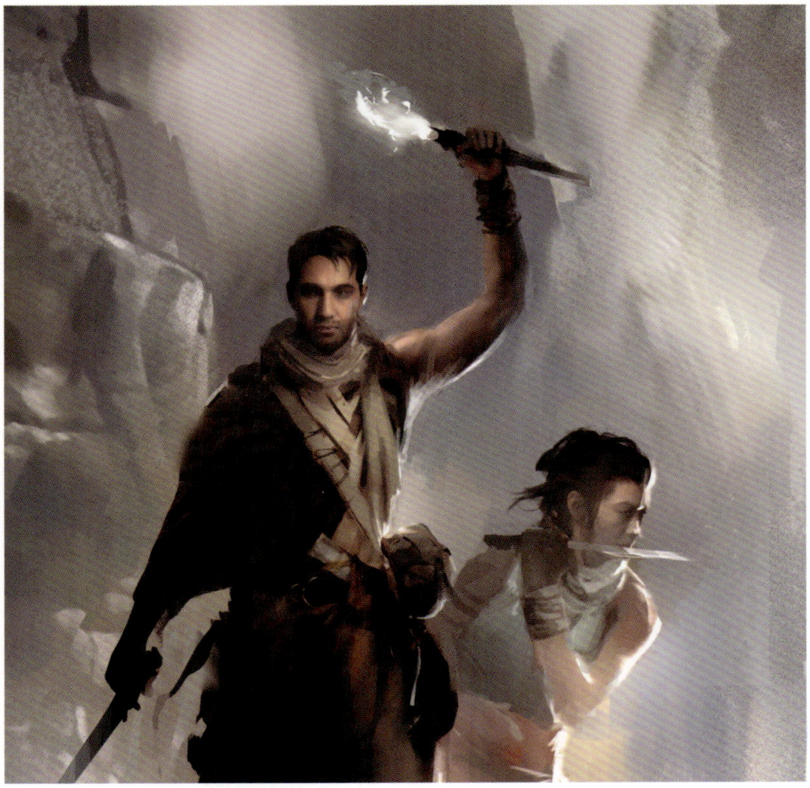

14 Adding more detail

The values are still a bit too bright in the background, so I darken them even more to illuminate the foreground. This creates a stronger sense of the light highlighting the characters' faces and clothes. I begin fine-tuning details, adjusting the flame on the torch and adding a satchel to the main character. I add more wrappings to his clothing and legs, making sure to maintain the overall values of the piece, thinking of the 'light on dark' and 'dark on light' that Frazetta often implemented in his paintings.

Adding contrast can push the silhouettes of elements, however we never want to overdo it

15 Final touch-ups

Now I can finish wrapping up any remaining details. I adjust a few more bodily proportions on each character, making sure to zoom out so I can see if everything is anatomically correct overall. Adding an orange hue to the torch gives it the effect of glowing fire, and I bump up the brightness on the characters' faces accordingly, accentuating the areas of illumination. Last of all, I add a few more touch-ups to the clothing, such as belt pieces and further rendering on the cloth.

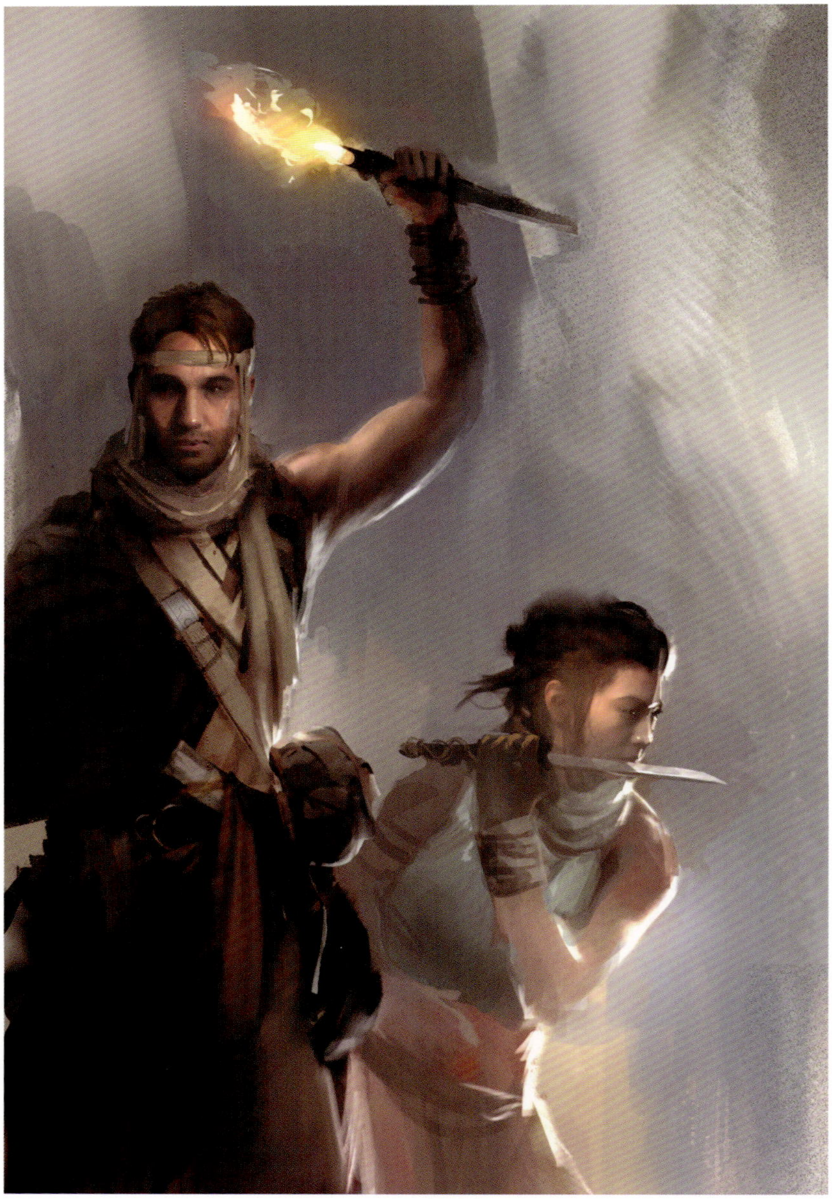

Placing the final detail touches is necessary to complete the whole piece

Conclusion

This piece was an absolute pleasure to create. I believe this way of translating another artist's approach into an original piece allows you to inject your own taste into the image, rather than just duplicating the same brushwork or finished quality. With this in mind, I have been inspired by some of Frazetta's techniques to formulate a few of my own compositions that have that classic energetic flow. He is by far one of the great masters that every beginner artist should study.

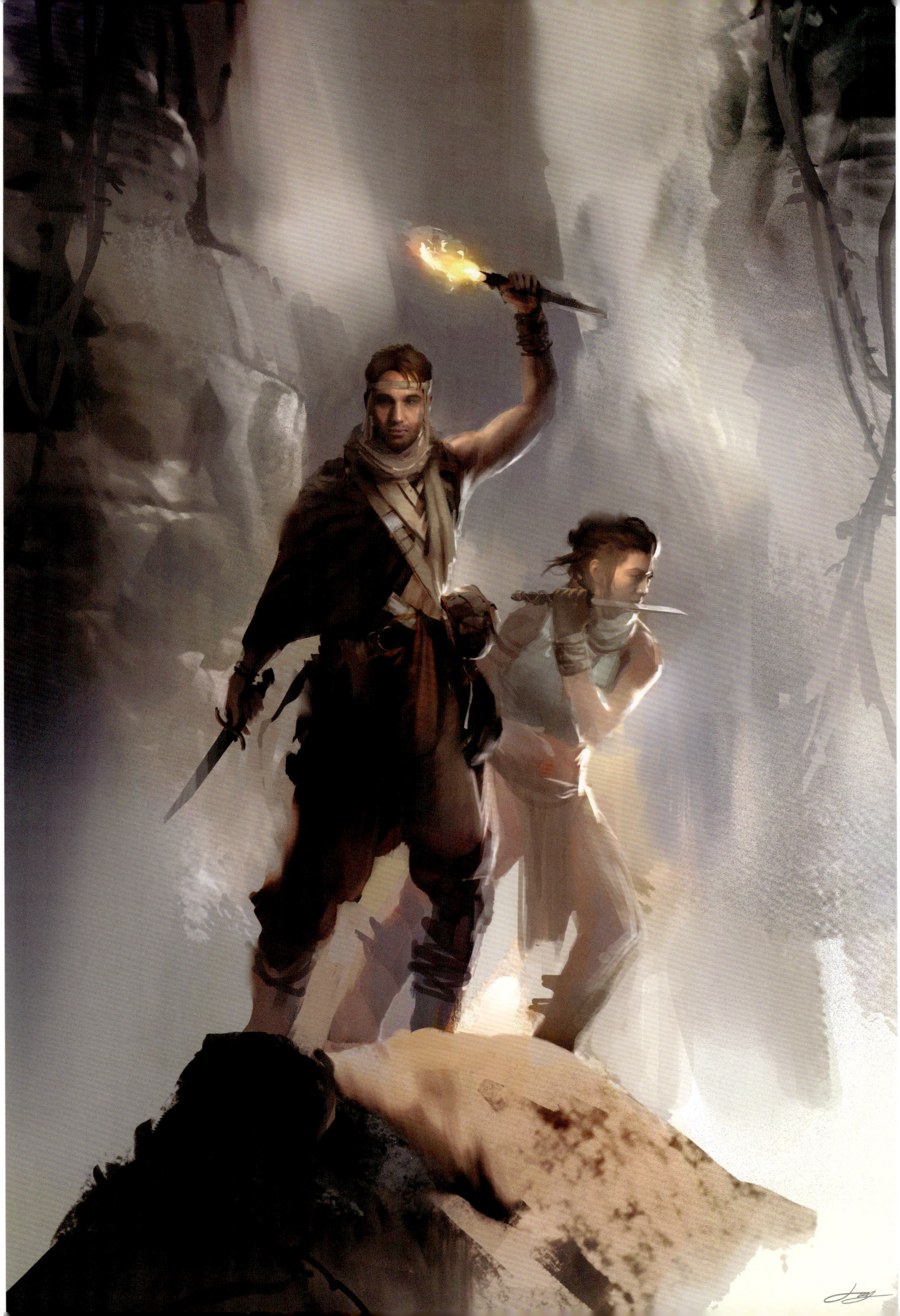

Final image © Dom Lay

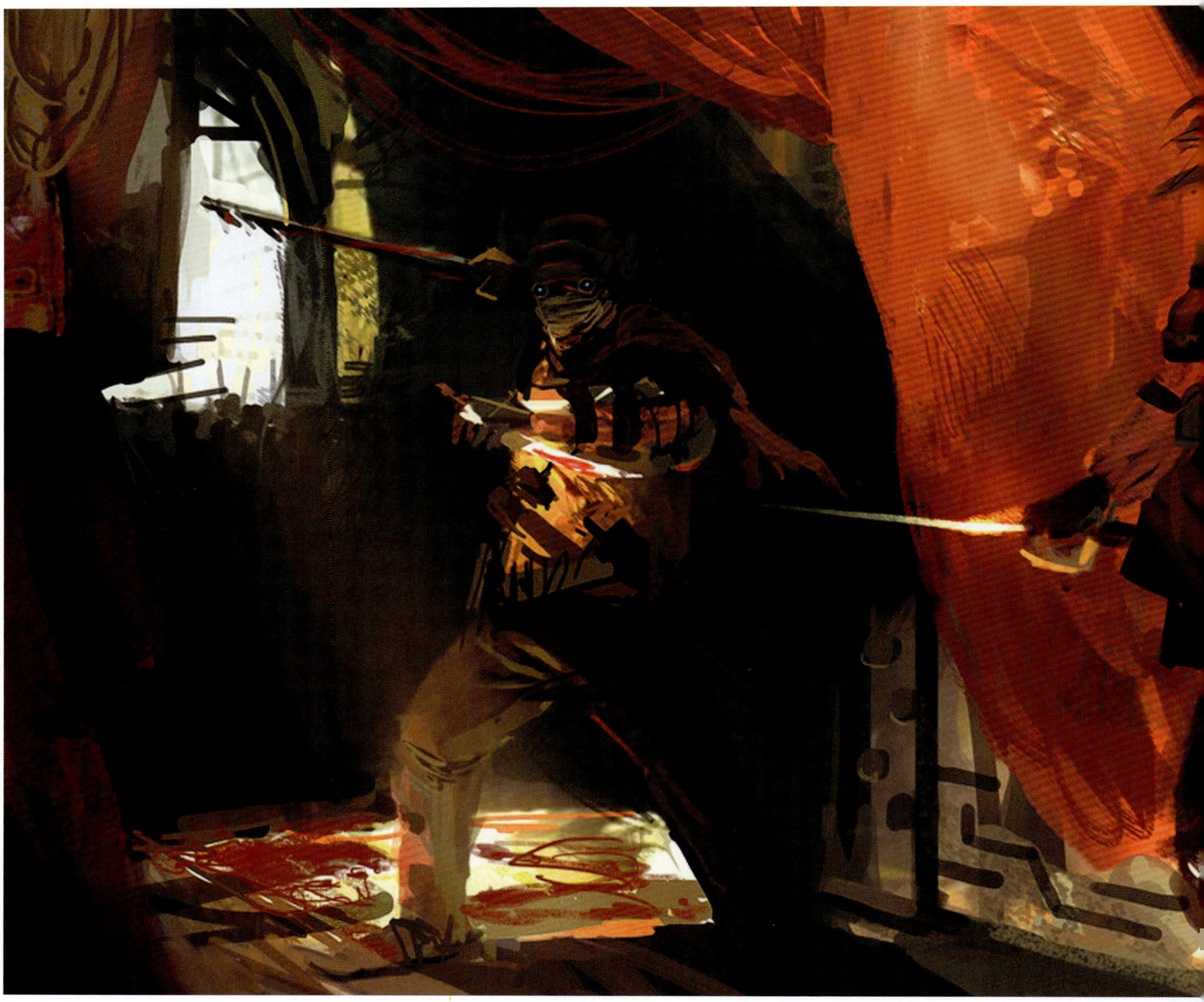

Gallery

by Dom Lay

A Tense Encounter © Dom Lay

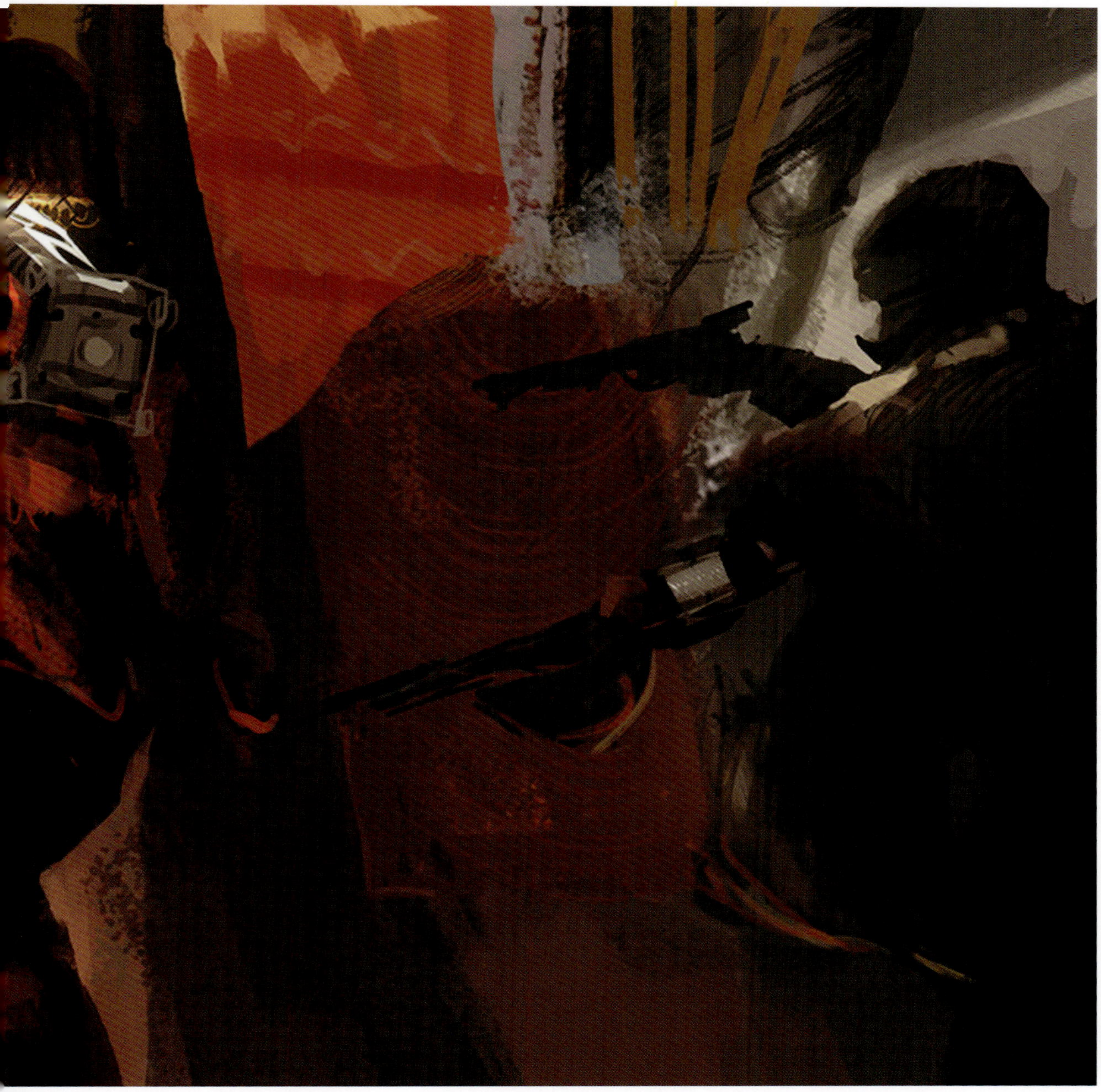

A Tense Encounter — *In this piece, I wanted to connect the characters together in this flow of their gesture, similar to how Frazetta uses a powerful energy in his work.*

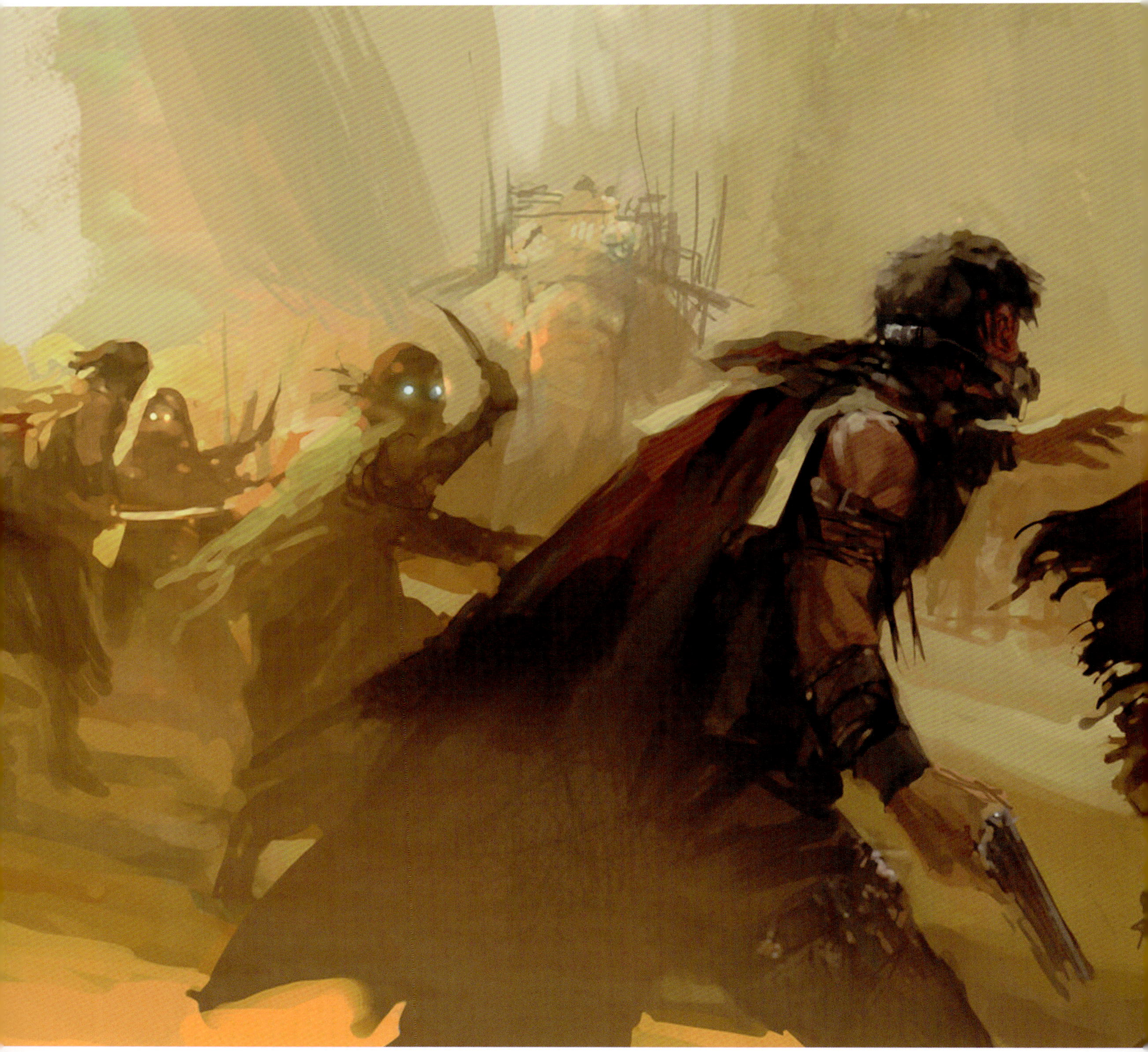

Visions of the Past © Dom Lay

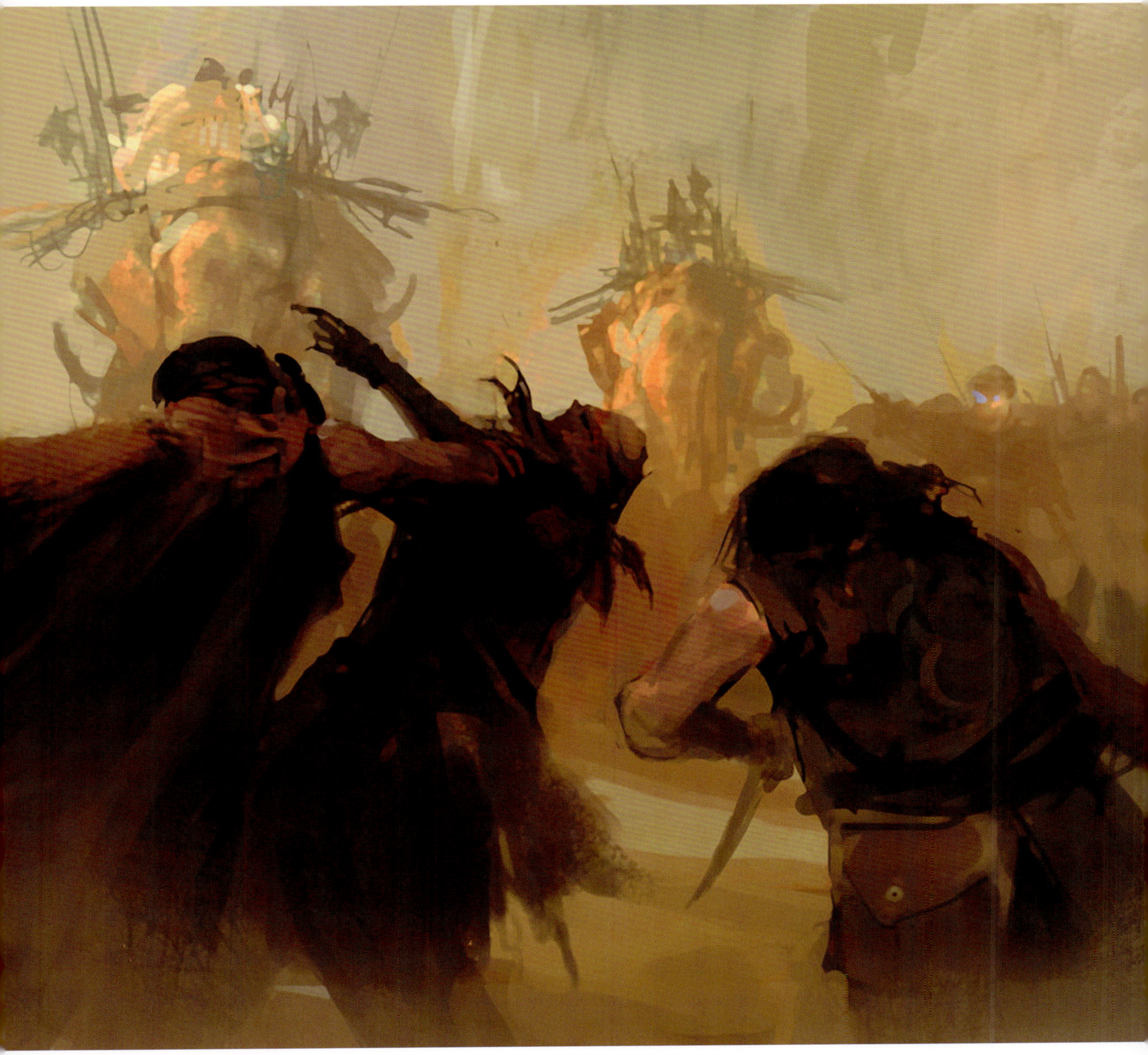

Visions of the Past — *In much of Frazetta's work, he illustrates some kind of conflict between his characters. Here I wanted to illustrate a grand battle scene that evokes a similar feeling.*

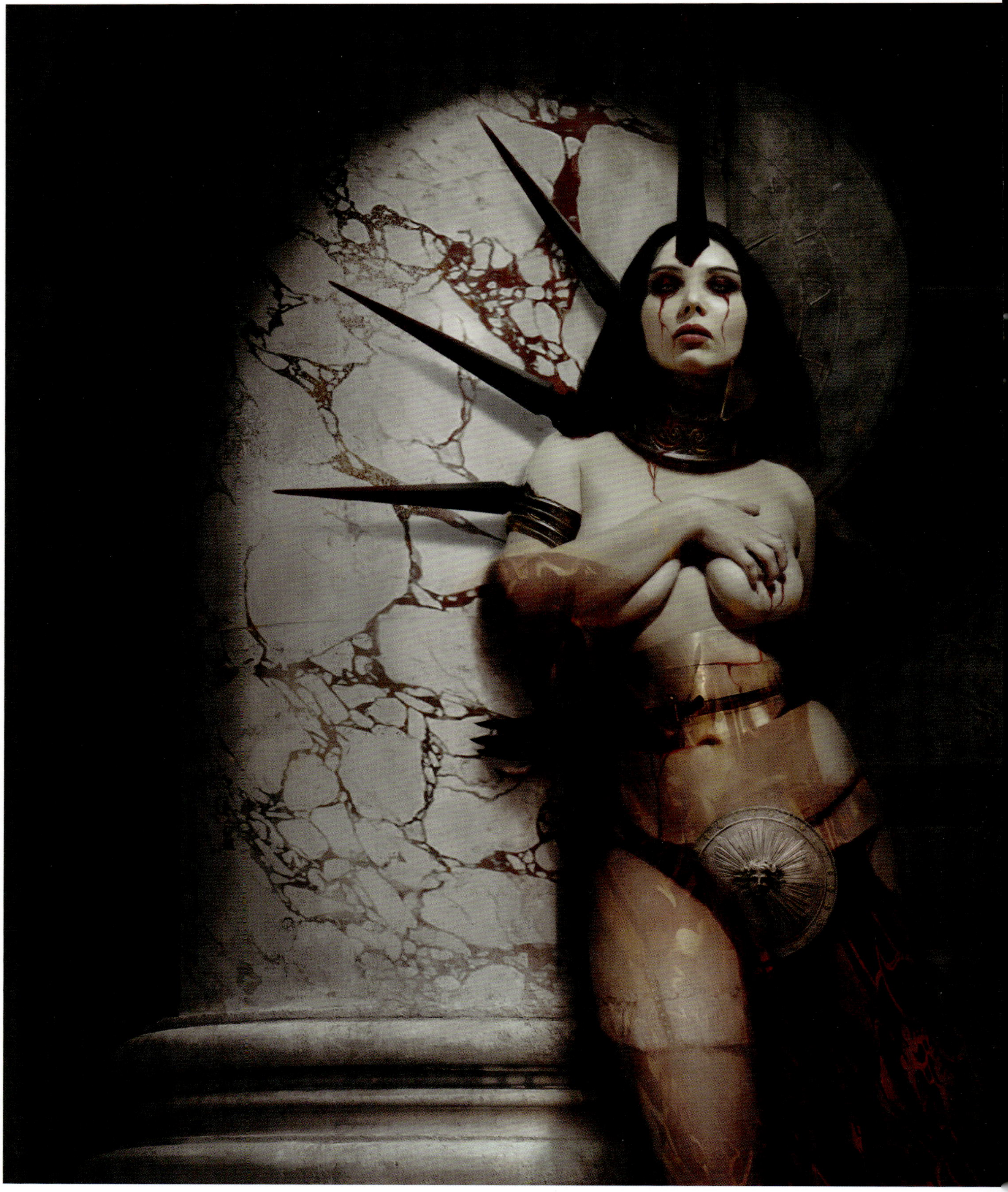

Final image © Bastien Lecouffe Deharme

The Death Queen

by Bastien Lecouffe Deharme

Creating *The Death Queen*

Working on this piece will be an excellent exercise in style – an opportunity to gather the elements within Frazetta's work that have influenced mine over the years. It feels like the right option is to jump straight into it, in confidence that Frazetta's presence will unavoidably pierce through. So here is *The Death Queen*, referring directly to my favourite Frazetta pieces, *Egyptian Queen* and *Death Dealer I*, but created using my usual digital techniques. I will go through the process with both eyes open, looking closely at the way I work and explaining it, while trying not to fall from the shoulder of a giant!

01 First sketch

This initial sketch is only here for me as a statement of intention. It's not made to be used in the process, at least not directly, but all the information here will be a reminder for the future steps. I want the character to be standing in light, body and blood, projecting strength and defiance, staring at the viewer just like in a Frazetta piece. The environment will be built around her, using contrasts of light and shadow, and line and direction, to complete and highlight her presence.

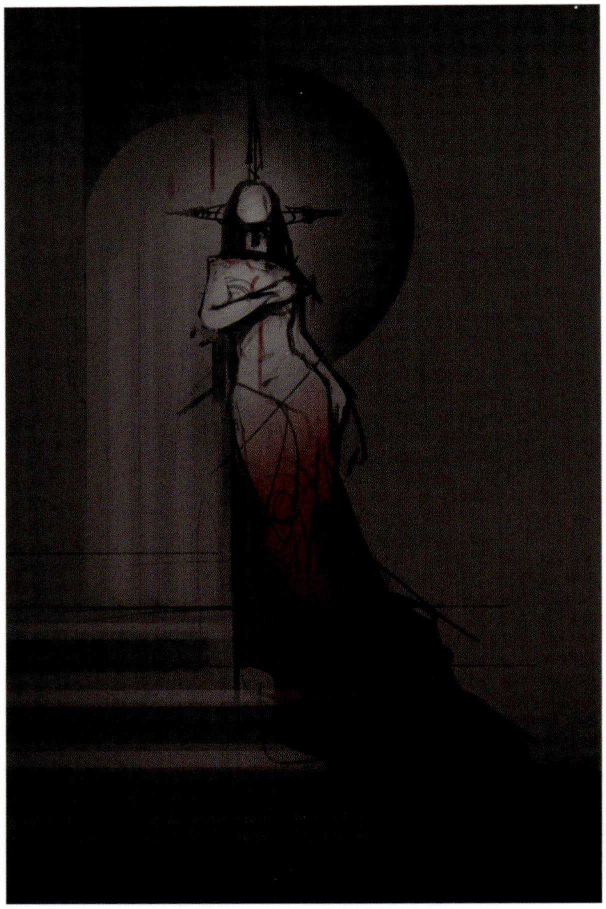

An initial quick sketch of my intentions

02 Model photoshoot

Once I have a clear idea of where to start, I set up a photoshoot with a model. More than just being references, models bring a specific energy to an image; a photoshoot will generate many new ideas, based on the model's poses and attitude. It's an opportunity to explore options for the project far beyond what I had initially imagined. So the sketch is pretty much just a guideline made to trigger everything that comes next. I shoot hundreds of photos, then assemble bits and pieces with Adobe Photoshop to build the reference I will work from.

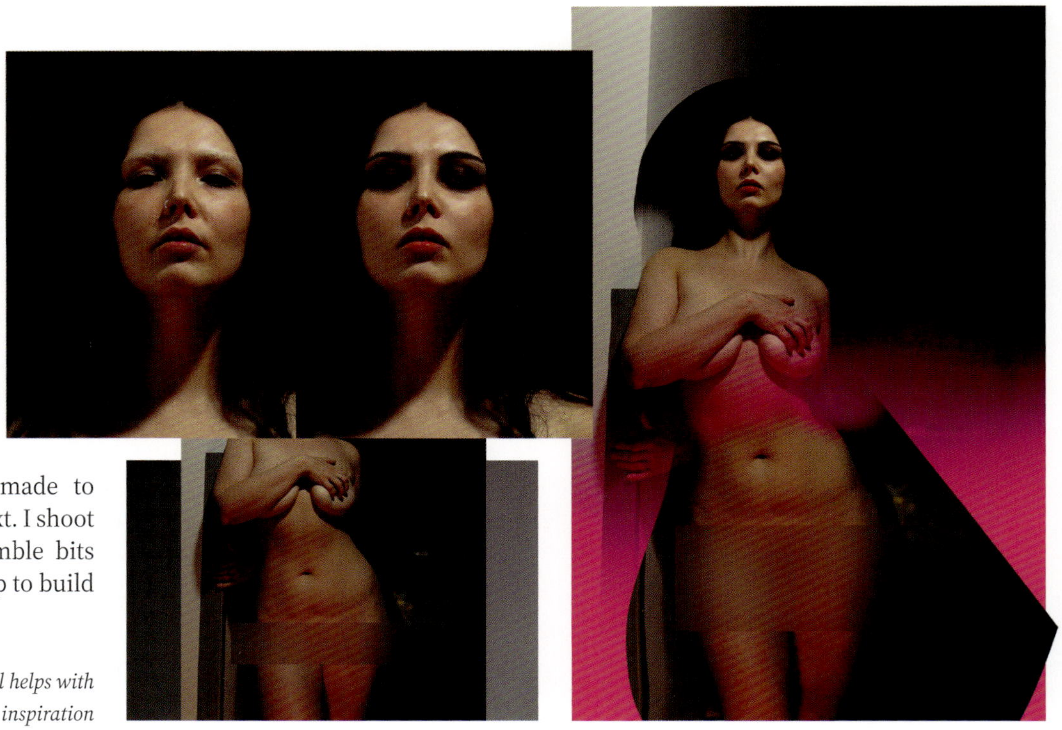

A photoshoot with a model helps with reference and inspiration

Using a grid for this particular process

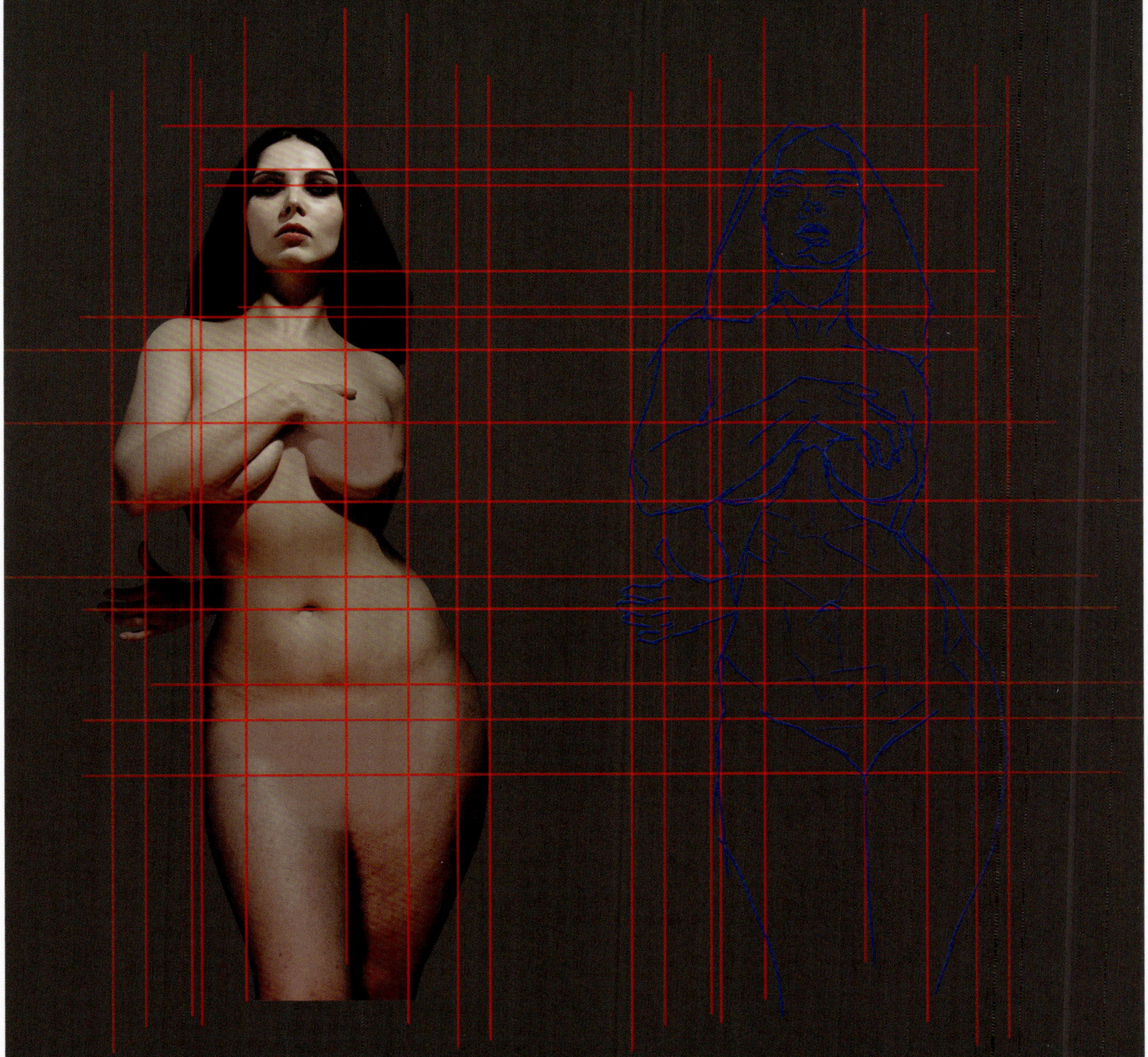

03 Gridded drawing

For the sake of speed, I grid the canvas, which enables me to recreate the model's pose with a high level of accuracy. I don't always work this way – sometimes I will just sketch and paint with the reference on another monitor. I teach and practise figure drawing, and I have learned that some of the best drawings are made from looser sketches, not aiming for accuracy but for flow and energy. I assume that this is also how Frazetta worked, embracing the dynamics of a pose instead of aiming for total accuracy.

04 Rough painting

These are some of the steps of my painting process. I work directly in colours, but my focus is on values – painting in blocks of shadows and lights. As long as the values are correct, the colours can divert from the reference and the result will still be stable. I do not erase and do not undo – I just paint directly over the sketchy blue lines. My relationship with the work, at this stage, is similar to what I would do on a traditional canvas. During this stage, I am being patient and taking the time to work through the 'ugly' phase of the painting.

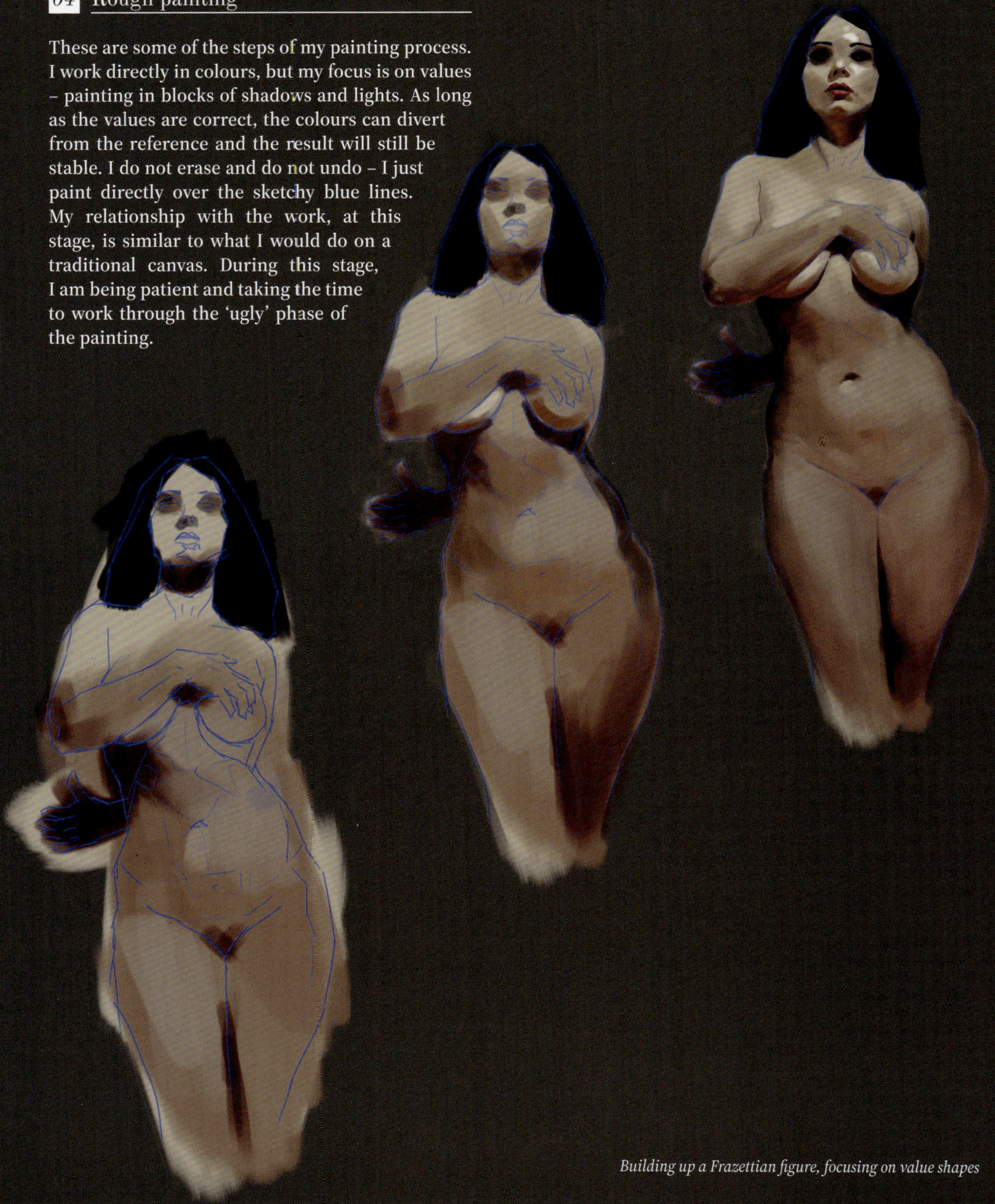

Building up a Frazettian figure, focusing on value shapes

05 Building up detail

Depending on the projects and the final render I need, I sometimes work directly with photographs; my painting skills still come into play, as painting is not only about brushstrokes but also about understanding values, composition, contrast, detail, and visual rhythm. However, for this piece, I really want to take the time to paint the character and enjoy it. This project is a perfect excuse for me to dive into the painting process of the figure. For the skin, I alternate soft and hard brushes and textured ones. They merge and overlap, helping me achieve a render reminiscent of traditional painting.

Pushing the character's details using a range of digital brushes

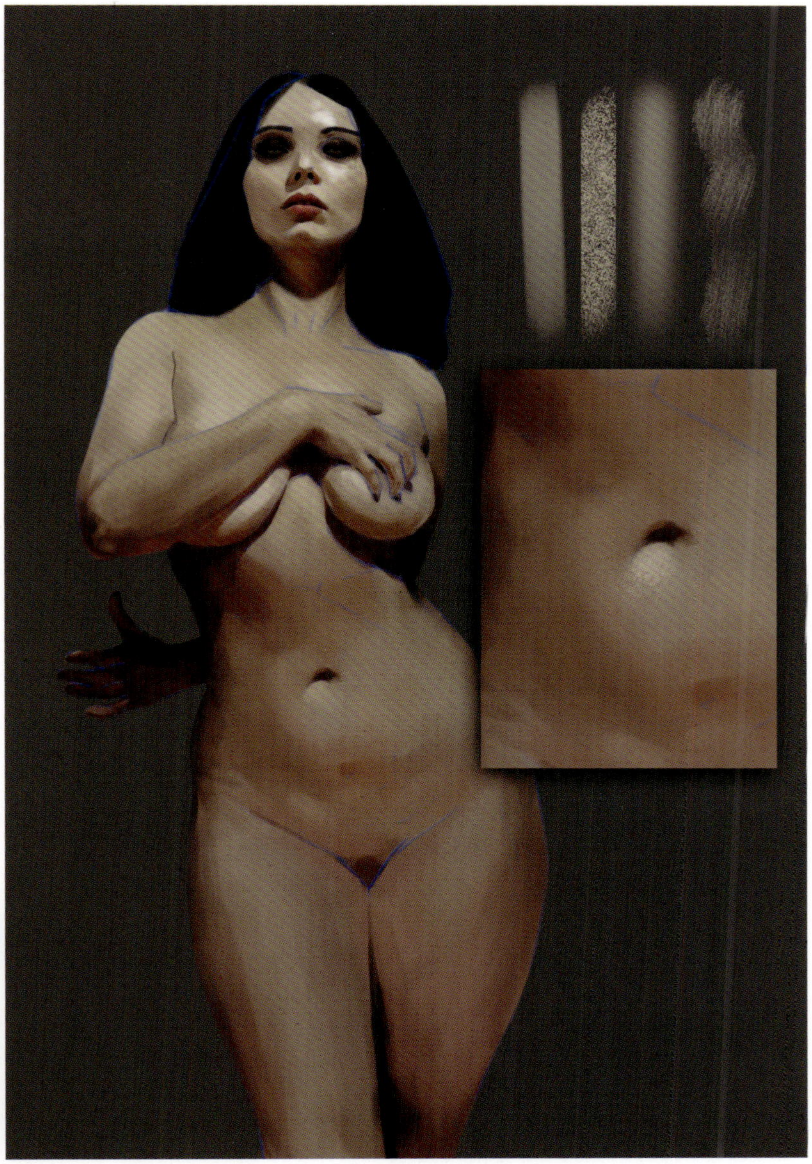

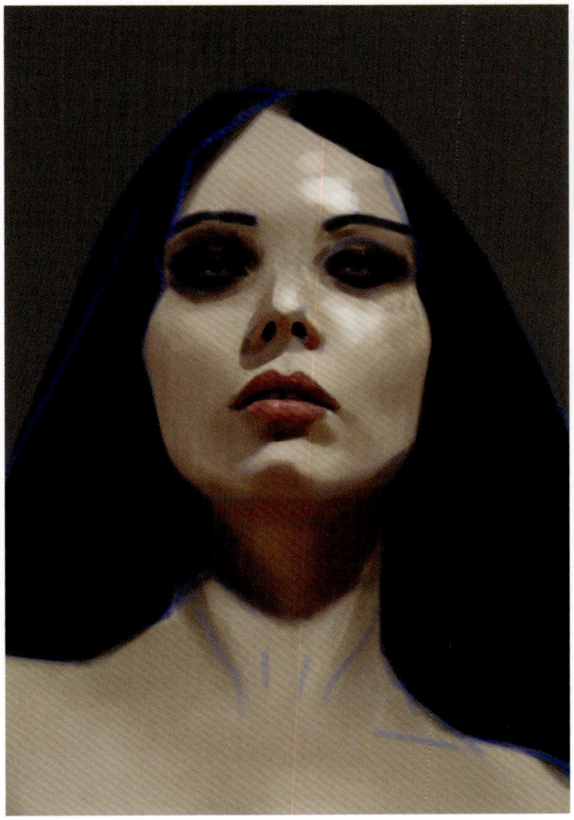

06 Eye contact

Frazetta's art is fantasy at the human level, which is also my personal preference – imaginary worlds being a playground for metaphors of the human condition. It's why I have always been attracted by the fate of characters like Conan, Elric of Melniboné, or Rick Deckard, rather than larger-than-human types of fiction. In *Egyptian Queen* or *Death Dealer I*, the main character looks at the viewer's soul, straight through the eyes. We are invited into the piece. I want this character to do the same.

The character holds eye contact with the viewer

07 Developing the scene

At this point I am starting to build the overall scene: placing the painted character on the canvas and pushing the values, establishing the composition further. I try making decisions to see if they work or not; if they don't, I adjust them until they do. I want the character to be at the centre of the piece, catching and reflecting the light. That's another thing I learned from masters like Frazetta and Rembrandt.

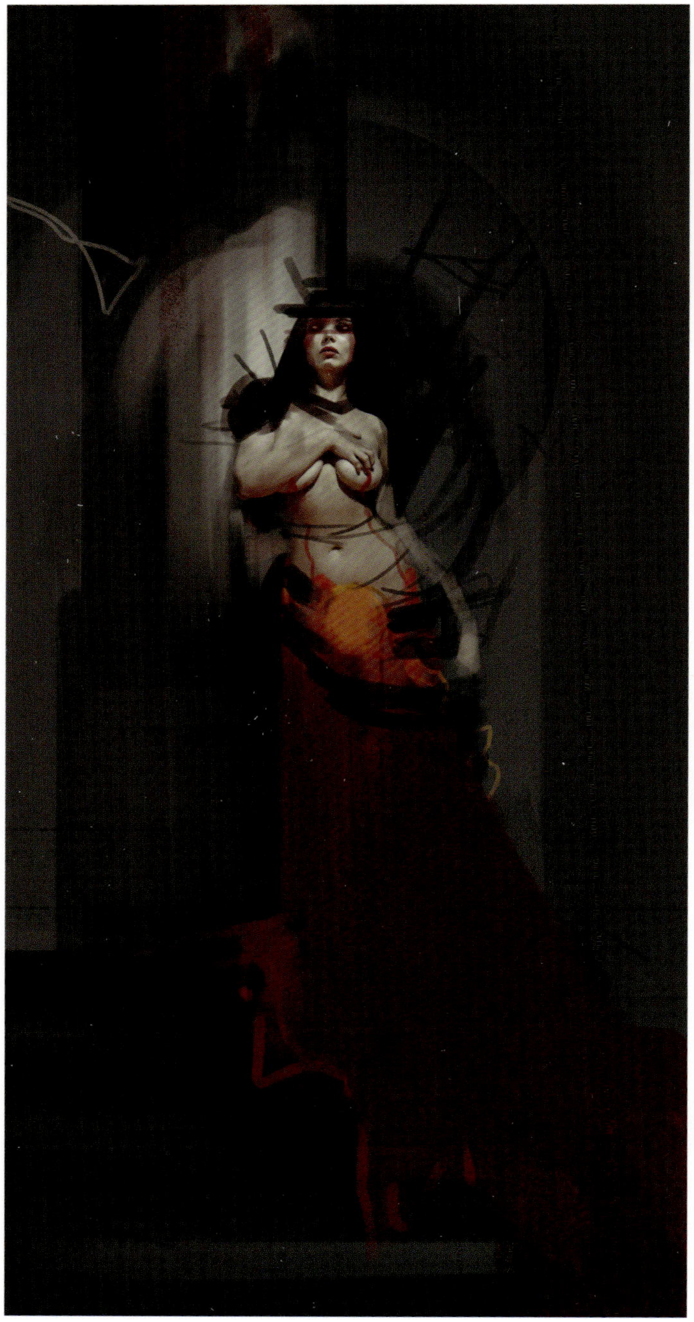

Building up the scene

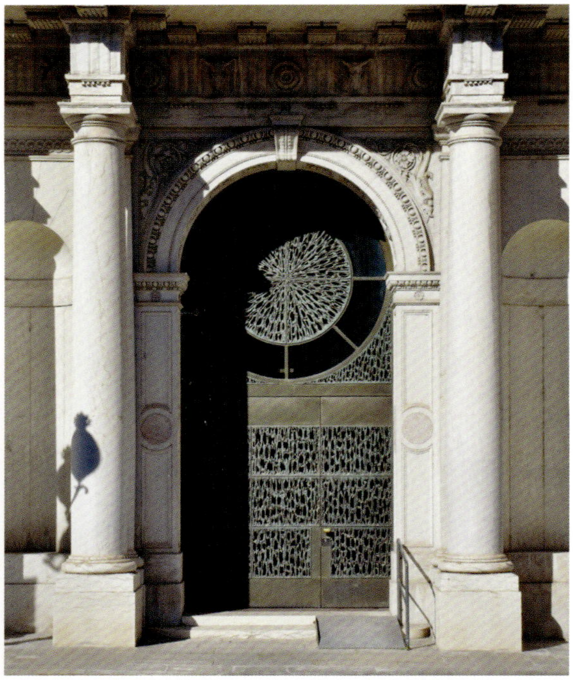

Photo by Arno Senoner on Unsplash

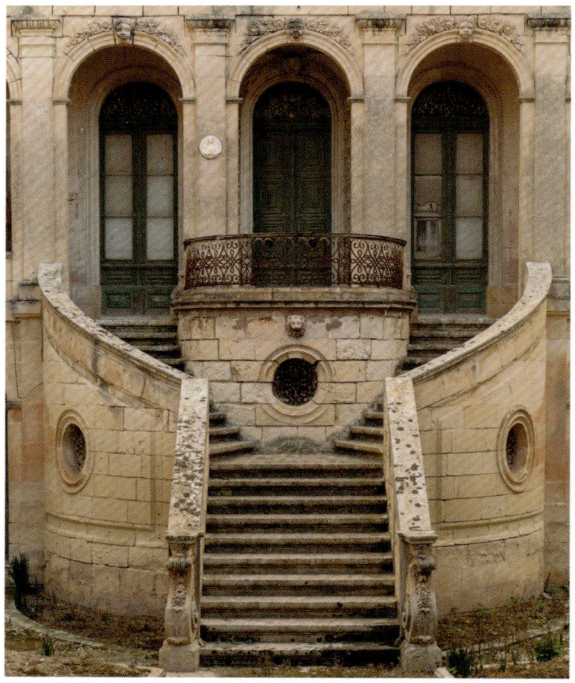

From the photobash.co 'Sandstone City' pack

08 Finding photo material

I need to find a few more references to serve the project. I try to take my own photos as much as possible, as I like to 'own' every part of my process. However, I can't find what I need in my photo library in this specific case. Instead, I turn to specialized resource websites such as photobash.co and Unsplash for two images that contain plenty of usable elements, such as a staircase, columns, and textures.

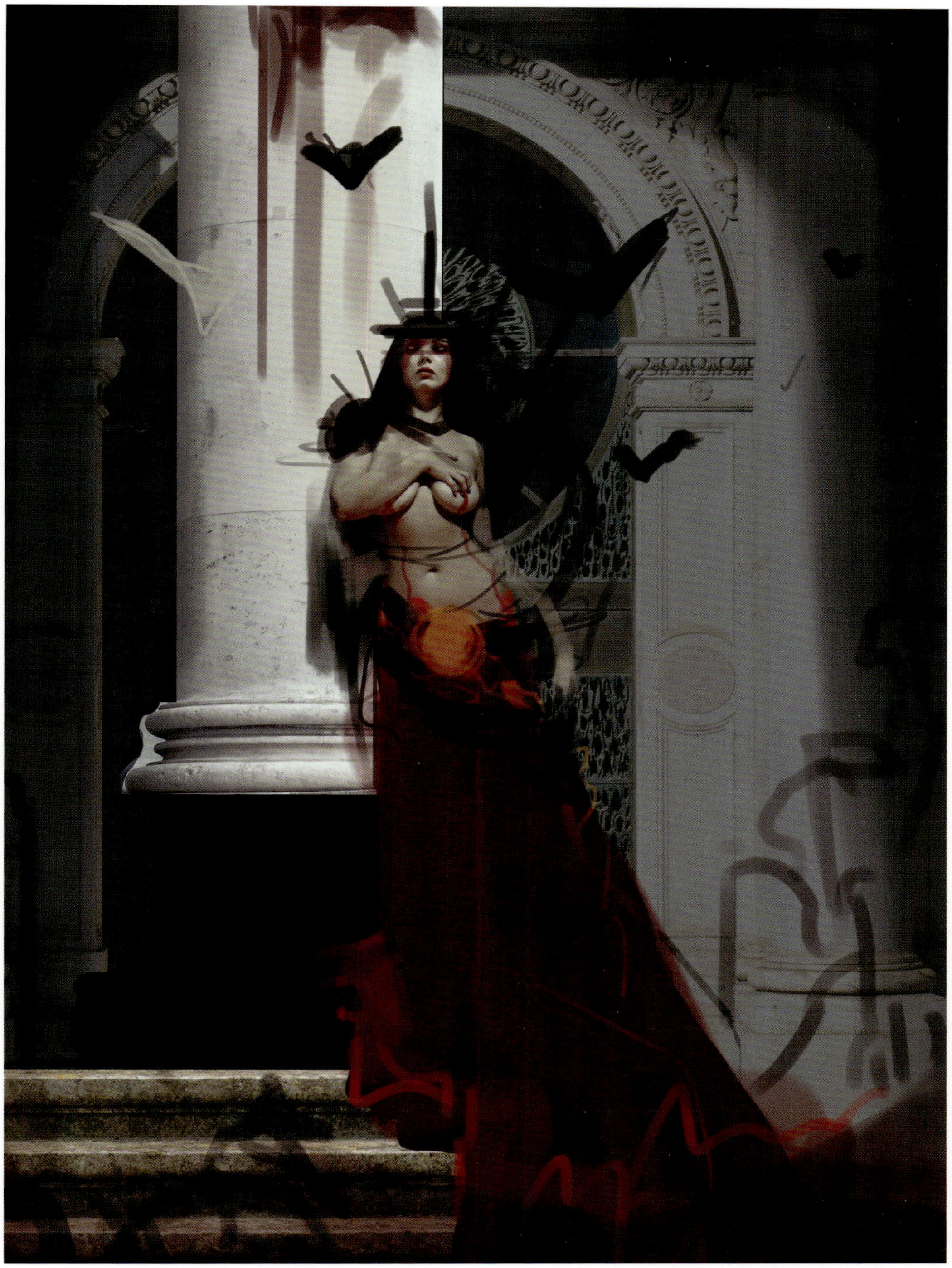

Painting and piecing together the photo elements

09 'Photo-sketching'

I place the photographic elements exactly where I need them to reflect the intentions of my initial sketch. I call this part 'photo-sketching'. I adjust, paint, and manipulate the photo elements in order to set up the overall image as closely as possible to its final form. Working this way, with photographs, allows me to test everything fast, to keep or discard. It helps me visualize and quickly decide what works and what doesn't for the mood and composition. This can take a while, with lots of trial and error, until everything is stable.

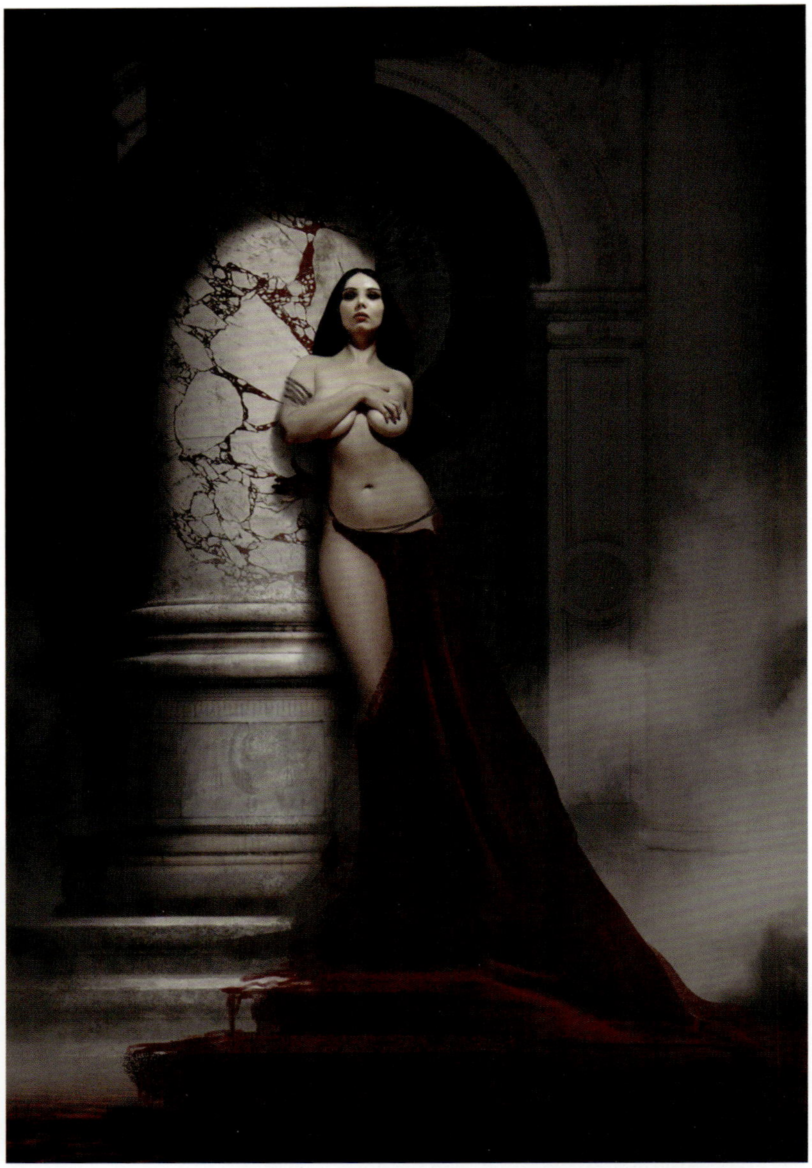

Emphasizing the focal points and dark mood

10 Spiral composition

I want to have a spiral-shaped flow in the composition – a strong diagonal leading to the character. The rest of the image is based on verticals and horizontals, which gives it a stable and calm feel, contrasting with the dress's diagonal form. The circle shape behind the character gives her a sort of sacred dimension. I emphasize some important aspects of the image: the dress, the column with the red marble texture, and the general mysterious mood. The pale colours around the character strongly contrast with the sharp, vivid red of the narratively essential blood.

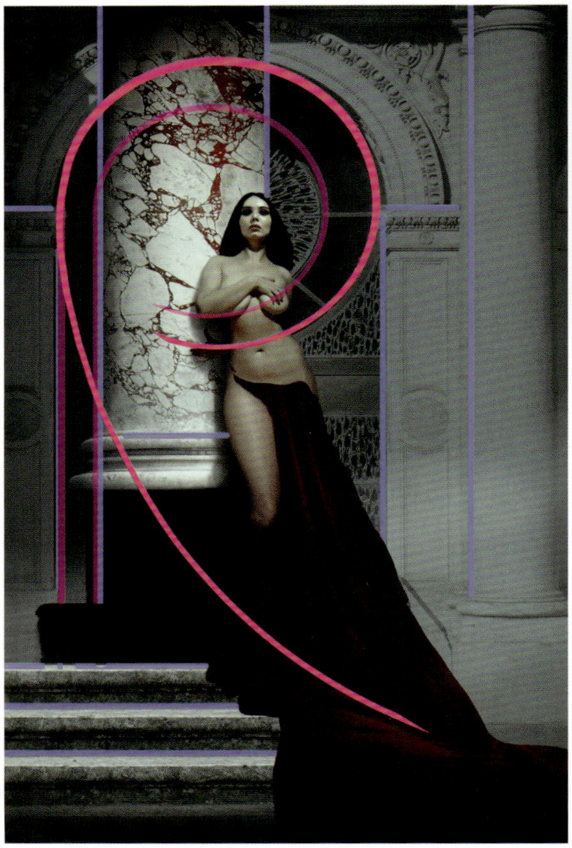

Cleaning up and affirming the composition

11 Mood & focus

I continue painting and pushing the mood. The dress turns to blood, dripping down the staircase. With *Egyptian Queen* in mind, I add a circular shadow on the column. Adding fog helps reduce the details where they don't matter, making sure nothing acts like a hook that could snag the viewer's eye away from the character. Frazetta taught me this: a finished piece isn't a piece that shows everything in detail. Instead, it's a piece that is built with balance, knowing when to be evasive and when to focus.

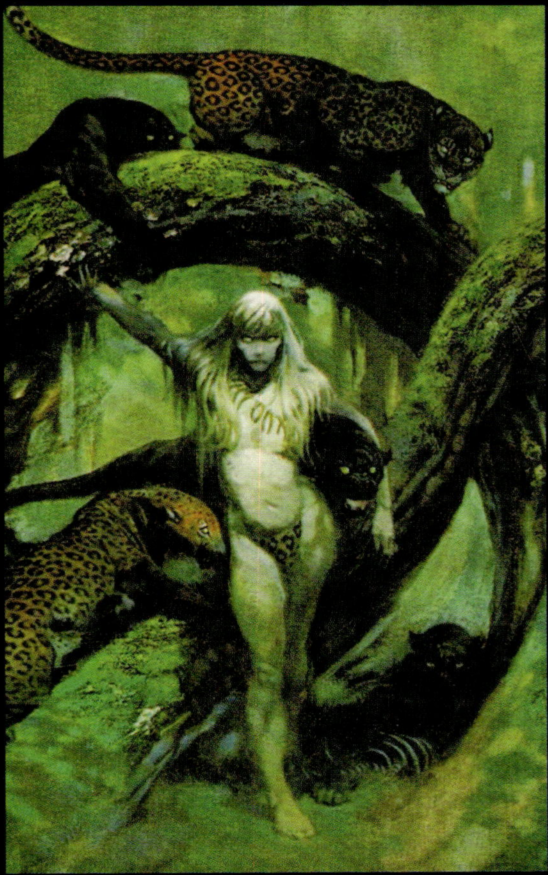

Cat Girl © Frank Frazetta

Discovering Frazetta

I don't remember which I saw first – maybe the Death Dealer, printed on the cover of a French dark-fantasy role-playing game, or the covers of the Conan novels. Along with *Egyptian Queen*, *Cat Girl*, and *Silver Warrior* (see on page 243), those are the Frazetta pieces that impacted me the most at an early age. In fact, they have been essential visual milestones on the path I took in life, from the dreaming kid escaping into imaginary worlds to the professional artist creating his own today.

Frazetta's paintings are raw – dark, crude, and brutal. I always found a sincerity in his work, setting his images apart from the oiled bodybuilders and stereotypes of painted bodies in the 1980s. It felt real. Honest. Full of tension and danger, muscles and curves, desire and strength.

Many of his pieces have something 'Rembrandtian' in their lighting. The character seems to be the light source, and the surroundings are only there to affirm, enforce, complete, and assist the focal point. From Frazetta, I learned to place details where you want the eye of the viewer to go. The rest can and should remain loose, to not distract from the main focus. Everything in his work is a masterful use of contrasts, focused on characters with strong stories. Stories that we don't know but we suspect.

These themes and the way Frazetta painted them have always been part of my work. When I started to teach art, later in my career, I realized how much he and a few other artists nourished my internal library, because I knew their work even before I started to draw and paint.

▸▸ *For image in full, turn to page 238*

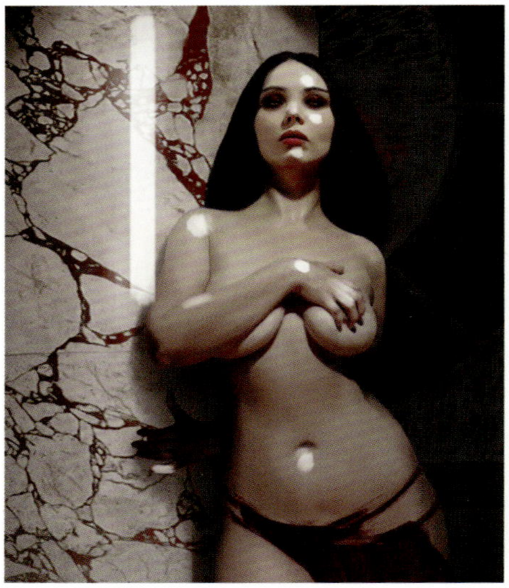

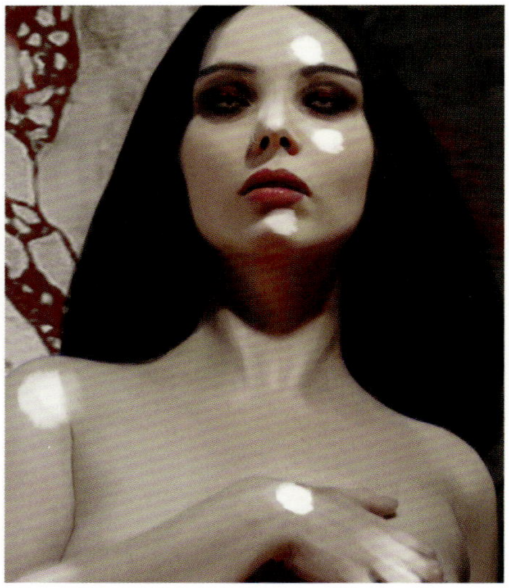

12 Fine-tuning light sources

One danger with working on characters and scenes from different sources is that they can easily appear mismatched. Adjusting colours is a simple process, but lights, shadows, angles, and perspective are a completely different deal! This is why I always work with photographic materials that share similar light sources and angles. During this step, I fine-tune the light and shadows to ensure the character appears as though she belongs within the scene.

Adding light that matches both the character and background

13 Generating chaos

I continue painting and adding more photographic elements and textures. I focus on the dress, neck, and waist-piece, adding more blood and painting more details. I notice a triangle under the jaw has appeared for some reason – a 'glitch' that looks cool, so I keep it. This process generates some chaos and accidents, opening the door to surprises that enrich the creative experience. It's my favourite part of the process, because I get to make decisions with unexpected results, leading to unplanned outcomes. In other words, I discover the piece as I build it!

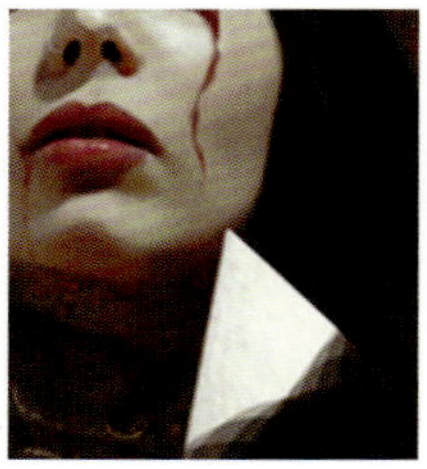

Adding detail while allowing for accidents, with textures courtesy of the photobash.co 'Medieval Armor' pack

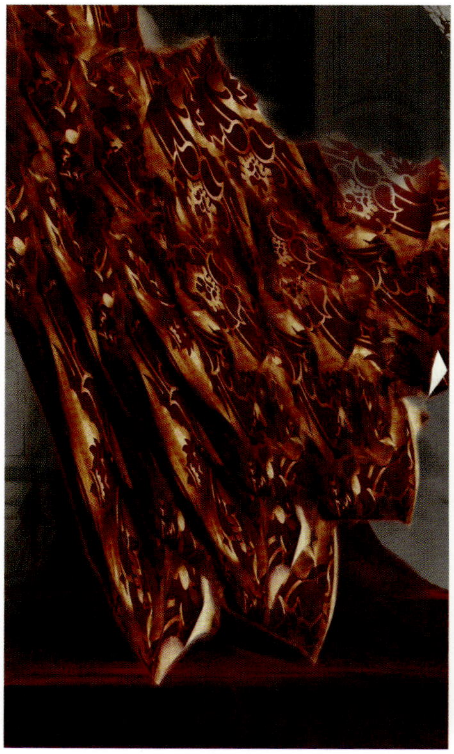

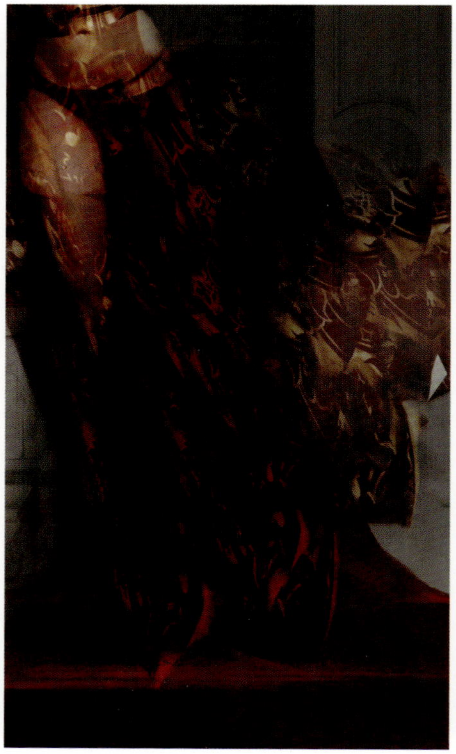

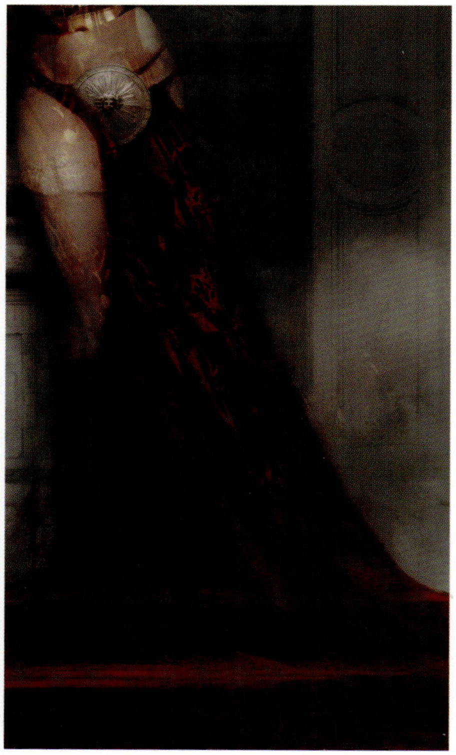

14 Mixing mediums

At this point, it's hard to tell what is painted and what is photographic, which is an effect I don't mind. Instead of trying to paint over everything, I look at this 'photographic render' technique as a great way to attract the eye of the viewer. It brings in details that I like to keep as they are, as marks of the process itself, which are pleasing to look at. Not everything needs to be blended and polished. The dynamic between painting and photography is a visual dance, and I like to find the right balance within it. It has become a trademark of my work.

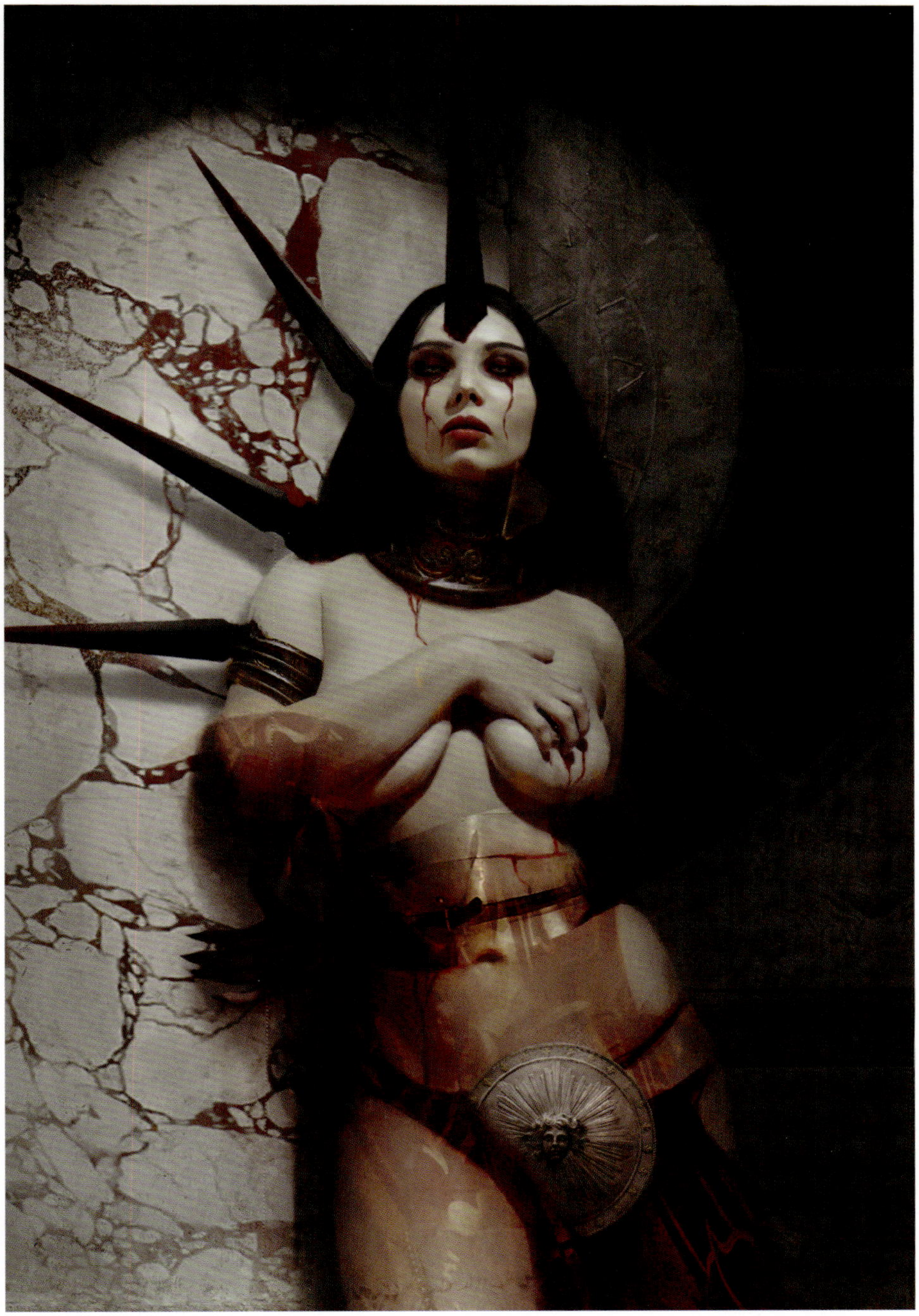

Zooming in on the blend of photographic and painted detail

15 A final close-up

In close-up, you can see another example of how painting and photography interact. The painted blood runs down the face, merging with the semi-photographic neckpiece. I use the red of the blood to tie together the multiple elements it crosses as it drips down the image. As the very last final touch, I add a subtle cross design that discreetly but directly references an element of *Death Dealer I*.

Blood is the key to tying the image together!

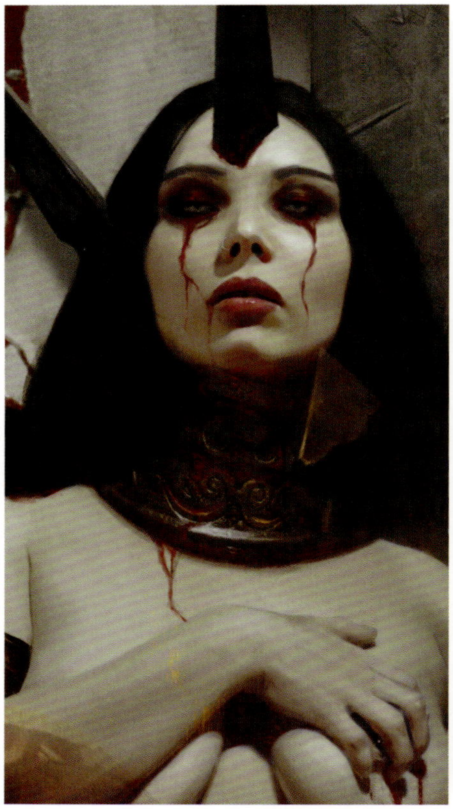

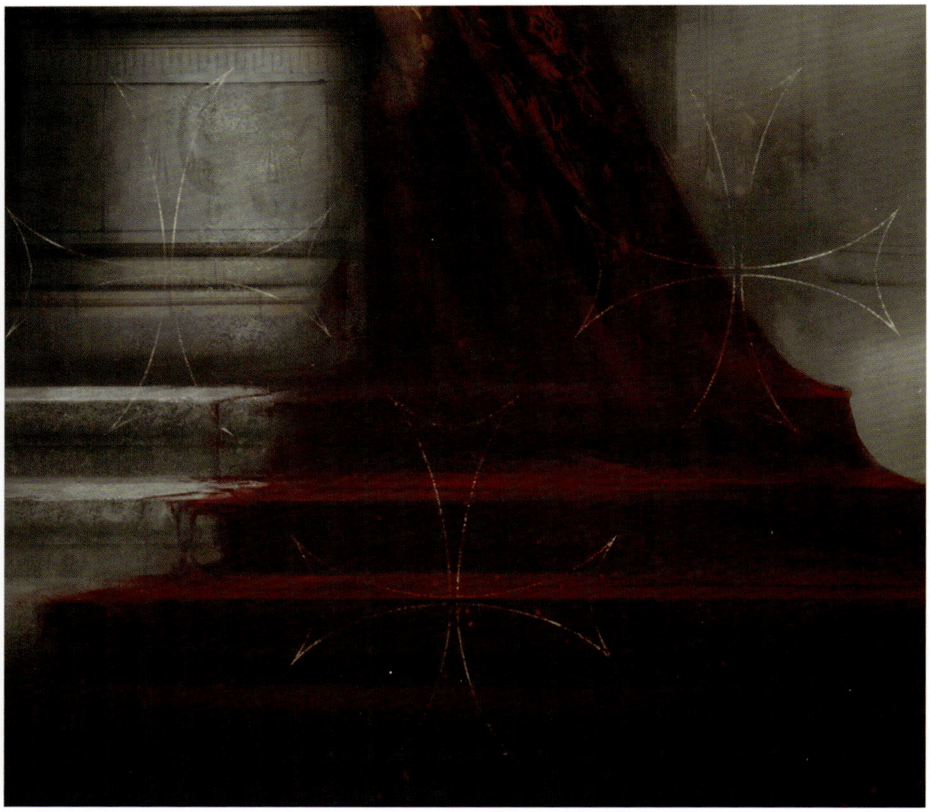

Conclusion

For this project, I made some playful moves, with open references to Frazetta's pieces, while staying true to my visual identity. I feel that the result really works! I cannot stress this enough: a successful image is all about contrast and choosing where to spend your energy. All of Frazetta's paintings have this quality. When you tell a story, you never want to lose yourself or your audience in details that do not matter, and the same is true of images as well.

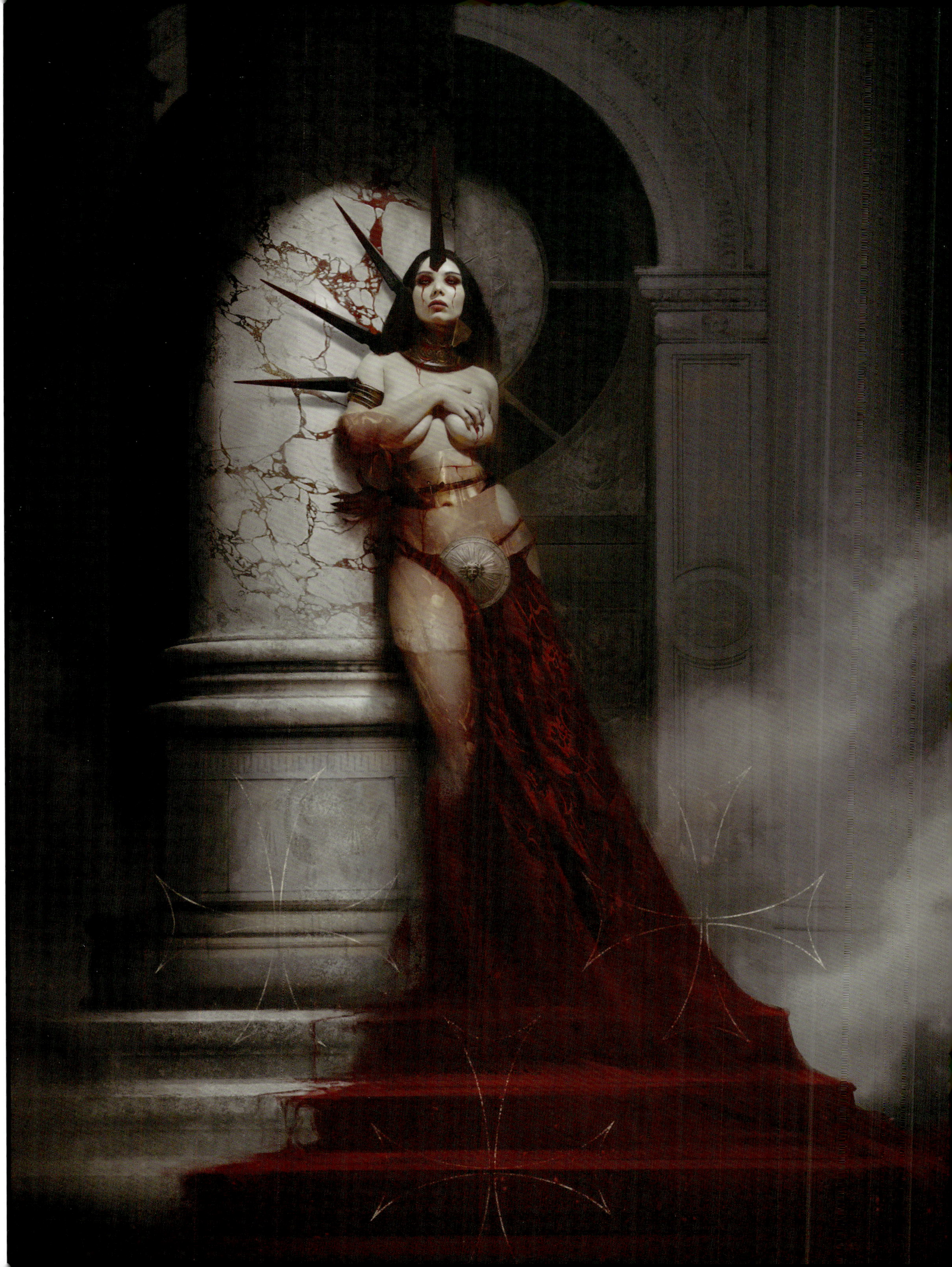

Final image © Bastien Lecouffe Deharme

Gallery

by Bastien Lecouffe Deharme

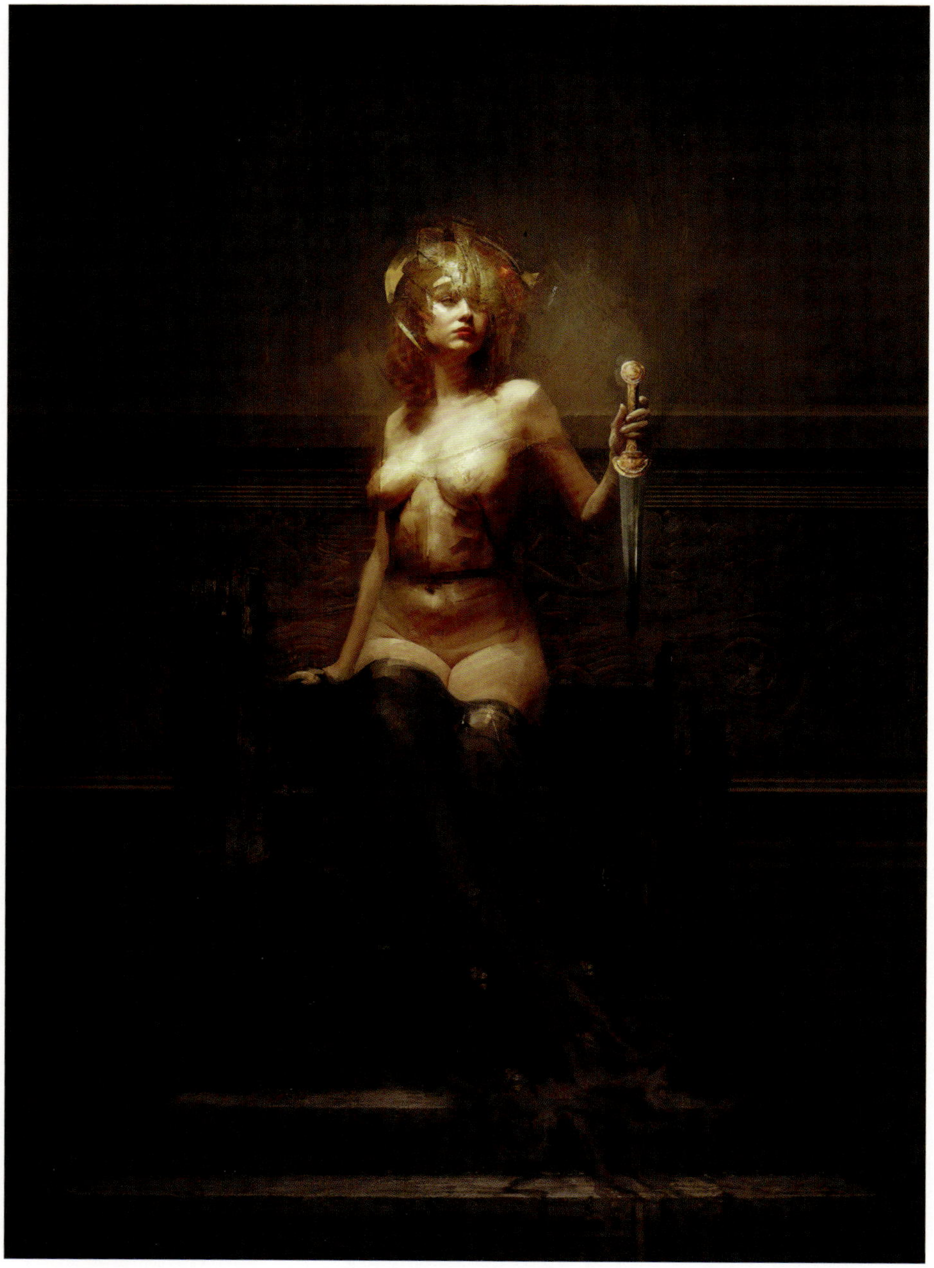

The Light Bringer © Bastien Lecouffe Deharme

The Light Bringer — *A piece focusing on light and ornamentation, showing as much expression as possible with the simplest pose and composition.*

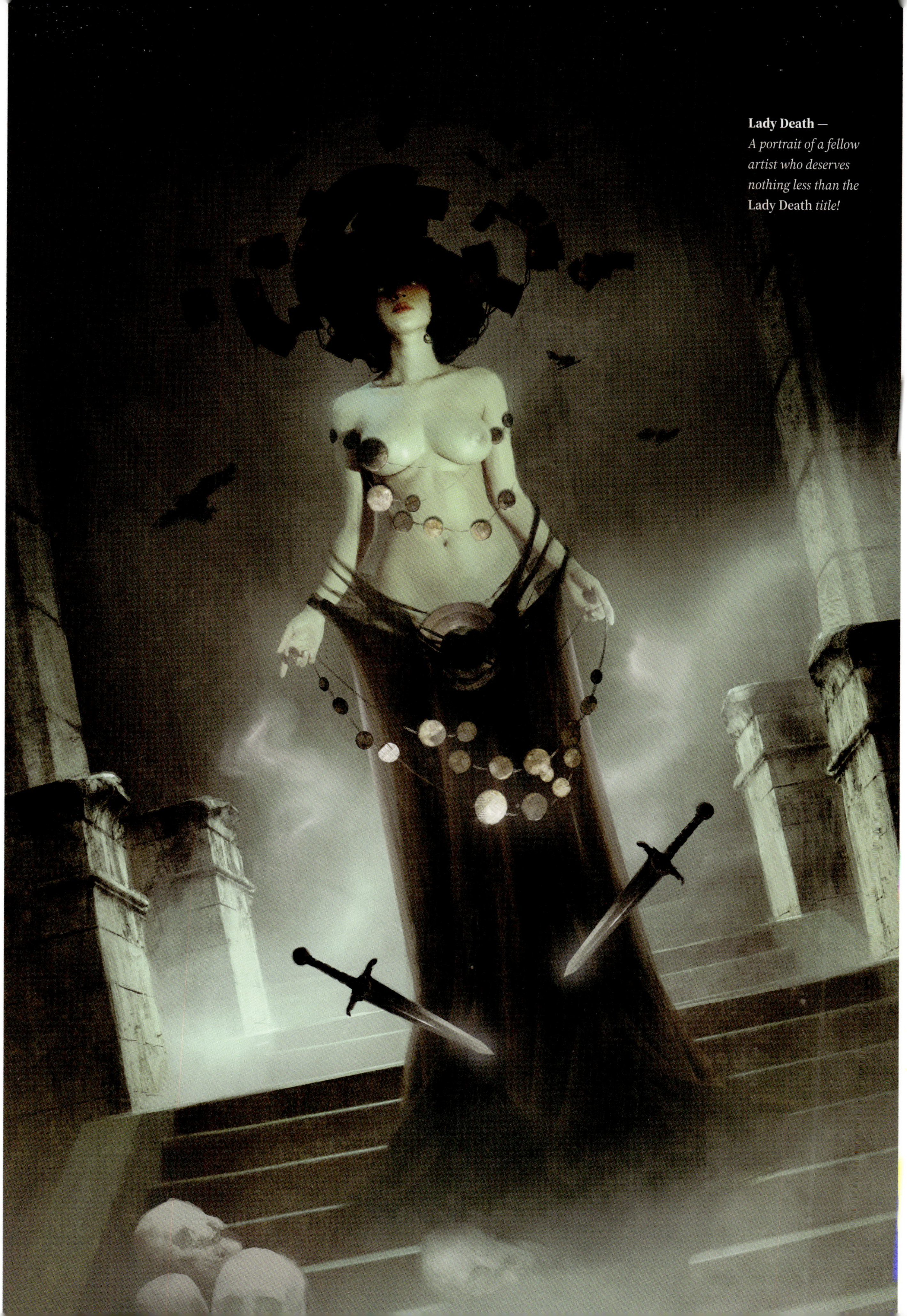

Lady Death —
A portrait of a fellow artist who deserves nothing less than the Lady Death *title!*

Lady Death © Bastien Lecouffe Deharme

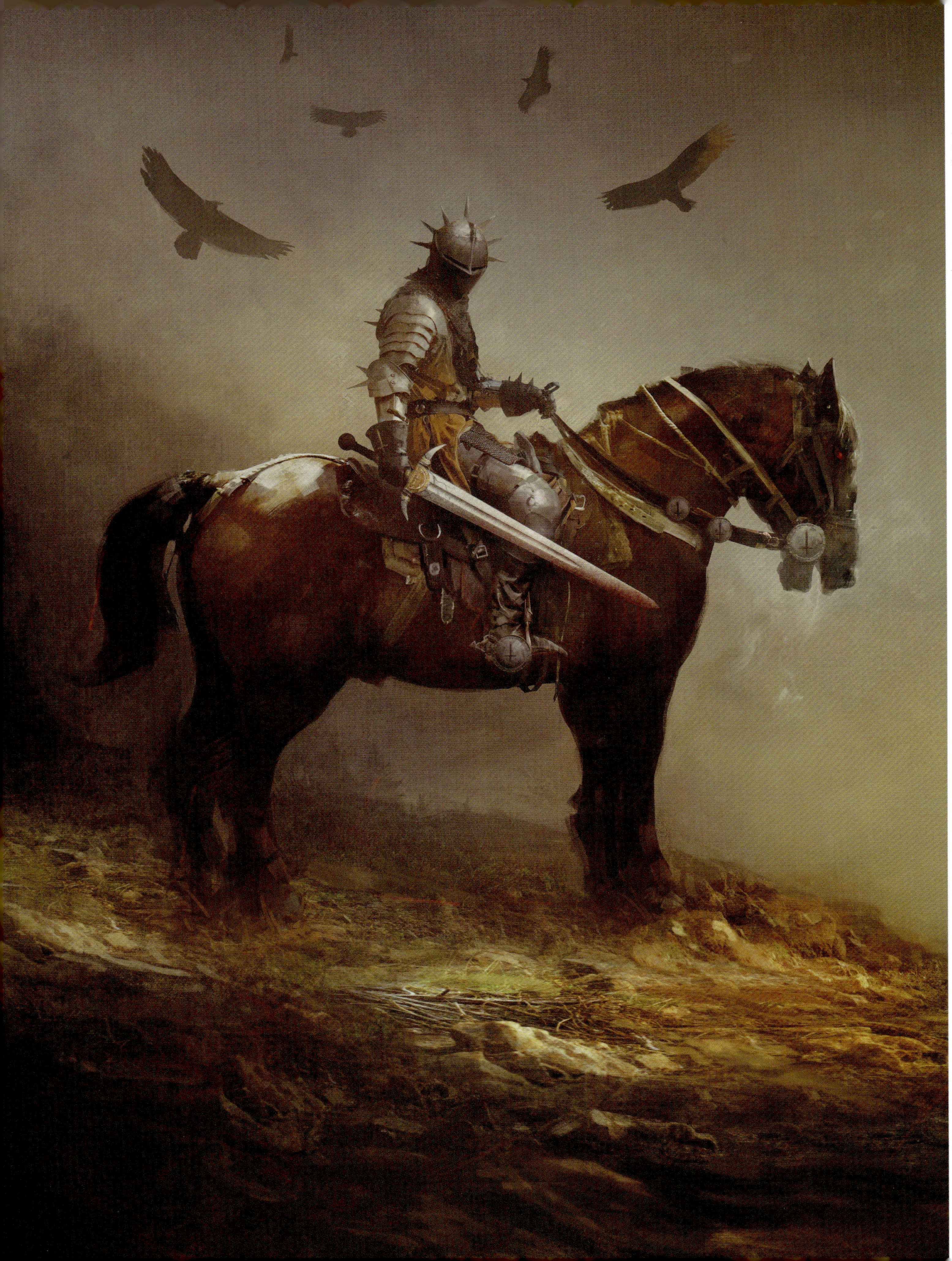

Night's Blood © Bastien Lecouffe Deharme

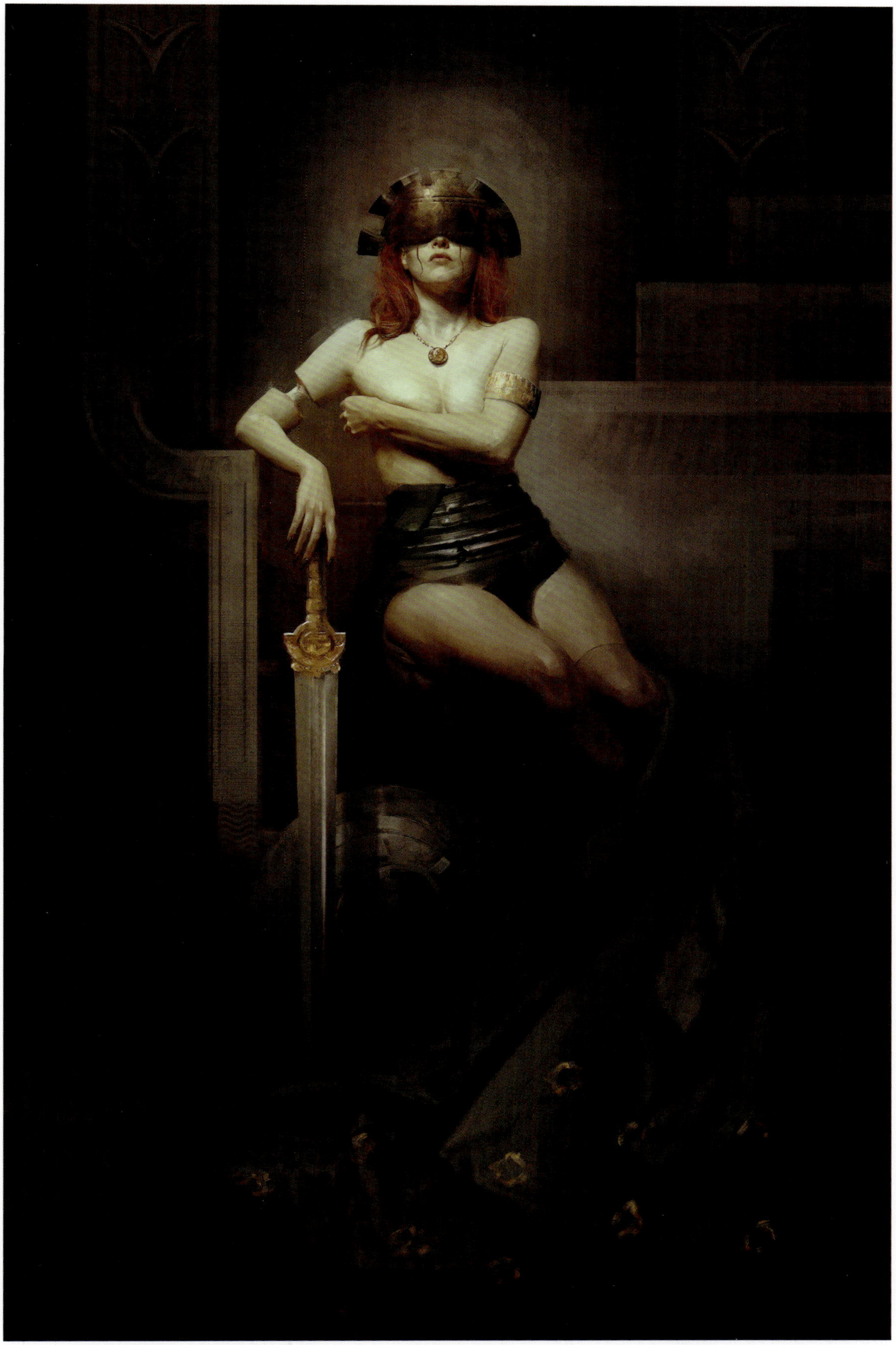

Shaparaah © Bastien Lecouffe Deharme

Gallery

by Frank Frazetta

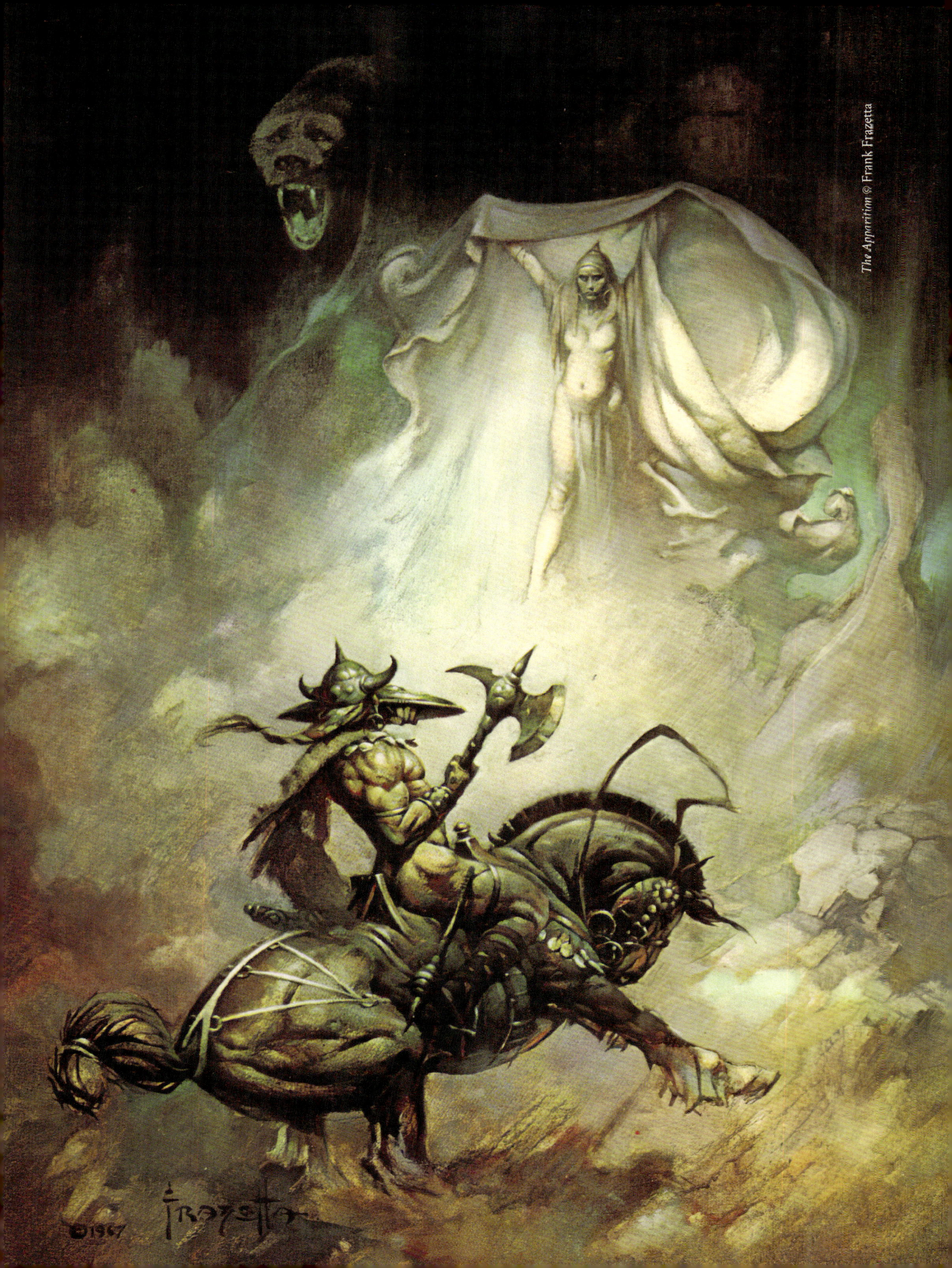

The Apparition © Frank Frazetta

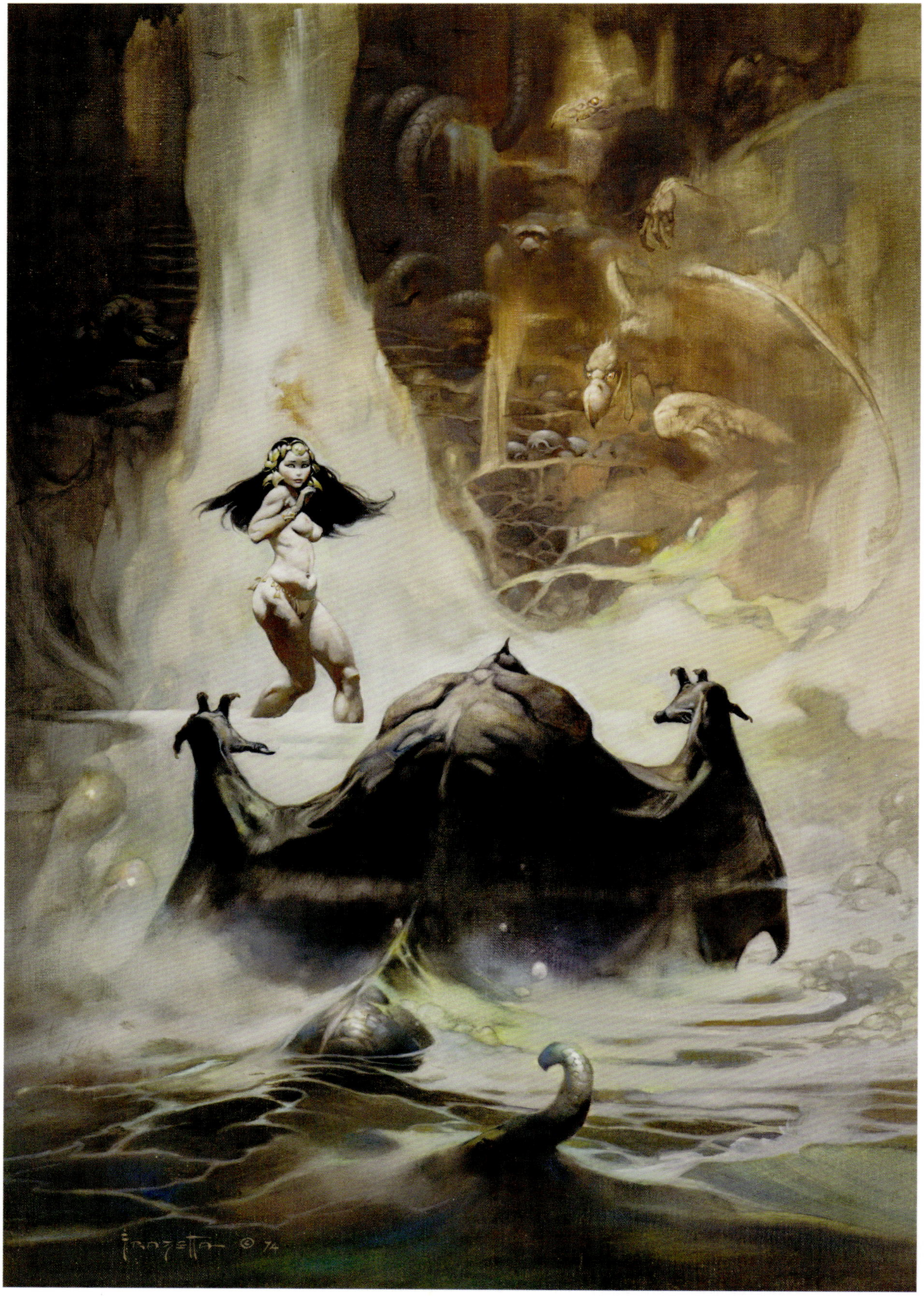

At the Earth's Core © Frank Frazetta

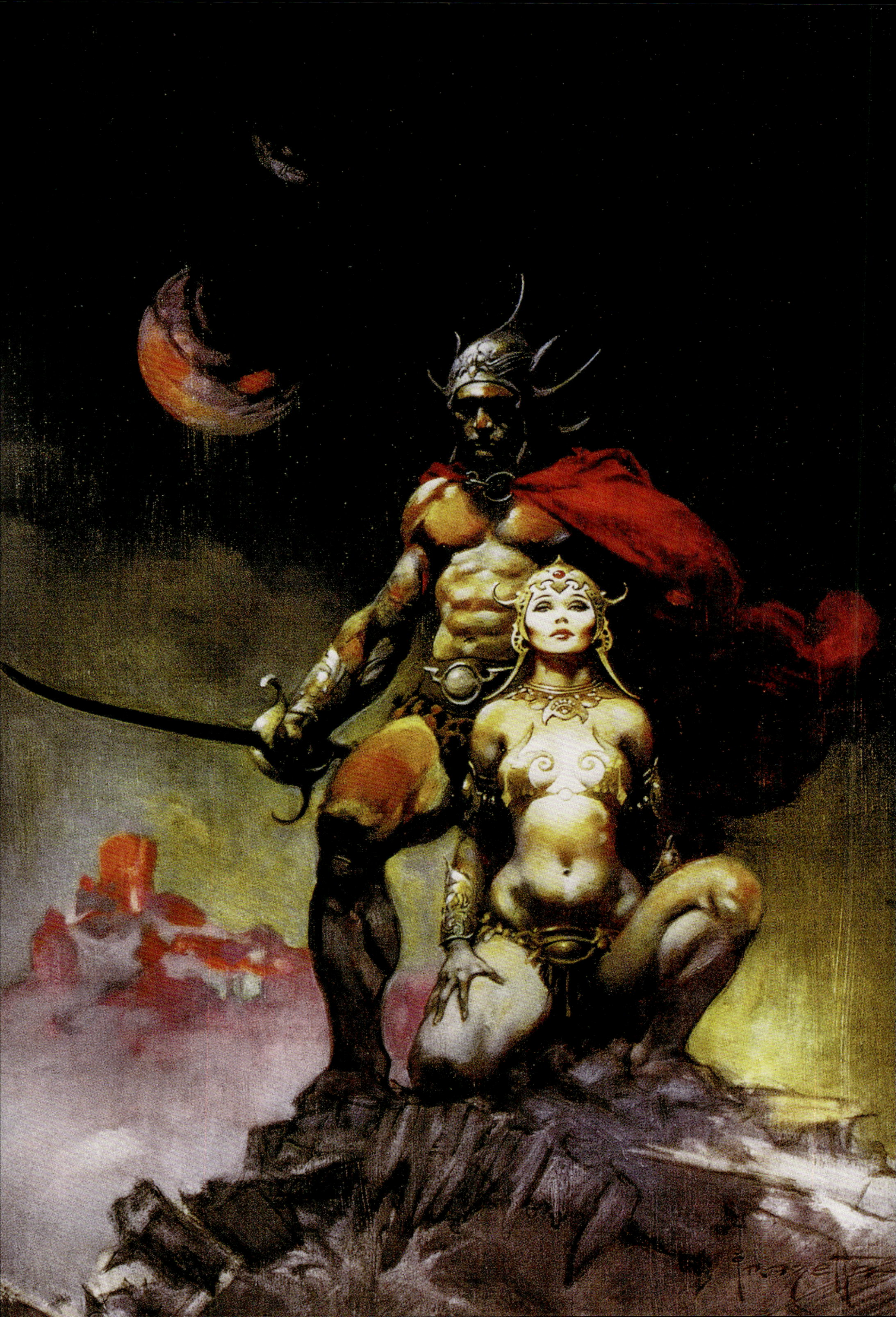

Mastermind of Mars © Frank Frazetta

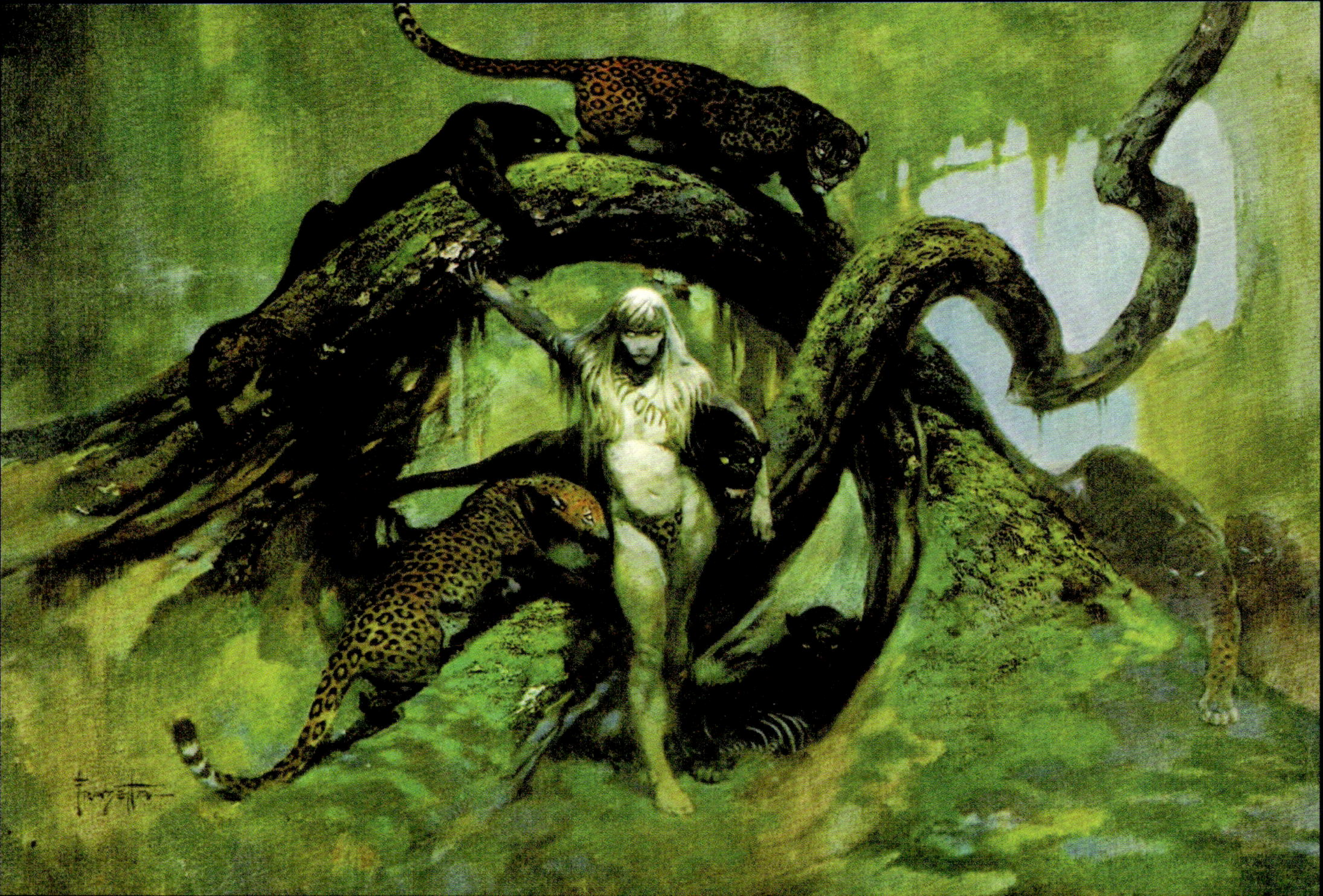

Cat Girl © Frank Frazetta

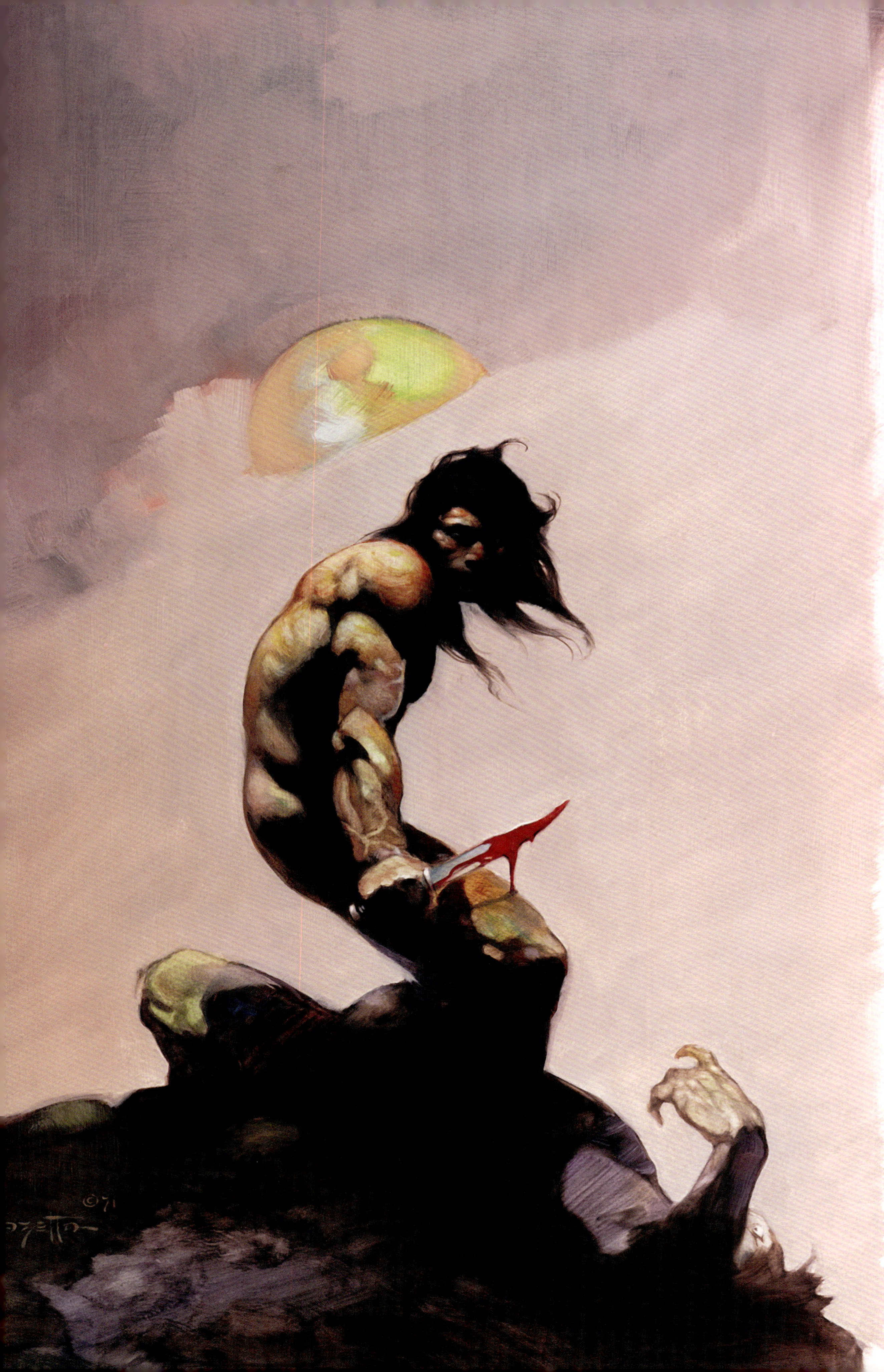

Tanar of Pellucidar © Frank Frazetta

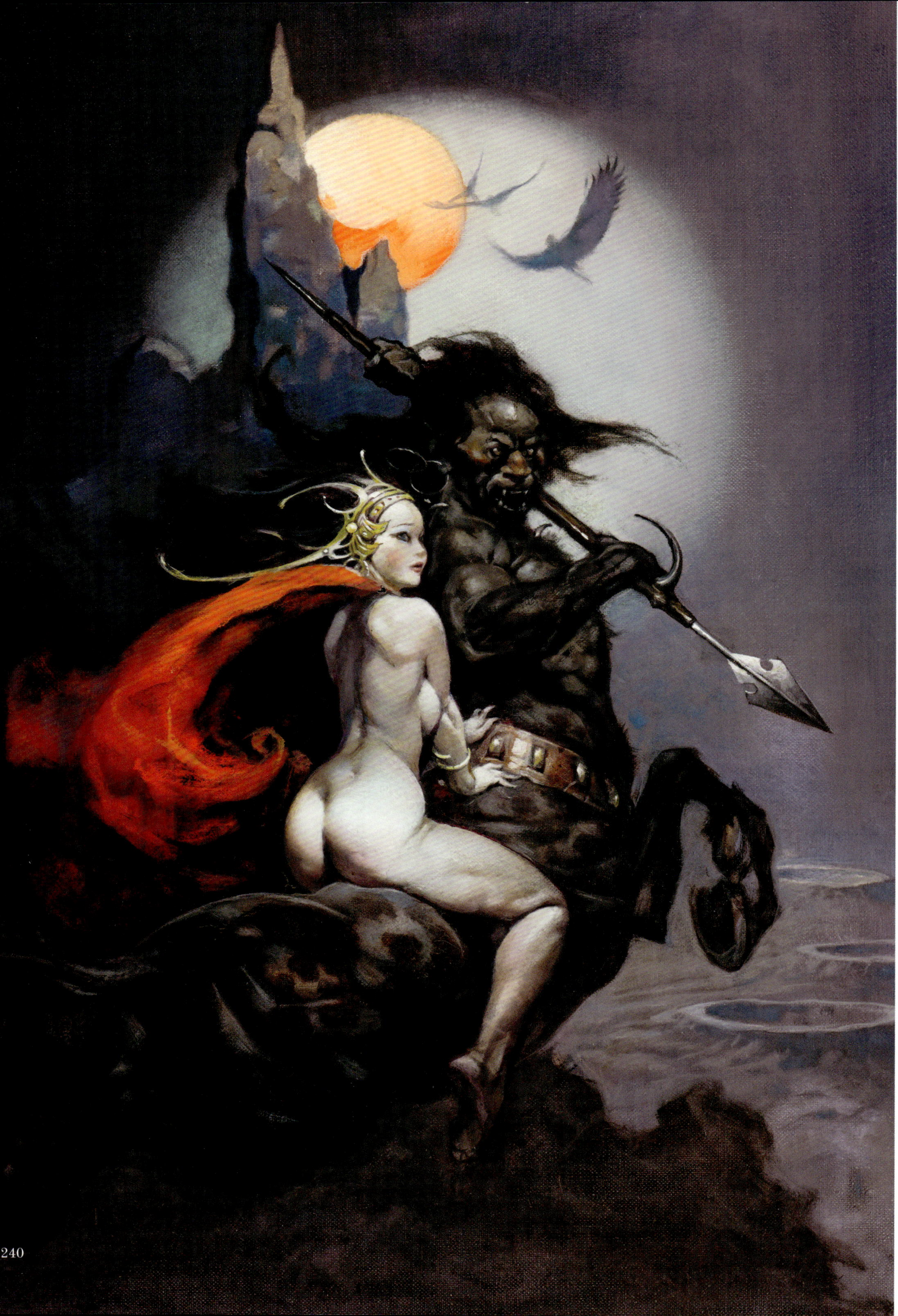

Moon Maid © Frank Frazetta

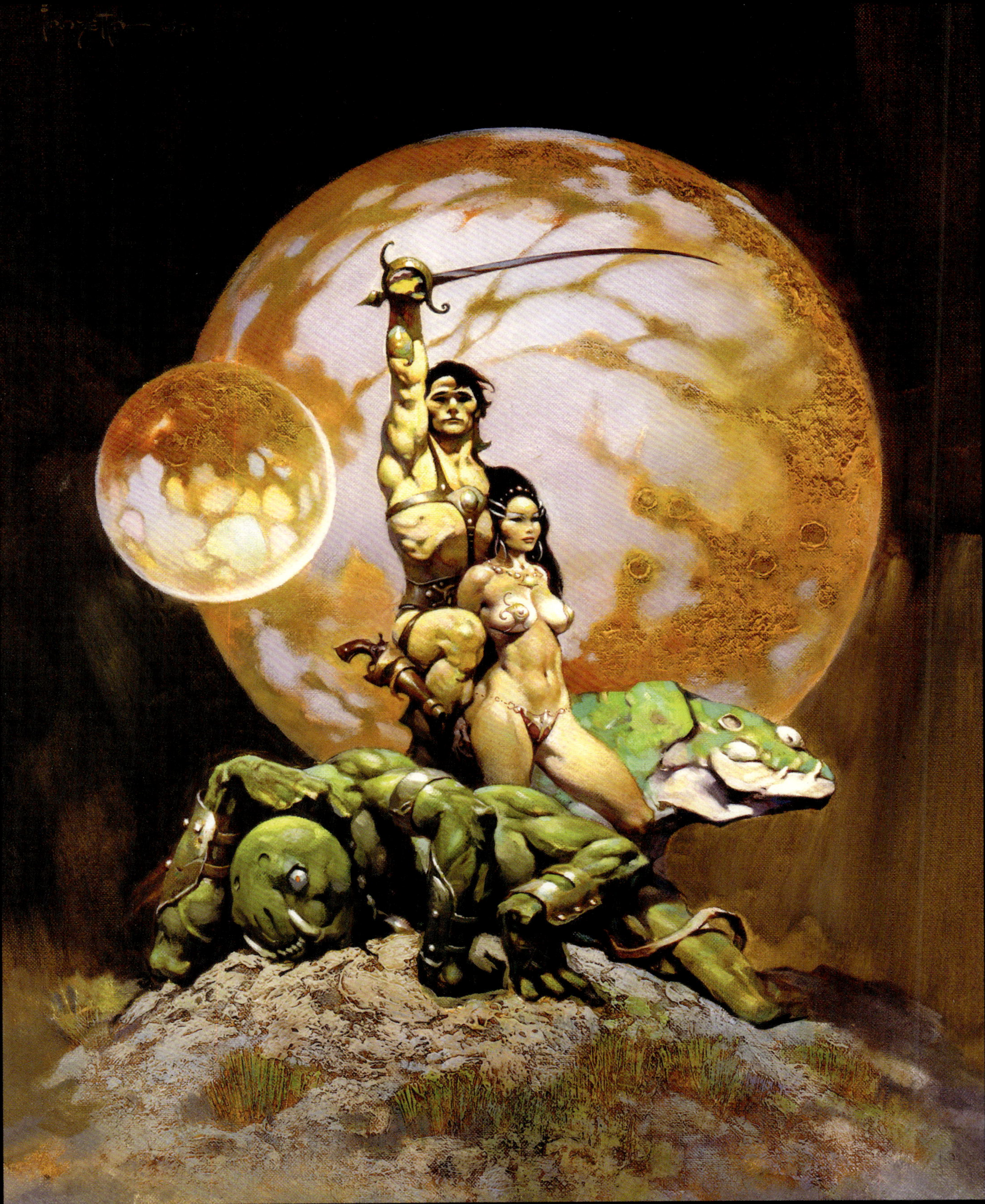

Princess of Mars © Frank Frazetta

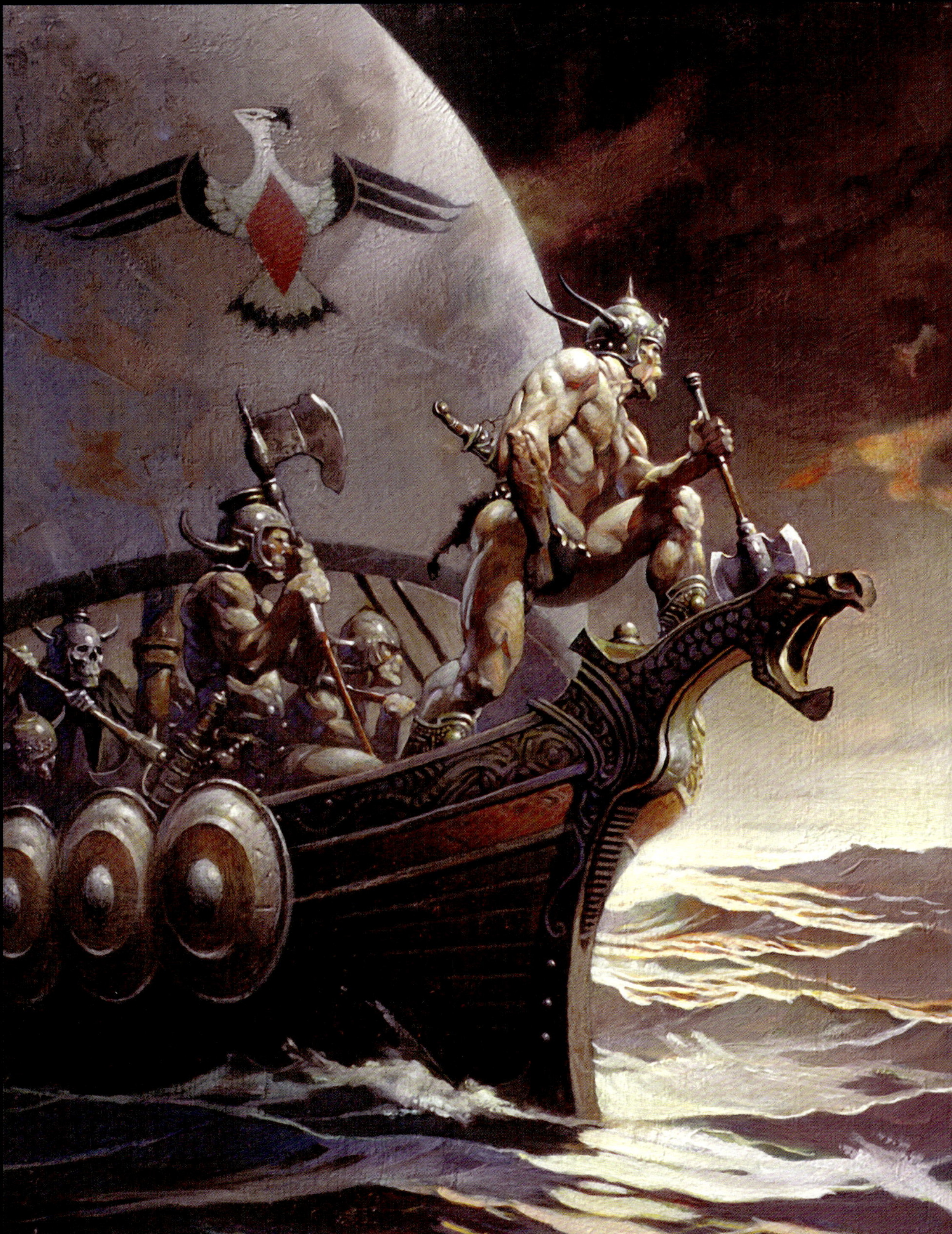

Kane on the Golden Sea © Frank Frazetta

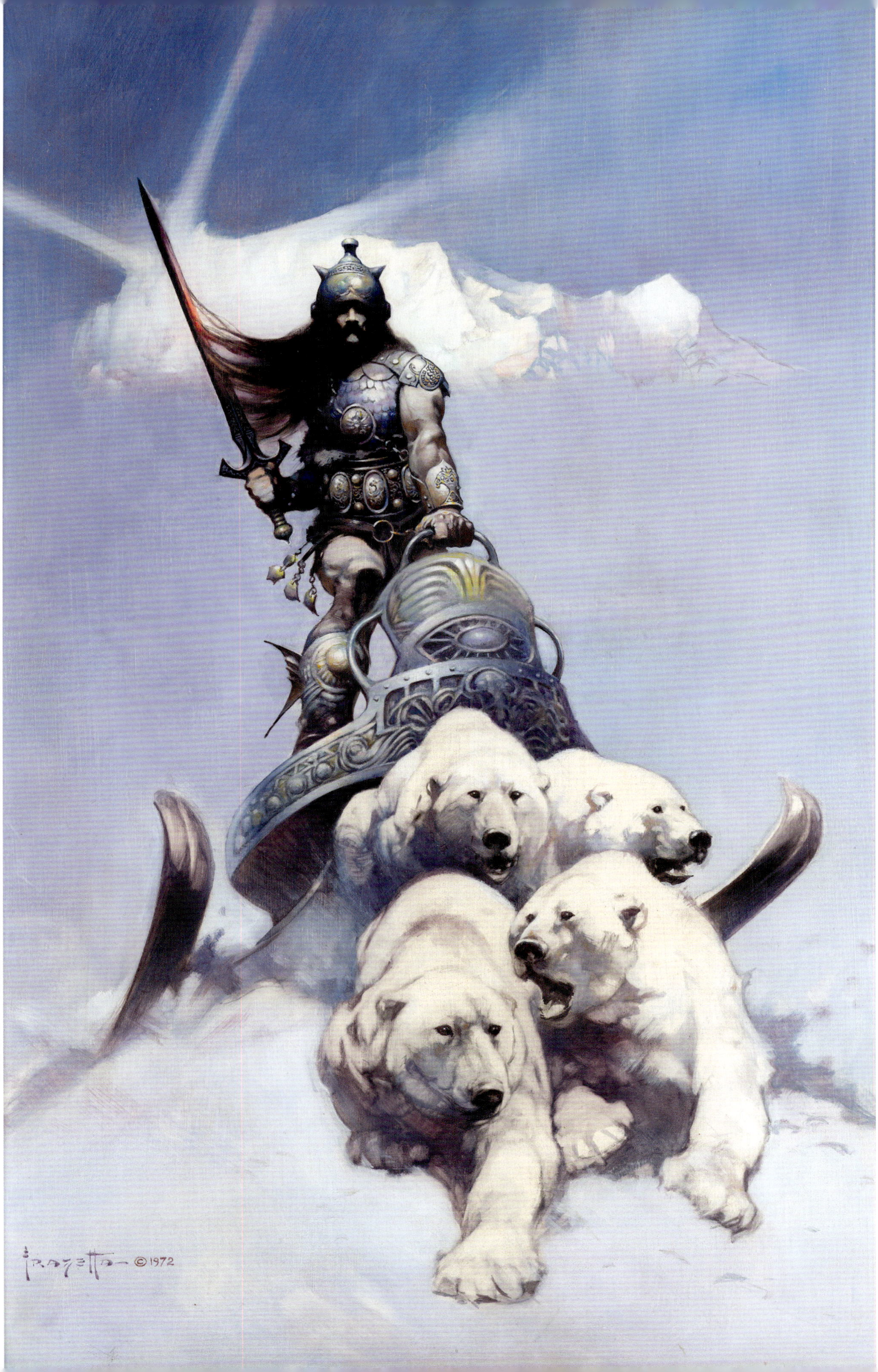

Silver Warrior © Frank Frazetta

Contributors

A very special thank you to Frazetta Girls and all the artists who took part in this book.

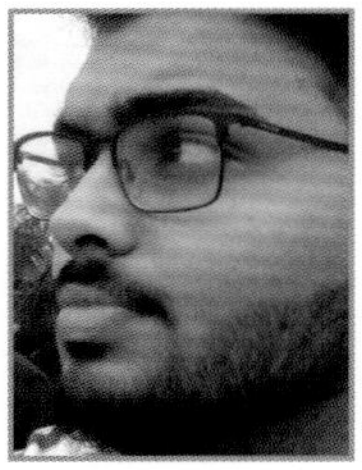

Hazem Ameen

artstation.com/caninebrush

Hazem Ameen is a freelance artist based in Kerala, India. When he's not working for clients, he is busy working on his own stories and worlds.

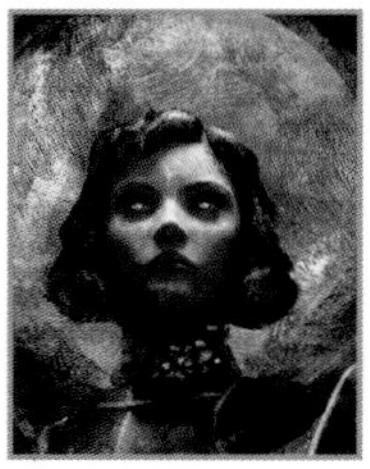

Anato Finnstark

finnstarkillustration.com

Anato Finnstark is an illustrator based in France, specializing in fantasy art and working on *Magic: The Gathering* and *Dungeons & Dragons*.

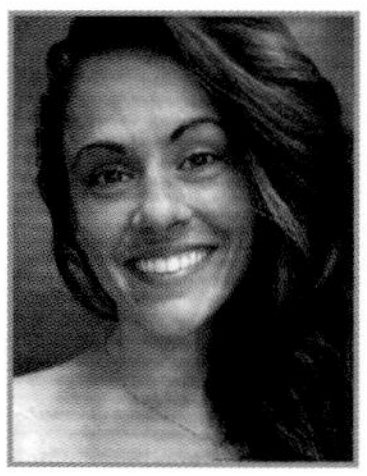

Sara Frazetta

frazettagirls.com

Sara Frazetta founded Frazetta Girls, an online platform for celebrating and preserving her grandfather's art, dedicated to offering official merchandise and ensuring the authenticity of his works for fans worldwide.

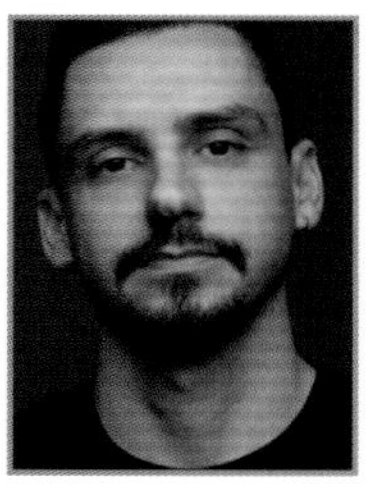

Rafael Grassetti

rgrassetti.com

Rafael Grassetti is an award-winning artist who has worked in the entertainment industry for over twenty years. Currently based in Los Angeles, he is working as an art director at Netflix, as well as creating art for comic-book covers, personal projects, and exhibits.

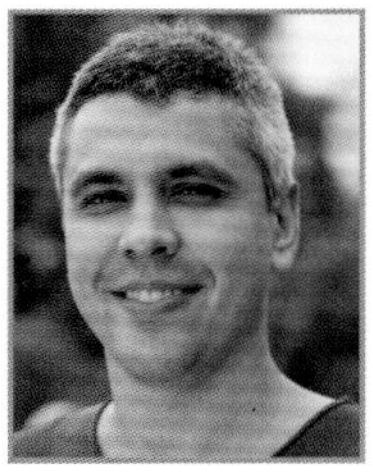

Jama Jurabaev

artstation.com/jama

Jama Jurabaev is a concept artist, illustrator, and art director working for movies and games. His credits include *Prehistoric Planet*, *The Mandalorian*, *Jurassic World: Fallen Kingdom*, and many others.

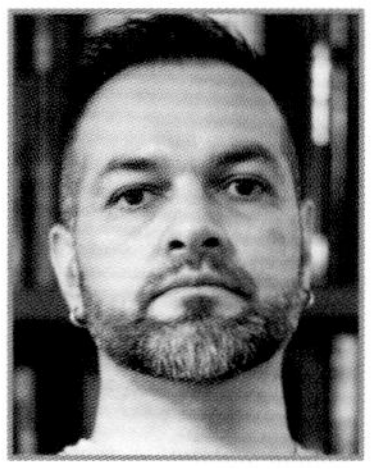

Daniel Landerman

danieland.art

Daniel Landerman is an illustrator and creative director based in Los Angeles, California. He has been working in the entertainment advertising industry since 2008, helping to design key art for film, television, and video games.

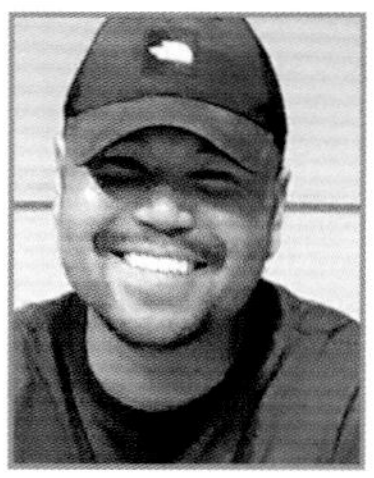

Dom Lay

artstation.com/dlartistry

Dom Lay is an artist based in California, USA. Producing art for almost fifteen years, Dom has created personal projects as well as working freelance and with AAA studios.

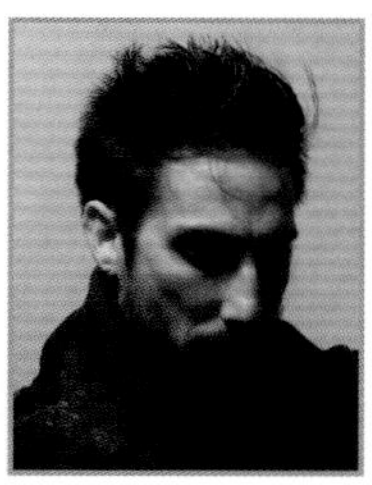

Bastien Lecouffe Deharme

deharme.com

Bastien Lecouffe Deharme is a French-American artist who creates dark and symbolic pictures. His artwork can be seen worldwide, including on *Magic: The Gathering* cards and many book covers.

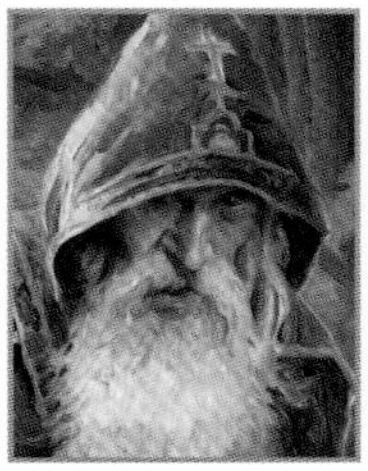

Petar Meseldžija

petarmeseldzijaart.com

Petar Meseldžija was born in 1965 in Serbia and has lived in the Netherlands since 1991. He is a fantasy artist, painter, writer, and illustrator of books, whose artwork has appeared in exhibitions and private collections worldwide.

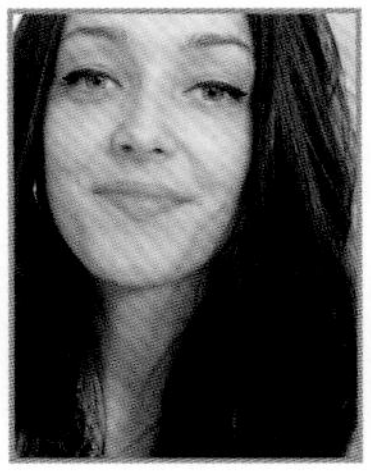

Jodie Muir

jodiemuir.squarespace.com

Jodie Muir is a freelance illustrator based in the UK, specializing in dark fantasy. Past clients include *Magic: The Gathering*, Black Library, and TKO Studios.

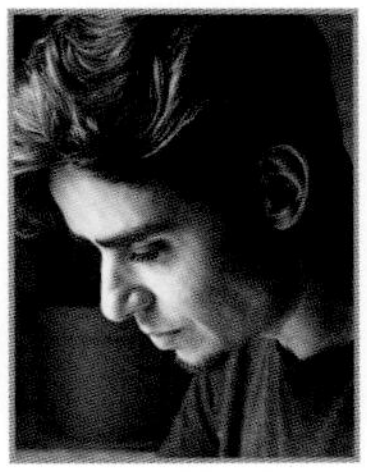

Dibujante Nocturno

dibujantenocturno.com

Fran Garcés, aka Dibujante Nocturno, is a Spanish artist specializing in fantastic art. He is passionate about sketchbooks and dark, elegant aesthetics.

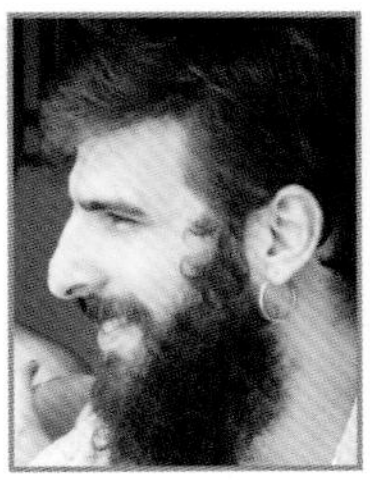

Gustavo Pelissari

artstation.com/gustavopelissari

Gustavo Pelissari is an artist based in Brazil, who has worked as a professional illustrator since 2010. He has experience working with fantasy themes for bands, book covers, and roleplaying games.

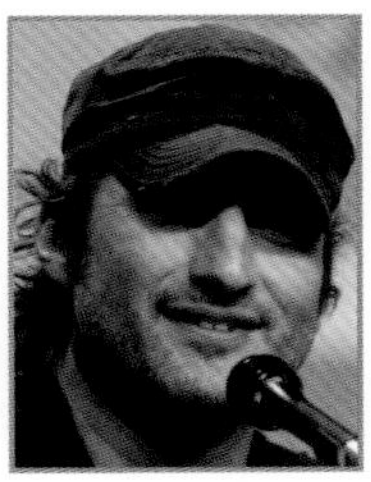

Robert Rodriguez

instagram.com/rodriguez

Robert Rodriguez is a director, writer, producer, and composer based in Austin, Texas, known for films including *From Dusk Till Dawn*, *Sin City*, the *Spy Kids* franchise, and *Alita: Battle Angel*.

Robert Rodriguez at SDCC 2014 by Gage Skidmore

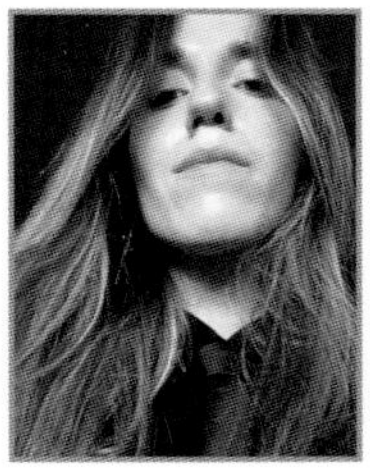

Valentina Remenar

valentinaremenar.com

Valentina Remenar is a traditional and digital illustrator, concept artist, and graphic designer from Croatia (currently based in Slovenia), who works primarily on game concepts, book covers, posters, character design, and digital illustrations.

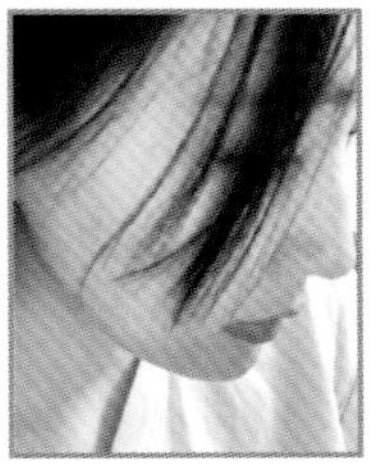

Entei Ryu

artstation.com/badzr

Entei Ryu is a concept artist and digital sculptor based in Tokyo. She graduated with a degree in architecture, but now mainly works on character and creature design for video games and movies, as well as creating sculptures and jewellery designs as a freelance artist.

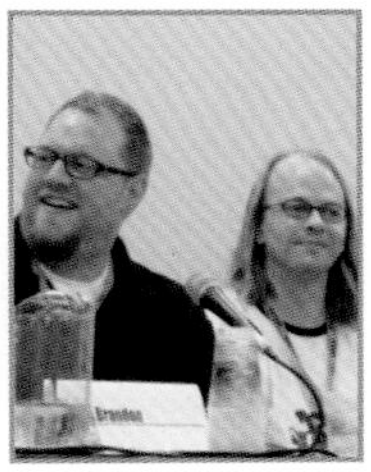

The Shiflett Brothers

shiflettbrothers.com

The Shiflett Brothers, Brandon and Jarrod, are traditional clay sculptors from Texas who have won the Spectrum Gold Award for Dimensional Work. Their book *Clay Sculpting with The Shiflett Brothers* is available everywhere.

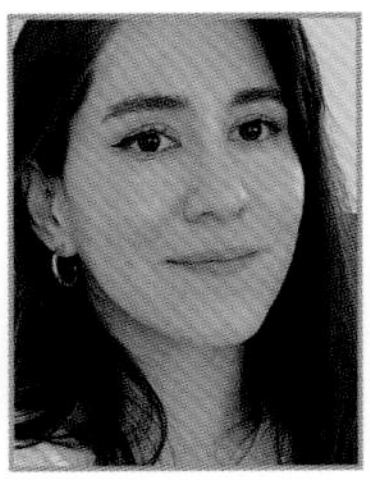

Fernanda Suarez

fernandasuarez.net

Fernanda Suarez is a digital artist who has been drawing and painting her whole life. Her passions are character design and telling stories through painting. Past clients include Paizo Publishing, Penguin Random House, and Blizzard Entertainment.

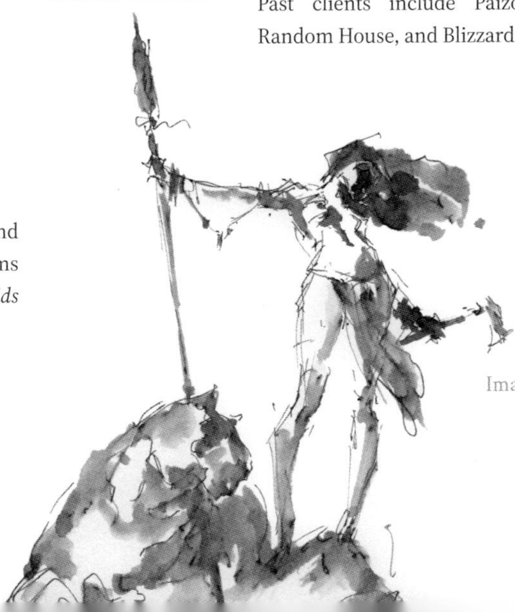

Image by Daniel Landerman

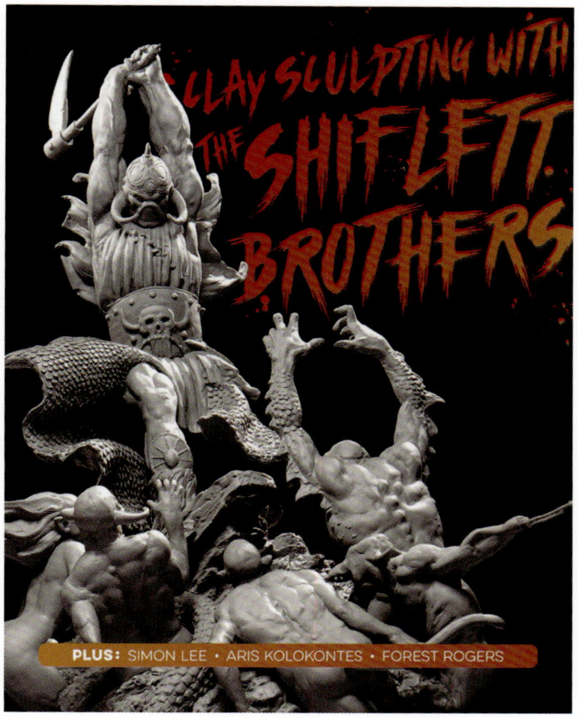

Clay Sculpting with the Shiflett Brothers

Clay-sculpting royalty 'The Shiflett Brothers' guide us through their creative journey as well as sharing in-depth insight into the processes behind their captivating fantasy sculpts. Joined by fellow esteemed sculptors Simon Lee, Aris Kolokontes, and Forest Rogers, the Shifletts bring together a collection of step-by-step tutorials that are sure to broaden your creative horizons and add an expansive set of practical skills to your sculpting arsenal, including studio-quality photography and a how-to on creating the Shifletts' very own tools.

Dibujante Nocturno

The Art of Fran Garcés

Turn the pages of this lavishly produced book to discover a collection of monsters, creatures, and characters created by illustrator and digital artist Fran Garcés, AKA 'Dibujante Nocturno'. The talented artist shares how his skills across traditional and digital media have evolved over the years, resulting in the darkly epic and exquisite style that has earned him over 440,000 followers on Instagram. In addition to a curated showcase of his past work, the book is packed with exciting new artwork and exclusive content, including step-by-step tutorials and vast galleries of previously unseen sketches.

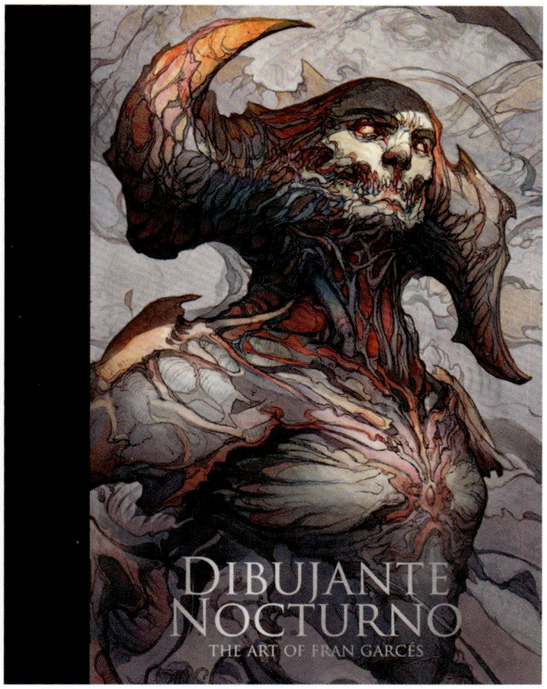

store.3dtotal.com

3dtotal Publishing

3dtotal Publishing is a trailblazing, creative publisher specializing in inspirational and educational resources for artists.

Our titles feature top industry professionals from around the globe who share their experience in skilfully written step-by-step tutorials and fascinating, detailed guides. Illustrated throughout with stunning artwork, these best-selling publications offer creative insight, expert advice, and essential motivation. Fans of digital art will enjoy our comprehensive volumes covering Adobe Photoshop, Procreate, and Blender, as well as our superb titles based around character design, including *Fundamentals of Character Design* and *Creating Characters for the Entertainment Industry*. The dedicated, high-quality blend of instruction and inspiration also extends to traditional art. Titles covering a range of techniques, genres, and abilities allow your creativity to flourish while building essential skills.

Well-established within the industry, we now offer over 100 titles and counting, many of which have been translated into multiple languages around the world. With something for every artist, we are proud to say that our books offer the 3dtotal package:

LEARN • CREATE • SHARE

VISIT US AT STORE.3DTOTAL.COM

3dtotal Publishing is part of 3dtotal.com, a leading website for CG artists founded by Tom Greenway in 1999.

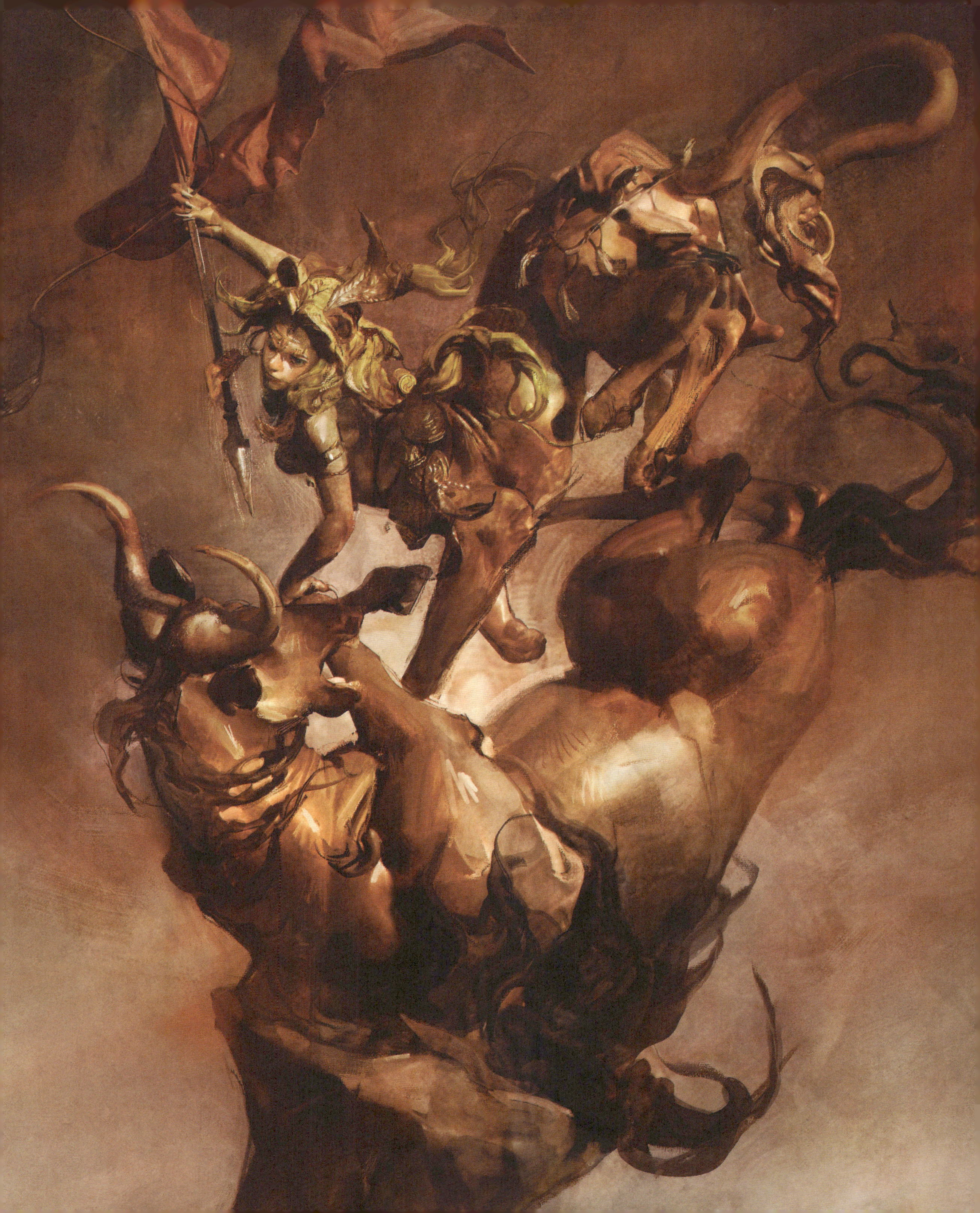